THE Pet ENCYCLOPEDIA

THE Pet ENCYCLOPEDIA

GENERAL EDITOR
FRANK MANOLSON, DVM, FRCVS

ADVISORY EDITORS

LEONARD BLACK, BSc, PhD, FRCVS
WENDY BOORER, BA
GEORGE CUST, MB, ChB, DPH, DTM, MFCM
HOWARD LOXTON
RITA VANDIVERT

THE VARSITY COMPANY
NASHVILLE, TENNESSEE 37203

Planned and Produced by Elsevier Publishing Projects
(UK) Ltd., Oxford © 1981. Elsevier
Publishing Projects,
SA, Lausanne.

Library of Congress Cataloging in Publication Data
Main entry under title:

The Pet encyclopedia.

  1. Pets. I. Manolson, Frank.
SF411.5.P47   636.08′87   81-1851
ISBN 0-8407-4079-4   AACR2

Published in Nashville, Tennessee, by The Varsity Company

Printed in the United States of America.

GENERAL CREDITS

Project Editors: Graham Bateman PhD
                           Anne Bosman BA
                           Dimples Kellogg MA

Assistant Editor: Bill MacKeith

Managing Editors: Ben Lenthall
                           Giles Lewis

Arts Editor: John Brennan

Picture Editor: Anne Davies

Design: Adrian Hodgkins

Origination by Art Color Offset, Rome, Italy.

CONTRIBUTORS

P.L. Bird

Michael Boorer BSc, DIP ED

G. Byott BSc, FLS, DIP ED

L.A. Byott BSc, DIP ED

J.A. Dawes BA, FZS, FLS, LIBIOL.

Ken Denham

Angus Dunn PHD, MRCVS

Malcolm Ellis

Jim Evans MRCVS

Bruce Fogel DVM, MRCVS

Allistair Fraser MVO, PHD, BVSc, MRCVS

Robert C. Gooden

Lexi Hishcocks

C.N.S. Lakin MRCVS

A. Livingstone PHD

T.G. McLeod McIntyre, CD, BA

Richard Mark Martin

Jacqueline Nayman BSc

John Norris-Wood ARCA

A.R.W. Porter MA

P.R. Ricketts

Clive G. Roots

Nina Sanders

Caroline Silver

Blanch V. Smith

Michael R. Thomas BASS, MIMF

Alan Walker ACIS, MIBIOL, FRIC, FIFST

Preface

A pet might be described as any tamed or domesticated animal which is kept as a favorite and treated with affection. This encyclopedia has cast its net extraordinarily wide in deciding what animals should be included. It will be a very unusual pet indeed if you cannot find it here for not only have we included all the more usual household pets, we have ranged through the whole animal kingdom—mammals, reptiles, birds, fish, and insects—to present the information that you need on every kind of creature that you are likely to keep.

For every animal you will find valuable advice on its suitability as a pet, several aspects of its care, information on its natural way of life, and help in understanding its needs. But this is much more than an encyclopedia of pet care. You will also find all kinds of other information about the animals you love, including advice on showing, breeding, and the law with regard to animals. Whatever your interest or your problem concerning your pet this book will guide you to the answer.

We believe that few people limit their interest to a single animal and that many keep more than one kind of pet. Children, as they grow up, may have a variety of different animals each of which may need a special form of care. All of us at one time or another are captivated by an animal about which we know very little and need to know more before deciding whether it makes a suitable pet for someone in our circumstances. That is why this is a book about *all* pets instead of being just about dogs, or cats, or canaries. It will enable you to choose pets wisely, to care for them properly, and to keep them safely; it will prevent you from keeping the wrong pet or treating the right one badly. If reasons of space, food supply, leisure time, or finance prevent your keeping a particular animal you will have the pleasure of finding out about the many kinds of pets that other people have in their homes.

The editors and authors are experts in their field, and most of them work with their sorts of animals at a practical rather than at an academic, theoretical, or research level.

This encyclopedia is divided into three sections—"All about Pets," "Pets of Every Kind," "The Healthy and Sick Pet." In the first section we give general background information on choosing, caring for, feeding, training, breeding, rearing, and exhibiting pets. "All about Pets" also introduces you to the history of petkeeping and working animals, gives an insight into the behavior of pet animals and outlines the laws governing pets and petkeeping. "Pets of Every Kind" is a comprehensive guide to all those animals that are likely, or unlikely, to be kept as pets—from dogs to wolves, from cats to lions, from goldfish to dolphins, from butterflies to snakes. The main aim of the "Healthy and Sick Pet" is to give detailed advice on the care of sick and injured animals and to set forth the vast number of ailments that can affect them. However, to help in the understanding of illness we have also included an introductory chapter on the biology of the healthy pet.

Contents

Introduction:
PETS & PEOPLE

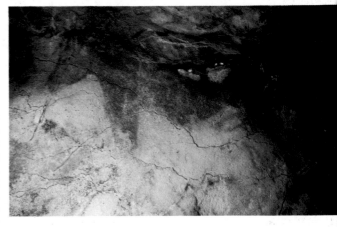

The dog has been domesticated longer than any other animal. Bottom. *Apparent several thousand years ago were distinct breeds, such as these Assyrian Hounds shown walking in the grounds of the Royal Park, Nineveh (dated about 640 B.C.).* Facing Page. *Today the dog is the most popular of pets, and the bond between mankind and dogs is the strongest of all pet relationships.*

Top Right. *A prehistoric painting of a horse from the walls of the Altimira caves, dated between 10,000 and 50,000 years ago, indicates the early importance of animals in the rise of humankind.*

Nigerian villagers have a tale about a boy who adopted the pup of a wild dog and brought it up as a pet, despite its mother's attempts to lure her offspring back into the wild. In time the grown bitch attracted a wild dog to the village, and the resulting litter grew up as tame animals and began to hunt with the men with such success that other villagers nearby began to adopt dogs—and the practice spread. Though only a tale, this story suggests that the actual transition from wild to tame and then to domestication was undoubtedly brought about by keeping young animals as pets.

Domestication can be defined as the process of taming and bringing animals under human control. However, successful domestication includes one other factor: that the species remains capable of reproduction. Thus the hare, which is a relatively easy animal to tame and which has been kept by mankind for many centuries (early Romans held them in walled enclosures called *lepuraria*), has never been successfully domesticated because it does not breed readily in captivity. The rabbit, by contrast, is easily bred in captivity and is widely kept. Sometimes domestication has been the means of saving a species from extinction. Both the alpaca and the llama are known only rarely in the wild, but both survive as domesticated animals. It is not

known for certain if the hamster still exists in the wild in the Middle East, but as a domesticated creature its survival is assured. Similarly, some scientists believe that some species of popular tropical fish no longer exist in the wild.

Domestication is not limited to the higher orders of animals. The honeybee, the silkworm, and the fruit fly are now commonly considered to be domesticated creatures. Many people mistakenly consider that a domesticated animal which is easily kept in captivity is neither dangerous nor likely to escape. As a result, people are still gored and killed by Jersey bulls or lose forever a golden pheasant which they have reared with loving care. On the other hand, a pet turtle kept in the garden is not likely to escape nor is it dangerous. It can hardly, however, be called a member of a domesticated species. Bears have been successfully tamed and trained, and many bears have been born in captivity; but the bear family as a whole is not likely to be domesticated.

So what is a pet? Agreement on a definition is almost impossible. For one thing, distinguishing between pets and working animals is difficult. The ubiquitous dog, most versatile and intelligent of the lot (who therefore occupies more space in this book than any other animal), is not only the premier companion but also a hunter, a herder, a watchdog, a pack-carrying and draft animal—and at times it has been considered a culinary delicacy.

The goldfish is one of the most highly "domesticated" of all animals. The cat shows little divergence from the wild type in both form and personality, and indeed has been associated with humans for only a relatively short period. Its independence, due to its ancestors' solitary habits in the wild, endears it to all true cat lovers. The Murena Eel, eaten in enormous quantities by sophisticated Romans, was also kept as a pet. (Visitors used to flock from far and near to admire one such eel, owned by a noble lady, Antonia, who used to adorn it with golden earrings.) As this book will show, representatives from nearly all forms of animal life have been made into pets at one time or another.

Most simply stated, a *pet* is any animal for which a human being has formed an emotional and social attachment. This simple definition, however, does not explain pet keeping; for in a deeper sense, a love of animals is rooted in people's basic involvement with

The cat was a sacred animal in Egyptian religion. Top Left. *This bronze figure of a cat representing the goddess Bast, was made about 30 B.C.* Top Right. *Mummified cats, carefully embalmed and wrapped, were sometimes entombed in great numbers along with their owners.*

the natural environment and with their need for companionship. The great pleasure many people derive from the companionship of their pets may supplement or replace human companionship.

The importance of animals in the life of mankind is shown by the prevalence of animal themes in folklore, myth, legend, religion, and the arts, and even in the terms we still use ("a greedy pig," "a clumsy ox," or "he's a pussycat"). Humans have always looked upon animals with a curious mixture of love and fear, of attraction and repulsion. There are the monsters with powers of death, chaos, and evil—the werewolves, vampires, dragons, centaurs, and the minotaur. But there are also animals representing powers of life and of good, such as the Apis bull god of ancient Egypt, the bison and horses of the prehistoric cave paintings, the animal totems of native American Indian tribes, and the beneficent creatures of Aesop's fables and Disney's cartoons. Attitudes toward the same animal have differed from time to time and place to place. While in ancient Egypt the cat was a most sacred animal, in the Middle Ages the cat had a precarious existence, being regarded as an emissary of the devil and the "familiar spirit" of witches; cats were killed, roasted alive, and thrown into bonfires. Even today, some people hold superstitions about black cats.

We owe a great debt to animals, especially to those we have domesticated, many of which have also become our most constant pets; in turn, these animals have made great contributions to human progress. They have been our hunters, guardians, and beasts of burden. Much of history until recent times has been influenced by the animals that people have kept. (See **Working Animals.**)

An even more fundamental service rendered by do-

mestic animals in very early times was the role they played in humanity's crucial transition from nomadic hunting and gathering of food to a settled farming life. The dog was probably most important; with its natural herding instinct, the dog helped its owner to round up herds of wild goats (and then sheep), which provided milk, meat, skin, fat, and bone. The then-tamed animals provided a key motive for human beings to settle in established communities. Once people were settled, there was opportunity to begin the domestication of crop plants. Small patches of grains were grown to supplement hunting and the gathering of food. The next great step in the taming of animals was to subjugate the great wild bovines that were raiding the newly planted fields. Once domesticated, cattle provided meat and milk in greater abundance, with hides for leather and dung for fuel and fertilizer. They also became beasts of burden and began to pull plows and the first crude carts. With the help of animals, people were now set on the path to civilization.

The later history of domestication—how the pig, the horse, the elephant, the donkey, the camel, the cat, fishes, and even insects (e.g., the silkworm moth) were tamed by mankind—does not concern us here. But some of these developments are fascinating. For example, the guinea pig was domesticated by the Incas of Peru as a succulent table dish and the cormorant in Japan and China as an aid in fishing. The Egyptians of the Old Kingdom went through a phase of experimental domestication, trying to tame and utilize all sorts of odd animals—many species of the gazelle, the hyena, the ibex. Of course, many of these animals became pets too.

The long history of pet keeping runs parallel with the story of the domestication of working animals.

10

Both stories are concerned with the development of tame breeds from the original wild stock, and the movement of these breeds from their point of origin around the world. Most farm animals seem to have originated in either Asia or the Middle East; but other parts of the world have made their contribution to both pets and working animals. The guinea pig spread through the Spanish Empire after the conquest of Peru and finally seems to have reached Europe as a pet via West Africa. The peacock, moving west from India, may have graced the famous Hanging Gardens of Babylon and was, it seems, brought to Europe by the Crusaders. From the Middle East came the first long-haired cats; goldfish were imported from China; turkeys originated in the New World. The hamster, discovered in Asia Minor in 1839, was scarcely known until 1930, when it was first bred in captivity. The gerbil from Mongolia has only been kept as a pet in very recent years.

Recorded history and the arts afford only occasional glimpses of animals that can really be called pets. Homer says little about pets, except for Odysseus' famous dog, Argos, who alone recognized him when he returned home from Troy. Another early pet story is about the dog that belonged to Xanthippus, the father of Pericles. Following his beloved master's galley, the dog managed to swim across the Bay of Salamis. The place where he was buried is still known as Cynosema, which means "the dog's grave." Another famous pet in antiquity was Bucephalas, the fierce stallion which Alexander the Great had tamed at the age of twelve, though no one else could do so. Alexander rode Bucephalas for twenty years in all his campaigns; and when the old horse was killed on the borders of India, Alexander founded the town Bucephala in his honor. Traditions say that parrots and parakeets were first brought back to the West by Alexander's armies.

In Egypt, as we have seen, cats were highly regarded. The sacred cats of the popular cat-headed goddess Bast lived in the courtyard of her temple at Bubastis, and their care was a special honor which passed from father to son. Temple and household cats were treated with great respect; they were mummified and buried with honors at death. In the nineteenth century a cache of 300,000 mummified Egyptian cats was discovered; they were ranged tier upon tier in underground tunnels. The Romans imported cats from Egypt and kept a wide range of exotic pets, from monkeys to turtle doves and peacocks.

Charlemagne the Great, ruler of the Franks, fancied exotic animals. Other rulers sent him presents of wild animals. In subsequent centuries, many kings, nobles, and princes assembled menageries of wild animals. The royal collections in France and England eventually became the first two public zoos—but these animals were curiosities, not pets. As sailors and explorers extended Europe's knowledge of the New World, new species were brought back to their homelands to become pets. For instance, when Spanish sailors landed on the Canary Islands in the fifteenth century, the natives taught them how to tame the little birds, known ever since as canaries. Soon there was a lively trade in these birds, reaching Europe, America, and India. Renaissance paintings show pet monkeys on leashes or colorful birds in the background of family portraits.

In Europe, as elsewhere, the dog never lost its place as humankind's favorite animal companion. In medieval France, special breeds of dog were developed for sport hunting. The St. Hubert Hound, for example—ancestor of the packhound breeds of Europe—was

developed in the Abbey of St. Hubert in the Ardennes.

Largely because of the chase, man and dog became inseparable. The hound ate beneath the table, slept in its master's bedchamber, and followed him everywhere. When church officials ordered that no dogs should be taken into church, their owners often stayed outside to hear the Mass; thus the custom developed of giving the blessing outside the church doors. Later, small dogs became popular as household pets. Lapdogs increasingly appear in the pictures, tapestries, and even the stained glass of the later Middle Ages. Mary Queen of Scots (whose lapdog is said to have emerged from beneath her skirts after her beheading) used to dress her pet in a suit of rich blue velvet. Henry II of France had bread especially baked for his dog.

The enormous difference between the smallest lapdog and the largest and most ferocious hound illustrates what drastic changes have taken place in domestic animals through centuries of breeding. The breeding of dogs and pigeons to produce varieties started at least 5,000 years ago, and it appears that breeding for pleasure and fancy, especially among pets, began long before any organized breeding of the larger animals for utility. Zoologists have shown that domestication in itself almost inevitably brings changes in animals—such as shortened skulls, weakened teeth, lengthened tails, and piebald (black and white) coloring.

Since the time of the first domestication, the human community has interfered with the natural process of adaptation, speciation, and selection by selecting the traits in animals that are beneficial to it, rather than those which help animals live in the wild. Thus people

Many pet animals have been domesticated because of their ornamental value. Shown here is an eighteenth-century Indian princess in her garden with peacocks and other birds.

which he could mistreat as he pleased. The first attempts at humane legislation concerned working animals. A measure to protect all beasts of burden from cruel treatment in public places was passed by the English Parliament in 1822. A Society for the Protection of Animals was formed soon afterwards; and when Queen Victoria took an interest in it, this became the present Royal Society for the Prevention of Cruelty to Animals (RSPCA).

Meanwhile in 1866 the American Society for the Prevention of Cruelty to Animals was created; originally based in New York alone, the ASPCA is today active in most major American cities. In 1878 the American Humane Society (which protects both animals and children) was organized as a nationwide body. Many other humane societies followed, together with charitable organizations to provide inexpensive or free medical care for animals whose owners could not afford to pay veterinary fees. These organizations have done much to make people aware of the cruelty that is still inflicted on many animals, and the pain which thoughtlessness can cause.

Organized efforts are now being made to educate the public and encourage humane treatment of pets. Small animals are taken into classrooms where children can get acquainted with them, learn to handle them properly, and develop a sense of responsibility. Some public libraries have special areas where animals can be petted and enjoyed by young visitors. At many amusement parks and state fairs, petting zoos featuring goats and similar animals are made accessible to both young and old animal lovers. For a number of years, the Animal Rescue League of Boston has held an "Animal Friends Summer School" supervised by a state conservation official. At this school on Cape Cod, children are taught to wash dogs and remove ticks from fur, monitor the hatching of duck eggs, handle live snakes, and perform various tasks involving competent pet care. Many museums now have special children's sections with live animals, reptiles and birds, and guides to lecture on the various species, their habits and needs. Zoos are also now being questioned as to adequacy and humane conditions. Although some species adapt to confinement, others (including wolves and animals who roam in natural habitat over wide areas) do not. Game farms in which animals are kept in areas duplicating their habitats and providing more space are becoming increasingly popular among animal lovers.

It is true, of course, that when humans lack contact with nature, they lose concern, which is one very important reason that keeping pets is not just a minor hobby. Not only can the activity be educational, but there is evidence that pets supply an emotional need in people. They fill the hours in the lives of lonely people, giving them a sense of relationship with another living creature. It is also a fact that when pets are brought into a mental institution, the inmates show a marked improvement in their outlook on life. Pets are a challenge and a responsibility which serve to draw humans out of themselves.

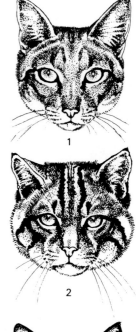

Top Left. *Working animals (horse, dog, falcon) are shown in a painting (dated about* A.D. *1000)*

Top Right. *The facial characteristics of the Domestic Cat have changed little with domestication. (1) African wild cat—probably the primary ancestor. (2) European Wild Cat. (3) Domestic Cat.*

have selected animals that yield more milk, more and better meat, or have better riding qualities. Up to the eighteenth century, breeding techniques were very simple. Man simply identified individual animals showing desirable traits and selected these for further breeding. Later, more sophisticated breeding techniques such as inbreeding were employed; although these had the immediate effect of perserving the desired traits, they also weakened the animals in other respects. More recently, researchers have realized that breeding must be conducted more carefully if people are to conserve the genetic riches of wild animals and old domesticated breeds. These animals contain a pool of variation that will form the basis of future breeding programs, and they must be conserved if human beings are to continue to "adapt" animals to their future needs.

Some scientists have been slow to recognize their responsibility to the animals they have domesticated. The first recorded rules for the care of working animals are found in the Old Testament. Until recent times, common law allowed a man to do what he liked with his "property"—including his family and his animals—

Bottom. *Domestication has had a greater effect on the facial characteristics of dogs than of cats. Predominant changes from (1) the wild ancestor—the wolf—are (2) dropped ears, (3) shorter and rounder forehead, and (4) a shorter muzzle, as in the Border Terrier shown here.*

12

According to the American Humane Association, there are more than fifty million pets owned by Americans. This has spawned businesses involving veterinarians, pet medications, grooming, breeding and training. Another byproduct is the growing number of pet cemeteries. At latest count, there were more than four hundred in the United States. In England, pets are sometimes buried with full ceremonies in graves with headstones.

An unhappy byproduct, however, is the failure of too many pet owners to curb the breeding of unwanted animals. The Humane Association offers the slogan: "If you can afford to keep a pet, you can afford to spay it."

CHOOSING A PET

An animal that you bring into your home may become dependent upon you for life. Before obtaining a pet of any kind you should therefore think hard about why you really want a pet and whether you are prepared to accept the responsibilities that come with having one in the home. Careful thought before you choose an animal will save you much unhappiness and could save the animal's life.

What Kind of Pet

You are free to select any kind of animal you like, but if you are leaning toward a particular species or breed, find out all you can about its needs, its advantages, and drawbacks. And then, perhaps, think again.

If you want a pet for a companion, you will be more interested in animals that can actively share your life. If you are likely to become very emotionally attached to them, you might also check their life expectancy.

Never give a pet to someone as a surprise gift. Giving pets should be restricted to occasions in which the

Remember that caring for a pet can take up a lot of time.

Do not give a pet as a surprise present.

job, you will need at least three hours a day to look after a stable-kept horse; a large dog like an Afghan or a German Shepherd needs at least a three-mile run each day. Remember that you will either have to take an animal with you on your vacations or arrange for its care, unless it is one of the few species that eats very rarely or is in hibernation. (See **Care of Your Pet.**)

Having considered your own needs, the feelings of the rest of the household, and the amount of time you are prepared to put into pet ownership, you can start to think about the pet itself. If you already have animals in the household and would like to acquire more, try to think of how they will react. Some species do not mix well and long-established pets may resent a newcomer on their territory. It may be safe to have both a cat and a caged bird, but a rabbit is not a wise choice for a household with a small dog. If you are obtaining another pet of the same species its sex will be important. In some species competition for mates will impose a pattern of one male to a number of females. In others, neutering may be considered advisable if you do not wish to allow breeding. (See **Breeding and Rearing.**)

recipient has chosen the gift, mindful of the responsibilities involved. Children should not be given pets; seldom is a child able or willing to care for the pet across the months—even years—of any pet's life span. If the child becomes bored, who will care for the animal? When a teenager has to leave home to start a career or go to college, who will be responsible for the pet that he or she leaves behind?

Make sure everyone in the household will welcome a pet before acquiring it. Some people cannot bear mice or snakes or yapping dogs, and they may be allergic to cats. If it is a house-proud home, then think of the havoc some animals can wreak.

Bear in mind the demands which exercising, grooming, and tending even the adult pet will make on your time, not to mention the expense of feeding and caring for it. Unless you intend to have someone else do the

Try to think how new pets will mix with existing ones.

As a general rule females tend to be easier to manage and usually smell better than males.

Another early decision must be whether you want a pet in the domestic sense or whether pets in the natural sense will fill your needs; that is, whether you want to bring an animal into the human environment, or want to alter a small part of that environment so that a wild creature can thrive on its own in a relatively natural setting.

If the choice is for a domestic pet, then it is necessary to consider the human environment carefully in order to discover what types of pet will be compatible. For example, budgerigars and parakeets suit housebound people living alone.

If the choice falls toward pets living in a natural environment, you should make sure that you can provide the space, temperature, shelter, and foodstuffs which will vary enormously from one animal to another—anything from a treehouse for a chickadee to a pond and an acre for a completely natural community. Sometimes these animals need attention from trained specialists so be prepared in advance to deal with such problems. (See also **Wild Animals as Visitors and Pets.**)

CHOOSING FOR THE HOME

There is one absolute requirement in choosing a family pet and that is "only domesticated species for the domestic environment." The interpretation of the term *domesticated* is broad and usually includes all those species which through human intervention have become, to a greater or lesser extent, dependent upon people (such as white mice) and all those species which, although able to survive on their own, have become relaxed in their relationship with humans (such as domestic cats).

PETS FOR CITY DWELLERS

The surroundings of the urban dweller dictate and restrict the selection. Usually the greater the area of land available the greater the diversity of animals from which to choose pets.

In a city, the choice is best made from those species which can live indoors virtually all year around and require a minimal area for exercise. Suitable pets are cats, small dogs, small rodents, small birds, and pets

This appealing and cuddly puppy will soon grow into a large adult, which will need plenty of space to exercise and will eat a lot of food. Any prospective owner must bear in mind these long-term needs.

which can be housed in compact environments such as aquaria and terraria, including fresh and saltwater fish, terrapins, and small snakes.

Of course some people do have large animals in the heart of a city, but keeping them healthy requires a lot of effort on the part of the owners.

OUT IN THE SUBURBS

Although leisure time and money may be no greater than for inner-city dwellers, people in suburban areas usually have more space available and can provide facilities for a wider range of pets needing outdoor runs or room for exercise. Outdoor aviaries, ponds, or rabbit runs become more possible, and larger breeds of dogs are easier to keep in the suburbs. There may be enough garden space to grow fresh foodstuffs for herbivores, and some form of wildlife may be induced to visit or even live in the garden. However, local regulations and consideration for neighbors may prevent you from keeping some species, and few homes will have gardens big enough to provide grass for a horse or other grazing animals.

Fish make ideal pets for town and city dwellers.

Top. The time taken in the maintenance of a healthy aquarium is fully compensated by the contribution the aquarium makes to the decor of any room.

16

PETS IN RURAL AREAS

The advantages of more available space and access to fields greatly increase the ease with which some of the larger animals can be kept, but you should realize that shelter from heat or cold may still be required. In country areas there is also a greater risk from predators, and houses and runs must be made secure against foxes, coyotes, and the like. They must also be secure enough to prevent your pets' escaping and upsetting the local ecology. Gray squirrels, coypu, rabbits, and mink are among the creatures which have had disastrous effects in countries where they were not indigenous.

Horses, ponies, donkeys, and farm animals are obviously much easier to keep in the countryside. Chickens, ducks, and geese can be kept in sufficient quantities for their eggs to be a useful contribution to the household. Working breeds can fulfill their proper function.

Sometimes it may be possible to establish a small breeding colony for a threatened species. By carefully choosing the plants you grow you may be able to attract particular butterflies and moths. You could even obtain eggs of a disappearing species and release them when hatched. If you have land at your disposal, you could organize a small wildlife reserve or, at least, provide environmental conditions which will attract wildlife.

OTHER CONSIDERATIONS

Even if you have carefully matched your choice of animal to the environment you can provide, you may still end up with a pet that is not really compatible with your own personality. If you expect action all the time, a sluggish animal like one of the constrictor snakes may prove boring. If you value peace and quiet, a peacock

"In a city, pets must be able to live happily indoors for most of their lives".

Top. *Cats are ideal pets and playful companions for people living in suburban and country areas where these small animals are less likely to come to harm when wandering alone outdoors.*

Page Center. *Even a single goldfish can be an important household pet.*

Gardens have to be large to keep grazing animals at grass.

17

or a colorful macaw will shatter your tranquillity with its raucous cries. If you are particularly fastidious, make sure that your choice of pet does not entail too much cleaning of its living quarters. If you are of a nervous disposition and want an animal to guard and protect you, do not choose an aggressive breed of dog which you may not be able to control.

Always think what the adult animal will be like since almost all young creatures are irresistible. Remember that unless you know the parentage, a mongrel dog may turn out to be a giant when you thought it was a pigmy. If you find you are attracted to an exotic animal or the pet currently most in fashion, then resist the urge, for you will still be responsible for a living animal when fashions change.

Thousands of animals are turned out as strays each year. They either meet a painful end or have to be destroyed because their owners became bored with them, or they grew too big or they were not cared for while the owners went on vacation. An owner's initial enthusiasm does not guarantee a lifelong house for a pet.

It is a misconception that abandoned dogs and cats can fend nicely for themselves. Sometimes people "dump" them in rural areas near farmhouses, assuming that the animals will be welcome additions to these homes. Or they assume that the dog and cat can live off the land as hunters. The truth is that the animals usually starve to death or die from exposure. At best, the dog may survive to run wild attacking livestock,

Top. *The pleasure gained from riding and owning a horse or pony is greatest in a rural environment where the horse will also get the best feed and all the space and exercise it needs.*

Resist the urge to buy pets that are just fashionable.

ACQUIRING A PET

There are occasions when we do not choose a pet at all but are adopted by a stray, or we are given a pet by someone who has bred more young animals than can be kept. In both cases the urge to keep the animal should be resisted until you have come to terms with the responsibilities involved. If you are being given a pet, you have a much greater chance of knowing its background and the conditions in which it has been bred and reared than when you obtain an animal from an unknown source. However, familiarity with the donor should not prevent you from making the same appraisal of the animal as you would if purchasing it.

and sometimes even people. It is kinder to have a pet put to death humanely by a veterinarian if no other home can be found, but if the animal is reasonably healthy, the owner can usually find it a good home. Most veterinarians encourage notices of pet "giveaways" on bulletin boards in their clinics. This is an excellent method because people who utilize services of veterinarians are pet lovers.

Most communities also have humane shelters where persons can adopt the pet of their choice for a small fee. Unfortunately, not all the animals will be adopted, and some city pounds serve merely as temporary quarters for the unwanted animals who will be killed. An even better solution is for the owner of a pet to have the animal spayed or neutered so that unwanted offspring will not be born.

Take a careful look at a pet shop before buying from it.

18

Top. *Apart from their obvious beauty, butterflies and moths, such as these Giant Atlas Silk Moths, have a short generation time and require no extra attention when young or old.*

PET SHOPS

There are extremely good pet shops from which to choose your pet, but unfortunately these are not in the majority. In most countries there is rarely any control over who can run a pet shop or the condition in which animals for sale are kept, beyond the protection offered by laws against cruelty to animals. Take a careful look at the shop before buying from it. Does it seem well run and hygienic? It is all too easy for a pet shop to become a focal point of disease. Do the animals appear confident and happy in their surroundings?

Even in the best run shops a cage or section of the window does not provide a suitable environment for a puppy or kitten. Some dealers will therefore arrange an introduction to a breeder or for a particular breed to be brought in especially for inspection. For birds, fishes and small animals which spend their lives in cages, shop housing does not create such hardship. Indeed you will often find specialty stores for birds and aquarium fishes.

Be aware that in the United States many species of animals are protected by law and are not to be sold as pets. If you have any doubts about an animal's legal availability on the market, contact your local authorities. These laws vary from area to area. Pet shops often sell chicks, ducklings, and goslings during the Easter season (although some states now ban this). Buying these creatures is unwise because small children often abuse and abandon them.

Bottom. *It is always best to buy a pet from a specialized breeder or establishment, such as this pet market stall which obviously specializes in cage birds. However, always carefully check any prospective pet to make sure it appears healthy.*

BREEDERS

Buying from a knowledgeable breeder is usually the best way to acquire a pet. You may be able to find advertisements in pet journals or in your local paper. If you visit shows, you can see the animals and meet the breeders. Sometimes the animals will be for sale and the potential of a breeder's stock can be assessed on the spot from his exhibits. If possible, visit the breeder's establishment and apply the same criteria as you would to a shop. Notice the way in which the breeder treats the animals and try to judge their temperaments.

CONDITION

As a general rule animals should look bright-eyed and clean. If you do not want to be saddled with a lot of worry and a pile of veterinarian's bills, leave sentiment behind and resist the appeal of the pathetic loner in the corner of a cage or the weakling of a litter. Choose a healthy strong animal. Do not look for bargains: the little you save could soon be eaten up by medical bills.

If you are not sure whether an animal is healthy, ask for an inspection by a veterinarian before your purchase. If the dealer refuses to comply with this request, then you should go elsewhere. Do not, however, take any pet on a trial basis. After a day or so you may find yourself emotionally committed, even though your better judgment tells you that you have made a mistake.

More detailed information on what to look for when choosing a particular species is given in the following chapters on the various kinds of pets.

HOW OLD AN ANIMAL?

Most people like to acquire a pet when it is very young so they can have the pleasure of seeing it grow and of influencing its development. With species that start wholly independent, such as insects and tortoises, it does not matter how young the animal is when you acquire it—indeed you could start by incubating the egg. But mammals and others which need parental care should not be taken from their mother until they are fully weaned and able to feed themselves. Breeders will often have their own opinion about when a pet should go to its new home and will insist on keeping it until it has reached that stage.

Do not, however, believe that a young animal is the only possible choice. Animals with long life expectancy, such as turtles and parrots, may well be older than you are when you acquire them. Working animals may be preferable if they are old enough to be fully trained. Many legitimate reasons may arise to prevent an owner's keeping an animal and leave it in need of a new home. If you like the animal and find it has no habits which make it unsuitable, you will probably soon feel it has always been yours.

National animal organizations will give information on how to obtain a pet that is no longer wanted by its owner. An adult animal from one of the humane shelters will be a stranger to you, and its previous treatment may have produced defects in behavior. On the other hand you will have the advantage of judging the mature animal, and with care and affection its behavior may improve. Some people are happier if they adopt a fully grown pet and avoid the strain of a boisterous youngster. Moreover, most mature dogs and cats have already been housetrained, are less susceptible to diseases, are easier to feed, and require less attention.

CARE OF YOUR PET

All pets are kept to some extent under artificial conditions and are dependent upon their owners for food, congenial surroundings, and protection. The degree of their dependence is related to the differences between their natural habitat and the environment provided by the owner, as well as the difference between the domesticated type and the wild animal. A pet living within its natural climatic range requires only the shelter it would seek in the wild, but an exotic animal calls for the creation of a mini-environment with the correct temperature and humidity. A domesticated animal can rarely obtain for itself all the food it needs, and in many cases it must be taught to accept alternatives to its natural diet. (See **Feeding Your Pet.**)

The artificial selection of domestic animals often results in coats that make additional grooming necessary. Some animals which relied on the mutual grooming of others in their natural habitat may also need grooming in captivity and if housed alone. To avoid smells and messes, toilet training and facilities are important. Control of mating and reproduction may be necessary if you do not want to be overrun by an increasing population.

This chapter deals primarily with the general needs of those mammals most often kept as household pets. The specific requirements of individual species and of birds, fishes, reptiles, amphibians, and insects are dealt with under their individual sections in **Pets of Every Kind.**

Introducing a Pet to its New Home

Before introducing a pet to its new home, you should have already prepared housing and bedding, obtained food, bowls for food and water, and everything necessary for grooming and exercise. Animals which have been brought up with people, or which are being separated from their mother and litter mates, should be introduced to their new surroundings at a time when you can give them plenty of attention. Faced with a strange new world, all creatures will be happier if they are able to adjust to it calmly. Avoid loud or sudden noise, too many people around, and excessive handling. If the journey to your home has taken some time, it often helps to place the animal's traveling container within its new housing arrangement. In the case of an uncaged animal, leave the container freely available. The pet will already be familiar with the container and, however much it was resented while traveling, it will be impregnated with the animal's smell and may seem the safest spot in alien territory.

A tempting meal, its usual sleeping basket, or favorite toys will reduce the distress of change for an adult dog or cat. With a puppy or kitten, plenty of affection from you and its own inquisitive interest in new things will probably keep it happy until nighttime comes, and it suddenly realizes that its mother and litter mates are not there. What you do at this point must be the same as what you intend to do in the future. Some owners may feel that the youngster must be shut up in the

Top. *"When introducing a new pet to the home allow the newcomer and established pets to sort out their own relationships."*

Bottom. *Many domesticated pets, such as this Chinchilla rabbit, require a lot of grooming if their artificially long coats are to remain in good condition.*

kitchen, or wherever its sleeping place is to be, and left there alone no matter how plaintive or loud it cries. Having made this decision, any lack of resolution, such as creeping out of bed to comfort the animal, will show it how to get its own way. On the other hand, some owners may be pleased to have a puppy curled up on their bed or a kitten pushing a wet nose under the sheets and snuggling up against a substitute mother. Choose the approach which you intend to stick by. Of course, if you take two or more pets from the same litter the problem will be reduced with their having each other's company. If you already have established pets, they may also be prepared to take charge of the newcomer.

MEETING ESTABLISHED PETS

In some species, such as gerbils, the male will not tolerate the presence of another male in its territory, and consequently they should not be placed in the same housing. Most established household pets will be possessive about their territory, even when the newcomer is a female. Often a token fight will take place to establish dominance between the animals. If the new pet is a young animal, it will usually make signs of submission and all will be well.

Do not make a great fuss over the new pet at the expense of the established animal, and do not place either under restraint or you may increase the initial antagonism. It is usually wise to be present at this first meeting until both animals have had a chance to sniff at each other and become acquainted. Sometimes the established animal seems frightened even if the new pet shows submission. You should leave the animals alone

since your presence will intimidate their natural responses. It is rare for one animal to seriously injure another in this situation, although the noises they make may sound like a bloodbath! Dogs and cats will often welcome a new playfellow but still want to retain such rights as sleeping on the bed or the attentions of a particular member of the family. Older cats can be helped to accept new kittens by rubbing a little urine or used litter from the cat's dirt tray onto the kitten's fur. By impregnating the newcomer in this way the established cat will identify the kitten as its own and make itself responsible for the younger animal. If the older cat is already well trained, it will probably teach the youngster the rules of the house.

Introductions between species

Animals of different species which are natural enemies in the wild will often curl up together happily if they have been brought up together. But this should not give you the idea that such animals can be easily mixed. Carnivorous fishes may regard any newcomers, even those of the same species, as a tasty meal. Similarly, dogs and cats will instinctively chase small rodents that run away and may look upon them as prey.

ACCLIMATIZATION

Animals brought from a different climate must be provided with conditions as close as possible to those from which they have come and should be exposed gradually to local conditions. This applies particularly to birds and reptiles, such as terrapins, taken from a tropical to a temperate climate, and vice versa.

Speaking generally every pet has to make some

Quite different species, even those that are natural enemies such as this kitten and guinea pig, can establish a friendly relationship in the domestic environment raised together.

adaptation unless you intend to keep it in exactly the same way as its previous owner did. When you buy an animal, find out exactly how it has been fed and treated and follow this pattern at first to reduce the stress of changes for the animal. Gradually introduce any alterations of diet and timetable. Some species, which only eat live food in the wild or have diets which cannot be provided in captivity, must be coaxed into accepting a substitute. This applies particularly to some birds and reptiles, and the process is known as meating-off.

General Care

ROUTINE

Almost all pets, especially cats and dogs, prefer a regular pattern in their daily lives. Regular times should be established for meals, exercise, grooming, and games. If your cat or dog is allowed out on its own, or your cage pet is given an exercise period outside its cage, it is wise to establish a mealtime as the time when it must return. If an animal knows that it can expect certain things at certain times, it will return happily and you will not be pestered for food or attention. If you always give food in the same place, there is less chance of its being dragged all over the cage or home.

GROOMING

All furred animals benefit from grooming. Frequency of grooming will depend on the coat of the individual animal. The grooming of dogs and cats that are allowed outdoors will be also determined by the mud, dust, and burrs they have collected. Bathing is rarely necessary

If you follow a number of simple rules your pet will remain healthy, and a healthy pet is a happy pet. (1) Pets need plenty of exercise. (2) A fat pet is not a healthy pet; do not overfeed. (3) Long-haired breeds need plenty of grooming. (4) In old age pets deserve more care and attention. (5) A healthy mouth denotes a healthy animal; dental care is vital in many pets. (6) Establish a relationship with a veterinarian before problems arise.

for cats and rodents, but dogs sometimes become dirty enough to need shampooing. Some birds benefit from being sprayed with water, and most require either water or dust baths in their quarters.

Breeds with unnaturally long hair have been developed among dogs, cats, goats, hamsters, guinea pigs, and rabbits. These animals cannot groom themselves effectively and require regular attention from their owners. With pets that have the run of the house regular grooming is to the owner's advantage since it reduces the amount of hair being shed on carpets and furniture. Most furred animals molt to decrease the thickness of the coat during warmer seasons when the lengthening days act as a natural "trigger mechanism," but house pets exposed to an even amount of daylight throughout most of the year will shed fairly constantly, with extra loss at the seasonable periods.

With most mammalian species grooming is a relatively simple procedure demanding no special skill. The grooming of a horse is somewhat more complex and is dealt with separately in the chapter on **Horses and Ponies**. It is traditional for certain dog breeds to be clipped and groomed to particular patterns which set off the features preferred in show competition. (See **Dogs**.) However, such treatment is not actually necessary for the well-being of the dog, except when a hot climate makes a heavy coat uncomfortable.

Simple Grooming Techniques

To avoid a mess, groom your pet on a table covered with newspaper. Dead hair can be loosened by massaging the animal's skin with your fingers and much of it may then be removed by stroking from head to tail with the palm of your hand. Dogs and cats enjoy a vigorous brushing and combing. This process also removes dust

and dirt from the coat, reduces the risk of fleas and skin parasites and, in the case of short-haired dogs, minimizes the need for bathing. For animals such as the guinea pig, gentle blowing on the coat against the lie of the hair may be all the grooming that is required.

The stiffness of the brush should be matched to the animal's coat. There are a wide variety of brushes and combs suited to long- and short-haired dogs and care should be taken that the different breeds are treated appropriately. For example, a pin wire brush is most suitable for breeds such as poodles, the Afghan, and Pekingese whereas a dandy brush is best for gundogs. Gloves made from a variety of materials are commonly used in grooming animals with really short coats, and chamois leathers can be used to finish the coat. A velvet pad is sometimes used to give a final sheen to the coat of cats. Also there are special combs and brushes for cats, whose coats need gentler treatment than dogs' coats. Keep all brushes, combs, gloves, and other tools clean and disinfected.

The feet also need care and grooming. Excess hair between a dog's toes and between the foot pads collects dirt and should be cut away. Cats too sometimes collect dirt and sticky substances on their pads that they cannot wash off. Claws and nails should be checked for splits and trimmed if necessary. Be sure to inspect ears for mites, clean their eyes, and look for any general indication of ill health. (See also **Ailments Charts, Glossary of Ailments.**)

When cutting a cat's claws, use a strong pair of nail clippers, not scissors. Be very careful to avoid cutting

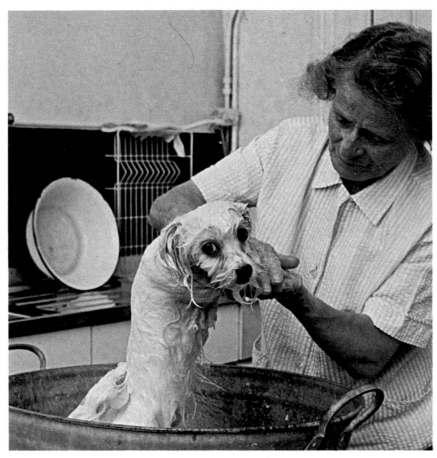

into the quick—the live part of the claw. You will be able to see the blood vessels of the claws clearly in good light and thus can judge how much to trim.

Some species of birds also require occasional trimming of their claws, but it is more difficult to see the blood vessels and not cut into the quick. Since a bird has proportionally much less blood, a bleeding claw can lead to a serious loss.

DENTAL CARE

It is essential that the teeth of carnivorous animals be kept as healthy as possible. A sensible diet without

Top. *Bathing is an important part of a dog's routine, more so if it is a show animal. White breeds, such as this Maltese, quickly show the dirt.*

Bottom. *Important equipment for the care of cats and dogs. (1) and (2) Plastic feeding bowls for cats. (3) and (4) Plastic feeding bowls for dogs. (5) Glazed pottery feeding bowls. (6) Cat scratching post. (7) Plastic litter tray. (8) Two-grade comb (coarse/fine). (9) Medium wooden-handled comb. (10) Double-sided brush. (11) Slicker brush. (12) Oval brush with strap.*

Center Left. *The claws of cage birds need to be cut periodically—a task that must be left to a veterinarian or to an experienced owner since it is easy to damage the claws.*

many unnatural sweet tidbits will help, but most carnivores develop a deposit of tartar on their teeth as they get old.

Teething can sometimes cause problems in puppies when the permanent teeth do not erupt through the sockets holding the milk teeth and therefore do not push them out. A double row of teeth results, and the milk teeth have to be extracted. Sickness during the teething period can lead to faulty development of the tooth enamel, so great care should be taken to maintain good health at this time. Cats rarely have this problem and often the milk teeth are swallowed without the owner's being aware of the process.

In dogs of about two years of age and cats of about three years, a buildup of tartar can lead to gingivitis and bad breath with subsequent deterioration of the teeth. Tartar can be removed with a clean fingernail during normal grooming, but if it develops as a hard crust which does not come off easily, the teeth should be scaled by a veterinarian in the same way that dentists treat human teeth. In dogs this requires some restraint or even an anesthetic.

Herbivores like rabbits and hamsters have long incisor teeth that are naturally kept short by the wearing down action of gnawing. Some, however, grow too long and the animal has trouble eating. It may paw at its mouth or rub its face against the side of the cage. A veterinarian can relieve the condition in minutes by carefully snipping off the overgrowth. Because there are no nerves in these extended tips, the cutting is usually done without an anesthetic.

Many elderly sheep and some very old goats lose so many teeth that they simply cannot survive on their normal rough diets. Some veterinarians advise substitute diets which require no mastication. In the case of valuable breeding stock or pets, stainless steel false teeth are sometimes implanted. The majority of sheep and cattle, however, have their lives cut short well before they develop geriatric dental problems.

Top. Many dogs and cats suffer from a buildup of tartar on the teeth. Periodic inspection and descaling by a veterinarian is important in older animals.

The molar teeth of horses may wear unevenly. The sharp irritating edges which usually result are injurious to the delicate linings of the mouth. Proper grinding of foodstuff is impossible. The horse may pass entire undigested grain kernels in its droppings and show signs of poor condition. The veterinarian uses a long instrument that looks like a wood file (called a float) or rasp to smooth the rough edges away. He will give the owner an idea of when the horse should be treated again; individual horses vary considerably in this respect.

It must be emphasized that this is merely an outline of common dental problems. Animals can, and do, get as wide an array of tooth problems as we do and these problems can be just as painful. It is the owner's responsibility to recognize the problem and arrange veterinary attention as soon as possible.

A range of collars and leashes for dogs and cats: (1) Cat collar with elastic insert. (2) Puppy/cat harness and collar. (3) Puppy collar and leash. (4) Leather dog harness. (5) Plaited leather leash. (6) Round collar. (7) Studded flat leather collar. (8) Plaited flat leather collar. (9) Welded chrome leash. (10) Welded chrome choke leash. (11) Kennel chain. (12) Leather hand loop. (13) Nylon braid leash. (14) Cord slip leash. (15) Chain end leash. (16) Check chain.

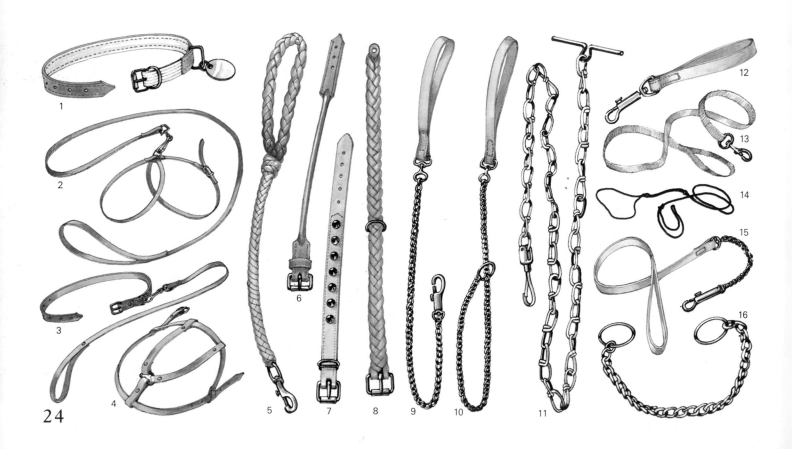

24

Inspection of a pet's mouth at grooming time is a good way of checking on the general state of health, for a healthy mouth usually denotes a healthy animal. While handling the animal during grooming, the owner should also clean the eyes, check for mites in the ears or for any unusual lumps or swellings which may indicate physiological disorders. (See also **Ailments Charts, Glossary of Ailments**.)

EXERCISE

When an animal is not using energy to obtain food, it needs exercise to keep fit. Dogs enjoy long walks and, depending on the breed, require a considerable amount of exercise. Dogs of the same breed may vary in their exercise needs but, generally speaking, small toy dogs may get enough exercise running around the house. On the other hand, larger dogs should start with approximately twenty minutes of road walk each day at about four months of age and increase to thirty or more minutes by the age of six months. Road exercise is important in hardening the pads of the feet, strengthening the toes and keeping the nails short. Dogs of the hunting and coursing breeds need a lot of exercise, but the average adult house dog needs two good walks a day.

If the dog can be safely exercised off its leash it will cover a much greater distance with less wear on the owner. Ball games and stick retrieving help the lazy owner keep a dog fit, but some dogs develop an enthusiasm for these games which is difficult to stifle.

Stabled horses need one to one-and-a-half hours of exercise each day, although most will benefit from one day of rest each week. On the day following a hard day's hunting or other heavy riding, a short quiet walk to ease stiff muscles is generally all that is needed.

Cats will usually take the right amount of exercise on their own, provided that they are not overfed. An overweight animal finds that exercise requires more effort and therefore puts on even more weight until a serious obesity problem develops. This problem is seen in many domestic pets, and the owners are usually to blame. A lean and lively animal is a healthy animal—keep your pet that way. (See **Feeding Your Pet**.)

With many pets, exercise depends upon having enough space in the run or cage, although mice and gerbils also seem to enjoy running around inside exercise wheels.

VETERINARIAN ATTENTION

Choosing a veterinarian is very much a matter of proximity, recommendation, and your own reaction to his or her personality. It is worthwhile to determine first of all that the veterinary practice is experienced in the species you intend to keep. Make a note of the veterinarian's name, address, telephone number, and office hours, and keep it by the telephone or where you keep your pet's medical supplies. You should also start a record card for the animal, recording, if known, its date of birth and its medical history. This will prove invaluable not only in providing information in case of sickness but as a reminder of when vaccinations are due, or of the pattern of estrus in mammals.

Vaccination can give protection against dangerous diseases in many animals. Frequency of vaccination, and the preferred age for innoculation will vary according to the vaccine used and the individual veterinary practice. The accompanying table is a guide to the main diseases requiring vaccination. Also check with

Top. *Most pets need daily exercise to keep them healthy. For hamsters this can be achieved by having a play wheel in the cage, which also helps prevent boredom.*

your veterinarian about any localized diseases within your district against which protection should be given.

Travel and Vacations

TRAVELING WITH PETS

Well-disciplined dogs can safely be taken on public transportation (provided it is authorized). Small or dangerous pets must be kept in an escape-proof box or carrier, but larger, obedient pets, such as dogs can be kept on a leash. Never risk letting an animal run uncontrolled. Even in a private automobile such restraint is advisable, particularly if the pet's only companion is the driver. Some sudden distraction or escape through a window can have dangerous consequences for occupants of the car and the pet. Some dogs will sleep

Bottom. *If you have to leave a dog in an automobile, always make sure that the car is in a shaded spot and leave a window partly open. Remember heat stroke can kill!*

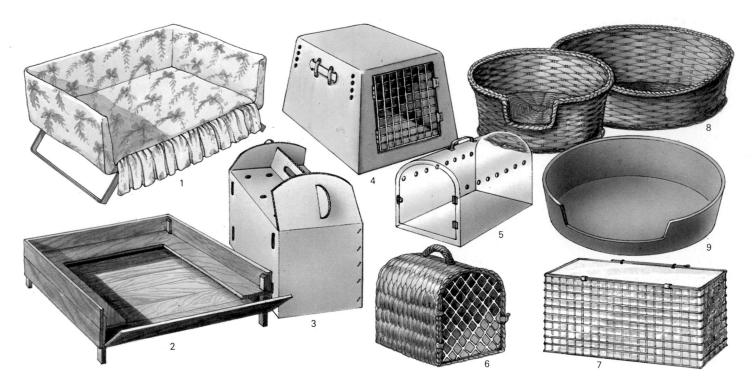

happily in a car while their owner is visiting or shopping. Your host or other shoppers may well prefer this, but it is often better to leave the dog at home. If you do leave an animal in an automobile, make sure that it has plenty of ventilation. Do not leave the car in sunshine where it will rapidly turn into an oven, and remember that shady places do not stay that way long. Heat stroke is extremely serious and often fatal.

EXCURSIONS AND VACATIONS

Most species suffer to some degree by being moved from one place to another, and it is better to have them cared for at home. On the other hand many pets feel disturbed at being separated from their owners. Most dogs, many cats, and sometimes animals of other species become more closely involved with people than with places.

Traveling cages for small animals should be a complete environment in themselves. Provided there are no loose fittings which could harm the animal, the normal housing may serve for transportation by automobile. For cats and small dogs, rabbits, and similar mammals there is a wide choice of carriers available. The traditional wicker-type basket is popular but difficult to disinfect in case of illness. Cages constructed of plastic coated wire are most hygienic for traveling by automobile, but they are not suitable for carrying in bad weather.

It is usually easier to get an animal in and out of a carrier with a top opening, but a front-opening type gives a better view of the animal and allows it to feel more involved in the situation. For short journeys perhaps the most preferable container is one which enables the pet to see what is happening outside in order to maintain its interest. However, on a long journey with a sick pet, or with some shy animals, it is better to have a well-ventilated container without windows so that the pet is in a darkened atmosphere and is encouraged to sleep. One useful type has a wire-covered window at one end with a flap that can be rolled up or pulled down like a blind.

Some animals, especially dogs, suffer from travel sickness. If you know that your pet is likely to be travel sick, do not feed it before the trip. Puppies and dogs need an eight-hour lapse between feeding and travel. Young puppies which are fed immediately on arrival home after a short trip begin actually to look forward to going in the car. In the case of a long journey, and with animals that do not overcome this problem, tranquilizers may be helpful but they should not be given without a veterinarian's approval. Sometimes a light chain attached to the rear axle of the automobile and allowed to drag on the roadway will prevent a buildup of static electricity which is thought to be one of the causes of travel sickness.

It is not a good idea to take your pet on vacation if you are going to leave it shut up in a hotel room. Your pet deserves at least as much freedom and attention as at home.

LEAVING PETS AT HOME

Ideally, you should ask someone your pet already knows to stay in the house when you are away. But whatever the arrangement it is important that the pet's routine be maintained as closely as possible. Sometimes even then a pet may sulk for a few days before making the best of the situation!

Careful instructions should be given on what and when to feed your pet, on how much exercise it requires and what kind of games, grooming, and special attention it is used to. A pet accustomed to a lot of personal attention will be much happier if the person providing care does not merely come in and put down food, change the litter, and perform other similar chores, but also spends time with it and plays its favorite games. Most important of all, make sure that you give the person your veterinarian's address, telephone number, opening hours, and some means of contacting you in case of an emergency. You should also warn against over feeding and spoiling an animal. After two weeks of overindulgence it may take many more weeks to reestablish proper discipline and a healthy weight.

A range of baskets and transport carriers for dogs and cats: (1) Luxury metal-framed dog basket. (2) Wooden whelping box for dogs. (3) Cardboard transport box useful for all small animals. (4) Air transport dog box. (5) Transparent plastic transport cage for small dogs and cats. (6) Side-opening wickerwork transport basket for cats. (7) Top-opening wire mesh transport cage for cats. (8) Wickerwork dog sleeping baskets. (9) Plastic sleeping basket for dogs.

BOARDING PETS OUT

There are many boarding establishments which provide care and accommodation for horses, dogs, and cats. If you do not know any, a veterinarian, breeder, or pet shop may be able to recommend one. Exotic pets cause greater problems, and this is a factor which should be kept in mind before obtaining such animals.

In many countries boarding kennels and stables have to be licensed and must maintain certain standards to keep the license, but routine inspection is rarely frequent or thorough enough to ensure that badly run establishments do not exist. Never leave your animal at a kennel without inspecting it yourself. Owners of a good establishment will be glad to show you around and will be concerned about the health and vaccination certificates of your pet. Some establishments provide special separate facilities for sick animals. Look for

cleanliness and efficiency in both premises and staff; make sure that the accommodation is light, well ventilated but free from drafts, dry, heated adequately and safely, and gives the animal sufficient space—preferably with an outdoor run. The feeding dishes should be clean, and each animal should have its own drinking bowl filled with clean water. Animals should be separated as much as possible, with space between each run or kennel. Provided there is a solid partition between them, alternating cats and dogs is sometimes a safeguard against the spread of disease.

Make sure that your pet has all its inoculations in good time before being boarded. If you have several pets of the same species, arrange for them to be

Always make proper arrangements for your pets when you are away on vacations. Top Left. *Cats can be left at home so long as someone calls in daily to look after their needs.* Center. *The best solution, however, is to place them in a well-run boarding cattery, particularly if you have an expensive purebred that cannot be left to roam.*

Bottom. *If you cannot take your dog away with you on vacations, it is best boarded out at good kennels where it will be cared for properly. Always check the kennels carefully before leaving your pet there.*

boarded together. They will be happier with their friends, and most places have facilities for shared pens. Take along a favorite cushion or a special toy. If your pet has a special diet for medical reasons, explain this in detail along with any other peculiarities it may have.

Pets that are kept in the house all the time and have no contact with other animals are more likely to become ill when boarded, since they have not had the opportunity of building up resistance to disease. If an older pet has never been boarded, make some other arrangements for its care. An animal that has been boarded regularly in younger years will know what to expect and probably will have some resistance to infection. Remember that in the older animal disease can be more serious.

TRAVELING LONG DISTANCE

Regulations and facilities for transporting animals vary from country to country and from one railroad or airline to another and should be carefully investigated before a pet is subjected to a journey alone.

Special horse boxes and cattle trucks are made for taking large animals long distances, and stalls are usually provided for railroad, sea, and air transportation. In many countries transportation accommodation must meet strict legal requirements, both for safety and the animal's well-being. For the transportation of large animals, the services of specialized shipping agents should be used. Unaccompanied small animals must be housed in strong crates clearly labelled with the name, address, and telephone number of both sender and receiver so that either can be contacted rapidly in case of emergency. Facilities must be included in the crate for food, water, and toilet area and, if possible, arrangements should be made for the animal to be exercised. Animals traveling in the hold of an aircraft suffer enormous changes of temperature and pressure which few species can tolerate. Even small animals need plenty of space to ensure an adequate

oxygen supply and room to stretch their limbs.

Most of the states of the United States, most provinces of Canada, and many other countries require health and vaccination certificates before an animal can be transported across borders. Great Britain requires that animals be placed in quarantine on arrival for six months to reduce the risk of rabies and other diseases. (See **Pets and the Law.**) Six months of confinement is harsh treatment for any pet, and animals often pine and die in such circumstances. Certificates of origin and health and export licenses may take some time to obtain, so plan any journey to another country well in advance.

Caring for Aged Animals

As animals reach old age they become more prone to physical disorders and more vulnerable to disease. The decline will not be so noticeable in species with short life spans; you may hardly notice a mouse or a gerbil living at a slower pace. You will be able to observe, however, that a dog can no longer run so fast or walk so far without showing strain, that a horse tires more quickly and that a cat loses its liveliness. There will also be obvious physical signs of aging in many species such as gray hairs and a less compact shape. Sight and hearing may begin to fail.

Horses should be retired from active work to enjoy the leisure they have earned during their working life. Dogs and cats deserve patience and consideration if, in their later years, they sometimes become incontinent or need more care. Since aging animals usually exercise less but continue to enjoy their food, obesity is a common problem. Kidney conditions, arthritis, heart diseases and tumors are all more likely to occur in the older animal. Fleas can be more troublesome, and eczema and other skin conditions are more persistent, especially if caused by parasites. Dogs often suffer gum diseases. If teeth are lost, chopped and mushy food

Perhaps this retirement home for horses and ponies is a luxury few owners can afford, but all animals deserve extra care, attention, and consideration in old age.

should be given to them. Cataracts and glaucoma can sometimes be treated, but blindness and deafness are usually the result of a gradual deterioration. Yet a blind animal may be perfectly happy and able to find its way about if no major changes are made in its living conditions. Blind and deaf pets should not be allowed out on their own for they are extremely vulnerable to attack and accident. Do not subject an elderly pet to unnecessary strain. Children should not be allowed to tease it or encourage it to tax its energy.

Elderly animals should be given regular checkups at least every six months. The records of the animal kept by you and the veterinarian will be extremely valuable in showing what stresses and diseases it has experienced, and this information will help warn of any danger areas. Your veterinarian may recommend changes in diet, vitamin and other supplements, or even hormone injections for some geriatric conditions.

Extra care should be taken over grooming since the older animal needs more help. Above all, you should handle your pet with patience and consideration.

EUTHANASIA

All animals derserve the chance to live out their natural lives as long as they are not in pain or distress. Although many simply go to sleep and do not wake up, there often comes a time when an owner must make the decision that the animal's suffering has become too great. Your veterinarian will give you advice about the animal's condition, but the decision is yours. Do not pass a death sentence simply because you cannot be bothered to care for an aging and difficult pet, nor should you condemn a creature to prolonged agony because you cannot bear to lose it. (See also **Pets and the Law**.)

29

YOUR PET'S BEHAVIOR

There are three main preoccupations in life for all wild animals: to breed, to eat, and to avoid being eaten. By domesticating animals we have done little to reduce the first two instincts, but we have almost entirely removed the third.

An artificial system of selection imposed by human beings has also resulted in an alteration of many of the characteristics found in wild animals. With many centuries of domestication, an animal's sense organs have become dulled and its defensive weapons weakened. Horns and teeth of domestic animals are smaller and weaker than those in the wild species, and the pricked ear, which can be turned in the direction of the source of any noise, has been lost in many domestic animals, notably in certain breeds of dog.

Sometimes exaggerated species have been bred in which the ability to move has been greatly reduced, as in tumbler pigeons, creeping hens, and the Ragdoll cats bred in the late 1960s in the United States. In the wild, these animals would not survive infancy. Many characteristics considered endearing to humans have been bred into dogs, especially the toy breeds. The shortened face and high domed forehead found in such breeds as the Chihuahua, the Pekingese, the Pug, and Bulldog are typical examples. Although highly desir-

able for show purposes, the breeding of such characteristics often affects the health of the animal. On the other hand, artifical selection has often increased the efficiency of certain bodily organs, such as the Bloodhound's super sense of smell. Selective breeding has also emphasized a certain propensity such as the German Shepherd's ease in training for guiding the blind and for police work. Although the household pet may look far removed from its wild counterpart, the differences are more superficial than real. The inherited reactions of millennia are stronger in animals than the conditioning of life with humans. In order to understand your pet, it is useful to know that instinctive behavior, however deeply submerged, will sometimes surface, paticularly during stress. Sometimes knowing what kinds of behavior you might expect from your pet will enable you to handle an unforeseen situation.

Bottom Left. *In the wild, animals have many means of protection from predators. Even though this fawn was born in captivity it retains its instinct to remain motionless while camouflaged in undergrowth until its mother returns.*

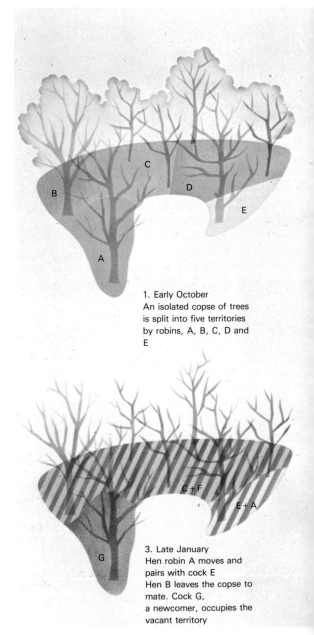

1. Early October
An isolated copse of trees is split into five territories by robins, A, B, C, D and E

3. Late January
Hen robin A moves and pairs with cock E Hen B leaves the copse to mate. Cock G, a newcomer, occupies the vacant territory

Means of Protection

Some animals depend on camouflage to hide from their prey or their predator. Although natural colors and patterns have been lost in domestic breeds and pets are kept in artificial settings which minimize the usefulness of their camouflage, you have only to try to spot a tabby cat in the evening light, which is its natural time for hunting, to realize how effective its disguise can be. An animal exhibiting the ability to camouflage itself is the chameleon which can readily adapt its color.

Extreme fear causes many animals to suffer a kind of paralysis, or an inability to move, known as akinesis. This "freezing" is sometimes seen in mice and birds cornered by a cat. It has survival value for these animals because a cat's eyes can best see moving objects. If the prey remains still long enough, the cat will get bored with the search, lose sight of its prey, and move away. Paralysis can also be seen in other domestic animals such as the rabbit. Fear can sometimes bring about urination as a nervous reaction, as in dogs, cats, and monkeys.

Territorial Behavior

In the wild most animals have specific territories in which they spend most of their lives. Their reactions to intruders depend on whether the intruder is a human, another species, or a member of the same species.

FLIGHT DISTANCE

Most animals have an escape or flight distance which they maintain between themselves and human beings for protection. Invading this area of separation will trigger the animal's flight reaction, and it will run away. Since some species are more efficient at escaping than others, each has its own specific flight distance. Generally speaking, small animals have a shorter escape distance than larger animals, and birds a shorter one than mammals. If you go out on a country walk, wild birds, mice or lizards will allow you to approach fairly near, whereas a rabbit sensing you on the other side of the field, will make for cover. You will rarely even catch a glimpse of a deer.

The length of the flight distance depends on the

TERRITORIAL BEHAVIOR

Like other songbirds, the European robin has strong territorial instincts. In autumn each cock robin establishes its territory and drives out other robins that enter it; some hens also hold territories. The birds sing to inform other robins that the territory is occupied. In late December and early January, pairing begins. Resident hens move to share the territories of their mates. New hens also enter the district from outside. About mid-march, the hen builds a nest. Mating takes place and eggs are laid.

The diagram shows the territorial behavior of a group of robins in South Devon, England and is based on a study by David Black.

2. Late December
Cock robin C drives out D from his territory and pairs up with a newcomer, F

4. March
Cock E is killed by a cat. His mate, A, moves back to her old territory and pairs with G. The pair C and F expand into the vacant territory

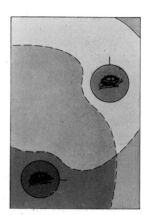

Territorial behavior is admirably demonstrated in the European Robin.

Parts of a home range may be occupied by two or more members of a species, whereas a territory is defended against others of the same species.

31

environment as well as the species. Thus the European Robin, which in Great Britain is a friendly garden bird, is wild and very shy of people in the Continental countries where it is killed for food. The flight distance becomes shorter if the danger is reduced. On certain islands where there are no predators, the native animals have no flight reaction and are fearless of humans. This is what made the Dodo such an easy prey for sailors visiting the island of Mauritius.

By domesticating animals we have reduced and finally eliminated their flight distance altogether, and as a consequence we can touch and handle our pets. However, the domestic animal is not entirely free from flight reaction. In spite of the blinders, bridles, and bits that have been invented, a horse will still bolt if a sudden noise or unexpected movement triggers its flight reaction. Even a pet cat or dog will flee from sudden and unusual noises such as a gun shot or fireworks, or from an unexpected movement.

CRITICAL DISTANCE

When a wild animal, which would normally flee from people, is cornered and cannot escape, it will attack. If the flight distance is seen as a large circle drawn around the animal, then the critical distance is a smaller circle within which the animal will attack any trespasser. The attacks are not agressive but are born of fear and desperation. This instinctive behavior is the cause of many of the bites which domestic animals inflict upon people, especially children, who from ignorance or impatience suddenly stoop toward a cornered pet. The animal may regard the person's gesture as an attack and defend itself with tooth and claw while the owner wonders why a usually docile pet has suddenly turned vicious.

TERRITORIAL DEFENSE

Animals have a geographical living area or home range which they defend with territorial behavior. By this means the members of one species are dispersed so that each animal has sufficient food. A carnivore must have a larger territory than a herbivore since its territory must include the territories of enough prey-animals to provide food without seriously depleting the prey in the area. Animals of different species which do not use the same food supply are tolerated or ignored when they enter a territory. Thus a bear does not attack a wolf, nor does a robin attack a sparrow.

The animal feels most confident and is therefore most aggressive at the center of its territory. As it gets farther away it becomes less agressive and more fearful. If another animal of the same species trespasses into the center of the territory, it will get a fierce reception, but if it only wanders onto the outskirts it will be chased off with far less aggression. The boundary of a territory, therefore, is formed where two animals meet and each is far enough away from its center to feel equally unsure. At this point, neither animal is sufficiently confident to chase the other away, and so territorial defense is limited to threatening behavior. This can take the form of mock attack with open mouth, which is the case with some species of cichlid fishes, or of a singing match with songbirds and howler monkeys.

In most mammals, however, territory is not so clearly defined. Territory may take the form of a large home range with fixed points of interest—places for hunting, resting, and sunbathing—all of which are joined by an elaborate network of paths. There is a

certain amount of overlap of home range, and an animal spends most of its time in a smaller area known as a first order home. In the case of domesticated animals this would be the house, or one room, or one corner of a room. A cat or dog will often repel any other animal that attempts to usurp its favorite place or share its rights.

Dogs are essentially pack animals and, like wolves, will defend both the home range and pack members from intruders. They accept us and our families as their pack and defend us as well as our homes. It is most likely in this connection that dogs have been bred to bark. Wolves, wild dogs, and other canines can bark but rarely do so. By choosing dogs which are more inclined to bark and breeding from them, humans have the advantage of an early warning system. In hunting, however, the bark is a disadvantage. In some hunting dogs such as the Basenji, there is virtually no bark. Hounds only give tongue when the odor of the prey becomes particularly strong, and gundogs are trained not to bark.

The cat is a solitary animal, not a pack animal, and is not nearly as territory-conscious as the dog. It has a first order home and a home range, but the home ranges between cats greatly overlap, and the paths through them are used by many cats, although not simultaneously. Colonies of feral cats show considerable mutual tolerance, and a cat may even be induced to share its first order home with another. Normally, however, adult cats avoid each other. They seem to rely on vision in waiting until the other cat has left the path or hunting area before venturing onto it. They may also judge by smell how recently other cats left marks on prominent features such as posts and stones along their paths. If they do come upon each other unawares they may fight, although in cities and other areas where many cats live in a small area they will usually try to settle the matter through displays of aggression. However, if a fight does ensue it may be long and bloody or even fatal. Two individual cats will probably only fight once; next time they meet head-on the weaker cat will flee. Thus a hierarchy will be established. Occasionally, at night, cats gather in fairly large numbers. They will sit close and groom each other, but these peaceful get-togethers are not properly understood.

Not all animals are territorial. Starlings and swallows are nonterritorial birds. The Cape Hunting Dogs roam in packs and move continually from one area to

Facing Page. Body gestures in horses: (1) Muzzle-sniffing when two horses meet is often followed by (2) striking out with a foreleg—which can be dangerous to handlers. (3) The gray is showing the most common threat gestures—swishing tail, laying back of ears and lifting of a hindleg—and the bay displays another threat gesture—extension of her head, threatening to bite while the nostrils and ears are laid back. Wrinkling of the nostrils is often the first sign that a bite threat is coming. (4) The skewbald is signalling alarm—trotting with a highly elevated and extended action, head and tail held very high, muzzle up and nostrils distended. The horse usually will snort very loudly in these circumstances.

another. Nevertheless these animals have an individual distance which they defend. Swallows, for example, always keep a distance of a few centimeters between each other when they are gathered together on telegraph wires. You will never see them huddled so close that they touch, and the same is true of starlings roosting on a ledge or of seagulls resting on the sea wall. This individual distance may also be related to the space needed for takeoff.

TERRITORIAL MARKINGS

Many males mark out their home range by scent. Some mammals use the secretion from special glands to rub on trees and other landscape features while others mark with urine or feces or, in the case of the hippopotamus, both. The bushbaby wets its front and back paws with urine in order to mark its territory. The dog marks chiefly with urine; the cat with urine and a viscous liquid from the anal glands, which has a most unpleasant odor to human beings. Cats also possess marking glands on the tail and side of the head, although the liquid excreted cannot be smelled by humans. When a cat rubs against you or the furniture, it is probably marking you or the table as its own.

The marking seems to have two functions: it marks the animal's home range, thereby showing ownership, and it identifies the animal or, in other words, acts as a calling card. Thus, when you take your male dog out for a walk he will stop every few paces to sniff the places where other dogs have urinated, and then he will lift his own leg to show he has been there too. He will also urinate at key points in his territory such as the gate post. He may then scratch up earth. This is not an attempt to cover up his excreta, as with the cat, but an

additional visual sign that this is his territory.

If a wolf smells the urine of another wolf not belonging to its pack and in its home range, it will become extremely excited; if this stranger is found it will be driven off aggressively by the leader of the pack. Dogs of most breeds are less aggressive, but they always examine a strange dog olfactorily around the groin and anal regions. The dogs circle each other, and they either exchange a friendly greeting in which the face is smelled and licked or they fight.

Neutering of domestic male dogs before they reach sexual maturity may inhibit the showy territorial instinct and the marking procedure.

Although not territorial birds, starlings will always keep a distance of a few inches between them when gathered on telegraph wires.

1

2

3

4

33

Appeasement Signals

Most animals, except the domestic cat, do not stare each other or humans in the eye unless they are going to attack. If you look your dog straight in the eye, it will look away. The avoidance of eye contact and the turning away of the head are the most common appeasement signals. Many other signals can be noticed when a young animal meets an older or stronger dog, or when a dog has been reproved by its owner. In some dogs, these signals are seen whenever they come into contact with human beings.

Appeasement signals are universal in dogs and in their wild counterpart, wolves. They include a typical "friendly" face with the corners of the mouth pulled back horizontally into a grin and the ears held back flat against the head. These gestures are accompanied by a crouching body position and the tail tucked down between the legs. The dog may roll over onto its back, at the same time raising its legs and, finally, it may urinate. By these movements, it is exposing the belly and genital region—the most vunerable part of its body—in just the same way that a puppy will present this area for licking to parents. This gesture inhibits the attack of another dog. The inhibition ceases once the underdog rolls back onto its feet, and the aggressor may renew its attack. Sometimes, the underdog may have to go through the appeasement ritual several times before it can slip away and escape.

You may have to intervene if your dog cannot appease an attacker in a blind rage. You can recognize a really serious attack by the victim's typical yelp of fear which is different from other dog noises. The yelp has the effect of bringing other dogs into the fight on the side of the aggressor. If you want to save your dog you must act quickly—but take care! In separating fighting dogs even the most adored owner stands the risk of being bitten by his or her dog, for a fighting dog is out to kill and will not know its owner from its enemy.

Understanding Other Signals

Some or all of the appeasement signals already mentioned can be seen in your dog when it comes to greet you. However, its tail will not usually be tucked between its legs but held high and wagged. The tail and the ears are the most obvious parts to watch in order to understand your dog's body language. Generally speaking, the higher the tail is held, the more confident the dog. Confidence can also be seen in the forward-pointing position of the ears.

Thus, as your dog approaches you in a friendly and confident mood, it will have its ears pointing forward, its teeth covered by its lips and its tail held either horizontally, or raised and wagging. It will probably try to lick your face for this is the dog's social greeting and the way in which both the dog and the wolf greet a friendly member of the pack. Since human beings' faces are much farther from the ground, dogs make a habit of jumping up on people.

A dog which is in an aggressive mood will show a different set of signals. As with most animals that wish to intimidate, the body movements are designed to make it look as big as possible. The legs will be straight and stiff, the neck arched, the hair of the neck and rump will be raised, and the tail will be held high and the tip may be wagged. Beware of this type of wagging for it is not a friendly signal. The expression on the dog's face will be obviously aggressive. The eyes will stare directly at the cause of its aggression and the lips

Body signals in dogs: Dog (1) is standing in a normal, neutral position. It receives a "friendly" greeting from (3) whose slightly crouched body, low tail wag, "grinning" expression, and flattened ears while attempting to lick the face of (1) indicate submission. (2) shows another typical submissive posture. (4) is directing an aggressive threat to (5)— with legs stiff, head and tail high, ears pricked and hackles up he stares at (5), who is abandoning his aggressive threat by looking away while lowering his ears and tail. (6) slinks away in an extremely submissive posture.

will be drawn forwards and upwards into a snarl, baring teeth, and crinkling the skin of the nose. This will probably be accompanied by growling. The ears, which at first point forward, will twist outwards and downwards, and finally will be plastered back against the head as the dog attacks.

The behavior signals that a dog gives may not always be as clearcut as described above because a dog, like a human being, may have conflicting emotions. It may be curious about a new person or object in its environment, but at the same time nervous. These conflicting emotions will result in a mixture of signals and can be most clearly seen in a fear biter, where the snarls will be aggressive but the tail and ears are held in a submissive position. Where there is a very strong conflict of emotions, movements completely inappropriate to the situation, known as displacement activities, come into play. Displacement behavior is found in most animals, including humans. Thus an angry person prevented from attacking by fear or social convention may suddenly scratch his or her head or yawn. An animal gripped by the same conflict may break off its actions to groom or preen itself.

Your cat will show a different set of signals. It will probably greet you with its tail raised straight up in the air. It will also hold it in this position when rubbing against you or when it is soliciting food. The same tail position is seen in kittens when they greet or follow the mother.

The tail wag of the cat is a sign of intended attack and is also seen, to a lesser degree, when it is stalking prey. Accompanied by hissing and extended claws, the tail wag is a sign of danger. Although the cat does not have such a clearly defined appeasement ritual as the dog, it can show a passive acceptance by crouching still and turning its head down or away and thus removing its

direct stare—a posture which may also serve to inhibit attack by other cats.

The two main characteristics of a cat's behavior are offensive threat and defensive threat. The advance warning of attack is simply a direct stare with the pupils of the eyes small, the body poised for attack, and the ears turned slightly outwards and backwards. The defensive threat, familiar to most people, is seen when a cat is attacked by a dog. The hair stands on end, the back is arched, and the animal stands sideways so that its enhanced size can be properly seen. The ears go back and down until they are almost hidden behind the head, the pupils of the eyes dilate, and the cat opens its mouth to spit and hiss. The tail is arched and, if the attack continues, it becomes upright and fluffed out. If this intimidating display does not succeed, the cat will lash out a paw at the dog with the claws extended. It may turn and run, depending on its speed and its ability to climb out of reach.

Cats have a far greater range of vocal signs than do dogs. Apart from the meow, which is only used to communicate with humans, there is a large vocabulary of other noises and calls. The noise a mother cat makes as she approaches her kittens is different, for example, from the noise she makes when courting. In many bird species the male attracts the female at mating time by a specific song. Communication among birds is always heard when the mother warns her young of a predator. The sound she makes will vary depending on whether the predator is grounded or flying.

Of course dogs also communicate by barking and growling, but their visual signals make up a far more subtle language which tell much more to other dogs, and to human beings once they have learned to interpret them. Because we rely on speech to communicate our feelings, we tend not to be conscious of body and

Body signals in cats: (1) is standing in a friendly greeting posture with head and tail high and ears pricked. (2) is standing in a normal, neutral stance while (3) is a female in heat in a receptive posture—back hollowed, tail to one side and treading with hind legs. (4) is showing the offensive threat—legs stiff, tail curved towards opponent, hair partly raised, head swinging side to side, ears back and pointing upwards and pupils constricted. (5) is showing an extreme defensive threat—claws extended, ears flat and pupils dilated. (6) is crouching in the more usual defensive posture. (7) is showing the defensive threat reserved for other species.

35

Top. *The position of the tail indicates social rank when a group of wolves interact—the higher the tail is held, the more dominant or higher ranking the animal. The wolf in the background is showing the normal resting tail-carriage.*

Bottom. *This dog is not showing a fully aggressive threat, the drawn-back ears indicating a certain amount of fear and submission.*

facial signals. Nevertheless, we do make such signals to each other and understand them readily. Animals are particularly attuned to understanding body language—both theirs and ours. One often hears people making statements such as "my cat always knows when we are going away," and "my dog can tell, when I go out the door, if I am going into the garden or to take it for a walk." Of course animals know because we give ourselves away in a hundred ways without being aware of them. Konrad Lorenz, an eminent zoologist, has a story about one of his dogs which could sense whether

he liked or disliked his visitors. However much he attempted to disguise his dislike of a particular man the dog would sense it and reward the unwelcome visitor with a bite from behind.

Breeding Behavior

Many wild animals are so strongly territorial that they chase any animal of the same species, including females, out of their territory, unless it is mating season. The robin is a good example of this type of mating behavior. The female protects herself from attack by the male by following a ritual in which she flutters her wings and begs for food in such an infantile way as to inhibit the male's attack long enough for him to discover that she is a female and a potential mate. With spiders, on the contrary, the male protects himself from the larger female's attack with a distinctive way of plucking her web so that she will recognize him as a potential lover, not as a meal.

Many male animals, however, have a uniform inhibition preventing them from injuring a female of their own species. Male wolves and dogs will not normally attack a female.

Domestication, however, has affected the breeding habits of animals in many ways. It has, for example, increased the number of sexually receptive periods, or heats per year. Wild canines have only one heat each year while the domestic dog has two or even three. Domestication has also accelerated the onset of sexual maturity and contributed to promiscuity in pets. Wolves show mate preference and are monogamous; dogs rarely care what bitch they mate with, although some bitches will refuse to mate with dogs they do not like.

In many animals, especially birds, there is a complicated sexual ritual peculiar to the species which makes it impossible for the animal to mate with any animal other than one of its own species. With domestication, these rituals have been lost and some very bizarre crossings can take place such as the mating of canaries with finches to produce "mules," or of a stallion with a female ass to produce a "hinny." From the human point of view, the domesticated animal's lack of discrimination is convenient since it permits the owner to choose the animal's mate.

Behavior Of The Young

The behavior of the very young puppy or kitten is instinctive and is similar to that of wild cats or dogs. At first, the young may lie close together for mutual warmth. If it is hot, they spread out. A kitten lifted out of its nest will open its mouth wide and hiss, but a puppy will show no unfriendliness. Later, when their eyes are open, the young will start to play.

PLAY

Play is seen in all young animals. It is essential to their healthy development, and animals deprived of play will grow up socially and psychologically deprived. (Puppies do not thrive when kept alone in experimental establishments with no play material, and no human contact except with the person who feeds them.) Play is most likely a method of learning and practicing new skills. The kitten will chase and pounce, and the puppy chase, pounce on, and shake its imaginary prey. Through play, young animals also learn the limits of aggression with each other. The play bite of young puppies can be painful, but by the time they are about three months old most have learned to control their bites. As the pup grows up, a hierarchy will develop in the litter—with the weaker appeasing the stronger.

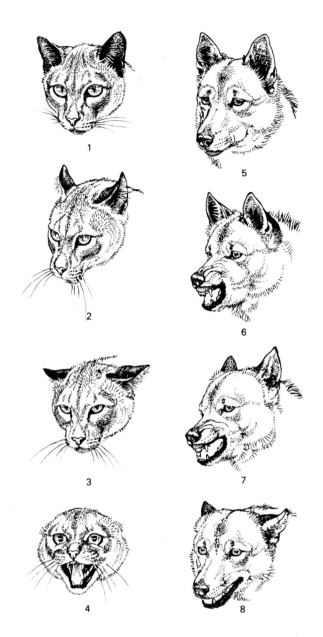

A dog will show typical signals if it wishes to play. Its tail, ears, and mouth will stay in the friendly position, and it will seem to bow by bending its front, but not its back legs. It may then make its intentions clearer by sham attacks on its owner or on another dog, or by suddenly running away, thus soliciting a chase. Both cats and dogs may bring favorite toys to you to show they want to play a game. A small animal may adopt a begging position without any conscious training, in order to ask you to play.

Top. *Facial expressions in cats and dogs: (1) Normal, alert. (2) Offensive. (3) Defensive. (4) Extreme defensive. (5) Normal alert. (6) Offensive. (7) Defensive. (8) Submissive or friendly.*

Bottom Left. *A familiar cat posture—this is a defensive threat reserved for species other than cats.*

Hunting

Moving objects trigger the chasing instinct in both cats and dogs. The kitten's reaction to a moving object seems to be innate. It will chase the object, be it mouse, bird, or ball of yarn; it will crouch and stalk it and finally pounce. The kitten's first attempts at catching mice are not usually successful, and presumably it learns by watching and hunting with its mother. A mother will also bring back live prey for her kittens. A kitten that does not come across live prey until it is a few months old may never learn to kill, although the

stalking, chasing and pawing reactions are there. A kitten that is brought up with tame rats or mice will rarely kill these species. Therefore keeping a cat hungry in order that it may kill vermin is not necessarily a successful ploy. Experienced cats will kill more often, but inexperienced or well-fed cats do not make the connection between killing and the prey as food. A still object seems to inhibit the cat's hunting instincts, and the cat will paw the unfortunate prey into action before finishing it off.

This play with a prey animal is found to a lesser extent in dogs, and a confused prey which runs towards its persecutor will make the dog retreat in defense. However, as the prey turns to run away, the dog will pounce upon it. If the prey animal is badly hurt or frightened, it will go into a state of shock and will neither seem to see, hear, nor feel pain. Small animals die more easily from shock than do humans.

Infantilism

There is a definite trend for domesticated animals to retain infantile characteristics in adult life. This phenomenon, known as neoteny, shows itself physically in the shortening of the face, weakening of the jaw mus-

cles, reduced size of teeth, and development of a high, domed forehead. Infantile behavior also is typical of certain varieties of adult dogs and is most noticeable in toy breeds. If a dog is to be a house dog and its only function, as far as its owner is concerned, is to be either a companion or dependent, the qualities required are obedience and love towards humans, especially its owner. Therefore, over the years, dogs showing the

Top Right. *This playful stalk by a kitten is all part of its preparation for adulthood, when hunting may be vital for survival.*

universal friendliness of a puppy have been chosen for breeding. The house dogs we approve of do not attack or even bark at our visiting friends, although we expect them to attack a felon and to protect our home from intruders.

Purring may be an infantile habit which has continued into the adult life of the domesticated cat. Why a cat purrs when it is content is not clearly understood but may be connected with the fact that kittens purr when they are suckling. Purring at that stage is accompanied by a kneading of the paws on the mother's side which probably helps the milk to flow. Kneading sometimes accompanies purring in adult cats when they are extremely contented, for example when they are being stroked. Some cats will also salivate at such times, and there are cats which actually try to suckle furry or wooly objects or an owner's hair. A possible explanation for these infantile habits is that these cats have been taken from their mothers too early.

Inbred Characteristics

The different behavioral characteristics bred into the various types of dog are even more striking and interesting than the differences in color or body form. For instance, hounds, which have been bred to live and work in packs, are not aggressive with each other and will even accept strange hounds into their pack—something no wolf nor wild dog will do. But terriers, which have been bred to work singly flushing rabbits, badgers, or foxes out of burrows, have had so much aggression bred into them that it is often impossible to keep more than a pair of these dogs at a time, since their aggression extends to the members of their own breed. Some breeds hunt by smell and some by sight; different breeds retrieve, herd, point, or flush game. Some

Bottom. *Camouflage and silence are essential elements of a successful stalk. Dogs and cats achieve the stalk in similar ways.*

have been bred to guard while others are merely lap-dogs. Yet the potential for doing all these jobs is present in every dog.

Imprinting

The way in which animals become fixated on a parent is recognized as a definite behavioral phenomenon among animals and is known as imprinting. The primary function of imprinting seems to be ensuring that the young animal develops a following response to its parent. In the vast majority of cases the parent-object is the appropriate one, and this attachment promotes survival. Sometimes, however, animals grow up regarding themselves as one of our species, so that their own species seem alien. This is particularly true of animals which are born fully furred or feathered and

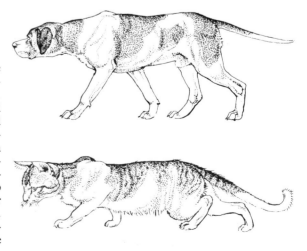

39

able to walk, such as calves, foals, chicks, and goslings. It is extremely important for their survival that these young animals follow their mother from the moment of birth.

A number of experiments have been conducted with birds which show that the young do not instinctively recognize their own species, but follow the first moving object they see or, in the case of ducklings, hear. Konrad Lorenz proved this point by inducing a row of ducklings to follow him as he imitated the mother's quacking. They regarded him as their mother since his voice was the first they heard after hatching. Of course, in normal circumstances the first object to be seen or heard is the mother, but it can be a completely different animal, a human being, or something as bizarre as a table-tennis ball.

There is a critical time for imprinting in young animals. If chicks are kept blindfolded for the first few days of their lives, and the blindfold is then removed, they will run away from any moving object, whether it be hen or human. Fixation on humans can be seen in birds which have been taken from the nest and hand reared. These birds, which have included the budgerigars, jackdaws, crows, starlings, and sparrows, show no interest in their own species as mates but court their chosen human assiduously. If hand reared by humans without contact with their own species, puppies and kittens also may become fixated on humans and liable to consider people as their proper mates, although this

does not usually prevent them from breeding. The attachment of lambs to their human nurses is well known, and an attachment to inappropriate parent-objects has also been noted in the young of moose, buffalo, zebra, and mouflon.

Socialization

There seems to be a critical time for socializing in puppies and kittens. This is approximately between the fourth and tenth weeks of their lives. During this period they should have contact with humans and with other dogs or cats. In the case of dogs being trained as guide dogs for the blind, the pups have to be taken away from the mother at an early age and hand reared in order to strengthen the human attachment.

The dog will regard human beings as members of its "pack" provided it has human contact while it is a pup. It is important that it should look upon you as the leader of the pack or "alpha animal"; an aggressive dog brought up in a permissive way may see you as the subordinate, and then you are in for trouble!

If a pup has had no social contact with people until after it is three months old, it will regard you as a potential enemy and will be extremely shy. Such dogs do not make good pets. Puppies, and kittens as well, should be handled before this age so they can become used to people. Domestic animals brought up only

Top Left. Imprinting can result in bizarre happenings, as in the case of these Muscovy ducklings who immediately after hatching followed what they believed to be their mother—a Labrador retriever!

Above and Facing Page. In poorer areas of large cities groups of scavenging house dogs are increasingly common during the day. Truly feral or "gone wild" city dogs however, form small groups of two or three and are active at night when human activity is at its lowest.

Feral cats, such as are often found in farmyards, become shy, wary and fierce as a result of their lack of contact with humans.

with women or only with men may dislike or be frightened of the other sex. On the other hand, if a puppy, for example, is hand reared from a very early age and has no contact with other puppies and dogs, it may show fear of other dogs and have some initial difficulty in mating and breeding. This phenomenon is seen in other animals as well; hand-reared apes and monkeys make very poor mothers themselves, and if they have been brought up in complete isolation from their own species they may never learn to socialize with them. Mother love and the opportunity to play with peers seem to be very important to the normal pyschological development of young animals.

Both domesticated dogs and wolves kept in captivity exhibit a fear of new places and of new objects in familiar places at about the age of four to five months. This characteristic probably means that in the wild these animals would have learned the topography of their home range by that age. Whereas dogs come to terms with these fears, wolves remain wary on their own range all their lives—even if they have been hand reared. The domestication of the dog has reduced some of its instinctive curiosity and its need to investigate every object within its range.

For a wild animal to be moved from its home ground is an unimaginable trauma. This is why wild animals,

such as monkeys, which are caught as adults for the pet trade, have such a high death rate in the first few weeks of their captivity. In zoos the movement of an animal from one enclosure to another is done with the utmost care. First, the traveling cage is left in the animal's enclosure for several days before actually moving. Once the animal is in its new enclosure it is allowed plenty of time to investigate its new quarters. This will probably take some hours and it may even return to the traveling cage if it is frightened in any way.

The fact that you can take your dog on vacation with you or change your parrot's cage with impunity shows to what extent humans have altered animals by domesticating them. The longer the history of domestication, the more marked is the change in the animal's natural behavior. The cat which has been domesticated in comparatively recent times, sometimes shows more attachment to its home range than to its owner. Dogs, however, are usually more attached to their human "packmates" than to their home range.

Species which are more recently domesticated will retain much more of the natural behavior. If dogs and cats are abandoned by humans, they will become feral and will tend to revert to their wild habits in order to survive: cats become shy, wary, and fierce and dogs form themselves into hunting packs.

41

FEEDING YOUR PET

Whatever the type of animal—carnivore, herbivore, insectivore, omnivore—food must fulfill the same basic needs: provide energy, furnish building materials for the body (either replacement tissue or new growth), and supply the micronutrients (e.g., vitamins and trace elements) essential in small quantities for the thousands of body processes. In feeding our pets, however, we are as much concerned with differences in feeding behavior and taste preferences as in food requirements. Some animals, such as lions, gorge and sleep between infrequent meals while digestion takes place. Others, such as chipmunks, eat busily all summer in order to store nutrition for a winter hibernation. Snakes need to eat only once every seven to ten days, while shrews must eat their own weight in food every day or die. Ruminants feed nearly all day to support life on a low energy diet. Although some animals are highly selective, every species must obtain the nutrients it needs in amounts and proportions according to the life processes and activities involved.

There are two extremes of diet found in animals. First (Bottom) there are the carnivores or meat eaters, such as the Domestic Cat, and second (Top Right) there are the herbivores, such as the Golden Hamster seen here stuffing its cheek pouches with seeds and biscuit.

Feeding Habits

CARNIVORES

The zoological order Carnivora includes the dog, bear, raccoon, weasel, civet, hyena, and cat families. Anim-

als of this order live mainly on the bodies of small mammals, reptiles, birds, and fishes, although individual species may be omnivorous, such as most bears, or mainly vegetarian, such as the Giant Panda. The wider term *carnivore* embraces many whales, dolphins, seals, the flesh- or fish-eating birds and numerous reptiles.

Carnivores have relatively large but simple (single pouch) stomachs and usually have powerful jaws with teeth adapted for tearing flesh and gnawing or cracking bones. The digestive juices are well supplied with enzymes to break down protein, but they can also assimilate some starch, especially if it has been precooked or predigested in the stomach of the prey. Some carnivores prefer their prey's organs, notably the liver and stomach, but in general the whole body is consumed except, in most cases, fur, feet, and large bones. Examination of the stomach contents of wild animals classified as carnivores often shows they have eaten plant foods of many kinds when their prey became scarce.

HERBIVORES

The animals within this group include horses, sheep, cattle, goats, and rabbits. Herbivores feed wholly on plants, including the flowers or fruit as well as the leaves and stem. Many herbivores have digestive systems especially suited to deal with their bulky and rather indigestible diets, and teeth adapted to breaking off and chewing vegetation. The most specialized herbivores are the ruminants, which include deer, antelopes, giraffes, cattle, sheep, and goats. In these species the stomach is divided into sections or pouches—a rumen and true stomach—which have separate functions. Ruminants may graze plants and grass at ground level, or browse the leaves, bark and cambrium (inner bark) of trees. Whatever the source, the lightly chewed vegetation passes first to the rumen, where it undergoes bacterial fermentation and becomes more digestible. The bacteria in the rumen also synthesize vitamins which the animal uses in its body processes. Later, particularly at night, the fermented mass is regurgitated from the rumen in lumps which are chewed at leisure before being reswallowed and digested by the usual mammalian processes.

Some herbivores, such as the horse and the rabbit,

lack a rumen but have an enlarged cecum (a pouch branching off the large intestine) in which fermentation can occur, although utilization of the nutrients is probably less efficient than in rumination. Other herbivores, including many monkeys and apes, assimilate an herbivorous diet without having either a rumen or an enlarged cecum.

OMNIVORES

This group includes humans, pigs, and rats—three of the greediest creatures within the animal kingdom! Many animals traditionally regarded as carnivores, for example the dog, are fed as omnivores. Omnivores are characterized by the ability to digest a wide range of foodstuffs of both plant and animal origin and have teeth and digestive systems adapted to both types of food.

INSECTIVORES

This group feeds almost exclusively on insects. Shrews, hedgehogs, lizards, frogs, toads, and many birds devour a variety of insect forms—beetles, flies, caterpillars and grubs—while the Aardvark has a highly specialized diet consisting of termites.

BIRDS

Birds show a remarkable diversity in diet. Some common species such as robins and wrens are omnivorous, while others restrict their intake to a particular insect or plant food. If insectivorous birds are regarded as a type of carnivore adapted to food with a tough external skeleton, seed-eating birds may be thought of as vegetarians which cope with a hard seed or grain by ingesting grit to grind or macerate the food in the bird's gizzard. In addition to these types, some birds eat mollusks or worms.

ESSENTIAL NUTRIENTS

Before discussing the different foods in detail, consideration should be given to the essential nutrients required by nearly all species and to their food sources.

WATER

This nutrient is second only to oxygen as an essential to animal life. It makes up about two-thirds of the body weight of most animals. Losses through excretion, respiration, perspiration, and other body secretions must be replaced, or death from dehydration quickly follows. Many foods have a high water content, such as fresh green vegetables in which the total weight is 90% or more water. Some water is also available from the digestion of food but, if the water intake from food and its digestion is insufficient to maintain a balance, an animal must drink.

The water requirement varies widely depending on the species and the climate. Some desert animals, such as the gerbil, rarely urinate and thereby conserve water. Provided it has some wet food this rodent rarely needs to drink. Nevertheless, clean drinking water in an appropriate container should always be available to all pets. In many cases the natural environment of the animal has been altered, and the owner has no way of knowing when it needs to drink.

ENERGY

All living things—plant or animal—must obtain energy from the environment. Animals produce ener-

gy by eating and digesting food. Through a complex series of chemical processes in the body, energy is released and used, appearing ultimately as heat. The most convenient way of measuring and comparing the energy value of foods is in terms of this heat equivalent, or calorific value. There are various ways of expressing energy content. Dieticians use the term *calorie* to stand for kilocalorie (abbreviation kcal) while the biochemist expresses energy in terms of joules (J). The energy-yielding parts of food are digestible carbohydrates, fats, and proteins. Carbohydrates such as starch and sugar can yield up to 16kJ/g (3.7kcal/g; 106kcal/oz) if fully digested. Protein gives slightly above this amount but fat produces over twice as much: 37kJ/g (90kcal/g; 250kcal/oz).

The amount of energy used by an animal depends on several factors, the most important being the animal's size and degree of activity, followed by its individual nature and the environmental temperature. Breeding females usually have a higher energy requirement.

Top. *In warm, even climates exotic birds, such as these parakeets, can be allowed to fly free since they are still dependent on food provided by their owners.*

Bottom. *Teeth in various mammalian groups: (1) Carnivores. (2) Insectivores (3) Pinnipedia (seals, etc). (4) Rodents. (5) Lagomorphs (rabbits). (6) Cloven-hoofed herbivores.*

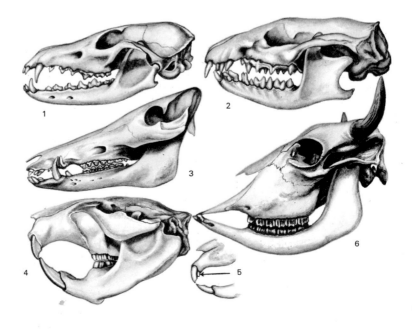

Calorie needs are not directly proportional to body weight because the surface area, and therefore heat loss, becomes proportionately less as bulk increases. For the mathematically minded, it has been shown that basic energy needs at constant body temperature are proportional to body weight raised to the power of 0.75. This relationship applies to mammals ranging from shrews to elephants. In practice the equation means that a 70kg. (150 lb.) Great Dane needs only about five times as much food as a 7kg. (15 lb.) terrier, not ten times as much.

CARBOHYDRATES

In theory, carbohydrates are not essential nutrients since their function is to provide energy and they can therefore be replaced by protein or fat, both of which have other necessary functions. However, many species, especially herbivores, cannot digest a diet rich in fat and protein so that carbohydrates are essential for these animals. There are many carbohydrates present in plants—some of which are easily digested by nearly all animals and others that require special enzyme systems in order to be digested.

The most widely distributed carbohydrates are the sugars: sucrose (cane or beet sugar), lactose (milk sugar), glucose (grape sugar), fructose (fruit sugar).

The other chief carbohydrates are the glucose polymers, starch and cellulose. Starch is digested almost as easily as glucose, but cellulose is not broken down by the digestive juices of any higher animal. It is assimilated in part by herbivores through the fermentation action of bacteria in the rumen or cecum. Cellulose also provides roughage to give bulk to excrement and reduce the risk of constipation.

PROTEINS

This nutrient is the basic substance from which the animal body is constructed. Protein provides the material for such diverse tissues as muscle, hair, blood, and the internal organs. Even the skeleton, although owing its rigidity to mineral matter, is based on cells rich in protein. Unlike plants, animals cannot synthesize protein from nonprotein foodstuffs and other materials. They must therefore obtain sufficient protein in their diets. The quality of the protein is also important. Apart from being digestible it must also have a composition suitable for the needs of the animal. All proteins are built up from about twenty simple substances called amino acids combined in different numbers, orders, and proportions. Some of these amino acids can be made in the animal's body but about nine of the essential ones cannot. In general, proteins from animals sources such as eggs, milk, meat, and fish are richer in essential amino acids and are of a higher biological value than plant protein. However, some legumes, notably the soybean, contain a high propor-

Opposite Page. All dogs enjoy bones, which should be large and uncooked if they are not to cause digestive trouble.

The Minimum Nutrient Levels Recommended in a Balanced Maintenance Diet for Healthy Adult Dogs.

NUTRIENT REQUIREMENT (PERCENTAGE OR QUANTITY PER KILOGRAM OF FOOD)					
TYPE OF DIET		DRY BASIS (0% WATER)	DRY TYPE (10% WATER)	SEMI MOIST (25% WATER)	CANNED OR WET (75% WATER)
Protein	%	22	20	16.5	5.5
Fat	%	5.5	5.0	4.0	2.0
Linoleic or arachidonic acid	%	1.6	1.4	1.2	0.4
Minerals					
Calcium	%	1.1	1.0	0.8	0.3
Phosphorus	%	0.9	0.8	0.7	0.25
Potassium	%	0.6	0.5	0.45	0.2
Sodium chloride	%	1.1	1.0	0.8	0.3
Magnesium	%	0.05	0.04	0.03	0.01
Iron	mg	60	54	45	15
Copper	mg	7.3	6.5	5.5	1.8
Cobalt	mg	2.4	2.2	1.8	0.61
Manganese	mg	5.0	4.5	3.6	1.2
Zinc	mg	20	18	15	5
Iodine	mg	1.54	1.48	1.16	0.39
Vitamins					
Vitamin A	mg	1.5	1.4	1.2	0.4
Vitamin D	mg	0.007	0.006	0.005	0.002
Vitamin E	mg	48	43	36	12
Vitamin B12	mg	0.02	0.02	0.017	0.006
Folic Acid	mg	0.18	0.17	0.13	0.04
Thiamin	mg	0.73	0.65	0.55	0.18
Riboflavin	mg	2.2	1.9	1.6	0.5
Pyridoxin	mg	1.0	0.9	0.75	0.25
Pantothenic acid	mg	2.2	1.9	1.6	0.54
Niacin	mg	10.6	10.0	7.5	2.5
Choline	g	1.2	1.1	0.9	0.3
Vitamin K	mg	1.4	1.3	1.1	0.4

tion of protein which is similar in quality to meat protein.

FATS

Fats are such a storehouse of energy that the bulk of food needed can be reduced by increasing the fat content of the diet. This may be important in very cold climates. Depending on its source, fat contains certain necessary nutrients called essential fatty acids or polyunsaturates which keep the skin and coat of fur-bearing animals in healthy condition. Apart from being a source of energy, fat also transports some dissolved substances (fat-soluble vitamins), within the bloodstream to points of need. From a practical viewpoint, fat increases the palatability of food for many carnivores and omnivores.

VITAMINS

These are natural substances which are essential in very small amounts to the proper functioning of the body. In association with proteins called enzymes, they catalyze basic processes such as respiration, digestion, and growth. There are about fifteen vitamins, although several occur in different forms. The fat-soluble vitamins A, D, E, and K can be stored in the liver or elsewhere, while the vitamin B group and vitamin C are water-soluble and must be supplied almost daily to an active animal.

Vitamin A protects tissues from infection, helps to control the formation of bones, and is involved in the mechanism of vision. Some species such as humans and dogs can convert an orange-colored plant pigment called ß-carotene into vitamin A. Vitamin D is mainly used in the formation of bone tissue, although an excess can cause bone to dissolve. Vitamin D is produced by ultraviolet rays acting on substances which naturally occur in the skin of many animals. It is considered an essential dietary requirement and should always be given to rapidly growing animals. Vitamin E is involved in muscle action and in the reproductive process. Vitamin K is necessary for the clotting of blood, but in many animals it is produced by bacterial synthesis in the gut.

The ten or so vitamins of the B group are vital to the basic processes of respiration, digestion, and cell metabolism. Best known within the B group are B_1 (thiamin), B_2 (riboflavin) and, the most recently identified, B_{12} (cyanocobalamin, or cobin) which is remarkably effective in preventing pernicious anemia.

Vitamin C (ascorbic acid) catalyzes certain fundamental processes. However, nearly all species make their own vitamin C from glucose, which is a closely related substance. The exceptions, species which require a dietary intake of vitamin C, include humans, some other primates such as monkeys, cavies, and some birds and insects.

MINERALS

Like vitamins, minerals are needed in relatively small amounts. Yet they differ from vitamins in being composed of immutable chemical elements instead of organic, biological substances. The list of known essential minerals grows almost yearly, but only a dozen or so are of practical importance in compounding diets, since the remainder occur in almost any natural diet in sufficient quantity.

Most domesticated animals depend entirely upon their owners to provide their daily food requirements. The ultimate source of this food is normally quite different from the natural source of food eaten by wild animals. To emphasize this the food chains for a domestic cat and for a wild cat or a feral (gone wild) domestic cat are shown here.

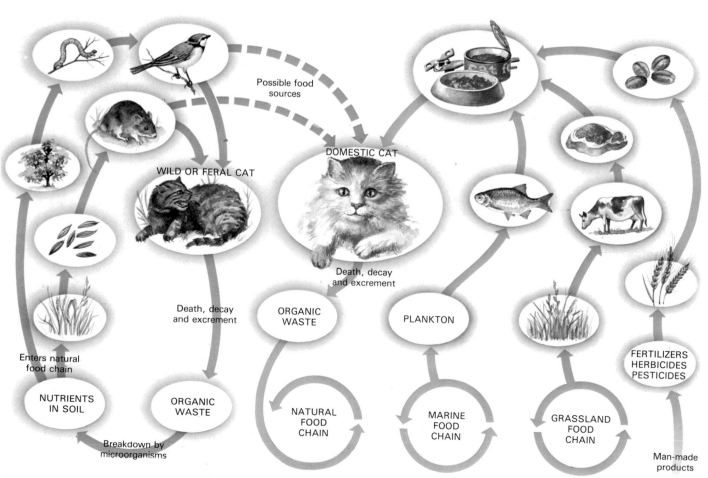

46

Calcium in the form of calcium phosphate is the major constituent of bones and teeth. Phosphorus, as phosphate, has an important function in the basic processes of digestion and growth and is essential to the release of energy. Sodium and chlorine are combined as sodium chloride (common salt), which helps regulate the movement of water outside the tissue cells. Magnesium is a minor component of bone and, together with potassium occurs in the form of salts inside tissue cells where it regulates water-transfer control processes. Iron is an essential part of the red pigment of blood and of enzymes controlling respiration. Copper, manganese, and zinc are also enzyme constituents. Cobalt is part of the large vitamin B_{12} molecule. Fluorine occurs in minute amounts in teeth and helps to protect them from decay. Sulfur is a constituent of the essential amino acid methionine. Iodine is found in the thyroid hormone in the molecule of its key component, thyroxin.

The important minerals listed above are sometimes poorly absorbed from food, and supplements may be necessary to achieve optimum growth or breeding performance.

Foods and Their Composition

Although every foodstuff used for human consumption can be used for feeding one or more pet species, many pets thrive on food not commonly eaten by their owners, including a wide range of feeds especially manufactured to meet their needs.

CEREALS

These are cultivated grasses whose seed is harvested as grain. All the usual pet species, with the exception of most snakes and terrapins, will accept and digest a certain amount of cereal in their diet. Precooking is advisable in the case of carnivores and primates in order to increase the digestibility of starch. The best-known cereals include barley, canary seed, corn (maize), the millets, oats, rice, rye, sorghum, and wheat. All cereal grains contain a concentrated source of energy in the form of starch. Cereal protein, which ranges from 5 to 15 percent by weight of the grain, is also an important factor in the diet of many omnivores, herbivores and even semicarnivores, although the quality is lower than that of animal protein. Cereals also contribute some B complex vitamins—especially B_1 (thiamin)—and essential fatty acids.

FARM PRODUCTS

These include milk, the milk products of butter and cheese, and eggs. The three main components of mammalian milk are lactose (milk sugar), fat, and protein which is itself a mixture primarily of casein and lactalbumin. The proportions of these three ingredients vary widely in the milk of different mammalian species. Cows' milk is a valuable food for most mammals, although some individuals cannot digest the high level of milk sugar while others are allergic to the protein.

Milk also supplies minerals (notably calcium) and vitamins (especially A, D, and B_2) but is too dilute for optimal growth after infancy or for adult maintenance. Milk is accepted in small amounts by many birds and reptiles. Moribund or exhausted creatures belonging

Feeding time is when young owners should realize the responsibility they have for the well-being of their pets, as do these children with their pet mice.

to these groups will often revive after a small feeding with lukewarm milk. Glucose water is as effective, but less readily available. (See below: **Suckling Mammals and the Value of Milk.**)

Butter consists mainly of milk fat and is a rich source of vitamins A and D. Cheese contains most of the fat and protein of milk, but not the lactose or the mineral- and vitamin-rich watery part (whey). Skimmed milk lacks vitamins A and D and tends to be laxative, but it still contains the valuable milk protein.

Hens' eggs are a rich source of high quality protein. The yolk also supplies fat and fat-soluble vitamins. However, raw white of egg contains an antivitamin factor and therefore should be cooked.

MEATS

Whether flesh or offal, meat is an important source of protein for all carnivores and some omnivores. The biological value of the protein varies: it is high in carcass meat and liver but very low in connective tissue (gristle). The fat content of meat varies from very little in some offals to 50 percent or more in fatty cuts. Lean carcass meat consists of about 70 percent water, 20 percent protein and 10 percent fat. Meat is also a source of the B complex vitamins.

Liver has a similar composition to carcass meat. It is a rich source of all vitamins including the fat-soluble group, vitamins A, D, and E. Liver tends to be laxative. Lung (lights or lites) and trimmed tripe (rumen) contain less protein and fat although both are valuable protein foods. Spleen (melts) has less protein value. Heart is of similar quality to muscle meat (flesh) but is very lean. Kidney, in addition to protein and fat, usually contains significant amounts of vitamin A and C. However, a deficiency common to all meat and offal is the serious lack of calcium. Supplements in the form of bone or inorganic calcium salts must be given to all carnivores, first of all to support the rapid growth of the young and then to maintain the adult skeleton.

Provided that the animal will accept it, meat should be cooked as a precaution against food poisoning and parasites. Meat obtained from slaughter houses is always suspect for it may carry harmful germs or be contaminated with drugs used to treat or kill horses and farm animals. Finally, poultry offal, especially the head and neck may contain hormones which lead to sterility in a male animal. Cockerels are sometimes castrated by implanting a hormone pill under the skin of the neck. If another animal accidentally eats this pill, it too can be affected.

FISH

Although traditionally a food for cats, fish is also accepted by dogs and many other carnivores and omnivores. In nutritional terms, fish can be divided into two main groups depending on the fat content of the fish. Herring, mackerel, salmon, sardine and related species have a moderate to high fat content, while the white fish, which include cod, flounder, and whiting are very lean. Both groups provide high quality protein.

Whole fish, containing the liver, is a good vitamin source, but it should always be cooked in order to destroy germs, parasites and substances harmful to digestion, notably thiaminase in herring. The waste from processing frozen fish fillets, fish fingers, and the like is often surprisingly nutritious and therefore widely used by pet food manufacturers. Fish liver oils have an extremely high vitamin A content and should be measured carefully when administered.

VEGETABLES

A great bulk of green foods must be consumed by ruminants, including deer, cattle, sheep, and goats. Rabbits, cavies, and tortoises live mostly on green plants, and some greenstuffs should be made available to rodents and birds. Fresh green vegetables are important for their water content, which sometimes reaches 97 percent by weight. Green vegetables also provide minerals and vitamin C.

Leguminous vegetables such as peas and beans, which are the seed of the plant, are more nutritious than other green vegetables due to their large amounts of protein and starch. Root crops usually contain 80-90 percent water and the extra solid matter is starch. Carrots, kale, and spinach contain ß-carotene, which many animals can convert into vitamin A. The tops of trunips provide more vitamins and ß-carotene than do the roots.

FRUITS

These vary widely in composition, from the citrus type with a high water and vitamin C content to dates with 15 percent water, a high energy value and vitamin content. In general, fruit is a poor source of protein and fat. It is much liked by many monkey and rodent species. Carnivores are not very fond of fruit, but will sometimes eat berries and other fruit with a relatively high sugar content.

NUTS AND OILSEEDS

These foods, which are really a type of fruit, have a high fat content in the form of vegetable oil. It is in fact this high fat content which makes them particularly palatable. As well as being of high energy value, nuts and oilseeds are usually a rich source of essential fatty acids. More important still is that most of the nonfat solids in such foods as groundnut, cottonseed, rapeseed, and soybean have a high quality protein. Defatted oilseeds like soybean, rapeseed, peanut, or cottonseed are the protein source in compound feeds

for cattle, sheep, pigs, and poultry. In the wild, nuts and oilseeds are eaten by many rodents (eg., squirrels) primates and birds.

SCRAPS

Given in moderation, table scraps make a useful contribution to the feeding requirements of pets. The value of these scraps depends on the composition of the original foodstuff and how it has been processed or cooked. Scraps which are usually discarded by humans for aesthetic reasons tend to be the most nutritious. These include the outer leaves of vegetables, meat trimmings, and fish heads, although the bones must be removed before the latter is given to pets.

ADDITIVES

The various supplements—tonics and vitamin or mineral mixtures—which are available for pets of all kinds are unnecessary for a healthy animal that is fed a

Top. Tortoises are basically herbivores, but enjoy the occasional earthworm to supplement their diet.

Bottom. A pet fruit-eating bat has its lunch.

properly balanced diet. Much harm can be done by administering such preparations, especially if young animals are given unbalanced amounts of vitamins A and D, calcium and phosphorus.

There are a few occasions, however, when nutritional supplements can be added to the diet. A sick or convalescent animal may be assisted in its recovery if given vitamins under veterinary supervision. A breeding female may become anemic because of the metabolic strain of gestation and lactation. The coat, skin, or general condition may suffer as a result of nervous strain, in which case additives could help.

Suckling Mammals and the Value of Milk

By definition a mammal receives its mother's milk as its sole food from birth to weaning. The first milk secreted by the mammary glands generally differs in composition from the rest of the lactation since it is higher in protein and contains less fat and lactose. This early milk is known as the colostrum and contains protein antibodies which give the young animal protection against some of the harmful microbes in its environment. Colostrum is secreted for only a day or so in bovine species, but for a week or more in the dog and cat. The later true milk varies greatly in composition between species. Fast-growing species in cold climates have the richest milk and slow-growing primates, the poorest. The fat content of the milk of seals and other marine mammals exceeds 50 percent.

Animals, whether fed naturally or hand reared, are rarely weaned under the age of three weeks. The object of weaning is to effect a smooth transition from milk to an adult diet without interrupting growth and development. In some species, for example dogs, the parent assists this transition by regurgitating its own partially digested food. (See **Breeding and Rearing.**)

Food Acceptability

The first essential in feeding an animal is to be sure that the food is eaten. Perfect nutritional balance is useless if the animal starves to death by refusing to eat. Acceptability depends on a great many factors, some of which do not stem from the food itself. Climatic conditions, intensity and pattern of illumination, noise level, privacy, extraneous odors (especially of other animals), type of food receptacle, change of ownership or dietary regime, sexual stimulus, state of health, and degree of hunger are all factors affecting appetite. Changes of routine and diet are the most common causes of refusal to eat in household pets.

PALATABILITY

This agreeable property of food arises from the original ingredients, although it can be affected by processing and storage. Odor and taste are the main sensations involved, but color, brightness, and texture can also be significant. The temperature of the food is also important—a cat, for example, will not readily accept food straight from the refrigerator. The basic sensations of taste are often separated into sweet, sour, bitter, and salt. But the sense of taste is a complex mechanism closely allied to smell and touch, and no one knows

with certainty whether these categories can be applied to the sensations experienced by any particular animal species.

One of the characteristics of mammals is the production of milk—the sole food required from birth to weaning.

Practical Feeding

A regular feeding routine should be established as soon as possible for a pet. The number of meals each day, the time of day for each meal, and nature of these meals must be considered. When you find a dietary regime on which your pet thrives, do not make changes for the sake of change. Variety may be the spice of human life, but it is a condiment that most pets can do without. Always beware of overfeeding your pet, but make sure that all nutritional needs are being met. Watch the condition of fur or feather, brightness of eye, and general alertness as an indication of overall health. You will find details about individual diets required by the various types of pets under their separate headings in **Pets of Every Kind.**

Without becoming fanatical, you should observe a reasonable degree of hygiene in food preparation and serving. As a general rule and provided that the animal will accept it, all fresh meat, meat offal, poultry, and fish should be cooked in order to destroy germs, parasites, and antinutritive factors. Leftover wet food and opened cans should be refrigerated promptly or discarded within twenty-four hours (twelve hours in hot weather). Dry foods are usually stable for several weeks unless contaminated or allowed to become damp. Food that has gone bad can usually be recognized by its odor or apparent signs of infestation. If you do suspect contamination, do not take chances; throw the food away. Water containers and food receptacles should be cleaned out daily. Cartons and packets should be stored in a cool dry place. Deep-frozen or refrigerated food should be allowed to reach room temperature before being served.

Sick animals frequently need special diets as advised by the veterinarian. During convalescence do not encourage overeating by excessive attention. The aging pet usually needs less food because of lower energy output, but protein, vitamin, and mineral requirements may increase due to a less efficient metabolism and tissue wasting. Any necessary diet changes should be made gradually. An abrupt change of diet should at all times be avoided.

TRAINING & OBEDIENCE

Confidence in handling, consistent and considerate treatment, and a regular timetable will engender trust and a pattern of reaction in most species. Even fish will swim to a regular feeding place when familiar footsteps approach the pond's edge. Taming an animal involves teaching it to trust you and to be gentle towards you. This is a prerequisite for further training. With animals from the wild, taming may be a protracted process, especially if they have been captured and previously ill-treated by humans. However, with young animals born in captivity and with domesticated animals growing up with regular and close human contact, trust should develop more easily. Nevertheless, natural instinct will be strong and any threat, real or imagined, may produce a dangerous reaction; sharp teeth and claws, strong jaws and hooves should always be respected.

Most animals will respond to the provision of food and come forward more readily to receive it as they become more certain that you offer no threat. They will be more likely to accept handling and even welcome it if it is combined with some grooming activity which they enjoy. If they associate something pleasant with the sound of their names, they may learn to come when called. Many gregarious species will come because they want company and will welcome yours if there is none of their kind. However, the level to which animals can be trained will differ widely according to species and there will be considerable variation between individuals. As a general rule, an animal's amenability to training and the kind of behavior it learns is closely related to the pattern of its life in the wild, or to that of its ancestors.

Praise, not punishment, is the key to animal training, although reproof is sometimes necessary. Indeed, we can learn a lot by watching mother animals with their young; they rarely do more than growl or administer a gentle pat to discipline their young. Some people maintain that physical punishment should never be administered, and this is a good basis from which to start training your animal. However, if there is an occasion when you feel physical punishment is necessary, *never* set out to hurt the animal. It is all too easy for a slap to do serious damage to a young animal. Firm verbal disapproval or withdrawing attention will be punishment enough for many dogs and cats. A tap on the nose or the sound of a rolled newspaper being struck nearby will make a strong impression with cats, and a light slap across the flank will get the message across to even large dogs. Animals respond to a particular tone of voice so that praise and positive instructions should be given in a pleasnat tone. Rebukes and prohibitions should be voiced in a stern, harsh manner.

The primary training needed for any household pet will be toilet training and restriction of territory.

Toilet Training

From the start you must accept the fact that toilet training is impossible for many species since they urinate and defecate almost involuntarily, and there is no behavior pattern on which training can be based. Large animals must be kept out of doors or else their stabling must be regularly cleaned. Smaller pets which do not produce so much waste matter can be kept in an indoor cage which can be cleaned easily. They should be released at regular times for exercise in a larger area. You must be prepared for wet and messy droppings from the fruit-eating birds and some other animals if you let them free in a room. Fortunately, dogs, cats, and their close relations have considerable control over their excretory functions and can be easily trained to go outdoors or use a little tray.

Cats are particularly fastidious and kittens are usually trained by their mother to use a litter tray. On introducing a new cat to the house keep it in a restricted area with a water bowl, its feeding dish, a bed, and a litter tray. It may decide to sleep in the litter tray and dirty its bed. Try a variety of materials in the litter tray until it gets the idea. If there is the occasional accident in the house, it will probably be a protest that you have let the tray get too dirty. If you have an orphaned kitten or one whose mother has failed to train it, you should simply pick it up and put it in the tray whenever it messes on the floor. After a couple of times, you will probably be able to sense when the animal is about to relieve itself and can get it to the tray in time. The kitten will soon get the idea. If, later, you want the cat to go outside, begin by putting the tray out in the selected area and when the cat is used to going to this toilet spot, remove the tray. Most cats will quickly learn to relieve themselves when you desire but, if your pet is one of those rare ones that learns slowly, try not to become impatient with it. Gentle and persistent guidance will accomplish far more than displays of anger or frustration.

The housebreaking of puppies is best done by taking them out after every meal. If they have to remain indoors, place them on a litter box or several layers of newspaper when they seem about to perform. When you start taking them outside, use a set expression such as "hurry up" and keep it for such occasions, so that they do not think this is a major outing. Praise them when they have finished and when they return indoors. If a puppy looks as if it is about to make a mess in the wrong place, transfer it to the proper area so that the

One of the first training programs is toilet-training, although in the case of a house-trained female the kittens are usually taught by their mother to use a litter tray.

right location is established by the smell. No young animal should be punished for using the wrong place.

Cats and dogs are not the only animals which can be housebroken. All species which use regular toilet places are susceptible to training. Even rabbits have been successfully trained, but this is the exception rather than the rule.

Restricting Territory

The only way to define the territory of some pets is to erect physical barriers. Cats and dogs which are allowed reasonably free movement have to be taught that there are some places where they may not go whether it be into certain rooms or onto chairs, tables, shelves, or kitchen surfaces. Cats have a strong sense of their own territory and learn to respect that of others. They should be reproved if they start toward or go into a forbidden area, removed and then petted when they return to their proper place. Some cats learn this is a way of attracting attention, however. Dogs will often desist at a word of rebuke, but if they continue to go where they should not, they should be ordered back to their beds and petted when they obey.

It is unreasonable to let a young puppy or kitten have the run of the house and then expect it to keep off the furniture as it gets bigger. Establish your rules from the start, and do not change them. Consistency is an important rule to follow in training an animal.

Collar and Leash Training

The simplest way for an animal to carry an identification label is by means of a collar. Puppies—and kittens too if they are to wear them—should be taught to wear a collar as soon as they have been innoculated. Remember to replace the collar with a larger size as the animal grows. Goats and other animals which have to be tethered should be introduced to a collar or halter when they are very young. Horses, donkeys, and mules can also be trained to accept a harness collar when young but should not be saddled or bridled until they are fully developed.

Some animals enjoy wearing a collar from the beginning and will even bring it to be put on. If an animal shows irritation, however, start with short periods of wear until it becomes accustomed to the collar. When

Begin training that you intend to continue. Once you have allowed a habit to develop, such as allowing your pet to eat from the family table, then it will be difficult to cure should you change your mind later.

51

first taken for a walk on a collar and leash, most puppies and almost all cats will need very patient coaxing and may refuse to budge. Try standing or crouching in front of your pet within the length of the leash and calling it to you. If the animal comes, try repeating the process but move backwards as it comes to you. In many cases you may simply have to drag your pet along, but coax it and encourage it all the time as you do so. Cat owners may never succeed in leash training their pet, although the younger the animal, and the more frequent and playful the lessons, the better their chance of success. Most cats, and some small dogs, will find a harness more comfortable to wear than a collar because the harness prevents the whole pull of the leash being taken on the neck. Animals should not, however, run free when wearing a harness for it can catch on something and trap them. A cat collar should always include an elastic section so your pet can wriggle out of it if it gets hooked through a twig or other protrusion.

A number of small animals such as monkeys, parrots, and ferrets will accompany their owner on a restraining chain. Others will perch on a shoulder or travel happily in a pocket because they feel safe and secure with a particular human. Such animals must be gradually exposed to disturbing noise, traffic, or strangers. Great care should be taken to avoid any sudden alarm that would cause them to take off on their own beyond your care and protection.

Detailed information follows for the training of dogs, horses, pigeons, and singing and talking birds. The training methods suggested may also be successful with other animals if reinterpreted to match the pet's natural behavior patterns. A pet may do something spontaneously which, if encouraged and praised, it will repeat to please you on future occasions.

Training Dogs

Successful dog training, for whatever purpose, is simply a matter of knowing more than the dog and patiently applying this knowledge with a modicum of common

sense. Scientists rate a dog's intelligence above that of a horse and below that of a pig. The dog's ability to solve problems is extremely limited, but it does have an excellent memory and behavior once thoroughly learned (good or bad) is seldom, if ever, forgotten. Proper training is therefore essential from the day a pup is brought to its new home.

According to the latest research on dog behavior the second and third months of a dog's life are critical: what happens to it in this crucial period will influence its future development for better or worse. Socialization with humans begins when a dog is weaned at about four or five weeks and the breeder begins not only to feed it but also to stroke and play with it. Contact with the breeder creates a firm bond with humans and is a valuable prelude to future training.

Opposite Page. *Many different types of dog collars have been used over the centuries. Top Left. This Pug is wearing a belled collar fashionable in the nineteenth century.* Top Right *The spiked collar of the Pyrenean Mountain Dog protected its neck from the jaws of wolves it hunted.* Center. *Fighting dogs, like these Staffordshire Bull Terriers, wore wide, studded collars when fighting.*

Intelligence varies within a breed and even within a litter. Rating the intelligence of different breeds is a debatable matter, but certain breeds do react more readily to basic training, are more obedient, and are more versatile in responding to owners' demands than other breeds. With only a few exceptions, breeds originally developed to work closely with their owners, such as retrievers, sheep dogs, guard and rescue dogs, respond faster to obedience training than do most hounds or terriers in which strong-willed independence and/or aggressiveness is purposefully bred. Hound and terrier owners must be prepared to put in a little more effort for a civilized and devoted pet.

THE NEW PUPPY

Ideally a puppy is trained by the breeder and its mother. If not, training should begin at the moment a puppy reaches its new home. If the journey from the breeder's has not been too long and the puppy was exercised before leaving, there is a good chance that it will not have soiled—but it will now be bursting to do so. Carry the puppy into the predetermined toilet area, wait for it to relieve itself and praise the dog in glowing terms.

You should establish from the beginning the area where the puppy is to be allowed. If on reaching home, the pup is first allowed in the kitchen, it will soon discover everything at or near its eye level, including the garbage can, and will be eager to chew and paw things for further investigation. It will also discover the way out of the kitchen. At this point, all but one of the family should leave the room and the remaining person should discipline the puppy. It will be too much for the newcomer if more than one person gives commands.

At first, a puppy's behavior can be corrected by saying the dog's name together with a sharp "No!" The puppy will quickly learn that certain things on or near the floor and leaving the room are prohibited. As soon as the puppy tires of exploring the area and wants to rest, place it in a prepared basket in its confined area.

The puppy should be allowed out of its kennel or basket when it signals, for example by howling, a need to eat and drink. Immediately after a period of activity and food it should be taken to its toilet area. It should always be allowed out after any long period of confinement in a basket or kennel. The last thing a puppy wishes to do is to mess its kennel, but a young animal cannot control itself as well as an adult dog.

Bottom. *Dogs trained for Red Cross work have been used in both world wars to find wounded and to carry medical supplies.*

Punishment and Reward

Like a young child, a pup does not know the difference between acceptable and unacceptable behavior. If the new owner is only concerned about housebreaking the puppy and scolding it when it misbehaves, the animal will never hear words of approval. A solid week of reprimands can turn the boldest pup into a cowed, cringing creature afraid to do anything. Situations must be provided for lavish amounts of praise which is the best possible training method. Give the dog very brief but consistent obedience lessons during which it is praised for walking on a leash, heeling, sitting, staying, coming when called, and going into its kennel or basket when ordered. The puppy has made its owner happy and is therefore happy as well. It does not always need tasty tidbits as a reward; affectionate praise and petting is sufficient.

Physical punishment has absolutely no place in training a puppy, even for such habits as nipping people. Proper discipline for this bad act includes clasping the head firmly around the muzzle at each attempt, giving the puppy a short shake, and saying "No!" sharply. The owner who resorts to physical punishment is demonstrating an ignorance of proper training methods, an inability to handle frustration, or possibly a trace of sadism in his or her personality.

However, if the puppy obstinately persists in unacceptable behavior, use the more extreme measure of withdrawing affection. After the initial scolding the puppy should still be allowed the run of the room but should be ignored totally for an hour or so. Such periods of being rejected are as successful with dogs of all ages as they are with children. A naughty puppy should not be confined to its kennel or basket when it misbehaves, because of the unpleasant associations this may create.

GIVING COMMANDS

The first thing a dog must learn in order to obey further commands is its name. Choose a name that the dog will not confuse with a command, either in obedience training or in the hunting field "Joe" is too close to "No"; "Whoa" and "Rhum" to "Come." A retriever enthusiast would not use "Jack" because it is too similar to "Back" or "Get back." There is no need to bellow commands like a drill sergeant issuing orders across the parade square, but the military method of preceding an executive command with a precautionary word is helpful when giving instructions to dogs. You should catch the dog's attention by stretching out the name; then pause and give the specific obedience command. Failure to obey promptly and correctly means that the dog has not been sufficiently trained and that more drill is required.

Every member of the puppy's human family must learn to give and to enforce the same commands in exactly the same way each time. Not being consistent simply confuses the dog. Commands should always be given in soft but firm tones, except for "No"! The puppy will have enough trouble adjusting to its new surroundings without having to cope with orders being screamed. This only increases its feelings of insecurity and slows down the training process. Men with deep, throaty voices may find it helpful to speak a tone or two higher when addressing the puppy. Some people automatically kneel down when talking to a puppy. This is a good idea since the person is closer to the dog's eye level and therefore presents a less menacing figure. It is advisable initially to issue most commands from a kneeling posi-

tion. In addition to creating a closer bond with the animal, it will allow your dog, with all the distractions vying for its attention, to concentrate better on what you want it to be learning.

Many people accompany a verbal command with a physical gesture. This is also a good idea since a dog responds readily to its owner's movements: the accusing, wagging finger when it misbehaves, the arm motion or clapping when it is to come, the upraised palm when it is to stay. When training a young puppy, physical gestures should definitely be used to reinforce voice commands. This feature is particularly effective with younger dogs.

JUMPING ON PEOPLE

Although this natural and friendly action of a puppy may be tolerated when it is small, it should be discouraged at an early age so it will not become a nuisance as the animal grows larger.

When a puppy jumps on your leg, you should back away, bring your hand forward with the palm facing downwards and gently order "Down" or "Get down." If the dog fails to understand your gesture, you can let your hand come forward onto the pup's shoulders so pushing the animal down. It is best to use a gentle approach initially so the puppy does not feel its friendly intentions are being rejected.

In the case of older puppies it may be necessary to push with your knee and command more firmly, "Down," or "Get down!" You should never follow the advice of those who suggest stepping on a young dog's feet because such action can cause pain and could possibly inflict injury to the delicate bone structure of the foot.

FORMAL OBEDIENCE TRAINING

The whole object of training is simply to prevent your dog from being a nuisance to you, your family, and friends. When training the six-to twelve-week-old pup, use gentle commands and actions and brief, frequently repeated lessons which are presented as play. No pup should be expected to perform like a seasoned trouper, even though surprisingly good results may sometimes be attained in a short time.

Training sessions for older dogs or pups older than nine months should be limited to fifteen minutes. Sessions may, of course, be repeated several times during the day.

The gentleness or severity of approach should be adjusted to the age and personality of your dog. An animal working with its tail down is not happy. It is either being pushed too hard and fast or not being given enough affection and praise during training, or is suffering from a combination of both. Regular practice is the key to success; with every command and action repeated in the same way each time.

For basic training, the necessary requirements are a chain slip collar and a leather or flat nylon leash 180 cm. (6ft.) long. For a puppy, a rolled leather collar may be used instead of the chain link one. Chain leashes are so heavy and unwieldy that they may hurt the owner's hand and should never be used in obedience training. The slip collar should be placed around the dog's neck so that the running end attached to the leash rides freely through the other ring. Thus applied, the collar will only tighten when pulled or jerked and will loosen immediately when these actions cease.

54

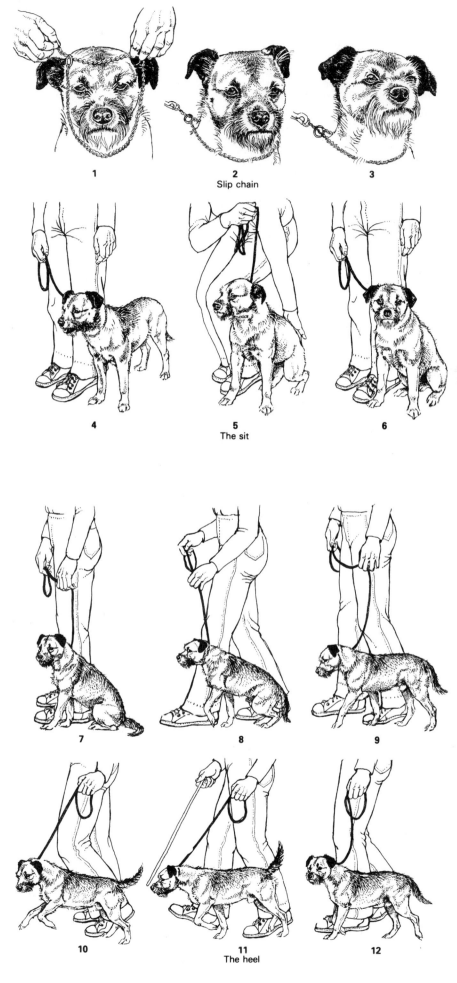

1   2 Slip chain   3

4   5 The sit   6

7   8   9

10   11 The heel   12

In the early stages of training, you should reinforce voice commands with the appropriate hand signals. Later, you may use either. Traditionally, dogs are worked on the owner's left side. However, the owner can adapt the training instructions to work the dog on the right side.

The Sit

Immediately after saying the animal's name and the command "Sit!" you should apply downward pressure to the dog's rump with the left hand and, with a shortened hold on the leash, pull your right hand upwards. The dog has no choice but to sit. You should now move along with the dog a half dozen or more steps, stop, and repeat the command and the actions. In time, and with sufficient praise and petting the dog will sit automatically when you stop. Under no circumstances should the dog be allowed to jump up on you when it is being praised and petted.

The Heel

Start teaching this command with the dog in the sit position on your left side and the leash held across your body with both hands. Then, call out the dog's name and the command "Heel!" Follow this action with a gentle tug of the leash in the right hand and a corresponding loosening with the left which will have the effect of pulling the leash forward. At the exact moment that the jerk is administered, you should step forward with the left foot and begin walking at a normal pace.

The left hand grasping the leash should hang naturally within the animal's vision. When the dog lunges against the leash so that its muzzle is no longer in line with your knee, jerk it back with the left hand and simultaneously order "Heel!" The jerks on the leash should be decisive; weak and ineffectual little tugs will not do. If the slip chain collar has been applied properly, the dog will suffer only momentary discomfort since its furred hide is about five times less sensitive to pain than the human skin. If the dog continues to forge ahead past your knee, its muzzle can be tapped lightly with a long, light stick. If such a stick is not handy, the loose end of the leash may be twirled like a propeller in front of the dog's nose to keep its head level with your knee.

Doubling Up

Once the "Sit" and the "Heel" are properly understood they should be combined into one movement. If you have done the job well, you will only have to command "Heel!" and the dog will sit automatically when you stop walking, and you can dispense with jerking the leash on the "Heel" command. However, if the dog begins to sit crookedly or fails to react immediately when you stop or command "Heel!" you should take your dog back to basic orders and actions for a time.

The Stay

This command is generally given with the dog in a sitting or lying position. It may, however, be given when the dog is standing, in which case owners of pointing dogs used to hunt birds may prefer to substitute "Whoa" or some other such word. The forewarning of the dog's name may be omitted in the "Stay" command.

You should both face the same direction so that the dog's head is in line with your left knee and the leash held only in the right hand. As you give the command "Stay!" you should sweep the left arm back full length so that the palm of your hand—with fingers close together—stops just short of the dog's nose. Then, walk forward to the

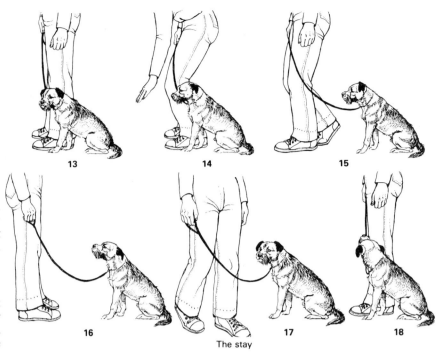

The stay

end of the leash, turn to face the dog and challenge it, with intensity of manner and hard-eyed stare, not to move an inch.

This lesson will have to be repeated a few times until the dog understands. When it is staying well, walk towards it with the leash still in your hand. Then, starting from the dog's left side, circle around the animal and stop when it is at the correct left-hand, side-knee position to you. During this circling maneuver, hold the leash so that it remains in front of or above the dog without ever touching the animal.

The "Sit," "Heel," and "Stay" may now be combined during a training session with plenty of petting and praise. At this stage, having several sessions each day to reinforce the dog's behavior is helpful.

The Come

This should be the easiest lesson of all for a young pup. However, for older dogs with little early training it can prove difficult, particularly if they are worked off the leash.

When the dog is in the Sit position, you should order "Stay," walk to the end of the leash, turn to face the dog and after a short time, call out its name and the command "Come!" If the dog comes, gather in the leash so that it does not become entangled. If the dog does not obey, you should haul in the leash hand-over-hand. The puppy will soon learn to come, and you should then substitute a long training cord for the leash so that it will come when called from a longer distance. The training cord can be of any flexible material with a diameter the same or preferably greater than that of a clothesline.

Once the dog comes, it should be ordered to sit directly in front of you and await the next command.

The Down

While dogs spend the better part of their lives in the supine position, ordering them to lie down on command is often quite difficult. For whatever reason,

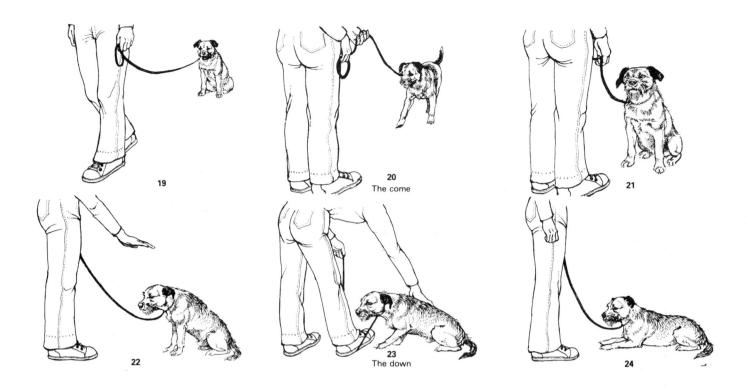

19

20
The come

21

22

23
The down

24

dogs initially feel they are being punished when ordered to lie down.

Call out the dog's name and then the command, "Down!" and accompany this by a forward sweep of your arm from head to waist level or lower, with the palm of your hand moving toward the dog. If the dog refuses to obey the verbal command and hand signal from the Sit–Stay position, you should step on the leash with your right foot close to the dog's collar. The leash should be under the arch of your shoe so that you can pull it with your left hand and push the dog's back down with your right hand. This will force the animal to lie down whether it wishes to or not.

These actions usually have to be repeated a number of times before the dog will respond solely to the voice command and hand motion. Once success is achieved from the Sit–Stay, you can command the dog from the Stand–Stay position. The dog may still be reluctant to lie down, but this will be overcome.

Combining the lessons

When all five lessons have been learned, they can be combined during a fifteen minute training session. When Heeling, the dog should always be made to work with its head close to your left knee, even if you turn abruptly or if it has to circle people, posts, or other obstacles. The dog's Sit positions should be close to you and square rather than crooked or on one haunch. Finally, the dog should learn to obey all these commands off the leash. However, not even dogs that reach this level of training should be trusted off the leash in an area with traffic. A single distraction or forgetful moment could result in injury or death.

It is relatively easy to train a dog alone in your garden or in a deserted parking lot. Yet it is more challenging and ultimately more valuable to train your pet in the distracting presence of other dogs. Only the dog that goes through its paces in company can be considered thoroughly trained. To achieve this perfection, it is advisable to attend an obedience-training course. Some

dogs are harder to train than others, and both dogs and owners can learn from each other in such a class.

Other useful commands

The command, "Kennel!" tells the dog to go into its kennel. You should accompany this order with a sweep of the hand in the direction of the desired movement.

"Leave it!" can mean a host of things: Do not touch that Sunday dinner! Do not roll on that dead fish! Do not chew on that slipper! Do not chase that animal! It seldom needs to be prefixed with the dog's name. Indeed, when this command is needed, there is seldom time for anything but the words "Leave it!"

TRAFFIC TRAINING

Dogs should not be let off the leash in a congested area or where there is likely to be traffic. It may be against the law to allow your pet to wander without a leash. Your dog should be taught to stop on reaching a curb and not to cross a road until ordered to do so. This is not difficult when the basic obedience lessons have been learned. Conditioning to traffic should be gradual, and you should correct any tendency to wander onto the road by jerking the dog back decisively onto the sidewalk whenever any traffic approaches. If you live in an area where you feel it is safe to let your dog out without a leash, you should still teach it to be wary of traffic at an early age by allowing it to roam on a long leash and jerking it back as a vehicle or cyclist approaches. For safety's sake this kind of training should be carried out with the collaboration of a motorist: relying on random traffic could lead to an accident.

Dogs that chase vehicles can sometimes be cured of the habit in the following way. You should ask someone to drive slowly past your dog and as it rushes towards the car, the driver should shower it with screams of rage and a barrage of empty cans. Carry out such a procedure on private property and not on a public highway! This method may require several attempts, but its success will be worth the effort.

56

Top. Police dogs are taught to attack on command and—perhaps more important—to stop when told to do so.

Bottom. You must train your dog to be obedient when traffic is around lest it causes a serious accident or harms itself. Chasing cyclists is extremely dangerous.

WATCHDOG

You may wish your pet to do double duty as a watchdog, and bark when people come to the door or onto your property. Most pups will do this naturally once they begin barking at about six months of age. All you have to do is encourage this tendency and, when the stranger has been identified as friendly, order the dog to cease by saying something like "Good dog. Quiet now. Friend."

The dog's sense of territory and of its owner's property is so strong that sometimes it will block a stranger's approach instinctively. Some dogs will even threaten attack with menacing growls. If you encourage such behavior you should be mindful of the lawsuit that may result from an attack on a child who wanders onto your property or a stranger, such as a postal employee or delivery person, who comes to your property legally. Discouraging the dog's overly aggressive behavior or its needless barking is just as important as encouraging it to bark when a stranger is present.

GUARD AND ATTACK DOGS

Some breeds and certain individual dogs can be trained to attack intruders or hold them at bay and attack on command. Few dog owners would or should wish for such a dog; they are primarily for the police, military, or private security organizations. Both the dogs and their owners or handlers must be trained by reputable and experienced professionals, and it would be dangerous and irresponsible for you as a pet owner to train your dog in this way. During periods of increased crime, people are naturally inclined to want guard dogs for protection, but it is not a wise idea.

SHEPHERD DOGS

If you want a dog to herd cattle, sheep, or even turkeys, you should acquire a promising pup from the best of the local working shepherd dogs and have it trained professionally. Although many of the popular show breeds still have some herding instinct, this does not mean that they or their descendants will naturally turn into first-rate herding dogs.

Training Horses and Ponies

A horse or pony takes longer to train than most other domestic animals because of the complex nature of the tasks required of it and the dangerous accidents that may result from inadequate training. Assuming that it has a kindly disposition, a young horse may become an enjoyable riding animal for an experienced rider within six months. However, it will not normally develop into a safe ride for a novice for several years after that, nor can it be expected to cross country smoothly and reliably until it has three to four years of training behind it.

The number of months or years spent training a horse depends upon the degree of sophistication required by the trainer. A racehorse may be running on the track six months after breaking in because galloping on a level surface is the only requirement. On the other hand, a quality dressage horse can take six years to come into its prime and will then stay at its peak only as long as regular practice training is continued.

Before any attempt is made to train a young horse or pony, the psychology of the animal must be understood. A horse is a herd animal, lonely and nervous away from its fellows. Its natural survival instinct is deeply embedded and manifests itself in fear of any unknown object, movement or sound and in the tendency to run first and ask questions afterwards, to buck a predator off its back and to gather reassurance from the company of others of its species (the greater the numbers the greater the odds against any one individual falling victim to an attacker). These hereditary traits are signs of common sense more than cowardice, and without such instincts the horse would not have survived.

The horse, then, should be handled gently but firmly. The absence of sudden movements or noise and a soothing tone of voice will do much to reassure a young horse. Familiarity with the human race and with some of our peculiar demands should begin as soon as possible. A foal can be taught almost from birth to wear a tiny harness collar. In the first few months of its life it can be taught elementary lessons, such as to come when called and to pick up its feet on request.

The horse learns by association. Praise for its efforts will encourage it to do better and a kind word or a pat for a task well done are the best rewards. A young animal rewarded with food can become a menace when it is older and stronger. Harsh voices or loss of temper affect horses adversely and may cause permanent damage because the horse has an excellent memory. If punishment must be administered it should be given at once for better association with the crime and should be limited to a single light lick with the whip or hand.

To train your horse successfully you should keep to a regular timetable. If the horse is brought in from the field daily at four o'clock it will soon learn to wait at the gate at that time. Exercise during the same period every day will result in an animal that is eager to work, whereas irregular hours frequently cause an anxious horse that does not know whether to settle down or stay alert.

A gradual process of teaching always produces the best and most permanent results. New commands should be introduced singly and practiced daily until they are thoroughly understood before another skill is attempted. Routine practice of lessons already learned should be part of the daily program to reinforce the basic training and give opportunities for praise and reassurance. This helps the horse to build up confidence before beginning new work with a trainer.

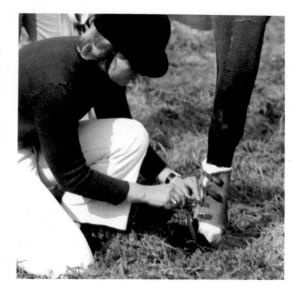

Brushing boots are fitted to protect a horse from striking himself; this is especially important during longeing.

Regardless of whether early handling has taken place or not, physical work with the horse should not be started until it is at least three years old. A horse does not stop growing until it is four and too much work at an early age can strain bones and muscles permanently. Racehorses appear to be exceptions to this rule because many are earning a living at two years of age. However, they are fed on special high protein food from birth and usually suffer some damage to the spine from carrying weight before the bones are hardened.

Years spent training a young horse slowly are repaid by a prolonged working life and by the pleasure of riding a thoroughly trained animal. A horse that does not enjoy its work shows it through a sullen or disobedient response to its rider. A good riding horse is one which is alert, fearless and obedient, comfortable in all its paces, physically able and willing to carry out all its rider's commands, and shows pleasure in the execution of its job. The training of a horse requires expert knowledge and experience and should not be attempted by the amateur. If you have only limited experience, you can do real harm by working unsupervised with the horse. The value of expert training cannot be overly stressed.

LONGEING

The common, and best, method of initiating the young horse to harness and to commands is to work it on the longe in circles to both sides. This work in hand—where the trainer stands in the center of the circle around which the horse is moving—is the foundation of balance and fluidity in the horse. Most horses turn to one hand more readily than to the other so that regular longeing on the horse's stiff side does much to adjust its balance. An assistant is needed during the first few lessons to lead the horse around the circle until it understands what is required of it. Expert longeing, carried out daily over a period of weeks, will teach the horse to shorten its overall profile by moving with its hocks well under it, its neck arched, and the plane of its face carried vertically while "taking" the bit. A horse that has thus been taught to balance itself correctly will be able to use its muscles to the best advantage and be a comfortable ride. In addition, the horse trained in this manner will be less likely to injure itself.

Longeing is the first stage of formal training for a horse. The longeing attachment (caveson) is worn over the top of the bridle. Before the exercise starts, the side reins must be adjusted to the correct length.

In the initial stages of longeing the young horse is led in a circle by an assistant who holds the longeing reins near the head, while the trainer works from a slightly shortened longe.

The trainer moves to the center of the circle, and soon the young horse trots happily on the longe. The rein is straight, and the trainer keeps the horse between the rein and the whip.

Incorrect longeing: The horse is being disobedient and has broken from the trot into the canter. The rein has gone slack, and the trainer has momentarily lost control.

BACKING

Mounting the horse for the first time should be attempted only when the horse is obedient to commands from the ground. Verbal instructions to "Walk on" or "Halt," if learned in hand, make the transition to associated signals with the rider's hands and legs much easier. The safest time to back a horse is when it has finished its normal work and is settled and tired. The area chosen for the lesson should be a confined space, such as a stable or small paddock, with a surface of peat or grass that minimizes danger from slipping.

As in the initial stages of longeing, when a helper is needed to lead the horse until it becomes obedient to voice commands, an assistant is also invaluable in backing. While the assistant holds the horse's head and talks to it soothingly, the trainer progresses slowly from leaning his or her weight on the animal to lying across its back with the legs off the ground. If the animal remains calm, the trainer may slowly move a leg across its back and mount it. Slow and deliberate movements are important once the trainer is on the horse because the animal will be extremely nervous and unsure about what is happening. The wise trainer will

Top Left. *Backing (mounting) the horse for the first time has to be done slowly, carefully and quietly. The rider is usually given a gentle leg up.*

Top Right. *The rider should then lie across the horse's back to accustom it to a rider's weight.*

Center. *Once mounted, the horse is gently walked with an assistant holding a side rein.*

Bottom Left. *When a young horse first finds himself carrying a rider he can be difficult to handle.*

Bottom Right. *The first stage of training a horse to jump is to get it to trot over poles that are lying on the ground.*

take special precautions in order to avoid unnecessary excitement that could lead to injuries of himself or the animal.

During backing the trainer and assistant must stay constantly on the alert. Although the horse may appear to take the unfamiliar weight on its back without concern, this apparent calmness is often because it has not realized what is happening. Thus it may panic when asked to take a step or two forward or when catching a glimpse out of the corner of its eye of the trainer sitting above and behind its head. The need to be alert and careful cannot be overemphasized because, once the animal has been unduly frightened, some time may be required before it will allow the trainer to mount it again.

TRAFFIC TRAINING

Familiarity with traffic is essential for horses which are to be used on the road. If you have access to a field beside a road or railroad, pasture your young animal there, preferably in the company of an older animal which is not alarmed by the honks and rumbles of passing vehicles. Introducing the young horse to the road itself is most safely done with either a calm horse or a person between it and the traffic. Riding a green or novice horse in a motorized society without protection from the ground or from another horse can be extremely dangerous. It can also lead to sizable legal expenses.

JUMPING

When the horse is going smoothly in all its paces, is balanced and obedient, and is thoroughly used to being ridden, you can introduce it to jumping. This should not normally be attempted until it is four years old because of the horse's physical immaturity. You should begin lessons by walking and trotting the horse, either ridden or on the longe, over poles on the ground. Then, progress very gradually to raised poles and different types of obstacles. When it is going freely and confidently, you can introduce it to the hunting field or equivalent. A young horse gains confidence from being taken alongside an experienced jumper and will soon meet a variety of obstacles at speed. But you should not try to rush its development as a jumper. It takes much time and encouragement before a horse is ready to jump large obstacles, and any attempts to speed up its progress could result in crippling injuries.

Training Birds

TALKING BIRDS

Parrots are renowned for their ability to talk, a talent they share with only a few other birds such as members of the crow and starling families. The popular African Gray Parrot is an able performer, while the tiny budgerigar is charming with its ability as a talker. The most skillful talker however is the Hill Mynah which looks rather like a smart, miniature crow, but belongs to the starling family. These birds can be trained to talk and often become accomplished mimics with amazing vocabularies, capable of repeating whole nursery rhymes or singing songs. They are also adept at whistling tunes and imitating the sounds around them, such as a squeaking door or a dripping tap.

The best age to start teaching a budgerigar to talk is soon after it has left the nest and is feeding itself. A Hill Mynah must be obtained when it still begs for food. The color-variety of the bird is not relevant, although young cock budgerigars are generally better for training as talkers than hens. It is probable that male Hill Mynahs are better talkers than the hens, but it is difficult to be sure due to the problem of sexing this species.

Top Left. *You can easily teach a pet bird to come by offering choice of bits of food, as with this cockatoo.*

Top Right *A racing-pigeon owner places his pigeons in a transport basket before a training flight.*

Birds which are not tame seldom become good talkers. The bird should be housed separately, out of sight and hearing of other birds. Only one member of the household should act as the teacher and the first phrase taught should be a short, simple one. Repeat the phrase slowly and as often as possible. When the first phrase is mastered, start teaching another short one in the same manner. A bird should never be expected to learn more than one phrase at a time. A tape or cassette recording machine is best employed as an additional aid, as birds benefit from personal attention and instruction.

COMING WHEN CALLED

You can teach your pet bird to come by offering it inducements in the form of choice tidbits of food. Fruit is especially good as a reward and mealworms are relished by many birds. A handful of grain will tempt pigeons, domestic and ornamental fowl, and waterfowl.

Like other types of training, teaching birds to come when called is best done by one person whom they learn to recognize and trust. The trainer should wear similar clothes and behave in the same way each time the bird is being taught to come. Entice the bird with food so that eventually it will come to the same spot at the same time to receive its tidbit. Calling "Come on, come on" will usually be sufficient to make it come. Some birds will also answer to a whistle or the rattle of their food dish.

RACING PIGEONS

The methods used to train racing pigeons are many and varied, as most fanciers develop their own theories. However, the following method has been well tried and is suitable for the novice. You should either have bred the birds yourself or else have acquired them at about five weeks of age, that is, as soon as they are able to fend for themselves. They should not have been allowed to fly freely. From the outset, you should spend as much time as possible with them so that they recognize you as a friend and are not frightened each time you enter the loft. The birds should be placed on top of the loft before they can actually fly in order to become familiar with the surroundings and the kind of traps used for entering the loft.

Around the age of six weeks the pigeons will start to flutter about. At this stage the feeding system should be changed so that they are only allowed out for exercise when they are hungry. They should be released fairly late in the evening and, after a few skirmishes around the loft, they will enter the traps clamoring for food. If they are given their freedom after a meal, there is no incentive for them to return quickly to the loft and speedy trapping is essential if they are to win races.

Put the fledglings in a basket, place it inside the loft, and let them remain there all night. This will teach them to become used to being in a confined space and to being fed and watered while in the basket. Repeat this exercise on two or three occasions. By the time the pigeons are nine or ten weeks old, they should be flying for periods of an hour or so and covering a large area around the loft. The home range area often extends to several kilometers or more.

Real training begins now. Select a fine day and in the evening before feeding, place the pigeons in the basket. Take them about 3km. (2mi.) away from home and then release them. This exercise is usually referred to as a training toss. On the first occasion, the pigeons will probably take an hour or so to return home, but the experience gained will be invaluable. Extend the distance by stages to approximately 8, 16, 24 and 32km. (5, 10, 15, and 20mi.) in the direction from which they will be raced. The time taken to return will be greatly improved. They should then be released from about 48km. (30mi.) on one or two occasions and they will be ready for their first race, which is usually about 80km. (50mi.). Young birds are not usually raced beyond 320km. (200mi.). Older birds, which are familiar with the course, should be given a few tosses of 80km. (50mi.) to get them fit before their racing season be-

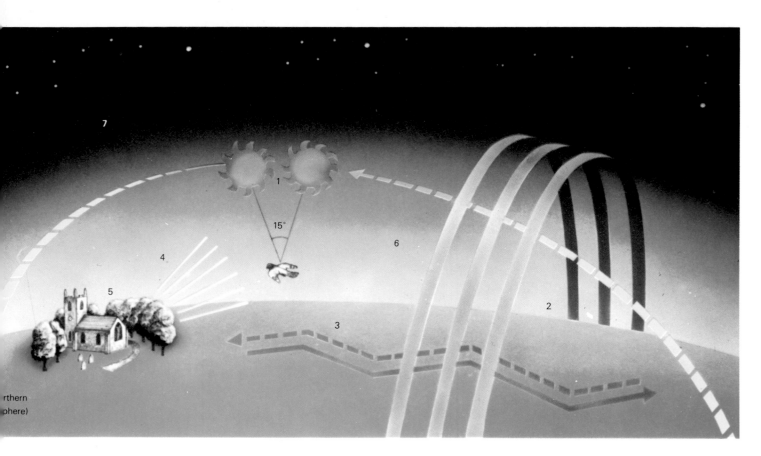

gins. These races often extend beyond 965km. (600mi.) and flights of 1,600km. (1,000mi.) have been achieved, but seldom more than 800km. (500mi.) is covered in one day.

How do pigeons navigate? We cannot pretend to understand fully how the "homing" ability of the pigeon works, but scientific studies of pigeons suggest that some or all of the "navigational aids" shown in this diagram play a part. The diagram shows a Northern Hemisphere location.

1. The Sun used as a compass to determine orientation in terms of North to South and East to West position. This hypothesis assumes that pigeons have some kind of internal clock to compensate for the changing position of the Sun (15° per hour). Under cloudy conditions there is some evidence that sunlight reflected from a patch of blue sky can be used, even if the Sun itself is obscured. This hypothesis assumes that the pigeon has an ability to detect planes of polarized light—a skill already shown to exist in honeybees.

2. The Earth's magnetic field used to determine position. This hypothesis assumes that the pigeon has an interpretive ability not found in other animals.

3. Inertial guidance used. This hypothesis assumes the ability to remember changes of course during the outward journey and to repeat them in reverse during the homeward journey. There is little evidence to support this theory.

4. Navigation by olfactory information. This hypothesis assumes that the pigeon has a sophisticated recognition of smells and smell gradients—as has been shown to exist in salmon. There is little evidence to support this theory.

5. Recognition of landmarks to guide navigation. There is little evidence to suggest that this comes into use except during the last few hundred yards of the journey.

6. Pressure pattern used. This hypothesis assumes an ability to recognize small changes in barometric pressure. There is some evidence to suggest that pigeons are able to do this.

7. Navigation by recognition of stellar positions. This hypothesis assumes that the pigeon has an internal clock and can correct its course.

WORKING ANIMALS

From the first time dogs came into the human domain, civilizations have made use of the skills, superior senses, and strength of animals. Although the dog was the first and most versatile working animal, fulfilling most of the functions animals have performed for the human community, it has been supplanted by other species in many of its roles.

Hunting

Early man observed the ability of a pack of wild dogs to drive a herd of prey while waiting for the right moment to single out a victim. At what point the dog became an actual companion to men as hunter or as herder cannot be specifically stated. Domestication is a gradual process, and facts and figures concerning the early domes-

tication of animals are constantly being revised. Dogs still play the part of hunting help today.

The highly skilled sheep dog can work closely with its owner following instructions given by whistle or by gesture, or else operate entirely on its own. The appearance of sheep dogs varies considerably because different kinds have been developed to meet the particular demands of regional areas. Of course, some types are bred for showing where looks are paramount. Even when kept as a pet, a sheep dog retains its herding instinct and will busily round up stragglers when out for a walk with the family. A wide range of other dog breeds have been developed through the centuries to match specific tasks in the hunting field. Among these breeds are hounds, terriers, pointers, setters, spaniels, and other retrievers.

In the Middle Ages, when hunting deer was the

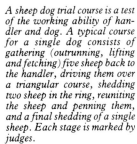

A sheep dog trial course is a test of the working ability of handler and dog. A typical course for a single dog consists of gathering (outrunning, lifting and fetching) five sheep back to the handler, driving them over a triangular course, shedding two sheep in the ring, reuniting the sheep and penning them, and a final shedding of a single sheep. Each stage is marked by judges.

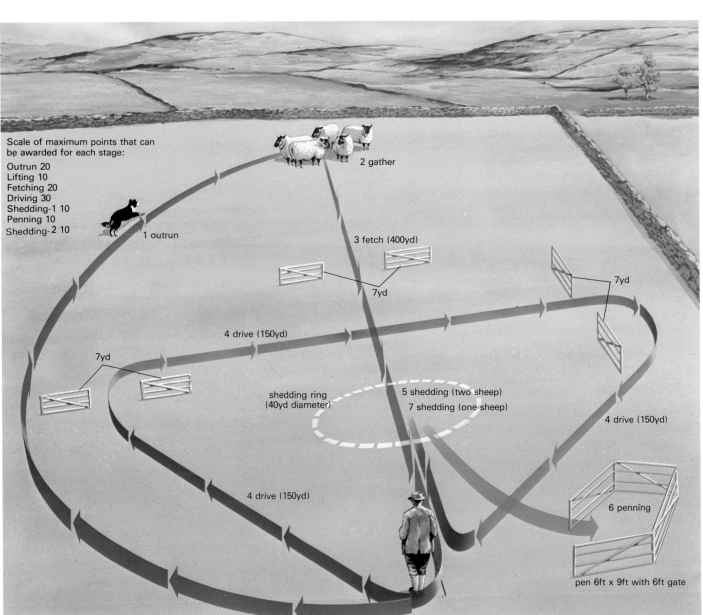

Scale of maximum points that can be awarded for each stage:

Outrun 20
Lifting 10
Fetching 20
Driving 30
Shedding-1 10
Penning 10
Shedding-2 10

1 outrun

2 gather

3 fetch (400yd)

7yd

4 drive (150yd)

7yd

7yd

4 drive (150yd)

shedding ring (40yd diameter)

5 shedding (two sheep)
7 shedding (one sheep)

4 drive (150yd)

6 penning

pen 6ft x 9ft with 6ft gate

Top Left. *An unusual working animal is the pig, shown here hunting for truffles.*

Top Right. *Falcons and hawks have been used for centuries to hunt small birds and game. Although now primarily a sport, falconing has its roots in working situations.*

prerogative of kings and a select number of lords, people living in or near the king's forests were not allowed to keep large dogs lest they should poach. Since the forest laws prohibited common people from keeping hunting dogs, pigs were trained to hunt game instead. Individual pigs are still kept for hunting purposes, and in France they are widely used to find the delectable fungus, the truffle, which grows beneath the soil.

Even the domestic cat was taught to retrieve by the ancient Egyptians while another member of the cat family, the cheetah, is still used to hunt antelope. A cheetah trained for hunting is taken into the field blindfolded. The moment antelope are sighted, its eyes are uncovered and the cheetah released. Although they have less staying power than greyhounds, cheetahs can reach a speed of up to 100kmph.(62mph.).

For centuries, falcons and other birds of prey have been used to hunt smaller birds and small game, and in the Far East, cormorants are still trained to fish with their necks constricted by a cord or ring so they cannot swallow their catch. In recent years some urban dwellers have trained falcons to hunt among the large pigeon populations plaguing various areas.

Guardians

The word *watchdog* has become synonymous with the word *guardian* in our language, but many animals apart from the dog will give warning of the approach of strangers or of known danger and will make as much noise as any barking dog. Most famous perhaps were the geese whose shrill voices warned the ancient Romans of an attack upon their city. Geese are still kept on the Capitoline Hill in commemoration of this fact. They have often been kept by those too poor to own a dog because they can also be extremely vicious if they have reason to attack.

Many animals have a strong territorial sense and will defend their owners and home range against threat. Even the domestic cat has been known to pin an intruder in a chair and, on one occasion, an Abyssinian cat sprang at the face of a man who persisted in giving unwanted attention to its young owner when they went out for a walk! Nevertheless, the dog is the traditional protector, whether of house or flock. A Roman book on farming claims that anyone could train a dog to be a faithful guard by giving it a roasted frog to eat!

Warfare

Dogs and even lions were trained in early civilizations to take an active part in battle, and the elephant was used as a living armored vehicle, trampling the enemy underfoot. Seated in a howdah on the elephant's back, an archer had a vantage point better than the horseman's, and far superior to that of the foot soldier. The camel has also been widely used in warfare. The Dromedary Camel was a significant factor enabling the Arabs to overrun the Middle East in the seventh century A.D.

However, throughout the ages the horse has assumed the greatest role in warfare. The Mongol conquests of half the world in the Middle Ages can be attributed to the rugged strength and agility of their ponies used for transportation and in cavalry units. The possession of new equestrian aids such as the saddle and the stirrup, the horseshoe and harness, gave superior strength to an army. Although modern methods of warfare have deprived horses of any active

Bottom. *These Chinese Geese make ideal guardians, producing considerable noise when strangers approach.*

role, they were used in Europe as recently as in World War II. Thousands of mules were also used in Burma in World War II.

Dogs have also played a part in war. Frederick the Great and Napoleon used dogs as sentries and ammunition carriers. At the outbreak of World War I, a century later, the German army had a force of 5,000 dogs trained to carry out sentry, messenger, guard, and ambulance duties. During World War II, the United States forces trained over 20,000 dogs. They were also used extensively by the Australians and Japanese in jungle campaigns. More recently, they played an active role in Vietnam where they were trained to give advance warning of a hidden enemy, to save a patrol from ambush, to smell buried mines, and even find arms caches. They have saved many lives by guiding stretcher bearers to the wounded.

Law Enforcement

Even in the Middle Ages, many European villages kept a Bloodhound to track down thieves. Today, dogs are trained to follow the scent of criminals and to find missing people.

German Shepherd dogs are usually used as military guard dogs. On active service in the field, they are trained to attack intruders but on home bases, especially airfields, they are taught to seize and hold an attacker until their handler arrives and takes control. Police forces throughout the world use dogs in similar ways. They accompany patrolmen on the beat and thus provide their handlers with an extra pair of eyes and ears and a much more sensitive nose. Specially trained dogs are being increasingly used to "sniff out" dangerous drugs and explosives.

Many countries have a mounted police force similar to the well-known Royal Canadian Mounted Police; their role is varied and includes the suppression of smuggling and traffic in narcotic drugs. Many police forces use horses to contain possible insurgencies or disperse demonstrators. Some cities are starting to use more mounted policemen in efforts to reduce crime.

Guiding the Blind

Ironically, one of the dog's most peaceful roles had its origin in wartime. The use and success of highly trained dogs in World War I, together with the alarming number of men blinded in war injuries, encouraged the wide scale training of dogs as guides in Germany. A training school was set up in Potsdam. But the practice was not taken up elsewhere until 1925–1926, when an American breeder, Mrs. Dorothy Harrison Eustace, visited the Potsdam school and founded an organization in Switzerland called *L'oeil qui voit* (The Seeing Eye). An article she wrote for the *Saturday Evening Post*, coupled with an American tour by one of her dogs and its blind master, led to the establishment of the first guide dog organization in the United States and inspired the first training school in Great Britain. There are now training centers in Italy, Sweden, Belgium, Holland, Israel, Australia, South Africa, and elsewhere.

The character of the dog rather than its physical characteristics is the more important factor in the training of many breeds as guides. However, through artificial selection the necessary traits of character have been inbred to produce animals even more suitable for this work. No other animal has fulfilled this role unless of course, the legendary account of a wolf in the sixth century is taken into consideration. After having killed and eaten the dog that acted as guide to a Breton hermit, the wolf was compelled to take on the dog's duties!

In Harness

It was the dog once again, which was probably the first draft animal. In the Stone Ages, it was used to pull a simple sled consisting of two poles with crosspieces like the letter A, the ends of which trailed behind. A similar dogsled, the travois, was adopted by the reindeer herders of northern Europe and Asia. It may be assumed that other animals, as they became domesticated, were also used to carry loads. Cattle were probably harnes-

The mule (the result of crossing a horse with a donkey) remains an important working animal, particularly in the Mediterranean region. This mule is working on the waste tip of a coal mine in Spain.

person very far. A bigger, stronger animal was needed for a satisfactory mount and so the selective breeding of horses for riding purposes began among the nomadic tribes of Central Asia. Over the centuries, the horse has been carefully bred to produce strains suitable for certain terrains and particular jobs until, today, most regions of the world have a local breed of horse and an indigenous pony type. The Mongol pony is perhaps the most versatile of pony breeds and is essential to the Mongol economy. In addition to its endurance as a transportation and cavalry animal, it has also been bred for herding, riding, pulling carts, carrying a pack, and for farming. It also supplies milk, cheese, and kumis (a fermented drink.)

The mule (a cross between a horse and a donkey) and the domestic ass or donkey (*Equus asimus*) itself have taken over many of the working roles of the horse in Mediterranean agriculture, since they are stronger for their size than a horse and much cheaper to maintain. For these reasons, there are far more working donkeys and mules in the world than all other working animals combined. They are still used as pack animals in many countries. The mule was once the favorite mount of ecclesiastics. In desert regions of North Africa and Asia, the camel, with its ability to store water, takes the place of the mule and has become both baggage animal and mount. The South American relative of the camel, the llama, has been domesticated by Andean peoples for over 1,000 years, and it is still used for its wool and as a beast of burden by the Peruvian Indians.

All kinds of exotic creatures have been tried as mounts but most unusual perhaps was the crocodile. According to the Roman writer Pliny, the Egyptians perfected a method of riding the crocodile. The dolphin, which science has shown to be one of the most intelligent creatures, has always displayed an affinity with humans. Greek myth endowed dolphins with the benevolent role of guarding and caring for people, and Greek art portrayed them being ridden. There is no evidence to prove this, but, it is not unbelievable when we recall that modern underwater explorers have gotten a free ride on a shark!

It is not only for riding and drawing wagons that these hardworking animals have earned their keep. When human beings needed energy to raise water from wells or to turn machinery, they turned to the horse, the donkey, the mule, the ox, the camel, and even the dog and set them to work again, plodding around a circular track or moving back and forth drawing up a bucket. A particular kind of small dog was developed to run inside a treadmill that turned a cooking spit. It was also proposed that horses operating a treadmill could power the early railway locomotives.

Messengers

Animals have been used to carry messages when other forms of transportation proved unsatisfactory. A single rider and his mount have been employed to carry messages from the time of the Assyrian Empire. A coach and horses gave speedy and efficient service in the days of Wells Fargo. But if the roads were not accessible or the terrain was poor or in enemy hands, the pigeon excelled as message carrier. The story of Noah and the ark reminds us how long the pigeon's homing instinct has been understood, and the use of pigeon mail service goes back to ancient times. Pigeons had been kept for centuries in Assyria, where they also had a religious significance, to carry military intelli-

sed from very early times and, in ancient Egypt, the ox was used to pull a plow that was too heavy for one man to pull alone.

The elephant, due to its great strength, can be harnessed directly to a load and is also employed in lifting timber with its trunk. It is still used for this purpose in several parts of the world, such as the hardwood forests of Southeast Asia. Since elephants do not breed readily in captivity, each has to be individually trained after capture. One man, known as the mahout, is usually responsible for the training of the animal and works with the same elephant for the rest of its life, developing a close relationship with it.

Pigs have been put to work as draft animals, and the ancient Egyptians used them as a kind of plow by driving them over the mud left by the retreat of the Nile floodwaters. The furrows made by the pigs were just the right depth for sowing seed.

With the invention of the wheel, carts and carriages came into use and were first drawn in Mesopotamia by onagers—wild asses. Onagers, however, were no longer domesticated by the time of Alexander the Great.

The horse began its working life as a status animal about 300 B.C. and was used to draw the chariots of kings. When people first discovered how to ride the wild horse, it did not have the strength to carry a

mercial value as a messenger. Nevertheless, Paul Julius Reuter, founder of the first news agency, used them in 1850 to bridge the gap between the end of the new German telegraph line at Aachen and the beginning of the Belgian and French system at Brussels.

Pigeons have maintained their importance during wartime since they are more difficult to intercept than other message carriers. During the seige of Paris in 1870, they carried messages reduced photographically to a tiny dot which, when projected upon a screen, kept the outside world aware of developments within the Prussian-encircled capital. During both World Wars they were used by German, British, and American forces. The record flight for a United States Army signal corps pigeon is 3850km. (2400 mi.) while flights of 1600 km. (1000 mi.) are routine. During the Korean War groups of United States agents were parachuted behind enemy lines and for four months used pigeons to keep in touch with their base. Not a single message was lost.

The dog was used as a messenger conveying vital intelligence through the trenches in World War I. In beseiged Stalingrad in World War II, a cat carried messages from scouts to base with information on enemy gun placements.

Top. Elephants are still vitally important working animals in the hardwood forests of southeastern Asia. They are able to work in situations where machines are unable to go.

gence messages. They were released by the ancient Egyptians from their ships to give advance notice of arrival at their home port. Rameses II used pigeons in 1204 B.C. to announce his accession to the throne. Julius Caesar is said in some traditions to have relied upon pigeon mail carriers to convey news of his campaigns in Gaul back to Rome; Nero used them to send out the results of sporting events to friends who lived in the countryside. The Sultan of Baghdad set up a pigeon mail system in A.D. 1150, and Genghis Khan, the Mongol ruler, established a network as his conquests spread.

Pigeons were faster than any other message system and could get through when visibility was too poor for any beacon signal or semaphore system to operate. In 1815, pigeons carrying the news of Napoleon's defeat at Waterloo reached the Rothschild banking house in London long before the official dispatch. The invention of the electric telegraph, and then of telephone and radio communications, put an end to the pigeon's com-

Entertainers

All kinds of animals have been trained to appear in circus acts, in plays and films, and in advertising campaigns. Advertisements sometimes make use of a particular habit, like that of a famous cat in England which would dip its paw into its food and scoop it up. This idiosyncrasy was used for many years to promote a brand of cat food. Doves sometimes earn their keep as subjects in traditional magic acts while small birds, particularly budgerigars, perform tricks upon command as a street entertainment.

Natural kinds of animal behavior are usually required in movies but sometimes, especially in circus acts, an animal is taught to perform a routine which is not based upon usual behavior patterns. Of course, it is easier to train an animal to do something related to natural behavior. In the typical big cat circus act, for instance, it is more difficult for a lion to stand on a stool than it is for a leopard which climbs naturally in the wild. There is a question in many minds about our right to subject animals to such unnatural training for the sake of human entertainment.

Research

Bottom. *The ring on the leg of this pigeon can be used to hold messages. This service is rarely used today, but remains a resource that could be used in an emergency.*

Animals of different species are widely used in medical, scientific, and cosmetic research. Everyone who loves animals would agree that unnecessary suffering should be prevented and that the codes which govern the keeping and use of experimental animals should be strictly enforced. Human beings owe a large debt to the many and varied animals that work for a living.

Some members of the ape family are presently being taught to use sign language in experiments designed to learn more about how language is acquired. Psychologists have used various animals in behavioral studies dealing with such subjects as the innate need for touch or the effects of noise pollution. Animals are being used in research areas for which they were not previously considered suitable. As advances in science are made in the coming years, research with animals will continue to contribute to our body of knowledge.

69

BREEDING & REARING

We all know the joys we share with our pets or the quiet pleasure we obtain by simply observing them. We sit for hours talking to a bird in a cage or watching fish in a tank, throwing a ball for a dog, or simply sitting with a purring cat. This is all of course a complete waste of time, but there must be some basic drive that makes us do it!

Observing and assisting our chosen pets as they reproduce themselves adds a new dimension to the relationship we have with them. Our reasons for this interest are as diverse as we are and as varied as the species we call pets. Some of us are quite happy to buy a dozen roses and enjoy them in a vase. Others prefer to grow them. A few go into the complicated business of actually breeding new varieties. Similarly many of us are quite happy to buy a half grown hamster and simply enjoy its company for its two- or three-year life span, while others wish to rear their own. It may be a bit more work and involve more expense but many feel that the satisfaction of bringing new lives into their orbit is well worth the effort.

The emergence of any new form of life is a miracle of nature, whether it is the slow unfolding of a butterfly,

For many owners there is no greater enjoyment than to breed and rear a group of purebred kittens, such as these Siamese.

the chirp of a damp chick as it struggles from the egg, the apparently effortless release of tiny guppies like bubbles in a stream, or the prolonged and often painful parturition of many mammals. Human observers watch this process with endless fascination.

The purposeful selection of mates for obtaining new or better offspring has long been a preoccupation of those of us who take the keeping of pets seriously. Thousands of clubs and societies composed of breeding enthusiasts proudly exhibit their planned progeny as proof of their singular dedication. There are clubs whose members breed mice; others rear guinea pigs and many are interested in cats, dogs, and horses. Each tends to have people who talk a language of their own, and who seem enthusiastic or boring, depending of course on whether you yourself have a compelling interest in the species. People also get involved in breeding because they sincerely believe that their dog or cat possesses desirable characteristics that should be passed on to the offspring.

Some people get into breeding because they think it is an easy way of making money. A person who pays a large price for an expensive Yorkshire Terrier may

multiply that figure by four (possibly an average litter) and multiply that by two (litters per year) and decide that breeding is a good investment. Several million-dollar schemes based on the same theory have gone bankrupt breeding animals from rabbits to pigs to horses. In fact the majority of breeders barely cover expense. Many subsidize their breeding program from other income. An amateur pet keeper should start out on a small scale and spend no more than he or she can afford to lose. After a few successful seasons and the invaluable experience gained, one is in a better position to assess whether or not it is worthwhile expanding.

Most pet owners become involved in breeding almost accidentally. A pair of white mice or a female cat may present offspring that were not planned, and this can happen repeatedly in a short period of time for some species. It must be considered irresponsible, if not cruel (and in some places the law says so), to permit the birth of unwanted creatures. There are ample veterinary services to prevent such occurrences. (See **Cats; Dogs.**)

Many amateur pet keepers who want to get into breeding start with buying a pair of animals. This is valid with many of the smaller pets, but many people will buy a pair of dogs or cats or even horses because they have become enthusiastic about the idea. Generally speaking, the beginner should keep only females and use the stud of a professional breeder. This also provides more control over the breeding process.

A common mistake is to think that one cannot embark on a breeding program in an apartment or a small house. The majority of breeders everywhere live in unpretentious circumstances. In many parts of the world racing pigeons are successfully bred by people in lofts on roofs of tenements or garages. Practically all caged birds can be bred—and on quite a large scale—in the smallest home. Common sense dictates that domestic poultry are better kept in an outdoor run, but cats and dogs can be managed in a small area. After all, many breeders with acres at their disposal bring their gestating females indoors to have their litters. Until the kittens or pups are four or five weeks of age they can be reared in a corner of any room. Aside from accessibility, this has the added advantage of socializing the youngsters. Increased contact with people enables the young animals to be more readily handled.

With a little extra trouble it is quite easy for the amateur aquarium owner to breed and rear tropical fish such as these Discus which are shown guarding their young.

SPECIES	WATER (%)	PROTEIN (%)	LACTOSE (%)	FAT (%)	MINERALS (%)	ENERGY (KJ (kcal)/100g)
Cat	73	9.5	10	7	0.5	585 (140)
Cow	87.5	3.5	5	3.5	0.5	270 (65)
Dog	78	8	3.5	9	1.5	520 (125)
Donkey	89.5	2.5	6	1.5	0.5	140 (45)
Goat	86	4	4	5	1	310 (75)
Horse	91.5	1.5	5.5	1	0.5	170 (40)
Human	87.5	2.5	6	3.5	0.5	270 (65)
Pig	84	5	3	7	1	400 (95)
Sheep	81	6.5	5	7	0.5	460 (110)
Fur Seal	47	8	0	43	2	1,500 (420)

This table illustrates the varying milk composition between species. (See also **Feeding Your Pet.**)

Donkeys, ponies, and horses will require more space, but it was not so many years ago that horses were kept in stables in backyards just as we now keep automobiles in garages.

This outline of the basic principles and the common pitfalls involved in breeding all our common pets needs the addition of the owner's enthusiasm and dedication. How to put these breeding hints into practice will vary from species to species, and this information is included in the general entry for each pet in **Pets of Every Kind.** You provide the enthusiasm and dedication. **Pets of Every Kind** aims to provide additional knowledge of others' experiences. The rest is up to you. Let us hope the experience is both fruitful and pleasurable.

The remainder of this chapter deals with a type of rearing which is different from the planned and controlled rearing of pets, that is, the raising of orphans.

Raising Orphan Mammals

The majority of animal species are more or less independent soon after birth. They neither need nor seek

With the correct equipment it is quite easy to rear butterflies and moths, such as this female Privet Hawk Moth shown laying eggs. Within a short time span the complete life cycle from egg to larva to pupa to adult can be observed.

parental care. But many of the more familiar and popular household pets require considerable help during their early growing period. If a mother abandons or attacks her offspring, or is too weak to rear all her young, or dies before she can do so, they must be fostered or hand reared in order to survive.

FOSTERING

Provided that a few precautions are taken, fostering can often be surprisingly simple. Many animals are unable to resist the appeal of a helpless young creature which often transcends the usual inhibitions between species. With mammals the most successful method of fostering is to find another female of the same species who has just lost one of her young or who can cope with an addition to her litter. A foster mother of a different, even though similar, species can present complications.

A nursing mammalian mother often needs little persuasion to accept a needy youngster, even of another species. Some of these interspecific relations neither tax the foster mother's capacity nor impose drastic changes on the orphan. Cats, rabbits, dogs, rats, mice, lions and tigers, wolves and foxes have all figured in recorded instances of fostering. Legends and myths abound of more unusual combinations. Over the centuries shepherds, herdsmen, and breeders have learned that the nursing female does not care about the looks of her prospective sucklers or brood. If they smell familiar, she will usually accept them.

When the orphan is introduced, keep a sharp eye on the adult because nursing mothers have been known to turn on foundlings and kill them quickly. A prospective foster cow may butt or kick at the head of a begging calf. Rats may reject strangers, no matter how young, by efficiently severing the jugular vein and carotid artery. In the expensive world of the racehorse each foster introduction is attended by at least two people. One keeps a firm hold of the nursing mare's halter while the other guards the colt.

Experienced people recommend that fostering introductions be made at night. In many species it eases the situation if the foster mother is removed for a short while from the area where they are to meet before introducing the orphans. With domestic poultry and many other species who must regularly leave the nest it has often been shown that the ideal time for introducing orphans is during the normal dusk forage.

Once the foster mother allows the orphans to nurse she seldom rejects them later; that single acceptance often appears to bond them as firmly as blood.

At the beginning of their lives mammals reared on their mother's milk receive a protection from many common illnesses which is denied to orphans. The milk for the first few days, and particularly for the period from twenty-four to thirty-six hours after birth, is rich in antibodies which confer immunities until the young animal is able to produce its own antibodies. This early milk, known as colostrum, is also a laxative. The loss of colostrum's benefits is the factor responsible for the majority of deaths of the smaller animals which people try to rear. Whether the orphan or foundling be a dormouse, a field mouse, a hedgehog, a skunk, a badger, or a rabbit, the possibility of obtaining colostrum, either from the mother or other female of the species, is remote. The chances of successful rearing are correspondingly less and the majority succumb to illness within the first fortnight. If an animal is being hand reared (see below) or fostered on a different species, you should work in close consultation with your veterinarian. In larger and generally more valuable species colostrum may be obtained from a mother who has recently given birth and then stored in a freezer until needed; this is a common practice on thoroughbred stud farms and in some zoos.

The best foster mother is obviously one who most closely resembles the orphan. If she is at the same stage of lactation as the mother would have been, so much the better. Simple methods will endow the orphan with an odor which will make it acceptable. Some experts say the mother's feces or urine should be used, others say they should be rubbed with milk from the foster mother. Some successful breeders who have had considerable experience with fostering say the only prerequisite is placing the foundlings in the nursing area while the foster mother is absent. With horses and sheep a common practice is to skin the hide or pelt of the dead colt or lamb the mother has just lost and tie it around the orphan before presenting it to the mother. Some people have successfully used the same method with cats. A highly strung prospective mother calls for more care in introducing the orphan. Hands must be washed in strong soap and well rinsed, lest they trans-

fer other strange smells and animals are far more sensitive to smell than humans. If the skin of another animal is used, place it carefully on the orphan using a large curved needle and thread to stitch the edges together quickly. Urine, feces, or milk should be smeared on with a cloth or tissue, *not* with the hands, to avoid smell contamination. In whatever way the familiar odor is conferred, the takeover is often facilitated if the foster mother is not allowed to nurse for some hours beforehand. As the pressure of milk in her mammary glands builds up to the point of discomfort she becomes less discriminating about the means of relief. In most species discomfort escalates to pain in about twelve hours; so do not allow the udder to become so painful that the foster mother will reject all advances.

HAND REARING

In economically useful species human communities have developed artificial rearing to an astonishing degree, deliberately taking young from their mother. The sight of a brood of chicks following their mother about a farmyard is now unusual in developed countries, but we take for granted large buildings containing thousands of chicks who never in their entire lives will see a chicken older than themselves. Indeed, they will have been artifically reared from the time the egg was laid. Similarly the vast majority of calves of dairy cows are separated from their mothers within a day or two of

Top Right. *There is a lot to be learned from fostering parents in nature, as exemplified by the cuckoo whose young are always reared by foster parents.*

Bottom Left. *Abandoned or orphaned young can be placed with foster mothers that have young of the same age. These two Springer Spaniel pups have been adopted by a Smooth Fox Terrier with her own pup.*

73

birth. This system of artificial nurturing has been perfected to ensure us a steady supply of cow's milk, butter, and cheese.

Such methods of rearing animals without their mothers are applicable in general terms to all the dependent orphans among household pets. It is necessary to provide the basic conditions of:

    (1) freedom from disturbance,

    (2) temperature control,

    (3) suitable food and a constant supply of water.

In some species grooming and cleaning must also be prime considerations.

Ponies, calves, and most of the herbivores which in the wild are born in the open are able to stand and move quite soon after birth—often astonishingly so—for in the first minutes of life they are at their most vulnerable to predators. Those species which remain immobile and often unseeing in the nest require more help from their mother, so that artificial rearing of carnivores usually involves more trouble.

The rearing of animals, whether orphaned or not, is as much an art as a science. In the case of motherless young the art comprised of caring must be provided by the person who has undertaken the task. Scales and thermometers are not a substitute for personal observation. Animal husbandry at every level requires constant appraisal. Whatever kind of animal is being reared, the signs of discomfort or difficulty—and of well-being—must be noticed and acted upon. Chilled birds, for instance, huddle together. Overheated birds scatter to corners away from the source of heat. Frightened lambs can suffocate in a heap of panic. Underfed kittens cry piteously. Overfed puppies lie in bloated discomfort. Constant observation rooted in devoted care is imperative. The science is the proven method which can be detailed. The art lies in the devotional care of the human agent acting as foster parent.

Bedding

A comfortable nest prepared for the birth may not give the accessibility which hand rearing requires nor provide the heating and temperature control which would have come from the mother's body. Bedding may be of any soft absorbent material. Cotton wool is useful for very small orphans, particularly during the first ten days. Finely shredded paper or strips of rags have been successfully used. Hay and straw are generally too prickly for the comfort of very small animals. Some successful breeders suggest that it is better not to provide any bedding. They say that it adds little to the animal's comfort and may be a hazard as some young eat their bedding. Absolute requirements include shelter from drafts, protection from other animals *and humans*, quiet, and a controlled temperature.

Sometimes members of an orphan litter will attempt to suckle upon each other's tails or fur causing sore patches. It may be necessary to separate them and rear them in small boxes which should be about four times the size of the youngster, big enough for it to turn around but small enough to keep uniformly heated, and deep enough to prevent escape. These smaller containers can be grouped together in a larger box.

Temperature Control

Cats, dogs, and many other species cuddle close to their mothers to maintain their body heat. This should be 35°C. (95°F.) for the first few days, reduced to about 30°C. (86°F.) by the tenth day and gradually down to 24°C. (75°F.) by the end of the fourth week. Chilling is the most common cause of death in orphan kittens and puppies, and this part of the rearing program must be frequently checked. A maximum–minimum greenhouse thermometer is invaluable. So is a thermostatically controlled source of heat. Neither need be expensive. However, in the initial emergency with orphans it may be easier to keep the whole room warm or to provide heat from an ordinary electric light bulb hanging over the orphan's box. A bright light is harmful to the still blind eyes, and this method should not be continued for longer than it takes to be replaced. An infrared lamp will give a radiant heat source with a much lower level of illumination and was until recently frequently recommended. However, thermostatically controlled heating pads—similar to electric blankets—are preferable and are becoming increasingly popular. They are inexpensive and safe, provided they are properly installed with well-protected cords.

Grooming and Cleaning

The animal mother keeps her offspring clean by grooming and washing them with her tongue. She cleans the face after every feeding and makes sure no stain remains after elimination. The vigorous massage of grooming the abdominal area helps to stimulate the discharge of waste. The human foster mother must replace this devoted care with the judicious use of damp cloths or cotton wool. The youngster should first be wiped clean, then the abdominal area should be massaged vigorously. If the massage stimulates excretions it should be cleaned again and replaced in its heated box.

Hand Feeding

The orphan must be given a milk as close as possible to that of the natural mother. Substitutes can be mixed, but if at all possible obtain one of the commercial milk substitutes specially manufactured for kittens and puppies. These are sterile, easily reconstituted powders and have proved widely successful. At least four companies with worldwide distribution manufacture these products, which have simplified the rearing of orphan carnivores.

Absolute sterility is necessary while reconstituting and feeding milk and milk substitutes because milk is an ideal medium for bacterial growth. Leftovers may be given to adult animals but should not be kept for later use.

The feed, whatever it is, should be given at blood temperature. It can be offered with a medicine dropper provided the rubber bulb is used only to fill the plastic tip which the animal can then suckle. If the bulb is squeezed to force the contents down the animal's throat, some may go down the lungs. Choking from this type of forced feeding is a common cause of death for orphan carnivores. There are other safer ways using appliances which offer a teat-like substitute for the nipple of the mother.

Having prepared the milk, heated it to 38°C. (100°F.), and transferred it to a preheated sterile feeding bottle, the human foster feeder should be seated comfortably with a thick towel to protect the lap. With small animals lifting them to a comfortable level is easier than attempting to feed them while kneeling on the floor.

The crucial initial feeding can be started by putting a few drops of the formula on the orphan's nose and lips. The slight taste will trigger the suckling reflex in the hungry baby, unless the animal is too young. Some are

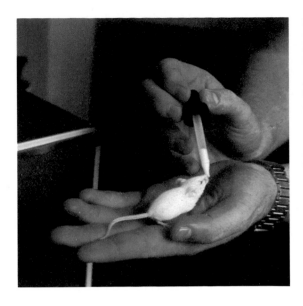

not ready to suckle until they are several hours old. Keep the milk warm and make another attempt about four hours later. If it is still refused, discard that feed and mix a fresh one later.

For most animals five or six minutes of an unhurried bottle should be sufficient. It used to be the practice to offer a feeding every couple of hours, gradually reducing the number of feedings to four a day over a period of three weeks. Recently people claim to have successfully raised carnivores with gaps of six hours between feedings. Scientifically speaking, 200kcal per kilogram of body weight should be supplied during the first week, increasing to 250kcal per kilogram after the first month. In simple terms that means between two and three teaspoons per feeding of most formulas for kittens and toy dogs. A Saint Bernard orphan or a foundling lion cub can easily accept half a pint.

Many puppies and kittens will attempt to lap with their tongues shortly after their eyes open at ten days of age. Some actually succeed by fourteen days but two-and-one-half to three weeks is more usual. At this stage the usual weaning diet can gradually be introduced, as natural mothers do in rearing their young. It is at this point also that a separated litter can be reunited for the benefit of mutual play, or there may be a nonnursing female or a tractable male who will accept the youngster's company. Such a foster parent can teach the orphan through play and example many of the facts of life they would have learned from a natural parent.

Orphan Birds

The fostering or hand rearing of birds presents different problems from those of fostering mammals since birds lay eggs that must be incubated before the young emerge rather than giving birth to live young. If a bird abandons its eggs, it is unlikely that any other bird will be willing to take over the entire nest, but it is sometimes possible to give the eggs to other birds to hatch out. There are also some excellent incubators for hatching eggs. Birds generally accept only those eggs which closely resemble their own, but this is by no means always so. Foster parents do not have to be paired birds—unmated females often become broody and can be extremely good at fostering. Birds that have no eggs of their own will sometimes accept other eggs to incubate, especially if they have recently lost some, but birds already incubating their own eggs are more likely to accept additional ones. The eggs can be put with those already in the nest if the bird can cover them all comfortably. If not, some of its own eggs must be removed and the others put in their place. The new and the original eggs need to be at a similar stage of incubation so that they all hatch about the same time.

Fostering eggs works most successfully with the domesticated species that have been bred for many generations by mankind. Birds such as canaries, budgerigars, pigeons and doves, and farmyard fowl will usually foster eggs laid by others of their kind and will frequently accept those of their exotic kin. The Bengalese or Society Finch is a particularly devoted foster parent and is commonly used to hatch and rear Australian finches and other small cage birds. Owners of ducks and geese, pheasants, and some other gamebirds regularly collect the eggs and hatch them in incubators or under brood hens specially kept for this purpose. Silky bantams are ideal for all but the biggest eggs. Some of the more unlikely examples of fostering include Barbary Doves hatching the eggs of Bobwhite and Japanese Quail, and budgerigars the eggs of the tiny Painted Quail.

If the birds are very different, the foster parents will probably not feed the strange young when they hatch. They may simply desert, or possibly attack, them. Because of their different feeding habits, some foster parents may not feed the young an adequate diet. More suitable foster parents must be found to raise them or they must be hand reared. This also applies to young birds abandoned by their own parents and to those hatched in incubators. Birds are guided by the appearance and responses of the young, and the principles for finding foster parents willing to raise them are similar to those for finding birds to incubate. Usually birds are more ready to accept naked or downy young. When the young have begun to grow feathers the adult's attitude can change, and even birds that have once doted on their foster young may suddenly reject them.

GROUND-LIVING BIRDS

Fortunately the young of most ground-living birds are well developed when they hatch and soon leave the nest. After a day or so, newly hatched ducklings, goslings, pheasant chicks, and the like can be placed in a coop, along with their foster mother if they have one. In an emergency any suitable box or even a strong cardboard carton with some wire netting across the top will do for a short while to house young on their own. The container should have a dry, clean sack or towel on the floor and be kept in a light, airy space free from drafts. For the first week at least, the birds must be kept very warm by using an infrared lamp or some other heat source. If they have no mother to brood them, the temperature needs to be around 35°C. (95°F.), with access to a slightly cooler area. The heat can gradually be reduced as they grow bigger, until eventually the coop can be put outside during good weather. Move the coop to a fresh spot of very short grass each day. In addition to the rather obvious esthetic benefit for your lawn, this will provide the young birds with fresh grass to eat and will avoid the possibility of contact with disease-producing organisms that may have attached themselves to their droppings of the previous day.

With a little encouragement most young birds quickly learn to feed themselves. At first they should be offered dry chick starter mixed with finely chopped hardboiled egg yolk and lettuce or some other greens. Finely crushed grain, seed, and crumbled biscuits can be used if starter feed is not available. Most young birds also need some live food, which will encourage them to investigate the inanimate food with which it is mixed. Chicks require drinking water in a shallow container that they cannot walk into or tip over. Ducklings and goslings should be given some water in a shallow dish. Unbelievable as it may seem, ducklings can get too wet and easily become chilled and die. So give water sparingly at first and be sure they can dry off quickly when they leave the water. A little finely chopped lettuce and duckweed dropped into the dish

During the late spring and summer, fledgling birds leave their nests. They often appear lost, helpless, and are remarkably tame, as is this young European Robin. However, do not be tempted to catch and rear them—their mothers are usually quite near and looking after them. Most will die if you try to rear them.

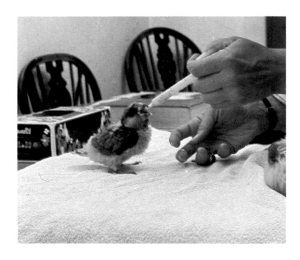

of water will be readily gobbled up. Indeed, they will soon feed with great enthusiasm.

PERCHING BIRDS

The young of most birds that perch are born helpless and remain dependent on their parents for some time. In many cases it is not possible to find suitable foster parents, and they must be hand reared—an extremely difficult task that requires a lot of time and the utmost patience. Several baby cereals and foods for invalids, as well as foods for insectivorous birds sold by pet stores, can successfully be used as a basis for rearing many species. For others, such as members of the crow family, dog meal is more suitable. Depending on the age and type of birds, finely chopped hardboiled egg yolk, lean minced meat or canned dog food, mashed fruit or shelled seeds can be mixed in with the basic feed. (See **Birds.**) The food should be moist enough to be made into small pellets that can be fed with forceps or tweezers or be given in a more liquid consistency using a medicine dropper. In addition, the young of most perching birds require some live food. For very small birds maggots and mealworms can be chopped up and added to the prepared food or they can be fed whole to larger birds. As a temporary measure a little moistened bread can be a handy food. The young birds need to be fed whenever they beg or at intervals of not more than two hours throughout the day. If they do not beg, a light tap on the beak is often sufficient to persuade nestlings to open their mouths. Otherwise the beak must be carefully pried open with the thumb and forefinger and the food gently pushed down the throat. Until they are well feathered they must be kept very warm and will prefer a snug homemade nest in a box or cage. As they get older a dish of food should be left with them to encourage them to feed themselves.

Ground-living birds are relatively easy to rear. Top Left. Pheasants can be hatched by a broody hen. Top Right. Once hatched, young, such as these Muscovy ducklings, can fend for themselves but beware of allowing them near deep water before they are able to swim and before their down is waterproof—ducklings can easily drown. Center Left. Perching birds, such as this Green Parakeet, need a lot more care and attention, since they will not feed themselves (and must eat every few hours).

EXHIBITING & SHOWING

Human beings are competitive. It cannot have been long after they started keeping and breeding domestic animals and pets before individual owners began claiming that their particular animals were better than anyone else's of the same breed.

An animal's competence at work probably formed the basis of the first competitions. For example, the owner of the best sheep dog in any area found that his dog was admired not only for its working ability but was also in demand as breeding stock. Other dog owners would soon challenge the title of best local dog and this competitiveness formed the basis of the first formal local competitions. With this competitive spirit having developed between owners of working animals, it is easy to see how shows originated for the exhibition of "pet" animals which competed on the basis of their form or beauty. Even today there is a clear distinction between shows that exploit either the working prowess or visual appeal of pets. Many dog shows simply judge the animals on the "ideal" for a breed, a type of show quite distinct from, for example, sheep dog trials and gun dog trials, where working ability is still tested. Perhaps the best known and most popular "working" trials of today test the working ability of rider and horse either in show jumping, dressage, or three day events.

Long before Gregor Mendel published his complex observations on heredity in the common garden pea in 1866, the early animal breeders were finding their own way down the same road to selective breeding. The dog breeds we know today were mostly developed centuries ago to fulfill local working needs. Little attention was paid to Mendel's work until this century when its application to animal breeding was recognized. Breeders of all kinds of animals and plants could recognize their freaks and breeds as genetic mutations and use them deliberately to create even more variations. These breeds are now the basis of the whole cult of show or exhibition pedigree pets.

The "ideal" is a standard formulated by the governing body which all breeders aspire to meet, whatever their personal opinion. From time to time, the "ideal" may change as a result of grass roots pressure or new advances.

However, shows are more than events for the benefit of professionals or spectacles for the general public. Beginning breeders are encouraged to go to most shows, to compare their animals against those of the professional and to actually compete in classes for beginners, giving them a chance to step onto the bottom rung of the exhibition ladder. Shows are thus a great meeting place where many with common interests can exchange views. Most exhibitors are pleased to answer questions and will encourage newcomers.

In the following sections we discuss aspects of the showing and exhibiting of dogs, cats, horses, birds, small mammals, and fishes. Much of the advice is either general or applies to specific shows run in particular countries governed by the relevant ruling bodies. If you wish to enter the showing world at any level, it is essential that you obtain from show organizers or governing bodies all the specific rules and regulations that will apply to shows in your area for your particular pet.

What then are the objectives of holding shows today? There are a number of reasons, many of them interrelated and overlapping. Primarily shows are held to provide an opportunity to assess the relative merits of individual animals in specific breeds by qualified judges. This enables breeders to compare their own stock with that of rival breeders, to assess the qualities of others' stock which they may wish to buy or use at stud, to consider the judges' placings in relation to those of other judges, and so build up an assessment of the merits of the competing animals of the breed. Showing fosters healthy competition which spurs breeders to improve their stock.

Shows also provide competition between breeders for prizes and recognition among their peers. Those whose animals win most consistently are likely to attract more business than the less successful. At the same time shows provide a "show case" for people who wish to choose suitable breeds for companionship or breeding, or to replenish their stocks.

Although well-staged shows present a spectacle of interest to the general public and usually provide a profit for the promoting society, they are not just beauty contests. For the dedicated breeder the principal interest is to watch over the years, the developments, successes, and failures. This process of continuing comparison is a virtual necessity for the maintenance and improvement of type, quality, and breed character. The opportunity to see other breeders' animals in the ring helps in the selection of stud and replacement stock.

All animal shows, whether for birds, mammals, or fish, have roughly the same structure, the competitors are divided into classes of breed, variety, age, size, color, and sex (where this can be ascertained). The precise definition of each division and the subdivisions within them varies according to the peculiarities of the species as a whole and is drawn up by the governing body for each species. These definitions are not always consistent around the world since the governing bodies in various countries differ on some points. Such differences in opinion determine each country's "ideal" for the species.

Showing Dogs

The first recorded dog show was held on June 28 and 29, 1859, in the Town Hall at Newcastle-on-Tyne, England. There were only two classes, one for Pointers and the other for Setters and the event drew an entry of sixty dogs. Obviously dogs had been matched against each other before this date, but it was usually their ability to perform some task that had been tested, with wagers often being laid on the outcome. Thus dogs had fought against each other, had tested their courage against formidable adversaries such as bears and bulls, had killed phenomenal numbers of rats in rat pits or raced each other to find the fastest animal, but it was not until 1859 that the first beauty competition took place; the idea was an immediate success. Not only did the number of shows increase very rapidly but so did the number of breeds being scheduled in each show. Catalogs of these early events contained few of the details which are now considered essential because the breeding of most of these show dogs had not been well documented.

GOVERNING BODIES

A certain amount of deception seems to have taken place at these early shows with the same dog being entered in several events under different names and making a clean sweep of all the prizes. Ownership too was often in dispute and it was for these sorts of reasons that the English Kennel Club was founded in 1873 to provide a framework of regulations for the running of all shows and to keep a Stud Book which would record both the breeding and the ownership of dogs being shown. Today in every country where the purebred dog is valued there is a kennel club to safeguard its interests and to enforce the rules and regulations which govern shows in that particular place, for the classification and definition of classes differ throughout the world. All kennel clubs, however, record the registration of purebred dogs, maintain a Stud Book (entry to which is automatically given to any dog which wins a

certain minimum classified standard), and license all the shows held within their area of jurisdiction.

The English Kennel Club is the oldest of these organizations and has absolute power in the pedigree dog world in Britain. It licenses some three to four thousand shows and matches each year as well as three to four hundred field trials and working trials, and a Stud Book has been issued annually since the inception of the club.

The American Kennel Club issued its first Stud Book in 1878 and licenses and supervises dog shows, obedience contests, and a variety of field trials. It also registers over one million dogs annually. There is a separate organization, the United Kennel Club, which is chiefly concerned with the registration of Coonhounds and the licensing of Coonhound trials.

The Canadian Kennel Club was founded in 1888 and now works in close cooperation with the American Kennel Club. Both these clubs recognize the registrations of the other making it easy for dogs to compete across the border between the two countries.

The Australian Kennel Club works on an entirely different system being a purely advisory body made up of delegates from the eight state canine administrative bodies each of which is autonomous.

Another large organization concerned with the running of shows and the maintenance of Stud Books is the Federation Cynologique Internationale. Most of the European countries belong to this body, and European shows are run under its rules. It is also concerned with gaining mutual agreement of breed standards amongst its members.

ENTERING SHOWS

The structure and type of shows vary from country to country, but the most coveted title to be gained by a show dog is that of the champion. The United States, Canada, and Australia award this on a points system, the number of points a dog gains being based on the type of show, the nature of the dog's wins, and the number of competing animals. In Great Britain a dog has to win three challenge certificates under three different judges at championship shows, and even then a judge may withhold this award if he feels that there is no exhibit of sufficient merit. For a number of reasons it is often harder to attain the rank of champion in Great Britain than elsewhere in the world.

Obviously, then, the biggest and most important shows are championship shows (where challenge certificates are offered) or points shows where points can be gained towards the necessary total of fifteen for the title of champion. Shows like these are often spread over two or three days and may attract up to ten thousand dogs. The best known of these is Crufts held in London and the Westminster held in New York, while the Sydney Royal is Australia's best-known show.

Types of smaller shows vary from country to country; some are limited to the dogs belonging to the

Top Left. *At dog shows each dog must be judged carefully, and some judges will have more than one hundred individuals paraded before them each day.*

Top Right. *A Smooth Fox Terrier stands on a table ready to be judged—every dog must be trained to behave well if it is to catch the judge's eye.*

members of whichever canine society runs the show, some are shows devoted to one breed alone while others cater to a group of breeds and also add "variety" classes where different breeds compete against each other. Each kennel club publishes its own book of regulations listing the types of shows which can be held within its own area of jurisdiction.

In Great Britain most dogs are exhibited by their owners, but in the United States and Canada, because of the greater distances involved, most dogs are prepared, trained, and exhibited by professional handlers who make their living this way. For the same reason, shows in these two countries tend to be run in circuits with five or six shows scheduled on consecutive days in the same district. Any owner whose dog has been correctly registered with the presiding kennel club may enter shows, which are announced by the two weekly dog magazines in Great Britain and in the *American Kennel Gazette*, which is the official publication of the American Kennel Club. Individual entries must in most cases be received by the show secretary by a closing date which is several weeks before the show. Schedules and entry forms can be obtained from the show secretaries and are self explanatory.

If you are a novice exhibitor, plan to visit one or two shows before entering a dog at one. This will enable you to see the techniques used in showing your particular breed. A dog show is a beauty competition, and the aim must be to present a sparkling, well-groomed animal in the bloom of health, and trained to show itself to the best advantage. The training is important and should be started early with a show puppy. You must always bear in mind that the judge will have at the most two or three minutes to assess the worth of each entry and if your dog is not showing itself to full advantage during that vital time it is unlikely to win.

Dogs are judged on their overall appearance, their structure and conformation, and their movement. The judge first directs all the animals to move around the ring together before examining each individually. Your dog must be taught to gait at an even pace beside you without pulling on the leash, both in a circle with the distraction of other dogs, and in a straight line to and from the judge. You will also have to pose your dog so that the judge may run his hands over the animal to assess make and shape. During this time the dog's teeth will also be examined so you must accustom your dog to having his mouth touched. Toy dogs and other small breeds are normally examined and posed on a table so this too must become a familiar process.

Show preparation for some breeds must start months in advance because the trimming of the coats is a skilled and lengthy process. Different grooming techniques are needed for the various types of coat found in different breeds and the best style for your breed can be learned from a book on grooming or from an experienced breeder. However it should be emphasized that all dogs benefit from daily coat care which aids cleanliness and stimulates circulation.

There is certainly a divergence of type between dogs

Preparing dogs for a show requires considerable time and care. Bottom Left. A Shetland Sheepdog receives its final brush. Bottom Right. The coat of a Yorkshire Terrier has to be oiled and wrapped in paper to maintain its length.

that are bred for work and those that are bred for the show ring, and shows have been criticized for producing beauty without brains. On the other hand in an increasingly urbanized society few dogs are ever required to have any working ability, and many breeds have been standardized and improved greatly in appearance by being shown.

Showing Cats

Cat shows are popular throughout the world, and an increasing number of shows are being staged each year. In North America there were some 350 shows and 81,000 entries from 1976 to 1977; these numbers are expected to grow to 400 shows and 100,000 entries by 1980.

The United States and Canada have the largest and most active groups of cat fanciers in the world.

GOVERNING BODIES

As with all animal shows there are strict standards and regulations laid down by the various cat clubs and societies, although the conditions and the methods of judging varies from society to society and from country to country. In Great Britain there is just one governing body, the Governing Council of the Cat Fancy (GCCF), to which all other British societies seek affiliation. Many of the clubs in the Commonwealth follow the standards and practices of the GCCF. Although it was founded with the advice and personal help of English fanciers in the late 1890s, the structure of the North American organizations and its show patterns have diverged widely from those of most other countries. Eight different North American organizations present the exhibitor and breeder with eight different philosophies, political structures, and codes of regulations covering cat registrations, breed standards and show rules.

The largest body in North America today is the Cat Fanciers' Association, Inc. (CFA). It consists of more than 550 clubs whose members lack direct voting power, but are represented by delegates at annual meetings and by regional directors at quarterly directors' meetings. Among other things, CFA pioneered computer registrations, rigid requirements for judges, and the "unisex" cat show which is now the North American norm.

The second most popular American cat organization is the American Cat Fanciers Association (ACFA). It broke off from CFA in 1955 over the issue of individual, rather than club, voting power. ACFA practices an advanced form of democracy. Its members vote by mail ballot on all important issues including elections and breed standards, and all officers are subject to recall. Among ACFA's other innovations have been the multiple four-judge cat show which is now standard. (Before 1955, North American shows consisted almost invariably of one allbreed and two speciality events.) Written scoring sheets for judges point scoring were introduced by ACFA. Every exhibitor at an ACFA show receives a scoring sheet showing what percentage of perfection the judge believes each cat to have earned on each of its features.

Only CFA and ACFA are truly continental associations. They are represented by clubs in Canada and throughout the United States.

Next largest in number of cat shows is the Cat Fanciers Federation, Inc. (CFF). It sprang from CFA in

1919 and holds shows in the eastern and midwestern United States. CFF is a club-membership organization.

Five smaller groups make up the balance of the North American cat fancier organizations. The oldest of all is the American Cat Association (ACA), founded in 1901. It has both individual and club memberships, and its shows are distributed along the eastern and western seaboards. A recent conflict of personalities has resulted in the formation of a new West Coast registry, the American Cat Council (ACC), composed almost entirely of former ACA members. ACC's structure is similar to that of ACA.

The Canadian Cat Association (CCA) was founded in 1960 to serve Canadian cat fanciers only. It is an active progressive organization which has been in the forefront in the acceptance of newer breeds and colors, such as Sphynx, Blue Burmese, Egyptian Maus, and Tonkinese.

The United Cat Federation (UCF) dates from 1946. Centered on the West Coast, it is small but has been a strong liberal voice, favoring the acceptance of newer breeds and unusual show formats.

Crown Cat Fanciers Federation (CROWN) was founded in 1965 with the revolutionary idea of being primarily a show-sanctioning body. It is an individual-member association and continues to be liberal and progressive in outlook. Any registered cat of any association is welcomed to its shows. Despite its relatively small size it has considerable impact on the community of cat fanciers.

Official cooperation between these North American organizations is minimal, and there is a basic cleavage between CFA and the seven smaller "independent"

Top. *A Turkish queen is judged while an assistant takes notes.*

Bottom Left Opposite. *Before show cats are allowed into the showing and judging area they must be inspected for signs of disease.*

associations. The member clubs of the independents are linked by their support of the All American Cats—a scoring system developed by *Cats Magazine* which is used to select mathematically every year the winning cats across the country of every breed and color, from all those exhibited in the shows of the seven organizations.

ENTERING SHOWS

Geographical differences dictate various patterns of shows. In Great Britain, where few exhibitors need to travel very long distances, shows last one day only. In the United States they are usually two-day affairs, held on a weekend if possible. On the European Continent some shows spread over three days, although the judging is completed on the first day if possible.

In Great Britain, cats may not be exhibited at two shows within fourteen days. This is to prevent the spread of any possible infection and results in a schedule of shows with an interval of two weeks between each to enable cats to be entered in as many shows as their owners may wish.

You will find a calendar of shows regularly announced in the publications *Fur and Feather* for Great Britain and *Cats Magazine* for the United States. Write to the organizer for entry forms, list of classes, and show rules. Your cat must already be registered with the appropriate authority if you plan to enter one of the pedigree classes. You will have to pay an entry fee for each class you enter which is sent, together with the completed form, to the organizer. If everything is in order you will then receive all the necessary documentation, including a vetting-in card and a numbered tag to tie around the cat's neck.

On arrival at the show each exhibit is examined by a veterinarian. Any suggestion of disease may mean that entry will be refused and your fee forfeited because no risk of infection can be allowed with so many cats gathered in one place. The vetting-in card is designed to speed up examination. Once passed you may make your cat comfortable in the pen corresponding to the number on your cat's tag. If judges are to visit the pens you should provide the cat with a white blanket and a litter tray, and food and water dishes will be needed when feeding is allowed. Some owners fasten clear plastic sheeting across the front of the pen to prevent any visitors from touching the cat through the bars.

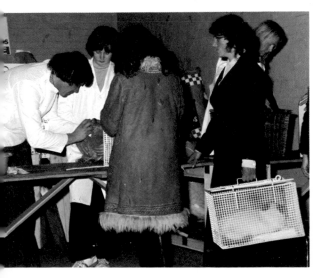

Top. *The largest cat show in England is the National, held at Olympia Exhibition Center each year.*

Competitors will usually be asked to leave the hall or to watch from a gallery when judging is actually in progress.

All the cat associations require their judges to be experienced with cats and to meet specified qualifications. The way of assessing each cat varies from organization to organization. Under British GCCF rules there are strict allocations of points for different aspects of each breed which are laid down in the breed standard. The ACFA also uses a point-scoring method, but many other associations use an overall evaluation by the judge. There is another big difference in approach: At North American shows and most Continental ones the cats are taken to the judges whereas in British shows the judges visit the pens and only for the final "Best in Show" judging are cats taken up to the platform.

In Great Britain there are three categories of show: championship shows, where challenge certificates are given to cats who win the adult open classes and are considered worthy by the officiating judges (premier certificates are the equivalent for neuters); sanction shows, similar but where challenge certificates are not awarded; and exemption shows which have less stringent rules and are intended for beginners. If a cat is awarded challenge certificates at three different shows under three different judges, the owner can apply to the GCCF to have it recognized as a champion. Some shows select Best in Show, the best adult, kitten, and neuter being chosen from Long-hairs, Short-hairs, and Siamese or other type. Others choose Best of Breed for each variety.

In North America, a cat winning in one class qualifies to go forward to be judged in the next until eventually, a Best in Show Cat is chosen, together with a

Second Best and Best Opposite Sex. Best of each variety and best neuters will also be chosen. Kitten classes do not go forward for judging against others. The ACFA omits selecting a Best Opposite Sex but selects Best Cat down to Fifth Best.

Continental practice is similar to that in Great Britain. The winner of an open class is given a Certificate d'Aptitude au Championnat (qualifying certificate for the championship). Three such wins qualify to become a champion and enter the class for champions only where a winner is awarded a Certificat d'Aptitude de Beaute (award for the best cat). Three wins at this level qualify to compete for a Certificat d'Aptitude au Grand Championnat International (qualifying certificate for the Great International Championship) and three such wins will take a cat to the highest European award and entitle it to the title Grand Championnat International (Great International Championship).

PREPARING A CAT FOR A SHOW

Not all cats have the temperament to endure many hours confined to a show cage after the disruptions of a journey while hundreds of people stare at them and strangers handle and inspect them. A cat that is upset will not be feeling or looking its best and may even show symptoms of developing an illness and fail to pass the vetting-in. A cat can become accustomed to traveling and to the restricted show pen by being placed in a cage about two feet square for a few minutes each day and then for gradually longer periods until it can accept confinement for a whole day without distress.

If a cat is to look in peak condition it requires a little more than its regular grooming. A dry shampoo a few days before the show, with a commercial shampoo, will improve the coat of light-colored cats. Use oven-warmed bran for dark ones. Powder should be used about three days before the show and bran about five so it will all be brushed out. Be sure there is none left in the coat at judging time.

You will need a carrier for transportation of the cat and a clean blanket, water dish, food bowl, brush and comb, and litter tray, together with a cloth and disinfectant to wipe out the pen before putting your cat in it. Pens are disinfected by the show organizers but it is worth taking every precaution against the risk of infection. For short-haired cats a piece of velvet will be useful to polish the coat after you have given the eyes and ears a last minute cleaning and the fur a final grooming just before the judging.

Showing Horses and Ponies

For thousands of years horses have been selected and judged on their beauty while horse competitions including ridden events and chariot racing formed an integral part of the classical Greek Olympic games originating over 2,500 years ago. Today, horse shows provide a broad selection of classes for horse breeds and various displays of horsemanship.

GOVERNING BODIES

International horse competitions are governed by the rules enacted by the Federation Equestre Internationale (FEI) which determine the contents and specifications for all international competitions. The American Horse Shows Association (AHAS), governs National shows in the United States and Canada, and

sets the standards, tests, routines to be performed and entry requirements for all in-hand (breed) and ridden classes. The major organizing bodies in Britain are the British Horse Society (BHS) and the British Show Jumping Association (BSJA). In each state of Australia, each regional Royal Agricultural Society organizes the major shows and stipulates the entry requirements.

CLASSIFICATION OF SHOWS

Horse shows in the United States are classified as either recognized, approved, or local. Recognized shows are governed by AHAS rules; approved shows are sponsored by specific breed societies such as the American Quarter Horse Association; and local shows, which include gymkhanas, are sponsored by area associations, riding (pony) clubs, hunting clubs, and riding schools. Horse shows may last from one day to one week.

Horse shows differ considerably from other animal shows in that horses are judged both on beauty and performance. Horse show competitions therefore consist of two main categories: in-hand (breed) classes and performance classes. For in-hand classes a particular breed of horse is led on halter for judging on its conformation to the ideal standard set down by its breed society. Performance classes are numerous and are based on the horse's versatility as a mount on the flat, over jumps, and in harness. There is also a wide range of competitions on the flat and over jumps which judge the rider's skill.

There are classes for both horses and ponies. The distinction is made by the animal's height as measured at the withers (shoulder). Horses must be over 14.2 hands high and ponies are not to exceed 14.2 hands. One hand equals four inches. In order to qualify, each entrant must produce a measurement certificate, which is issued by a veterinarian, either before the closing date for entries or on the day of the show.

Pony classes are usually divided into three categories: ponies up to 12.2 hands, 12–13 hands, and 13–14 hands. Horse classes are for animals exceeding 14.2 hands but no more than 15 hands and 15–15.3 hands. Apart from a height stipulation, classes are also divided according to breed or type of horse, age of the rider, and previous winnings. A horse or a rider that has not won a first ribbon at a recognized show may compete in what is termed maiden classes. If no more than three first ribbons have been won, the entrant may compete in novice classes, and if no more than six firsts have been gained, in limit classes. A horse or rider of any age or experience may take part in open classes.

As many as eight awards can be made in each class although for hunter, show jumper, and hack divisions, only three or four placings are usually made. In the United States and Australia, a blue ribbon signifies a first place and a red ribbon, a second. In Great Britain and Canada, a red ribbon is first and a blue, second. For all countries, a yellow ribbon is third, white is fourth, pink is fifth, green is sixth, purple is seventh, and brown is eighth place.

Championship and reserve championship awards for both horse and pony divisions are made to winners in certain classes in each division. The champion (and reserve champion) hunter and show jumper is the horse with the highest number of points accumulated throughout the show. Each ribbon denotes a certain number of points from five points for first place to one point for fourth place. The selection of the champion (and reserve champion) in hack divisions is made in a

Opposite Page. *Dressage requires peak coordination between rider and mount. The rider must sit immobile, his signals so slight that they are not noticeable to the observer.*

84

Show jumping is a popular sport for rider and spectator. For the horse and rider, the show jumping course is a test of all-round ability.

separate class where first and second place winners are judged on performance and conformation. In-hand (breed) championships are selected from a class in which place winners may compete. Supreme championship involves the selection of one animal from many different types or breeds.

CLASS REQUIREMENTS

A description is given below of the main requirements for horse and pony classes. Classes are divided into in-hand, on the flat, over jumps, and in harness competitions.

In-Hand

The ultimate aim of in-hand or halter classes is to guarantee the quality of a given breed because prize winners are highly sought as stud animals. Animals that are selected are judged on conformation to the standard for that breed. In-hand competitions include classes for Thoroughbreds, Arabs, Morgans, American Quarter Horses, American Saddlebreds Appaloosas, and native pony types. Each entrant must be registered with its particular breed society in order to qualify. Classes are for mares and stallions, fillies and colts.

Horses may be shown in bridle, show headcollar, foal slip or stallion bridle, and a web lead rein. Head gear, whether headcollar or bridle, should be the type which most flatters the animal. Horses are either led around the ring at a walk and required to halt and trot, after which a selection is made, or else all entrants are

considered for awards after an individual run-out (performance). The run-out consists of walking out and trotting back past the judge in order to test overall performance, manners, and gait. Colts and fillies must be squarely balanced, under control at all times, and able to stand still at command. When led out, they should walk forward freely and smoothly. General presentation of both horses and person are important and are taken into consideration.

Although some horses that are entered in breeding classes may also qualify for ridden classes—as is often the case with Morgans and American Quarter Horses—they are usually kept exclusively for stud purposes.

On The Flat

All classes in this division are ridden competitions.

Hack (Saddle Horse) The performance, manners, balance, and conformation of the horse are judged in this type of competition. Show hacks are usually Thoroughbred or part-bred Arabs (in Great Britain) and Saddlebreds (in the United States) and measure up to 15.3 hands for horses and up to 14.2 hands for ponies. Formal attire on the part of the rider is required.

Horses are usually shown with single reins (plain snaffle bit) or double reins (double bridle). All entries are required to form a ring around the judge and walk, trot, and canter to command. Horses that are selected for a further test are called into the center of the ring, although the judge also has the right to thin out the ring and call into the center those that are not to be considered further. After a number of entries have been selected, each is required to give an individual performance. This test usually consists of walking in a straight line, performing a simple figure eight, and trotting back past the judge and halting squarely. The horse may also be called upon to display both extended and collected paces and a hand gallop. In some cases the judge may ride the horse himself and put it through its paces to test for smoothness of performance and a comfortable ride. The horse's gait, suppleness, and willingness to go forward are important factors in hack classes. Much emphasis is also placed on the horse's conformation and soundness. Blemishes such as splints, spavins, and curbs may disqualify the animal. However, the judge has the right to place a horse with perfect performance and minor blemish over another with an uneven performance and clean limbs.

In the United States Saddlebreds are shown in either three-gaited or five-gaited classes. In the three-gaited class, the horse is required to perform at walk, trot, and canter while in the five-gaited class a more sophisticated training is called upon, requiring the horse to go through its pace at a walk, trot, canter, rack and slow gait.

Equitation (On The Flat) The rider's performance forms the basis of equitation classes on the flat. The essential points on which the rider is judged are posture, use of aids, control on the mount, turn-out (presentation), suitability of the horse to rider, and finally, the horse's conformation.

Horses form a ring around the judge and walk, trot, and canter to command. A first selection is then made and an individual performance is required; consisting of a walk, trot (extended and collected), a simple figure eight, and a halt. After completion of the test, the turn-out of both horse and rider and conformation of the horse is inspected.

Dressage Dressage represents perfection in horse training. It involves the execution of complex movements within an enclosed arena. Dressage tests vary in complexity from test A, the simplest, through to B and C, the most difficult, which most approximates the Grand Prix de Dressage of Olympic Games complexity. The test is learned from memory and performed in front of a panel of three judges, each of whom has a score card for awarding points ranging from 10 (perfect) to 0 for each figure that is completed. The entry with the highest number of points is the winner. International Dressage competitions, as well as those of national shows, usually follow the requirements set down by the International Federation of Dressage.

At the most elementary level, the horse must be able to perform both collected and extended gaits, make smooth transitions at the canter from one leg to the other, back, and turn on the fore and hind limb. More advanced levels call for lateral and diagonal movements, half-pirouette, and counter-canter.

Judging is based on the horse's suppleness, balance, fluidity of movement, and eagerness to go forward. The saddle seat is required: the rider must sit erect and straight in the center of the saddle and give the aids effortlessly without being apparent. Formal riding attire is compulsory.

Dressage tests are also combined with show jumping and hunting events to form a one- or three-day event.

Western (Stock) Horse

Although not recognized in Great Britain, Western Horse competitions are popular in the United States and form a part of some shows in Australia. Western Horse events include classes for stock horses, cow ponies, cutting horses, roping horses, Pleasure horses and half-bred Arabian Pleasure (Western) horses.

Working ability is the essential criterion. Work clothes, western saddles, and any type of hackamore bit are acceptable. Stock horses are required to perform a figure eight, gallop, halt from a gallop, and execute sharp turns of direction. Other competitions include steering-roping events and cutting events, where one animal is separated from a herd. Pleasure horses and part-bred Arabian Pleasure horses are judged on performance, manners, suitability to rider, and conformation. They should be able to work on a loose rein at all paces (walk, jog-trot, lope, and hand gallop).

Over Jumps

Show-Jumping. Show jumping is judged on the horse's ability to clear a given course of obstacles. As well as completing a clear round, the horse must, in some classes, compete against the clock, penalties being allotted for each second in excess of the limit. Competitions in accordance with FEI rules are against

Three-day eventing is the supreme test of all the skills of riding combined with durability. In the cross-country stage the jump from water is one of the most spectacular obstacles for onlookers.

a buggy—a two wheeled wagon. Fine and heavy harness horses pull a viceroy—a four wheeled show wagon. There are also harness classes for pairs, tandems (three horses), and four-in-hand. Combination classes are popular and incorporate both harness and performance requirements. After being shown drawing a vehicle, the horse is unhitched and shown under saddle as a hack.

GYMKHANAS

Gymkhanas are a type of show sponsored by riding clubs, aimed at promoting horsemanship and care of the horse and pony. A gymkhana provides an assortment of ridden classes (on the flat and over jumps) and includes equitation, hack, hunter, and novelty events. In the United States and Australia, turn-out classes judged on the suitability of horse and rider, and presentation of both horse and rider, are popular. Points are allotted to the cleanliness of the horse and tack, and correctness of the rider's attire.

Novelty events, either for teams or individuals, are an important part of the gymkhana. Great skill is required in some of these events—bending races, where the horse must wind its way at speed through a number of poles set in a straight line, demand skill and agility. Baton races depend on team coordination and speed. Other popular novelties are sack races, obstacle, and barrel races. As for major shows, gymkhanas also have a selection of novice classes in equestrian, hack, show jumping, and hunter divisions.

Showing Birds

Since the sixteenth century, European breeders of cage birds have been in the vanguard of the movement towards scientific intensive breeding, and now the ordinary canary exists in a bewildering variety of strange mutations—the characters of which can be preserved from one generation to the next. Thus, today, we have not only all the different types of canary but all the further subdivisions of feather-types, shapes, colors and markings which so intrigue the fancier and which in the end make up variety for the showbench. Showing is primarily concerned with the judging of such distinct type-breeds as, in the canary, the Belgian, Lizard, Norfolk, Border, Gloster, Yorkshire and Scotch Fancy (the European and particularly English influence on the development of canaries is evident from this list). Besides such positive type-breeds, there are also "mules" (hybrids between canaries and other finches) and the Roller or Song Canaries—which are judged solely on the merit of their songs with absolutely no attention being given to their appearance. Song canaries used to be judged in special rooms of their own at the big bird shows so that their songs remained unimpaired by the inferior calls of other canaries but now, since these facilities are no longer available, special shows are sometimes staged.

More recently, as knowledge of genetics progressed and breeding techniques became more sophisticated, new color varieties have appeared. This quest for new colors has been the main driving force in budgerigar breeding since the 1870s; similarly canaries have also been subjected to color-breeding, and a whole new group (New Color Canaries) has arisen. This is a different practice from that of feeding artificial color agents to enhance the colors of type-breeds like the Yorkshire.

Although color is the main difference between one

the clock while those under AHAS regulations stipulate a clear round with no time limit.

A jumping course consists of both high and wide obstacles and includes such jumps as a brick wall, post-and-rail, double oxer, three-in-one, and a water jump. Penalties are handed out for the knock down of a jump (10 points), first refusal (10 points), second refusal (20 points), and fall of horse or rider (20 points). After three refusals at the same jump, the horse is disqualified.

Hunter Hunter divisions are numerous, consisting of classes such as working hunter, handy hunter, open hunter, and hunter hack. Obstacles within the course resemble those encountered in the hunting field and may therefore be set up in the show ring or outside. Hunters are judged on the ability to clear jumps, evenness of pace, suitability to rider and, also, on conformation. For working hunters, conformation is incidental as ability and movement are the important criteria. Hunter hacks must combine the qualities of both hack and hunter. They are first judged according to their performance at a walk, trot, canter, and hand gallop. After a first selection is made, each horse is required to jump a given course.

Equitation (Over Jumps) In equitation classes (over jumps) the skill of the rider in negotiating a given course of obstacles is tested. Usually, a combination of a clear round and the rider's performance, including posture in the saddle, use of aids, and control of the horse, determine the winner and runner-up.

In Harness

Harness classes are divided into fine (Saddle-breds), light also known as roadsters (Standard-breds), and heavy (Hackney horse and pony, Morgan, Shetland, and Welsh) harness. Fine and heavy harness horses are judged on action (an animated walk and showy trot), conformation, and manners. Roadsters are judged on speed at an ordinary trot and at a pace. Roadsters draw budgerigar and another, configuration and physical condition have an overall importance when it comes to the awarding of points on the showbench, and all exhibition budgerigars, irrespective of variety, should be as near the "ideal" as possible.

Budgerigars and canaries are the backbone of the cage bird showbench but alongside them are many other classes covering Bengalese Finches, Zebra Finches, Foreign Birds, Parrots, Hardbills, Softbills, and Talking Birds. All these categories and the subdivisions within them have a following in addition to the band of devotees for each variety of budgerigar and canary.

The presentation of birds for judging in organized cage bird shows at both local and national level is of continuing interest to all enthusiasts whether amateur or expert. It fosters healthy competition between breeders which spurs them to improve their stock. Shows are generally held in the winter months, after birds have finished breeding and are in prime condition.

A bird wins its class in a show when it accumulates more points than any other competitor. A proportion of the total available points—usually one hundred—is awarded for each of such features as feathering, color, markings, shape, size, stance or posture and wing-carriage (the requirements of the "ideal" vary from species to species). But irrespective of its inherent quality a bird must not be entered for a show unless it is in the prime of health—pert, bright eyed and sprightly; it has to be well trained so that it is steady and shows itself to the best advantage; it should be displayed in the correct cage for its type and entered in the correct class. Neglecting any of these points will mean rejection, as can a dirty or untidy cage or one without the correct perches and equipment.

The same basic principles outlined here for the showing of cage birds also apply to the exhibition of poultry, although it remains an entirely different discipline. Poultry, which includes all geese, hens and bantams, are prepared for shows with as much meticulous care as cage birds. They are bathed, groomed, and maintained in carefully controlled conditions. The showcases used for poultry are similar to those for cage birds but are obviously larger and lack perches.

Poultry shows are often staged as features of agricultural shows although their aims are the same as in shows devoted to cage birds. Perhaps it should be mentioned here that many of the so-called cage birds seen at shows are, strictly speaking, aviary birds. The majority of wild birds—all those not domesticated—should be housed in aviaries which encourage breeding, even though they may be transferred temporarily to cages for the purpose of showing.

Showing Small Mammals

The exhibition of small furred livestock may not be as universally popular or well known as the organized shows of large domestic beasts, dogs, cats, cage birds or poultry, but to the enthusiast it is just as important. Apart from the competitive element, these shows provide an opportunity for comparison, discussion, and the contact which is essential to the health and progress of every group favoring specific animals.

Of all the many hundreds of species of small wild mammals found on every continent, the vast majority are rodents, and it is from the Rodentia that all the

traditional pet mammals smaller than a rabbit are derived. Many wild mammals are, of course, kept as pets from time to time, but only those with some special indefinable quality become thoroughly domesticated and subject to the specialist breeding programs that sustain and enrich the separate disciplines. Rabbits, mice, cavies (guinea pigs), hamsters, gerbils and, to a lesser extent, rats and chinchillas are those which have so far reached this advanced stage of development.

Judging at small mammal shows is always done on a points system, whereby each entrant begins with its full complement of points (usually one hundred). A proportion of points are allocated for each of such considerations as color, markings, condition, type, fur, and size (these generally carry the most points), and also for specific features such as ears, eyes, tail, etc. Each animal loses points for every deviation from the "ideal." Animals are also penalized for other faults like obesity, sores, nervousness, molting, and dirty housing. Disease will obviously disqualify an entrant, but so can intractability, improper caging, and incorrect class selection.

Small mammals of all types are prepared for shows in much the same way. Handling is an important part of the show bench routine, and all prospective show animals should learn to accept being picked up, handled, and examined. Intensive "training" starts about a week before the show. Groom animals larger than mice with a soft brush or the hand, which removes loose hairs and stimulates the oil gland giving the coat a nice gloss.

No amount of final preparation, however, will turn a mediocre animal into a good one. And conversely even a potential champion must always be maintained in prime condition. Only continually correct feeding will keep an animal in good health and ready to be brought into top show condition.

You will want your entrant to arrive at the show in good time and in the same condition as it left home. Traveling boxes should correspond to the size of the animal. If they are too large, the inmates can panic and damage themselves; if they are too small, the animals will be cramped. The correct size cage for most rabbits, for instance, would be about 45cm. (18in.) long, 30cm. (12in.) wide and 35cm. (14in.) deep. Boxes and cages have to be sturdy, contain appropriate bedding and food, and be clearly and correctly labeled.

There are numerous breeds of rabbits which range in size from the Flemish Giants, weighing over 5kg. (11lb.), down to the Polish, weighing less than 1.4kg. (3lb.). Other exhibition rabbits include the Dutch,

Bird shows can include a wide range of cage birds from the highly domesticated canary with all its varieties (Top) *to wild species such as the gold-finch* (Center).

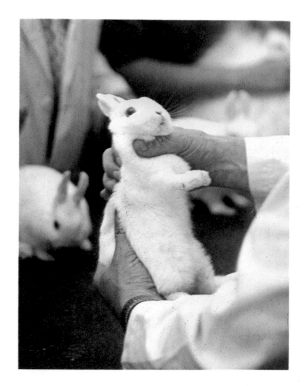

English, Himalayans, Lops, and the exceptionally beautiful Angora. Along with the Dutch, the Belgian Hare breed is ideal for beginners. The different breeds are shown in classes determined by a wide variety of colors and further subdivided by age and sex.

Guinea pigs (or cavies) probably form the second most popular branch of small mammalian pets, and shows are well organized and taken very seriously. Cavy and rabbit shows may be either small independent exhibits or part of a large agricultural or livestock show. The smooth-coated varieties can be groomed by first rubbing the coat the wrong way so as to dislodge dirt and expose unwanted guard hairs, and then grooming normally with a dampened cloth. The rosettes or cowlicks of the Abyssinian Cavy can be placed with a toothbrush quite easily but the Peruvian needs days of exacting preparation.

There are twenty recognized colors of the American, English or Bolivian Cavy, of which white (or albino) is the most common. An exhibition cavy must be true to the color of its type; it should also have a round nose, droopy ears, bright prominent eyes, feet tucked well under the body, and a round sloping rump.

Hamsters, despite their very recent appearance, have rapidly gained popularity and are available in a variety of mutations. A champion hamster could probably be described thus: *Color* (for which 30 points are allocated) correct for its class; *Type* or *Body* (15 points) broad, head large, nose blunt; *Fur* (15 points) short, dense, and soft; *Size* (15 points) large without being fat; *Condition* (15 points) alert, fit, and healthy; *Eyes* (5 points) large and set well apart but not protruding; and *Ears* (5 points) large and erect.

Preparation of hamsters for the show bench is again very important. Diet is temporarily changed to omit carrot, which can stain the fur, and cabbage which fouls the urine. Any stains on the fur can be removed by lightly dampening the area and rubbing in chalk or cornflour, which can be lightly brushed out when dry. No trace of chalk or cornflour is allowed at judging.

Mice have their own groups of fanciers. Mouse shows are held in Great Britain under the auspices of the National Mouse Club (NMC); although it is not binding, it is advisable for all exhibitors to be fully paid-up members of a recognized small livestock club affiliated with the NMC. The ten main classes for adult mice are: Self White (pink-eyed and black-eyed), Red or Chocolate, Self Blue or Black, Silver Gray, Fawn or Brown, Dutch, Champagne, Broken, Variegated, Tan, and a mixed class for any other variety.

Considering the small size of mice, it is fortunate that they do not often need much preparation for shows. A few gentle strokes with a piece of silk will usually put the finishing touches to their coats. Traveling rations must be as dry as possible (a piece of carrot is sufficient to provide moisture), and sawdust should liberally cover the floor. Most mice travel very well if they can make themselves a nest.

The ideal show mouse must conform to the color of its class. The coat for most varieties should be short, smooth, glossy, and soft. Its shape should be long, slim, and racy; the tail straight and about the same length as the body, tapering to a point from a thick root. Ears should be large, erect, set wide apart, and free of creases. Eyes should be large and prominent.

Gerbils, chinchillas, and rats are seldom exhibited at present, although interest in showing the gerbil has greatly increased. There are only a few varieties—of which the Albino Standard, White Spots, and Dilutes are main ones. Basically a good exhibition gerbil should be alert and tractable with a healthy, soft coat. It should be large but not fat, with a tail as long as the body. The head must be short, broad and set well into the body, with widely set eyes which are large and bright. The ears should be quite small, erect, and not too rounded. Coloration is extremely important and must comply to a detailed code.

Perhaps more than any other variety of small mammal, the gerbil, chinchilla, and fancy rat provide the best scope for the pioneering breeder who wants to concentrate on developing a new branch of small mammal keeping.

Showing Fish

The showing and exhibiting of fish takes place on a number of different levels: within local clubs, between local clubs, and at regional and national shows. The regional and national shows, which may only be held annually, are open to anyone who wants to enter and are well advertised in the aquarist press. Local club or interclub shows are usually for club members only and are often small informal events held frequently. A beginner can learn a lot by visiting the regional and national shows as many species of excellent fish are on display.

Most shows are for fish only, but there are classes for plants and for furnished aquaria at the larger shows. In the furnished aquarium class the exhibitor has to set up, in a 60 x 60 x 30cm. (24 x 24 x 12in.) tank, a complete aquascape with gravel, rocks, plants, and fish. The judge gives marks under the following headings:

    (a) design and character of aquascape
    (b) selection, quality, and condition of fish
    (c) selection, quality, and condition of plants
    (d) technique

Showing fish themselves is, however, the most popular form of competition. In smaller shows fish are entered in a limited number of show classes such as Carps, Barbs, and Minnows; Characins and related families; Livebearers; Anabantids; Cichlids; Killifishes; Catfish and Loaches; and AOV (any other variety). In larger shows there are many more classes and there may be classes for individual species. Another popular class is the breeders class where the exhibitor shows up to six fish which he has bred. A number of specialist aquarium societies, such as The Guppy Society and The Cichlid Society, sponsor shows for fish in their own particular interest families. When entering a fish show it is important to know what the classes are, the rules, and judging methods. These can be obtained from the show secretary.

Staging a fish show involves a great deal of work both for sponsors and exhibitors. Many shows ask the exhibitor to bench the fish in a standard-sized sweet jar with plain sides. The fish is usually brought in a show jar which saves work for everyone. Judging at national shows is carried out by very experienced and approved judges, and even at local club level there is usually an experienced judge for most classes. Show standards have been laid down for some fish, but a standard method of judging is also used. Marks out of a possible twenty are given under each of the following headings: size, color, fins, body shape, condition, and deportment (the way the fish sits and swims in the water).

Many of the regional and national organizations which have fish shows publish information about their show standards or have lists showing the marks which should be given to various size fish in the more common species. The judge relies upon experience in allocating marks.

To be a consistent winner at shows means that the aquarist must have a stock of good fish and have learned the techniques of exhibiting fish to their best advantage. On the other hand the person with only one tank may have a good fish presented with care which,

Exhibiting fish poses many problems including getting them to the show and then providing tanks with the correct conditions there. Despite this, as well as competitive categories for fish (Center) at bigger shows there are also those for plants (Top).

against local competition can win best in the class.

Obviously the aquarist will choose his best fish. Remember that in a Livebearer Class a half-grown swordtail will only score 10 out of 20 for size no matter how good it is in other ways. Fish which have been fighting and reveal missing scales or torn fins will lose points. Fishes with abnormalities, for example a missing gill cover, will be marked down severely by the judge.

An aquarist who is an avid exhibitor may buy twenty or more of a particular species of fish and raise them separately under first class conditions with the best feeding possible before finally picking the one to be shown.

It is a good idea to select the fish for exhibit about four weeks before the show and place it in a separate tank without plants or gravel. Feed this fish small amounts at short intervals to improve its alertness and to become accustomed to close observation. Always use water from the fish's own tank in the show jar. Do not put it into strange water which may disturb it. Make sure the jar is sparkling clean and the water is crystal clear. Placing the fish on the show bench as early as possible gives it more time to settle down and resume normal coloring after the journey from home. The judge can only judge the fish as seen and if it has been roughly caught then dumped in a show tank it will not be at its best, no matter how good it normally looks in the tank at home. The very best way to learn about exhibiting fish is to enter them in local shows. Every winner of national events started in this way.

PETS & THE LAW

The extent to which legislators have passed laws relating to pet animals varies considerably from country to country. Countries in which the keeping of pet animals is less common obviously find it less necessary to enact legislation, whereas in countries like Great Britain and the United States where most families keep a pet of some kind, legislation is essential. Legislative rules and regulations normally fall into five broad categories: welfare measures, disease control provisions, measures designed to provide a degree of control over the animals themselves, the treatment of sick and injured animals, and finally euthanasia and the disposal of animals after death. These laws differ so greatly from country to country, or even from state to state, and are being amended so frequently that it is impossible to generalize on an international scale. However, by considering each category of legislation separately we can understand most types of law applicable to pet animals in modern society.

WELFARE MEASURES

Some countries maintain that since a pet animal is the sole property of its owner, the owner should have absolute rights over it, and no other authority should have cause to intervene. In other countries, however, it is acknowledged that with rights go responsibilities, and the dominion over animals carries the obligation not to abuse that power. These countries frequently enact legislation making it a criminal offense for anyone to treat an animal cruelly. What constitutes cruelty is often a matter for debate—principally because animals cannot speak for themselves and it is not always accurate to assume that a cause of suffering for a human being will necessarily have the same effect upon an animal. In a case heard by the English courts some years ago, the opinion rendered the definition of cru-

In many areas it is against the law to let dogs roam free, and dog catchers are employed to capture the strays.

elty as "the unnecessary abuse of an animal." Thus, to beat, kick, wound, starve, or otherwise affect the physical well-being of an animal is commonly a criminal offense and comes as no surprise to most pet owners. The abandonment of an animal is also an offense in some countries, but unfortunately this law is hard to enforce.

Laws which prohibit the breeding and keeping of animals to fight against each other in such sports as cock fighting may have less acceptance. Most developed countries do have welfare legislation which could be invoked if animals were set purposely to fight each other, and many countries also have legislation which controls the use of animals in circuses and filmmaking, in order to prevent such fighting for public entertainment.

The breeding and selling of animals attracts some people whose sole interest is to make the maximum amount of money with little concern for the conditions under which their animals are reared. The only possible course, to cover such circumstances, is the enactment of legislation to control breeding establishments and pet shops. Boarding kennels for pets also need to be of a high quality. The wise pet owner will always determine whether or not he is dealing with a breeding, selling, or boarding establishment which meets the requirements of national legislation and local regulations.

In preparing a pet for competition with others, a pet owner may sometimes consider surgical correction for minor defects—for example in the teeth, the tail, or the ears of dogs. Very few countries have legislation specifically banning such procedures (provided they are performed under anesthesia and with due regard to the avoidance of cruelty), but show clubs often ban animals whose faults have been corrected in these ways. In some countries, certain other procedures such as the docking of puppies' tails and the cropping of their ears is often advocated before showing particular breeds.

On the other hand owners will sometimes request veterinarians to carry out operations such as declawing cats, debarking dogs, or pinioning birds solely for the owners' convenience. In some circumstances these operations may prove to be illegal, but in any event members of the veterinary profession will frequently be unwilling to perform these operations.

Finally, it should be noted that great distress and even death can be inflicted on an animal if it travels without the greatest care being given to its feeding, watering, and physical well-being during the journey. There are now stringent international regulations concerned with the transportation of animals by air, and there is also, in most developed countries, strict legislation regarding the transportation of animals by road, railroad, and sea.

DISEASE CONTROL

Legislation designed to restrict the movement of animals, in order to prevent the spread or introduction of disease, exists in most countries—sometimes for the benefit of farm livestock. In New Zealand, for example, restrictions are placed upon the dog population to

prevent the spread of disease within the cattle of the national herd. More often, however, disease control legislation is promoted in relation to zoonosis—diseases which are transmitted from animals to humans. Psittacosis, for example, can be transmitted from parrots and certain other exotic birds to humans, causing a pneumonia-like illness which can sometimes prove fatal. The most dangerous common zoonosis transmissible by a pet to its owner is rabies. Once a human being shows the signs of rabies the disease is always fatal, although it can be successfully treated in the first few days after infection.

The laws to control such diseases vary from country to country, depending largely upon whether the disease in question is endemic, occasionally present, or not present at all. Countries with land boundaries are in a more vulnerable position, since disease may often be transmitted by wildlife crossing the borders, but a country which is an island will normally have strict requirements regarding the importation of animals which might carry a disease not currently present in the country in question.

Requirements for taking pets into foreign countries are many and varied. They can include various kinds of health certificates, proofs of rabies and/or distemper inoculation. They can prohibit the import of all animals except with special permission from the right government department, as in Norway. In West Germany special permits are required for dogs. And in Australia, New Zealand, and Great Britain there are long periods of quarantine in official kennels. In fact Australia and New Zealand will only allow domestic animals into their countries after six months isolation in Great Britain plus six months further domicile there. Since import measures differ from country to country, you should check with the official body of the country concerned, such as its embassy or consulate, well in advance of your planned journey. Attempts to violate the provisions of the legislation can lead to heavy fines or imprisonment as well as the destruction of the animal in question.

In countries where a particular disease is already present, the law is more likely to require prophylactic measures. Thus, in countries where rabies is found dogs and cats are normally required to be vaccinated, and failure on the part of the owner to see that this is done can result in penalties.

CONTROL OF ANIMALS

Control over animals is needed to prevent the spread of disease, but pet animals are controlled for other reasons, particularly in countries with large urban populations. Most countries require a dog to be licensed and to wear a collar bearing the name and address of its owner. In theory, this should limit the dog population (by taxing the ownership of a dog) and provide a measure of control (by permitting the identification of the owner of a dog which causes trouble). In fact, dog license fees are seldom high enough to deter potential owners and any attempt to set them at a prohibitive level might also prohibit the poor from

The barbarous sport of cock-fighting has been banned for many years in most Western countries and now survives legally only in parts of Asia.

93

Rigid regulations govern the import and export of animals, and most international airports have facilities to monitor such traffic. For air transportation special cages are required, such as those shown here for birds (Left) and bees (Right).

ownership. Moreover, leash laws prohibiting dogs from running loose and collar-tag laws are frequently not enforced.

In several countries the control of the urban dog population is passing from the owner to the dog catcher or dog warden, who is given power under national laws or local regulations to "arrest" any stray dog, keep it in an appropriate pound, and then either to find the owner and return the dog (still with the possibility of court action against the owner), or to destroy the dog in due course. As the dog population increases, the problem of the stray dog in the urban area is becoming more acute every year. More and more people live in houses or flats with no gardens or other exercise facilities for their pets, and the human population and their motor

vehicles demand an everincreasing share of the available space. As the problem magnifies, people who do not own dogs become less tolerant of pavements which are fouled or of children's playgrounds littered with dog excrement which may carry disease. Laws therefore often ban the fouling of public places by dogs but fail to provide areas in which the dogs may legitimately micturate and defecate.

Laws, although in this case more often of a civil than a criminal nature, also often provide that the owner or person in charge of an animal shall be liable for damage caused by the animal. For example, in England an owner who takes his dog for a walk, allows it to escape from its leash, run into a busy road and cause a traffic accident with resulting injury or damage, may find that he has to compensate those who have been injured or have suffered damage. The test, under the Animals Act of 1971, is whether the person in charge was or was not negligent in his or her control of the animal. In many other countries the owner will also be liable for the damage his animal causes to either property or person, as in the case of a bite.

One area in which a dog owner will certainly be liable to heavy penalties—and the animal concerned subject to death—is in cases of attacks on sheep or other kinds

Many animals have to be quarantined before being allowed into certain countries. Center Left. Quarantined animals must be handled with great care to prevent any possible contamination. Bottom Left. Quarantine facilities have to satisfy strict regulations; often one must pass through three sets of doors to reach each individual animal.

Bottom Right. *Rabies is not present on the British Isles, and every effort is made to keep infected animals out. Measures include the exhibition of these posters at airports and ports which warn of the dangers of the disease and the legal penalties for importing animals without quarantine.*

of livestock. Damages to the livestock owner in these cases can be considerable.

In an effort to limit the keeping of unsuitable pets in apartments and other urban accommodations, some authorities have local regulations completely banning pets. In justification for such legislation the authorities point to the problem of dogs roaming loose and in packs, knocking over children and old people. They point also to the fact that continuous confinement inside an apartment can border on cruelty to the animal. Nevertheless, such regulations banning the keeping of pets are frequently criticized on the grounds that it interferes with the rights of the individual citizen.

TREATMENT OF SICK ANIMALS

Most countries have long recognized that the proper person to treat the ailments and injuries of animals is the professionally qualified veterinarian, and it is for the protection of animals and their owners, rather than the benefit of the veterinary profession, that the law in many countries gives veterinarians a virtual monopoly in treating animals. There are some exceptions, the most common being the right of the farmer to treat his own livestock. And there is general acceptance of the right the individual animal owner has to treat a pet. It would clearly be nonsense to bar an owner from anointing a sore or sprinkling powder on an itch from which the pet is suffering—and normally the pet owner knows when the pet's illness or injury is serious enough to warrant calling in the veterinarian.

EUTHANASIA AND THE DISPOSAL OF ANIMALS AFTER DEATH

There is at least one important difference in the approach of death for an animal from that situation for a human being. Members of the medical profession are under an obligation to do all they reasonably can to prolong a human patient's life, and any suspicion that the death of the patient has resulted from euthanasia will lead to an inquiry and possibly to court proceedings. In the case of an animal, an owner has a positive moral duty in certain situations to consider whether it would not be kinder to have the animal put to death. Thus in cases of irreversible illness, serious injury, or extreme feebleness due to old age, it is sometimes more cruel to try to maintain life. The law does, of course, normally permit euthanasia but sometimes it goes further. Sometimes the law will define cruelty to an animal not only as a positive act of cruelty, but also as *the omission* by the owner of any act which consequently results in unnecessary suffering to the animal. Therefore, failure to have a sick or injured animal put to

death when the suffering cannot be adequately relieved could, of itself, be a legal offense.

When euthanasia is decided upon, it should be carried out as painlessly as possible. There are humane, quick, and painless methods of euthanasia such as an injection by a veterinarian. Whatever method is used, the law will expect that all reasonable precautions are taken to avoid unnecessary suffering.

When the animal has been put to death or has died naturally, there may be problems in disposing of the body. In urban areas in particular, an owner may have difficulty in arranging for burial. In country areas such difficulties are not as prevalent and in sophisticated communities there may be crematoria and burial services. Leaving the body in some unsuitable and unauthorized area must be avoided at all costs, not only because the law in all probability makes this an offense, but because of the health hazard which this action could cause. These problems can cause disproportionate worry to the average owner simply because of inexperience. Your local veterinarian, however, will be dealing daily with the problem of disposing of bodies and a short consultation with a member of his staff will provide the sensible and legal solution.

ENDANGERED SPECIES

Throughout the world, new laws are frequently being enacted to deal with endangered species of animals. (Not all the animals can be considered as pets, but some of them may be.) Some countries, such as Great Britain, have developed wildfowl sanctuaries in order to attract migrant birds, and others are setting aside lands for native wild animals, such as elephants, rhinoceroses, and big cats. Similarly, illegal trade in endangered species is coming under strict control. Laws now protect trade in exotic animals, butterflies, hawks, falcons, owls, eagles, and more. Trade in goods made from skins of animals and other animal products (such as ivory) is regulated in some countries. United States' federal and state laws prevent people from catching and keeping native wild birds, and even some types of turtles, fish, and rabbits have been protected. Not all species have been saved, but significant progress is being made. Since laws vary greatly from state to state and country to country, consult local authorities if you have any questions.

Pets of Every Kind

DOGS

Probably no other animal has been more shaped by human design than the dog. Thus we have ferocious creatures called Pekingese who can fit into women's purses and we have ponysized Irish Wolfhounds whose tails are more dangerous than their teeth. Unless we were told, would we suspect that the bullet-shaped Bull Terrier and the elegant Whippet were both developed on the tiny island called Britain? The very diversity of breeds is a testimonial both of mankind's consuming passion with his oldest animal friend and to the canine's remarkable flexibility.

Choosing a Dog

How does one choose a puppy from the many available sorts? If we humans were completely rational beings it would be impossible. There are simply too many possible choices. Of course we have a rough idea of the size and shape and temperament we want. And some of us have an idea of why we want a dog. It may be as an aid to hunting, as a guard, or simply as an incentive to go for regular walks. It may be that we want a dog to lend prestige to our otherwise unprepossessing presence. An awful lot of us get dogs simply because we think it is a good idea for the children to have one. But of course the vast majority of us get a dog because we love the creatures and want to share our lives with theirs. Basically that is why our choice is often, in objective eyes, quite irrational. Why choose a smooth-haired Fox Terrier, for example, which is likely to be noisy, aggressive, and difficult to train when for the same amount of money one could have a Labrador who with very little effort can be taught etiquette up to university level. Or why get an Afghan which will require lots of grooming when Salukis are available? The answer is quite obvious. It is simply a matter of personal preference.

But here a slight word of warning. Exercise your personal prejudices by all means, but before you make your final decision make sure that the breed you buy bears some resemblence to your conception of the breed.

Facing Page. Dogs have been domesticated for so long that there are many hundreds of breeds, most of them developed as working types. Dogs like to join in family activities. They make good pets because they accept family life as a substitute for pack life.

You need plenty of space if you want to keep a dog as large as a Great Dane. Remember when you see an appealing little puppy it may grow, in only a matter of months, to be a very large dog which will require plenty of exercise and cost a considerable amount to feed.

Some people, for example, think that because a Bull Terrier is such a strong, ferocious-looking beast it would be an ideal guard dog. Indeed most of them will effectively deter other animals, but many of them would wag their tails encouragingly while a thief carried away your valuables.

So how do you find out? Narrow your field of choices by reading all about the breeds you fancy. Then go to a couple of dog shows. If you are looking for a children's dog see how many children are sitting among the exhibits. You might, for example, have one of your misconceptions upset when you see the number of children cuddling Chows. You might find that the breed of your choice is surrounded by signs warning people to watch from a distance.

Talk to the exhibitors. Almost all are genuine enthusiasts. They would rather not make a sale, most of them, than see one of their pups go to an unsuitable owner. Many exhibitors will have nothing for sale but will be able to recommend someone who has a pup of "pet" quality. There is a vast difference in price between these and pups who have breeding or show potential. For your purposes the "pet" puppy might well be more than good enough.

One must remember that puppies are not produced on a year round assembly line. Many people decide that Christmas is the best time to get a puppy. Nature does not agree. So you should be prepared to wait until a good breeder or someone he has recommended has a litter to offer.

Any reputable breeder will agree to a veterinarian's examination of the puppy before the sale is completed. You, of course, will have to pay for it. In many cases, however, the puppy will have had one or more prophylactic inoculations, and the breeder's vet may be willing to confirm that he found nothing wrong at that time.

If your nose is offended by the odor of the puppies or you see a lot of sniffling or scratching or loose motions among them, either leave the whole place alone or insist on a veterinary certificate of health.

Wherever there are dogs inevitably there will be many who are not purebreds. In the main they are testimonial to human beings' irresponsibility. People who care and people who know breed purebreds. Those who allow their dogs to roam and to reproduce indiscriminately are ignorant or callous or both. Quite rightly in many places these people and the nuisances they create are being legislated out of existence. Everyone can tell stories of the wonderful mongrels they have known. One must agree. Lots are, but one seldom hears of the vast majority who uncared for and unwanted are rounded up and destroyed. The statistics make depressing reading.

However, if one wants to give one of these mongrels a home how does one choose? Unhappily it is very much a gamble. You really cannot have any idea how it will turn out—and that is the whole point about pure breds. That is why men of all races and classes from the humblest shepherd to powerful sheiks and kings have selectively bred to produce the breeds we have today. They were not breeding for snobbery. They were selecting for the characteristics they wanted in a dog.

One must mention crossbreds or hybrids. These are usually the result of accidental mismatings between purebreds. Occasionally people match them deliberately. Lindy the Brussels Griffon absolutely adores Bonny the Chihuahua. The owners decide to allow that affection full expression. That first generation cross may well have the best characteristics of both dogs plus a factor that scientists call hybrid vigor. There are all sorts of possible combinations. Naming them can be quite amusing. Many spoodles (spaniel cross poodle) are charming. Some are downright nasty. Some of the nastiest canine misfits are German Shepherd cross Labradors. Yet some turn out superbly. Advice? Try to avoid accidents. Leave the experiments to the experts.

Finally one may be offered a mature dog—purebred or otherwise. Usually they are free and one is, of course, told the reason for giving up the family pet. Sometimes the reason is genuine. The family has to move to Timbuctu or some place where dogs are not allowed. Sometimes people fail to mention that they would have taken the dog had it not acquired the habit of biting the children or urinating on the sofa. In all such cases, it is best to have a written agreement covering all possible contentions. Before you finally decide, have it at home for a couple of days or a week. You might discover that its owners are very sound sleepers and did not realize it howled every morning from three till five. The agreement should also state that the owners have no right to reclaim their dog on their return from Timbuctu. It is amazing how many people do try exactly that. But by that time you have grown attached to the creature. Ugly it may be. Smelly it certainly is. But you love the dog and it loves you and no way will you be parted. And that's what it's all about!

Feeding Your Dog

Dogs share the basic nutritional needs of all animals. (See **Feeding Your Pet**.) Although dogs belong to the zoological order Carnivore, they are almost as omnivorous as humans. The dog's digestive system copes efficiently with sugars and cooked starch which can form over half of the dry matter of a balanced canine diet.

Like most other mammals, healthy dogs do not need dietary vitamin C (ascorbic acid) because they make it in their own bodies. Unlike cats, dogs can use the orange pigment (ß-carotene) found in carrots, tomatoes, and other vegetables to make their own vitamin A. They can also make the vitamin niacin of the B group from the essential amino-acid tryptophan if the diet contains sufficient good quality protein. Dogs need essential fatty acids (linoleic and arachidonic) for a healthy coat and skin and are one of the few species in which a requirement for vitamin E in the diet has been clearly demonstrated.

WHAT TO FEED

Since the dog is so omnivorous, innumerable diets can be devised to meet its needs. However, the diet should not be varied unnecessarily as this can lead to digestive disturbances. The sensible method for maintenance feeding is to find a diet which the dog likes and thrives on, and to vary this as little as possible. Most dogs do well, for example, on a diet of meat, water, biscuit, and an occasional bone. Milk, fish, cheese, and eggs are available protein foods as alternatives for the few dogs which either dislike or cannot be given meat.

Canned food for dogs is readily available. Most brands are supplemented with cereals, vitamins, and minerals to provide a complete and balanced diet. Some of the more expensive brands contain no cereal and are customarily fed mixed with dog biscuits, whole or coarsely ground. Biscuits help to meet energy needs at a relatively low cost and also contain fiber which adds bulk to the stools. They are frequently supplemented with vitamins and minerals and thus help to balance a meat-based diet. Whole biscuits can be fed separately to provide the owner with some amusement and the dog with dental exercise. Bread, cooked potatoes and other cereals can be given as they are easily digested and provide energy with some protein and minor nutrients.

Completely dry or semi-moist foods for dogs have been available for some years. They are formulated from cereals, vegetable, and animal protein concentrates and vitamin/mineral supplements. The semi-moist forms contain about 26 percent water and have a somewhat rubbery or chewy texture.

The completely dry food can be given either as it is or moistened in water or gravy. Although there is no objection to dry feeding, a dog used to wet food may require some time to become accustomed to the change. A dry crunchy food may assist, by abrasion, in keeping teeth and gums in healthy condition but wet food is usually more palatable. If dry feeding is adopted it is essential that drinking water be freely available, especially for some hours after meals.

Bones provide nourishment, help keep the teeth clean and, of course, give most dogs a great deal of enjoyment. The bone should be as large as the dog can carry comfortably and it should first be boiled for a few minutes. A piece of shank bone is ideal. Smaller bones may splinter and lodge in the throat, or even cause internal injury. Fish and poultry bones should never be given. Do not provide too

Examples of Diets for Adult House Dogs

	SMALL DOG 4.5kg (10lb) REQUIRING 1,700KJ/DAY (400 kcal)	MEDIUM DOG 13.5kg (30lb) REQUIRING 3,800KJ/DAY (900kcal)	LARGE DOG 27kg (60lb) REQUIRING 6,300 KJ/DAY (1,500kcal)
DIET 1	*1st meal* 115g (4oz) whole cow's milk 60g (2 oz) brown bread *2nd meal* 115g (4oz) minced lean beef 30g (1oz) grated carrot	340g (0.75lb) cow or sheep tripe 170g (6oz) plain dog meal 15g (0.5oz) sterilized bone flour 5 drops cod liver oil	115g (0.25lb) cow liver 340g (0.75lb) cow or sheep tripe 340g (0.75lb) plain dog meal 28g (0.25oz) sterilized bone flour
DIET 2	*1st meal* 1 small can 200g (7oz) dog food 60g (2oz) fortified dog meal *2nd meal* 2–3 small dog biscuits 85g (3oz) whole cow's milk	1 small can 200 g (7oz) dog food including cereal 200g (7oz) *fortified dog meal 5–6 small dog biscuits	1 large can 425g (15oz) dog food including cereal 340g (12oz) *fortified dog meal
DIET 3	*1st meal* 85g (3oz) complete dog meal *2nd meal* 60g (2oz) complete dog meal	280g (10oz) complete dog meal	510g (18oz) complete dog meal
	*that is with added vitamins and minerals Fresh drinking water should always be available.		

many bones as an excess of gnawing can lead to severe constipation or even blockage in the lower bowel.

A healthy dog's diet does not need to contain fruit or vegetables. Nevertheless, all dogs eat grass at times as an emetic or purgative, and a small proportion of green vegetables in the diet may be of value for the laxative effect. Any diet with a reasonable proportion of cereals contains sufficient roughage for the excretion of well-formed stools.

The feeding of table and kitchen scraps is unlikely to have ill effects if the amount does not exceed 25 percent of the total diet. However, some foods are best avoided. Chocolates, sweets, and sweet biscuits may unbalance the diet and are probably as bad for a dog's teeth as for ours. Sudden changes of diet can be almost guaranteed to upset the digestive system.

Finally, fresh water must be supplied every day. A heavy earthenware bowl is the most suitable container. It should be replenished as necessary during the day and washed out once a day.

WHEN TO FEED

Healthy adult dogs usually thrive on one meal a day. A toy dog needs more food for its size and should be fed twice daily. Some of the large breeds such as Bloodhounds and Boxers are prone to indigestion if the stomach is overloaded and consequently should also be given two meals a day. Indeed there is no harm in giving any dog two meals a day if the amounts are adjusted to avoid overfeeding, and most dogs will overeat if given the opportunity. A convenient system is a main meal of meat with cereal and a second light meal of a few dog biscuits and a milk drink.

Meals can be given at any time convenient to the daily routine. It is important to keep to the established hour: the dog's digestive system expects no less! Working dogs should be fed in the evening but should be given a light meal such as biscuits, before a heavy working day. Avoid snacks between meals. They can easily result in overfeeding and may make the dog a begging nuisance. Rewards given in training should be small.

HOW MUCH TO FEED

The amount to feed is controlled by three main factors—body weight, individual nature, and the amount of exercise or work. Shape, coat, health, age, breeding, and climate are also relevant. The accompanying table gives the average energy needs of healthy pet dogs ranging in weight from 1kg.–90kg. (2lb.–200lb.). This energy must be provided in a balanced diet. Examples of typical diets for adult house dogs are also shown in a separate table.

The surest indication that an adult animal is receiving the correct amount of food—provided that the diet is balanced—is the maintenance of its body weight. Dogs should be weighed about twice a month. With dogs up to about 23kg. (50lb.) this is easily done by weighing yourself on a bathroom scale, first alone and then carrying the dog, and noting the difference. Owners of large dogs need to observe condition more closely or use an industrial platform scale to weigh them. The aim is to maintain the dog in lean, firm-muscled condition.

FEEDING THE PUPPY

The puppy should be weaned by first learning to accept cow's milk as a substitute for the mother's milk, then after a few days it can be introduced to solid foods in the form of pellets, crushed biscuit, or a cereal baby food. Continue to offer milk.

The weaned puppy should be receiving two substantial proteinaceous meals a day, morning and evening, with light milky feeds at midday and late evening. The puppy should be weighed at weekly intervals. The amount the puppy will eat varies with its breed and temperament.

The late evening meal can be omitted within a week of weaning and the midday meal at three months, but milk should still be given, in the quantities indicated in the accompanying table, either separately or mixed with the main meals, up to six months of age. Meat should be introduced, mixed with the puppy meal, at about eight weeks unless it has already been incorporated into the diet. (This is not neccessary if a "complete" food such as an expanded meal is being given.) Any type of meat, if cooked, is suitable but too much at once may cause a gastric disturbance. Continue to feed two main meals a day. If the puppy cleans up the dish and is obviously not satisfied, give more at the next meal. A healthy puppy usually eats its fill in less than five minutes. Rate of gain should be about 100g. (4oz.) a day for puppies of Labrador-size breeds, 50g. (2oz.) for Beagles, and 25g. (1oz.) for Miniature Poodles.

At about six months of age (sooner in small breeds and later in the larger) the rate of growth slackens and overfeeding a greedy puppy must be avoided. As with humans, excess weight is much more easily acquired than lost again. Throughout the puppy stage it is beneficial to provide large pieces of cooked shank bone for gnawing. This helps with the change of teeth at four to five months—and may save the furniture from attack!

Dietary regimes for some popular breeds during the puppy period are suggested in the accompanying table. Owing to the great variation between individuals, even of the same weight, it must be used with discretion. The surest guide is the dog's condition. Note that from the age of about three months to the end of the rapid growth period, a puppy needs more food than it subsequently does as an adult animal (unless it is a working dog).

FEEDING OLDER DOGS

Dogs grow rapidly, spend most of their lives as active adults, and decline through a relatively short old age. With proper care a healthy dog of medium size requires no change of diet until at least ten years old. As activity diminishes you should take care not

Energy Requirements For Adult House Dogs

APPROX WEIGHT kg (lb)	REPRESENTATIVE BREEDS	ENERGY REQUIREMENTS kJ (kcal)
0.9 (2)	Chihuahua	625 (150)
2.3 (5)	Maltese Terrier, Yorkshire Terrier	1,050 (250)
3.6 (8)	Miniature Dachshund, Toy Poodle	1,450 (350)
4.5 (10)	Papillon, Pekingese	1,675 (400)
6.8 (15)	Cairn Terrier, Miniature Poodle, Shetland Sheepdog	2,360 (550)
9 (20)	Corgi, Dachshund, Fox Terrier, Whippet	2,925 (700)
11.3 (25)	Cocker Spaniel, Irish Terrier	3,350 (800)
13.6 (30)	Beagle, Kerry Blue, Schnauzer	3,750 (900)
18 (40)	Bull Terrier, English Springer Spaniel	4,600 (1,100)
22.6 (50)	Airedale, Bulldog, Chow Chow	5,500 (1,300)
27.2 (60)	Boxer, Greyhound, Retrievers, Setters	6,275 (1,500)
36 (80)	Alsatian (German Shepherd), Rhodesian Ridgeback	7,550 (1,800)
45 (100)	Bloodhound, Bullmastiff, Pyrenean	9,600 (2,300)
68 (150)	Great Dane, Mastiff, Newfoundland	13,400 (3,200)
90 (200)	St. Bernard	16,750 (4,000)

Because of individual variation the figures should be treated as a guide—most dogs will come within ± 20%. Young dogs usually need more food than suggested and old dogs less. A particularly active dog, or one that is used also in a sport, may need up to 30% more than the figure indicates. Dogs kenneled outdoors need more food in winter, the amount depending on the severity of the climate. Very short-coated breeds like the Whippet and Smooth-haired Dachshund lose more body heat and have greater energy needs in cool climates than shown.

BREED	AGE	WEIGHT	MORNING MEAL	MIDDAY MEAL	EVENING MEAL
Miniature Poodle	8 weeks	1.8kg (4lb)	40g (1.5oz) puppy meal 55g (2oz) milk	30g (1 oz) milk	30g (1oz) puppy meal 55g (2oz) milk
	3 months	2.7kg (6lb)	55g (2oz) puppy meal 30g (1oz) meat	85g (3oz) milk	30g (1oz) puppy meal 55g (2oz) milk
	4 months	3.6kg (8lb)	85g (3oz) puppy meal 55g (2oz) meat	—	2 small dog biscuits 140g (5oz) milk
	6 months	5.4kg (12lb)	115g (4oz) puppy meal 85g (3oz) meat	—	3 biscuits 140g (5oz) milk
	9 months	6.3kg (14lb)	85g (3oz) dog meal 115g (4oz) meat	—	4 biscuits
Beagle	8 weeks	3.6kg (8lb)	85g (3oz) puppy meal 85g (3oz) milk	115g (4oz) milk	85g (3oz) puppy meal 85g (3oz) milk
	3 months	5.4kg (12lb)	115g (4oz) puppy meal 5g (2oz) meat	140g (5oz) milk	85g (3oz) puppy meal 140g (5oz) milk
	4 months	7.7kg (17lb)	170g (6oz) puppy meal 115g (4oz) meat	—	5 small dog biscuits 285g (10oz) milk
	6 months	11.3kg (25lb)	255g (9oz) puppy meal 170g (6oz) meat	—	5 biscuits 285g (10oz) milk
	9 months	13.6kg (30lb)	170g (6oz) dog meal 170g (6oz) meat	—	5 biscuits

to overfeed. Gradually reduce the energy, content of the food (usually by cutting down on biscuits), but maintain protein, vitamin, and mineral intakes. Be sure the food is not too hard or lumpy for old jaws and worn teeth. If digestive ability is impaired, divide the daily amount between two or more meals.

FEEDING PROBLEMS

The ease in feeding healthy dogs can lead to the common problem of obesity. Obesity is rarely a consequence of an unbalanced diet or a defect in the animal's metabolism. Most dogs overeat if allowed more food than is needed to maintain health and body weight. One small biscuit a day too many can produce a weight gain of 4–5kg. (10lb.) in a year. The remedy is obvious but hard to implement. Meals must be reduced until the dog is losing weight gradually: not more than 0.5kg. (1lb.) a week for a dog weighing 18kg. (40lb.) whose proper weight is 13.5kg. (30lb.).

When the correct weight is reached, the diet should be increased just enough for that weight to be maintained. Unfortunately the dieting dog may seek food on its own and develop bad habits such as thieving and coprophagy (dung-eating). Prescription diets are available and may satisfy hunger while pro-viding all essential nutrients. Alternative activities should be provided, such as long walks, ideally off the leash, or a really hard bone to gnaw. If the prescription diet is not used, reduce the carbohydrate part of the daily ration (biscuits and chow) and give a vitamin/mineral supplement in the quantity prescribed.

Coprophagy (dung-eating) is common in dogs. Usually they are attracted to the droppings of other species, especially cattle, horses, and cats. The latter normally bury their excrement but nothing can be done about cow and horse dung except to keep the dog away from temptation. In moderation the habit is not basically injurious but there is a risk of infection from parasites or harmful bacteria. A smaller proportion of dogs eat their own and other dogs' stools. The owner can help to correct the habit by removing stools as soon as possible. Often the cause is boredom or stress, and the owner should ensure that the offender is adequately exercised and not left alone for long periods.

Looseness is another common problem. True diarrhea (liquid feces) will lead to serious dehydration if persistent and veterinary advice must be sought. There may be an infection or a defect in the digestive system. Soft, shapeless stools, particularly following a change of diet, are not usually serious. Adding a little bone flour or providing a bone to gnaw may correct the problem but neither should be given in excess. Sometimes looseness is a form of incontinence brought about by stress. It is evident in nervous dogs, dogs which have changed ownership, or those undergoing strict obedience training. The problem is then behavioral rather than nutritional, requiring considerable patience for its solution.

Lack or loss of appetite (anorexia) can be caused by sheer satiation, the most frequent sufferers being overweight small dogs. Usually these dogs become extremely fussy about their food. The only effective solution is starvation until the dogs learn to be less picky. Failure to eat well over a long period, leading to serious loss of weight, must receive veterinary attention. Loss of weight associated with normal appetite can be caused by worm infestation or a defect in the digestive system, and professional advice should be sought.

*Average **Daily** Food Consumption of Six-week-old Puppies*

BREED	BODYWEIGHT	*METHOD 1		*METHOD 2		
		Puppy meal	Milk	Scraped beef	Baby Cereal	Milk
Labrador	3.6kg (8lb)	100g (3.5oz)	350ml (0.75pt)	115g (4oz)	56g (2oz)	350ml (0.75pt)
Beagle	2.5kg (5.5lb)	70g (2.5oz)	250ml (0.5pt)	80g (2.75oz)	42g (1.5oz)	250ml (0.5pt)
Miniature poodle	1.4kg (3lb)	43g (1.5oz)	120ml (0.25pt)	40g (1.5oz)	28g (1oz)	120ml (0.25pt)

*The amounts given should be divided between at least two main meals.

A number of dog breeds, such as poodles and wire-hairs, are traditionally barbered both for comfort and appearance. For show purposes, the accepted styles differ from breed to breed. Terriers are more usually plucked or stripped. Right. You can trim a dog's coat yourself, provided you purchase the proper clippers, but you may prefer to take your pet to a dog beauty parlor to be dealt with by professionals as here. Remember, while giving a "beauty" treatment the parlor will not be responsible for dealing with any medical condition.

Poodle Clips. *Although poodles are known today largely as fashionable pets they have a long history as working gun dogs, particularly used for retrieving ducks from muddy lakes and ponds. Their hind quarters were frequently shaved in the past to make swimming easier. This resulted in what is now known in Great Britain as the Lion Trim* (Center Right) *and in the United States as the Continental Clip. The hair of the dog's head used to be tied up, often with a brightly colored rag, to make the animal more easily seen when swimming, and it is still the custom to tie up the topknot with ribbon. This trim is compulsory for show dogs in the United States, except for dogs under one year which may be shown in Puppy Clip.* (Bottom Left) *The Lamb Trim* (Center Left) *is the most popular clip for pet poodles.* (Bottom Right) *The Dutch Clip is popular with nonshow dogs but is more difficult to maintain because the style leaves hair where it most easily collects dirt.*

101

Breeding and Rearing Dogs

There are more than one hundred breeds of dogs. The smallest is the Chihuahua. Very large ones include Great Danes, Irish Wolfhounds, and Mastiffs. In addition to the breeds recognized by official kennel clubs there are reckoned to be about seven hundred true breeding types scattered over the globe. Dogs can successfully breed and produce fertile hybrids with the coyote (Canis latrans), the jackal (C. aureus), the dingo (C. dingo), and the wolf (C. lupus). The permutations are endless. Although there are no recorded examples of Chihuahua–Great Dane crosses, there is no scientific reason why they should not occur. Certainly there are many instances of crosses that are only slightly less bizarre.

Most canines are indiscriminating and promiscuous. Most bitches come on heat twice a year, and it lasts about three weeks. An old saying is that a dog (term for male of the species) comes on heat only once a year, and it lasts 365 days. That is true of some breeds and of many mongrels. There are many notable exceptions. Some may be due to selective breeding over the centuries. Some types and breeds are inherently different. The Basenji, for example, normally comes on season but once a year. Many Salukis simply will not mate with any canine that is not a Saluki. The English Bulldog may be pantingly willing but often cannot perform without some assistance both before and after mating. Some of the toys scarcely consider themselves to be dogs. They are so people-oriented that their only reaction to other canines is a rapid retreat to their owner's arms. Strangely enough some dogs who have been reared with cats rather than other dogs will, in later life, be sexually interested in cats but not other dogs.

There are other subtler differences in sexual development and proclivities. Greyhounds, for example, are rather late developers. Beagles and Alsatians (German Shepherds) by comparison achieve puberty quite early. In many breeds the male is able to mate at a younger age than the female. Chow males, however, often do not achieve sexual maturity until two or three years after the female. Many breeds, particularly most of the terriers, are so aggressive that it is impossible to keep two males in one pen. Schipperkes by contrast, although sexually quite willing and capable, are often kept happily in large mixed groups.

There is only one way for a novice breeder to find out about the idiosyncrasies of a chosen breed. That is to ask questions at shows and kennels. Do not go to shops or dealers. Quite often the proprietors know little or nothing about breeding and rearing. The enthusiastic specialist breeder, however, will patiently answer even the simplest questions. The novice does better to admit total ignorance but a willingness to learn rather than pretend knowledge or experience.

To describe sexual behavior (or any other sort for that matter) in the canine world one must choose a breed as a prototype. Otherwise every statement must be qualified. Many veterinarians and animal behaviorists, zoologists, and other more formal students of animal science use the Beagle as a model. As dogs go it is neither too large nor too small. There are no outstanding faults associated with its shape or temperament. It is easily reared and kept under a variety of conditions. It is a remarkably uniform breed and most individuals are easily handled. They have large trouble-free litters. They are not picky eaters. Possibly most important is the fact that over the years more knowledge has been gathered about this breed than any other. Unless stated otherwise the information that follows has mainly been gleaned from observations of Beagles.

PUBERTY

Male puppies may show sexual activity as early as five weeks of age. It is, of course, unproductive activity and consists of grabbing a litter mate and mounting it. There is no sexual discrimination. If the litter mate stands passively, the sexy male will execute vigorous pelvic thrusts whether the object is male or female. When the male is a bit older, it will display exactly the same pattern against pillows and children. For social reasons this behavior with children must be firmly discouraged.

Most males do not mature sexually until they are ten or twelve months of age although many a Beagle has fathered a litter at six or eight months. If neutering is to be performed, it should be undertaken by the veterinarian at about that stage of the dog's development. Castration at an earlier age is thought to retard other aspects of the dog's development.

The female does not usually reach puberty until she is about nine months of age. Many do not come on season until after their first birthday. Although the average period between seasons is usually about six months, many normal bitches have quiet intervals of as long as nine months or one year. Some individuals will cycle twice yearly for two or three years and then for no apparent reason have a long quiescent period. By contrast it is relatively rare for a female to have a period shorter than six months between heats except at one particular point in her development. She may have a relatively short or slight heat at about six months and then two or three months later have a normal three week heat with all its attendant signs.

The female puppy does not display juvenile mounting behavior as does the male. She demonstrates her femininity by standing passively as the male mounts and thrusts. Only with her first season does she assume a more active role. This "courtship" behavior will be described later.

As most of us have observed one of the other main differences between dogs and bitches is that the latter squat when they urinate. Young dogs also squat but they do not bend their legs so much. As they approach puberty they begin to twist their bodies slightly and attempt to lift one hind leg. These initial attempts are often awkward, sometimes amusing, and occasionally embarrassing for the human observer within range. Within days or weeks the dog is able to lift one leg and unerringly direct a stream horizontally. Dogs use this skill to mark their territories. They take a particular interest in places where other dogs have freshly urinated. They also respond to various oils, tobacco, and to the excreta of other animals. Most dogs are happy simply to urinate on these areas. Others insist on rolling in the stuff.

The only time the female shows such avid interest in the discharges of other animals is when she is on heat. In addition to being attracted she becomes attractive to all the males in the neighborhood. The owner must exercise constant vigilance for three weeks to guard against an undesirable mating. The most fertile time is often during the last day or two when the outward signs of heat have all but disappeared.

BIRTH CONTROL METHODS

Spaying

Many owners decide after consultation with their veterinary adviser that spaying is the simple solution. In the United States particularly it is now almost a routine operation—in spite of being a major abdominal one. It involves total removal of the ovaries and the uterus. Hence it is called an ovariohysterectomy. Even in Great Britain where the operation is not performed as commonly as it is in the United States such experts as the Guide Dog for the Blind Association have their trainee dogs neutered.

In both countries people debate about the best time to have it done. Certainly it is an easier, less traumatic operation before the onset of the first period. However some suggest that bitches spayed too young retain too many undesirable juvenile features. They say that the first heat allows a fuller development of the female's real character. Some go even further and say she should be allowed to have one litter, but that has certainly not been scientifically proven. Others suggest that it really depends on the breed. It may be wise to discuss the problem with an experienced breeder as well as a veterinarian.

Pills

Birth control pills and injections are far more complicated. There is no doubt that they work when properly administered. They can and do postpone the onset and symptoms of heat. There is some evidence that given before the onset of the first season they may impair normal development, particularly in some breeds like Scottish Terriers which are prone to reproductive problems even without interference. There is also a school of thought that suggests all interference with hormonal balance has possible adverse side effects. Yet the average breeder is often faced with a problem that cannot be solved without the use of these progesterone-based drugs.

Abortion

Abortion completes the list of common interferences with the natural reproductive processes of the female dog. Almost always the reason for this drastic step is that despite constant vigilance by the owner the bitch has escaped or a dog has found its way past the barriers, and the mating was not judged a desirable one. Surgical abortion of the bitch is difficult. The operation often causes a septic birth canal necessitating a hysterectomy. Chemical abortion is simple. An injection or two of stilbesterol or a similar hormone almost always works provided it is given within a day or two of the misconception.

MATING

Heat

The normal breeding bitch in controlled surroundings comes on season and is either mated with a selected male or kept firmly under control.

Most bitches go through quite a dramatic cycle. Their external sexual organs swell. In the early stages there may be a clear discharge. Later it becomes bloody. The bitch urinates more frequently and is more purposeful in selecting sites. Fastidious females may lick their hind quarters to such an extent that the owner never sees any discharge. However, some bitches show so little change that the veterinarian must take a vaginal smear to determine the best time to mate her. The fact that this is not a common procedure indicates that the vast majority are easily mated by following the dictates of common sense and the inclinations of the dogs involved.

Generally the bitch will only accept the male during the estrus. The discharge by this time is usually less bloody and more straw colored. The external sexual organs become softer and more pliable. This stage often occurs from the fourth to the twelfth day of heat but may vary from as early as the third day to as late as the twenty-eighth. Because canines vary more than any other pet, many experienced breeders suggest that the bitch should be mated on alternate days from the twelfth day that she shows signs of heat and that these matings should be continued until the bitch refuses to stand. If the bitch does not stand at the twelfth day, she should be tried daily until she does.

The Stud

In assessing potential sires prior to mating, the female's owner should discuss all eventualities with the owner of the stud. Questions involving money must be included. What is the stud fee? Does that include boarding the bitch? If conception does not occur during one heat, does the fee include a return mating the following heat? Who does the paper work for registering the pups? If the stud fee is "choice of litter" at what age must the choice be made and at what age is the puppy taken away? Who pays the damages if there is a nasty fight during mating? Who pays if the bitch escapes from the kennels or in transit? Who pays if a person gets badly injured during the mating? All of these accidents can and do happen. Remember that some animal insurance policies carefully exclude breeding hazards.

Courtship and Mating

The actual mating can be a very simple matter or it may require a lot of clever help from two or three human handlers. The Beagle male usually indicates courtship by wagging his tail and nosing about the head of the receptive female. The female may stand quietly or she may run in short playful spurts. The male will run alongside. They may then turn and face each other with forelegs bent in the classical posture indicating a prelude to play. The dog may pause to urinate, but he always faces the female while doing so. The male will continue to pay attention to the head of the female, but gradually his focus will switch to her hindquarters. As he licks her vulva she will lift her hindquarters and hold her tail to one side. If she is ready to accept mounting, she will stand quietly while he grasps her hindquarters with his forelegs. Some dogs grip the neck of the female with their teeth.

As the male mounts, his hindquarters thrust forward in sporadic jerks. Some males either through lack of experience or an excess of excitement mount from the front or the side. A calming human hand may be needed to guide those efforts in the correct direction. With some breeds it is best to protect the hand with metal-lined leather gloves.

The female too may need human help. Some resist attention by crouching or turning their hindquarters away. Some simply run away. Others will viciously attack the dog and human attendants, including their owners. Generally, however, toward the end of estrus most females become increasingly receptive. Older bitches are usually more receptive and for a longer time than younger ones. Some are so forward that they mount the male and thrust with their hindquarters. This is more likely to happen when the female is experienced and the male is a novice or frightened. However, within minutes the roles can be easily reversed, and normal copulation proceeds.

The posterior part of the dog's penis rapidly swells as it enters the female. In turn the muscles of her vagina constrict. This results in the classical lock which breeders describe as the "tie." The male stays mounted for a short minute then swings one foreleg over the female so that although still "tied" he is standing alongside. They may stand tied in this position or they may move about and even face in opposite directions. Actual ejaculation starts at about the same time as the initial "tie" and may continue for several minutes. The whole "tie" may last from ten minutes to as long as half an hour. Although there may be gyrations during this period, including attacks by the female on the male, the penis is remarkably not injured in this process. Afterwards the male usually licks his genitals and loses interest in the female. Virile males of most breeds show renewed interest within hours. Many have been known to perform successfully five or six times in a day. However, if they are presented with bitches on several successive days their interest and ability wanes.

Dog breeding has not been as well documented as horse or cattle breeding. We do not know the dog's capacity. For most breeds it is suggested that a maximum of twenty to thirty bitches be mated annually with appropriate rest intervals. However, in normal circumstances in the purebred dog world there are seldom enough bitches to prove the dog.

PREGNANCY

The bitch reverts to her normal behavior and appearance within a few hours or days of mating. The novice breeder needs to be aware that although she has been properly bred by a selected male, there is a short period during which she can be successfully mated by an unselected male. It has often happened that someone with, say, a Cocker Spaniel bitch has taken it off to reputable kennels with a proved sire. Four or five days later they are told that the bitch has been mated. They pick her up, pay the stud fee, and take her home to resume her normal life. Nine weeks later she presents a litter of Spaniel cross Terriers, and the owners cannot believe that the mismating occurred after the bitch returned home. The safe rule is to continue surveillance for about a week.

There are few changes in early pregnancy. The female may be fed and exercised as usual. Prior to mating it should be determined that the bitch is clear of parasites both external and internal and that her inoculations are up to date. This can be checked again at the first veterinary examination three weeks after mating.

It is at that stage that the signs of pregnancy are most easily seen or felt by the veterinarian. Pregnancy diagnosis in the bitch is not an exact science. It is more of an art in that it is dependent on experience, judgment, and sometimes just plain instinct or "a feel for the bitch." At the three week stage the nipples, particularly those of the bitch that has been bred for the first time, will swell slightly, become more sensitive or full, and assume a pinkish tinge. The gentle experienced hand can feel the circular shapes of the developing feti within the uterus. They vary in size from that of a walnut to a tennis ball or larger depending on the breed. Later these circular masses seem to "merge." Only the enlarged horns of the uterus can be felt and these may be indistinguishable from the

For controlled breeding the stud and in-season bitch are introduced to each other under supervision. They may appear to play initially, the stud indicating his courtship by nosing around the head of the bitch.

Once the first meeting has been successful, the stud will switch his attention to the hindquarters of the bitch. If she is inexperienced or frightened she may require some comfort and reassurance from her owner.

If the bitch is ready to accept mounting she will stand quietly while the stud grasps her hindquarters with his forelegs. He will then mount and may remain for only a short while.

The "tie." The two animals are so firmly locked together that the stud is able to turn around and face away from the bitch. "A "tie" may last from ten minutes to half an hour.

outline of other internal organs, such as the bowel.

There are no simple laboratory pregnancy tests for the bitch, probably because there is no great demand. In the horse or the cow the longer gestation period and economics dictate knowing as soon as possible. In the bitch one knows one way or the other in a couple of months. X-rays, however, are sometimes used by veterinarians in the later stages of pregnancy particularly if there are any complicating factors.

Some bitches show signs of pregnancy although they have not been bred. They mope about or "mother" objects. Some build nests by burrowing into things like laundry baskets. Some lose appetite. The most pronounced sign is a buildup of milk in the mammary glands. Sometimes the abdomen swells. The condition is called "false pregnancy." Mild cases need no treatment except time. Like true pregnancy they are self-limiting in duration. Most cases, however, are treated with injections of male hormone. Persistent sufferers are usually spayed. Allowing the bitch a normal pregnancy is thought to prevent future attacks. Under no circumstances should the afflicted bitch be allowed to suckle herself. Many are prone to

do so possibly to relieve the pressure. A restraining harness or "many-tailed" bandage may be needed as well as drugs to dry up the fluid. Those cases obviously must be treated under veterinary supervision.

Normal pregnancy proceeds in a gentle, undramatic way. The body accommodates the growing lives within. The bitch should be allowed—even encouraged—to go through her normal activities. The healthy normal bitch can remain active right up to the time of giving birth. Border Collies have been known to pause while herding to whelp a litter.

Less active females or those confined to concrete become very awkward during the final few days. Many need three equal-sized meals rather than their usual small breakfast and large dinner. Those meals must include adequate minerals. Supplements may be needed, particularly for the larger breeds. Bonemeal (cooked crushed bones) is still considered the best supplement. Cod liver oil, if used at all, should be given sparingly. A teaspoonful twice a week for a Labrador is usually adequate.

A day or two or three before the impending birth the mammary glands swell. A bitch in good condition may leak a few drops of milk. In larger breeds it may be easy to induce quite

a flow. Although the swelling may be obvious in smaller breeds there is little discernable flow and in some they do not swell until the puppies have been born.

BIRTH

Three important signs of birth are: a slackening of the muscles in the pelvic area; an enlargement of the external genitals; and a drop of about one degree Fahrenheit in body temperature as determined by a rectal thermometer.

The experienced breeder does not become too concerned. The bitch will be confined in a suitable maternity area as her time approaches. The size, location, and layout vary widely. The determining factors are the size, temperament, history and breed of the bitch, the time of the year (heat in winter, air conditioning at the height of the summer), the size of the home or kennels, and the bank balance of the owner.

Many a champion Papillon has been born in a cutout cardboard box sited near the stove in a kitchenette. Whatever the breed the maternity area should be secure, secluded and of an even, easily controlled temperature. One of the prime causes of death in newborn litters is a rapid change of temperature. Aim for a comfortable 18° to 24°C. (65° to 75°F.) overall. One may provide additional heat in the form of a properly insulated electric blanket. Tiny breeds can easily bear a litter in an area the size of a pillow. Very large breeds need much more space. It is often best to install guardrails within the area which afford the puppies protection while a cumbersome bitch moves.

Again this is a facet of dog breeding where a ten minute visit with an experienced breeder is more important than any reference book. Because unlike any other pet the canine has dozens of distinctly different types and may have their own patterns of whelping.

Most bitches follow a familiar pattern of sleeping and resting more during the last few days of pregnancy. Be sure she is in the designated whelping area at this point. The bitch usually becomes very restless in the last few hours and constantly shifts position. She may attempt to hollow out a nest—even on a linoleum floor.

When the actual contractions start she will strain. The intervals between straining are about ten minutes. She may rearrange her carefully made bed. Most bitches, particularly of the working breeds, simply sit with their heads in a position that can only be described as tense. Others, particularly those commonly described as lapdogs, may whine or tear up everything within reach as the contractions increase in intensity and duration. It is very important to note that a bitch almost never cries out or howls during these contractions or the subsequent delivery. The whining, if any, is low pitched and not sufficient to wake an owner who has nodded off in an adjacent chair. In the intervals between contractions the bitch pants, licks her external genitals, and may urinate.

The bitch takes about three hours to produce an average litter of five puppies, but the amount of time may vary for a number of reasons. Some bitches have internal abnormalities. Some simply do not have enough strength to continue pushing. Of course some have only one puppy, but there is a documented instance of a bitch who produced a record twenty-three!

Usually the puppies emerge at half hour intervals, but they may emerge every five minutes or every hour. The mother immediately tears the sac with her teeth and removes it by vigorous licking. Some of the breeds with shorter heads require human assistance. After she has completed that task—usually within a couple of minutes—she bites off the umbilical cord and swallows the lot. When the afterbirth is expelled, she will swallow that as well. This is normal and beneficial and is not to be discouraged. The mother may then pause to clean herself. Most, however, spend the time between contractions diligently licking the puppy. When she is satisfied that the puppy is all right she will encircle it and await the next one.

This normal pattern may be disrupted if the bitch is placed in unfamiliar surroundings when whelping begins. Nervous bitches also may require the presence of the owner to reassure them. The instinctive pattern of whelping in many females is disrupted if these common sense factors are neglected.

If there is any difficulty, veterinary attention is imperative. The rule of thumb is to call the veterinarian after twenty minutes of unproductive straining. It is good practice to establish a relationship with the veterinarian well before the event. At the twenty-first day post-mating checkup he should tell you how he handles routine whelping and the sort of emergency service available. Veterinarians should not be expected to offer courteous service when called at three in the morning by a total stranger with a bitch who has been straining since noon.

THE NEWBORN PUPPY

The mother does not leave the puppies for the first few days except to eat or pass feces or urine. Feeding should be done by a familiar human who can clean the bed at the same time. Some mothers, but particularly terriers, will leave the nest to attack outsiders whether animal or human. Common sense dictates that these disturbances should be avoided. About ten or fourteen days later the mother may leave the nest for longer periods of up to three hours.

During the first couple of weeks the mother usually lies on her side to allow the puppies to suckle. Large breeds may sit and straddle the puppies while they suckle. She spends a lot of time grooming them or investigating any cries of distress. While grooming she licks their hindquarters with extra vigor. This stimulates their elimination processes. Many mothers immediately clean up the mess by swallowing it.

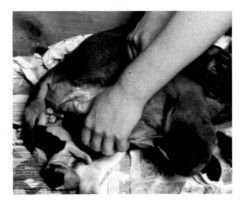

Birth of a beagle pup in a whelping box lined with newspaper. The first pup has just emerged from its mother; the fetal membrane has burst, but is still visible around the pup's hindquarters.

The pup is now fully free, and the mother immediately turns around to vigorously lick away the remains of the membrane before she bites off the umbilical cord. She will then turn her attention to the puppy again.

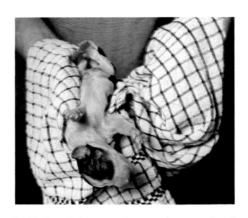

At this time a helper may take away the pup to clean it up and clear the fluid from its lungs so that it can breathe freely. When this is done the pup should be returned quickly to its mother.

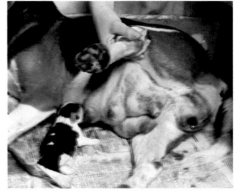

Within half an hour, or even sooner, the next pup is about to arrive. By this time the firstborn is already showing some interest in suckling from its mother.

The puppy who rolls away from the nest may not be retrieved by the mother. She may decide that if nature does not want it neither does she. That statement is borne out by the sad experience of many breeders. It is best to avoid the problem by using a well-designed bed in which there are no hazards like water dishes or corners in which a puppy can roll or crawl. A bitch who decides to reject a puppy may either ignore it completely or attempt to bury it. Sometimes she may accept it a few hours after being tranquilized. More often it is better to try and rear it as an orphan.

Docking is an emotional subject. Many people think that dogs should be allowed to keep the tail that nature provides. Some countries, such as Norway, have banned the practice of docking. The British Veterinary Association has come out strongly against docking, yet breeders of Yorkshire Terriers and Poodles, among others, are adamant that the tail is a nuisance if not a hazard. Everyone, however, is agreed that if it must be done at all, it is best done when the puppy is three days old. Obviously it should be done by a veterinarian or an experienced breeder. Also it is best to remove the mother from the area during the operation; otherwise the human attendants may suffer mutilation as well.

Almost everyone agrees that dewclaws should be removed, particularly from the hind legs. There are some exceptions; breeders of Pyrenean Mountain Dogs, for example, attach some importance to the retention of these hazard-prone appendages. Again if it is to be done the best time is at about three days of age.

WEANING

Weaning should be a gentle process. Gradually the puppies take less from the mother and more from the bowl as they gradually learn to play, explore, and assert their own independence.

Some puppies will take solids from the time they are two weeks old. Many a litter has been weaned to solids at two and one-half weeks simply because the mother has dried up.

Most puppies feed on the mother until they are four or five weeks or older. Indeed it is not uncommon for a puppy of four or five months to continue suckling. This is more likely if there are but one or two left in the litter. The mother may aid in the weaning process by regurgitating food for the young. This is more common in working and hunting breeds which are absent from the young

Weaning usually starts around four or five weeks, although it may occur earlier in some circumstances. The puppy is too young to cope with a real bone, but he is certainly enjoying a trial run on a bone-shaped hard biscuit.

for long periods. The mother may also encourage her young to share her bowl. It is particularly important, therefore, at this stage that the mother has plenty to eat. A hungry or underfed bitch may turn on her own puppies when they try to get at her food. The amounts of food and supplements required are outlined in the feeding section of this chapter.

The worming program for the puppies should be worked out with the veterinarian. Many consider that roundworm pills should be administered at three, five, and seven weeks of age but this varies widely according to the area, the breed, and the condition of the litter. Administered wrongly or in excess, worm pills can do a great deal of harm. Many litters are set back for a week or more.

It is important to get puppies used to adults, children, other animals, and a variety of objects as soon as they begin exploring. The first injection for protection against distemper, canine hepatitis, and the two sorts of leptospirosis may be given at seven and one-half or eight weeks of age. It is usually at about that age that the puppies go off to their new homes.

The new owners of a puppy should be given a sheet detailing: (1) the worming program, (2) the inoculation program, (3) the diet, and (4) the general regime including sleeping arrangements, housebreaking progress, and words that the puppy recognizes.

Some bitches continue to produce milk after the last puppy has gone. Veterinarians can prescribe safe, effective pills to relieve the condition. If it is only a mild buildup, curtailing liquids for a day or two usually effects a cure.

Most bitches, however, have dried up completely well before this stage. Some will be bored. Most will be tired. All will enjoy a well-deserved rest before the next cycle. Some bitches can easily produce and rear two litters a year. The vast majority of our domestic dogs should not be bred to that extent. Their wild cousins generally only have one litter a year—and skip the odd year. The dog has been domesticated for longer than any other pet. Nevertheless it is still more subject to the rules of nature than the dictates of human beings. (For details of behavior see **Your Pet's Behavior,** of training see **Training and Obedience,** for showing see **Exhibiting and Showing,** and for working roles see **Working Animals.**)

Dog Breeds

There is no universally accepted classification of the many breeds of dog, although many authorities have devoted much attention to devising one. The wide variety of shape, the diversity of origin, and the sheer guesswork involved in the history of many breeds, precludes their relationship to each other ever being fully traced. The kennel clubs, the organizing bodies for the registration and exhibition of pedigree dogs in each country where they are shown, divide the breeds into groups for administrative purposes, but the composition of these groups differs from country to country. (See **Exhibiting and Showing.**) Breed standards are the blueprints with which breeders work, a verbal description of the ideal in each breed which is lodged with each kennel club. Unfortunately breed standards are not universally the same and differences in a breed can occur from country to country, so it is always wise to check the regulations applicable to your chosen dog.

A dog's height is always measured at the withers, the highest point of the shoulder. All the heights and weights quoted are the maximum for a male dog of that particular breed. Bitches always tend to be smaller. In this book the breeds dealt with have been divided into seven groups, based either on similarity of type or on the kind of work for which the dog was originally bred. Ear cropping was banned by the English Kennel Club in 1895, and no cropped dog may be exhibited in Britain. Where a breed is described as cropped, it will be shown in Britain either with a dropped ear or with a naturally bred erect ear.

TOY DOGS

Toy dogs, as the name suggests, are the tiny members of the canine race, and many of these breeds are scaled-down versions of larger types. They are active, vivacious little dogs which, although not large enough to be guards, often make excellent watchdogs. Developed solely to amuse and befriend, these dogs usually have a marvelous personality which makes up for their small stature. They have small litters, sometimes with difficulty, and this tends to keep the prices of puppies high. Treated sensibly, toy dogs make hardy, long-lived companions.

Affenpinscher

This is an old German breed whose name means "monkey terrier." A pair of roguish dark eyes set in a tangle of bushy eyebrows and whiskers, give the dog its required simian expression. Always playful and alert, the breed has a long history and has been used to create at least two better known descendants, the Brussels Griffon and the Miniature Schnauzer. The coat is harsh and wiry, and the dog is usually both cropped and docked. Most are black in color, although there are a few red specimens in the United States. The maximum height is 25.5cm. (10in.) and the maximum weight is 4.5kg. (10lb.). The Affenpinscher is relatively rare.

Bichon Frise

This breed belongs to a group of small toy

dogs with long, silky white coats. Dogs of this type have been known since before the Christian era, and they were often clipped and shaved in the manner associated with Poodles. The best known of the group is the Maltese, but recently the Bichon Frise has gained popularity in the United States and is known in Great Britain. The Bichon should be up to 30cm (12in.) at the shoulder and have a body slightly longer than its height. The coat is a double one with the profuse outer coat of silky loose curls. The color is white with cream, apricot or gray markings permissible on the head.

Brussels Griffon

Also known as **Griffon Bruxellois, Petit Brabaçon,** and **Belgian Griffon,** these are small, terrier-like dogs, usually with a harsh rough coat. There is a less popular, smooth variety known as the Brabaçon. They developed from the small ratting dogs kept by the cab-drivers of Brussels about a century ago. Traveling with their masters, their pompous air caught fashionable attention. The breed was smartened up and reduced in size and their willful, impudent character has gained them a steady circle of admirers on both sides of the Atlantic. The rough variety are trimmed to leave a bushy beard and whiskers which emphasize the pugnacious jaw. They are usually both cropped and docked and can be up to 4kg. (9lb.) in weight. Permitted colors vary from country to country but include red with or without a black mask, black, and black and tan.

Cavalier King Charles Spaniel

These are one of the larger of the toy breeds, being up to 8kg. (18lb.) in weight. They are popular in Great Britain but rare elsewhere. They were virtually recreated in the 1920s by breeders who wanted to revert to the type of toy spaniel so often shown in sixteenth and seventeenth century paintings. The result is an active, graceful, well-balanced little dog showing marked sporting inclinations. Docking is optional so most have a graceful plume of a tail carried low. They come in four color varieties; black and tan, ruby or rich, whole red, chestnut and white, and tri color.

Chihuahua

This breed claims to be the smallest dog in the world and is widely known and popular. The name comes from a Mexican city and state, and the dog is properly associated with Mexico. Evidence indicates the Chihuahua's ancestors were known to the Toltec and Aztec civilizations. The first Chihuahua was registered with the American Kennel Club in 1904, and there are two recognized varieties, smooth and long-coated. Any color is permitted and the maximum weight is 3kg. (6lb.), but the smallest typical specimen is preferred. They are alert, brisk little dogs with large, upstanding ears which help give the impression of alertness. The tail, rather flat and furry in the smooth and plumed in the long-coat, should be carried up over the back.

Chinese Crested Dog

These remarkable creatures belong to a small group of hairless dogs all of which are very rare and which have always been regarded as great curiosities. The **Mexican Hairless Dog,** the largest of the group, is now extremely rare, but the small Chinese Crested is established in Great Britain. The name comes from the crest of hair on the dog's head which, together with the plume on the tail, are the only furnishings it possesses. With upright ears and a long muzzle, they resem-

External features of the dog. (A) Forequarters. (B) Middlepart. (C) Hindquarters. (1) Nose. (2) Muzzle. (3) Stop. (4) Occiput. (5) Withers. (6) Back. (7) Loin. (8) Croup. (9) Tailroot. (10) Cheek and throat wart. (11) Breast bone, (12) Fore chest. (13) Brisket. (14) Shoulder. (15) Upper arm. (16) Elbow.

(17) Forearm. (18) Wrist or pastern joint. (19) Front pastern. (20) Paw. (21) Upper thigh. (22) Second thigh or gaskin. (23) Knee or stifle. (24) Hock joint or point of hock. (25) Dewclaws.
Height is measured from the withers and width of chest over the deepest point of the chest (blue line).

Affenpinscher

Bichon Frise

Brussels Griffon

Cavalier King Charles Spaniel

Chihuahua

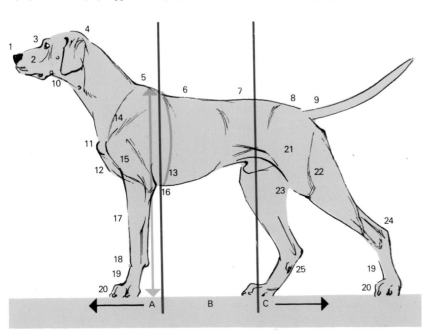

Chinese Crested Dog

English Toy Terrier

Japanese Chin

King Charles Spaniel

Maltese

ble the English Toy Terrier in shape. The skin shades can range through bronze to elephant gray, and the color is often mottled and speckled with pink.

English Toy Terrier

Also known as **Black and Tans** and **Toy Manchester Terriers,** this breed was fashionable a century ago but is now very low in numbers in both the United States and Great Britain. They must be under 5.5kg. (12lb.) in weight in the United States and under 3.5kg. (8lb.) in Great Britain. Originally used as ratting dogs, they still exhibit the spirit of a true terrier. The breed first diminished when the English Kennel Club banned ear cropping. Many breeders of these then fashionable toys turned to other dogs, leaving it to a few devotees to produce the breed with the natural upright ear that English Toy Terriers have today. The color is black and tan, and the placing and the shade of the tan markings is considered very important.

Italian Greyhound

This miniature greyhound is one of the most delicate and graceful of all breeds. It should weigh under 3.6kg. (8lb.) and have a high stepping, prancing action, like a hackney horse. The hair should be thin and glossy like satin, and most colors are acceptable. This dog has been widely known, if not widely kept, for centuries. The elegance and aristocratic air of the breed have made these dogs court favorites in all the capitals of Europe since the sixteenth century, and they are shown dancing in attendance with their noble owners in many historical portraits. Being very delicately boned, they are perhaps more prone to injury than some of the more sturdily built breeds.

Japanese Chin

A short-faced toy dog of Asian origin, also known as the **Japanese Spaniel**, it is probably related to the Pug and the Pekingese. It appears to have a longer leg than the latter and is more sprightly in appearance. The breed seems to have been known in Japan in the homes of royalty for at least 1,000 years, during which time they were highly valued and carefully bred. The American naval commander, Commodore Perry, brought two of these dogs back to the United States in 1853, thereby starting a wave of importations and popularity. They were soon eclipsed, however, by the Pekingese, and have not been widely kept since. The height is about 25cm. (10in.) and the weight 4.5kg. (10lb.). The profuse silky coat is either black and white or red and white.

King Charles Spaniel

The King Charles (also referred to as the **English Toy Spaniel**) takes its name from the English king, Charles II, who was extremely fond of toy spaniels. They were known long before this by the affectionate name of Comforters. In the nineteenth century the breed changed greatly, becoming a short-faced, dome-headed toy dog and losing the spaniel-type muzzle. The weight should be up to 6.4kg (14lb.) and, as in the more popular Cavalier King Charles, there are four color varieties: the black and tan or King Charles proper, the tricolor or Prince Charles, the ruby, and the red and white.

Lowchen

Also known as the **Little Lion Dog**, this breed appears to be related to the Bichon family and is increasing in popularity. They are shown with their hindquarters, legs and tail shaved, bracelets of hair being left just above the paws, and a long tuft being left on the end of the tail. Paintings from the fifteenth century suggest that a small dog clipped in this fashion has been known in Europe for a long while. The mane should be fairly long and inclined to wave but not curl and all colors including dapples and particolors are permitted. Height is up to 35cm. (14in.) and weight up to 3.6kg.(8lb.).

Maltese

This is the best known of the Bichon group and has a better documented history than most. It has been known in the Mediterranean since the first century but whether it comes from Malta or the Sicilian town of Melita is uncertain. A gay, volatile, and good-natured dog, it has enjoyed moderate but steady popularity in most countries where dog showing is a sport. The weight should be under 3kg. (7lb.) and the height under 25cm. (10in.). Obviously, the white silky coat needs care if the dog is to look its best, but underneath the flowing locks there is an animal with sound body construction.

Miniature Pinscher

Papillon

Pekingese

Pomeranian

Pug

Shih Tzu

Miniature Pinscher

A German breed, known in its native land for at least 300 years, the Miniature Pinscher is one of the smartest and most spirited of toy dogs. The cropped ears and docked tail emphasize the compact, well-balanced body. This is another breed which is required to have a high stepping action adding to the animated appearance. They are widely popular in Germany and the Americas, less so in Great Britain where a dropped or an erect ear is permissible. The smooth, short coat is usually red or black and tan. The height must not exceed 30cm. (12in.) at the withers.

Papillon

The French word meaning butterfly is the name for this member of the toy spaniel family. They have long been popular in France and Germany and are well-known elsewhere. The name refers to the large, upstanding ears—heavily fringed and obliquely carried—which suggest the half-opened wings of a butterfly. The clearly defined white blaze on the face represents the body of the insect. A rarer type in this breed has a completely dropped ear and is known as a Phalene (moth). Along with their dainty appearance, Papillons have plenty of intelligence and are easy to train. The height is up to 27.5cm. (11in.) and the flowing coat should be white with patches of any color except liver. The head markings should be symmetrical around the white blaze.

Pekingese

This sturdy, heavily-boned dog is one of the best known and most loved of the whole toy group. Having been bred exclusively in the Imperial courts of China for centuries, they were first seen in the West after four were looted at the sacking of Peking in 1860. A few more were smuggled out by less extreme methods a little later, and it is from this handful that all the dogs in the Western Hemisphere are descended. This dog which is so remarkable both in character and shape says much for Chinese skill in breeding lap dogs. The profuse coat is matched with individuality and independence of spirit. Any color is acceptable and the dog's weight should be between 3–5.5kg. (7–12lb.).

Pomeranian

This is a dwarfed form of the German Spitz which was produced in Great Britain at the end of the last century. In a surprisingly short space of time the German Spitz, weighing about 11kg. (25lb.), was selectively bred to a race of toy dogs weighing about 2kg. (5lb.) and carrying the name of the German province where its ancestor was so widely kept. The standard describes in detail the wide range of permitted colors. The harsh, long, stand-off coat frames an alert, foxy, little head. These are energetic, vivacious dogs which, even at the end of a long hard day, still call for attention and applause. They make excellent small watchdogs and are moderately popular everywhere.

Pug

The Pug is another short-faced, sturdy, and compact breed which is believed to have orig- inated in China. This is one of the larger toys. It is decidedly chunky in appearance and weighs up to 8kg. (18lb.). Pugs became extremely fashionable in England in the nineteenth century and, though their popularity has declined somewhat, they are still widely known and kept throughout the world. They have the advantage of a short, smooth coat that is particularly free of odor and requires little in the way of grooming. Originally, fawn dogs with black masks were the most popular, but when the first blacks were shown they created a great deal of interest. Silver and apricot fawn dogs should have a black mask and ears, as clearly defined as possible.

Shih Tzu

This small dog is claimed by its devotees to be more than a toy because of its arrogance and courage. The name is Chinese for lion, although the breed is the Tibetan version of a lapdog produced as a symbolic representation of the mythical Buddhist lion. Weight can be up to 8kg. (18lb.), and the very shaggy, coarse coat makes the dog look even heavier. The long, profuse hair falls forward over the eyes, and the plumed tail is carried over the back. All colors are permitted, but a white blaze on the forehead and a white tip to the tail are highly prized. The standard claims that the hair on the head should have a chrysanthemum-like effect, and the dog should be heavily boned and muscular. This is the best known of the Tibetan breeds, but it is still not numerous.

Silky Terrier

This Australian breed was developed in the early 1900s in Sydney, New South Wales, and it is also known as the **Australian Silky Terrier** and the **Sydney Silky**. Though popular in its country of origin, it is only otherwise exhibited in Canada and the United States and not greatly known elsewhere. The Australian Terrier and the Yorkshire Terrier were among the breeds used to create the Silky. The head is wedge-shaped with pricked ears, and the standard insists on the breed's terrier character and spirited action. The coat is flat, about 15cm. (6in.) long and of a very fine, glossy, silken texture. The lower half of the legs and the muzzle are smooth-coated. The color is blue and tan. Weight is up to 4.5kg. (10lb.) and height is up to 25cm. (10in.).

Tibetan Spaniel

This breed is rare everywhere except Great Britain, where it seems to have established a permanent foothold since the late 1940s. Though their breeders and exhibitors would question the description, Tibetan Spaniels look very much like unexaggerated Pekingese. Their flat, silky coat, with a distinct mane over the shoulders, is shorter and less profuse than the Peke so that they appear higher on the leg. The muzzle, though short and blunt, is longer than that of their cousin, and the mouth is slightly undershot. The origin is obscure but, like all Tibetan breeds, these are dogs of strong character. Most colors are permissible, but shades of fawn and cream are the most common. Dogs can be up to 27.5 cm. (11in.) in height and 7 kg. (16lb.) in weight.

Toy Fox Terrier

Although this breed is only known in the United States it does not receive official recognition from the American Kennel Club. Despite this, the dog is both numerous and popular, having been developed as a miniature of the Smooth Fox Terrier in the early years of this century. The dogs must be under 3kg. (7lb.) in weight and are white with either black or tan terrier markings. The muzzle is narrow and relatively long. The ears are erect and the tail carried high and docked very short. These dogs are easy to keep as well as being hardy and energetic.

Toy Poodle

The Toy Poodle, a descendant of the Standard Poodle, has been bred down through the Miniature Poodle. The breed requirements for the Toy are the same as for the Standard and Miniature except height which must be under 27.5 cm. (11in.) in Great Britain and 25cm. (10in.) in the United States. (See **Poodle**.)

Yorkshire Terrier

This diminutive animal is widely known and very popular. Though it was produced a little over a century ago by working men in the weaving towns of northern England, very little is known about the forerunners of the breed. The early specimens, though larger and coarser than today's dogs, found a ready sale to the fashionable and wealthy who were

Australian Silky Terrier

Tibetan Spaniel

Toy Poodle

Yorkshire Terrier

attracted by the length, color, and texture of the coat which, even then, was of paramount importance. Underneath all the hair is a game little terrier with a sound unexaggerated shape which probably accounts for its popularity as a pet. For the coat to attain its full glory, as seen in the show ring, a great deal of time and care has to be taken. However, the result is so glamorous that the dog has always been a favorite with exhibitors. The color must be a dark, steel blue relieved by rich, bright tan markings. Kennel Club standards permit a weight up to 3kg. (7lb.). As with many toy breeds, the smaller dogs are preferred in the show ring but the larger ones make better pets.

TERRIERS, PINSCHERS, AND SCHNAUZERS

Most of the terrier breeds originated in Great Britain and are a group of dogs distinguished by their plucky temperament. They were mainly developed as vermin killers and, as such, did not attract the attention of fashionable society. Being dogs of the stable and the yard, they were selected for their working ability alone and thus have no well-documented history. When travel was arduous and communications bad, many local types were produced to suit local conditions. Many terrier breed names are taken from the small areas where they were first produced and it is only in the last one hundred years that so many pure breeds have been established and recognized. This group in general is very robust, energetic, and fun loving. They can also be too noisy and aggressive. However, their courage and gaiety will always guarantee them many admirers.

The pinschers and schnauzers are German in origin, "pinscher" being the German word for terrier. As a group they were more general purpose dogs than the British terriers, adding droving and guarding to their duties as well as hunting vermin and small game. The guarding instinct is very well developed in some of these breeds and they are easier to train than some of the more independent terriers.

Airedale Terrier

This is the largest of the terriers and, like most of the terrier breeds, is a British dog created during the latter half of the nineteenth century. Among the Airedale's ancestors may be numbered the now extinct **Black-and-Tan Terrier** which was a harsh coated, vermin-killing dog. The Otter-hound may also have played a part, giving the Airedale a sweeter and more placid nature than some of the smaller terriers and also giving it a love of water. Whatever the combination, the name and type did not become firmly established until the 1890s. Today the Airedale is a docked, wirehaired, black and tan animal up to 60cm. (24in.) at the shoulder and weighing about 22.6kg. (50lb.). As with all wirehaired dogs they need trimming (not clipping, which will ruin their coat) to look smart. They are courageous dogs as befits their ancestry and are used quite extensively on the continent of Europe for police and guard dog duties. They are firmly established but not numerous.

Australian Terrier

This is an industrious little terrier first shown in its native land in 1899. It is a low-set, compact dog, very agile and an excellent ratter and vermin killer. The average height is about 25cm. (10in.) and the weight about 5kg. (11lb.). The coat is straight and hard, about 5cm. (2in.) long. The color is silver gray with tan markings, or red. Popular in Australia, this breed has recently become quite well-known in the United States but is rare elsewhere. ·

Bedlington Terrier

The Bedlington has a beguiling lamblike appearance with an expression that should look mild and gentle in repose. Around 1800 it was used for catching vermin but later became higher on the leg and more streamlined when it was used for catching rabbits and poaching. These are speedy dogs with a light, springy action at the slower paces. The thick, linty coat is trimmed with scissors for the show ring to emphasize the pear-shaped head and the roached back. The color is blue, blue and tan, liver, or sandy. Though darker pigment is preferred, it is rarely to be found. Height is about 40cm. (16in.) and weight up to 10.5kg. (23lb.). This has never been a popular breed but they are in no danger of disappearing.

Border Terrier

The Border Terrier remains one of the most natural of the terrier group. They are not docked, nor does the harsh, dense coat need trimming. They look as if they could come straight into the show ring from doing their original job, which was bolting hill foxes from their dens in the Border country between England and Scotland. With long legs and enough stamina to keep up with horses and hounds, the Border is a working dog which is both game and courageous. The head is like that of an otter with a short, strong muzzle. The color can be red, wheaten, grizzle and tan, or blue and tan. The weight is up to 7kg. (15.5lb.) and the height about 30cm. (12in.).

Bull Terrier

This is considered the gladiator of the canine race, being a breed that was developed in the nineteenth century for the barbarous sport of dogfighting. A jaunty dog, smooth-coated, active and powerfully muscular, the Bull Terrier has a distinctively egg-shaped head and a punishing jaw line. Like many of the fighting breeds it has a sweet disposition toward the human race. In the United States, white and colored varieties are shown separately but no distinction is made between them in Great Britain. Miniature Bull Terriers are rare but recognized in Great Britain as a separate breed. These should be under 35cm. (14in.) in height and 9kg. (20lb.) in weight.

Cairn Terrier

One of the most popular of the small working terriers, the Cairn is a Scottish breed that has successfully made the grade from a purely working dog to that of a well-loved pet. They

Airedale

Bedlington Terrier

Australian Terrier

Border Terrier

Bull Terrier

Cairn

Dandie Dinmont Terrier

Doberman Pinscher

Smooth Fox Terrier

Wire Fox Terrier

came originally from the west coast and islands of Scotland where they were expected to tackle foxes, martens, and wildcats. Though small in stature, they are hardy, adaptable, and less aggressive than some of the other terrier breeds. The tail is naturally short and carried gaily. The head is broad, the ears erect, and the profuse harsh coat, which needs no trimming, can be almost any shade except white. The height is about 25cm. (10in.) and the weight about 16.4kg. (14lb.).

Dandie Dinmont Terrier

This is a little-known terrier of distinctive appearance which also comes from the Border country between England and Scotland, an area that has produced a large number of tough, hardy breeds. The Dandie has a long, strong flexible body set on heavily-boned, muscular short legs. Perhaps their most striking feature is their large, dark liquid eyes which give them one of the most appealing expressions in dogdom. The eyes are set off by pendulous ears and a head covered with very soft, silky hair. The rest of the coat should be about 5cm. (2in.) long and feel crisp to the touch. The official colors are pepper (ranging from dark, bluish black to silvery gray) and mustard (ranging from reddish brown to pale fawn). The height is about 27.5cm. (11in.) and the weight near 8kg. (18lb.).

Doberman Pinscher

These dogs were the creation of Herr Louis Dobermann, a German who wanted a dog that combined the agility of a giant terrier with excellent guarding instincts. They are also simply referred to as **Doberman**. Between 1865 and 1890 he produced a breed that became justly famed for its fearlessness. Since then the Doberman has become a working animal and is extensively used as a police and guard dog. A very intelligent dog, the Doberman is now both more elegant and more tractable than it used to be. The smooth, glossy coat is usually black and tan, though brown or blue with tan markings are allowed. Dogs stand about 67.5cm. (27in.) at the shoulder.

Fox Terrier

Fox Terriers, both smooth-coated and wire-haired, have been among the most popular of breeds in times past, but have now declined considerably as pets, though still retaining a remarkable success in the show ring. As the name suggests, they were expected to bolt foxes from their dens, but this working past is far behind them. The modern Fox Terrier should have a keen expression and be alert at the slightest provocation. White coloring should predominate with black or tan patches. Coat in the **Smooth** is hard and short. The **Wire** should have a coat like coconut matting which needs extensive barbering

before the dog appears in the show ring. Its decline in numbers as a pet dog may be explained by the rather scruffy appearance it has without this artful trimming. Fox Terriers tend to be restless and noisy dogs, weighing about 8kg. (18lb.). The Toy variety is described separately in the section on toy dogs.

German Hunt Terrier

A breed of recent origin, the German Hunt Terrier was created in Germany less than fifty years ago. It is popular in Germany and established on the Continent but is generally unknown elsewhere. The aim in developing this breed was to create a general purpose sporting dog with all the terrier pluck but also with the ability to track and retrieve from both land and water. The dog is expected to give tongue when following a scent or sighting game. The coat can be either smooth or coarse and dark, solid colors are preferred. The ears are dropped, and the tail docked to about two-thirds. The height is about 36.5 cm. (14.5in.). This is a keen sporting dog which is not really suitable as a pet.

German Pinscher

This is a long established German breed which is not well known elsewhere. It is famed as a ratter and is still bred more for work and guard duties than as a pet. It is one of the ancestors of the better known Doberman Pinscher. The coat is short and smooth, the ears cropped, and the tail docked very short. The preferred colors are black and tan or brown and tan and the height is about 40cm. (16in.). In 1958 the **Harlequin Pinscher** was recognized as a separate breed, which is 5–7.5cm. (2–3in.) smaller and is pied, dappled, or brindle in color.

Glen of Imaal Terrier

This small working terrier is virtually unknown outside its native country of Ireland. The Irish Kennel Club recognized it in 1933 though it appears to have been already known in County Wicklow in the sixteenth century. This is a hard-bitten, tough little dog, used in the past for dogfighting and badger-baiting. It has a plucky, pugnacious character and is seemingly impervious to pain. The Irish Kennel Club, anxious to keep these qualities in the breed, stipulates that no Glen of Imaal Terrier can claim the title of Champion unless it has been tested for gameness in going to earth. These are short-legged terriers, comparatively long in the body, with a moderately long, untrimmed, soft coat. The color is blue, brindle, or wheaten. Dogs weigh about 16kg. (35lb.) and stand 36.5cm. (14.5 in.) at the shoulder.

Irish Terrier

The Irish Terrier, though known quite widely, has never been a popular breed. Nicknamed the Red Devil, for the color must always be red, it has all the virtues and vices of a fighting breed. A tough venturesome and cocky dog, it is very sweet tempered and loyal to its human friends. It is a taller, racier dog than the Fox Terrier and the wire coat needs less trimming. Those who want an inquisitive, spirited dog of this size can probably find no better companion. The height should be approximately 45 cm. (18in.) and the weight about 12.2kg. (27lb.).

Jack Russell Terrier

Though not recognized by the English Kennel Club, the Jack Russell is enormously popular as a pet in Great Britain. It is a readily identifiable type—although not meeting the genetic continuity required of a breed—which adapts equally well to urban or country life. The name comes from a well-known sporting parson whose hunt terriers were renowned in the nineteenth century. It seems very unlikely that his dogs bore any resemblance to today's Jack Russell, which is a short-legged dog usually with dropped ears and a docked tail. The coat can either be smooth or wiry, and it is basically white with black or tan markings. This is a dog that has had to make its own way without the benefit of show ring publicity, and it seems to have done so mainly because it is an independent, tough little character with a wicked sense of fun.

Kerry Blue Terrier

This is the largest of the Irish terrier breeds and is a compact, powerfully built dog standing some 47.5cm. (19in.) at the shoulder and weighing up to 16.7kg. (37lb.). The puppies are born black and are expected to have attained the desired dark blue coloring by the time they are eighteen months of age. This has always been an exhibitor's dog rather than a pet owner's favorite since the breed was first given official recognition in 1922. The coat is soft, silky, thick, and wavy. The outline of the dog as viewed in the show ring has been sculpted by the exhibitor's scissors. The history of the breed is obscure.

Lakeland Terrier

This is another medium-sized terrier expected, in its working capacity, to find and and kill foxes. Again, this is a breed that has made a great deal more impact in the show ring than it has on the pet owning public. It is an alert, lively animal, less aggressive than many of the other terriers. The commonest color is black and tan, which makes it resemble the Airedale and the Welsh Terrier to the uninitiated public. Obviously a sound breed with much success at top level shows, the Lakeland should weigh about 7.7kg. (17lb.) and be 36.5cm. (14.5in.) in height.

Manchester Terrier

This dog is rare in Great Britain and the United States and relatively unknown elsewhere. It is a smooth-coated ratting terrier which was created at a time when killing rats in a pit was a gambling sport for gentlemen. Wagers were laid on how long it would take a dog to kill a certain number. The record was held by a dog called Billy which is reputed to have killed one hundred rats in six minutes thirteen seconds. When ear cropping was banned by the English Kennel Club, the Manchester Terrier nearly died out, and it is probably only due to American influence that the breed still survives. The color is black with very precise tan markings, and the weight should be not more than 19kg.

German Hunt Terrier

German Pinscher

Glen of Imaal Terrier

Irish Terrier

Manchester Terrier

Kerry Blue Terrier

Lakeland Terrier

(22lb.). Height at the shoulder is 40cm. (16in.).

Norwich Terrier

These small dogs, usually red in color, have a modest following on both sides of the Atlantic but are unknown on the Continent. They seem to have originated near Cambridge, England, and are described in their standard as a demon for their size but of lovable disposition and not quarrelsome. Originally the ears were either pricked or dropped, but in 1965 the English Kennel Club allowed the two varieties to separate into different breeds, the drop-eared ones being known henceforth as **Norfolk Terriers.** This distinction was not followed in the States. Both types are small, untrimmed, rough haired terriers with medium docked tails. The ideal height is 25 cm. (10in.).

Schnauzer

These dogs come from Germany, the name being derived from the mustache on their muzzles. They are known in three sizes, the **Giant,** the **Standard** and the **Miniature,** of which the Standard is by far the oldest breed. Although they look very much like a terrier, particularly when trimmed, the Schnauzer temperament has little of the excitability or aggression found in many terrier breeds. Like many of the German breeds, these were general purpose working dogs used as cattle drovers and guard dogs, with a little ratting on the side. The Standard Schnauzer can be up to 50cm. (20in.) in height. The Miniature Schnauzer appeared in 1900 and has far outstripped its larger relatives in popularity. The size was reduced by crossing with the Affenpinscher, and the dogs should be over 30cm. (12in.) but less than 35cm. (14in.) at the shoulder. The Giant Schnauzer has had a more checkered career, having had several disastrous declines in number. It now seems to be well established in Germany, where it is used for police work, and is beginning to be known elsewhere. The height can be up to 67.5in. (27in.). All Schnauzers have strong, wiry coats which are heavily trimmed to emphasize the eyebrows and mustache. Colors include black and pepper and salt (a gray brindle).

Scottish Terrier

This breed was very popular in the early 1930s but has since declined in numbers. It is still however well represented at shows throughout the world. Black seems to be the color that is always associated with the **Scottie** but they can also be wheaten or any shade of brindle. The dogs were first used to chase vermin, which accounts for their tough character and their thick weatherproof coats, which however, need a lot of trimming. This is a low-set, sturdy terrier suggestive of great power and activity in a small body. The beard and whiskers are made more pronounced by the stripping of the rest of the head, giving the dog a rather dour expression. The height is up to 27.5cm. (11in.) and the weight up to 10.4kg. (23lb.).

Sealyham Terrier

One of the breeds that was created by one

Norwich Terrier

Scottish Terrier

Schnauzer

Sealyham Terrier

Skye Terrier

man for a specific purpose, the Sealyham Terrier has changed a great deal since the days when it was expected to tackle polecats and otters without showing the slightest hesitation. Some bad-tempered individuals are reminders of their former fighting qualities, but most today are peaceful little dogs with a comical turn of mind. Their low-slung appearance is stressed by the way they are trimmed, and the breed needs a certain amount of coat care if it is to look smart. It is a breed which has never really caught the limelight. The color should be white, though lemon, brown and pied markings are acceptable on the head. Height is 30cm. (12in.) and weight should not exceed 9kg. (20lb.).

Skye Terrier

The Skye Terrier is not very common and is today almost entirely an exhibitors' breed. Basically it is a rather large dog on very short legs and entirely curtained in hair. Underneath the flowing coat on the head are a powerful pair of punishing jaws, a legacy from its working past. The length and profuseness of the coat are a modern development which would have been decidedly

impractical in a working terrier. It is possibly the Skye Terrier's disinclination to be friendly toward strangers that has kept it such a specialists' breed. The color should be gray or cream with black ears and nose. The height is 25cm. (10in.) and the weight about 11.3kg. (25lb.).

Soft Coated Wheaten Terrier

This terrier is indigenous to Ireland where it was used as a guard and a vermin killer. It came perilously near extinction but now has a modest following in its native land and Great Britain and the United States. It is a hardy dog with a strong constitution and would appeal to those who like a medium-sized, sporting terrier with a coat that requires little or no trimming. The color must be a good clear wheaten, though this may not be achieved until maturity, the puppies often having black masks. The coat is soft and silky with large, loose curls. The height can be up to 47.5cm. (19in.) and the weight up to 20.4kg. (45lb.).

Staffordshire Bull Terrier

Organized dogfighting, with bets being laid on the result, has been conducted in all parts

Staffordshire Bull Terrier

Boxer

Soft-coated Wheaten Terrier

Bullmastiff

Bulldog

MASTIFFS AND ALLIED DOGS

Sheer size is always impressive, and this group of dogs contains some of the largest of the canine race. Broad-mouthed, large powerful dogs have been known for as long as we have had historical records. The Assyrians, the Romans, and the early Britons all had dogs remarkable for their size and ferocity. The same is true in the Far East where the Tibetan Mastiff gave rise to a number of large fighting and guard dogs. From this group of dogs descended the bull- and bear-baiting dogs of the Middle Ages, and some of these in turn have become the most exaggerated canine types today, with excessively foreshortened muzzles, thick bodies, and heavily wrinkled skin. This is not a very homogenous group, and it contains a number of breeds that require a great deal of money and space if they are to be kept properly. The fighting instinct has successfully been bred out and most of these breeds are peaceable, loving companions.

Boxer
This medium-sized, powerful, and boisterous dog was developed in Germany at the turn of the century and has been used extensively there as a police dog and frontier guard. This breed remained relatively unknown outside its native land until 1945, when returning servicemen introduced the breed to both Great Britain and the United States. Then suddenly the Boxer became popular, and it has retained its worldwide status. Though tractable in temperament, this is a vigorous dog whose exuberance needs discipline. Boxers have a deep, square muzzle, but not so short that it interferes with breathing ability. Their tails are docked short and, in most countries, their ears are cropped. Height is up to 60cm. (24in.) and weight up to 30kg. (66lb.). Colors are red and brindle, with a black mask and white markings.

Bulldog
The modern Bulldog is one of the caricatures of the canine race, proving just how far breeders can go in exaggerating various features. The original bullbaiting dogs were much more like the modern Staffordshire Bull Terrier than the modern Bulldog. The broad, squat body gives an appearance of great power, while the large, heavily wrinkled head radiates a certain ugly charm. All the ferocity of the past has been bred out and they make amiable, if wheezy, companions. The smooth coat can be almost any color and the weight is about 25kg. (55lb.).

Bullmastiff
While the Boxer has rocketed to success, its somewhat larger British counterpart has declined in popularity. This is another black-masked, broad-muzzled breed developed in the nineteenth century by crossing the Mastiff with the then more agile Bulldog. These dogs were bred by gamekeepers—and first known as "Gamekeeper's Night Dogs" —to help them with their increasingly bloody battles against poachers. The Bullmastiff is a

of the world. Staffordshire Bull Terriers are one of the breeds that has successfully outlived its bloodthirsty past. Originally this type of dog was kept by miners in the industrial heart of England who prized courage above all in their dogs. The breed was recognized by the Kennel Club in 1935 and has considerably increased in numbers, possibly because of their friendly attitude to the human race, particularly to children. They are exceptionally strong dogs for their size and need firm training when they are young if they are to turn into good mixers with other dogs. The coat is short and can be any color except liver or black and tan. Height is up to 40cm. (16in.) and weight up to 17.2kg. (38lb.).

Staffordshire Terrier
This is an American breed which comes from the same root stock as the English Staffordshire Bull Terrier. It was bred for the same purpose, namely dogfighting, and has the same very pronounced jaw and cheek muscles. The American breed is cropped and is a somewhat larger, more upstanding dog. Height can be up to 47.5cm. (19in.) and

weight up to 22.6kg. (50lb.). Like many dogs with a fighting past, they are very friendly with both adults and children which make determined guards should the need arise. White, black and tan, and liver are not acceptable colors.

West Highland White Terrier
This is one of the most popular terrier breeds today wherever terriers are shown. It is also widely kept as a pet, adapting easily to a suburban existence while retaining all the cheeky, sporting character which is such a feature of the terrier group as a whole. Westies and Cairn Terriers spring from the same root stock. The early Cairn breeders discarded the occasional white puppy that appeared in their litters as untypical. One family, the Malcolms of Portalloch in Scotland, reversed the process, believing that white dogs were more readily seen when they were working among the rocks and heather. The Westie in fact was recognized officially in 1907, two years before the breed that produced it. This is a happy little dog which is not too flighty or aggressive. The height is about 27.5cm. (11in.).

large dog which still combines symmetry with agility. Bred for silent attack where they used their weight as much as their jaws, these dogs make powerful guards as well as gentle companions. The short coat can be any shade of brindle, fawn, or red. The height is up to 67.5cm. (27in.) and the weight up to 59kg. (130lb.).

Boston Terrier (Boston Bulls)

This breed was first developed for pitfighting in the Boston area, and by the 1920s was one of the most popular breeds in the United States and Canada. They are known but are not very common elsewhere. They have a square skull and short muzzle, and the precise placing of the white markings is of importance in show specimens. The coat is short and lustrous and the ground color either brindle or black. Three weights are recognized: heavyweights, 9–11.3kg. (20–25lb.); middleweights, 6.8–9kg. (15–20lb.); and lightweights, under 6.8kg. (15lb.). Boston Terriers are not easily bred. The desired head structure, combined with narrow hips, tends to cause whelping complications which often necessitate a Caesarian delivery.

French Bulldog

After many efforts to dwarf the Bulldog, the French succeeded in producing a smaller version albeit with very distinctive, upstanding bat ears. When first shown in Great Britain at the turn of the century they excited a great deal of ridicule, but their alert disposition and robust constitution soon made them a number of friends. They became popular in the United States where the somewhat erratic ear carriage was standardized and improved. The short coat, handy size, and "ugly mug" expression seems likely to ensure a steady stream of admirers. Colors are brindle, white, pied, and fawn. Top weight for dogs is 12.7kg. (28lb.).

Dogue de Bordeaux

This is the French version of the Mastiff, a dog whose size and power creates an impression of awe in the observer. They exist on the continent of Europe but are little known elsewhere and sheer size alone must prevent them from becoming a very popular dog. Despite a past which includes fighting wolves, bears, and bulls, this dog has great warmth of character, is gentle with children, and devoted to its friends. The skull is large with wrinkled chops and dewlaps and a black mask. The coat is short, fine, and soft to the touch, and the color can be any shade of red, fawn or golden. The height for dogs is up to 67.5cm. (27in.) and the minimum weight is 49.8kg. (110lb.)

Leonberger

This is a rare continental breed, few of which survived World War II. It is a large, imposing dog whose official standard was only published in 1949, though the breed had been in existence for some time previously. It is the product of selective breeding by a resident of the town of Leonburg in Germany, who is believed to have used St. Bernards, Newfoundlands, and Pyreneans in his breeding program. The result is a dog with a minimum

French Bulldog

Old English Mastiff

Leonberger

height of 75cm. (30in.) and a head and skull without the excessive skin—or the tendency to dribble—shown by the St. Bernard. The coat is quite long, slightly wavy, and fitting closely to the body. The color is red-brown through a golden, or occasionally wolf-gray. White is not admissible.

Mastiffs

The Old English Mastiff has been known in Great Britain since before the Christian era. It is of a type which was very widespread and famed in the past for baiting wild animals. As with most of the massive, ponderous breeds, the aggression has been bred out. Two World Wars decimated the breed in Great Britain where it was only reestablished by the importation of American stock. It is a magnificent dog combining grandeur and good nature, courage, and obedience. Height and substance should be as great as possible provided both are proportionately combined. Such an animal needs a great deal of upkeep and space, and their numbers are therefore small on both sides of the Atlantic. The short coat can be apricot, fawn or brindle with a black mask.

The Tibetan Mastiff is claimed by some to be the prototype of all the mastiff breeds, but this cannot be substantiated by fact. A handful exist in the United States, but it is difficult to estimate how typical these are to the original. They stand 70cm. (28in.) at the

shoulder and are suspicious dogs. The coat is medium in length, and black, or black and tan, are the usual colors. Like all the Tibetan Breeds the plumed tail is carried over the back.

The Japanese Tosa is a mastiff exclusive to Japan where it has been developed in the last hundred years solely for the purpose of dogfighting. It is somewhat smaller in size than other mastiffs, the minimum height being 59cm. (23.5in.) and the minimum weight 37kg. (82lb.).

The Neopolitan Mastiff appeared in 1946 at a Naples dog show, or perhaps it would be better to say officially appeared, as the breed is certainly a very old one. Another massive dog, males can be up to 71.5cm. (28.5in.) and weigh up to 68kg. (150lb.). The ears are cropped and the tail docked to two-thirds of its length. The distinctive colors of the short, harsh coat are black, lead, mouse gray or mahogany. The Neopolitan Mastiff is not numerous anywhere.

Newfoundland

This breed is included here more for its massive size than for any proven connection with the mastiff group. It is the only really big dog to have come from the New World, though little is known about its origins. Three breeds come from Newfoundland and the coasts of Labrador: the Newfoundland, the Labrador

Saint Bernard

Tibetan Mastiff

Newfoundland

Neopolitan Mastiff

Retriever, and the Chesapeake Bay Retriever. All are excellent swimmers, and the Newfoundland has a legendary reputation for rescue work in water. Certainly, they were also used for hauling and like all draft dogs, they are capable of towing their owners about. They are dignified, benevolent dogs, which make ideal companions. The color of the dense, waterproof, moderately long coat is usually black but can also be black and white (known as a Landseer), or bronze. Height can be up to 70cm. (28in.) and weight up to 68kg. (150lb.).

St. Bernard

The legendary St. Bernard, while present in modest numbers in Great Britain and the Continent, is established among the ten most popular breeds in the United States. They are descended from the Alpine Mastiff and have been kept by the monks of the Hospice du Grand Saint Bernard since the beginning of the eighteenth century. Though many romantic tales are told of the dogs' rescuing travelers buried in snowdrifts, it is most likely that their role was that of a trained guide, finding paths obliterated by snow. Their benevolent expression accords well

with their traditional reputation. The minimum height for dogs is 69 cm. (27.5 in.). The rough-haired dogs are by far the most common, but a smooth-haired variety also exists. The colors are orange, mahogany brindle, red brindle, or white with patches of any of the above colors.

SHEEP DOGS AND OTHER HERDING DOGS

From the time human beings first became herdsmen, dogs have been used to protect and drive domestic animals. There are over seventy different breeds of sheep and cattle dogs in the world. Some of these are now kept solely as companions. Many, however, are still very much working dogs and, as such, do not adapt easily to the somewhat idle life of a pet. These working breeds have been evolved specifically for the local conditions and the local types of domestic animal, and this accounts for the wide variety of shape and size. A very rough division can be made between dogs expected to control flocks and herds, keeping them in one specific area or moving them from one spot to another, and

dogs which even today are expected to guard the flocks from predators such as wolves. Of course there are also many general purpose farm dogs, expected to guard the yard, keep down the vermin and bring in the cows for milking.

As a group, the herding dogs tend to be particularly responsive to human company. Many seem to have an air of responsibility as if they realized their own value in farming economy, and they are both sensitive and highly intelligent. They are readily affected by the moods and mentality of their owners, and bad handling can spoil the temperament of some of these breeds more easily than with less perceptive dogs. Conversely, the bond between this type of dog and its owner can be particularly strong and satisfying to both.

Anatolian Karabash

This is a Turkish guard dog of which a handful are present in Great Britain and recognized by the English Kennel Club but are not recognized by the American Kennel Club. They are large, probably related to the mastiff group, and are still used by Turkish shepherds to guard sheep and goats against larger predators. On duty they present a fear-

117

Anatolian Karabash

Briard

Bearded Collie

Bernese Mountain Dog

some sight wearing a heavy, iron spiked collar and having their ears cropped by cutting straight across. They are blackmasked dogs with a short, dense, fawn or brindle coat and a gaily carried tail. The height can be up to 60cm. (24in.) and the weight is about 56kg. (124lb.).

Australian Cattle Dog
This is a rugged working breed, also known as the Heeler, whose job is to round up, drive, and pen the extremely wild range cattle. For this job they must have great endurance, toughness to dart in and bite, and agility to avoid the flying hooves of the steers. They are dogs with wedge-shaped heads and upstanding ears, believed to have, among other things, Dingo blood. The short dense coat can either be blue or blue-mottled, or red or red-speckled. They are about 45cm. (18in.) at the shoulder and weigh some 18kg. (40lb.). Though they are mainly a working breed, they are shown at Australian shows, and a few have reached the United States.

Bearded Collie
An old Scottish sheep and cattle dog, the first Bearded Collie was registered with the English Kennel Club in 1949. Since then the breed has made considerable progress in

Great Britain and is becoming increasingly widespread throughout the world. These are medium-sized dogs, very active in both mind and body, but adaptable enough to fit into family life because they enjoy human company. They are lithe, muscular animals with a long tail and a shaggy coat that includes a profuse beard and whiskers. Height can be up to 55 cm. (22in.) and weight about 20kg. (45lb.). The colors include black, all shades of gray, brown and sandy, with or without white collie markings.

Beauceron
The Beauceron or **Berger de Beauce** is a smooth-haired French sheepdog, which is relatively unknown outside its native land. The ears are cropped but the tail is left long. The color is very often black and tan. Since the dog presents a powerful, muscular but not heavy appearance, there is some resemblance to the Doberman. They are credited with an inborn herding instinct and make good guards. The height is up to 69cm. (27.5in.).

Bernese Mountain Dog
One of the four Swiss Mountain breeds, the Bernese is the only one known outside its native land and even then it is a rarity. This is

a very handsome, long-haired, good-natured breed, used in the past for draft work and for taking cattle to their summer Alpine pastures. It is a heavily built dog and, though easygoing in nature, needs regular and sufficient exercise and training. The silky coat is black with rich tan markings and white on the chest, foreface, tail tip and feet. The dogs can be up to 69cm. (27.5in.) and the weight is about 54kg. (119lb.).

Border Collie
This is one of the finest and most widespread working sheep dogs. Border Collies are recognizably a type but are not shown as a pedigree breed anywhere except Australia and very recently in Great Britain. This does not mean that they are not bred with the greatest care, but their tractability and their intelligence are the prized characteristics rather than their looks. The International Sheepdog Society maintains a stud book which records the breeding of dogs of proven working ability and also conducts the sheep dog trials which have done so much to raise the standard of the working collie. Most Border Collies have a dense, moderately long coat, usually black, gray or merle, with white markings. The dog can be up to 45cm.

118

Smooth Collie

Rough Collie

Cardiganshire Welsh Corgi

Pembrokeshire Welsh Corgi

Bouvier des Flandres

fine short-haired muzzle is framed by the mane and frill of a dense, long, harsh coat. This breed has always had plenty of publicity in books and films which have brought it even further into public esteem. Though color is stated to be immaterial most are sable, black and tan, or blue merle, each set off by snowy white markings. Dogs are 60cm. (24in.) in height and up to 29.4kg. (65lb.) in weight.

Smooth Collie
This smooth version of the collie breed has never achieved much popularity. Their history is closely woven with that of the Rough Collie, and occasionally they may both appear in the same litter. The Smooth Collie has all the virtues of collie temperament, allied to a short, trouble free coat. Though in all essentials it is the same as the Rough, the Smooth Collie presents a more competent exterior, appearing almost angular beside the glamorous, sweeping curves of its heavily coated relation. Size and weight are the same as for the Rough, but blue merle and tricolor are the commonest colors in what is a rare breed.

Cardiganshire Welsh Corgi
There are two breeds of corgi, both originally Welsh cattle dogs, and both recognized separately in 1934. They are both short legged dogs, but the Cardigan is slightly larger and heavier. Dogs had to be low to the ground so that they could fly in and nip the heels of cattle without getting kicked in return. The facial expression should be foxy, and the erect ears are rather large in proportion to the dog. The body is long and strong, and the line of the back is continued in that of the tail, which is bushy like that of a fox. The coat is short and hard textured, and the most usual colors are tricolor, blue merle (blue and gray mixed with black), or dark sable. Height is 30cm. (12in.) and weight up to 11.7kg. (26lb.).

Pembrokeshire Welsh Corgi
The Pembroke Corgi began a remarkable rise in popularity when King George VI of England bought one as a family pet. Since then they have always been important members of the English royal household and have received a great deal of publicity. The breed is now known worldwide and is particularly popular in Australia. The Pembroke Corgi has slightly smaller ears than the Cardigan and has a tail which is docked short. The expression should be foxy, and the short coat is most often red or sable. The height is from 25–30cm. (10–12in.) and the weight up to 10.8kg. (24lb.). The Pembroke Corgi now far surpasses in numbers what is probably its older relative, the Cardigan.

German Shepherd Dog
Now probably the most popular and the most useful dog in the world, the German Shepherd (or **Alsatian**) was virtually unknown outside its native land before 1918. Returning servicemen introduced them from Germany to Great Britain where, in six years, they rose to being the most popular dogs. This rapid rise was followed by an equally

(18in.) and weigh 20.4kg. (45lb.). These dogs can become neurotic if denied the opportunity to work. They are often used by obedience enthusiasts and are noted for their success in obedience tests. The abilities of these dogs make them a pleasure to own.

Bouvier Des Flandres
This is a Flemish drover's dog of large imposing appearance and a rugged, hardy constitution. The breed was almost extinguished by the reduced need for droving cattle dogs and two World Wars. However, enthusiasts built up the number again, and they are now well represented at Continental shows and in the United States and Canada. This is a large powerful dog with a square body shape and a sensible, stable temperament. Their ears are cropped and the tail docked very short. The bushy eyebrows and whiskers give the dog a rather dour expression. The coat is very thick and wiry and comes in dark shades, brindled gray, or tawny. Dogs are up to 67.5cm. (27in.) in height and 40kg. (88lb.) in weight.

Briard
The Briard, also known as the **Bergerde la Brief,** is a shaggy French sheep dog that is currently enjoying a wave of popularity in Great Britain and is shown regularly in the United States. This is one of the breeds that proved itself invaluable as an army and Red Cross dog in France where it is highly regarded as a worker. They are entirely natural dogs, neither cropped, docked, nor trimmed. They are said to be slow learners but very retentive of a lesson once mastered. The Briard has a very shaggy appearance with a coat that is long, slightly wavy, stiff, and strong. Two dewclaws must be present on each hind leg. All solid colors are allowed, but dark colors are preferred. Dogs can be up to 67.5cm. (27in.) at the shoulder.

Rough Collie
The Rough Collie is one of the most popular of this group as a pet and companion dog. It is no longer used for work. It comes orginally, as do all the collies, from Scotland. They are one of the breeds that benefited from royal patronage as Queen Victoria admired the working Rough Collie and installed some in the royal kennels. Spotlighted thus they became fashionable, and great breed improvements took place. The "improved collie" took its place in the show ring, while the "unimproved collie" remained a working farm dog. The Rough Collie is now one of the most beautiful and graceful of breeds. The

rapid decline as dogs with bad temperaments in the wrong hands gave the breed an increasingly bad name. The same thing happened in the United States, but in both countries the breed made a slow, steady, and irreversible recovery. These are strong dogs, active in both mind and body needing owners who appreciate this fact. They are highly trainable and a correctly bred, properly handled German Shepherd is one of the most stable dogs under stress. They are the most popular choice for organizations which train guide dogs for the blind and are also the mainstay of the canine section of many police forces in the world. In fact wherever there is work for a dog, there will be a German Shepherd, ready and willing to do it. The only color barred from the show ring is white, and the commonest colors are black and sable or gray. Dogs should be up to 65cm. (26in.) in height.

Groenendael

One of the shepherding breeds from Belgium, the Groenendael (also known as the **Belgian Shepherd,** has made the most progress in popularity outside its native land. It is widely kept in France, regularly shown in the United States, and beginning to be known in Great Britain. They are alert, attentive dogs resembling the German Shepherd in shape but appearing more slight in build. The head carriage should be proud, and the dog's expression shows intelligence, courage, and devotion to its owner. The coat is moderately long and fairly harsh. The color is always black. Dogs may be to 65cm. (26in.) in height.

Kelpie

This is a working Australian sheep dog not known outside the Antipodes. Like the other Australian breeds, it is a tough dog able to work strenuously under grueling conditions. It seems very likely that Smooth Collies imported into Australia in the 1870s were used as foundation stock in the Kelpie's development. These are smooth-coated dogs with erect ears and a brush of a tail. The colors are black or red (with or without tan), chocolate and smoke blue. Dogs are up to 50cm. (20in.). It is estimated that there are about 80,000 Kelpies working on the sheep stations in Australia. They are regular competitors in sheep dog trials, and a few are also shown at Australian dog shows.

Komondor

The Komondor is a large, powerful, white herding dog of the Hungarian plains. There the dog has been selectively bred and highly prized for centuries because of its abilities as a guard dog. It is a rare dog outside Hungary but is appreciated in Germany, and a few specimens are shown in the United States and Great Britain. The Komondor's most remarkable and distinctive feature is its coat which is extremely long in the mature dog and somewhat coarse in texture. It cords very easily, tending to cling together in long tassels and mats. A mature Komondor looks very much like an enormous old-fashioned floor mop. Underneath the hair is a dog with

Kuvasz

Pumi

Puli

Komondor

German Shepherd

a wide skull, blunt muzzle, and square muscular body. This is the sort of dog that must have an experienced owner, especially since they can be as big as 77.5cm. (31in.) at the shoulder.

Kuvasz

The Kuvasz is another white Hungarian herding and guard dog, but there the resemblance to the Komondor ends. The Kuvasz is a handsome and majestic dog in appearance, which, though powerfully built, is very agile and light-footed. The black eyerims and lips are set off in a beautifully proportioned head by a moderately long coat of pure white. The dogs are up to 72.5cm. (29in.) in height and 52kg. (115lb.) in weight. They are fairly widely kept and shown in Hungary and have a breed club

looking after their interests in the United States but are practially unknown elsewhere.

Lhasa Apso

Probably a misfit in this group, the Lhasa Apso, or **Tibetan Apso,** is nevertheless considered by some authorities to be related to some of the smaller varieties of herding dogs. What little is known about its Tibetan origins suggests that it was used there as a small indoor watchdog. Like all Tibetan breeds it is extremely hardy, has a long, heavy, dense coat, and carries its plumed tail curved over its back. In the early 1930s, when both the Lhasa Apso and the smaller Shih Tzu reached the West, there was a great deal of confusion in distinguishing between them. They are now very recognizable as two different breeds with the Apso being up to 27.5cm.

Lhasa Apso

Old English Sheepdog

Pyrenean Mountain Dog

Malinois

Rottweiler

(11in.) at the shoulder. The preferred color is golden or lion tawny, but any color is acceptable. They are kept and shown both in the United States and Great Britain.

Maremma

The Maremma is the sheep dog of Central Italy and appears closely related to the Kuvasz and the Pyrenean Mountain Dog. It is fairly widely kept and shown in Italy but there are only a handful elsewhere. The coat is plentiful, rather harsh and white or pale in color. This breed does not have the bulk of its relatives, dogs being up to 70cm. (28in.) and 43kg. (95lb.) in weight.

Malinois

This is the short-coated version of the Belgian Sheepdog and is little known outside its native land. It is built on the same lines as the Groenendael but the dense, close coat is fawn to mahogany, including gray and brindle. The dog should have a black mask and preferably black ears.

Old English Sheepdog

This massive shaggy animal is currently enjoying a wave of popularity in Great Britain and the United States, due partly to its appearance in a number of advertisements. Known as the **Bobtail,** they were originally droving dogs whose tails were bobbed as a sign that they were tax-free working dogs. Despite their somewhat lumbering appearance and lethargic ambling gait, they display surprising agility and elasticity at speed. They need plenty of exercise and plenty of grooming; points not always appreciated by their owners. The minimum height is 55cm. (22in.), and most dogs are a good deal larger

than this. The coat color can be any shade of gray, grizzle or blue, with or without white markings.

Puli

The Puli is one of Hungary's smaller sheep dogs and is a nimble lively dog of great stamina. It is known as a show dog in the United States and Great Britain, but the unique coat would seem to preclude it from being widely kept as a pet. Due to its versatility and intelligence, it was used as a police dog in Hungary. It is also used there as a watchdog and a hunter of small game. The most acceptable color is black of a peculiar rusty or weather-beaten shade. The coat is remarkable for its matted, corded length which completely shrouds the dog from nose to tail. Their trailing hair combined with their quick and bouncy movement make some Pulis seem in danger of tripping themselves. Height may be up to 45cm. (18in.) and weight up to 15kg. (33lb.).

Pumi

The Pumi is also Hungarian and, as yet, not known elsewhere. The dog has semipricked ears, a docked tail, and a shaggy gray coat which is not as exaggerated as the Puli's. It is an extremely lively and energetic dog with many of the terrier characteristics. It makes a noisy guard dog and a keen hunter of vermin. The height should be about 42.5cm. (17in.) and the weight about 12.7kg. (28lb.).

Pyrenean Mountain Dog

The Pyrenean Mountain Dog, or **Great Pyrenees,** is the most popular of what might be called the large white guarding dogs. This is a very old French breed and has a well

documented history going back to the fifteenth century. In the seventeenth century the size and magnificence of these guard dogs impressed French royalty, and it became fashionable for every noble to have his chateaux guarded by a number of Pyreneans. Such a large dog is too expensive for many pet owners to keep, but the Pyrenean enjoys a modest and steady popularity on both sides of the Atlantic. The flat, long outer coat is principally white although lemon, badger, and gray markings are permitted. The height can be up to 80cm. (32in.) and the weight as much as 56.6kg. (125lb.).

Rottweiler

When Roman invaders crossed the Alps, the armies took their food with them in the form of beef on the hoof, and these herds were driven by cattle dogs. The Rottweiler is believed to be descended from these dogs. The town of Rottweil in Germany was for many centuries a livestock marketplace, and the

121

Shetland Sheepdog

Tervueren

butchers and drovers there used powerful, mastiff-type dogs to drive and guard the cattle. With the development of the railroads, cattle droving became a thing of the past, and the Rottweiler almost became extinct. Luckily their worth was recognized by the German police and army. Now they are firmly established in the United States, Great Britain, and the Continent. The Rottweiler is a broad, powerful compact dog with a short, black coat and clearly defined tan markings. Dogs can be up to 67.5cm. (27in.) at the shoulder.

Shetland Sheepdog

All the domestic animals of the Shetland Islands are diminutive compared with their mainland counterparts. Whether this is due to the environment or to inbreeding of an island population is not known, but the Shetland Sheepdog is no exception to the rule. These small working sheep dogs were brought back from the Outer Isles by tourists at the turn of the century. There was immediate controversy on two counts. Collie breeders did not want the word "collie" (by then synonymous with Rough Collie) attached to these miniature nondescripts, and the original sponsors of the breed fought hard to retain the dog's working appearance. The collie breeders won, and the dog was called the

Shetland Sheepdog, but the working faction lost and the Sheltie was bred to resemble a small version of the elegant Rough Collie. Though they no longer work, Shetland Sheepdogs make charming and very trainable pets and are well known on both sides of the Atlantic. The ideal height for dogs is 30cm. (14.5in.).

Tervueren

This breed of Belgian Sheepdog is similar in structure to the Groenendael. It is present only in small numbers outside Belgium. Tervuerens share all the virtues of the other Belgian Sheepdogs, the color of their coat being their most distinctive feature. This is a rich fawn overlaid with black. Each fawn hair is tipped with black adding depth and richness to the basic shade.

Tibetan Terrier

The Tibetan Terrier is established in Great Britain but is not numerous. Some authorites believe these dogs were used as watchdogs and herding dogs by nomadic Tibetan tribesmen. They are higher on the leg and present a squarer outline than the other Tibetan breeds known in the West. The coat is long and profuse, and the heavily feathered tail is carried over the back. Any colors are acceptable, and the height is up to 40cm. (16in.). This shaggy dog is presented naturally in the show ring and resembles a miniature Old English Sheepdog.

COURSING DOGS

Coursing dogs are those which follow their swift moving quarry by sight, overtake them by superior speed, and pull them down with slashing bites from long, powerful jaws. Coursing is one of the oldest bloodsports, and this group of dogs contains the most ancient of the clearly differentiated breeds in the Mediterranean greyhounds. All the coursing breeds are built for speed and are a delight to the eye. Most are now kept as pet and show dogs only, and any would-be owner of these breeds should appreciate their need for space and exercise. Many are gentle and dignified dogs in the house, but obedience is not their strongest feature.

Afghan Hound

This bizarre and beautiful dog is one of the most popular of the coursing hounds. It was used for coursing gazelle and desert fox by Afghanistan tribesmen. The powerful loins, wideset hip bones and large padded feet make the Afghan unequaled in negotiating uneven ground at top speed. British Army officers were responsible for introducing the breed to Great Britain at the turn of the century, though it was not until after World War I that their numbers began to increase. The dog can be up to 47.5cm. (29in.) in height, and the long silky coat can be any color. The proudly carried head and aristocratic appearance correspond to the Afghan character of complete independence and a certain aloofness towards strangers.

Borzoi

A stylish dog, the Borzoi, also referred to as

the **Russian Wolfhound,** has always had aristocratic connections. Borzois, owned by the tsar and nobility in Russia, were used in a rather ceremonial and traditional form of coursing wolves. The first Borzois reached the West as ceremonial presents to British royalty from the tzars of Russia. The English aristocracy admired and exhibited the breed in the late nineteenth century, and the breed reached the United States from Great Britain at about the same time. Though they are dogs whose size limits their potential ownership, their air of good breeding and their beautiful, springy gait will guarantee them many admirers. The coat is long and silky and rather flat on the body. The color of the coat is unimportant. The minimum height for dogs is 47.5cm. (29in.).

Deerhound

The Deerhound or Scottish Deerhound is one of the tallest of the greyhound family. The decline of deer coursing in the Highlands of Scotland parallels the development of the sporting rifle. The Deerhound nearly disappeared as deer stalking took the place of coursing, but it was saved by a handful of enthusiasts. This gentle and dignified hound seems to have changed remarkably little over the centuries. Always a dog for discerning owners its registrations are low but steady in numbers. The dogs are usually dark blue-gray, though sandy is not unknown. The coat is harsh and wiry. Dogs should not be less than 75cm. (30in.), and weight can be up to 47.5kg. (105lb.).

Greyhound

Due to the sport of greyhound racing, the Greyhound remains today as prominent a breed as it has ever been. One of the oldest purebred types of dog, this breed has been depicted on carvings, pottery, and paintings from the time of the pharaohs to the present day. Bred for the chase for so long, the modern Greyhound is extremely fleet-footed and capable of reaching speeds of nearly 65kmph (40mph). Few are kept as show dogs or pets, though they are just as suitable in these respects as the other coursing breeds. The short, fine coat can be any color. Dogs can be up to 75cm. (30in.) at the shoulder and weigh about 31.7kg. (70lb.).

Irish Wolfhound

The Wolfhound claims the distinction of being the tallest breed and is also powerfully built. A very ancient Irish breed, the Wolfhound has always commanded respect and admiration. It was expected to do battle beside its master, pulling the enemy from his horse, and the dog was also used, as the name suggests, for killing wolves. The Wolfhound did not long survive the extermination of the wolf in Ireland, but a certain Captain Graham, who made it his life's work, reconstructed the breed in the nineteenth century. The coat is tough and wiry and is usually gray or fawn. Truly a gentle giant, the minimum height is 80cm. (32in.) and the weight near 54kg. (120lb.).

Lurcher

The Lurcher is not a true breed and is never

Borzoi

Deerhound

Irish Wolfhound

Greyhound

Sloughi

Saluki

likely to be officially recognized. It deserves a place however in any canine list of coursing dogs as it was, and is, a type bred for illegal poaching. The Lurcher was a poor man's dog, the gypsy's friend, bred to catch meat for the pot. A dark, speedy silent dog was needed and a terrier/greyhound cross was often used. The name is used for any sort of greyhound cross that is good at its job. Today they remain popular as pets.

Saluki
The Saluki is a desert greyhound from the Mediterranean basin. Owned and bred with the same care as the Arab horse, the Saluki traveled with its nomadic masters and coursed the gazelle, often in conjuction with trained falcons. The breed did not really become established in the West until the late 1920s. The soft, silky coat can be nearly any color, but creams and fawns predominate. The legs and ears are feathered, and the low set tail is curved and fringed on the underside. The height can be up to 70cm. (28in.).

Sloughi
Another of the desert greyhounds, the Sloughi is well established in France but little known elsewhere. The breed is smooth-haired and was bred for coursing antelope, jackal and smaller desert game. Rather sur-

prisingly for such a speedy dog, it has rather an upright shoulder. The Sloughi's head is the feature which distinguishes it most clearly from other similar hounds. It presents a domed appearance and the expression of the eyes can be described as nostalgic. The light colored dogs (creams and fawns) have a velvety dark eye; dark brindles and blacks have a burning, topaz one. There is a wide height range but it can be up to 75cm. (30in.).

Whippet

When one considers that both the Greyhound and the Italian Greyhound have very long histories, it is surprising to find that the Whippet is little more than 100 years old. This was a workingman's dog, developed in northern England. Nicknamed the poor man's greyhound, the Whippet was used for a primitive form of coursing where rabbits were released in an enclosed space and the dog's performance timed. When anticruelty laws brought this to an end, Whippet owners raced their dogs instead. This sport got a bad name and died out when more stringently controlled Greyhound racing became popular. Meanwhile the Whippet was being appreciated as a pet and show dog, and it is now very widely established. Recently, amateur Whippet racing has enjoyed a revival in many places, and this is one of the few breeds where there is no dichotomy between racing and show type. English whippets can be up to 46.5cm. (18.5in.). Structured like miniature Greyhounds, they can be any color.

SPITZ BREEDS

The spitz breeds are one of the basic dog types and are known in one form or another throughout the world. There is a great variety of color, texture, and length of coat, but the basic shape is unmistakable. These are dogs with wedge-shaped heads, erect ears, a short compact, body and a curled tail over the back. As a group they are alert, hardy, individualistic dogs, which have been used for every conceivable type of job.

Akita

The Akita is the largest of three spitz types known in Japan and is the only one recognized outside its native land. Throughout their history they have been used mainly for hunting, anything from deer and sable to wild boar and bear. Being a courageous and determined dog, the Akita has been used more recently as a guard and army dog. The coat is harsh, of medium length, and can be most colors. They have recently become established in the United States where they were taken by returning servicemen who were impressed by their size and guarding ability. They can be up to 69cm. (27.5in.) and weigh as much as 50kg. (110lb.)

Alaskan Malamute

Few purebred sled dog breeds have survived apart from the Alaskan Malamute. Used by the Eskimos on the Seward peninsula as a sledge dog and a pack animal, enough Malamutes survived the indiscriminate breeding

of the Yukon gold rush era to form the nucleus of a breed which is now widely kept as a companion dog in Canada and the United States. A few are shown, and teams of Malamutes are occasionally raced. They have a coarse, thick outer coat and a thick, woolly undercoat. They are usually a shaded gray in color. Distinctive black head markings in the shape of a cap or mask are desirable. This is a strong dog that needs firm handling. Males can be up to 62.5cm. (25in.) and 38.5kg. (85lb.) in weight.

Canaan Dog

The Canaan dog is indigenous to Israel where it was used as a sheep and guard dog. Often living a pariah-like existence in the Middle East, they have been more carefully bred since the 1930s. This is a medium-sized, vigilant dog which is distrustful of strangers. The coat lies close to the body, and the most desirable color is white with large markings of either black or brown. The breed has gained a foothold in the United States and Canada but is practically unknown elsewhere. The height can be up to 60cm. (24in.) and the weight up to 27.2kg. (60lb.).

Chow Chow

The Chow is well known as a show dog and as a pet. They tend to be one-man dogs which is perhaps indicated by their aloof, scowling expression. They are a very ancient breed known for many centuries all over China. They reached England from China as long ago as 1780 when the famous naturalist, Gilbert White, remarked on their unique blue-black mouth and tongue. The Chinese bred them for their flesh, their fur, for haulage work and for hunting. The coat is one of this breed's glories; it is long, profuse and stands off from the body. The breed is also peculiar in having an almost straight hind leg which gives a stilted hind action. Whole colors are desirable, the commonest being red, black, or blue. The minimum height is 45cm. (18in.).

Elkhounds

At least three Elkhound breeds are known in Scandanavia, where hunters developed local types to suit their needs. The elk (moose) is a large, ungainly animal of the deer family that prefers flight to fight, but can be very formidable if cornered. Elkhounds are expected to track and hold this animal at bay until the hunter can get within shooting range.

The best known of these breeds is the **Norwegian Elkhound** which is regularly shown and kept as a companion in most parts of the world. A typical spitz dog, it is compact, powerfully built for its size, and bold in temperament. The coat is coarse and weatherproof, medium in length, and any shade of gray. Dogs are about 51.5cm. (20.5in.) and weight approximately 22.6kg. (50lb.).

The **Swedish Elkhound (Jamthund)** is the national dog of Sweden and well established in Scandanavia, if not elsewhere. It is similar in shape and coloring to the Norwegian breed but, being 60cm. (24in.) at the shoulder, considerably larger.

The **Black Elkhound** which used to be

quite popular in Norway is the rarest of the three Elkhound breeds. It is rather more rangily built than the other two and the coat, as well as being black, is more close-lying.

Finnish Spitz

The Finnish Spitz is popular in its native land, known in adjoining countries and established in Great Britain. As well as for general farm work, they are used as bird dogs in Finland and their hunting ability is tested at field trials. The shortish coat is dense and semierect and the color is usually red, giving a fox-like appearance. Dogs can be up to 50cm. (20in.).

German Spitz

The German Spitz or **Great Spitz** comes in three sizes; the silver gray **Wolfspitz** with a minimum height of 42.5cm. (17in.); the **Standard Spitz** which is 39.5cm. (15.75 in.) in height; and the **Small Spitz** which should be under 27.5cm. (11in.). Except for the shaded Wolfspitz, these dogs are self-colored, either black, white, or brown. They are very striking to see because of the length of the profuse, standoff coat. They are popular dogs in Germany and known elsewhere on the Continent. This breed was the root stock from which British breeders created the Pomeranian.

Husky

This type, also known as the **Eskimo Dog** or **Greenland Dog,** is not so firmly established as the other two sled dog breeds, the Alaskan Malamute and the Siberian Husky. In the remoter parts of Greenland some are still used for their original purpose of haulage in subzero conditions. They were also used to search for food and still have a strong hunting instinct. A handful are established in Great Britain and on the continent of Europe. Being tough dogs in every respect, they need patient and persevering owners prepared to give them an immense amount of exercise. Color is immaterial, and there is a wide range in height which can be up to 67.5cm. (27in.), and weight up to one 47.5kg. (105lb.).

Iceland Dog

This breed is very near extinction and is relatively unknown in most countries. The breed has been indigenous to Iceland for a very long time and was used to guide the caravans of Iceland ponies and to fetch the sheep down from mountain pastures. They are comparatively lightly built for a spitz breed, and are up to 45cm. (18in.) at the shoulder and weigh 13.6kg. (30lb.). The coat is harsh and usually a black-tipped fawn in color.

Keeshond

Although it is not one of the most popular dogs, the Keeshond is well established in many parts of the world. It bears a more than passing resemblance to the German Wolfspitz, but comes from Holland where it was used as a farm dog and as a guard on the barges of the Low Country canals. The wolf, or ash gray coat stands off from the body, and a valued feature is the black pencilling marks around the eyes which give the appearance of spectacles. Height is up to 45cm. (18in.).

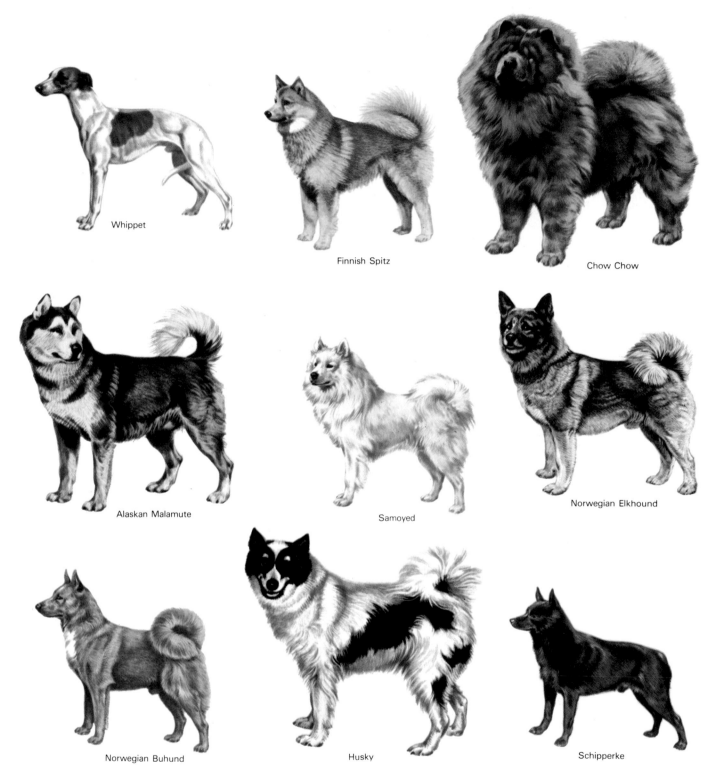

Whippet

Finnish Spitz

Chow Chow

Alaskan Malamute

Samoyed

Norwegian Elkhound

Norwegian Buhund

Husky

Schipperke

Laika

The Russian spitz breed, the Laika varies widely in coat color and size according to the region that it comes from. They were certainly used as gundogs and in this respect resemble the German Spitz varieties. Breeding information for the modern Laika is unavailable, but they are still in use as evidenced by the fact that the first dog in space was a small version of this Spitz type.

Norwegian Buhund

Though established in Great Britain and Australia, the Buhund is not a common dog in most parts of the world. It is a farm dog in Norway, used for guarding and herding and for killing vermin. The coat is fairly short, and the usual color is wheaten or biscuit. Height may be up to 45cm. (18in.).

Samoyed

The Samoyed takes its name from the nomadic tribe who first used them in Siberia. There they controlled the herds of reindeer, hunted small game, harried larger predators, hauled sledges, and had their fur and skins used as clothing by their masters. The modern Samoyed is snow white in color. A feature of the breed is the slightly upturned black lips which gives the dog a smiling expression. The breed is popular in the United States for sled dog racing and is well established in Australia, Great Britain, and the Continent. The height can be up to 52.5cm. (21in.) and the weight up to 30kg. (66lb.).

Schipperke

The Flemish name means "little skipper," and this spitz breed is firmly established worldwide without attracting great publicity anywhere. They are small jet black dogs, used as guards on Belgium barges (hence the name), and now popular as house dogs. The hair is short, harsh and straight, lengthening to form a mane and cape round the shoulders. The docked tail gives the rump a rounded appearance. These are very lively and alert little dogs that weigh about 7.2kg. (16lb.).

Siberian Husky

In 1909 the first team of Siberian Huskies was imported into the United States to take part in the fast growing winter sport of dog sled racing. They proved outstanding, and their numbers grew rapidly in the United States and Canada, particularly when it was found that they adapted easily to being companion dogs. They are established in Great Britain and Germany but are not well known. The Siberian Husky is a lighter, smaller dog than the Alaskan Malamute and often has striking blue eyes. The coat is medium in length and very dense. All colors are allowed but various shadings of gray are most usual. A striking variety of black head markings are a feature of the breed. Dogs can be up to 59cm. (23.5in.) with a weight of up to 27.2kg. (60lb.).

Wallhund (Vastgotaspets)

This Swedish herding dog, also known as the **Vastgotaspets,** is a short-legged spitz type with a docked tail. It resembles the Welsh Corgi and does similar work to that they used to do. The preferred color is gray, and the height can be up to 40cm. (16in.). Weight is about 14kg. (31lb.). They are popular in Sweden and the Baltic area, and there are a handful in Great Britain.

Norwegian Buhund

Siberian Husky

HOUNDS

The hound group contains all the breeds which hunt their quarry mainly by scent. They are more diverse in type than the coursing dogs and hunt more slowly, wearing their victims down by persistence rather than overtaking them quickly with superior speed. As they track their game many of the hounds give tongue, and the sound of the hounds is most exciting to followers of the chase. They are not particularly aggressive dogs but they are independent and following a scent is often more attractive to them than home comforts.

Basenji

The sharply distinctive Basenji comes from the Congo basin and did not become established in the West until the late 1930s. This is a lightly built, gazelle-like animal with a tireless, swinging stride. The upright ears and tightly curled tail are reminiscent of a spitz, but this is a smooth-coated dog, bright red, black, or black and tan with white markings. The wrinkled forehead gives the dog a quizzical expression and it has the habit of cleaning itself with its paws like a cat. They are a breed which do not bark, communicating by a number of other sounds which are not always musical to the human ear. The height is up to 42.5 cm. (17in.) and the weight up to 10.8kg. (24lb.).

Basset Hound

Basset Hounds, originally French pack hounds, have increased remarkably in numbers since the 1960s. They are large dogs on short legs. New Basset owners must keep in mind that they need a great deal of hard exercise and that they can be noisy if left alone. The Basset Hound is credited with as fine a nose as the Bloodhound. The wrinkled skin on the head and the enormous pendent ears give the dog a soulful, dignified expression which entirely belies its energetic, active nature. The smooth coat can be any recognized hound color. The height is up to 37.5cm. (15in.) and the weight about 22.6kg. (50lb).

Basset Griffon Vendeen

France developed more hound breeds than any other country because the French nobility regarding hunting as an art. Many of these breeds did not survive the French Revolution, and those that did are often few in numbers. The Basset Griffon Vendeen is one of the latter. A low-to-ground dog, this hound is much less exaggerated than the more widely known Basset Hound. It is a robust, active dog entirely covered with moderately long harsh hair, giving it a beguiling whiskery expression. They are rare in Great Britain and otherwise little known outside their native land. Height is up to 41.5cm. (16.5in.).

Beagle

The Beagle is one of the oldest of the British hounds. Beagle packs were used for hunting hares. Today the Beagle is kept very widely as a pet and companion. In the United States and Canada, Beagle field trials are very popular. Numerically they are one of the strongest

hound breeds in the world. Beagles are also widely used for research purposes. They are smooth-coated, medium-sized dogs with a stylish appearance. Height limits vary in different countries with a 37.5cm. (15in.) maximum. Any true hound color is recognized.

Bloodhound

The Bloodhound is a breed that is familiar to many but kept only by a few. These are large hounds with the most remarkable scenting powers of any domestic animal. They are gentle, affectionate animals whose instinct for tracking does not seem to be allied in any way with a desire to attack their quarry. Bloodhounds are smooth-coated and either red, black and tan, or liver and tan in color. Their head is remarkable for the amount of loose skin falling in folds and wrinkles, giving a dignified and solemn expression. Dogs average 65cm. (26in.) in height and weight up to 50kg. (100lb.)

Coonhounds

The American Kennel Club recognizes only the **Black and Tan Coonhound,** but there are at least five other coonhound breeds engaged in what is one of the roughest and toughest of American sports. The raccoon is a nocturnal animal which the dogs trail and tree. As this is done in darkness the hunter relies on the voice or bay of the coonhounds to indicate where they are, how hot the scent is, and whether or not they have treed their quarry. A large number of coonhound trials are held annually. The Black and Tan Coonhound is the largest breed, being up to 67.5cm.(27in.) in height and has some Bloodhound ancestry. The other breeds are the **Redbone,** the **English Coonhounds,** the **Bluetick,** the **Treeing Walker,** and the **Plott Hound.** Most of these have been developed from the American Foxhound and they are all strictly working dogs.

Dachsbracke (Drever)

The Dachsbreche is a popular hound in Sweden and the Baltic area. It was officially recognized for show purposes in 1953 but has been working in Swedish forests for centuries. It is a low-legged, smooth-coated hound about 35cm.(14in.) high, with an excellent nose. It has always been trained and used to drive game towards the guns, a job for which it is ideal since it is a slow moving, tracking dog with a great deal of persistence. It is used today mainly against Roe Deer. The color may be red and white, yellow and white, or tricolor. The standard states that the white must be visible from all angles as it minimizes the chances of the dog being shot at by accident.

Dachshund

The well-known Dachshund comes in six varieties which in some countries, such as Great Britain, are registered as six distinct breeds. Dachshunds are German dogs, used originally to burrow after badgers, which is why they have short legs allied to long flexible bodies. Despite the fact that they have been kept more widely as pets and show dogs than for working, Dachshunds still retain a

Basset Griffon Vendeen

Bloodhound

Beagle

Coonhound

Basset Hound

Dachshund-Shorthaired

Dachshund-Longhaired

Dachshund-Wirehaired

Vallhund

lot of their hunting instincts and, given the chance, are very sporting dogs. There are three types of coat; the **Smooth-haired,** the **Long-haired,** and the **Wirehaired.** Basically there are two sizes for each coat type, the **Standard** and the **Miniature,** though Germany recognizes more, with very small Dachshunds being used for hunting rabbits. Different countries tend to have different size regulations for each variety, but Standards should not weigh more than 11.3kg. (25lb.). The commonest colors are red, black and tan, and chocolate and tan, but dapples and brindles are also permitted. Smooth-haired Dachshunds have tended to be the most popular over the years, but are now being overtaken by the Long-haired variey. The Wirehaired Dachshund has never attracted the same attention as the other two.

Harrier

The Harrier is best described as a hound intermediate in size between a Beagle and a Foxhound. Old established packs of Harriers exist in Great Britain for hunting hares but their numbers are declining. In the United States one or two packs are used to hunt foxes. They are also used in South America for trailing the mountain lion and in Sri Lanka for hunting leopards. The Harrier is strictly a working dog, possessing a good nose and obvious versatility. The smooth coat is often tricolor and the dog stands up to 52.5cm. (21in.) in height.

Foxhound

Fox hunting has been an English blood sport since the thirteenth century and shows no signs of diminishing in popularity. Since the masters of foxhound packs kept their own stud books, the detailed ancestry of most English Foxhounds can be traced back further than any other purebred dog. English Foxhounds are bred for good nose, good voice, and great stamina. Type may vary slightly between packs, since the hounds are bred especially to suit their particular terrain, but the average height is 60cm. (24in.). English Foxhounds are unsuitable as pets because of their strong hunting instinct, and because their toughness makes the discipline of pack life an essential. They are shown only at Hound Shows which are not under the jurisdiction of the *Kennel Club*. The **American Foxhound** is of a racier build than the English and is used in a wider variety of ways. Though often descended from English bloodlines, the American Foxhound is much more an individualist in trailing the fox and less of a pack animal. Field trials for American Foxhounds have been held for nearly 100 years and are a popular sport. The individual voice of each hound is recognized by its owner, who can tell the progress of the chase by the timbre of the baying. Some of these hounds also appear in the show ring where they have been known to win Best of Show, although it does not occur often.

127

Otterhound

Dalmation

Pharaoh Hound

Rhodesian Ridgeback

Ibizan Hound

Ibizan Hound

The Ibizan Hound comes from the Balearic Islands and is popular in Spain while a few are exhibited in Great Britain. It is a strongly built greyhound, with large upstanding ears. They hunt as much by scent and hearing as by sight, and are extremely agile. They are expected by their owners to point, flush, and retrieve game, such as partridge, or they may be used for rabbit hunting, either alone or in packs. The coat can be smooth or wirehaired and the height about 40cm. (26in.). The colors permitted are white and red, either as a parti-colored or as a whole colored dog.

Otterhound

The Otterhound bears some resemblance to a harsh-coated Bloodhound and is credited with the same sensitivity of nose. To follow the scent of a swimming mammal, as Otterhounds were bred to do, calls for great perseverance as well as great scenting powers. The coat is oily and waterproof, enabling the dog to swim for hours in the kind of fast flowing, icy streams frequented by otters. Otterhounds cover the ground surprisingly fast with a lumbering gait, again reminiscent of a Bloodhound. The dog is rare, one purebred pack alone being known in Great Britain. In America Otterhounds are bred for show rather than work purposes, but are still not very numerous. The colors are grizzle

and sandy, with some black and tan markings. The height is up to 65cm. (26in.).

Pharoah Hound

Of similar build and probably similar descent to the Ibizan Hound, the Pharaoh Hound is a rather smaller dog, some 62.5cm. (25in.) in height. They are smooth-coated, glossy dogs, chestnut or rich tan in color with white markings and a flesh or fawn nose. The eyes are amber and the expression alert and keen. Playful and active, they are avid hunters that need a lot of exercise. They are recognized and shown in small numbers in Great Britain.

Rhodesian Ridgeback

This South African breed is remarkable for the ridge of hair along the spine, lying in the opposite direction to the rest of the coat. They are red-coated, robust dogs, popular in Central Africa and well established as show dogs in the United States and Great Britain. The nickname "lion dog" has been given to the Ridgeback, not because of its appearance but because they were used to track and harass lions until they presented an easy target for hunters. The height can be 67.5cm. (27in.) and the weight about 34kg. (75lb.).

GUNDOGS

Many of the breeds classified as gundogs no longer work in the field and seem to have

made a smooth transition to the more idle life of companionable pets. Most of these breeds retain the tractability which made them valuable as hunting dogs. Gundogs perform a number of separate functions when working. There are some, like the pointers and setters, that are expected to crisscross the ground, ranging widely ahead of the sportsman. When they scent game they freeze, indicating by their immobile stance where the hidden birds are. The retrievers find and pick up both wounded and dead game and bring it back to the sportsman. They are expected to carry birds without crushing them and a "soft" mouth is valued in these dogs. The spaniels search through cover, flushing the game for shooting, and then retrieving it. Finally there are the dual purpose breeds which are expected to find the game, point, flush it on command, and retrieve it tenderly when it has been killed. All these dogs must work silently, as opposed to the hounds which indicate when they are on a scent by baying.

American Cocker Spaniel

Though both Cocker Spaniel breeds originally came from the same English root, the American Cocker Spaniel has diverged widely and is now a very distinct and popular breed. The skull shape is domed and the muzzle shorter than in the English variety.

The coat is extremely long, in some cases touching the floor and completely obliterating the body line. The skull, neck, and back are clipped short. The ideal height is 37.5 cm. (15in.) and much attention is paid to color with different color classes provided at shows. This is an extremely popular show animal and pet in the United States and Canada and is established in Great Britain. It no longer works in the field.

American Water Spaniel
Known only in the United States and Canada, the Water Spaniel is used for wildfowl and duck shooting along the Mississippi flyway, the migratory route of waterfowl from Canada to the Gulf of Mexico. It is chocolate or liver in color, up to 45cm. (18in.) at the shoulder and 18kg. (40lb.) in weight. The coat consists of dense tight curls and the long tail is covered with short thick hair. This is not a very common working dog although it has a small but steady following.

Brittany Spaniel
One of the most popular sporting dogs in the United States, the Brittany Spaniel originates in France where it is still well known. This is one of the few breeds that has so far managed to combine successfully both working qualities and show type. It has proved very adaptable in working all types of game birds, retrieves well on both land and water, and is the only spaniel required to point. It is rangy in build, up to 51.5cm. (20.5in.) in height, and with a dense, flat coat with little or no feathering. The color must be orange and white or liver and white.

Chesapeake Bay Retriever
The Chesapeake Bay Retriever is well established only in the United States and Canada, where it is valued as an extremely tough dog for hunting wild fowl. These dogs are rugged individualists showing great determination and endurance when swimming in icy, heavy seas. The coat is very oily and dense and the deadgrass color varies from faded tan to dull straw, an ideal camouflage for a duck shooter's dog. The eyes are yellow. The height is up to 65cm. (26in.) and the weight up to 34kg. (75lb.).

Clumber Spaniel
The Clumber is the most massive of the spaniels with strong, heavy bones, a square body and a massive head with a thoughtful, dignified expression. They are no longer working dogs though they wre originally bred for slow methodical working in thick cover. One of the six British Spaniel breeds, the Clumber has never been very popular and its numbers are declining. The sparkling white coat has lemon markings and the weight can be up to 31.7kg. (70lb.).

English Cocker Spaniel
One of the best known of the spaniels, the English Cocker either is or has been one of the most popular breeds in many countries. It is one of the merriest and friendliest of dogs with a stump of a tail that never stops wagging. There are fewer working Cockers existing today than previously, but the breed

American Cocker Spaniel

curly-coated Retriever

American Water Spaniel

English Cocker Spaniel

Clumber Spaniel

Chesapeake Bay Retriever

remains a compact, active one, built on lines that enable it to participate enthusiastically in a day's shooting. The flat, silky coat comes in a wide variety of attractive shades. Height and weight standards differ in different parts of the world but a general guide is 40cm. (16in.) and 12.7kg. (28lb.) respectively.

Curly Coated Retriever
The Curly Coat is no longer numerically strong, though it was at one time a gamekeeper's favorite. The coat, consisting of tight crisp curls, shows up in sharp contrast the smooth velvety face. This is a robust dog, an excellent swimmer, and a good family animal with a strong guarding instinct. The color is solid black or occasionally liver. The height is up to 67.5cm. (27in.) and the weight up to 36.2kg. (80lb.).

Dalmatian
This strong active breed is somewhat a misfit in this group, though the Dalmatian has been used in a variety of sporting ways for years. It is shown, together with hawks, greyhounds

and spaniels, in a picture by Jan Fyt (1609–1661) called the *Hunting Party*. Built on the lines of a retriever and with similar stamina, Dalmatians have been used as guard dogs, draft dogs, vermin killers, and stable dogs. They are well-known dogs because of their distinctive spotted coats and make ideal family dogs for those of an energetic disposition. The coat markings must be round, distinct and well defined, either black or liver on what is otherwise a basically white dog. The height is about 57.5cm. (23in.) and the weight around 25kg. (55lb.).

English Setter
A breed popular everywhere because of its beautiful coloring and gentle soulful looks, the English Setter is now primarily a pet and show dog in most parts of the world. However in the United States and Canada, smaller working strains exist which are popular for hunting and field trials. The head of the English Setter is long and lean with dark hazel eyes that have a sentimental expression. The

German Short-haired Pointer

Poodle

English Springer Spaniel

Flat Coated Retriever

Field Spaniel

slightly wavy coat is long and silky. The ground color is usually white, flecked and softly freckled with either black, orange, lemon, or liver. The height can be up to 67.5cm. (27in.) and weight up to 29.5kg. (65lb.).

English Springer Spaniel
The English Springer is probably the oldest established breed of spaniels and the taproot from which most of the other spaniel breeds sprang. It is a popular, well-established breed which seems to have equal success as a rough shooter's dog prepared to find, flush, and retrieve any sort of fur or feather, as an exhibitor's dog shown widely in Great Britain and the United States, and as a loyal, devoted family dog. It is a well-balanced dog in every way: a good size, an attractive coat, and a sensible temperament. The coat is close and straight, either liver and white or black and white. Height is 50cm. (20in.) and weight about 22.6kg. (50lb.).

Field Spaniel
The offshoot of the Cocker Spaniel and now near extinction, the Field was bred to an exaggerated length at the turn of the century, until it looked like an overfed Basset and had lost any pretense at working ability. By the time this had been rectified, the Cocker was extremely popular, and the Field Spaniel's numbers have remained low ever since. They are self-colored dogs, usually black or liver. Height is about 45cm. (18in.) and weight about 22.6kg. (50lb.).

Flat-Coated Retriever
The Flat Coat was the most popular of the working retrievers in the 1900s and has since declined drastically in numbers for no apparent reason. It is built on the same lines as the Labrador and has the same calm, sensible temperament. The coat is dense and flat with feathering on the ears, back of the front legs and tail. The color is either black or liver, and the weight should be between 27.2–31.7kg. (60–70lb.).

German Short-haired Pointer
Like many of the Continental gundogs, the German Short-hair is a dual purpose dog, obedient, and an extremely keen worker. Though the breed was created less than 100 years ago, this is now one of the best known sporting dogs in the world, being particularly appreciated in the United States and Canada. The dog is versatile and yet has the style and pace for field trials. Though the coat is short and coarse, the dog will face icy water or thick cover without any qualms. The color can be solid liver, liver and white, or black and white. The height is (62.5cm.) 25in. and the weight 31.7kg. (70lb.).

German Wirehaired Pointer
This pointer now resembles the German Short-hair in every way except coat. Though its working qualities seem to be of an equally high order and it is popular with German sportsmen, it has only recently become established in the United States and is not widely kept elsewhere. The outer coat is harsh and wiry, and the head of the dog has bushy eyebrows, beard, and whiskers.

Golden Retriever
This popular retriever is successful in many fields. Some still work with the guns and can perform brilliantly. They draw large entries at shows and are equally well known as good-tempered, biddable family dogs. They are also used extensively as guide dogs for the blind. They are descended from a yellow sport (mutation) that cropped up in a litter of black Flat Coat Retrievers. The wavy coat with good feathering can be any shade of gold or cream. Height is 60cm. (24in.) and weight up to 31.7kg. (70lb.).

Gordon Setter
The Gordon Setter is the most heavily built of the three setter breeds and has always been the least popular. It is no longer much used in the field and, but for the enthusiasm of some exhibitors, might have disappeared altogether. The Gordon Setter is a handsome dog with a shiny black coat relieved by rich chestnut markings. The head is deep with rather heavy jowls, and the dog should be built on the lines of a weight-carrying hunter. The height can be up to 67.5cm. (27in.) and the weight as much as 36.2kg. (80lb.).

Irish Setter (Red Setter)
This flashy, stylish Irish dog is known the world over. The breed has been popular for so long on both sides of the Atlantic that there is now a divergence of type between the American and the English bred dogs. The

Golden Retriever

Gordon Setter

Irish Setter

Labrador Retriever

Irish Setter's high spirits and good humor, as well as its rich mahogany red coloring, guarantee it a host of admirers, though it is seldom worked in the field. This is a streamlined dog that can be up to 67.5cm. (27in.) in height. The flat, silky coat· has abundant feathering on the ears, tail, and forelegs. Originally red and white Irish Setters were in the majority but today these are never seen, the color always being rich chestnut. White markings on the chest, throat, forehead, and toes are acceptable.

Irish Water Spaniel

This is the largest of the spaniels and totally unlike the others being more closely allied in looks and probable ancestry to the Poodle and the Portuguese Water Dog. The appearance is distinctive, the color being a rich dark liver and the coat consisting of dense tight ringlets except for the face and tail which are smooth. The breed is particularly suited for hunting wild birds since it is an excellent swimmer whose oily coat insulates its skin against cold and wet. Although these are dogs with plenty of personality as well as an unusual appearance they have never become very popular. The height is 54–59cm. (21–23in.) and they weigh (50–65lb.).

Labrador Retriever

Known and respected the world over, both as a worker and a companion, the Labrador Retriever is a robust, yet patient, and gentle dog. It is still a great worker, the black variety being favored by shooting men. It is also well known as a companion, a police dog, and a guide dog for the blind. The breed came from Newfoundland, where it was used by fishermen to take to shore the ropes holding the nets used for retrieving anything that went overboard accidentally. The fishermen sailed the Atlantic to sell their catches in English ports, and sometimes sold their dogs at the same time. These sturdily built dogs have a short dense coat which is either black, yellow or more rarely, chocolate. Height varies in different countries from 56.5–61.5cm. (22.5–24.5in.) and weight is up to 34kg. (75lb.).

Large Münsterländer

The Large Münsterländer is a well-established dual purpose gundog in Germany and is beginning to be known in Holland and Great Britain. It is a medium-sized, setter-like breed with a sleek, slightly wavy coat and a long feathered tail. The color is white with a black head and large black patches on a flecked body. The height can be 62.5cm. (25in.).

Poodle

The **Standard Poodle,** the oldest variety, was first known as a gundog, used for retrieving waterfowl in the same way as water spaniels, and these dogs may share a common ancestor. This fun-loving, clever dog has now colonized the whole world and is known in a variety of colors and sizes. The Standard Poodle, the largest size, is now rarely used as a retriever, but still retains its love of water.

Breeding down from the Standard Poodle has produced two smaller versions, the **Miniature** and the **Toy.** These have far outstripped their larger relative in popularity. Clipped in patterns either to suit the show ring or suit their owners, poodles delight in attention and praise. Standard Poodles can be up to 60cm. (24in.) at the shoulder; Miniatures up to 37.5cm. (15in.); Toys up to 52.5cm. (11in.) in Great Britain or 50cm. (10in.) in the United States. Parti-colored poodles are not allowed, but there is a wide range of solid colors.

Pointer

The Pointer is built for galloping, head held high, seeking the scent of game birds in the air. When the dog finds this scent, it freezes, literally pointing the way to the quarry. With the diminishing open spaces in Great Britain this breed is rarely worked, but it remains a popular field trial dog in the United States. It is regularly exhibited wherever dog shows are held, but is too energetic and rangy to be suitable for town life. The short coat is white with orange, lemon, liver, or black markings. The height is up to 70cm. (28in.) and the weight up to 34kg. (75lb.).

Portuguese Water Dog

These are not gundogs but are included in this group because of their obvious affinity to the water spaniel and the poodle. Their work is similar to the original use of the Labrador for they act as fishermen's couriers between boat and shore. Sadly, few are exhibited on

Sussex Spaniel

Wirehaired Pointing Griffon

Weimaraner

Small Munsterlander

the Continent, and their numbers are low. The colors are the original poodle colors, black, white, or brown. The height can be 55cm. (22in.), and the hindquarters are often shaved.

Small Münsterländer

This is a smaller, more lightly built gundog resembling a long-tailed spaniel. A popular working dog in Germany, the Small Münsterländer is the recreation of a very old breed used when hawking was a fashionable sport. The wavy coat is brown and white. The height is up to 50cm. (20in.).

Sussex Spaniel

The Sussex Spaniel, like the Field Spaniel, seems on the verge of extinction. Their color is unique, a rich golden liver, and they are among the heavyweights of the spaniel breeds. Though they are among the oldest and most distinct of the land spaniels, their low numbers seem to have created fertility problems. The height is about 40cm. (16in.) and the weight about 20.5kg. (45lb.).

Viszla

The Viszla is a dual-purpose gundog from the plains of Hungary. It resembles a lightly built Pointer, though the tail is docked to two-thirds of its length. Also, it is not as wide ranging as the Pointer when hunting. It is a versatile dog, adapting easily to different conditions and to different games, whether fur or feather. It is respected as an all-round sporting dog in the United States, where it is well established, and it is beginning to be exhibited in Great Britain. It is a smooth-coated dog, russet gold in color. Height is up to 62.5cm. (25in.) and weight up to 30kg. (66lb.).

Weimaraner

The Weimaraner was developed in Germany as an all-purpose hunting dog whose breeding and development was closely controlled by a club devoted to the breed's interests. They were recognized by the American Kennel Club in 1943, when they had already excited a great deal of interest by their success in obedience tests. They are now widely used in the United States and Canada and are well established in Great Britain and the Continent. They are smooth-coated, silver-gray dogs with amber or blue-gray eyes. Height can be up to 67.5cm. (27in.).

Welsh Springer Spaniel

The Welsh Springer, midway in size between the English Springer and the Cocker, has existed in Wales for a long time. Though not one of the most numerous of the spaniel breeds they are now well established as a rough shooter's dog and as a show dog. They are compact, strong dogs with comparatively small ears. The coat is silky and flat without too much feathering. The color is always rich dark red set off with sparkling white. The weight can be up to 20.5kg. (45lb.).

Wirehaired Pointing Griffon (Korthals Griffon)

The Wirehaired Pointing Griffon is a popular gundog in its native land of Germany but is making slow progress in the United Sates and Canada. They are methodical, careful workers, easily trained but without the style and dash required for field trial dogs. The distinctive coat is short and bristly and the color a mixture of grayish white with chestnut patches. The height is up to 59cm. (23.5in.).

CATS

A cat will fit into almost every home. It is a clean animal with a strong sense of personal hygiene, and its care is comparatively easy.

There are many popular fallacies about cats. They may "walk alone," but they are nevertheless capable of close rapport with their owners. They do *not* all like milk; sometimes it can be bad for them. They do not instinctively balance and regulate their diet; some can be tremendous gluttons and easily become overweight. They need plenty of exercise and a constant supply of fresh water. Some breeds have a reputation for being spiteful or stupid. Certain traits do seem to go along with certain breeds, but intelligence and personality are much more due to the character of the individual cat and the way in which it has been reared. The average lifespan of a cat is from thirteen to seventeen years, but some have been known to live to thirty years and to produce kittens when twenty years of age.

Choosing A Kitten

There are many breeds to choose from as well as plenty of nonpedigree kittens that desperately need a good home. Whatever your choice, pedigree or mongrel, the same criteria apply for choosing the right animal.

All kittens should be inoculated against panleucopenia (feline infectious enteritis) at eight to ten weeks of age and given booster injections at the dates prescribed. If the kitten has been inoculated, make sure that the breeder or pet dealer gives you the vaccination certificate so you will know what kind of vaccine was used and when the booster injections will be required. If the kitten has not already been vaccinated, you should arrange for it to be done as soon as possible.

Cat flu (pneumonitis) in the form of feline viral rhinotracheitis or feline picornavirus infection can also be dangerous. Never purchase a kitten that is sneezing or has runny eyes, or even one that has been in contact with an infected animal as this disease is highly contagious. Vaccines are now available against cat flu, but many veterinarians question their value and safety.

You should watch for black specks or small hard granules like sawdust on the coat; they may be flea droppings or lice. Check the ears to make sure the insides are clean and free of mites—a cat that is continually shaking its head or scratching its ears may have an infestation. Take a look inside the kitten's mouth which should be a rosy pink color. If it

Cats have a reputation as fussy eaters. Avoid this by giving your cat a variety of foods early and by being firm about not replacing unwanted food with the cat's favorite.

does not have all its teeth, it is too young to be sold. The eyes should be clear and bright. If the inner eyelid (haw) is partially closed, it may be a sign of sickness. Above all, the kitten you choose should be lively, playful, and curious.

You should have the kitten neutered at this point if you do not propose to breed it.

Feeding Your Cat

The domestic cat is almost wholly carnivorous and must receive a high proportion of good quality protein in its diet. Fat should make up about 15 to 20 percent of the total

diet. After all essential nutrients have been supplied, the remainder of the food (approximately one-third on a dry matter basis) can consist of cooked starch which the cat is able to digest efficiently. (See **Feeding Your Pet.**) Cats have high vitamin needs which can be met by giving up to 10 percent liver in the diet. Higher levels are potentially dangerous as the cat may become addicted and suffer from an excessive intake of vitamin A.

A balanced feline diet consists mainly of animal protein foods—meat, offals, and fish, plus some cereal. Many cats like to crunch dry cereals: breakfast food or even dog biscuits. Otherwise, dry cereals can be soaked in milk or mixed with protein foods. Milk fur-

DIET 1	DIET 2	DIET 3
200g (7oz) whitefish	70g (2.5oz) dry cat food	1 small can of meat and cereal cat food.
30g (1oz) liver	120ml (0.25pt) milk	120ml (0.25pt) milk
14g (0.5oz) cereal		
120ml (0.25pt) milk		
A large active tomcat may require over 1,650kJ (400kcal)/day, while queens require 1,000–1,250kJ (250–300kcal).		

nishes the intake of minerals. If refused in any form or not tolerated in digestion, you should give a proprietary supplement. Bones provide calcium, but rabbit, chicken, and fish bones are dangerous.

Reputable manufactured foods provide a balanced diet in various convenient forms: canned, soft-moist, and dry. These are similar to the corresponding dog foods but usually have higher protein and vitamin levels. Soft-moist cat foods contain little if any sugar since most cats do not like it. Dry cat foods are nutritionally complete but require some caution. Cats have unusually concentrated urine and if fed dry food without enough liquid, they can develop stones and suffer a blockage in the urinary tract. Therefore dry food should never be given as the sole diet. If you are not sure whether the cat is drinking enough, either soak the food or change to a wet diet. Given in moderation these manufactured dry foods are a convenient, reliable, and palatable addition to a cat's menu.

Cats may need only one meal a day, but they prefer two or more, particularly if they are family pets. They like to be offered food when they see family food being prepared. Also, smaller quantities given more often will not get stale or spoil. The quantity required does not vary too much between cats since their weights occupy a fairly narrow range. Drinking water should always be available.

In the wild, cats eat the stomach contents of their prey and thus obtain some vegetable food. The house cat should occasionally be offered cooked vegetables or a little shredded lettuce with their food.

If they do not have access to grass, some should be grown indoors for them to nibble from time to time. The cat uses grass as roughage and sometimes as an emetic to bring up balls of fur which accumulate from the hair swallowed when washing itself. Cats particularly like Cocksfoot grass (*Dactylis glomerata*). Do not grow philodendrons or dieffenbachia as house plants since both are poisonous to cats.

A healthy aging cat needs no special changes in feeding. The general principles described in the chapter **Feeding Your Pet** apply.

Feeding the Kitten

Kittens grow fast and should be kept on a high protein diet with adequate vitamins and minerals. All types of meat, offals, and fish are suitable but should be cooked and have all bones removed. Offer a variety to avoid addiction to one food, particularly liver. Canned foods are quite suitable. Some cereal can be mixed with the meat or fed separately. Cow's milk should be provided, as long as it is accepted. (Some orientals never acquire a taste for it.) Fresh water should always be available. Feed to appetite, three times a day from weaning to three months and twice a day to six months of age. During this period of rapid growth, total intake exceeds that of an adult cat.

FEEDING PROBLEMS

The most common difficulty in feeding cats is their tendency to be picky and develop narrow food preferences. They should be trained from an early age to accept a varied diet to ensure a balanced intake of essential nutrients. Picky eating is nearly always the consequence of an indulgent owner overfeeding the cat so that it becomes obese and is never really hungry. The remedy is obvious but requires a firm hand. Nutritious food should be put out once or twice a day at regular times and removed in an hour if not eaten. Cats tend to be nibblers, but a hungry cat is as voracious as any other species.

Owing to the cat's clean habits, diarrhea is often not recognized until the cat is seriously ill and veterinary help must be sought immediately. Mild looseness is usually not detected and will correct itself if the cat continues to be generally healthy.

Breeding and Rearing of Cats

Felines are perverse creatures. If you simply can not stand the feel of a cat you can be sure that one will leap into your lap. Call a cat for breakfast, and it may not decide to appear until dinner time. Similarly you may have a purebred queen which you have introduced to champion toms all over the country without successful mating. One day you leave the back door open, and nine weeks later she presents you with a litter of unwanted mongrels.

Feline nature may be perverse, but it is

Cats can be prolific breeders, and control measures are required to stop breeding altogether or (Above) to prevent the result from being a mixed bag of kittens. Right. The breeding of purebreds such as these Siamese requires great care but has its reward when the result is a perfect batch of kittens, some of which may reach show standard.

certainly fertile. The domestic cat has not changed appreciably over thousands of years. Unlike many breeds of dogs, even the most exotic of purebred cats retains the essential vigor, the sexual proclivities, and the survival instincts of its feral cousins.

THE FEMALE CAT—THE QUEEN

The female shows the first signs of puberty at about six months of age. A couple of month's variation either way is determined by the weather and the type of cat. During a warm early spring, for example, many an oriental cat has been found to be pregnant at four or five months. On the other hand, a domestic cat like the British Short-haired Blue or a Long-haired Chinchilla born in the early part of the winter may not achieve puberty until it is eight or nine months of age.

If one does not wish to raise kittens veterinarians advise spaying or neutering at five or six months of age no matter what the season or the breed. There are, of course, injections and pills that may postpone the whole cycle. Aside from the fact that they are but temporary aids, many veterinarians suggest that they cause undesirable side effects particularly when administered to pubescent queens.

There are many terms used to describe the receptive queen. Some say she's "in season"; others that she's "on heat"; or "she's calling" or "on call." Owners of orientals often say, "She's driving me crazy. I haven't slept for three nights." Indeed most oriental cats come on season more often and less subtly than other cats. They cry, they roll about, they rub against objects, people, and other animals. They present their receptive posteriors to all within their restricted world. If there is no response they will make every effort to escape to find a mate. There are thousands of slim and lithe black half-Siamese cats resulting from these efforts. It is said that orientals are always either on call, pregnant, nursing, or about to call. Many are of course less promiscuous. In cold weather, particularly, the oriental that lives a semi-outdoor existence may have relatively long periods of sexual quiescence.

At the other end of the sexual display range we have the other sorts of purebred cats—the longhaired and the domestic and the non-purebred cats. These cats are meant to be seasonally polyestrous and, given the correct weather, they will have several heat periods. If they are mated and become pregnant these periods stop.

The heat periods last three or four days if there is a male available and ten days or longer if there is not. The female usually accepts a male most readily during the last day or two of her heat. There is a two or three week period of comparative calm between heats.

As stated earlier the number of heats and the time of the year in which they occur depends on both the climate and the make up of the individual cat. In England, for example, some authorities say that spring and early fall are the usual prime time for cat breeding. Another authority says that in the northern United States few cats are in season between September and January. Obviously nature does not want kittens born in the depths of winter. One report on two hundred cats in an English laboratory states that most of the cats came on season many times during January and February, then again (but less frequently) in June and July. The average duration of heat was three days and the interval between heats about ten days. The average period of pregnancy was sixty-two days, and the average size of a litter was four.

To prove the perversity of felines, one family which owned a British Short-haired Blue queen noticed that she displayed signs of heat and was receptive to the tom for only four hours. As a result when she approached her time they penned him in an adjoining pen with an open passage to hers. Otherwise they would have had to keep a constant watch—and that in itself would have probably put her off. More than likely your female cat will not exhibit similar behavior.

THE MALE CAT—THE TOM

The tom cat, on the other hand, matures more slowly. At six or eight months of age he is still a kitten. He may have almost reached his full size, but in sexual matters he remains physically and mentally incapable. Although many males of that age may attempt to mount a queen or other object and may indeed go through the thrusting motions of the mating act, these are but adolescent imitations of the real thing.

If the owner wishes to prevent the tom from achieving sexual maturity, the veterinarian will advise castration between five and seven months of age. Although the operation is slightly easier and less traumatic at four or five months of age, many advocate delaying the operation until six or seven months of age. They suggest that the benefits of the male hormones during those crucial months may prevent urinary, skin, or other medical problems in later life.

The neutered male is quite happy to live for the pleasure and convenience of his owner. He may, if allowed, become incredibly overweight and lazy but the vast majority live healthy, active lives. The full tom gradually develops a life of his own. His head and shoulders develop the massive strength we

135

associate with males of many species. His tentative forays into the outside world become confident nightlong circuits as his sexual drives parallel his physical development.

Most full toms stake out their territory and vigorously reject intruders. They do this (among other means) by urinating along the outer borders of their home range. Few people would actually choose to live with this odor. As a result most full toms live completely feral lives, or they live in the outbuildings of farms, factories, or warehouses. Pedigree toms in the main are confined in kennels or areas of the home in which the owners do not eat or sleep.

It is not impossible to keep a full tom. Thousands of people do. But one must remember that queens and neuters can learn to share our mundane lives and largely to ignore the cries in the night. The full tom, though quite willing to be part of a human household, cannot. No creature that shares our lives is still so much a part of the wild.

MATING

The vast majority of cats reproduce without any help from human beings. The queen on season attracts males. In rural areas there may be only one available male. But in most places two, three, or even more males may be within her orbit. A tom can travel two or three nocturnal miles without pause. When they hear or smell a queen on heat they swoop down on her. They may have to cross a couple of main roads, climb a fire escape, and traverse a bridge, but they will find her. As the toms converge on the queen, they circle around her keeping an eye on each other and on the chance to mate. As one tom moves in another may attack him. These squabbles produce some of the sounds we hear in the night. During the melee the quickest or strongest tom darts in, mounts the ready queen, and with a quick thrust inseminates her. He rolls off immediately to protect himself either from her or from his fellow toms. As he dismounts another tom is ready to take his place. A queen may accept several toms during a session. She may have a kitten or two from each mating. This is called superfecundation. The whole affair including the preliminary infighting and intercourse with three or four toms can take as little as ten minutes if the queen takes fright and dashes off, or it can last the entire night. That is why some people at the appearance of a litter of kittens honestly have no idea when it could have happened.

The Stud

The essential difference between that sort of mating and scientific breeding is human selection of the partners in the latter. It is not left to chance or nature. Almost always the queen is taken to the stud. The stud is kept in his own room or kennel. Ideally this should be large enough so that he can easily escape the unsheathed claws of an unwilling queen. If the stud is to be kept permanently in his quarters (as many are), common sense and good husbandry dictate that those quarters should contain room for feeding, sleeping, and toilet areas as well as a large and, preferably, interesting run. Skillful stud owners bring the tom into the house for certain periods as well as spending a lot of time with the animal in its own quarters. Toms still benefit from human companionship.

Few toms are able to perform satisfactorily before they are about one year old. Experienced cat breeders usually do not try them until they are sixteen or eighteen months of age. But again this varies with individuals, with breeds, and with the weather. Many a seasoned tom at the height of his virility—between three and four years of age—may prefer his heated bed to a beckoning queen during a protracted cold spell.

These arranged matings involve an agreement between the owner of the stud cat and the owner of the queen. The preliminary step is for the queen's owner to check the tom's credentials. He should have many desirable features or have fathered many litters who have done well. Most experienced breeders will not try to economize by using an inferior or an unproven sire. He will contribute 50 percent of the kittens' characteristics, and there is no economy in rearing inferior kittens. Most queen owners agree that it is worthwhile to pay a bit more for the services of a proven and recognized sire.

Most owners of pedigree stud cats are conscientious people who will do their best to guide the amateur or first time breeder. However, it is common practice for them to suggest that, in lieu of a stud fee, they are willing to accept one (or sometimes two) kittens which they specify as "choice of litter." Such deals are usually best avoided, since the queen may have but one promising kitten.

Most stud owners will readily agree to a free return service should the first prove unfruitful. After a sterile return service to a proven sire the queen's owner must seriously consider whether the queen is at fault and seek veterinary advice. It is no longer the stud's problem; nor need the owner return the stud fee. In the case of unproven studs the owner may be more flexible.

The experienced stud owner will not accept a queen that is not healthy. The lack of a valid inoculation certificate for feline infectious enteritis indicates either profound negligence or parsimony. The queen will not be allowed on the premises. Any queen who sneezes or exhibits a discharge from the eyes or nose will not be admitted. Nor will one with any signs of diarrhea or skin infection. No stud fee can compensate for the misery and expense of disease. Some stud owners isolate an apparently healthy queen for a day or two as a precaution. Those same stud owners will be concerned about the temperament of the queen. A stud almost never injures a queen, but a queen in temper may cause terrible damage to the tom. Such incidents can be avoided by keeping a careful watch over the pair when they first meet.

Courtship and Mating

If the tom and queen have successfully mated before, the queen is usually put right in with the tom. But if the queen is a novice some breeders suggest putting her in an adjoining run for a few hours. When she shows some interest in the tom she is allowed to join him. The preliminary courtship is probably a kind of recognition ritual. He may croon and she may hiss or there may be a bit of mutual sniffing. Until he thinks he has been accepted he usually remains on the defensive and poised to leap away in case she turns nasty.

Copulation in the cat is initiated by the male firmly gripping the neck of the female with his teeth. As he does, the female automatically crouches in the receptive position. While mounted he may rub with his forepaws and the female may tread with hers. He may arch his back and begin pelvic thrusts before his penis emerges. It is then that the female swings her tail to one side to accommodate the male. The actual insertion, ejaculation, and separation takes less than ten seconds. The female may decide to take a swipe at the male, but he usually anticipates that by leaping away and diligently grooming himself. The female too may then groom herself. She may then begin to roll and rub her face against the walls of the enclosure or she may attempt to renew the tom's interest by pawing him. After a minute or so the whole procedure may be repeated. It is not uncommon for a half dozen insertions to occur in a short half hour. Some breeders suggest the process be repeated the following day to ensure a successful mating.

THE PREGNANT QUEEN

The queen is then taken back to her home and resumes her normal life. There are few obvious changes during pregnancy. A maiden queen will show enlarged, possibly pinkish nipples at about twenty-one days. At that stage it is much easier for the veterinarian to diagnose pregnancy. The developing kittens may feel like small ping pong balls to the experienced hand. Later they tend to merge and only the enlarged horns of the uterus can be felt. If the queen comes on season again, the mating was apparently not successful. Either way it is wise to arrange a veterinary examination about three weeks from the time of mating. The veterinarian may advise a slight change in the diet—usually additional calcium rich foods or bonemeal—and will check for parasites both external and internal.

Basically the queen will carry on as usual until about the eighth week of pregnancy. She might eat a bit more or be more interested in grass or unusual foods. She might slow down a bit and take more than her usual interest in warm corners of the home. During the final days, however, she will appear appreciably larger, slower, and more deliberate. Some queens become secretive; others unusually aggressive. Some go through rather elaborate nest-making rituals; most

Bottom. *A mother licks its newborn kitten. Most females can cope with birth without any human assistance, but some prefer company.* Top. *The mother will allow newborn kittens to suckle within minutes of birth. This first milk (colostrum) is vital in building up the kittens' resistance to disease.*

simply familiarize themselves with secluded areas.

The owner should offer three meals rather than the usual breakfast and dinner.

Children and dogs may be admonished to avoid the awkward creature. Most importantly the queen should be confined to the well-prepared area in which she is to have her kittens as the final hours approach.

THE BIRTH

An ideal kittening area is one which is free of hazards such as gas fires, unprotected electric cords, water receptacles, open toilets, open windows, chemicals, sprays, and heavy potted plants, but has adequate circulation and insulation from the elements. Some people still use infrared bulbs suspended from the ceiling for supplementary heat. Low wattage insulated electric blankets are less expensive, more efficient and, if properly protected, completely safe. They also have the advantage of not interfering with life's normal rhythms, and many are made of easily washable materials.

None of this need be expensive or elaborate. Many professionals place the heating unit and blanket in a cardboard box. When the kittens are old enough to scramble over the sides, it may need replacing. Needless to say in hot climates or during a hot summer an extractor fan or an air conditioning unit may have to be substituted for the heater. In temperate areas environmental control can be left to nature.

Few cats have difficulty giving birth. The vast majority of kittens emerge easily from the contracting uterus of the queen. Some authorities state that about half of all kittens come out backwards. Although there are few published tabulations, many owners agree that most kittens are born in the early hours of the morning.

If an owner finds the situation too nerve-racking, it may be better to hospitalize the cat during the period. Another indication for veterinary attention is unproductive straining of more than twenty minutes' duration. Quite obviously if the queen is going through the contractions of labor without results there must be some sort of problem. If you move the queen to the veterinary hospital, remember to confine her in a securely closed basket; otherwise in panic she will leap out and hide. She is following her instinct for solitude and security so necessary for the survival of the litter in the wild.

There are two further notes of caution. First, although many cats do give birth at exactly nine weeks it is not at all unusual for kittens to be early or late. Healthy kittens have been born at anything from fifty-seven to seventy-five days. The condition of the cat indicates more than the calendar. If there is any deterioration in condition or if she gets grotesquely large, a veterinary examination is advisable. Secondly, many cats will deliver four or five kittens and then after an interval of twenty-four or more hours deliver another lot. Usually all seem to thrive.

CARE AFTER BIRTH

Some novice breeders panic when a queen produces more than six kittens because some authorities suggest that she should not be allowed to rear more than four. There is no need for an early decision. Certainly during the first week or ten days even a very large

A mother will care for its kittens in the first few weeks without human help. When she is ready, the kittens will be allowed to become part of the human family.

litter will not place undue strain on a maiden queen. Quite often novice breeders will indiscriminately cull a large litter only to watch one or two of the selected four fail to develop well. It is wiser in those early days to leave culling to the mother cat and to nature.

In large, commercially run catteries where three or four queens give birth at about the same time, some kittens from large litters are put in with queens who have produced less than four. Four or five seems to be a universally acceptable litter.

Until about the third week the queen seems able to cope without much help. In fact some very successful breeders suggest that until the kittens display curiosity and exploratory behavior they simply do not handle them. Of course, some require handling and examination earlier; others are best left alone. Each queen and each litter are different.

Feral cats and wildcats may begin to eat meat before their eyes are open. Most breeders, however, do not offer solids to the kittens before they are three or four weeks of age. Many do not realize that the kittens are ready for solids until they actually see the kittens eating from the mother's bowl.

Suffice it to say that between three and five weeks of age kittens rapidly develop. They almost double in weight. They develop their own personalities. They learn to play as a preparation for survival. But they are not ready to leave the mother. Although they become increasingly dependent on the food

people provide and less dependent on the mother's milk, they still need her as a teacher and as a guide.

They should be allowed to stay with her until eight or even ten weeks of age. Toilet training, hunting, enemy recognition, social behavior, and grooming are some of the lessons the conscientious queen includes in her curriculum.

Ideally the kittens—if they are destined for lives in a human household—should be reared with people. No amount of pampering at a later stage can compensate for a period of early isolation.

Within a couple of months the kittens rapidly assume adult characteristics and imperceptibly achieve feline maturity.

Cat Breeds

New permutations of shape, color, and length of coat are continually being developed by breeders. The breeds given below are recognized by the main cat associations or, in some cases, are of particular interest as a breed development. If you want to enter your cat in a show, you should check on the standards required by the organizing body, for they differ from one organization to another and are frequently revised. (See **Exhibiting and Showing**.)

SHORT-HAIRED CATS

The wildcats from which the domestic cat developed and the cats of ancient Egypt and of Europe all had short hair. It was the short-haired cat which was taken to North America

by the early settlers from the Old World. The striped coat of the tabby is one of the most common among cats and its similarity to that of the European Wild Cat and to that of striped cats portrayed in Egyptian paintings, Roman mosaics, and medieval illuminations suggest that this was indeed the basic type.

Short-haired cats fall into two main groups: the svelte Foreign Short-hair and the Short-haired cat of Europe known variously as the British Short-hair or, in the United States and Canada, as the Domestic or American Short-hair.

Foreign short-haired cats are cats with slim bodies, long tails, and slender legs giving them an overall elegant and sophisticated appearance. (The description *foreign* has nothing to do with their origin.) They usually have large pricked ears and slanting eyes. They generally do not like a solitary life and need companionship of humans or other cats. They tend to mature earlier than other cats.

Sexing kittens. The male (right) *has more space between genitals and anus than the female* (left).

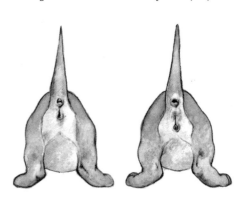

138

Some foreign cats, especially Siamese, Burmese, and Russian Blue, are particularly susceptible to panleucopenia. They should be inoculated against the disease as early as possible and receive regular boosters.

Separate development has led to differences between the American and British types, but they are minor compared to their similarities. In the **American Short-haired Cat,** for instance, the ears should be smaller at the base than in the European, and the muzzle should present a slightly more square aspect. But both types should have a broad head with well-rounded contours with the nose and face medium-short in the American, and short in the British. The cheeks, especially in stud toms, should be well developed and the small ears should be rounded at the tips. Eyes should be large and round and set well apart to show the width of the nose.

British or American Short-hairs are sturdy, well-boned cats. The body should be deep and full in the chest, the tail thick at the base and tapering slightly to the tip, and the short legs should be strong, muscular, and in proportion to the body with well-rounded feet. The coat is short, fine and close.

In Great Britain the coat may be white, black, blue, bicolored, cream, blue cream, silver tabby, red tabby, brown tabby, spotted, tortoiseshell, or tortoiseshell and white. In the United States black smoke, blue smoke, chinchilla, shaded silver, and blue and cream tabbys are also recognized.

Abyssinian

Although the Abyssinian has a reputation for intolerance, it behaves very well with friends. Abyssinians are intelligent and affectionate but do not like to be restricted to small areas. They like plenty of attention and involvement in the life of the household. Litters arc often small, and Abyssinians are extremely difficult to obtain.

Many owners like to believe that the Abyssinian is a direct descendant of the cats of the pharaohs. The present day Abyssinian

Red Abyssinian

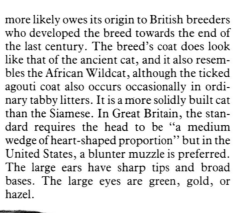
American Wirehair

American Shorthair

more likely owes its origin to British breeders who developed the breed towards the end of the last century. The breed's coat does look like that of the ancient cat, and it also resembles the African Wildcat, although the ticked agouti coat also occurs occasionally in ordinary tabby litters. It is a more solidly built cat than the Siamese. In Great Britain, the standard requires the head to be "a medium wedge of heart-shaped proportion" but in the United States, a blunter muzzle is preferred. The large ears have sharp tips and broad bases. The large eyes are green, gold, or hazel.

Each hair of the coat has two or three distinct bands of black or dark brown on the ground color which gives the distinctive agouti look. There should be no stripes or bars in the coat. The underside of the body and inside of the forelegs are a lighter shade, orange-brown, or deep apricot according to the main color. Although undesirable, a white chin is not a fault. A light area around the chin and mouth and around the eyes, which are rimmed in black, together with markings on the forehead gives an attractive puma-like appearance to many cats. Kittens often show heavy markings which fade as they grow. The characteristic coat does not usually develop until they are eight or ten weeks old. The **Ruddy-coated Abyssinian** (known simply as the Abyssinian in Great Britain) has a reddish brown ground color. The nose leather is red with a black outline, and paw pads are black. The back of the hind legs should be black. The **Red-coated Abyssinian** has a rich copper ground color. The nose and pads are pink. The back of the hind legs should be brown.

American Wirehair

This breed is the result of a chance mutation which produced a kitten with very coarse and wiry fur. The only difference between this breed and the American Domestic

Brown Burmese

Egyptian Mau

Japanese Bobtail

cat is that the coat should be of medium length, consisting of stiff, wiry hair on the head, back, sides, and hips and along the top of the tail. The coat should become less coarse on the underside of the body and on the chin.

Bombay
The result of crossing a Burmese with an American Short-hair, the Bombay is a medium-sized muscular cat with a rounded head and medium-sized ears. The eyes are yellow to deep copper in color, and the coat is a lustrous black.

Burmese Breeds
Although known in a wide variety of colors, not all of them are officially recognized as breeds. This is another cat whose name does not necessarily have any connection with its origin: the first American cat was imported from India. This particular animal proved to be a hybrid Siamese and was itself mated back to Siamese. Matings between its hybrid kittens produced dark-coated cats. However, the Burmese should not be dark-coated Siamese (although at one time the introduction of so much Siamese blood did produce this result) but a distinct type of its own with no suggestion, as the British standard puts it, "of either the Siamese type, or the cobbiness of a British cat." The chest should be rounded, the tail taper only slightly to a rounded tip, and the head should be slightly rounded on top with wide cheek bones tapering to a short blunt wedge. The ears are broad at the base and have slightly rounded tips. The eyes have an oriental slant at the top and a rounded lower line. They should be an intense yellow, the more golden-colored the better.

The **Brown Burmese,** known in France as the **Zibeline,** was the first of the type to be produced and is recognized by all European and American bodies. The body color should be a warm seal-brown shading to almost imperceptibly lighter coloring on the other parts. A slightly darker mask and ears are

permitted, but there should be no other markings nor white patches.

The **Blue Burmese,** recognized by many associations, has a soft silver gray coat only slightly darker on the back and tail. There is a distinct sheen on rounded areas like the ears, face, and feet. Pads and nose leather are gray.

The **Champagne,** or **Chocolate Burmese,** should be an overall warm milk chocolate color with chocolate nose leather and pink shading to chocolate pads.

The **Platinum Burmese,** known in Great Britain as the **Lilac Burmese,** is not recognised by many of the American associations. It has a delicate dove gray coat to which a pinkish tinge gives a slightly faded effect. Nose leather and pads are lavender pink (shell-pink in kittens).

In Great Britain a number of other color varieties are also recognized: **Red,** with light tangerine fur and pink leather; **Tortoiseshell, Cream, Chocolate Tortie,** and **Lilac Tortie (Lilac Cream).** Leather in the Tortoiseshell and in the Torties can be plain or blotched; in the Cream it should be pink.

Egyptian Mau
This breed began as an attempt by breeders

to reproduce the cat shown in the paintings and sculptures of ancient Egypt. The American strain was developed from cats imported from Cairo, but the English variety originated in tabbies of foreign type which occurred in the breeding of Tabby Point Siamese. This attractive spotted cat is recognized in **Silver** (sloe black markings on a silver ground) and **Bronze** (dark brown on a light bronze ground) by a number of American associations and is approaching recognition in several tabby colors in Great Britain, where mackerel tabby markings are also allowed. The British cat must also have a mark on the forehead patterned like a scarab beetle. The eyes can be green, yellow, or hazel.

Exotic Short-hairs
This is a recently developed American breed in which the body type of the Persian cat has been given a short coat. All the Persian colors and patterns are acceptable except for the Peke-faced Red.

Japanese Bobtail
This is an oriental cat geographically since it comes from Japan where it has been known for centuries. The Japanese Bobtail conforms

to neither foreign nor domestic body type but has a sturdily built, well-muscled physique while maintaining a comparatively slender look. The most distinctive feature is the short tail of 10cm. (4in.), which is carried curved so that it looks only about 5cm. (2in.) long. The hair of the tail grows in all directions giving the effect of a rabbit's bobtail, an appearance which is increased by the breed's long back legs. When the cat is relaxed, however, the back legs are usually kept bent. The coat is traditionally tricolored, but a wide variety of colors and patterns are accepted including solid, bicolored, and tortoiseshell. Siamese points and unpatterned agouti are not acceptable. This breed is claimed to shed its coat less than other types.

Korat

Originating in Thailand, this breed has been known for centuries in its native land as the Si-Sawat. Its silver-blue coat is exceptionally soft and close to the body. The leather is dark blue or lavender although the paw pads may have a pinkish tinge. The face is more heart shaped than in other orientals, and the tail is thicker at the base, of medium length, and tapers to a rounded tip. The ears are also slightly rounded, and the eyes are amber in color turning to green-gold as the cat grows older. Korats can be a little nervous, especially of sudden noises and disturbance and may be intolerant of cats outside their own family.

MANX CATS

The Manx is principally recognized as the cat without a tail. The Manx has a similar conformation to other Short-hairs but its head is larger, with a longer nose and chubby cheeks, and it lacks the snubby look of the Persian type. Its back is relatively short and its hindquarters very high with a deep flank, which gives it a characteristic bobbing gait. The long hind legs give it a powerful spring and make it a faster cat than most. A true Manx has no vestige of a tail, and it should be possible to feel a depression at the end of the backbone. But Manx do not always breed true, for kittens with tails and stumps (shortened tails) may appear in a Manx litter. Some Manx have a small tuft of fur on the rump. This is acceptable if it contains no cartilage or bone. Manx may be any color or pattern, but their eye color should conform to that laid down for the color of the coat.

Unfortunately the mutation which causes the Manx not to have a tail affects the entire vertebral column. Although the reduction of the length and number of vertebrae is usually concentrated at the rear, vertebrae may be missing from other regions causing malformation. As the malformation increases so does the risk of infant mortality and Manx bred to Manx through several successive generations may produce dead kittens. A malfunction of the sphincter muscles is sometimes associated with the malformation of the Manx and would obviously rule out such a kitten as a domestic pet. A stumpy (cat

Manx

Bicolored Shorthair

with a shortened tail) will be assured of a normal life and the introduction of non-Manx blood will prevent the concentration of the lethal factor.

Mixed color breeds

The **Blue Cream Short-hair** is recognized on both sides of the Atlantic, but standards for this comparatively rare breed are contradictory. While the British standard requires that the two colors should be "softly mingled, not patched" and a cream blaze on the forehead is favored by breeders, the American requirement is a clearly patched coat. Eyes may be copper, orange, or yellow but should not be green.

Bicolored (Parti-colored) Short-hairs are, in Great Britain, restricted to cats with a pattern of any of the solid colors and white distributed in even patches with not more than two-thirds of the coat colored and not more than one-half the coat white. In America, the colored part of the coat can also consist of mixed colors such as Blue-Cream or Silver Tabby. The face should be patched with color, and a white blaze is admired. Eyes may be deep orange, copper, or yellow but should not show any trace of green.

Tortoiseshell Short-hairs should be evenly patched with black, deep red and light red. Some American standards specify cream

Tortoiseshell Shorthair

141

Cornish Rex and head of Devon Rex

Seal Point Siamese

instead of light red. There should be no trace of white hairs, tabby markings, or brindling. Legs, feet, tail, and ears should be as well patched as the body and head. A red blaze running down the forehead to the nose is desirable and, in the United States, some standards require that the nose carry a different color on each side. The eyes should be deep orange or copper. In Great Britain, hazel eyes are also permitted.

Calico, or **Tortoiseshell** and **White Short-hairs** have the tricolor patching handsomely set off against white legs, throat, and belly, but cats with a predominance of white would not reach show standard. A white blaze is desirable. Eyes should be orange or copper, or hazel in Great Britain.

Ocicat

This is an American breed, developed by crossing a Chocolate Point Siamese with a half-Siamese, half-Abyssinian cat. The Ocicat still awaits full recognition as a show cat. A dark chestnut and a light chestnut variety have been produced and both have a spotted coat with tabby markings on the throat, legs, and tail. The eyes are gold colored.

Rex Breeds

These cats have an unusual kind of fur which has also appeared as a mutant form of coat in other animals. Instead of being made up of guard hairs, awn hairs, awned down hairs, and down hairs—the four kinds which constitute the usual feline coat—the Rex fur consists of only down hairs or a combination of awned down hairs and down hairs in the case of the German Rex. The result is a curly coat only about half the length of that of normal short-hairs and about two-thirds its thickness. Whiskers and eyebrows are also affected. They are of good length but are crinkled.

The **German Rex** was the first mutation to be recorded, and the strain can be traced to a female born in East Berlin before 1946 from

which a planned breeding program produced curly-coated cats.

The **Cornish Rex** first appeared in the litter of a Cornish farm cat in 1950. It seems to be the same mutation as the German Rex, since German and Cornish Rex have been successfully crossbred. The Cornish Rex has a medium wedge head which narrows to a strong chin, and the ears are large and conical, taller than they are wide, with a modified point at the tip. In Great Britain, the ears should be well covered by fur but in the United States, the standard mentions that the adult's ears should be naked on the outer surface. All coat colors are acceptable, and white markings must be symmetrical (except in tortoiseshell and white). Eye color should match the coat color.

The **Devon Rex,** although having a similar coat, is genetically different from the Cornish Rex. When the first Devon Rex was mated to a Cornish Rex female, only plain coated kittens resulted. The Devon Rex has a broader chest than the Cornish Rex, full cheeks, and particularly large eyes. Most coat colors are acceptable although white markings are considered a fault, and the oval eyes should be of a color to match.

The **Si-Rex** has, as the name suggests, Siamese points combined with the Rex curly coat. The eyes are chartreuse, green, or yellow in color.

An American form of the Rex mutation appeared in Oregon in 1959, but no pure American strain was developed. Some American organizations recognize only one type of Rex and sometimes the types are grouped together with the Cornish, German, and American type known as Gene I and the Devon type as Gene II.

Russian Blue

Previously known as the Foreign Blue or the Archangel this cat may have been taken to

Great Britain in the time of Elizabeth I. However, the type can appear as a natural mutation and blue cats have also been dubbed Maltese. It did not appear in the United States until after World War II by which time British and Scandinavian breeders had introduced the Siamese there. In 1950, the Foreign Blue standard required a full Siamese type, but there has now been a return to the earlier form, and a much shorter nose than in the Siamese is required. The coat is especially soft and silky with a silver tipping to each hair. This silvery effect is more noticeable in winter. The color on any one cat must be even throughout, but the breed colors may range from medium to a dark shade of blue. In summer, strong sunshine sometimes produces a brownish tint. Whisker pads are prominent and the ears, which have few hairs inside them compared with most cats, have exceptionally thin skin so that they are nearly transparent.

Russian Blues are usually very gentle cats with quiet voices. They can be extremely shy but become very attached to their owners. Queens do not call very loudly when in heat, and owners should watch an unspayed female's behavior for indication of when she is in season.

Scottish Fold

This breed resulted from a mutation which appeared in Scotland in 1961. They are the same as British Short-haired cats except that the ears are folded forward and downward in the adult cat. Although recognized by the Cat Fanciers Association in the United States in 1974, there is strong prejudice against this development in other organizations.

Shaded Coat Breeds

Breeds with shaded coats are not recognized in Great Britain. **Black Smoke** and **Blue Smoke Short-hairs** are recognized in the United States and provisional standards exist

142

on the Continent. They have white or very pale undercoats with appropriate dark tippings and deep copper or orange eyes. The **Chinchilla Short-hair** is recognized only in the United States. The Chinchilla has a silver coat tipped with black. Eyes are blue-green.

The **Shaded Silver Short-hair,** which is also recognized only in the United States, has a silver coat tipped with black which shades from dark on the back to silvery white on the chest, belly and chin and under the tail, while the feet and face are dark. Eyes are blue-green.

Siamese Breeds

This breed has been known in Thailand for centuries, although there is no evidence that this is where they developed first. The Thais often call them Chinese cats. Siamese are particularly susceptible to panleucopenia, and an inoculation program should be started early and continued with care. Some of this breed may have difficulty digesting milk and refuse it after the kitten stage. They tend to be sexually mature at an earlier age than other breeds.

At one time, crossed eyes and a kinked tail were characteristics of the breed. Both are now considered faults. The darker coloring of the Siamese is limited to certain areas: the face, where it spreads out from the nose and eyes over the cheeks and chin (the whole area is known as the mask), the ears (which are linked to the mask by delicate dark lines), the tail, feet, and legs. All these areas are known as the points. There is usually a darker shading on the shoulders and rump which becomes more noticeable as the cat gets older. There should be no dark color on the belly

and the chest should be very pale if the cat is to achieve show standard.

The body is long and svelte, the legs slim, and the feet oval. The tail is long, thin, and tapering. The head is long with narrowing straight lines to a fine muzzle and a strong chin. The ears are rather large and pricked, wide at the base and pointed at the tip. The eyes are almond shaped and slanting. All Siamese cats, whatever their color, have deep blue eyes.

The **Seal Point** was the first Siamese coloring to be recognized and is genetically a dilute form of black, not brown. The points should be a deep seal-brown and the pads and nose leather should be the same color as the points. The body color is cream shading to a pale fawn on the back.

The **Blue Point** should have a body of glacial white shading into a light blue with points in a darker, cold blue. The Seal and the Blue Point were the traditional colors for the Siamese, but since World War II a number of others have been developed.

The **Chocolate Point** is ivory coated with mask and points in a warm milk-chocolate color. The **Frost Point,** also known as the **Lilac Point** in Great Britain, has an off-white (magnolia) coat with a frost-gray mask and points which have a pinkish tinge.

The **Lynx Point,** known as a **Tabby Point** in Great Britain, has a body free of markings but a tabby pattern on the mask and points. Some American groups do not recognize this breed as a type of Siamese but call them **Tabby Colorpoint Short-hairs.** The mask has clear tabby stripes with dark rims to the eyes and black-spotted whisker pads. The

legs have broken horizontal stripes with the back of the hind legs solid color and the back of the front legs body color. The tail is ringed with a solid tip. The ears are dark with a light "thumbmark" on the back. All Siamese colors are permissible, and nose leather and pads should match those of the Siamese colors already mentioned.

Red and **Tortoiseshell Point Siamese** are also recognized in Great Britain, and they are known in the United States as **Colorpoint Short-hairs** since they are not recognized as true Siamese. A **Cream Point** has also been bred although it does not have breed status yet.

The **Albino Siamese** is recognized in the United States by only some associations. Its coat shows no pigmentation, and it has the pink skin and pinkish eyes usually found in albinos.

Solid color oriental: Breeds

There are several breeds which are developments of the Siamese type. The **Foreign White** recognized in Great Britain is not an Albino but a genuine White in which the genetic factors which restrict Siamese color to the points are so overriding that there is no trace of color in the coat at all. There were difficulties in the early development of this breed and, although the strains concerned were discontinued, many people feel that these cats have an inherent weakness to a number of diseases.

The **Havana,** or **Havana Brown** as it is variously known, is a Chocolate Siamese in which the dilution factor does not operate. In the United States, breeders have clearly separated it from the basic Siamese originals and require a less foreign type and may even penalize a Siamese head. The eyes should be a definite green. Some authorities claim that the Havana Brown does not suffer from the digestive difficulties caused by milk that afflict many Siamese, but that it is susceptible to cold and damp.

Blue Point Siamese

Havana

Chocolate Point Siamese

143

Black Shorthair

British Blue

The **Foreign Lavender,** known in Great Britain as the **Foreign Lilac,** is a self-colored cat of Siamese type produced when both parents carry genes for blue and chocolate. It is recognized by some groups only in the United States. The eyes are rich green and the paw pads pink.

The **Tonkinese** is recognized by one American organization, but has not been given breed status. It was produced by crossing a Siamese with a Burmese cat.

Solid or Self Color Breeds

Solid or self color breed are recognized in Black, White, Blue, and Cream and, in the United States, in Red. A pure white coat, with no sign of creaminess or colored hairs or, alternatively, a pure black coat with no white hairs nor a brownish tinge known as rustiness are not easy to achieve. Both Black and White Short-hairs require attention to keep coats in good condition for greasiness will soon produce stains and discoloration. In cat terminology, blue means a bluish gray and is genetically a dilute of black. The **Black Short-hair** must have a coat that is jet black to the roots. Sunbathing will give the Black Short-hair a rusty tinge; kittens with faint tabby stripes and a degree of rustiness may not lose these until they are fully adult. Most black cats are sleek-bodied animals with green eyes but the pedigree Black Short-hair standard requires a cobby body (the usual requirement for all short-hairs) and deep copper or orange eyes with no trace of green.

The **White Short-hair** is divided into three varieties according to eye color which may be blue, orange, or odd-eyed, that is, with one blue and one orange eye. Blue-eyed Whites are almost always deaf, a disability which is color-linked, and this, together with the conspicuous white coat, would hinder its survival under natural conditions. The popularity of white cats as pets, however, guarantees their continuance. Since all kittens start life with blue eyes, it is impossible to tell which variety of white a very young kitten will become; but if it has even the slightest smudge of dark hair (usually on the head between the ears), it carries a gene for black or blue and will not grow up deaf even though the dark patch may fade and the eyes remain blue.

The **Blue Short-hair** breed varies according to the American and British standard. A wide variety of blue cats used to be known as Maltese Cats, and at one time Blue Short-hairs were shown under this name in the United States although it is no longer used for a recognized breed. The **American Blue** follows the type of other American Short-hairs, but the **European** or **British Blue** has a plusher coat, a broader head, and more developed cheeks than other short-hair colors.

The **Exotic Short-hair** is the American breed which most closely resembles the British Blue in conformation, although it is recognized in the full range of short-hair colors. At one time the British Blue was not so massive and was clearly distinguished from the French breed, known as the **Chartreux.** Although the French standard allows a coat of any shade of gray or grayish blue, in Great Britain it should be from light to medium blue. Most judges now consider the two types almost identical. Eyes are copper, orange, or yellow. The Blue Short-hair has a reputation for gentleness, placidity, and intelligence.

The **Red Short-hair** is recognized as a breed in the United States but not in Europe. This breed frequently shows heavy tabby markings. The eyes are copper or orange in color.

The **Cream Short-hair** is, however, recog-

Spotted Shorthair

Brown Tabby Shorthair

nized on both sides of the Atlantic, the dilution of red having also reduced the strength of the tabby pattern which may still reappear in very hot or cold weather. The eyes should be copper or orange in color.

The Spotted Cat

The show cat must have a distinct pattern, but this does not have to consist entirely of circular spots. Markings can be round, oblong, or rosette shaped provided they do not give the impression of broken stripes. They may be any color, and eyes should conform to the color laid down for other short-hairs with the same principal coat color.

Short-haired Tabbies

The name *tabby* derives from the similarity of the pattern of the coat to that of watered silk or tafetta which was originally made in the district of Attibiya in Baghdad and known as tabby.

The basic tabby marking was a striped coat like that of the wildcat, but in many parts of the world a blotched pattern is now more common. The blotched pattern is a mutation of the striped coat which was already common in Europe by the mid-seventeenth century. In this mutation, now considered the standard tabby pattern in Europe and the United States, there should be three dark stripes running down the spine, a butterfly pattern across the shoulders, an oyster-shaped whorl on the flanks, and two unbroken narrow lines, known in Great Britain as the "Mayoral chains", on the chest. The legs and tail should be regularly ringed, the face should carry delicate pencilings running down to the base of the nose, and the cheeks should be crossed by two or three distinct swirls. A well-marked tabby will usually also have a clearly defined pair of "spectacles" around the eyes and an M-shaped mark on the forehead.

The striped tabby, now usually known as the Mackerel tabby, should have distinct narrow rings running around the body, legs, and tail. The stripes may sometimes be broken but should not break up into spots. Clear rings running from the spine to the belly are preferred. Cats with this pattern of clear, narrow, closely-spaced stripes are now comparatively rare in the West, the more common being the blotched form. There is no

Standard Tabby Pattern

Mackerel Tabby Pattern

indication that breeders or owners prefer blotched tabbies so it is difficult to understand why this mutation has proved so persistent.

It is rare for variants other than broken forms of the blotched and striped patterns to occur naturally, although the ticked or agouti

coat of the Abyssinian cat is genetically a form of tabby marking. A careful selection of tabbies with variant markings has led to the development of both the Egyptian Mau and the Spotted Cat breeds. The tabby marking persists in many other created breeds and shows in the first kitten coat, while parts of the tabby pattern have been retained in breeds such as the Lynx or Tabby Point Siamese.

Short-haired Tabbies may be Brown, Red, or Silver and, in the American Short-hair, Blue and Cream are also recognized.

The **Brown Tabby** is one of the oldest established breeds and although nonpedigree cats of this type are common, it is comparatively rare as a pedigree cat. This may be partly because pedigree pet owners look for something more unusual but it is also difficult to breed a cat of really good type and color. Distinctive markings without any brindling or smudging are not easy to develop and white patches, especially on the chin and lips, can be persistent. The markings, whether blotched or striped, should be a dense black and quite distinct from the sable or rich brown ground color. The eyes may be orange, hazel, deep yellow, or green.

The **Red Tabby,** with hazel or orange eyes, should be a rich orange-red with markings in a darker red—not the ginger or sandy

Silver Tabby Shorthair

145

color of the frequently seen "marmalade" cat.

The **Silver Tabby** should have a uniform ground color of pure silver with dense black markings. Eyes are green or hazel. Many owners claim that this beautiful cat is extraordinarily affectionate, and it has a reputation for being gentle and shy. Both Red and Silver Tabby kittens with good markings sometimes lose them during their first few weeks but regain both color and markings as they mature.

LONG-HAIRED CATS

There are no truly long-haired cats among the wild members of the cat family. The Northern Lynx and the Show Leopard have longer coats than the cats of warmer lands, but they are protected from the cold by thicker, rather than longer, fur and have a particularly thick undercoat. Long hair in the domestic cat seems to have developed from a mutant type whose preservation was made possible through domestication since a long coat would be a handicap to a wildcat. The breeds known today as long-hairs originated in Turkey and Iran. They were not seen in Europe until the end of the sixteenth century and were not properly established until 300 years later. The names Angora and Persian have both been used to indicate long-haired types, but they now refer to two different kinds of cats.

In the United States, Persian is officially used to describe all long-hairs except the Angora, Balinese, Birman, Himalayan, Maine Coon, and Turkish cats and a few recently created breeds. In Great Britain, the group is now officially known as Long-haired Cats, but the name *Persian* is still popularly used.

Angora

This was probably the first long-haired cat to be seen in Europe, and the name was originally used for all long-hairs. The Angora, which gets its name from Ankara, Turkey,

has a longer body and tail than the Persian, and its head is smaller with upright ears. The Angora was in danger of becoming extinct until the Ankara Zoo began a carefully controlled breeding program to ensure its survival. In 1963, the governor of Ankara gave permission for a pair to be taken to the United States and from this and a subsequent pair, the breed has been reestablished. It is not yet recognized in Great Britain. Only white cats are recognized in the United States, but there is no reason why other colors should not appear.

Balinese Breeds

These cats are a Siamese mutant with a long coat. They are the reverse pattern of the Himalayan. In everything except fur length it follows the Siamese type and has been recognized in **Seal, Blue, Chocolate,** and **Lilac (Frost) Point** colors. All should have vivid blue eyes.

Birman Breeds

First recognized in France, Birmans have a longer body than the Persian group and a rather long tail. The head is round and wide with full cheeks. The silky coat is creamy gold, slightly curled on the belly, and has a good ruff. Mask, tail, and paws are seal brown, and each paw is tipped with white like a glove which extends up the back of the hock on the rear legs. Eyes are blue. Nose leather should also be seal but the paw pads are pink. Birmans in **Seal Point, Blue Point,** and **Chocolate Point** have been recognized.

Himalayan (Colorpoint) Breeds

These are Persian cats with a Siamese coat pattern, although it does *not* have an oriental conformation. **Seal, Blue, Chocolate, Lilac (Frost), Red,** and **Tortie-Point** are recognized. A **Cream-Point** has been produced but has not yet received recognition. All have blue eyes.

Maine Coon

As the name suggests, these cats were once thought to be the result of matings between racoons and the domestic cats of the early

American settlers. There is however no truth in this belief since such a coupling is not possible. Maine Coons probably originated from crosses between American domestic cats and Angoras or other long-hairs brought from the East by New England sailors. Often seen in the eastern states until about fifty years ago, interest in the breed waned until it was revived in the 1950s by the Central Maine Cat Club. Maine cats have the small head and long-bodied, long-legged, and muscular look of the Angora with large ears and slightly slanting eyes. The fur is not as long as in the Persian, and the ruff is not as full. The coat is long on the stomach and haunches, where it forms a heavy pair of breeches. The Maine Coon's coat is easier to keep in condition than that of most other long-hairs and may be any color or pattern. Eyes should be green or in accordance with the coat color.

Peke-faced cat

This breed is not recognized in Great Britain. It was developed from the Red Self and Red Tabby Persian and may be of either type. It has a face resembling that of the Pekingese dog. The high forehead bulges over the nose to form a sharp stop and the nose is so short that in profile it is hidden by the cheeks. The muzzle is wrinkled and a fold of skin runs down from the inner corner of the eye to the outer corner of the mouth. Breeding for this extreme appearance has brought criticism from veterinarians. Emphasis on the short nose can lead to breathing difficulties, and the teeth do not always meet correctly. The fold of skin beneath the eyes can cause blocking of the tear ducts. Breeders must be careful not to perpetuate deformities with this breed.

Persian Cats

All the Persian breeds have cobby bodies set upon short, thick legs. The head is round and broad with full cheeks, a short, almost snub nose, and a distinct break known as a stop between the nose and skull. The ears are

Chocolate Point Balinese

Maine Coon Cat

146

Red Self Longhair

Smoke Longhair

small, neat, and spaced well apart, and the eyes round and large. The coat is long and silky, with no woolliness and the tail short and thick with a greater bush of hair at the tip than at the root. The head should be framed by a ruff of longer hair (on show cats brushed up and away from the body and neck to make it more noticeable) which continues as a deep frill between the front legs. There are long tufts of hair on the ears.

Persian cats have been bred in a wide range of colors, not all of which have been universally recognized as breeds. North American associations tend to prefer a more extreme type of Persian.

Solid or Self-colored Persian Breeds

These are recognized in **Black** (deep copper or orange eyes), **Blue** (copper eyes) and **White**. Blue eyed, orange eyed, and odd eyed Whites are all accepted as separate breeds but blue eyed Whites are almost always deaf. **Brown** and **Lilac** Persians have been bred but are not yet recognized.

Mixed-color Persian Breeds

Bicolored (Parti-colored) cats with orange eyes are recognized in Great Britain in any solid color and white but are not yet accepted by all the American groups. Tricolor cats of

black, red, and cream broken into patches are known as **Tortoiseshells** and have deep orange eyes. They are almost always female.

Tortoiseshell and **White Persians,** also known as Calico cats, have orange or copper eyes but the required patterning of the coat varies according to the cat association. In Great Britain the pattern should be black, red, and cream interspersed with white and well distributed. Various American associations require white with black and red patches, with white predominant on the underparts. There should be black, red, and cream patches on the head, back, sides, and tail. The underside and half the body should be white as though dropped into a pail of milk—the milk "should have splashed up the nose and halfway around the neck." **Blue Tortoiseshells** and **Whites** have also been bred but are not recognized.

Shaded-Coat Persian Breeds

The **Chinchilla** has a pure white undercoat with the hairs of the back, flanks, head, ears, and tail tipped with black giving a sparkling silver appearance. The legs can be slightly shaded but chin, ear tufts, stomach, and chest are pure white. The nose tip is brick red, but the paw pads and the visible skin

around the eyes is black, giving a ringed effect around the emerald or blue-green eyes.

The **Shaded Silver** has a pewter look compared with the silver color of the Chinchilla. It is not recognized in Great Britain because of the difficulty of distinguishing between the two types. A **Masked Silver,** identical to the Chinchilla except that the face is masked in a very dark color and the paws are dark, is recognized by some associations.

The **Cameo** cat, created in the United States, has an ivory-white undercoat which in the **Shell Cameo** is tipped with red (a more dilute cream is accepted in Great Britain). It has rose-colored leather and eye rims and copper eyes. A slightly darker version is known as the **Shaded Cameo** and darker still is the **Smoke Cameo,** also known as the **Red Smoke.** Tabby markings are a fault in these breeds, but some associations recognize a **Tabby Cameo** in American Short-hairs. Most American associations also recognize a **Tortoiseshell Cameo.**

The **Smoke** is a cat with an ash white undercoat with the tips of the hair shading to black. The feet and back are black shading to silver on the flanks and with a silver frill around the neck. The eyes are orange or

Peke Faced

Chinchilla

147

Somali

copper. The **Blue Smoke** is identical except that the tipping of the coat is blue instead of black.

Ragdoll Cat

This is a recently developed breed of passive and dependent cats having the peculiar quality of limpness. Ragdolls seem to feel pain much less than other cats and since they also seem to have no sense of danger, they are extremely vulnerable. They are not fragile but changes in behavior must be carefully watched for signs of sickness or injury. The Ragdoll is similar to the Birman but has a heavier body, broader head, and thicker fur. **Lilac** and **Seal** varieties have been developed and both types have a slight white nose streak and tail tip. They must have the white mittens of the Birman.

Somali

This cat is a long-haired version of the Abyssinian and, although it is generally larger, conforms to Abyssinian type in all respects except hair length. Both **Red** and **Ruddy** versions are recognized in the United States.

Long-haired Tabby Breeds

Tabbies of both standard and mackerel type are recognized in **Brown** (with hazel or copper eyes), **Blue** (copper eyes, mauve nose leather and pads), **Silver** (a pale silver coat, jet black markings and green or hazel eyes), **Red** (a rich deep red rather than orange coat, and copper eyes), and **Cream** (copper eyes and pink leather). The Blue and Cream Long-haired Tabbies are not recognized in Great Britain.

Turkish

First known in the West as **Van Cats** because they come from the region of Lake Van in Turkey, this breed is similar to the Angora although it has a more sturdy physique. Males in particular should be muscular on the neck and shoulders. Fur should be long, soft, and silky with a woolly undercoat and full tail. The body color is chalk white with auburn markings on the tail and on the face, which should also have a white blaze. The nose leather and paw pads should be shell pink.

First taken to Europe in 1955 there are not yet many in the West since litters are small. They have earned the name of **Swimming Cats** because they not only swim but enjoy being in the water.

HAIRLESS CATS

Bald cats have appeared from time to time and Mexican Indians are said to have had a hairless breed, descended from the cat of the Incas, the last of which were owned by a citizen of New Mexico at the beginning of this century. Accidental mutations have sometimes been preserved and bred. The lack of coat makes such cats extremely vulnerable to cold. One strain, the **Sphynx** or **Canadian Hairless** which was developed in Ontario, has been recognized as a breed by two North American bodies. Like all cats defined as hairless, the Sphynx actually has a covering of soft down but when adult, this is only noticeable on the face and points and along the back. The last two centimeters or so of the tail and, in males, the testicles, carry longer hair. Sphynx may be any color but solid-colored cats should be evenly colored and parti-colored markings should be arranged symmetrically. The body and tail are longish and the head neither round nor wedge-shaped but sloping back from the eyes with a short nose. The ears are large and very slightly rounded at the tips. The golden eyes slant and are set well back.

Silver Tabby Longhair

Sphynx

HORSES & PONIES

Choosing a Horse

Selecting the right horse for a pet requires more prior knowledge than choosing almost any other pet. If you are inexperienced, take a knowledgeable friend with you and, above all, include an examination by a veterinarian of your choosing who specializes in horses as a prerequisite to purchase. Look for a horse that is properly trained and five to ten years old—a beginner will be happier with an older horse which thoroughly knows its job. Color and size will also affect your choice but these should not be the most important factors.

The best pleasure horses have some good breeding, that is, they carry blood of a specific breed or type. Draft horses can look appealing but are not usually of riding quality, and horses being sold by riding academies have usually seen their best days.

When considering a particular horse for purchase, make an appointment and then arrive an hour early. If the horse is being exercised by the owner, it may indicate the animal is nervous, not well trained or lame—navicular disease, an incurable lameness, wears off in the early stages of exercise. Also ask to see the horse caught from a field; some horses although tractable enough in the stable can take hours to catch. You should ride the horse you are considering before making a purchase. Have it bridled and saddled in your presence to see if it is difficult to handle. Ride the horse as you intend riding it for at least half an hour. Take it away from its

normal surroundings to see how it will react, since some horses become nervous and more difficult to handle in a strange environment.

The horse should be examined unsaddled. Check all parts of the body and flex all limb joints. Find out if your potential purchase suffers from any bad habits such as eating its bedding, biting, kicking, wind sucking, and

Top. *When buying a horse or pony always have it bridled in your presence. Only then will you be sure that it is not head shy or afraid of human movements.*

Bottom. *Points of the horse.*

weaving. Then you should observe the horse's gait and general behavior, both trotting and walking. Finally, the horse should

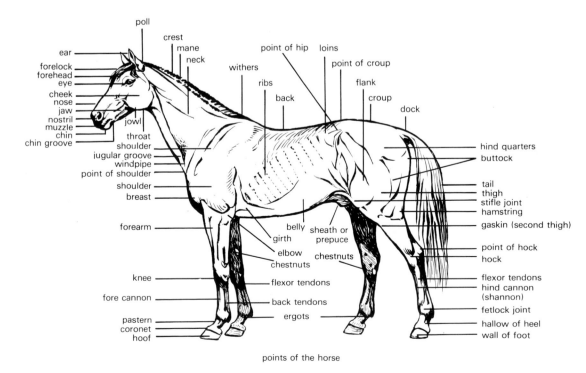

points of the horse

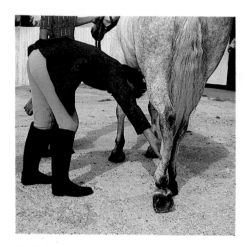

Points to check when buying a horse: Carefully run your hand down each leg and flex the joints. This will indicate whether the horse is accustomed to being handled and will also enable you to check for any signs of stiffness.

Check for splints, spavins, excess heat, and strained tendons. When lifting a hind leg, first run your hand down the hindquarters and then down the leg as a precaution against kicking.

The age of a horse is judged by its teeth. At five years it has six incisors and six cheek teeth. At ten years a notch called the Galvayne groove appears and gets longer with age.

be cantered for signs of strain or respiratory problems. Be willing to devote some extra time to familiarize yourself with the horse. (For basic training see **Training and Obedience**.)

Saddles, bridles, and bits vary according to the requirements of the rider and the function and strength of the horse. The racing saddle may weigh as little as 225g (8oz) and is used only for short periods. In contrast the armchair-like Western saddle gives comfortable support to a rider all day. The double bridle is often used in dressage. In the bitless bridle, or hackamore, control is effected through pressure on the nose.

Feeding the Horse and Pony

All horse and pony breeds belong to the same species and therefore need essentially the same food and dietary regime with adjustment for size, work, and individual nature. The horse, unlike the rabbit and the goat, has developed no special means for making the most of its bulky traditional diet of grass and other forage. The cecum is large, and bacterial growth therein produces vitamins and

other nutrients needed for reabsorption.

Grain and other concentrates can replace most of the natural grass diet, but fiber must then be supplied by hay or in the form of especially formulated pellets called nuts. An adult horse weighing 600kg. (12 cwt.) needs about 67,000kJ (16,000kcal.) a day for ordinary maintenance, but over 80,000kJ (20,000kcal.) if worked all day, even a walking pace. A 300kg. (6cwt.) pony uses about two-thirds this energy.

A protein level of 10 percent is sufficient if protein quality is satisfactory, as in fresh

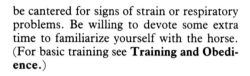

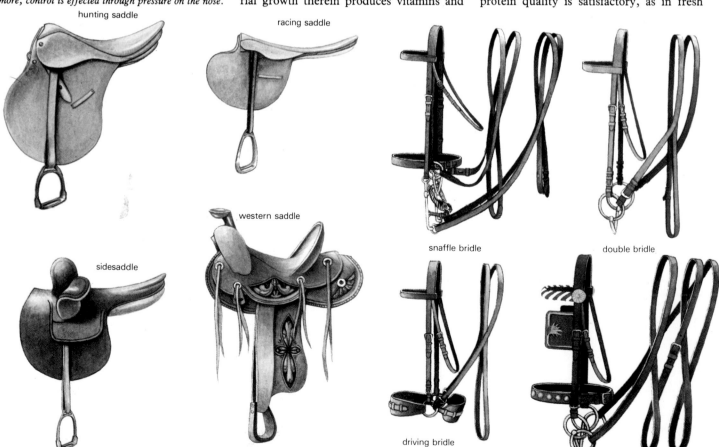

The horse's feet should be round and neat. Check that they are neither split nor cracked from the bottom of the hoof down. Examine the sole and frog for thrush.

A horse should always be mounted from the near side (the left). It should be trained to stand still and squarely balanced on all four legs during this procedure.

feet. The pasture must be free from poisonous weeds, such as bryony, hemlock, and ragwort, and the fence rows should not contain poisonous trees or shrubs, such as box, laburnum, laurel, privet, and yew.

If more work is required of the animal, more food must be given, usually in the form of crushed oats and barley or flaked corn (maize), offered two or three times a day. During the winter hay should be provided with grain and other concentrates at several feedings, according to the amount of work being done. The hay must be free from dust and mold to avoid respiratory problems and diseases. Root vegetables (carrots, potatoes, rutabagas, and turnips) are valuable and provide B-carotene which may be lacking in the winter. Pellets (nuts) have become popular with owners because of their convenience and their value as a foodstuff. Pellets are based on the traditional cereals with proteins, vitamins, and minerals added to make a balanced diet. Extra fiber should be provided in the form of bran and grass meal. It is now possible to feed a horse or pony entirely on such products, but an adult animal accustomed to hours of pasture feeding may in its absence become restless and bored and develop destructive behavior. It is wise to provide some hay for occupational value if no grazing is possible. The change from traditional diet to pellets must be made slowly, and frequent feeding (at least three feeds a day) is crucial. On such dry food, water must be offered frequently and, ideally, it should always be available in the stable.

grass or appropriate concentrates. The level of oil present in cereal grains and grass is adequate. Calcium and phosphorus are amply supplied in forage and there is no need for a vitamin supplement under good grazing conditions.

The horse has a comparatively small stomach for its size. Little and often is the most satisfactory way of feeding a horse in line with its natural habit. The day's food should therefore be divided among at least three, preferably four, meals. Traditionally, the largest meal is given at night, but a tired animal should not be expected to assimilate a

mullen-mouthed pelham bit

huge meal. Water should be offered frequently and should always be given before meals. Allow at least an hour after a meal before working the horse or pony.

In practice, feeding may vary considerably according to the time of the year, availability of foodstuffs, and the work required. Within the limits outlined above, the horse is extremely adaptable and lives contentedly in different parts of the world on widely varying diets.

In the spring and summer, a horse resting at pasture can obtain all the nutrients it needs by eating up to 90kg. (200lb.) of grass a day. The area of grass needed during the summer months depends greatly on the quality of the pasture. About 0.4 hectare (one acre) divided into two areas to allow rotational grazing is ample for a pet pony; more is needed for a horse. If less land is available, more supplementary feeding is needed. However, sudden unlimited exposure to lush grass should be avoided for this may lead to laminitis, a dangerous accumulation of fluid in the

FEEDING THE FOAL

Foals learn to graze alongside their dams and will nibble dry food from about one month of age. If properly fed by the mother, a foal does well on good grass with little, if any, supplement and is fully weaned by about six months. During the first winter both foal and dam should be given top quality hay and

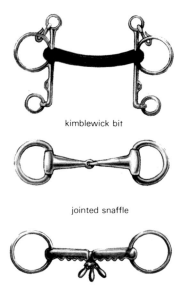

kimblewick bit

jointed snaffle

breaking bit with "players"

Approximate Daily Food Needs of Horses and Ponies

	5 Hours Each Day at Grass		Stabled		Energy Value
	*Concentrates	Hay	Concentrates	Hay	
600kg (12cwt) Horse					
Maintenance	0.45kg (1lb)	1.4kg (3lb)	2.7kg (6lb)	7.2kg (16lb)	64,900kj (15,500kcal)
Light work	1.4kg (3lb)	1.4kg (3lb)	3.6kg (8lb)	7.2kg (16lb)	77,450kJ (18,500kcal)
Lactation	2.7kg (6lb)	1.4kg (3lb)	5kg (11lb)	7.2kg (16lb)	96,250kJ (23,000kcal)
300kg (6cwt) Pony					
Maintenance	0.45kg (1lb)	—	1.8kg (4lb)	4.5kg (10lb)	41,850kJ (10,000kcal)
Light work	0.9kg (2lb)	0.45kg (1lb)	2.5kg (5.5lb)	4.5kg (10lb)	50,200kJ (12,000kcal)
Lactation	1.8kg (4lb)	0.45kg (1lb)	3.4kg (7.5lb)	4.5kg (10lb)	62,800kJ (15,000kcal)

*These amounts should be divided between three or four feeds.

concentrates; the pellet compound feeds are ideal for this purpose.

Care of the Horse and Pony at Grass

ADEQUATE PASTURE

The more land there is available for the horses the easier their management will be. They do best ranging widely over treeless pasture grazing from mixed herbage on a limestone soil. At the other extreme, it is possible to manage on far less suitable land with one pony to 0.4 hectares (one acre). A single mare kept for breeding will be lonely, which she will indicate by frequent whinnying, by walking round and round inside the pasture fence, and by trying to break out. Two mares are likely to be content. Odd numbers can be a nuisance as horses are inclined to pair up. Relationships become easier when there are foals or other young horses about. Small areas of land present two problems: keeping a supply of fresh young grass available for as long a grazing season as possible, and preventing the pasture from being heavily contaminated with worms. All horses have worms, and these lay enormous numbers of eggs which are eliminated with the horses' droppings. The eggs hatch, and the tiny larvae climb on to grass blades to be eaten and swallowed. They mature in the horse's bowel, to lay eggs in their turn. Control is by regular dosing of all horses with worm medicine and by arranging pasture management so that sunshine, drying winds, and frost can reduce the numbers of young worms on the grass.

THE GRASS

The best grazing for horses is meadow grass, a mixture of perennial grasses and a variety of herbs. This type of seed mixture can be obtained from seedsmen, but in most cases it already makes up the existing grassland and only needs the encouragement of an occasional dressing with fertilizer. The herbs in the grass, which in other locations might be called weeds or wild flowers, are the natural local ones that are much more likely to persist than those supplied in a seed mixture. They act as a condiment adding relish to the grazing.

Seedsmen are inclined to advise sowing land again to obtain a heavy crop. Such new grassland is suitable for hay or for cattle that are being pushed for fast growth and are receiving supplementary feeding, but is unsuitable for horses, which must not be encouraged to grow quickly. They do better on well-established pasture.

Hay fed in a hayrack under a shelter is the most economical method of feeding during the winter. Outside feeding usually involves some waste because food that is trampled into the ground will not be eaten. A horse will eat spilled food from a dry surface but will not touch it if it is mixed with mud.

PADDOCKS

Small fields for horses must be divided into paddocks allowing 0.4 hectare (1 acre per head). Depending on the quality of pasture each horse needs at least that much at any one time and can be expected to get through 1.2 hectares (3 acres) on a year-round basis. Ideally three paddocks should be used in turn for four or eight months, each on a one or two year cycle. This allows a portion of the available pasture to be grazed down and then allowed to grow again while the horses are occupying another area. Horses are untidy grazing animals. If left in one large field for a long time they become selective, eating off some parts, depositing their dung and urine in others and leaving some patches of grass and tall-growing herbs untouched. The land also becomes worm infested. With paddock rotation, the rough grass and herbs in the recently vacated paddock can be mowed or eaten off by cattle put in to follow the horses. The paddock should then be harrowed to spread out the droppings and to expose the worm larvae to drying winds and sunshine. The cattle will eat the grass down, considerably reducing the number of young worms which do not affect them. Each horse passes about fifteen droppings a day. If the labor situation allows, the droppings should be picked up daily and stacked away from the paddocks in a compost heap. This will eventually destroy all the worm larvae but some worm eggs will persist. The manure should not be spread back on the paddocks as a fertilizer but may be used elsewhere.

It is also possible with paddock grazing to keep some of the land entirely free of horses through the winter months. Such a spell, provided the grass is evenly short, is one of the greatest helps in ridding the land of worms.

Paddocks require fencing. Ideally this consists of a thick thorn hedge with oak post-and-rail fencing on each side. The hedge provides shelter from strong winds and driving rain while the fences keep the animals well apart from those in adjoining paddocks and protect the hedge from being overeaten by the horses, which are always ready to vary their diet by browsing. Simpler fencing is usually provided, such as a top rail and lower strands of plain wire.

Fences need to be well maintained. Horses will graze through them, and splintered rails or slack wires can lead to injuries. Barbed wire is too dangerous for fencing horses or ponies.

WATER

Horses need a regular water supply whether they are in open pasture or in small paddocks. Their demands vary a great deal, depending on the weather and the type of grazing, from very little up to 30 liters (8 gallons) or more on a really hot day. Horses are proverbially fussy about drinking. They like to choose their own time and to drink at leisure. Not only are they particular that the water should be clean, they dislike any change in taste or quality and may refuse unaccustomed water for several days to the point of becoming dehydrated. Working horses will lose condition in such cases, and suckling foals may find their milk supply reduced. If there is no natural running water supply, provision for fresh water must be made. A trough or bathtub is adequate if constantly filled with fresh water and scrubbed out weekly.

SHELTER

Horses need an open shed for shelter from hot sunshine and from flies. They seldom use a shelter against rain, but most horses kept as pets need stabling or shelter of some sort in snow or bitter cold. In continuing wet weather their coats may become water-logged, which can lead to skin disease or to severe chilling. If this should occur, it is advisable to stable them for a day or two to give their coats a chance to dry off.

Elaborate stables are not needed for mares and foals, but it is convenient to have stalls where they can be handled and fed separately and perhaps, depending on breed, location and climate, housed for part of the winter. Ponies that suffer from sweet itch, a wet eczema caused by midge bites, have to be stabled from mid-afternoon until well after dark when the midges are biting, which in some mild climates may be for more than half the year.

Care of the Stabled Horse and Pony

Stables should be tight but well ventilated, with a nonporous floor so angled that moisture drains off easily. The stable door should be in two parts so that the top half may be left open as a window. An interesting view, preferably of other horses, helps to prevent vices such as weaving and windsucking, which are caused by boredom. Projecting eaves over the stable door shelter the horse from rain and, in hot climates, protect its head from the sun, preventing sunstroke. Adjacent stable doors should not be close enough to allow horses to bite each other. A high ceiling promotes good ventilation. At its lowest, the ceiling must be high enough to allow the horse to throw up its head without injury. The roof should be pitched, constructed of tile or wood; a flat roof or a tin roof can turn a stable into an oven in hot weather.

The stable should be large enough for the horse to lie down stretched out and still have room enough to turn over without getting stuck against the wall. Windows should be protected by bars. Hayracks should be mounted on the wall at the height of the

horse's head—not above, as hayseeds will drop into its eyes. The manger should be mounted at a comfortable height for feeding, but should be high enough so that the horse does not bang its knees while eating. A removable manger installed into brackets is the easiest type to clean. Water buckets mounted on wall brackets are advisable so they cannot be knocked over.

Bedding should be thoroughly cleaned out at least once—preferably twice—a day. The horse should never be allowed to stand on wet or polluted bedding which may cause diseases of the feet. Wheat straw is the best bedding in temperate climates, but peat moss or wood shavings are acceptable alternatives and are preferable for horses which eat their bedding.

Unless the horse is turned out in a paddock during the day, it will need at least an hour per day of exercise. Exceptions are made for one day off a week and the day following a hard day's hunting, when the horse is simply led out for a short walk to ease its tired muscles and to check for any lameness or injury.

Routine in a stable is very important. If feeding, cleaning, and exercise come at set times the horse will adjust itself to stable life with little strain.

Grooming

Natural oils in the horse's coat protect it from the weather, so the horse should not be clipped or groomed thoroughly unless clothing and stabling are provided. If the horse is kept out in cold weather, a token removal of surface mud is all that is necessary. However, mud under the saddle and girth area should always be removed before saddling to prevent irritation. A side benefit of grooming a pastured horse, however lightly, is that areas of infection, small cuts, lice, or mange are discovered in the early stages.

A stabled horse needs daily grooming to promote circulation and to build and tone up muscles. (Horses at pasture do this themselves by rolling and through exercise.) Dirty eyes, nose, and genitals should be wiped clean with a damp sponge. Rugs and blankets should also be brushed clean of loose hairs, especially when the horse is shedding.

A sweating horse should be allowed to dry off before reaching the stable or field, as chills may result if the animal is left to stand with a wet coat. A stabled horse that has been exercised in the rain must be thoroughly dried off before the rugs are replaced. An easy way to do this is to pile the length of the horse's back with straw and invert the rug over it. This will dry the horse with air warmed by its own body while you attend to other tasks. When the horse is dry, the body hair should be brushed smooth before the horse is blanketed for the night; hair left matted with dried sweat may be an irritant, and the whorls and curls of a sweating neck will have set into permanent waves by the morning.

If the horse is clipped, all mud must be removed from its coat after exercise. Drying mud contracts, pulling the hairs on a thin coat and producing irritating little bumps known as mud fever. Mud fever is particularly common in the sensitive areas around the cleft of the heel which may become chapped and develop into the condition called cracked heels.

Whether the horse is being used or not, its feet should be inspected daily for stones and wear. If unshod and pastured on grass the hoof will grow naturally. Approximately every four to six weeks the wall of the hoof will require filing down; otherwise it will split. If the horse is running on rough terrain or is regularly led unshod on the road, the foot may become so worn down that shoes are required. Because of the natural growth of the hoof, shoes need to be removed and replaced every four to six weeks so that the wall of the hoof may be filed—even when the shoes themselves are not badly worn.

Routine inspection of the feet should include examination of the frog and heel for cuts and tears. Infection from cuts can lame the horse, since affected areas cannot swell in this area because of the restriction of the horny wall of the hoof. Other common causes of lameness are overreaching (the shoe on the hind foot cutting the heel of the front foot), a bruised sole from stepping on a stone, and cracked heels from standing with wet feet. If the feet are thoroughly examined and cleaned out every day—and always before and after exercise—and if cuts are cleaned and disinfected at once, much can be done to prevent lameness.

General Signs of Health

The base of the horse's ear should be slightly warm to the hand, since a horse's blood temperature, approximately 37.8°C. (100°F.), is a little higher than a human's. Legs should be cool and hard, the eyes liquid and alert, and the nostrils clean. A clear discharge from the nose is usually harmless, but a yellow one indicates an infection of the respiratory system. The horse's body should be free from lumps and bumps, from patches of heat rash, and from cuts, scratches, and parasites. A healthy sheen on the coat should be evident in sunlight. Droppings should be examined for consistency; if they are too liquid or too firm then the cause is probably in the horse's diet.

Daily inspection of the horse by hand and eye will accustom you to the feel of your animal, so that you will know at once if something is wrong. If the horse appears uncomfortable or listless and you are unable to find the cause, you should call the veterinarian. (For further details of illness and injury see **A Guide to Ailments** and the **Horse Ailment Diagnosis Chart**.)

Breeding and Rearing Horses and Ponies

Mares and their foals in summer pasture make a delightful picture for any observer, but only the breeder enjoys the sense of achievement after all the planning, hard work, difficulties overcome, and disappointments accepted.

Most people who consider breeding their own horses are neither investors who pay an occasional visit to the stables nor breeders who devote all their time to the animals. The middle course requires some land and stabling that can be under fairly constant observation, as many mares as may be reasonably accommodated, and some additional attention on an irregular basis. A joint family interest may be one approach. Experienced employees are expensive, and horse breeding is not usually a profitable project. Inexperienced helpers may learn fast, but their early mistakes can be extremely costly.

The detailed information needed to breed and raise foals can be accumulated quickly by those who like caring for horses. Horse ownership, especially with a breeding intent, creates contacts with other owners, riding schools and clubs, stud farms, veterinarians, farriers, and saddlers, most of whom are anxious to share their experience with another horse enthusiast.

THE SELECTION OF MARES

Breed

If the mare for breeding has not been selected, it would be sensible to choose a local type of horse or pony: Welsh ponies in Wales; American Quarter Horses in the United States; Manipuris in Assam. The regional favorite has several advantages; it is suitable to the locality, its characteristics are well known, and stallions are available for mating. If the chosen mares are crossbred, it is still a good plan to mate them to a horse of the local breed for the same reasons. Crossbred horses and ponies often turn out to be more suitable than purebred animals for particular requirements, especially in regard to

their size and the weight they may be required to carry.

Conformation

Heavily built, thickset animals are suitable for heavy draft work at slow paces. The present-day requirement is usually for a lighter and narrower horse designed for agility and speed. The Arabs and Thoroughbreds are the outstanding examples, but they require specialized care and are not easy to breed. There are many established breeds, often with a proportion of Arab or Thoroughbred blood, that are not quite as fast, but are more amenable and more readily adapted to a variety of activities.

The mares should be compact and balanced, with a straight action. Avoid animals that, whatever their height, give the impression of being tall, narrow-chested, or long in the leg. In most breeds the depth from the withers to the lower level of the girth should be slightly more than from that level to the ground. Well-sprung ribs are an advantage, the shoulders and pasterns should not be upright but reasonably sloping, while the distance from the knee to the fetlock should appear short with no pinching in below the knee. If some of the mares have faults of conformation, as they well may have since very few horses are perfect, care should be taken not to have them mated by a stallion showing the same defect or the fault is almost certain to reappear in the foals.

Size

After a particular breed is chosen, size is already decided within fairly narrow limits. Size affects susceptibility to disease quite significantly. The greater the height the more likely the horse is to develop roaring or whistling. In competitions, such as racing and jumping, size is an advantage. While many of the arthritic conditions from which these horses suffer are associated with the stresses of their work, the smaller and more compact animals are much less likely to suffer from splints, spavins, ringbones, sidebones, navicular disease, and spinal arthritis. Ponies, on the other hand, are more liable to develop chronic or acute laminitis, because they are so often overfed. They have a great capacity to thrive on poor quality grazing. Good grass gives them indigestion which leads to fever in the feet. If they are not getting plenty of work every day they require severe rationing, especially when they are out on spring or summer grass.

The mare controls the size of the developing offspring. If a small mare is mated to a large horse, the fetus will not grow beyond the size that she can produce satisfactorily at birth, though the foal will eventually grow a good deal bigger than its mother.

Age

The best time to breed from a mare is from three to twelve years of age. They come into season, indicating their readiness for mating, for a few days at a time, at intervals of about

three weeks from late spring until early fall. Two-year-old fillies and even precocious well-fed yearlings may come into season during the summer, and they can conceive. These youngsters would probably lose the foal early in pregnancy. If they do carry the foal to full term, it is likely to be a weakling and the strain of such early pregnancies interferes with the filly's growth and development. By three years of age most fillies are mature enough to breed successfully. Pregnancy lasts for eleven months, and mares may produce a foal each year for many years. Most of them miss a year now and again, and these barren years become more frequent as the mares grow older.

The chief reason for failing to conceive is womb infection. Infection carried in dust or dirt or from the mares own droppings gains access to the womb through the vulva which may become deformed by injuries from previous foalings or slackened in tone by advancing years.

Mares that have not been available for breeding because of other employment may be bred later in life. This is a routine arrangement with thoroughbreds which may race as two-year-old or three-year-old fillies and then be sent to stud at four years or later. In any breed the results are likely to be satisfactory up to a reasonable age provided that the mares have not been allowed to get overweight, a condition which interferes with the activity of the ovaries. As long as they are in good health and condition and coming into season regularly during the summer there is a good chance of successful breeding. The vulva does slacken with advancing years and may allow infection which has the effect of preventing conception. It may be of interest to refer to the exceptional case of a twenty-three-year-old hunter mare that had never been bred and was turned out in a field in honorable retirement. She broke out and paid a visit to some horses nearby. To her owner's surprise she foaled in her twenty-fourth year and raised her foal successfully. However, in most cases, it would not be advisable to purchase mares for breeding that are over twelve years old.

THE STUD FARM AND THE STALLION

It is customary for mares to be sent to the stallion to be mated at the stud farm. Mares which have a suckling foal take the foal along with them. This creates no problems if the stud is nearby, but some mares are transported long distances by road or air to a selected stallion. Such journeys can cause distress and illness in young foals. The problem is overcome by sending the mare to the stud farm a month before her foal is due to be born. At the stud farm she is in excellent hands for her foaling, and she remains at the farm until the next time comes for her to be mated. She will be sent home when the stud manager has good reason to believe that she is pregnant once again. By this time her foal-at-

The working surface of a horse's feet needs to be protected by a metal shoe, usually made of iron. This can be accomplished through the use of either hot shoes, available at a forge where each shoe is made to measure or, as shown, through use of a wide range of "ready-to-wear" cold shoes, which can be put on in the stable or on the farm.

foot will be two or three months old and well able to stand up to the rigors of the long journey home with its mother.

Stallions are widely advertised in the various horse magazines and papers as available for service at a stated fee, which may be from a few dollars to a few thousand, according to the breed and reputation of the horse. In some cases there is an arrangement of no foal, no fee, apart from boarding expenses. The decision as to the settlement of this fee depends on a veterinary report that the mare is

or is not pregnant by an agreed date, often the first of October.

It is important that the stallion should be healthy, fertile, and free from faults of conformation that might be transmitted to the foal. In many countries stallions are required to be inspected and rigorously tested before they are licensed for breeding. Federal, state, jockey club, and breed society regulations on horse breeding vary so widely that it is sensible to make inquiries on this point from veterinarians or stud farms when selecting a stallion. Some riding clubs and breed societies require and maintain stallions of high quality and encourage their use on a variety of mares in the interest of upgrading the quality of horses in their area.

It is sensible to select a stallion of the same breed as the mare or about the same size. If

the mare is crossbred, a horse of the breed of either of her parents is suitable. Mares of uncertain breeding are likely to produce foals of a good quality light horse type if they are mated to a Standardbred, an Arab, or one of the lighter pony breeds, a Welsh Pony, or a Pony of the Americas. If a heavier animal is required, the American Quarter Horse or Morgan breeds will supply bone and substance. For color, Pintos and Appaloosas will often produce pattern-colored foals from whole-colored mares.

The number of mares accepted for mating by a stallion is usually limited to forty per season, and fewer than that for horses in their first or second season. Consequently it is advisable to book a mare to the horse early in the year before his list is full. Really popular stallions may be booked up years ahead.

It is usual for mares to be sent to the stallion at the stud farm to be mated. A mare will only allow the stallion to serve her when she is in season, which first occurs in the spring.

MATING

A mare will only allow the stallion to serve her when she is in season. Mares first come into season, or on heat, in the spring. They remain in season for a few days and then pass into a phase when they are not interested in mating. They come into season again in about two and a half weeks, repeating this rhythm through the summer. Thoroughbred mares are warmly housed and well fed during the winter, to bring them into season in February or March so that they will produce early foals with a view to some advantage when they are racing as two-year-olds. Animals not under pressure to breed early first come into season in April or May and continue, unless they become pregnant, until September or October.

A mare indicates she is in heat by a change in temperament and by several behaviors. She repeatedly stands with the hind legs extended and the tail raised as if to pass urine and frequently opens and closes the lips of the vulva, which is referred to as winking. She is liable to squeal or kick and eject small quantities of urine if touched on the flanks or behind the saddle. These signs are exaggerated in the presence of the stallion. In the early stages of being in season she may squeal and kick viciously at the stallion; later she accepts his advances, turns her quarters towards him, and allows mating.

The mare's heat coincides with the passage of an egg cell from the ovary toward the womb. This egg cell becomes available for fertilization forty-eight hours before the end of her period in season, and the stallion's fresh and active semen should be waiting at this time to effect conception. Since the mare may remain in season for four to eight days, it is advisable to mate her every other day until she goes off heat and will no longer accept the horse. This routine is practical and is widely adopted.

It is usual for the mares to be lodged at the stud farm to obtain the best chances of conception. Some mares only show that they are in season in the presence of a stallion. At the stud farm the mare can be presented to the horse from time to time until she shows that she is on heat. The stud manager can then decide on the best time for her to be mated, and the mating can be repeated at forty-eight-hour intervals until she ceases to be receptive.

Some mares, especially in the early spring, remain rather vaguely in season over a longer period than usual. These animals may not allow mating and, if they do, conception is unlikely. Later heat periods will be shorter when mating will be more successful.

Mares that produce a foal from the previous year's mating are likely to come into season about ten days after foaling. This is the foaling heat and mating at this time is not advised because, if conception occurs, there is an increased likelihood that the foal will be lost by abortion.

THE PREGNANT MARE

Confirming Pregnancy

Mares that have conceived do not come into season again, and it is usual to assume that they are in foal if they have not shown in heat by three weeks after being mated. This assumption is not entirely dependable. After being mated some mares that are suckling their foals, and others known as shy breeders, may not show themselves in season although they are not pregnant. It is disappointing if a mare turns out not to be pregnant after all the trouble taken at the stud farm. At some stud farms a careful veterinary examination at about five weeks through the wall of the rectum can determine if conception has occurred and, if it has not, arrange-

ments can be made for mating again. If this expert detection is not available a laboratory test on a blood sample taken between forty-five and ninety days after mating can determine if the mare is in foal. A similar check from a urine sample can be made from 150 days after mating.

Abortion

A few mares that are known to be pregnant lose their foals during the first few months by a process known as resorption. The small developing fetus dies from some problem of nourishment and is simply absorbed rather than discharged from the womb. Even if this is known to have occurred it is almost impossible for the mare to become pregnant again in the same season. The mare is likely to breed normally in the following year. If a foal dies later than two or three months after conception, the fetus is usually aborted and may be found wrapped in its membranes lying in the stable or in the field. The mare may show some discharge from the vulva. A veterinarian should be called to check the mare for any needed treatment and to inspect the fetus to determine the cause of the abortion.

Twins

The most common cause of the loss of foals is twinning. In some breeds it is usual for as many as 5 percent of the mares to conceive twins. Almost always one robs the other of essential nourishment in the womb. The deprived fetus dies and, in rejecting it from her womb, the mother loses the other fetus as well. Sometimes the dead fetus is retained in the womb, and the stronger foal is born alive. Live twins are a rarity and they remain undersized.

Normal Pregnancy

Most mares carry their foals through the eleven months of pregnancy without trouble or complications. They require no more than the usual care and attention given to horses. If they are working animals there is no reason why they should not continue in their normal duties for the first seven or eight months of the pregnancy, but they should not be put to severe exertion. Feeding should be nourishing but not excessive. Overweight mares may have trouble at foaling and be difficult to get in foal again. The pregnant mares should be wormed like other horses with haloxon in June, benzadole in August, dichlorvos in October, and benzadole again in March. Another dose of benzadole should be given a month before the foal is due. It is important that foals should be raised in conditions as free of worms as possible. Foals and yearlings are particularly susceptible to damage to their internal organs by worms.

FOALING

Forecasting the day on which a foal will arrive is difficult. The chief sign of impending foaling, apart from the steadily increasing size of the mare's abdomen, is a distended udder with bulging teats carrying a crust of dried milk that looks like yellow wax. A thick sticky yellow milk can be drawn off between thumb and finger. If the udder contains a thin straw-colored liquid, the mare is not yet ready to foal. Mares prefer to foal alone, usually in the early hours of the morning. Mares in a field separate themselves from their companions to find a secluded spot to foal down. It is often sensible to let this happen. Bringing a mare into a stable to foal may distress her unless she is accustomed to being shut up alone. There is also a lot of hard work in preparing a stable for foaling and in keeping it prepared. The ceiling, walls, windows, and floor all need to be washed and disinfected, and a clean straw bed put down. If the mare is put into it a day or two before she foals, it all gets dirty again. If she is kept in another stable in preparation for the event, she is sure to foal there before she is moved to the clean box. A healthy mare and her newborn foal are quite capable of coping with all but the most severe weather conditions, and from the point of view of hygiene a green field and the open air are more suitable for the event than any building.

Foaling usually takes less than an hour from the first obvious contractions of the womb. These force the dull red placenta to bulge from the vulva. The placenta ruptures, discharging several gallons of fluid. Straining continues and, after a while, another membrane protrudes from the vulva. This one is white and closely covers the foal whose nose and one front foot can be seen within. This membrane also tears and the mare, usually lying down at this stage, forces out the foal's head and fore feet first in a series of rather violent thrusts. It is important that the mare should not be disturbed at this stage. The foal, taking its first gasping breaths, is still attached to the mare through the umbilical cord and will be deprived of a blood supply if separated at this time. After a period for rest from her exertions the mare gets to her feet and the cord separates naturally leaving a stump at a few inches dangling from the foal's umbilicus. It dries up and drops off after a few days.

The chief risk at an unattended birth is that the membranes may remain over the foal's nostrils and cause suffocation. If this is observed the membranes should be shifted to one side with as little fuss as possible so the mare will not be provoked by interference with her foal.

If a mare strains violently without making any progress after the placental bladder has appeared, there is probably some obstruction to the delivery of the foal and veterinary assistance should be called.

Induced Foaling
It is now possible, if a mare has carried her foal for eleven months and her udder is bulging with sticky yellow milk, to induce foaling with an injection of fluprostenol which acts

The birth of a thoroughbred in the luxury of a stable: the mare's tail is bandaged to keep the hairs from getting in the way. Top Center. The foal's forelegs have just emerged still enclosed in the fetal membranes. Top Right. Birth is all but complete with just the hind legs still to emerge. The membranes have broken so that the foal is able to breathe.

within a matter of three or four hours. There may be considerable advantages in being able to set a time for the foaling if it is to be supervised. Any extra risks in what is, in any case, a delicately balanced and complicated process, appear to be negligible.

CARE AFTER FOALING

The Umbilical Cord
When the foal is clearly separated from the mare, an antiseptic powder or lotion may be applied to the stump of the umbilical cord. No other attention is usually needed. The mare may be depended upon to clean the foal by licking it over.

The Afterbirth
The mare discharges the placental membranes, known as the afterbirth, within an hour or two of the foal's arrival. They should be examined to make sure that they are complete, in the shape of a Y. If the afterbirth has not been shed after twelve hours or if one of the branches of the Y appears to have been

Luxury births in stables are for thoroughbreds and other highly valued breeds. Most births, like that of the newly-born foal above, occur in the open, often without constant attention from owners.

A mare normally bears a single foal; twins are exceptional.

torn off and retained in the womb, veterinary help should be called.

THE NEWBORN FOAL

Colostrum
The mare's first milk, colostrum, differs from her later milk in that it contains antibodies, substances that protect the foal from infection. It is urgently necessary for the foal to receive colostrum during the first twelve hours of its life. Most foals can manage to stand and maintain sufficient balance to reach the udder and commence suckling within a couple of hours after birth. Weaker foals may need help to find the udder. Those that are not able to stand after a few hours should be given half a pint of colostrum every two hours, dribbled into their mouths from a

baby's bottle with an enlarged hole in the teat. This can be milked by thumb and finger from the mare's udder into a warm jug.

Meconium

The foal's first droppings are hard, sticky, and dark brown. They are known as the meconium and consist of waste products accumulated in the bowel during its growth in the womb. The meconium is usually cleared in the first twenty-four hours of life, after which the droppings are yellow from digested milk. This change in color may be noted with some satisfaction as a clear indication that the foal's bowels are functioning normally. Some foals have difficulty in passing the meconium and may develop a painful colic which must be treated with laxatives and enemas.

Maternal Care

The strength of the bond between mare and foal is very strong and must be respected. They need to be within sight and touch of each other and become upset if they are separated. The bond weakens gradually as the months go by and the foal becomes independent enough to play with other youngsters, but there are loud whinnyings if it goes out of sight. Weaning always presents some upset, no matter how carefully planned.

ORPHANS

Some tragedy at foaling may leave the foal an orphan. The idea of raising the foal by hand should be resisted if there is any possible means of fostering it with a mare that has just lost her foal.

Hand rearing foals involves feedings every two hours for several days and nights with freshly mixed powdered feed. Cow's milk is not the best nourishment for foals. Frequent and regular feeding at longer intervals is then required for two or three months. Antibiotics must be given to take the place of the colostrum and, later, there are liable to be digestive upsets, coughs, and colds. Human company is, unfortunately, an inadequate substitute for maternal care and instruction and may lead to fixation problems that prevent the foal from relating normally to other horses as it matures. Hand-reared foals seldom thrive.

Fostering a foal presents two major difficulties. The first is to find a mare deprived of her foal. Stud farms or the local branch of the Humane Society may be of help. In some areas there are established "foal banks" which specialize in introducing orphan foals to mares which have lost their foals at birth. The other problem is to persuade the mare to adopt the foal. She wants only her own dead offspring and no other. The dead foal's skin draped over the orphan may deceive her. Tranquilizers may help and strong-smelling ointments smeared over the foal and the mare's nose may sufficiently confuse her sense of smell, which is her chief means of recognition. It may take hours of patient persuasion, but once she has adopted the foal all should be clear sailing.

Bottom. *This mare seems to have accepted the orphan which is enthusiastically taking advantage of its opportunity.*

THE SUCKLING FOAL AND WEANING

The suckling foal needs little attention until it is weaned at about six months. For convenience of handling, the foal should be accustomed to being led in a rope halter or fitted with a head collar. If a head collar is used, it must be remembered that foals' heads grow very quickly. The foal will soon share whatever food the mare is receiving, whether this is just grass or supplementary hay and manger food. Supplementary foods should be limited to prevent foals and yearlings from growing too fast and developing upright pasterns which can lead to problems of lameness (See above: Feeding the Horse and Pony.)

Suckling foals should be given a benzadole worm dose when they are four months old and repeat doses at intervals of six weeks until they coincide, as yearlings, with the regular dosing of all horses, ponies, and donkeys on the premises.

If there are any peculiarities about a foal's feet, the advice of a farrier should be obtained early. It is advisable to ask the farrier to look at a foal's feet at four or five months old. Some minor attention with a foot rasp at regular intervals may prevent minor faults developing which could later throw the animal off balance when put to work.

Weaning is carried out chiefly to relieve the mare of the strain of suckling one foal and nourishing another in her womb through the winter. Weaning usually takes place when the foal is six months old. If the mare is not in foal, weaning may be delayed but she should be relieved of the foal in good time to build her up to reasonable condition for coming into season in the next spring. When several mares and foals are running together, weaning is simplified if the mares are withdrawn from the field one by one at a few days' interval. The foals, fairly independent of their mothers by this time, will scarcely miss them, having the companionship of the other foals and, if possible, the leadership of a barren mare or a gelding. This method is less traumatic than suddenly moving the mares to one stable and the foals to another, which may result in days of whinnying and refusals to feed. This is inevitable when mare and foal have not been kept with other horses. Separating them in paddocks, however distant, can lead to broken fences and injured horses.

YEARLINGS AND TWO-YEAR-OLDS

Yearlings and two-year-olds need little attention. Colts and fillies should be separated. Both can reach puberty while they are yearlings and, though mating is unlikely, their sexual play can lead to accidents. The young horses should be regularly haltered and led about, to accustom them to some discipline and the handling required for worming, foot care, and eventual breaking. Colts which are not needed for breeding purposes are usually castrated while they are two years old.

Having bred from your mares and enjoyed surveying your own young stock, it is difficult to part with any one of them, but some of them must go to earn their keep and make room for the next crop of possibly even more attractive foals. (See chapters on **Training and Obedience** for training and **Exhibiting and Showing** for showing horses.)

Horse and Pony Breeds

Roughly two hundred breeds of horse and pony exist throughout the world. Most, however, would not be described by their owners as "pets," though many fill that function. In deciding which breeds to include here, priority has been given to those breeds which are used mainly for pleasure; that is to riding animals rather than to work horses. Consideration has also been given to working breeds such as the Thoroughbred racehorse and the Shire which, in retirement, are often retained because of their owner's affection for them.

Breeds selected here are arranged according to their size and, where breeds are directly related, according to locality. Ponies and horses are classified as such according to their height, which is measured from the withers. A pony is up to and including 14.2 hands high (145cm.), and a horse stands more than 14.2 hands high. (One hand equals about 10cm. or 4in.) Horses can be described as warm-blooded and cold-blooded. Warm-blooded horses are fine-boned horses, suitable for riding purposes with, usually, a strain of Arab blood. Cold-blooded horses, such as the Percheron, are heavy bodied and suitable for farm and draft work.

Falabella

This Argentinian animal is one of the smallest horses in the world. It stands less than seven hands (70cm.) high and makes an ideal pet because of its quick mind and friendly disposition. The breed has become popular in the United States where breeders are concentrating on Appaloosa markings, although any color is acceptable.

In appearance and form it is more of a

Common face, leg, and body markings on horses.

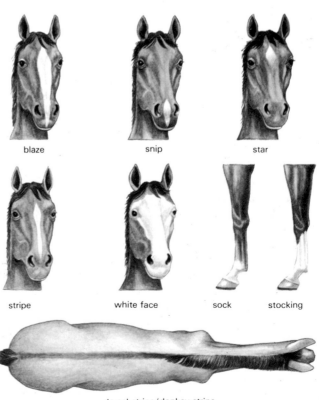

blaze snip star

stripe white face sock stocking

dorsal stripe/donkey stripe

Albino	Light Bay	Light Chestnut	Chestnut (blond mane and tail)
Dark Bay	Bright Bay	Cream	Blue Dun
Brown Bay	Black	Dun with black points	Light Gray
Brown	Piebald	Fleabitten Gray	Dappled Gray
Skewbald	Dark Chestnut	Liver Chestnut	Palomino

Common body colors and markings of horses and ponies.

miniature horse than a true pony type and lacks the physical strength needed for a serious riding pony. All Falabellas are descended from a small Thoroughbred stallion owned by the Falabella family who first developed the breed. Continued inbreeding to the smallest Shetlands and downgrading in size has contributed to the Falabella's physical weakness.

Shetland

For its size, the Shetland is the strongest of all breeds. It is capable of pulling twice its own weight (twice the power of most heavy horses). Although it averages only 9.3 hands (97cm.) high, it was often used to carry a man and his wife to market. The earliest remains of the Shetland, found in its native Shetland Islands off the northern coast of Scotland, date from about 500B.C., making it one of the oldest of breeds. It is an exceptionally hardy animal. Generations of exposure to a northern land with no trees and little shelter have encouraged it to grow a very shaggy winter coat. In addition to its extreme strength and hardiness the Shetland is probably the best-loved pony in the world.

Its distinctive head—small, often with a concave face, open nostrils, large kind eyes, and small, aristocratic ears—is cloaked with an abundant growth of forelock and mane. Its back is short and its legs firm with short cannon bones and small feet. Despite the density of the Shetland's strong body, it has a light, straight action. In character it is brave and gentle. Easy to train, surefooted and adaptable, the Shetland makes an ideal first pony for a child.

American Shetland

Descended from the British Shetland, the American Shetland is taller, measuring a maximum of 11.2 hands (115cm), and more delicately built. The head is refined and often dished. The American Shetland resembles the Hackney in its light-stepping action and proud carriage. Apart from being very popular as a child's pony, the American Shetland is also ideal in harness and in pulling lightweight sulkies for pony racing.

Caspian

The Caspian is thought, although not proven, to be the lost wild horse of Iran which was used by the Mesopotamians in the third millennium B.C. For more than a thousand years it was believed extinct, until

in the spring of 1965 a few animals of markedly Caspian-type that were being used for harness work were discovered in the towns beside the Caspian Sea. Subsequent comparative studies of structure have led researchers to believe that today's Caspian may be the ancient miniature horse of Mesopotamia.

The Caspian is more like a small horse than a pony. It is of slight build, with fine bones, a silky mane and tail and an Arab-type head. It stands 10–12 hands (100–120cm) high and is usually gray, brown, bay, or chestnut. In character it is quick-witted and tractable, perfect as a riding pony for a small child.

Gotland

This Swedish pony is thought to have run wild on Gotland Island since the Stone Age. It is believed to be a direct descendant of the Tarpan and may be the oldest of all Scandinavian breeds, protected by its island isolation against infusions of mixed blood.

It stands 12–12.2 hands (120–125cm.) high and is of lightweight build with a small, straight head, small ears, and a short, muscular neck. It has a gentle though stubborn nature. It moves well at a walk and trot,

Caspian

gallops badly, and is an outstanding jumper.

Today the Gotland is mainly used as a child's pony, as a jumper, and for trotting races, for which it is especially bred.

Iceland

The immensely powerful Icelandic pony of today was once the fighting horse of the Norwegian sagas. In the ninth century, Norwegian immigrants brought ponies with them to Iceland and amused themselves by staging fights between stallions. "Starkad had a good horse of chestnut hue and it was thought that no horse was his match in fight" starts off the story of the battle of that horse and Gunnar's brown described in the *Saga of Burnt Njal*, which began as a blood feud and ended in a massacre.

During the nineteenth century the Icelandic pony was much in demand in British coalpits, despite competition from native British breeds. It is a worker and has been used extensively as a pack and draft animal. Today it is in demand as a trekking mount. Since beef cattle cannot endure the bitter Icelandic winters it is also used for meat.

The Icelandic pony, averaging 13.2 hands (100–135cm.) high, is one of the toughest of all breeds. It has a stocky body and exceptionally good eyesight. It is remarkable for its homing instinct; it can be borrowed, ridden for great distances and turned loose to find its way directly home. Its docile temperament, its endurance, and its hardiness have made it popular outside its own country.

Dartmoor

This pony inhabits the wild expanse of open moorland called Dartmoor in Devon, England, and is hardy enough to survive snowy winters without shelter or extra food. It stands 12.2 hands (125cm.) high. White stars and socks are not uncommon, though excessive white is discouraged by the Dartmoor Pony Breed Society.

The Dartmoor's white markings, and the occasional appearance of piebald and skewbald members of a breed that is normally bay, brown or black, are the result of nineteenth century economy. When the demand for small ponies to work in coal mines was at its peak, Shetland stallions were loosed on Dartmoor to run wild and breed with the native ponies. That the purebred Dartmoor did not become extinct is due to the diligence of its breed society.

Dartmoor ponies are kind and sensible. They have a good action which is low and free as befits a riding pony. They make ideal first ponies for children.

Exmoor

This is the oldest of the British breeds, and its origin is uncertain. The Exmoor is closely related to the Dartmoor, being bred on a neighboring moor in southwestern England, and is equally hardy and handsome.

The Exmoor is distinctive for its mealy (cream-colored) muzzle. Its coloring is bay, brown, or mouse dun and, though it never shows white markings of any kind, it sometimes has a mealy underbelly and inside thighs. It has prominent eyes, known colloquially as "frog" or "toad" eyes, and its coat is of a peculiar texture, being hard and springy. In summer the Exmoor's coat lies close and shines like brass; in winter it carries no bloom.

It stands 11.2–12.3 hands (115–127cm.) high and is a splendid children's pony provided it is trained from an early age. It is intelligent, alert, and naturally wild, yet once trained is a kindly companion.

Shetland

American Shetland

Gotland

Exmoor

Dartmoor

Iceland

Welsh Mountain Pony

Pony of the Americas

Welsh Cob

Mongolian

Welsh

Ponies have run wild on the hills of Wales for thousands of years, varying in size and type according to the haphazard meetings of their parents. In order to distinguish between the differing abilities of these ponies, three types of Welsh are recognized and are divided into Sections A, B, and C.

Section A, the **Welsh Mountain Pony,** is thought by many to be the most beautiful of all the British mountain and moorland breeds. It stands about, or just over, 12 hands (120cm.) high and is a strong, graceful pony with a gay carriage and a small, Arab-type head. It is a fine boned pony, a beautiful mover, quick and free in all its paces. The head is set high and the neck is arched and proud. It has great intelligence and spirit.

The **Welsh Pony** Section B, is taller and stands 12–13.2 hands (120–130cm) high. Section Bs owe a genealogical debt to a small Thoroughbred stallion named Merlin, who ran wild on the Denbighshire hills less than a century ago. Section B ponies are often called "Merlins" to this day. This Welsh pony looks much like the Welsh Mountain, though without the Arab characteristics. Quality Section Bs are often seen at the head of ridden show ring classes, since the object of breeders of the Welsh pony is to produce the perfect riding animal for children, both in looks, movement, and in kind temperament.

Section C, the **Welsh Pony of Cob Type,** though not officially allowed to exceed 13.2 hands (130cm.) high, is a scaled-down Welsh Cob, smaller and lighter in build. It excelled in the days of the pony trap and might since have declined severely in numbers had it not been for the advent of trekking holidays. These ponies are substantial enough for adults to sit on without causing undue strain and are kind and hardy enough to work all day on relatively poor quality food.

Welsh Cob

The Welsh Cob, otherwise called Section D, is bold, energetic, and sturdy, with an even temper. The Cob's ancestry is uncertain, but the Welsh Cob of today and the Powys Cob of eight hundred years ago were similar in appearance. Standing 14–15 hands (140–150cm.) high, it is larger and heavier than the Welsh Mountain pony. It has a quality head and a powerful body. Its legs are strong, with plenty of bone below the knee and a little silky feather on its fetlocks.

The Welsh Cob is a versatile animal employed mainly in driving with an excellent trotting speed.

Pony of the Americas

The Pony of the Americas is a new breed with origins that are easy to trace. In 1956, Mr. Leslie L. Boomhower, a horse breeder living in Mason City, Iowa, crossed a Shetland stallion with an Appaloosa mare. The result was a very attractive miniature colt which was so successful in the show ring, so much admired as a potentially good children's pony, that it became the foundation sire of a new breed.

The ideal Pony of the Americas is a miniature Appaloosa horse standing 11.2–13 hands (115–130cm.) high. It should have style, substance, and symmetry. It has a willing and gentle character and is versatile enough to carry a younger rider on trail rides, over show jumps, and in races. It is especially popular in the western United States as a cow pony.

Pinto

The pinto pony is a general purpose riding horse of variable height with no specific conformation. Its name comes from the Spanish meaning "painted." Its color is piebald ("overo") which comes from a recessive gene predominating in South America, or skewbald ("tobiano") which is a dominant gene more pronounced in North America. The pinto pony appears all over the world but only in the United States is it recognized as a breed under the Pinto Horse Association founded in 1956.

Chincoteague

The origin of these ponies is difficult to trace since they come from Two American islands off the coast of Virginia where the horse is not indigenous. They are thought to be descended from partly Arab horses which survived a Spanish shipwreck in the sixteenth century. They stand about 12 hands (120cm.) high. Although these ponies can be of any color the most usual is pinto. Stubborn and still somewhat wild, some nevertheless make good family pets.

Mongolian

The pony loosely described as Mongolian, found all over the area covered by Mongolia, Tibet, and China is a variant animal bred for function rather than for the show ring. Mongolians are working animals, bred in large numbers by nomadic tribes, surviving as best they can on whatever they can forage. They are used for herding, riding, carting, in agriculture, and as pack ponies; they supply milk or meat for their masters. Mares' milk is made into cheese or fermented into *kumiss*, both practices dating from before the time of Genghis Khan, when nomadic tribes depended on their horses for their lives.

Mongolian ponies have, not surprisingly, enormous endurance. They vary greatly in appearance. In general they are between 12.2–14 hands (125–140cm.) high and are unprepossessing to look at. They are thickset, with a heavy head and a short neck. Common colors are black, bay, brown, and dun.

They can live on poor fare, and little of it, and their owners are more dependent on them than other horse owners are on their breeds. Even today Outer Mongolia has more horses per head of human population than any other country. Without the Mongolian pony many normadic tribes would not survive.

Asiatic Wild Horse.

The Asiatic Wild Horse (*Equus przewalskii przewalskii*) is a primitive pony believed to be one of the early basic breeds. It stands 12.1–14.1 hands (122–142cm.) high and is duncolored, usually with dark points and a mealy muzzle; it often has zebra stripes on its forearms, hocks, and gaskins. The ears are long, the head is large and broad, normally set on a ewe neck with a short, upright mane. The shoulder is upright and the hindquarters poor with a thin tail, but the back, loins and legs are strong.

Tarpan

Asiatic Wild Horse

The Asiatic Wild Horse is brave, sometimes to the point of savagery. In its feral state, stallions and even two-year-old colts will kill invading males long before they get near the mares. Because of its ferocity, and because of the rigors of its native habitat on the western fringes of the Gobi Desert where more domesticated types of horses could not survive, it has scarcely outcrossed and has remained almost unchanged.

The Asiatic Wild Horse has few qualifications as a pet. It is included here not only because it is one of the two pure primitive ponies (the other is the Tarpan) but also because people may have seen it in zoos. A couple of hundred of the few surviving members of its species (it was hunted almost to extinction in the Gobi Desert) are being carefully bred in European and American zoos.

Tarpan

Probably better known than the Asiatic Wild Horse, the Tarpan is another of the primitive pony breeds. There are two subspecies, the Steppe Tarpan (*Equus przewalskii gmelini*) and the Forest Tarpan (*E.p. silvaticus*).

Tarpans were once widespread in Europe and western Asia. Recently they have been restricted to Eastern Europe, especially to Poland. Controversy exists about whether they are actually extinct, since the last official Tarpan died in captivity in 1887. At that time the Polish government, poignantly aware of the probable extinction of the Tarpan, gathered together a number of Tarpan-like animals from peasant farms and let them loose in forest reserves. Thus there is an argument about whether the breed has been "preserved" or "restored."

The Tarpan's decline was due to the quality of its meat, which was regarded as a great delicacy. They were hunted ruthlessly, often dying after a ferocious battle in which a Tarpan stallion had attacked the mounts of his hunters. Their courage and tenacity in fight are legendary; but, though they are also stubborn and independent, they have been successfully caught and trained for useful work as a farm animal.

Their physical characteristics are like those of their Mongolian relative, though their winter coat is occasionally white, as in feral Arctic animals when living in a very cold climate. They also have better proportioned shoulders and a mane which lies down in normal pony fashion. Today's Tarpan owes its survival largely to zoos.

Bosnian

This compact mountain pony of the Tarpan type is the most widespread and important of the pony breeds in the Balkan states. About 40,000 of them work in Yugoslavia as farm and pack ponies and sometimes as riding ponies. They are sturdy, hardy, affectionate, and very intelligent.

Quality control is carefully exercised by the State so that only chosen stallions are allowed to cover mares. Pack pony stallions which are considered for stud work must first of all pass a test which consists of carrying a load of 100kg. (220lb.) for 16km (10mi.)

Fell

One of the strongest of the British working ponies, the Fell originates from the hills of Westmorland and Cumberland in northern

Fell

163

England. Its ancestors seem to have been the Friesian horse and the now-extinct Galloway breed of the Scottish lowlands. Now almost exclusively a riding animal, the Fell was formerly a harness pony and farm worker in the hill districts and a lead mines pack pony. During the seventeenth and eighteenth centuries there were no roads suitable for heavy carts to take lead from the mines to the coast, and the Fell regularly carried 100kg. (220 lb.) for 48km. (30 mi.) or more each day. It was also a famous trotter, moving at up to 32km. (20mi.) an hour for a considerable period.

The Fell is a handsome animal with a proudly carried head and a good, sloping shoulder. The body is muscular, with well-sprung ribs, strong loins, and hindquarters. The tail is thick and carried gaily, and there is light feather on the hard, strong legs. Its height is 13–14 hands (130–140 cm.) high and its color is usually black.

Dales
Stemming from the same region of northern England, the Dales pony is a bigger and even stronger version of the Fell. Some outbreeding has occurred with other British native strains. During the nineteenth century a famous Welsh Cob Stallion, Comet, that could trot 16km. (10 mi.) in 33 minutes carrying 76kg. (168 lb.) on his back, was bred to Dales mares with such success that today every Dales pony carries a trace of this great trotter in its blood.

Like many native British ponies, the Dales was nearly mechanized out of existence in the first half of the twentieth century. By 1950 it was almost extinct, but the boom in pony trekking saved it. The size and strength of the Dales pony make it a more suitable ride for adults than for children. It is now increasing in numbers.

The Dales stands 14–14.2 hands (140–145cm.) high and is black, bay or dark brown in color. It is sensible, quiet to handle, and thrives on work.

Fjord
The Fjord pony, also known as the Westlands, has changed little from the horse used by the Vikings for horse fights (see Iceland Pony). It originates from Norway, where it is likely to endure because it can work in high mountain areas that are too steep or too cold for motorized vehicles, but it is also popular all over Scandinavia and is especially loved in Denmark. It has many uses, being equally adaptable to packing, trekking, or to harness. It does well on poor fare, is indifferent to cold, and is a tireless worker. The Fjord is a stoutly-built, primitive sort of pony.

It stands 13–14.2 hands (130–145cm) high and has a smallish, well-shaped head, an immensely powerful body, and strong legs. It comes in all shades of dun, with the mane and tail a mixture of black and silver. The mane, which is upright, is traditionally cut on a crescent about 10cm. (4 in.) high at the peak, so that the black hairs at the center of the mane show above the silver cutside strands. The Fjord is fond of company and is charming in its appearance and personality.

Haflinger
This is the most popular Tyrolean pony and stands about 14 hands (140cm.) high. Haflingers are reared on mountain meadows and left to mature until they are four years old before they are broken in, which may account for their extremely long working lives. Some are reputed able to work until they are forty years old. The brand of the Haflinger is an edelweiss (the Austrian national flower), with an "E" in the center.

The Haflinger is almost always chestnut with a flaxen mane and tail. It has a medium-sized head with a pointed muzzle and small ears, a well-muscled body with short legs and hard feet, and the free, elastic action typical of a mountain pony. Haflingers are excellent for harness and pack work as well as for riding purposes.

Camarguais
The white horse of the Camargue, made famous by motion pictures, mostly lives wild in the Rhone delta (though it sometimes works as a cow pony or as a trekking pony). The breed is thought to be very old and to possess oriental blood because of its fine head and wideset eyes.

It is about 14 hands (140 cm.) high and has a short, strong body. The legs are fine, with good bone, and the feet broad and large—an asset on marshy ground, as the larger the feet the less likely the horse is to sink up to its elbows. It is near-black in youth and white in old age.

Highland
There are two types of Highland pony, both originating in Scotland. The **Garron** or **Mainland** stands about 14.2 hands (145 cm.), and the **Western Isles** 12.2–14.2 (125–145cm.) hands high. Both are normally dun in color with a dorsal stripe, but they can also be gray, chestnut, bay, and black. The Garron is stronger than the Islands type, though similar in physique.

The version traditionally associated with deer stalking is the Garron. It is surefooted enough to carry a deer's carcass on the steep slopes of the Scottish glens and is so docile and trusting that a hunter can fire a gun from its back. The Garron is the biggest and strongest of all the British pony breeds. It has been known to carry at a canter (in a circus act) seven adult riders at a combined estimated weight of 380kg. (840lb.) without apparent strain.

Both types of Highland are powerful, well-made animals with short, deep heads, open nostrils, intelligent eyes and short ears. Abundant mane covers a cresty neck and powerful shoulders. The chest and girth are deep and roomy, and the back short with well-sprung ribs and strong loins. Hindquarters are full, and the tail long and thick. The hard, short legs have plenty of bone and abundant feather at the fetlock joint. Action is straight and free, though there is a tendency to be on the forehand.

Notwithstanding its powerful appearance, the Highland is a sensitive pony, giving its trust generously to a good owner but tending to be wary of strangers and easily soured by ill-treatment.

Connemara
This famous pony from the Connaught Province of Ireland is renowned as a children's riding pony because of its exceptional kindness and intelligence. It possesses great natural ability as a hunter and jumper and makes an excellent show pony. Connemaras have been known in Ireland for many centuries. They are thought to be of the same basic family as the Western Isles type of Highland pony, and they have run wild in the mountains of the Irish west coast since before recorded history. Interbreeding with Spanish Jennets which survived the wreck of the Spanish Armada in 1588, and more recently with Arab and Thoroughbred blood, has altered the Connemara so much that it is questionable how many "Connemara" ponies of today really deserve the name. Dun, once the typical Connemara color, is becoming rare.

It is one of the taller ponies standing 13–14 hands (130–140cm.) high with a pleasing appearance. It carries its head well on its long, compact body, its shoulders and hindquarters are strong and sloping while its legs are short and firm, with good bone and hard feet. It moves freely and comfortably and is an excellent jumper. Outcrosses with the Connemara have produced good show jumping and hunting stock. The true Connemara loses its characteristically small wiry form if exported outside its native land and fed on lush pastures.

New Forest
More than 1,000 years ago the area of scrub common land called the New Forest extended throughout southern England from the borders of London almost to the west coast. Much of it is still common grazing land today. The New Forest pony is a mixture of many breeds that have been pastured on the common over the centuries. No serious attempt at breed control was made until 1938, so the name *New Forest* covers a wide range of pony shapes and sizes.

Whatever its outward appearance may be, the New Forest is the most tractable of all British riding ponies.

Height varies from 12–14.2 hands (120–145cm.) high. All colors are acceptable except piebald and skewbald. Though any pony bred in the forest may claim to be a New Forest pony, a definite type is becoming recognizable through the influence of the New Forest Pony Breeding and Cattle Society. Today's show ring New Forest has a rather large head well set on a shortish neck, a good, sloping shoulder, a short back and strong hindquarters. It is a hardy, thrifty pony with plenty of endurance and makes an excellent child's hunter.

Hackney
The word *hackney* comes from the Norman French *haquenée*, which was applied in the Middle Ages to ordinary riding animals. Later this word came to be applied to the highly prized breed developed in the eighteenth century from Blaze, the famous old Norfolk

Hackney Pony

Camarguais

Connemara

Criollo

trotting horse with help from Arab, Thoroughbred, Fell, and Welsh blood. Shortly before the dawn of motorized horsepower the Hackney-drawn carriage was the smartest form of transportation.

The most distinguishing feature of the Hackney is its stylish action. At the walk, it has a high, springing step, and even at a standstill it holds itself with great presence. The trot is a movement of magnificent animation: the forelegs are drawn up high with sharply bent knees and thrown well forward in a long stride, while the hind legs move with a similar exaggerated action. The movement is straight and true, with a tiny pause of each foot in mid air making the horse appear to float. Hackneys are used exclusively for harness. They vary in size from 12.2–16 hands (125–160cm.) high, but there are many more Hackney ponies than horses. In North America some, occasionally called "**Bantam**" **Hackneys,** have been bred as small as 11 hands (110cm.). Although the Hackney is assuming more of a pet function than other breeds of horse and pony, the delight that it brings to horse show audiences guarantees its future.

Basuto

This breed, developed in Lethoso, southern Africa, and accustomed to rugged climatic conditions, is one of the toughest and bravest in the world. It can carry a full-grown man for 100–130km. (60–80 mi.) a day despite its scrawny appearance, has been used for racing and for polo, and served extensively during the Boer War.

Its origins are Barbs and Arabs imported by the Dutch East India Company in 1653, strengthened by later injections of Persian and Thoroughbred blood. This quality ancestry was first bred in Cape Province and the result was called the **Cape Horse.** About 1830 it crossed into Lesotho, formerly known as Basutoland, largely by means of border raids. Here, lack of interest and the tough climate caused the Cape Horse to deteriorate into the Basuto pony. The deterioration, however, is only aesthetic. Were it not for the restrictions imposed by African horse sickness, a disease so lethal that no nation will allow the import of a horse from Africa, the Basuto pony would surely have enjoyed international popularity as a working animal. It stands about 14.2 hands (145cm.) high, often has a ewe neck and a longish back, and is fearless and exceptionally self-reliant.

Criollo

This compact, handsome horse is best known outside its native South America as the cow pony ridden by the gauchos. Its unique range of coloring—predominantly dun with dorsal stripe and white markings, roan, or sandy colors such as liver, chestnut, and palomino and sometimes mixtures such as blue and white—is thought to have evolved for self-protection in the wild during a short time. Horses were not known to South American peoples until the arrival of the Conquistadores in the sixteenth century.

The Criollo's basic blood is Andalusian, Barb, and Arab. Its smallness and toughness is due to three hundred years of natural selection during which it ran wild or semi-wild on the plains. Though it is bred with slight variations all over South America, it is in Argentina especially that people take great pride in its endurance. Stamina tests are held to choose the best Criollos for breeding. An annual ride is conducted by breeders during which the horses must cover 750km. (470 mi.) in 15 days carrying 110kg. (242lb.), with nothing to eat or drink along the way except such food as they can find for themselves.

The Cariollo stands 13.3–15 hands (137–150cm.) high. The head is short and broad, the ears small and the eyes large and expressive. It has a muscular neck set on strong shoulders. The chest is broad, the legs fine-boned, and the feet small.

Morgan

Few breeds of horse can claim descent from one common foundation sire, but Justin

Morgan, foaled about 1793 in Massachusetts, was a stallion of such astonishing prepotency that he stamped his offspring faithfully in conformation, character and height and thus established one of the truly American breeds.

The modern Morgan stands 14–15.2 hands (140–155cm.) high and is bay, brown, black, or chestnut in color. It has a short, broad head set on a compact, muscular body with strong loins and hindquarters and clean legs with plenty of bone. The Morgan is a tough, hardy horse with a high, free action and has enormous physical strength and endurance. It is kind, independent, and enduring. It can be ridden or driven, hunted or shown, or kept for family fun.

Barb

This tough little North African horse, standing 14–15 hands (140–150cm.) high, can live like a goat on small quantities of poor food. Nevertheless, it is docile, brave, and elegant. Its refined head is set on flat shoulders, its quarters are sloping with a lowset tail, and its legs are long and strong.

The Barb is one of the great foundation breeds which were widely used to improve other horses. It was exported from the Barbary region of North Africa as early as 800A.D. to Spain where, crossed with native horses it gave rise to the Andalusian. The Barb can be dark bay, brown, chestnut, gray, or black in color.

Arab

Allah said to the South Wind: "Become solid flesh, for I will make a new creature of thee, to the honour of My Holy Name and the abasement of Mine enemies, and for a servant to them that are subject to Me."

And the South Wind said: "Lord, do Thou so."

*Then Allah took a handful of the South Wind and he breathed thereon, creating the horse and saying: "Thy name shall be Arabian, and virtue bound into the hair of thy forelock, and plunder on thy back. I have preferred thee above all beasts of burden, inasmuch as I have made thy master thy friend. I have given thee the power of flight without wings, be it in onslaught or retreat. I will set men on thy back, that shall honour and praise Me and sing Hallelujah to My name."—*Bedouin legend.

This sort of exquisite mythology about the Arab horse originated in the teachings of Mohammed, who deeply understood how important the horse was to his nomadic tribes. In the Koran, written in the early 7th century, he reinforced his equine beliefs by religious creed. Among the injunctions of Mohammed, the military leader, are "the Evil One dare not enter into a tent in which a purebred horse is kept", and "As many grains of barley as thou givest thy horse, so many sins shall be forgiven thee."

The devotion of the nomadic Arab tribes goes beyond legend into fact. In contrast to Western ideas, the Arab tribes believed inbreeding reinforced good points. Courage and endurance of the resulting Arab horses suggests that they may be correct. The horses that they raised, often kept in the desert on dried meat and camel's milk, are among the hardiest and the most spirited in the world.

Though small, usually standing between 14.2–15.1 hands (145–152cm.) high, the Arab has an exquisite head, with a short and concave face, wide nostrils on an elegant muzzle, and large, sensitive, dark eyes wide set well below the small alert ears. The head is carried nobly on a gracefully arched neck. The body is compact and well muscled with strong hindquarters, and the legs are both delicate and strong, with small, hard feet. The whole effect is one of symmetry and grace, pride and exuberance. The action is free, straight, and airy. The colors are gray, bay, chestnut, and occasionally black.

Friesian

Keeping in mind that the horses of the past bear little resemblance to today's favored breeds, the Friesian is one of the oldest and most consistently popular horses in Europe. Descendants of this heavy native Dutch animal were valued as saddle horses by the medieval nobility and have been painted by many of the Dutch Old Masters. Probably by this time the Friesian had been strongly influenced by Andalusian blood and oriental influences were also likely.

The breed came close to extinction just before World War I and was revived by

Arab

Morgan

Head of Uracar Arab

Head of Shammar Arab

crossing with Oldenburg stock. In 1954, Queen Juliana of the Netherlands honored the Friesian breed society with the title "Royal."

The Friesian stands about 15 hands (150cm.) high, has feathers on its feet, a coach horse body, and a long, alert head. It moves flamboyantly and carries itself with pride. The Friesian has an exceptionally pleasant temperament. Black is the only color permitted—even white markings are undesirable.

Akhal-Teké

The prevailing color is gold, either golden dun, gold bay or gold chestnut, and its coat often has a metallic bloom. It can also appear in gray or bay, sometimes with white markings. It is known for its obstinacy and bad temper.

It is a bold horse, built like a greyhound, and its mane and tail are sometimes so short and sparse that they almost do not exist. Its action is magnificent—free and flowing in all its paces; it has a gliding, elastic stride. Height is between 14.2–15.2 hands (145–155cm.) high.

The Akhal-Teké comes from the Turkoman steppes of the USSR and is extremely resilient—one is even reported to have crossed 1450km. (900 mi.) of desert without a drink of water. Its supreme stamina has resulted from years of exposure to the extreme climate of the central Asian deserts, where it has been bred separately for centuries. There are indications of a horse of the Akhal-Teké type existing as long ago as 500 B.C.

Appaloosa

There are six basic patterns for the Appaloosa coat: frost, leopard, snowflake, marble, spotted blanket, and white blanket, though many variations exist. The basic ground color is roan, the skin around the nostrils, lips, and genitalia is mottled, and the eyes are ringed with white sclera. Hooves are usually vertically striped.

It is necessary to distinguish between Appaloosa as a color and Appaloosa as a breed. Horses and ponies with Appaloosa markings may appear in any shape or form all over the world. The Appaloosa breed, however, is American in origin. It is thought to have been developed initially by the Nez Percé Indians, who lived in the fertile area of northwest America watered by the Palouse river (hence "Palouse horse," "Palousy," corrupted to "Appaloosa.")

The Appaloosa breed is a tractable horse about 14.2–15.3 hands (145–157cm.) high, compact and hardy with a deep chest. It has an unusually wispy mane and tail and is sometimes called "rat-tailed" or "fingertailed." It has grown so much in national popularity that it now ranks as one of the largest and most popular breeds in America.

Palomino

The Palomino is commonly classified as a color/breed, but there is some controversy about applying the term *breed*. The Association of Palomino Horse Breeders of America recognizes horses ranging from 14.2–15.3 hands (145–157cm.) high, provided that they conform to a good saddle type.

The famous Palomino coat color on animals throughout the world is ideally gold rather than chestnut or yellow. No markings other than white should appear on the face or the legs. The mane and tail should be white with not more than 15 percent dark or chestnut hair, and the eyes should be dark. Palomino coloration appears most frequently among Quarter Horses, but the number of Palominos is dwindling.

Albino

This is another color/breed, like the Appaloosa and the Palomino. Unlike the Palomino, however, Albinos tend to breed true to color so that the establishment of an Albino breed is easier. Handsome, lightweight saddle horses with kindly, intelligent minds are beginning to set the standard in North America, where success is also being achieved in breeding out the weak blue eyes and the sensitivity of the skin to sun.

Albino horses, like other albino animals, tend to a complete absence of pigmentation in the skin. Coat color is snow white all over on a pink skin. Eyes are pale blue by nature and dark brown by careful breeding. There is no height specification for Albinos.

Waler

Horses are not indigenous to Australia. The earliest ancestors of the Waler (the name is derived from the early English-settled territories known as New South Wales) were brought from the Cape of Good Hope with the First Fleet settlers of 1798 and were of predominantly Spanish blood. Massive improvement with Arab and Thoroughbred blood during the first half of the nineteenth century, plus the rich pastureland and warm, dry Australian climate, produced a top-quality saddle horse closely resembling a large Anglo-Arab.

Then, in 1850 and for three decades to follow, lust for land gave way to lust for gold.

While the gold rush lasted, farming was neglected and horses roamed and bred at random. Quality saddle horses were less in demand than were small draft horses to pack the gold. But, by the 1880s, new fortunes needed new diversions and the Waler was regenerated as a luxury for racing and for riding.

The breed had its greatest and most tragic moments during World War I, when more than 120,000 Walers were exported for the Allied armies in India, Africa, Palestine, and Europe. Because of Australian quarantine laws, repatriation of these horses after the war was impossible. Thousands were destroyed in the desert by an Australian government order, and a bronze memorial in Sydney stands in memory of them today.

Walers are brave and enduring horses. They usually stand about 16 hands (160–160cm.) high and can be of any color. The head is alert, the ears fairly long, and the neck is well set on strong shoulders. The back and hindquarters are strong, and the legs clean with plenty of bone.

American Quarter Horse

This is the oldest of the American breeds. Numerically the most popular horse in the world, the Quarter Horse is possibly also the most versatile. More than eight hundred thousand Quarter Horses are registered in the United States and abroad, and more than forty different nations own specimens of the breed. The American Quarter Horse Association in Amarillo, Texas, must employ more than two hundred people to handle the largest equine registry in the world.

The Quarter Horse was selectively bred during the early part of the seventeenth century from Spanish imports (Arabs, Barbs, Turks) crossed with English animals of the early Thoroughbred type. It was bred for speed in the popular colonial sport of match racing, which usually took place over distances not exceeding a quarter of a mile and which were frequently run in the village

Appaloosa-Leopard

American Saddlebred

American Standardbred

American Quarter Horse

street. The name *Quarter Horse* comes from this horse's superlative performance over a quarter of a mile.

Later, it was used as a cow pony. It traveled west with the pioneers, excelling at every sort of work with cattle, and was soon said to possess a natural ability with cows. Today its major use is as a cutting horse on cattle ranches. It is also widely used in rodeos for the events of barrel racing, bulldogging, and roping because no other breed of horse can start and stop as quickly. The most lucrative race in the world belongs to the Quarter Horse—the All American Futurity Stakes, worth about $600,000.

The Quarter Horse is a compact, muscular, handsome animal standing 15.2–16.1 hands (155–162cm.) high. It comes in all solid colors, though chestnut predominates. It is an intelligent, highly adaptable, sensible, and active horse. It is built for sprinting—well muscled and short backed, with clean legs on a powerful body and massive hindquarters.

Tennessee Walking Horse

The Tennessee Walker has a unique gliding gait which makes it the most comfortable ride in the world. It is trained in three gaits: the flat walk, running walk, and canter. The movement apparently cannot be taught to any other breed, but in the Tennessee Walker it is now so much inbred that foals are sometimes seen to perform it simply from imitating their dams. The action of the forefeet is high and straight; that of the hind feet long striding. The horse moves with a four-beat gait, the forefoot touching the ground fractionally before the diagonally opposite hind foot, which oversteps the track of the forefoot. The effect is that of a steady, gliding movement which is emphasized by the rhythm of its nodding head.

It is a docile horse, willing and cheerful. It stands 14.2–17 hands (142–170cm.) high and carries its plain head nobly on an arched neck. The body is powerful, and the legs clean and hard. The abundant mane and tail is always worn long and full. The support muscles of the tail on show horses are nicked to give an artificially high tail carriage.

American Saddle Horse

This superb riding horse, known also as the Saddlebred, the Kentucky Saddle Horse and the Saddler, has great presence and a gentle, charming nature. It stands 15–16 hands (150–160cm.) high, and its action is extravagant and tremendously showy. The American Saddlebred is trained for five gaits—walk, trot, canter, slow-gait and rack—which it can perform with the grace of a ballet dancer.

The rack is an even four-beat gait in which each foot pauses in midair before coming down separately—a spectacular dancing movement that can occur at speeds up to 48kmph. (30mph.). The slow-gait is a slow and graceful version of the rack. As with the Tennessee Walking Horse, the original purpose in developing these movements was to give plantation owners a luxury ride. Now the purpose is usually the show ring, where

Saddle Horses compete in classes for three-gaited (walk, trot, and canter) and five-gaited horses according to their level of training. The three-gaited horse is distinguished by shaving the mane and the tail up to the breakover point.

American Standardbred

Conformation in the Standardbred varies somewhat, since its prime requirement is its speed, not its appearance. Standing about 15.2 hands (155cm.) high it is a small, muscular Thoroughbred type although of less refined appearance and is powerful in the shoulders, chest, hindquarters, heart, and lungs. Its legs and feet are iron hard. They are extremely tractable and well disciplined.

The name *Standardbred* applies to both trotters and pacers, and comes from a 1.6km. (1 mi.) speed trial standard requirement for entry in races. Entrants must attain standards of two minutes thirty seconds for trotters and two minutes twenty-five seconds for pacers. (Pacing is a gait in which both legs on the same side come down simultaneously). Although predominantly Thoroughbred, Standardbreds contain English and Canadian trotting blood as well as Arab, Barb, and Morgan.

Don

The Don was the favorite horse of the Cossacks and, as such, was an important cavalry mount. It was not a pampered animal. It was and still is herded on the central Asian steppes, where it must forage for survival during the heavy winter snows.

Today's Don has been refined by oriental blood from several of the quality Russian breeds. Standing 15.1–15.3 hands (152–157 cm.) high it is now used as a saddle horse and combines quality with unusual stamina. It has a calm temperament and is a consistent performer.

Irish Cob

Whether the Irish Cob is a specific breed is questionable although the type has existed in Ireland for centuries. Standing 15–16 hands (150–160cm.) high, it is an extremely capable and strong harness horse. It has a plain head with a convex face, a strong body, short, hard legs, and large, dense feet. It is sensible in temperament, active and a hard worker. The Irish Cob is an all-round animal, equally good in the shafts or carrying a heavy rider. All colors are acceptable although black, bay, chestnut and gray are the most common.

Cleveland Bay

The Cleveland Bay is one of the oldest of the current English breeds. It was formerly known as the **Chapman Horse,** named for the chapmen, or travelling merchants, who used it as a packhorse in the seventeenth and eighteenth centuries. Infusions of Thoroughbred blood in the late eighteenth century led to the now nearly-extinct Yorkshire Coach Horse, which was a taller and flashier version of the Cleveland model. The Cleveland Bay stands 15.2–16.1 hands (155–162cm.) high and is a handsome carriage horse, usually bay or brown in color. As a ceremonial coach horse it has few worldwide peers; as a cross with the Thoroughbred for producing hunters it is hard to find its equal.

Thoroughbred

The Thoroughbred is most famous as a racehorse and was bred entirely for that purpose. In the early seventeenth century, King James I of England, who personally preferred hawking and hunting to racing, began to develop horses for competitive speed because of the demands made by the Scottish nobles at his hunting lodge at Newmarket. In attempting to breed a fast horse, James I also recognized the military and civil importance of improving the speed and stamina of British horses, and he encouraged the importation of good foreign animals to strengthen the breed.

The three foundation sires from which all Thoroughbreds descend arrived in England in the eighteenth century. They were the Darley Arabian, which was sent to England in 1704 by Thomas Darley (the British Consul in Aleppo); the Byerley Turk (Colonel Byerley's battle charger); and the Godolphin Arabian (probably part of a gift of horses to the king of France from the Bey of Tunis which had been taken to Lord Godolphin's stud at Cambridge). These three were bred successfully with the fastest English racing mares. Every Thoroughbred registered in the General Stud Book of today has one or all of these sires in its pedigree.

The modern Thoroughbred racehorse differs greatly from its tough little oriental ancestors. It stands just over 16 hands (160cm.) high on average, and has the comparative length of leg of a greyhound (with attendant problems of bone and foot inadequate to its weight). The back is short and strong with a deep girth and well-sprung ribs. Its action is free and long striding. The Thoroughbred is the fastest horse in the world and one of the boldest.

Irish Draft

When crossed with a Thoroughbred or another quality lightweight horse, the Irish Draft produces the famous Irish hunters and jumpers. The Irish Draft is a big horse standing 15–17 hands (150–170cm.) high or more, and is bay, brown, chestnut or gray in color. Due to its quiet and sensitive temperament, active disposition and great body strength, it is an ideal working horse or mount for a large person.

Anglo-Arab

The qualities of the Arab and the Thoroughbred are displayed in differing measures according to the prepotency of the parents of this Arab-Thoroughbred cross. Nevertheless, an elegant lightweight saddle horse of charm and delicacy is sure to result. The brave, sweet-natured Anglo-Arab, usually standing around or just under 16 hands (160cm.) high, is a popular mount throughout Europe and throughout the United States. It excels as a show mount and is widely used in dressage, eventing, jumping, and hunting. Bay and chestnut are the most common colors.

Andalusian

The Andalusian was formerly the warhorse of lightweight cavalry. It was bred by the Spaniards for more than 600 years, the outcome of crossing Arab and Barb horses brought by the Moorish invasion with the tall, stout horses of the conquering Vandals. The result was a warhorse that influenced Europe during the Middle Ages.

The great breeders of the true Andalusian line were undoubtedly the Carthusian monks, whose obsession with purity of line was little short of fanatical. They even threatened to excommunicate followers who veered from the national equestrian style. Had it not been for the devotion of several Carthusian monasteries, who hid Andalusians away from Napoleon's acquisitive armies, and of the Zapata family who managed to conceal a small herd, the Andalusian strain would not have survived undiluted. As it was, a new stud was begun under King Ferdinand VII in the nineteenth century, and the breed has prospered ever since. Most of the Spanish horses which came to the New World were Andalusians.

The Andalusian is nearly always gray (though it can be black) and stands about 16 hands (160cm.) high. The Andalusian is a

Thoroughbred Racing

Irish Cob

Andalusian

Hanoverian

handsome animal and a superlative carriage horse. It is affectionate, intelligent, and proud in temperament.

Lipizzaner

The Lipizzaner is the mount of the famous Spanish Riding School of Vienna which was founded in 1758 "for the education of the nobility in the art of horsemanship." The Lipizzaner has been bred in Austria since the sixteenth century, the foundation stud being at Lipizza.

The original stock was pure Andalusian though at Piber, another famous Austrian stud site, Andalusians were mixed with Kladrubers, Neapolitans (a now-extinct Italian breed of predominantly Andalusian extraction), and probably with Fredriksborgs and Arabs. The result is a horse similar in appearance to the Andalusian.

Although usually gray in color, the Lipizzaner can also be bay, chestnut, or roan. Height is 15–16 hands (150–160cm.).

Kladruber

This is a taller but otherwise almost identical version of the Andalusian/Lipizzaner. It has been bred in Bohemia (now Czechoslovakia) since the sixteenth century, when the Emperor Maximilian II founded a stud of Andalusian horses at Kladruby. Like its cousin the Andalusian, it is almost always gray, though it can be black.

Today the Kladruber is still bred at the State stud at Kladruby, performing its ancestral function of drawing the State coach on ceremonial occasions. The famous Kladruby Grays are driven in teams of up to 16-in-hand, usually without postillions to assist the coachman. It is a majestic carriage horse. Height is 16–17.2 hands (160–175cm.).

Altér Real

This Portuguese horse is of basic Andalusian stock. Like the Andalusian, it was nearly decimated by the Napoleonic wars. The line was restored by the introduction of Andalusians from the Zapata herd. Intelligent management by the Portuguese Ministry of Economy has, during this century, brought about the great quality of the modern Altér.

It is a saddle horse capable of being trained to *haute école* standard. It has an aristocratic head and a strong body. It stands 15–16 hands (150–160cm.) and is usually bay or brown in color.

Hanoverian

The Hanoverian has been bred since the seventeenth century and descends from the Hanoverian Creams which were used as carriage horses for ceremonial purposes. There are great variations in this popular breed due to modification with Thoroughbred and Trakehner blood. The classic Hanoverian has a somewhat plain head, though individuals within this breed sometimes display an oriental head. The Hanoverian stands 15.3–17 hands (157–170cm.) high and is an indomitable, courageous animal that is both well mannered and versatile.

Balance, obedience, and physical power combine to make the Hanoverian a top-class dressage horse and show jumper, and in these two fields it justly commands very high prices. Besides its natural aptitude for sporting events (it is also an excellent hunter), it seems to have a genuine love of the game and sometimes an appealing sense of showmanship. Many of the famous German show jumpers of today are Hanoverians, and the breed is steadily gaining in international popularity. Any solid color is acceptable.

Oldenburg

This is the tallest and heaviest of the German warm-blooded breeds. Standing 16.2–17.2 hands (165–75cm.) high, the Oldenburg is a show hack or show jumper. It is charming, good-natured, active, intelligent, and loyal. It stands 16–16.2 hands (160–165cm.) high and is solid-colored.

Frederiksborg

This is a Danish horse of the strong harness type. It is usually chestnut in color, standing 15.2–16.1 hands (155–162cm.) high. It is active, tractable, and a hard worker. Although its head is plain, its eye is intelligent and its general expression alert. It has a powerful, well-muscled body, and good legs with plenty of bone. Modern requirements have changed its function; formerly an excellent light draft/harness horse, it is now used under saddle.

Einsiedler

The Einsiedler is the popular riding and cavalry horse of Switzerland. It is named for the Benedictine abbey of Einsieden, where records of a stud trace back to 1064. It is a bold, active horse with a gentle disposition and generally good conformation. It stands 15.3–16.2 hands (157–165cm.) high and is of any solid color, though bay and chestnut are the most common.

Einsiedlers are versatile horses that can show jump, often at international level, perform dressage, trot, and work in harness and on the farm.

Furioso

This is the elegant, versatile saddle horse of Hungary. Its handsome body is carried as a strong, all-purpose saddle horse. At the turn of the century it was the perfect coach horse, but subsequent crossing with predominantly Thoroughbred and Anglo-Norman lines has refined its massive body.

The Oldenburg has a powerful shoulder, a deep and roomy chest, deep girth and strong hindquarters. The legs are short with abundant bone, and the hocks are well let down. It comes in any solid color, though bay, brown, and black are the most common. It matures early and is sensible and kind in temperament.

Trakehner (East Prussian)

The Trakehner is perhaps the most outstanding of the modern West German breeds. Trakehnen Stud, now administered by the Polish Ministry of Agriculture, was founded by King Fredrich Wilhelm I of Germany in 1732, when the land was part of the province of East Prussia. The Trakehner was almost lost to the Western world in recent times. However, during the chaos at the end of World War II, some 5 percent of the 25,000 horses registered in the East Prussian Stud Book were filtered into the West. From these few refugees the modern Trakehner has been lovingly bred.

The Trakehner combines elegant looks and stamina with enormous versatility and has proved successful in all kinds of sport as well as in dressage, between the shafts, and on the farm. At its best it is a horse with a free, straight action which is sometimes exaggerated. This exaggerated action may be due to one of its foundation sires, a Norfolk Roadster called North Star. The other foundation sire was an English Thoroughbred named Furioso. During the nineteenth century these were bred to native mares of the Nonius type, a medium-heavy all-purpose horse of Hungary.

The Furioso excels at dressage and cross-country work, at jumping and eventing, and is also used for steeplechasing. Sometimes it also works as a carriage horse, since it has both great style and endurance.

170

Budyonny

The original cross which produced this superb saddle horse (named after its breeder, the famous Russian revolutionary cavalry leader, Marshal Budyonny) was Thoroughbred Don. The breed was selectively developed. Only the most handsome offspring of the stud were used and, of these, only those that passed tests for speed, endurance, and intelligence. The best results were obtained from Thoroughbred stallions crossed with Don mares rather than from Don stallions with Thoroughbred mares. By 1948 the new breed was established.

Originally developed as cavalry charges, Budyonnys excel at eventing, dressage, steeplechasing, and all equestrian sports. They stand 15.2–16 hands (155–160cm.) high and are usually chestnut or bay in color, often with the golden sheen on the coat that distinguishes so many Russian saddle horses.

Percheron

The Percheron is the most popular draft horse in the world. It is powerful, intelligent, graceful, and inexpensive to keep. Its fine head with widespaced eyes and open nostrils reflects the oriental blood that has helped refine its massive frame. Indeed, it is sometimes likened to an overgrown Arab.

It was first bred in the Perche region of France, where it is still excessively popular. It is now bred all over the world and is especially admired in Great Britain and the United States. There are slight variations from country to country; in Great Britain, for example, it is coveted as a horse to cross with the Thoroughbred to produce the perfect heavyweight hunter, and it is bred to exclude all feather from its feet. But no matter what the national fancy may produce in variation of detail, the Percheron remains universally constant in height, standing 15.2–17 hands (155–170cm.) high, and in color, which is gray or black.

Suffolk Punch

The Suffolk Punch, from the East Anglian region of England, is one of the purest of all breeds of draft horse. Its origins are the medieval Great Horse and the Norfolk Trotter and Norfolk Cob. A touch of Thoroughbred blood may also have been involved. All modern Suffolk Punches are descended from a smallish chestnut trotting horse called Blakes Farmer, which was foaled in 1760.

The Suffolk Punch is exclusively chestnut in color. Seven shades are recognized—red, gold, copper, yellow, liver, light, and dark. There are never any white markings, though a faint star or stripe is sometimes visible. The horse stands 16–16.2 hands (160–165cm.) high, and has a kind and honest nature. It is an active animal, moving especially well at the trot. It comes to hand early and can still work when well into its twenties.

Clydesdale

Clydesdale originates in Scotland, from the Lowland county of Lanarkshire through which the river Clyde runs. They were first bred in the mid-eighteenth century, when the development of the Lanarkshire coalfields led to a great improvement in road surfaces and, consequently, to a demand for shoulder-haulage horses rather than pack animals. Hardy native mares were crossed with heavier Flemish stallions, which were imported especially for the purpose. The result was the Clydesdale, an active, friendly horse standing around 16.2 hands (165cm.) high. It became a regular British export, going wherever horses were required for haulage work.

The Clydesdale's most distinguishing

Suffolk Punch

physical characteristic is the unusual amount of white on its face and legs, and often on its underbelly. The basic colors are bay, brown, roan, and sometimes black. The feathering on the legs is unusually silky. Clydesdales have a spirited bearing and snappy gait which is elegant for a draft animal.

Belgian

The Belgian horse is a massive Dutch Draft descended from the Brabant, produced by crossing the Brabant stallion (and to a lesser degree the Belgian Ardennais) with Zeelandtype mares. The Brabant is a massive horse with a pronounced square head proportionately small to its body, a very deep girth, and a short back with short, strong legs, which have much feather. The Belgian inherited these characteristics plus great stamina. It stands about 17 hands and weighs about 900kg. (3000 lbs.). It tends to be of a sorrel or chestnut color.

Shire

The central counties of England are called the Shires, and from these the Shire horse gets its name. It has a controversial history. Some authorities believe it stemmed from the Old English Black Horse, which was in turn a descendant of the Great Horse of chivalry. When the demand for horses to carry heavily-armored knights ceased, breeders were quick to recognize the merits of the Shire for heavy agricultural work. It has great strength—it can pull 4.5 MT (5 tons) and, though it is seldom used in agriculture today, its imposing presence and popularity at shows ensures its continuity.

Like all big cold-blooded horses, the Shire is gentle and docile. It is so kind that it can usually be trusted with a child. It averages 17 hands (170cm.) high, but sometimes exceeds 18 hands (180cm.) and is the tallest horse in the world. The most common colors are bay and brown with white markings, although gray and black are not unusual.

Shire

171

SMALL MAMMALS

Small mammals are probably the next most popular pets after dogs and cats. Small mammals available as pets can be divided into two broad categories: first the rodents and lagomorphs, and second the carnivores and apes. Rodents include the most popular small mammal pets—rats, mice, gerbils, cavies (Guinea pigs), hamsters, chinchillas, chipmunks, squirrels, and jerboas—while the lagomorphs, which differ from rodents only in the form of their dentition, encompass the rabbits and hares. This first category undoubtedly includes the best pets for children. They are easy to care for, their feeding requirements are simple to supply, they breed easily, and they quickly become tame. Children are in little danger from bites or injury from these animals although any abused animal can be dangerous. It is easy for children to look after such pets with a minimum of adult supervision. Pets of this type can be invaluable in developing a child's sense of responsibility and awareness of the animal world.

The second group of animals (the carnivores and apes) are quite a different matter. Examples of such animals are ferrets, mink, mongooses, skunks, bats, marmosets, tamarins, bush babies, galagos, lorises, and pottos. To these can also be added the bats. Without exception these animals can either be quite dangerous for children to handle or have such specific care and feeding requirements that they require more time and patience than many children are willing to give. Several, such as ferrets and mink, are primarily animals domesticated for their working abilities and commercial value and are only secondarily kept as pets, while others,

Rabbits and most small rodents are ideal pets for children since they are easy to look after with a minimum of adult supervision. Above all because of the size and mild temperament of these animals, children are generally quite safe when handling them, as in the cases of (Top) this gypsy boy with his pet guinea pig and (Bottom) the two sisters with their mice.

such as bats, skunks, and bush babies, are kept as "curiosity" pets and are basically animals captured from the wild.

Thus in the small mammals we have two extremes of animals suitable for pets—those that are ideal for children and those that should only be kept by adults. Of course, individual animals may have personalities that are opposite to those of the group as a whole which simply indicates the importance of always having some element of adult supervision.

Rodents

The name *rodent* is derived from the Latin word *rodere*, which means "to gnaw." The order of rodents (Rodentia) contains an enormous number (some 1,800) of species, nearly half of all mammalian species, and they all have characteristically sharp incisor teeth, one pair in both upper and lower jaw. (These incisors never stop growing, and any rodent in captivity must have enough hard food in its diet to keep the teeth sharpened.) The mouse-like rodents form a suborder of more than 1,180 species, relatively few of which are available to pet dealers; they include mice, rats, voles, hamsters, gerbils, and jerboas. The predominately South American suborder of rodents of the cavy or guinea pig type also includes the porcupines and chinchillas. The third chief group includes squirrels, marmots, chipmunks, and beavers.

Mice and rats chiefly eat seed and other tough vegetable matter, but can chisel their way into tough wooden barrels and casks to get at food. The front part of the incisors is stronger and slower to wear away than the softer rear part, so the front edge stays longer and retains a chisel shape. There is a gap (diastema), between the incisors and the cheek or grinding teeth, at which the mouth can be closed by specialized folds of skin on either side, so that inedible chips of wood or husks are kept out of the mouth while gnawing is in process.

MICE

Mice are widespread in their distribution and are considered pests to human beings in most parts of the world; they attack food sources and supplies from the Arctic to the equator, in forests and in desert regions. Although some still wild species are caught, the mice most commonly kept as pets are many hundreds of thousands of generations away from their wild ancestors. The House Mouse (*Mus musculus*) is now so highly developed in both color and coat condition as to be admired by many people who would normally be upset at the sight of a wild specimen.

Fancy mice have become so popular in recent years that there are now about forty different varieties to choose from, ranging from the pink-eyed white, once thought of as the only fancy mouse, right through black-eyed whites, creams, reds, blues (which are more of a slate color), to chocolates and fawns, champagnes and doves. More recently developed are the silvers, which are described as having the color of an old silver coin. There are pied varieties and some with chinchilla and agouti coats. Enthusiasts throughout the world breed and exhibit such fancy mice in competition. (See **Exhibiting and Showing—Small Mammals.**)

If kept properly, mice make good pets and

Modern plastic mouse cages are easy to keep clean and are quite acceptable within the decor of a home.

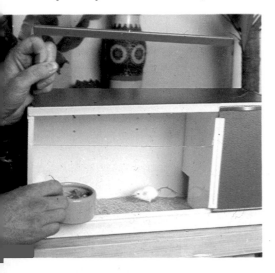

Brown and gray forms of the wild House Mouse, together with the albino form, which is the most common domestic variety.

are not a great disturbance to a household. They prefer a temperature of around 15°C. (59°F.) and can tolerate lower temperatures, but they dislike very hot conditions. If you are not going to breed but would like more than one, females can be kept happily together. It is male mice that are responsible for the distinctive "mouse" smell.

An undoubted attraction about mice is the ease with which they can be handled, particularly by children. They are most easily tamed by feeding from the hand. It is best to pick mice up by scooping them in both hands, but they can be lifted by the base of the tail, then quickly transferred to the other hand. They should never be carried around by the tail.

Housing. Metal cages are best for the average mouse since they cannot be gnawed. The cage should be cleaned once a week by washing it out with a mild disinfectant. After it dries, sprinkle a layer of clean sawdust on the bottom, but not enough to get into the food trays (which should also be washed weekly).

A sleeping box of wood or metal can be put into one corner and, if you wish to breed, this can serve as a nursery. A box with sides of 10cm. (4in.) is large enough for a small family. It should have an entrance hole 2.5cm. (1in.) in diameter and be raised above the floor of the cage with a ladder for access. A removable top will make cleaning easy. Use bedding of cotton waste and light wood shavings, which the mice will chew into little balls. An exercise wheel in the cage will be a welcome addition.

Feeding. The basic diet of mice has not changed in their development as pets. They need protein, and fat in lesser proportion,

but the bulk is made up from carbohydrates. Commercially prepared diets are available and have the right proportions of nutrients to keep the animals healthy. The more adventurous mouse keeper can provide a staple diet of whole or crushed oats—a teaspoonful for each mouse daily—plus a small cube of bread soaked in milk (although overfeeding with milk is dangerous since it can go sour). A pinch of salt and a little bird seed will provide extra vitamins and minerals. Once a week some fresh vegetables, such as grass, chickweed, apple, or cabbage, can be offered but not all mice will accept fresh food. Water should always be available and should be kept free from pollution with droppings and other cage floor dirt. The easiest way of keeping it clean is to supply it in commercially made drinking bottles. The best ones are glass with strong metal drinking tubes, and these can be hooked on to the side of the cage.

Breeding. Male and female (buck and doe) mate readily when kept together. The mother will suckle the four to eight young, which are born naked and blind after a three week gestation period. Their hair starts to grow immediately but the eyes do not open until about twelve days later, when they can start to eat solid food. The young are mature at two months.

Disease. Mice suffer from fleas and mites, which can be treated with pyrethrum powder. Fungus sometimes attacks the ears and requires treatment by a veterinarian, who will probably clip off the affected parts. Tumors occasionally develop, in which case

173

The domesticated rat makes a tame and easily-handled pet. Top Left. *The handler is showing the best way to pick up a rat—never hold one by his tail.*

Top Right. *Once confidence has been gained by both child and pet, a rat will happily crawl about on its owner.*

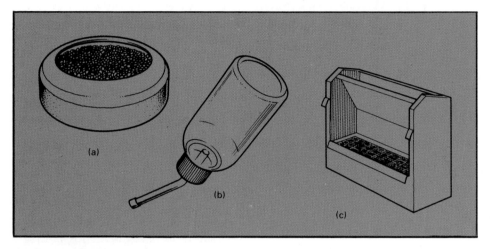

Center. *Feeding dispensers for small mammals include: (a) A solid, round bowl for holding grain nuts (pellets) and other food; this will not tip over when an animal feeds from it, so food is not wasted. (b) An animal drinking bottle which comes in a range of sizes*

suitable for mice as well as rabbits; these bottles ensure a constant supply of clean fresh water without spillage. (c) A nut hopper which is inserted through the wire so that it can be filled from outside.

it is usually best to have the animal painlessly destroyed and the cage sterilized or burned if it is of wood. A common ailment is a form of asthma, easily recognized by wheezing, which can be alleviated by adding a few drops of eucalyptus oil to the bedding. However, getting a veterinarian to examine your pet is advisable if an illness develops.

RATS

Size is the basic difference between rats and mice, though some species of rats are smaller than the larger species of mice. Rats share the same worldwide distribution and, despite every attempt by Man to destroy them, they are now so well adapted to life in towns and cities that it is doubtful they can ever be eradicated completely. The struggle to keep their numbers down demands a constant vigil by health officers aided by scientists. Many of the poisons created to destroy them have lost much of their effectiveness because rats have developed immunities.

The commonly kept pet rat has been developed from the Common Brown Rat (*Rattus norvegicus*) which reached Europe from

Asia, but it would be unwise to attempt to keep a wild Brown Rat, even if obtained as a baby, since it could carry disease. Rats have been extensively used as laboratory animals, and generations of pet and laboratory breeding have produced a tame and easily handled pet which, if properly kept, is much more attractive than its wild relatives. The most common variety is white, but others are piebald with black, brown, and cream markings and shades of all these colors in the overall body colors.

The tame rat will live in harmony with its cage mates and seldom, if ever, bites its handler, but their chisel-like incisors are larger than those of mice and a bite should not be ignored. Rat bites are not poisonous, but the bacterial content of the mouth could infect the wound.

Rats should *not* be picked up by the tail but can be gripped by the scruff of the neck or, better, by placing the palm of the hand gently on the back of the animal with the thumb and forefinger over the rat's shoulders and under its throat. The other fingers curl under the body and give support; the forefinger and thumb can control the head if necessary as

the rat is lifted. Sudden movements are likely to scare the animal, and a scared rat is likely to bite.

Housing. A rat cage should be made of strong metal bars to prevent escape. Although domestic rats are less likely to gnaw their way out of a wooden box than their wild relations, they are often capable of cutting through wire mesh. Rats dislike direct sunlight and prefer a shady position at room temperature, although they can withstand cooler temperatures if provided with bedding materials in the form of straw and newspaper. A layer of sawdust on the cage floor will soak up droppings, make cleaning easier, and provide some insulation. Depending on the number of rats and on space, their bedding will probably need to be changed twice a week and should never be allowed to get wet. The cage should be at least twice as long as the rat's body and preferably high enough to have two levels.

Feeding. Rats are fed the diet recommended for mice. Commercially-prepared food pellets are available but usually have to be bought in larger quantities than needed by anyone with just a few pets. Clean food and water should always be available and a bottle-type drinker with a metal tube is recommended for hygiene—rats will splash water from a bowl.

Breeding. A normal, healthy pair of rats, if kept together, will breed and raise young without any trouble (ten or more litters a year). It is wise to remove the male before the young arrive and to separate the young before they reach maturity; otherwise fighting may occur in the crowded conditions. The number of "pups" born after the three week gestation varies from six to twelve in each litter. Born naked, blind, and deaf, they develop very quickly. Ears start to function at three to four days and eyes open at fourteen to seventeen days. Sexing is not difficult since the testes of the male rat become noticeable at about forty days. At an earlier stage rats can be sexed by comparing the distances between the anus and the genital organs, the greater distance on comparison indicating a male. If possible the sexes should be separated at weaning, usually at about twenty days old.

GERBILS

Few of the 106 species of gerbil, which inhabit Africa and Asia, are available to pet keepers. The Mongolian Gerbil (*Meriones unguiculatus*), the Egyptian Gerbil (*Gerbillus gerbillus*), and the Libyan Gerbil (*M. lybicus*) have been the most frequently imported. They are fairly easy to breed once acclimatized, so dealers are now less likely to rely on imports. Gerbils are slightly longer than pet mice, have longer hind feet, and a coat as soft as that of a hamster. The long tail is covered with fur, unlike that of the mouse or rat. Color varieties have been developed; white is popular and pale-colored normals are available.

Top Left. *Similar to most small mammals, young gerbils are born blind and naked.* Top Right. *Gerbils breed freely if kept in a suitable metal and wire cage. They are playful animals and enjoy toys such as walking wheels.* Center. *A pair of adult gerbils have a mouse-like appearance, differing in the longer hind legs and hair-covered tails.*

Most gerbils are nocturnal desert animals and do not become active until the day is nearing its end—an asset for pet keepers who are away from home during the day and want a pet that is ready for attention when they return.

Housing. Cages that are recommended for mice will serve for gerbils, but they will scatter their floor covering through the bars of a metal cage. A glass aquarium with a wire top or the multi-compartment plastic housing now commerically available are better. Avoid housing with wooden frame members exposed, or the gerbils will soon chew into them. Cover the bottom with a layer of sawdust and wood shavings at least 25mm. (1in.) deep and provide a handful of hay to be used as bedding. Gerbils are playful animals and enjoy walking wheels and other toys, such as short pieces of plastic piping or a metal can with the ends removed and edges smoothed. They become bored if not able to exercise and need a large enough cage for running around.

Feeding. Various grains and seeds form the basis of the diet, together with fresh vegetables such as turnip, cabbage, kale, carrots, and spinach. The gerbil's water requirements are not determined; in the desert they get little chance to drink water and take their moisture from available vegetation. However, fresh water should always be available.

Breeding. Gerbils should be kept in pairs. They reproduce readily. The young should be taken away from their parents when they are weaned at about three to four weeks old. Males, if housed together, often fight and even members of the family community may be driven to fighting among themselves if they are kept in crowded conditions. Sexing gerbils is as easy as sexing mice and rabbits: the extra distance between the genital organs and the anus on the male compared with the female is a reliable guide and with practice can be judged on sight.

Nest boxes are not essential, but bedding of hay, paper, and other materials should be provided to be shredded for nest building. The young are born naked, blind, and deaf. They mature quickly, becoming miniatures of their parents within four weeks.

JERBOAS

Members of the family Dipodidae, all except three of the twenty-three species of jerboa are confined to Asia; the others, including the largest, occur in North Africa. They are not commonly offered as pets but are occasionally imported by dealers in other parts of the world. The different species vary from 4cm. (1.5in.) body length to more than 15cm. (6in.). Jerboas are best known for their jumping capabilities, and some small species can jump as far as 2m. (6ft.) at a single leap. Their rather large ears give them the appearance of a rabbit or hare rather than a mouse, yet their long tails with a tuft at the tip, and their very long hind feet, are not at all like a rabbit. They are sandy colored and in the wild spend much of the daytime in cool burrows below the hot desert. At nightfall they forage for food consisting mainly of seeds and dried vegetable matter. Little is known of their breeding and rearing habits. Pet keepers will require scientific identification of the species before gaining further information about habitat, feeding, and so forth from zoologists and museums. Even then only a small amount of information may be available.

Housing. Jerboas need a great deal of room to perform their spectacular leaps. Close-wired aviary-type cages with provision for burrowing suit them best.

Feeding. Give the same as for gerbils, if no specific information is available.

Breeding. Less profilic and longer living than most mouse-type rodents, jerboas have a gestation period of four to five weeks, producing a litter of three or four.

GOLDEN HAMSTER

There are sixteen species in the family Cricetidae but the Golden Hamster (*Mesocricetus auratus*) is the only one which is usually offered by pet dealers. Some authorities believe that all the Golden Hamsters available in the world today are descended from one group of wild specimens discovered in Syria in 1930 and taken to Jerusalem for study.

These small nocturnal animals are popular pets, require only a simple diet, have no really undesirable habits, and are easy to

Jerboas, such as Blandford's Jerboa (Jaculus blandfordi), *can perform spectacular leaps and should be housed in aviary-type accommodations.*

breed. When tame they may abandon their nocturnal habits. Hamsters, including the Common or Black-bellied Hamster (*Cricetus cricetus*), can be serious pests; Australia and New Zealand have banned the importation of the Golden Hamster.

Housing. Cages must be strong and escape-proof, preferably of metal. Hamsters in groups are inclined to fight and specimens are best housed separately unless mating is desired. (See **Breeding** below.) They need exercise and will make good use of a walking wheel. A normal room temperature is required, 15°–20°C. (59°–68°F.) being ideal. If kept for a period below 7°C. (45°F.) a hamster will hibernate for a month or more.

Feeding. Diet consists of commercial packets of hamster food or oats, seeds, and other cereals supplemented by greenstuffs such as cabbage, turnip, and carrots. Fresh water should be supplied from a drinking bottle. Hamsters have cheek pouches in which they stuff food before retiring to a quiet corner to eat. Do not overfeed, because hamsters will store surplus food which may then spoil.

Breeding. Mating involves a trial and error situation for the female only comes into heat for a few days at a time and there is no recognizable sign of her condition. Unless she is ready for mating she will attack and even kill the male. Normally, the female is taken to the male. If she stands on her hind legs and makes a frightening noise or turns around to face the male as soon as he approaches her, remove her before they start to fight. If she stands rigid while he approaches with ears erect, tail up and legs outstretched she is prepared for mating but do not leave them unobserved until you are sure that mating has begun. After about twenty minutes remove the female to her own cage. The young are born seventeen days after mating, and they remain naked and blind until about twelve days old. The mother should not be disturbed before that or she may eat her young. The baby hamsters can be taken from their mother at about twenty-four days.

CAVIES (GUINEA PIGS)

A South American species, the cavy (*Cavia porcellus*), was domesticated by the Incas and bred for food, as it still is in Peru today. The origin of the common name *Guinea Pig* is uncertain; it could be a corruption of "Coney Pig" or of "Guiana Pig." There are six species within the genus *Cavia*, and they were first introduced to Europe by Spanish sailors four hundred years ago.

Because of the roly-poly appearance, small size, and comparative hardiness, cavies are highly recommended as pets for children. Exhibiting cavies has become very popular with the development of many colored varieties and different coat lengths and patterns. There are long-haired, smooth- and short-coated animals and others with rosettes of fur along the length of the body. Self (overall) colors and agouti (banded) breeds offer a wide choice.

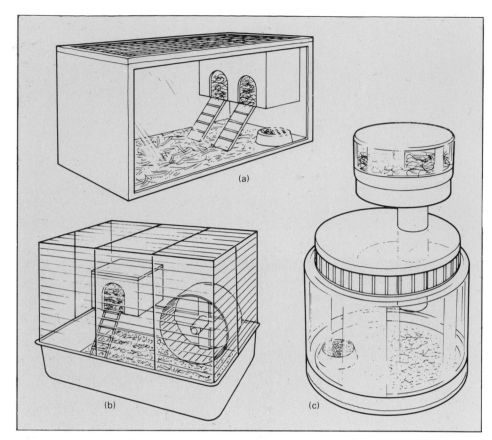

Cavies are easily tamed and seldom bite. Housed together, a pair will soon produce young who will themselves breed at about ten weeks of age. Cavies scatter their droppings indiscriminately, so their quarters require daily cleaning or the cage will become smelly. They are better kept outside.

Housing. Cavies are most commonly kept in wire-front wooden hutches measuring approximately 80 x 40 x 40cm. (32 x 16 x 16in.), together with a small enclosed area. Cavies have strong teeth, and the boards and wire front must be thick to prevent their escape. During the summer a movable hutch with a wire mesh bottom to the run can be put out on a lawn, but in the winter they should be housed in a frost-free garage or shed. Bedding of straw or hay (which forms a good diet additive should be heaped upon a 1cm. (0.4in.) layer of sawdust.

With good ventilation, cleaning should only be necessary once a week. Cavies can withstand variations in temperature from 14°–24°C. (55°–75°F.). Sacks laid over and around the hutch will help maintain the temperature in winter. Housing should be on one level only as cavies injure easily in falls because of their short legs and great weight.

Feeding. Oats, bran, and other cereals should form the bulk of the diet, with some greenstuffs such as cabbage, carrots, turnip, and kale. Pellets are available as alternatives, but these are dry and plenty of water must be taken to balance the diet. Vitamin C is also essential for cavies. Water should be supplied from a water bottle with a stainless steel metal tube, as cavies soon destroy soft metal tubes.

Hamster cages. (a) A homemade wooden cage. (b) Commercially-available all-metal cages. (c) Two units of the latest in plastic hamster cages, which can be extended by adding other units.

Breeding. The young are born fully furred with eyes open, are almost self-sufficient at twenty-four hours old, and can be handled after three or four days. The litter of two to four pups nibble at solid food very early in life but take milk from any lactating female

Cavies (or guinea pigs) are very popular pets, and many varieties have been developed. Shown here are a pair of multicolored long-haired cavies.

Chinchillas are normally quite tame and can make interesting pets. They hop around very quickly and can leap several feet in the air if startled.

Modern plastic golden hamster cages can be built into all sorts of shapes which provide entertainment for both owner and pet alike.

available and can cause a lack of milk in a pregnant sow if she is kept in the same hutch as their mother. Early weaning is recommended at fourteen to eighteen days by removing the young to other housing.

Diseases. Ticks and lice frequently appear but are easily treated with dusting powders.

CHINCHILLAS

The Chinchilla (*Chinchilla laniger*) is a nocturnal rodent famous for its long, soft bluish-gray fur but vastly underrated as a pet. They are about 20cm. (8in.) long (females always a little larger and heavier than males) with large ears that are more rounded than a rabbit's, and a long squirrel-like tail. Those liv-

ing at high altitudes have smaller extremities and a longer gestation period.

The fur's softness defies penetration by any fleas or similar parasites. The pelt was once the most valuable in the animal kingdom, and in its native Andes the Chinchilla was hunted almost to extinction in the nineteenth century. Following bans on their hunting and export, they were farmed in thousands on ranches in many parts of the world, thus aiding the protection of the wild populations. Today the wild Chinchilla survives only in the high altitudes of northern Chile, where it lives on coarse grass and herbs, relying on dew and moisture in the plants for water.

Chinchillas are almost always tame and can make interesting pets. They can be handled very easily, but hop around quickly and can jump several feet into the air if startled. Chin-

chillas should not be confused with Chinchilla Mice (a South American vole) or chinchilla rabbits, rats, and mice bred for their fancy chinchilla-like fur.

Housing. Most breeders would recommend that animals reared for their pelts be kept on wire floors, but clean sawdust spread across the cage floor and changed regularly is adequate for pets. Chinchillas live communally in the wild but mate for life. The cage for a pair should be as large as is practical. Height is important and thick branches for jumping and climbing will be appreciated. Although they are nocturnal animals and can withstand low temperatures, Chinchillas in the wild will bask in the early morning and evening sun. However, their enclosure should be shaded from strong sunlight. In the high Andes water is scarce, and they dislike damp conditions. Chinchillas like to take dust baths, so provide a dish or container about the size of a large baking pan and fill it with fullers' earth or pumice to a depth of about 8cm. (3in.). This bath can be put into their enclosure during the evening and taken out again at night. As the Chinchillas turn over and over in the container, the dust rushes through their thick coats and cleans them. Any droppings left in the bath can be sieved out when it is removed.

Feeding. Food and water should always be provided since these animals eat only a little at a time but often. A handful of hay for each animal in the early evening and a meal of rabbit pellets or similar food later will offer a good opportunity to see the activity that surrounds feeding at this time. Chinchillas enjoy some fresh fruit, such as apples, and also like chewing the bark from apple tree twigs, but do not use any that have been sprayed with pesticides. Chinchillas like seeds for a treat and can break open sunflower seeds with their sharp front teeth and extract the kernel with their front paws, very much like a squirrel.

During the summer, groups of guinea pigs can be housed outdoors where they can be given the benefit of a large run with a wooden hutch in which to shelter.

Chipmunks, or tree squirrels, make delightful pets that are at their best when kept in large aviary-type cages where they have plenty of space to run and climb around. They are easy to feed, requiring seeds, nuts, and vegetables.

Breeding. Chinchillas breed all year round but probably the best litters are born during spring and early summer (after mating four months earlier). They are born in litters of two or three, fully furred and able to run within hours. Provide straw in a nest box and let the young stay with their mother for about two and a half months. At that age the young should be separated by sex since it is unwise to allow them to breed for about six months. Usually parents mate for life and can be left together unless fighting occurs. They will breed for four or five years but will remain together until, at eight or nine years their teeth wear out and they can no longer feed.

CHIPMUNKS

Most of the sixteen species of chipmunk (or ground squirrel, a name also applied to other ground-living members of the squirrel family, *Sciuridae*) come from North America, with a few from Asia. These attractive small burrowing animals are close relatives of the East European and Russian Suslik, *Spermophilus (-Citellus) citellus*. The chipmunk has been popularized as a cartoon character due to their amusing habits.

Chipmunks are extremely attractive. Many have horizontal bands of white or dark brown along their fawn-brown bodies. The species most often kept as a pet is the Eastern Chipmunk, whose Latin name *Tamias striatus* means "striped steward." Chipmunks' tails are often equal in length to the body and slightly bushy.

Chipmunks inhabit areas just above ground level in forests and take refuge in rocks, small trees, and bushes while foraging for the nuts, seeds, and fruit which form their basic diet. They have cheek pouches and carry huge supplies of food to their burrows,

which they build with four or five chambers and line with grass and leaves, to provide sleeping quarters and storage facilities for the winter. They hibernate 1m (3ft) deep below the frost line.

Housing. In captivity, escape-proof quarters usually require strong wire netting on metal or concrete bases with provision for burrowing made in boxes of suitable size and layered with earth, peat, or dried leaves.

Feeding. Along with seeds and nuts chipmunks will eat insects, bird's eggs, mushrooms, and the tubers of fireweed (rose bay willow herb), carrots, and lettuce.

Breeding. Four to six young are born in spring and are weaned by six weeks.

TREE SQUIRRELS

Only the Eurasion Red Squirrel (*Sciurus vulgaris*) is widespread in Europe and temperate Asia, and while there are a number of tree squirrels in North America, over one hundred are found in the tropics. These lively bushy-tailed mammals vary in color from the small Red Squirrel, Pine Squirrel or Chickaree (*Tamiasciurus* species), and the Gray Squirrels (*Sciurus* species) of North America to the beautifully marked black, red, and creamy white Provost's Squirrel (*Callosciurus prevosti*) of Malaya. Another favorite is the Indian Giant Squirrel or "Tree Dog" (*Ratata indica*) the largest of its kind, measuring 80cm. (30in.) in length and having a chestnut brown coat with creamy white undersides. In some countries it is against the law to keep certain squirrels without a special license. In Great Britain the Red Squirrel is becoming rare, and the Gray Squirrel is a pest which may only be kept for scientific study, not as a pet.

One of the most commonly kept tree squirrels is the Eurasian Red Squirrel, which is, however, becoming rare in some parts of its native range and is a protected animal.

Housing. Squirrels are arboreal by nature and need plenty of room to climb and exercise. They are best kept in a large wire enclosure which includes one or two small trees. Native species can be kept in an aviary type of cage with strong weatherproof sleeping boxes at least 30cm. (1ft.) square and with an entrance 8cm. (3in.) wide. Furnish hollow logs for resting. Indian and other tropical species require some heating in temperate regions.

Feeding. Squirrels eat fruit, nuts, and vegetables which they may store for winter when they are less active. They also need hardwood or bark to wear down their incisors, as with other rodents. Squirrels drink water but may take milk as an alternative.

Breeding. Gestation varies between species. The female is easily agitated by intruders and may even kill her four to six young, who are born blind. They are weaned at about ten weeks.

Lagomorphs

Formerly classified with rodents, lagomorphs now form an order with two families which can be distinguished by pegteeth (or second incisors) in the upper jaw. Rodents have only one pair of incisors in each jaw. Out of the lagomorphs only the rabbit can be called a truly domesticated pet.

RABBITS

Rabbits and hares (which are *not* recommended as pets) belong to the family Leporidae. Species include the European Rabbit (*Oryctolagus cuniculus*) from which the domesticated rabbit is descended, the cottontails (*Sylvilagus*), and jack rabbits (*Lagus*) of North America, which are actually hares, and many regional forms. People have taken them to countries where they did not occur naturally. In Australia, for instance, just a few pairs were introduced which within a short while bred to such an extent as to be-

Top Left. *Rabbits are the most widely kept medium-sized mammals; despite their size they are extremely popular with children since they are easy to look after and like being handled.*

Rabbits have been domesticated for many centuries, and there are many breeds available. Exhibiting and showing rabbits is a growing hobby. Shown here are (Middle) a red Angora, the long coat of which requires a lot of grooming and (Right) a red short-haired Rex rabbit.

come a national pest. In ideal conditions one pair of rabbits can produce an average of eight youngsters every two months for two years, and with their young maturing at about six months old and breeding at the same rate, there will be many millions of individuals in only a few years. However, disease and natural hazards serve to keep the population down to a reasonable level in most areas.

Wild European Rabbits live in large colonies and burrow fairly deeply into the ground, forming complete systems of tunnels and larger burrows known as warrens or buries. The Eastern Cottontail (*Sylvilagus floridanus*) of North America lives more on the surface and digs a shallow nest much like that of the European Hare (*Lepus capensis*). Both species line their nests with soft fur plucked from their bodies and some dried vegetation to provide insulation and camouflage against possible predators such as foxes, cats, and dogs.

The natural food of rabbits consists mainly of vegetable matter such as grasses and small shrubs; new shoots are particularly favored. Such food is not always available in winter, and some species eat less digestible foods such as twigs and bark from trees which sometimes results in the death or stunting of the trees. For this reason foresters in many countries consider rabbits a major pest.

Rabbits are particularly well equipped to handle a tough diet with their chisel-like incisors and premolars and molars used to grind the food into a more acceptable state. The incisors are constantly in use and would wear down in a very short time if the teeth did not constantly grow, maintaining their strength and length for the whole of the animal's natural life. Pet rabbits should be provided with hardwood to keep the incisors exercised and worn to the correct length. Overgrown and misshapen front teeth need veterinary treatment.

Rabbit keeping is so well developed that anyone starting now can select from almost two hundred varieties and by selective breeding can establish a distinctive strain within a fairly short time, providing a continuous form of study for participants.

Rabbit breeds include a wide range of colors and different kinds of fur: **Chinchillas, Sables, Foxes, Rex** and many others. The coat of the Angora rabbit may be 120cm. (5in.) long, while Rex breeds have rather short, dense coats and are now produced in thirty different colors. There are clubs for almost all the breeds which have their own special breed shows and offer prizes for improving the breed. A breed such as the Angora needs special care to keep its coat in good condition and a breed less demanding such as the Dutch or the Belgian Hare (which is *not* a hare but a rabbit breed) is more suitable for the beginner.

Housing. Pet rabbits are best kept in hutches, usually placed in the yard or in a hut or shed. For most varieties a hutch about 1m. (3ft.) long and half as high and wide incorporating sleeping quarters is the most useful size, since it is sufficient for breeding and raising several young rabbits. Approximately the upper two-thirds of the whole front should be covered by wire with the remaining portion fixed as a solid door, forming a side of the sleeping quarters. Cleaning will be much easier if the floor consists of wire mesh with a removable droppings tray underneath. Slightly smaller hutches are acceptable for small breeds. An outdoor rabbit run, or a movable pen like that used for poultry with a netted floor and dry, weatherproof shelter at one end is even better, but bedding must not be allowed to get damp. Even tame rabbits burrow and precautions must be taken to prevent escape. All rabbit housing should be made secure against predators, especially foxes and coyotes and marauding cats.

Cleaning rabbit hutches calls for daily attention. Rabbits usually have a particular corner where they urinate and leave their droppings. If the hutch floor is not of wire, it should be covered with sawdust and the "used" part can be then be cleared away and replaced by a handful of clean sawdust in a matter of moments. Once a week hutches need a complete cleaning and replacement of the bedding, except in the case of a nursing mother who should not be disturbed.

Feeding. Feeding rabbits is very easy. Commercially prepared, mixed rabbit food is available at almost all pet dealers, but it can be expensive and wasteful. It usually consists of bran, corn, wheat, oats and nuts (pellets). Combined with plenty of drinking water, it offers a balanced but fairly boring diet. Many rabbits prefer some parts of the mix to others: if they ignore the bran or nuts this becomes wasteful. A better plan is to buy the items separately, discover the pet's preferences, and balance the diet yourself.

Green food, such as clean cabbage leaves, carrots, celery, and turnip, is much appreciated and should be given in small quantities daily. Fresh hay is useful both as bedding and food. Some wild foods, if not polluted or sprayed with chemicals, can be of equal benefit. Dandelion leaves are the best known of the wild foods and in some areas this plant is called "Rabbit Meat." Clover, coltsfoot, and plantains are also all very useful. Many plants should be avoided, including buttercups, poppies, and bluebells. Even garden lettuce can cause stomach upsets for the rabbit if too much is eaten; give only one leaf as a treat now and then. Commercial breeders do not go to these lengths: they maintain that balanced nuts plus water are sufficient. A pregnant or suckling doe should also be given milk to drink.

Water bottles with gravity feed tubes work best, and food bowls should be heavy so that they cannot be tipped over. Some breeders use metal hoppers fastened to the side of the

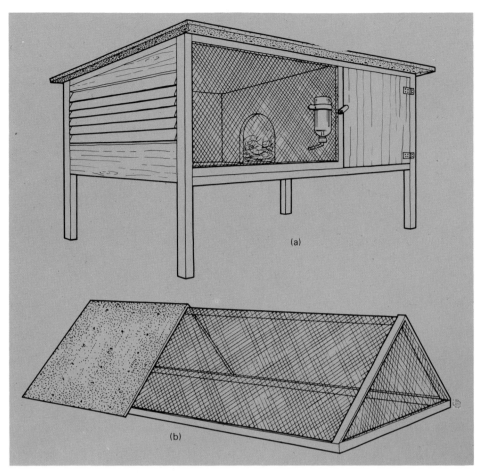

(a)

(b)

cage, and these only require inverting from time to time. They are very convenient for people with many animals and they help prevent the food from getting dirty.

Breeding. The doe is taken to the buck or dog for mating and then returned to her own hutch. Her food quantity is gradually increased to about double the normal amount by the time she gives birth. The doe will build her own nest of hay and soft fur plucked out of herself, usually a few days prior to parturition.

The blind young have only a light covering of fur and remain in the nest for about three weeks. During this time they should be disturbed as little as possible—and not at all in the first six days. The young begin normal feeding at this time and at eight weeks are fully weaned. At this point the doe is usually taken from the hutch, leaving the young in the environment where they feel secure.

Sexing rabbits requires skill and some instruction from an experienced breeder. The older bucks show a greater distance between the sexual organs and the anus than is found in does. Also, with a gentle pressure on either side of the sexual organ of the buck, the penis can be seen protruding: in the doe only a slit is present. Old animals should not be bred to young.

Diseases. The great scourge of rabbits is myxamatosis, an endemic disease of the South American Forest Rabbit (*Sylvilagus brasiliensis*). In this species it produces only a local tumor, but it is lethal in other species. Ear infection sometimes destroys the rabbit's sense of balance, and mites need rapid treatment. Rabbits are particularly susceptible to exhaust fumes and should not be kept in a garage.

Carnivores

The order Carnivora is characterized by animals with a system equipped for a flesh-eating mode of existence, i.e., large canine teeth, reduced and pointed cheek teeth, and sharp claws on all the toes. Best known carnivorous domestic pets are of course the domestic dog and cat, whereas the big cats, other small cats, wolves and bears are best kept only in zoos and wildlife parks. (See **Zoo Animals as Pets.**) Smaller species native to the temperate regions, such as the fox, badger, and raccoon, can be kept as pets but are best left to live in the wild. (See **Wild Animals as Visitors and Pets**). A few other smaller carnivores are kept as pets, but that is usually because of other uses to which humans have put them.

FERRETS AND POLECATS

Usually kept as working animals to control rabbits and vermin, ferrets also make reasonable pets. They are a long-domesticated form of the European Polecat (*Putorius putorius*) and are classified either as a separate species (*P. furo*) or a subspecies (*P.p. furo*). The ferret has now spread throughout Europe, interbreeding with the endemic wild polecat populations until it is often difficult to distinguish one from the other. Ferrets belong to the family Mustelidae, along with stoats, weasels, mink, martens, the Zorilla of Africa, the Wolverine of North America, badgers, skunks, and otters. Ferrets are 50cm. (20in.) long, including the 15cm. (6in.) tail, slender, and extremely quick to react. They range in color from the traditional pink-eyed albino (which becomes pale yellow in adult coat) to the dark brown "fichet" with buff underfur and cream markings.

They are not recommended as pets for children, who would find them difficult to handle and control. They can inflict nasty bites and often refuse to let go once they have obtained a good grip. They should never be allowed out alone with infants—they have been known to kill babies!

Wild polecats hunt small mammals such as mice, voles, and rabbits and will also take small birds, eggs, and insects. They may kill poultry, but they usually keep away from houses.

All mustelids have a scent gland under the root of the tail used for territory marking and for defense if injured or frightened. Although the hobs (males) smell stronger than the jills (females), the odor will not be offensive unless the ferret is under great stress. Ferrets have been successfully allowed in and out of the house along with domestic cats and dogs, but it is generally better to keep them in an outdoor sleeping place. Ferrets will usually defecate in a regular place and, if caged, this is frequently in the corner farthest from their sleeping place.

In ferreting the animal is taken to a known rabbit warren or rat hole and the entrance and exit holes covered with nets. The ferret is put down one hole and drives the occupants into the net traps, where they are killed by the hunters. The ferret is then called out and rewarded.

Taming requires handling and companionship and should begin when the ferret is still too young to do serious damage with its fangs. Caution should always be used when handling unfamiliar ferrets as they can inflict a severe bite. If bitten, even slightly, see a doctor as soon as possible for treatment. Gloves should be used with a new pet unless you know its history. Sometimes it is possible to slowly offer a clenched hand for it to sniff, with the skin drawn too tightly across the knuckles for the animal to get a grip with its teeth. If the animal fluffs out its tail, arches its back or spits and chatters, have no more to do with it!

Housing. Housing should be strong and secure. Large wooden hutches with a stone or concrete run attached are most suitable. A method of blocking the run from the sleeping quarters is desirable, so that the animal can be contained while cleaning is carried out. Dry, warm sleeping quarters should be provided. A sack partly filled with clean straw makes good bedding. If two sacks are provided the ferret will move to the second when it considers the first too soiled, and it can then be changed.

Feeding. Diet may be trapped mice and pieces of rabbit or poultry given uncooked and complete with fur or feathers. Occasional bread and milk mixtures can be offered as a treat to a nursing mother. Fresh water should always be available and, since ferrets tend to tip over open dishes, it is best given in a feeder bottle. If this is first filled with milk, the ferret will soon learn to use it.

Breeding. Mating takes place in spring and summer, and two litters each year is quite common. The six to eight kittens (more than in the wild polecats) are born hairless and blind. Ferret mothers are extremely nervous and should not be disturbed for at least four weeks, as cannibalism is a common reaction. The kittens' eyes open after twenty days, and they begin to eat solid food. Jill ferrets do not seem to prosper if unbred. They come into season in the spring, and their condition is easily recognized by the swollen condition of their genital parts. The jill should be placed with the hob, who demonstrates a violent courtship. The hob should be removed when pregnancy becomes physically noticeable.

Diseases. Ferrets suffer from dog distemper, influenza, pneumonia, and mites which cause foot rot, treatment for which demands the utmost cleanliness and application of ointment. They should be inoculated against distemper and in some countries, against rabies.

MINK

The mink is closely related and similar in shape to the polecats but slightly smaller and with darker, thicker fur. The two species, one from North America (*Mustela vison*) and the other, known as the European Mink (*M. lutreola*), which extends across Europe westward into Asia, are both prized for their fur; it is a deep chestnut color, with long soft guard hairs responsible for its lustrous quality. However, the American species has been highly developed for the fur industry by breeding on large farms and cross-matching to obtain various colors for the internationally known ranch-mink pelts.

The European Mink, which is rare except in Russia, does not extend its natural territory into Great Britain. However the North American species is well established there (as in Iceland, Scandinavia and Russia) due to importation and escapes from fur farms. Mink are excellent swimmers and prefer to live along river banks or at the sides of wooded ponds. They burrow into the banks or make tunnels through the roots of waterside plants and rushes. They hunt mainly in the evening or at night and seek out small mammals, frogs, crayfish, and even game fish—which make fisheries extremely wary of allowing mink to set up homes near their waters. Poultry farmers also claim to have lost stock to mink.

Mink kept as pets can be treated in much the same way as ferrets. Great care should be taken when handling mink; because of their greater size, gloves should *always* be worn. Some handlers advise wearing cotton or work gloves under leather ones since the mink find it difficult to penetrate two separate layers.

Housing. Provide secure, dry sleeping quarters and an exercise run with a concrete or similar escape-proof base and a strong wire enclosure. Both the run and sleeping quarters will need to be scrubbed with water and a mild disinfectant from time to time. At mink "ranches" these animals are restricted to wire and metal enclosures to help keep their precious coats free of soil from uneaten food and droppings.

Feeding. Fish and meat are required daily.

Breeding. Breeding is fairly easy. Born in the spring, the three to seven young open their eyes in about thirty days and are then ready to eat solid foods and to begin weaning.

A number of members of the carnivorous weasel family are domesticated and can be kept as pets, but these animals are strictly for adults since they can be extremely vicious. (Middle) The Ferret is a long domesticated form of the European Polecat originally kept for hunting rodents and rabbits. Bottom Right. The North American Mink is primarily kept for its pelt, but can be treated as a pet, albeit one that can inflict a nasty bite.

Disturbing a nursing mother may cause her to eat the young.

MONGOOSES

Members of the carnivore family Viverridae (which also includes the cat-like civets and genets), mongooses are almost always imported from Africa or parts of Asia. There are some forty-eight species. Some countries such as Hawaii and the West Indies have introduced and released mongooses to control pests, only to have the mongooses themselves become a serious pest of small native animals and poultry. For this reason it is illegal to import mongooses into the United States, even for zoos.

The most common species kept in captivity are the Egyptian Mongoose or Ichneumon (*Herpestes ichneumon*) from Africa and southern France and Spain, and two species from India.

In the home they become tame and attached to their owners, demanding a lot of time and attention, but they seldom tolerate other domestic pets and may kill an unwary cat or small dog if alarmed. Some have been trained to a leash and can be taken for walks like a dog. Plenty of exercise is essential: they are climbers and are extremely agile, so if an ample enclosure is not available they should be allowed to run loose around the house or trained to a leash.

Housing. During summer, outside housing similar to that for ferrets will serve with a warm, dry, straw-lined sleeping box. There must be protection from drafts and cold, which could prove fatal, and cold temperate winters demand indoor accommodation with a sleeping box and a wire cage at least 60cm. (2ft.) long from which they should be released as much as possible.

Feeding. Mongooses do not feed mainly on

An unusual pet is the mongoose, which can become extremely tame but will not tolerate other pets. A favorite food is eggs which the mongoose breaks open by throwing on the ground.

snakes, as is sometimes supposed, though they can catch and kill even venomous snakes in the wild. Their food mainly consists of small mammals, birds, and reptiles; some catch fish and frogs. One particularly favorite food is eggs, which they often break open by standing on their hind legs and throwing the egg to the ground with their front paws.

In captivity about 85g. (3oz.) of raw meat per day fed in lumps to keep their teeth healthy, plus such roughage as chickens' or rabbits' heads, form their basic diet. Some species enjoy fruit and a dish of milk. Clean drinking water is essential.

Breeding. This has proved difficult in the past. Mongooses seem to breed any time of year, with gestation lasting some sixty days. The Egyptian Mongoose has two to four babies in a litter.

SKUNKS

In the United States these members of the weasel family are kept both for their pelts and as pet and zoo animals. They are best known

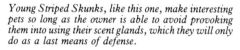

Young Striped Skunks, like this one, make interesting pets so long as the owner is able to avoid provoking them into using their scent glands, which they will only do as a last means of defense.

for their strong, unpleasant odor, which has made them a subject of humor for many years. Nevertheless, the nine species which inhabit North and South America are most attractive animals and make excellent pets. Most often kept are the Striped Skunk (*Mephitis mephitis*) and smaller Spotted Skunk (*Spilogale putorius*).

Skunks use their scent glands only as a last resort when cornered; they will turn on an enemy and squirt a fine spray which causes a foul smell and extreme discomfort to the attacker particularly if the fluid gets into the eyes. The distinctive black and white markings are used to attract a mate and to alarm an enemy by arching the big, bushy tail across the back to form a ball of fur with black and white stripes.

Skunks burrow and spend much of the day underground. The species vary in size, but most are about the size of domestic cats. Skunks can become tame and friendly pets, especially if trained from about eight weeks. Some have been housebroken and even learned to wear a collar and leash for outdoor walking, but this could be a dangerous practice where dogs are likely to be walked or let loose.

Young skunks are often descented with a surgical procedure performed by veterinarians which removes their glands. Since they are slow-moving animals and cannot climb easily, this operation takes away their only means of defense against attackers (including dogs) and must be set against the element of human convenience.

Housing. In captivity skunks may be kept much as ferrets, but their quarters should be larger.

Feeding. If taken at eight weeks, skunks will still need milk and liquid foods with vitamin additives for some time. Bottle feeding is often necessary several times each day.

Eventually the animal can be fed raw, lean bits of chopped meat mixed with egg, plus vegetables and some fruits. Milk is appreciated by most specimens and water should always be provided.

Breeding. A litter of about five is produced in the spring.

Bats

Bats are the only true flying mammals. The 1,000 or so species form an order (Chiroptera) second only to the rodents in size and grouped scientifically into two suborders: Megachiroptera, the fruit bats of the Old World tropics, and Microchiroptera, the insectivorous bats, with a worldwide distribution. The fruit bats are generally large, with dog-like faces (hence the name "flying foxes"), and they have good night vision. The insectivorous species are smaller with poor eyesight, but they compensate by having a well-developed means of echo location. By sending and receiving a series of supersonic sounds, they are able to locate obstacles and to navigate in flight.

All bats are nocturnal. They have comparatively large "wings" of a membranous tissue which extends from the long bones of the front limbs back along the body to the back leg ankle. Many bats hang upside down when not flying or feeding. In some cases they congregate in huge colonies, said to number millions. If viewed without prejudice, bats are attractive animals. For the pet keeper who wants to study an unusual animal few could be more rewarding than bats.

VAMPIRE BATS

The three species of vampire bats(family Desmodontidae) come from Central and South America. The vampire legends of Transylvania and elsewhere were not based on these animals but vampire bats do pierce the skin of a sleeping animal or bird and lap the blood flowing from the wound. The bite is carefully done so as not to wake the animal and the saliva of the bat contains an anticoagulant which prevents the blood from clotting in the wound. The amount of blood taken by an animal 8cm. (3in.) long is not harmful, but vampire bats are known carriers of rabies. Captive specimens may live longer than six years and have bred on rare occasions. When fed cattle or sheep blood obtained from a slaughterhouse, they soon learn to lap from a shallow dish.

INSECTIVOROUS BATS

Comprising fifteen of the seventeen bat families, these bats are not recommended for pets. Only someone with an extremely good supply of insects could maintain them in captivity. The prey is usually caught on the wing, either directly with the mouth and teeth or, sometimes, by scooping up the insect with the wings.

For the pet keeper who wants to keep and study an unusual animal few pets could be more rewarding than a fruit bat. Top Center. *This one has become hand tame but care has to be taken of the hooks on his wings.*

Top Right. *For most of the day he is quite happy to simply hang upside down on his portable "bat stand."*

FRUIT BATS

Fruit bats are relatively easy to keep and become interesting and entertaining pets. Some of the 150 species are frequently available from dealers. They vary in size from a wing span of approximately 150cm. (6in.) to the largest, known as Indian Flying Foxes, which may exceed 1.5m. (5ft.). Fruit bats are known for longevity: one at London Zoo is said to have lived for seventeen years. *Warning:* The importation of fruit bats is banned in some countries, particularly where fruit growing is a major part of the economy. Bats may be infected with dangerous diseases and great care should be taken to avoid being bitten; hands should be gloved and limbs covered. A bite should receive prompt medical attention.

Housing. Fruit bats inhabit tropical and subtropical areas and in cooler climates must be kept in large indoor aviaries, where they may hibernate. They need a temperature around 18°C. (65°F.), which can be provided by low wattage heating lamps *above* the cage if the room is not warm enough. Avoid strong lights, which disturb them. Branches and twigs in the cage will give them a perch for hanging and a place to suspend food dishes, though they may prefer to hang from the cage itself. If space is restricted, let them out to fly around the room each evening. Line the floor of the cage with newspaper to make daily cleaning easier. Protect nearby walls and floor coverings too, for they may be stained by the wet messy droppings.

Feeding. Natural diet varies from one species to another, so a little research is necessary. In general, fruit bats will accept most fruits: sliced banana, apple, pear, paw paw, melon, plums, but some will reject citrus fruits. Raisins and sultanas that have been soaked in water overnight and washed are a

good alternative, and they usually consider grapes a real treat. A few species will also take worms or maggots while others have a diet not based on fruit. Bats prefer to feed in the air and the food troughs sold for mynahs and other fruit-eating birds make useful containers, which can be hooked over branches in their cage. Water can be given in similar troughs but bats can also be trained to drink from a feeding bottle fitted with a tube. Extra vitamins can be given by adding a honey mixture to drinking water, but this should not be necessary if the available fruit has been fresh and varied.

Breeding. The smaller species are often bred in captivity, and tropical bats kept in constant temperatures may breed repeatedly throughout the year. Gestation periods and such data are scarce since not enough observation has been made by pet keepers and zoologists. Usually the young are born one at a time and cling to and feed from the mother until weaned onto solid foods. When first born, bats are nearly naked and quite small, and it may be some time before you realize a birth has taken place. The offspring may still cling to the parent even after twelve months, when the baby is as big as its mother and is feeding on a normal diet.

Primates

Primates, the order of mammals to which humans belong, include the apes, monkeys, tarsiens, bush babies, Pottos, and lemurs. Although many primates have been kept as pets, most apes and monkeys are unsuitable as household pets, and their keeping should be confined to zoos and wildlife parks. (See **Zoo Animals as Pets.**)

Marmosets and tamarins are probably the easiest of primates to keep because of their small size, but they are highly strung and will only become tame after careful handling. Shown here is (Top Left) *a Silver Marmoset.*

(Top Middle) *a Lionheaded Tamarin.*

MARMOSETS AND TAMARINS

These closely related primates (family Callithricidae) are all from the New World and in fact almost all are from South America. There are thirty-three species. "True" marmosets have shortened canine teeth in the lower jaw, while the "long-tusked" tamarins have fairly long canines.

The relatively small marmosets and tamarins are a possible exception to the difficulties of keeping larger monkeys because they can usually be handled after a short period of becoming used to their owner or the person who feeds them. (See **Zoo Animals as Pets.**)

Restrictions exist governing the importation of many of the primates. These laws change from time to time and should be checked by anyone wanting to keep primates (an established zoological garden would be able to advise).

Marmosets and tamarins are highly strung creatures and move around rather quickly in a jerky, uncertain style. They enjoy climbing and have claws rather than nails, a necessary adaptation for gaining a grip on trees. The long tail, which is not prehensile, is used mainly as a balancing organ. These squirrel-like dwarf monkeys have shrill voices often reaching a pitch which is inaudible to human ears, according to some authorities. Many marmosets have distinctive features such as banded tail colors, crown and ear tufts, mustaches and beards. The Lion Marmoset (*Leontopithecus rosalia rosalia*) and the Silky Marmoset (*Callithrix chrysoleucos*) both have long, lion-like manes which require grooming. Another species common in captivity is the Common Marmoset (*Callithrix jacchus*). Marmosets spend much of their time grooming themselves and other members of the family group with their fingers, teeth, and tongue, removing every speck of dirt they can find. They seldom seem to quarrel but may at breeding times.

Housing. These primates must have a long, secure aviary-type enclosure providing shelter from the rain and open space for sunbathing. In the winter they must be kept warm; only indoor enclosures should be considered suitable in northern climates, with possibly some additional heating.

Feeding. In the wild marmosets and tamarins feed mainly on fruits, berries, shoots, and other plant foods, plus insects and sometimes small birds. In captivity they are fed mixed vegetables and fruits with the addition of raw, minced lean beef. Vitamin additives may be needed because these monkeys are known to suffer from rickets if their diet is not carefully monitored.

Breeding. The gestation period quoted in scientific works varies according to species and observation, but is usually about twenty weeks. The pregnant female should be provided with well enclosed sleeping quarters and may produce two or three youngsters, whose care is shared to an unusual degree by the male.

BUSH BABIES OR GALAGOS

These extremely attractive "lower primates" or prosimians belonging to the family Lorisdae are found only in Africa. There are six species of which only three are normally kept: the largest, the Thick-tailed Bush Baby (*Galago crassicaudatus*), has a body length of about 30cm. (12in.) and a long, bushy tail; the smallest, the Dwarf or Demidov's Bush Baby (*G. dermidovii*), could fit into a teacup and is in popular demand when available; the best known is the Senegal Moholi, Common Bush baby, Galago or Night-ape (*G. sengalensis*) which can be tamed and has very beautiful, soft fur and a long tail. The wide-eyed look of the bush baby signifies that its eyes are adapted to night hunting and that its habits are nocturnal. It hunts for insects such as grasshoppers, mantids, and spiders and supplements them with fruit and eggs if available.

Bush babies are probably the most agile pets which can be kept in the home. Both owners and bush babies enjoy periods of free play for the animals outside the cage. Windows and doors should be shut, the room cleared of small, precious objects and possibly of other household pets. The long back legs of bush babies enable them to hop like Kangaroos, and their rapid leaps, up to 2m. (6ft.) or more, may make it difficult for the owner to get them back into their enclosure. They can be induced with their favorite food, live mealworms, or, if that fails, an agile owner can catch them gently in a trout landing net.

Bush babies do not like being held in the hand and prefer to sit on the hand or shoulder. Some people may find bush babies' habit of urinating on their own hands and feet at frequent intervals an undesirable characteristic since it may leave prints on surfaces they touch. This practice helps mark territory and the dampness on their pad-like fingers and toes probably affords a better grip when climbing. Beware of their sharp teeth; taming requires time and patience and temperamental individuals may bite. Bush babies are long lived, eight to ten years being normal for a properly treated pet, but sadly many succumb to illness at an earlier age due to inadequate care.

Housing. Bush babies cannot withstand drafts or sustained cold weather and in climates colder than their homelands they must

The Dwarf or Demidov's Bush Baby is the smallest of all bush babies; an adult could quite easily fit inside a teacup.

be kept indoors or in a warm outside enclosure at a temperature not less than 10°C. (50°F.). A spare room or attic is ideal; an aviary-type enclosure at least 2.75m. (8ft.) high is next best. Provide branches for climbing (bush babies are completely arboreal) and a snug sleeping box placed high up in the cage, with a branch or plank leading to an 8cm. (3in.) entry hole. Fresh hay makes good bedding and sawdust on the floor helps with the cleaning of the cage.

Feeding. Captive bush babies should be fed chopped fresh fruit and some vegetables, such as carrots. Some specimens will eat raw minced meat if mixed with egg, supplemented by live mealworms (about twelve each day), which are available at some pet shops, or locusts. (Blowfly maggots are *not* accepted as a substitute.) Offer fresh milk daily if they accept it. Water should always be available. Occasionally give a few drops of cod-liver oil on their favorite food, or on a piece of bread. Fruit eaters are messy feeders, and you must expect fruit smells and fairly soft droppings.

Breeding. After a four to five month gestation, single or twin (in which case only one normally survives) young are born. Bush babies are weaned at four months and reach maturity at about two years. They are at first either carried by the scruff of the neck in their mother's teeth or cling to her back.

LORISES, ANGWANTIBO, AND POTTOS

The true lorises live in South Asia, Southern India, Sri Lanka, Java, and Borneo. They include the Slender Loris (*Loris tardigradus*, which is *not* slender) and Slow Loris (*Nycticebus cougang*). The Angwantibo (*Arctocebus calabarensis*) and Potto (*Perodicticus potto*) are both African species. All, like the bush babies, are lower primates of the family Lorisidae.

Nocturnal by nature, these animals have large, front-facing eyes which are adaptations for night hunting. In the wild they feed on insects, small lizards, and sometimes small birds, supplemented with lots of fruit or berries when available. Unlike the related bush babies, these are slow-moving creatures, rarely coming to the ground and seldom

Top Right. *The characteristic wide-eyed face of the Slow Loris; this is a slow-moving mammal that rarely comes to the ground.*

Top Center. *The affinity between children and animals knows no international boundaries. This young Malay boy has adopted an orphaned Slow Loris.*

jumping from tree to tree. As an adaptation to climbing the thumb is widely opposed to the fingers, and the forefinger is much reduced. They have learned to hunt stealthily and kill their prey by grabbing it with a hand and delivering a series of quick bites in the head region. During the day they sleep curled up into a furry ball and are thus camouflaged against a tree trunk or dark leaves.

All have short, soft fur in various shades of fawn and brown and some have markings. They lack the long tails of their close relatives the bush babies, although the Potto does have a short, thick tail. In zoos they are often housed in a nocturnal house with day and night periods reversed. In a home environment outside their natural range they are mainly kept inside the house at normal room temperature and are awake in the evening when other members of the household are at home to enjoy them. Other household pets such as cats and dogs should be trained not to frighten them since these animals have no

defense to offer. The Potto does have extensions to several vertebrae hidden below the fur at the nape of the neck, which can be used in defense if the animal is in the right position. Like bush babies, all these animals urinate on their hands and feet to mark territory or to get a better grip when climbing. They also use a special cleaning claw for scratching through their fine coat to remove debris. The name *loris* is said to derive from the Dutch *loeris* which means "clown."

Housing. Spacious quarters and nest box facilities like those for a bush baby are required. Home pet keepers should provide a large cage with a sleeping box and hay for bedding and allow the animal to come out for exercise in the evening.

Feeding. Feeding these animals is relatively easy. The New York Zoo claims its Slender Loris "thrives on canned dog food, fruit, mealworms and the occasional lizard." This last item may prove difficult for most pet keepers to find; they might also offer raw minced meat instead of dog food.

FARM ANIMALS

Domestic creatures trained originally as draft animals or raised as providers of food are attracting increasing interest as family pets. Young animals which have been hand reared have often gained pet status on the farm. The current movements toward self-sufficiency and natural foods are encouraging the raising of food animals which, even when reared for practical reasons, become a center of family interest. Consequently, goats, sheep, cows, donkeys, and pigs now enter the category of domestic pets.

Although it is generally impractical, and possibly even illegal, to keep such animals in urban areas, country and suburban dwellers can usually provide for them.

Donkeys

A donkey is far more likely to become a pet than is a horse and is less expensive to buy, feed, or house than a horse or pony. The donkey or ass should only be considered for a pet if a small field is available

Donkeys are complex creatures, capable of many moods. They can be friendly, affectionate, independent, patient, and even sad, and there is no questioning their intelligence. But when a donkey would rather not do something, it can be the laziest and most stubborn creature in the world.

The domestic donkey is descended from three races of wild ass (*Equus asinus*) which evolved in Africa—the Nubian Ass, the Somali Ass, and the now extinct North African Wild Ass. It is known that the Nubian Ass was domesticated in the Nile Valley by 3000 B.C. and possibly earlier, which means it preceded the taming of the horse. There are fewer breeds of donkey than there are of other domestic herbivores. Donkeys range in build from the **Sicilian** and **Macedonian Donkeys** which are as small as a Shetland Pony, to the large **Poitu Ass** and the **Spanish Giant Ass.** Apart from variations in size and color the donkey's form or shape is unmistakable. They are primarily grayish-brown or dark brown in color, with lighter underparts and often with a dark line running across the shoulders. White donkeys are occasionally seen, while in the Middle East and North Africa sand-colored animals predominate.

Donkeys are slower in their movements than horses and are still used as beasts of burden, especially in areas where horses do not thrive or where poverty prevents their purchase. Donkeys pull carts, turn treadwheels to raise water or grind grain, and are capable of carrying a heavy person.

Female donkeys (jennies) and gelded males are likely to be more reliable with children than is an entire male (jack). Like horses and ponies, donkeys are capable of biting and

There is an immediate attraction between children and the newborn, whatever the animal. This newborn donkey has made friends with two children.

kicking with both hind legs, but such behavior is unlikely from an animal accustomed to children unless there is a great deal of provocation.

Donkeys are hardy animals and are remarkably resistant to disease. They are also long lived, reaching the age of forty years and sometimes more. Hoof care is extremely important to the well being of these animals. Donkeys originated in a hot, dry and often stony part of the world, where abrasive effects of sand and stone kept their hooves in trim. When kept on soft ground the hooves grow rapidly and soon become extra long. This puts great pressure on the pasterns as the animal's weight is no longer directly over its hooves. A farrier or veterinarian must be consulted long before the hooves reach this stage. In temperate regions, donkeys normally grow long coats for winter which should never be clipped. Regular brushings and curry combing is sufficient and will assist the shedding of loose hair when the winter coat is molted.

Even with a small field in which to graze, a donkey still needs exercise. If there is no one to ride it regularly and it is not put to some form of work, it should be walked on a halter.

Housing. A donkey requires a field of at least 0.4 hectare (1 acre) if it is to be kept on the same land all year. A donkey in good condition is practically impervious to cold weather since its thick winter coat provides excellent insulation against winter chills. Nevertheless, a shelter is necessary for protection from the sun, rain, and strong winter winds. The floor of the shelter should be covered with wheat straw or peat moss or wood shavings.

Page wire fencing, sometimes called pig netting, is the most suitable type for confining donkeys as they are adept at squeezing through barriers, even of barbed wire when the strands are only 45cm. (18in.) apart. When fenced land is unavailable, a donkey can be tethered in open pasture. The equipment needed for tethering is a leather collar (available from a harness supplier) a chain 9m. (30ft.) long and a stake and swivel. The location can be changed when the food supply dwindles. One disadvantage with tethering is that the animal cannot escape possible teasing by children or worrying by dogs. Also, donkeys, being clever creatures, may manage to escape.

Feeding. The donkey's digestive system and food requirements are similar to those of the pony. In the summer, provided that the

If you have the space to provide stabling for a donkey or a paddock in which it can be kept, you will have a delightful and amusing pet that can also be ridden.

donkey is kept on at least 0.4 hectare (1 acre) of reasonable pasture, supplementary feeding is unnecessary, although they will appreciate carrots and other such treats. Unlike horses, donkeys browse in addition to grazing so that hedges within reach will be trimmed if the grazing is insufficient. A donkey will eat weeds and even nettles, but special care must be taken to eliminate ragwort from its pasture as this is a highly poisonous weed. Fresh water should always be available.

In winter or if housed indoors, a donkey needs 3–3.5kg. (7–8lb.) of good quality hay a day and 1kg. (2lb.) of concentrates—oats, bran, and pony pellets. An occasional carrot, apple, or several sugar cubes make welcome additions to the donkey's diet and go a long way toward making friends too. However, a donkey can become a nuisance or hard to handle if it expects these tidbits regularly and they are not given.

The pregnant mare needs extra food in the final four months of her year-long gestation. Depending on the time of the year, the quantity of concentrates should be increased with care taken not to overfeed her.

Breeding. The donkey's gestation period is approximately twelve months, and jennies can be mated again eighteen days after giving birth. The foal should remain with its mother for at least five months, although it can be weaned earlier if this is desirable. The donkey can be crossed fairly readily with a horse

to produce a mule when the sire is a jackass, and a hinny when the sire is a horse. Hinnies and mules are usually sterile.

Goats

Goats are undoubtedly the easiest farm animals to keep as pets. Undemanding, hardy and simple to feed, they are suitable for most situations where a little space is available.

The domestication of goats commenced about 6000 B.C., and the animals were bred to provide milk, meat, leather, and hair. The wild goat *(Capra aegagrus)* of Asia Minor and the Greek Islands is considered the most likely ancestor of the many modern domestic breeds which show a great variety of form and color. In some breeds such as the Angora, both the male and female bear horns, while in others, such as the Saanea, both sexes may lack horns. Male (and in some breeds, female) goats have a beard and both sexes have appendages or tassles on the throat.

Switzerland has produced many of the milk producing breeds. The **Saanen,** from the Saanen Valley in Switzerland, is a large animal which is white or cream in color. It may be horned or hornless and, in both sexes, may be with or without a beard. The **Toggenburg,** from the Toggenburg Valley in Switzerland, is slightly smaller than the Saanen. It is light fawn to dark brown in color with white markings. The **Alpine** is a long-limbed goat that is black with white markings. The **Swiss Valais** goat is unusual in having both long horns and long hair. The front half of its body is black and the rear white. The **Nubian (Anglo-Nubian),** bred from Indian, African, and British goats, is a large animal with long drooping ears and a Roman nose. It can be horned or hornless. The Nubian produces milk that has a high butterfat content. The **Cashmere (Kashmiri)** goat from central Asia has very fine,

long hair that is whitish in color. The **Angora,** from Turkey, has long whitish fleece, a white face, and white feet. Both the Cashmere and the Angora are renowned for their fleece.

Goats are active, inquisitive animals but billies play rough, especially during the breeding season, and are capable of inflicting serious injury with a sudden unexpected butt. Goats have two major disadvantages: their destructiveness and the unpleasant smell of billies during the breeding season. This odor permeates everything, from the woodwork of their pen to the handler's clothing and skin, and is difficult to remove.

Unfortunately, goats have the habit of eating almost anything and many have died from consuming plastic bags and similar indigestible items. Goats are browsers and are capable of destroying trees and shrubs by continually barking and defoliating them. Some people have attributed to them the destruction of most of the ancient hardwood forests which once flourished around the Mediterranean.

Goats should be milked twice daily—in the early morning and then again in the evening—and the udder should be emptied on each occasion. They often object to being milked and a milking bench on which the goat stands at a convenient height, while eating from a trough, makes milking a much easier and calmer process.

Housing. Goats may be kept in the open in most countries. They are hardy animals and weather as cold as − 18°C. (0°F.) will not trouble a healthy specimen. When ample unfenced land is available, tethering by chain and stake is still the most acceptable means of restraining an individual goat. They must have access to shade during the summer months and should have a dry, draft-proof shelter in the winter.

Goats are the easiest farm animals to keep as pets. They are often found in children's corners of zoos and wildlife parks; the kids are tame and easy to hand feed.

Top Left. *One of the advantages of keeping a goat is the milk that it provides. However, goats often object to being milked, necessitating either a milking stand or, as here, two people to hold the goat.*

Top Right. *Goats are browsers and are quite capable of destroying trees, and shrubs. They are often accused of being the main culprits in the destruction of the original Mediterranean forests.*

Alternately, the pet goat may be kept in a sturdy concrete-floored shelter of about 3.2m. (35ft.) in area, with a larger fenced yard around it. All the grass and shrubs in the yard will be eaten so it should have a floor covering of coarse sand which is easier to maintain than an earthen floor.

Feeding. A goat with access to good grazing and browsing does not require supplementary feeding during the summer months. A tethered goat should be moved to a fresh area every day and should not be allowed to graze the same area again for at least two weeks to avoid infection with flukes and other parasites.

When confined in winter or housed permanently indoors, the goat should be given as much good quality meadow hay as it will eat, with a little added clover or alfalfa (lucerne). An adult animal should also receive 1kg. (2lb.) of chopped carrots, rutabagas, mangels, sugar beets, or cabbage, and 0.5kg. (1lb.) of concentrates such as sheep or dairy cattle pellets or a mixture of maize, oats, bran and linseed cake. Concentrates should be divided between two daily feeds. A mineral lick should also be provided, and fresh water should be available at all times. Secure the water container at an adequate height to prevent pollution with urine and feces.

A lactating nanny requires an extra ration of about 0.5kg. (1lb.) of concentrates for every .5 liters (3pt.) of milk she produces per day.

Goat kids must receive colostrum, the thick milk produced during the first four days of lactation, because it contains antibodies which provide resistance to infections. (See **Breeding and Rearing.**) Thereafter a kid can be bottle raised and should receive about 0.25 liter (0.5 pt.) of milk four

times daily at four hour intervals, but intake varies according to breed and size. Do not allow a kid to drain a bottle too quickly, for indigestion and diarrhea may result or milk may enter the lungs. Diarrhea can also result from overfeeding or making sudden changes in the diet, and an immediate reduction of milk intake is necessary. The use of glucose in water rather than milk for a few feeds should aid recovery, but if the looseness persists or if the feces become whitish or blood-stained, call a veterinarian immediately. Cows' milk is a good substitute for goats' milk as it has the same protein and water content, but slightly more lactose and less fat.

Soft meadow hay and lamb pellets should be available to goat kids from two weeks of age. When they are six weeks old the weaning process can begin. The amount of milk given at each feeding is slowly reduced, thus forcing the kids to rely more on the dry food. The milk supply can then be stopped completely when they are twelve weeks old.

Breeding. The goat's normal mating season is from the fall to the beginning of winter but this may vary according to circumstances and the environment. Goats housed indoors permanently may be receptive during other months while feral goats in New Zealand and the Galapagos Islands breed all year round. The goat's estrus period lasts three days and occurs at intervals of about two weeks. During estrus, the goat is restless, bellows frequently, and constantly twitches her tail. Male goats are capable of siring young at the age of six months, provided they are not weaned too early. The gestation period is 148–150 days. Female kids can be mated in the year of their birth without harm.

About ten weeks before a goat is due to

kid, start drying off her milk supply by gradually reducing the amount of milk taken, and then by reducing the frequency of milking. Without the stimulus of complete and frequent milking, the milk supply slowly dries up; but if the udder becomes swollen or uncomfortable prior to kidding, it may be necessary to milk the animal again.

At kidding time the goat should be left in its regular quarters to avoid any stress caused by moving it to special, but unfamiliar, kidding facilities. The pregnant goat must always be handled with care and she should not have to tolerate any roughness from other goats. Her regular companions can be left in the same stall if there is ample space, but strange goats should not be introduced during the later stages of pregnancy.

Goats seldom require assistance during kidding, but a veterinarian must be called when continual straining fails to produce the kid and if the placenta is not discharged within twenty-four hours of birth. Females of less than a year seldom produce more than one kid, but older animals are likely to bear twins or triplets. The lifespan of a goat varies between nine to eighteen years.

Sheep

Sheep are normally nervous, excitable animals that respond well to gentle handling, particularly when this is a regular occurrence started with bottle raising. It is frequently necessary to bottle raise lambs due to their being orphans or to the ewe's inability to care for them. In fact, hand-reared lambs often become so humanized that it is difficult to integrate them back into the flock, and they become a nuisance.

The many breeds of domestic sheep are believed to be descended from the Mouflon (*Ovis musimon*) of the Mediterranean region. There are well over four hundred breeds of sheep that can be classified according to their productive traits. The Australian **Merino** and the North American **Rambouillet,** classified as fine-wool breeds, are bred for their wool. These are relatively small, angular sheep with long thin tails. The legs and often the head are covered with wool. The **Hampshire** and **Suffolk,** known as medium-wool breeds, are usually bred for their meat. Medium-wool breeds are white in color although, as with the Suffolk, they may have a black or brown face and legs. The **Border Leicester** and **Romney Marsh** are members of the long-wool breeds and are raised for both their fleece and meat. The **Sardinian** and **Calabrian** from Italy, the **Basque-Bearne** from France, and the **Mancha** from Spain are used for dairy purposes. Dairy breeds are usually medium in size, angular in shape and sometimes have lop ears.

Some African breeds such as the **Masai, Cameroon,** and **Somali** sheep resemble goats as they have short body hair instead of wool, and the rams usually have a long neck mane. The most unusual domestic breeds are the fat-tailed sheep and earless sheep from the Middle East, the fat-rumped sheep from Central Asia, the **Zackel** sheep with long spiraling horns from Eastern Europe, and the four-horned sheep which, in Great Britain and North America, has become the most popular noncommercial breed. Ancient feral breeds such as the **Soay Sheep** from **St. Kilda** are also gaining popularity.

Sheep are a little more trouble to maintain and keep healthy than goats and donkeys. Shearing, for example, is an annual chore that has to be done early in summer. In some areas, the law requires sheep to be dipped as a precautionary measure against sheep scab or psoroptic mange. Sheep scab, caused by mites, is one of the worst sheep infections and health authorities in many countries require notification of its occurrence. Particular care must be taken during the early summer before shearing to prevent blowflies from laying their eggs on the long and often soiled fleece around the hindquarters. The maggots penetrate the skin beneath the wool and can cause considerable damage to skin and flesh before their presence is noticed. Fortunately, tame bottle-raised sheep are easier to observe for signs of infestation and are easier to handle than members of a hillside flock. The removal of excess wool on the sheep's rear, especially if this becomes soiled, will prevent this problem with maggots. The risk of maggot infestation can also be reduced by docking the lamb's tail soon after birth.

When it is necessary to lift or carry a sheep it should be grasped firmly in both arms, with one behind its hindquarters and the other across its front. A sheep should never be caught or held by the fleece as the ensuing struggle may damage the wool and can cause more serious injury. A sheep is best re-strained by holding it under the neck and chin with one or both hands, depending on the animal's temperament, and holding its head up, although not so high as to restrict its breathing.

Housing. The sheep's thick greasy coat provides good protection against cold and rain so that heated accommodation is unnecessary even in central Canada where the temperature may drop well below freezing. They do need a shelter with a bed of dry straw together with an adjacent yard. If the yard is too small to permit the growth of grass, the ground should be covered with coarse sand which can easily be cleaned and raked. Wooden floors in the shelter are unsuitable as they soak up and retain urine. A fence of wicker hurdles or page wire netting 1m. (3ft.) high is adequate to confine sheep.

Feeding. Like all herbivores, sheep need a high intake of bulk foods in the form of grass or hay. When a sheep does not have access to grazing land, it should be given as much good quality meadow hay as it will eat. Hay should be provided in a rack to prevent soiling from the ground. Commercial sheep pellets should also be given in the proportions recommended by the manufacturer. Feed the pellets from a trough with a rim to prevent them from being scattered and soiled. Mangels, rutabagas, carrots, and potatoes are necessary for animals that are fed permanently on a dry diet of hay and pellets but these should be thinly sliced for sheep sometimes choke on large pieces. A salt lick, a mixed mineral block, and fresh water should be available at all times.

Although hay can be supplied freely, the ration of concentrates and cereals must be controlled carefully. If food remains in the trough an hour after feeding, it is an indication that the ration is excessive and the food should be removed. Pregnant and lactating ewes need a larger ration of concentrates (approximately 25 percent more) than non-breeding animals.

Bottle-raised lambs drink between 170–230g. (6–8oz.) of milk per feeding initially, and this amount must be increased as they grow. (See **Breeding and Rearing.**) Five feeds daily at four-hour intervals are sufficient, and the milk should be warmed to body temperature. When the lamb is eight weeks old, one of the bottles should be canceled by increasing the intervals between feedings. Every two weeks thereafter another feeding should be stopped until, by the age of fourteen weeks, only one bottle daily is given. Milk feeding can be terminated when the lamb is four months old. Access to grazing or fine meadow hay and lamb pellets, must be available at all times after the first two weeks following birth to encourage the lamb to take solid foods. Overfeeding, feeding the milk too rapidly, or allowing an excessive intake of protein or fat is likely to cause diarrhea in which case veterinary advice must be sought.

Breeding. Sheep are prolific animals capable of producing up to three lambs each spring.

Lambs are perhaps the most popular of all pet farm animals—but don't forget they grow into full-sized sheep within a year and are very nervous animals as adults.

The Dorset Horn was unique among British breeds due to its natural ability to produce lambs twice yearly, but this breeding rate is now achieved annually from other breeds through the use of hormones. Lambs can be bred in their first year from the age of about 190 days. The gestation period for ewes is 144–151 days depending on the breed. The lifespan of sheep is generally seven to ten years although it can be more.

Pigs

Pigs may seem the most incongruous animals to keep as pets, but their reputation is much maligned. They are intelligent, emotional animals, capable of affection and devotion to people. Bottle-raised from a young age, a piglet develops an attachment for its foster parents which not only persists into adulthood, but can equal that of a dog for its owner. Wild pigs will also exhibit this devotion.

The most likely deterrents to keeping pigs as pets are the smell of their manure, their size when adult, and their destructive rooting habits. They enjoy wallowing in mud, but this does not imply lack of cleanliness. Pigs actually have very clean habits, keeping their beds clean, and soiling only one corner of the pen. However, the smell of their feces is objectionable to most people, and manure disposal is likely to be a problem. Pigs should only be kept, therefore, in a rural environment where there are no close neighbors to complain about the smell and where manure disposal can be handled.

Mature pigs are large animals, adults of the larger breeds weighing over 100kg. (220lb.). While bottle-raised females are likely to remain docile and manageable throughout their life span, boars are potentially danger-

Top Left. Top Middle. *Pigs and cows are the least likely of farm animal pets, but when kept on small holdings the individual animals can become as tame and as much pets as dogs or cats.*

ous animals that are capable of inflicting serious injury with their sharp teeth.

There are over three hundred breeds of pig throughout the world. Among the most popular commercial breeds are the **Large White,** which as the name implies is an all white pig, the **Wessex Saddleback,** which is black with a white saddle, and the **Landrace,** which is white with lop ears. Popular noncommercial breeds include the **Gloucester Old Spot,** a white pig with black spots and lop ears, and the **Tamworth** which is golden-red in color with a long snout and erect ears. Both breeds are suitable for small areas. A number of breeds have been developed in the United States, including the **Poland-China,** a black pig with a white face and feet and a white tip on the tail, the **Duroc,** an all red animal with fairly drooping ears, the **Hereford** characterized by a white head and red body color, and the **American Landrace,** which is white and yields a high quality carcass. Two of the strangest domestic pigs are the **Mangaliza Pig** from Hungary, which has a thick, curly coat and can be either white or brownish black with a white belly, and the small black **Pot-bellied Pig** from Vietnam, whose drooping belly almost reaches the ground.

Pigs can suffer from a variety of diseases. Anemia, due to iron deficiency, may occur in piglets which are raised indoors. Diagnosis and treatment of this deficiency should be carried out by a veterinarian or a knowledgeable breeder. After piglets begin eating pellets, the necessary iron will be supplied. If piglets are kept out of doors, they must be able to seek shelter from the sun since they are susceptible to sunburn, especially on the ears. Overweight adult pigs are prone to heat stroke at 32.2°C. (90°F.) and above.

Housing. Each pig needs at least a quarter of a hectare (half an acre) to range free; otherwise it must be housed in a pig pen. This should be in the form of a brick or concrete building, providing about 4.5m. (50ft.) of floor space, with an attached concrete surface yard approximately 1m. (11ft.) and surrounded by a sturdy fence. Oat or wheat straw should be provided for bedding, and the concrete floor must be constructed so that it drains to the front of the yard where well-secured water and feed troughs should be situated.

Warmth is most important to newborn piglets which lack subcutaneous fat and have very little hair to provide insulation. A damp or cold environment can prove fatal in short order, so a dry, heated building with an insulated floor is essential. The building should also be equipped with an infrared lamp under which the piglets can sleep.

Feeding. Unlike the other farm animals included in this section, pigs cannot cope with large quantities of roughage. They must have a diet which is fairly concentrated and therefore low in fiber and high in digestible nutrients. Diets especially prepared for pigs are available from animal feed manufacturers. Pig creep pellets, rearing pellets, and fattening pellets, all provide the special food composition required during all the stages of the pig's life cycle. Changes from one ration to another must be done very slowly. Commercial food preparations may be supplemented with a mash made from boiled household leavings such as potato peelings and other vegetable scraps. Fresh water should be available at all times.

Piglets rely solely on milk during their first two weeks, but thereafter must have access to creep feed. When five weeks old, the piglet should be eating appreciable amounts of dry food, and the milk intake can then be reduced slowly until the animal is completely weaned at the age of five weeks.

Breeding. Both sexes are ready for breeding when about eight months old. Females have a regular estrus cycle of twenty-one days all year round. The gestation period is 112–115 days, and a sow usually produces two litters annually. Six to twelve piglets are born in each litter. The lifespan of a pig is approximately ten years.

Cows

Cows should be the prerogative of country dwellers since these animals need plenty of grazing land. While it is possible for people in other situations to rear a calf to weaning age or just beyond, it is usually impractical to keep a mature animal unless land is available. The average lifespan of a cow is about twenty years.

There are two distinct groups of cattle from which all the modern breeds are descended: the Zebu or Humped cattle found in tropical regions, and the breeds which derived from the now extinct aurochs found in the temperate regions. The Zebu type includes such breeds as the **Brahman** from India, the **Boran** from Africa, and the **Indo-Brazil** from South America. The second group comprises the beef, dairy, and dual purpose breeds such as the **Aberdeen-Angus** (beef), **Jersey** (dairy), and **Simmental** (dual purpose). The most suitable breeds for the pet keeper are the small docile breeds such as the Jersey, **Dexter,** or even the exotic looking **Dwarf Zebu.**

Housing. Although cows are hardy animals and can be kept out of doors all year round, some sort of shelter should be provided against prevailing winds in the winter and excess heat in the summer.

Feeding. A cow should have at least 0.4 hectare (1 acre) of good grazing land. In winter or if the pasture is poor, a cow should be given as much good quality hay as it will eat, as well as concentrates in the form of cereals and oilseed meal. Concentrates can be fed in the proportion of 400g/1 (3.3lb/gal) of milk yield. Root vegetables such as mangels and rutabagas can also be given. Fresh water should always be available.

Breeding. Cows are polyestrus which means that they come into heat regularly and can be bred all year round. Heat lasts for less than twenty-four hours, however, but due to artificial insemination programs which have reached a high degree of perfection and are widely used on a commercial scale, the problems of mating are greatly reduced. The gestation period is 280 days.

BIRDS

Birds are the most successful warm-blooded animals alive today. They first appeared in the days of the dinosaurs, and since then they have conquered all continents: from mountain top to desert, from polar ice cap to jungle, and from freshwater lakes and rivers to the vast spaces of the oceans.

There are birds which can swim, dive, soar, sleep on the wing, live in caves, and migrate twice a year over several thousand miles. Among the nearly nine thousand species are carnivores, vegetarians, insectivores, and omnivores. This versatility coupled with a mobility that a terrestrial animal could never hope to equal has culminated in the high degree of tolerance, adaptability, and inherent toughness that makes many birds not only well suited to a life of captivity, but quite often revel in it—taking all that is good and tolerating much that is bad.

If you take all those physical qualities—not forgetting, of course, the basic power of flight, which humans have always envied and sought to emulate—and add to them the sheer beauty of birds, it is hardly surprising that they tantalize and beguile us as much as they do.

Despite their high degree of tolerance, it is important not to give the impression that *all* kinds of wild birds are suitable for captivity, even less as pets. The majority are still better off in the wild, even though they may survive under ideal captive conditions.

Careless and abusive treatment has endangered many species of birds. For this reason, new laws are being introduced to control the import, export, and sale of most birds. With very few exceptions, wild birds may not be kept in captivity or sold alive,

unless they have been bred from earlier captive birds.

The laws concerning pet birds are complex and constantly changing, so it is impossible to make a final statement of what is and what is not allowed. But it seems clear that the increasing number of protective laws will re-

Human beings began keeping birds simply for pleasure many centuries ago. The African Gray Parrot is intelligent, seldom noisy, and has a good temperament. It has a life expectancy of up to fifty years.

strict more and more the varieties of birds available to pet owners.

There are those, however, which seem tailor-made for a life as pets or under the care of an aviculturist. Apart from wild birds there are all the domesticated forms which were once wild, and in which human beings long ago recognized some special quality and

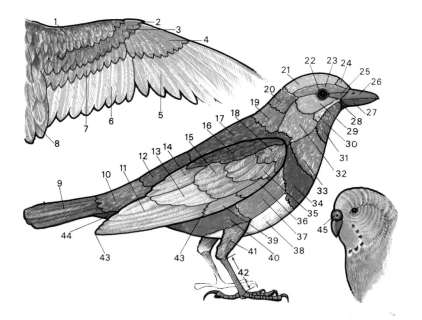

Topography of a bird	
1 Lesser wing coverts	23 Superciliary
2 Alula	24 Forehead
3 Middle wing coverts	25 Lores
4 Primary coverts	26 Upper mandible
5 Primaries	27 Lower mandible
6 Secondaries	28 Chin
7 Greater wing coverts	29 Ear coverts
8 Tertiaries	30 Moustachial stripe
9 Retrices or tail feathers	31 Throat
10 Upper tail coverts	32 Side of neck
11 Primaries	33 Upper breast
12 Rump	34 Lower breast
13 Secondaries	35 Middle coverts
14 Tertiaries	36 Aluia
15 Greater Coverts	37 Side
16 Scapulars	38 Belly
17 Mantle	39 Primary coverts
18 Lesser coverts	40 Flank
19 Hind neck	41 Thigh
20 Nape	42 Tarsus
21 Crown	43 Extent of remiges
22 Orbital ring	44 Under tail coverts
	45 Cere

set about turning it to their own advantage. Even the poor old battery hen has a barely recognizable wild ancestor in the Red Jungle Fowl of Asia, while pigeons were used to carry messages by the early Egyptians.

People began keeping birds simply for pleasure many centuries ago—for their songs, powers of mimicry, beauty of feather, or just their company. These types are less prone to genetic manipulation than the "working" species, and some birds like the Ringnecked Parakeet—introduced into Greece by Alexander the Great—can still be allied instantly to their wild cousins. Others like canaries and budgerigars have been the subject of such intensive breeding and experiment that even after a relatively short time, some forms are scarcely recognizable.

Generally, the wild birds best suited to life as pets are parrots, finches, and perhaps a few softbills. But in these days of heavy global pressure on all wildlife, no wild bird should be kept solely as a pet without proper regard to its natural propagation, and at least a pair or trio should always be housed together. If a single pet *is* required, choose a parakeet or canary, which can provide all the companionship and personality desired of any pet, while appearing not to mind living without a mate.

Principles Of Feeding Birds

The basic nutritional requirement of birds are similar to those of mammals: an energy source, protein, essential fatty acids, vitamins, and minerals. Birds do not have the womb and placental system for nurturing a fetus which is shared by all but the most primitive mammals. Instead, the embryo is supplied with a food store in an egg which is laid and incubated outside the mother's body. This food store sometimes feeds the nestling for a few days after hatching. The young of most species remain helpless in the nest for several weeks and must be fed by the parents. The mother has no milk glands, but some species project predigested food (called crop- or stomach-milk) into the youngster's beaks. In other species the parents provide small pieces of a suitable diet such as insects and worms. Details of individual feeding requirements will be given in each of the following sections.

Canaries

Canaries are popular cage birds because of their bright colors, sweet songs, and friendly ways. They make excellent pets and, if obtained quite young, frequently become delightfully tame. They thrive in small cages and are simple and inexpensive to keep. Canaries can also be fine aviary birds that prosper indoors or outside in garden aviaries, where they are often willing to nest.

The classic all-wire canary cage can be an extremely attractive furnishing in its own right.

The wild Canary (*Serinus canarius*) is a green-yellow, darkly-streaked bird, which in its natural form is indigenous to the Canary Islands, Madeira, and the Azores. It was introduced into Europe after the conquest of the Canary Islands by the Spaniards near the end of the fifteenth century. In 1709 a Frenchman, Hervieux, wrote what was to become the first standard work on this bird. His work contained descriptions of twenty-nine varieties, many of which were color variations rather than distinct breeds. In the nineteenth century, the keeping of canaries became popular, and it was during this time that many clubs and shows were created for the different varieties that had been developed. Early in the twentieth century, an attempt was made to cross red male Siskins with canaries in order to produce a red canary. This exciting innovation has resulted in the development of a wide range of new, brightly colored canaries.

When choosing a pet canary, it is always best to obtain a young cock bird. Hens do not sing, so a cock is essential if a pet is wanted for its singing ability. Some hens warble a little, but these are exceptions rather than the rule. Unfortunately, young birds cannot be sexed with certainty until they are several months old when the cocks commence to sing. Generally the smaller breeds of canary such as the Border, Gloster, and Red Factor, or one of their crosses, are the most suitable for a single household pet. The Roller can also be a good single pet although its song is sometimes too loud for a small living room. Color has no effect on a canary's ability to sing.

The average life span of a caged pet canary is about ten years, although some have been known to live twice that long.

HOUSING

Indoors a pet bird can be kept in one of the popular wire type of cages. The cage should be fitted with two or three well-placed and secure perches. One of the perches can be the swing type if it does not hinder the bird's movement. Although as a general rule canaries are not interested in toys and ladders, some do like a small mirror. The tray which slides out from the floor of the cage should be covered by a thin layer of clean sand or sandsheets sold for this purpose. The cage must

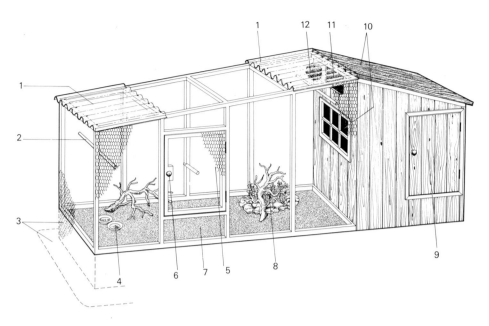

Aviaries should incorporate translucent covering (1) over main perches (2) which should be high and widely spaced. Netting (3) should extend 50cm. (20in.) below ground and 40cm. (16in.) outwards to deter burrowing animals. A water dish (4) can be located outside, but food is better positioned in the shed. Small doors (5), which deter escape, should be catch (6) operated from both sides. Floors (7) can be raked sand, soil, or concrete. Low perches and cover (8) are desirable. The shelter should have a door (9) with internal porch, windows and a roof that is solid and opaque (10). Nesting site (11) access should be high, except for ground birds such as quail which need ground access. Nesting sites (12) should be under cover.

be placed or hung in a well-lighted area, but it should not be near drafts and windows, where the temperature can fluctuate.

Canaries are extremely fond of bathing, and a plastic bath which hooks onto the open door is ideal for this purpose. These baths are totally enclosed to prevent water from splashing around the room. Whenever possible the bath should be provided early in the day, so there is plenty of time for the bird to dry off before it roosts.

A good cock canary will sing during about nine months of the year. It does not sing during its annual molt and may cease to sing if it suffers a soft molt (the sporadic or continual dropping of feathers outside the normal molting period). This may be caused by locating the cage in a draft or near a window, or leaving it uncovered all evening, so that the bird has to endure an unnaturally long day. Cages kept inside should be covered by a dark cloth daily around seven o'clock in the evening. Occasionally, after a year or two a cock fails to sing from a lack of competition with others. The obvious remedy is to place another cock within hearing distance, or play a recording of another bird.

Outdoors

Canaries are also easy to look after if kept in an outdoor aviary. Breeds such as Borders, Glosters, and Rollers quickly adapt to outdoor conditions. Canaries can usually be housed satisfactorily in aviaries with waxbills, finches, and other small seedeaters, and even with some of the smaller softbills.

The aviary should be large enough to contain a dry, enclosed shelter surrounded by a grassy area. The birds will benefit from picking about in the grass, and will probably destroy any growing vegetation. The aviary should be fitted with soft whitewood perches and dishes for food and water. Healthy canaries are quite hardy in a moderate climate and can usually remain outdoors without any need of artificial heat.

Breeding Cages

Most exhibition and special colored canaries are bred in box-type cages known as single, double, or treble breeders. The single kind is about 45cm. (18in.) long, 40cm. (16in.) high, and 30cm. (12in.) deep; the double is 90cm. (36in.) long, and the treble 120cm. (48in.) long, though these sizes can be varied to suit individual circumstances. Double and treble breeders have sliding partitions to enable them to be divided into smaller compartments. Most fanciers favor double breeders, though treble breeders are useful for mating one cock with two hens. The cock is placed in the center compartment and by removing one partition, the cock and one hen can be paired in a double breeder, while the other hen remains separated. Outside the breeding season, treble breeders that have the partitions removed make good flight cages for several birds together. Breeding cages must be fitted with soft whitewood perches running from the back to the front, and receptacles for food, water, and extras. When the breeding season comes, nest pans or other suitable receptacles should be installed. Earthenware, plastic, or wicker nest pans can

be bought, along with a wire holder for fixing them to the back or side of the cage at about the same height as the perches. Nest pans require a felt lining which can also be purchased. Otherwise an old piece of household felt can be used. The felt must be dusted with a safe insect powder and sewn or stuck inside the pan, which must also be dusted. Nesting material can consist of clean fine hay, moss, cow hair, combings from dogs, or other soft materials. Synthetic materials that can become entangled around the bird's legs and toes must be avoided.

FEEDING REQUIREMENTS

In the case of a pet bird, it is most convenient to buy commercially prepared canary seed. This contains a well-balanced mixture of seeds that will supply most of the bird's food requirements. In addition, fresh drinking water, a piece of cuttlefish bone and grit—if it is not already present in the floor covering—should always be available. A regular supply of fresh greenfood should be given, while a small piece of sweet apple, pear, or some other fruit, placed between the wires at the end of a perch, makes a very acceptable tidbit once or twice a week.

Except for the breeding season, a suitable diet for canaries housed outdoors is three part canary seed to one part red rape, with a small amount of tonic or condition seeds and greenfood once a week. About three months before the breeding season, however, the rape should be reduced by half and replaced by niger. Soft food which is needed for rearing the young must also be introduced at this time. At first soft food and greenfood should be given once a week, then gradually increased so that just prior to breeding it is given three times a week. The soft food can consist of finely chopped or mashed hard-boiled egg mixed with crushed plain biscuit, oatmeal, or one of the commercial canary rearing foods. During the incubation period the birds should be fed three part canary seed to one part red rape, with greenfood offered twice a week. A little soft food should be given the day before the chicks are expected to hatch and should be slowly increased as they grow. When the chicks are four to five days old, they need daily provisions of greenfood and soaked seed consisting of equal parts of rape, hemp, and teasel soaked in clean water for forty-eight hours, then thoroughly rinsed and well drained. Remove uneaten food at the end of each day during rearing as stale food will cause diarrhea. A diet that is too rich will also cause diarrhea and can be remedied by adding a little powdered arrowroot to the soft food. After about twenty-one days, the young must be removed from their parents and housed in a clean cage. Avoid overcrowding; four or five birds to a single breeder is ample. The cage should have clean paper on the floor which is changed at the end of each day. When the young are about six weeks old a little normal dry seed should be sprinkled on the soaked seed and soft food. The amount of dry seed should be gradually increased until the birds are successfully weaned, and continued until they molt at eight to twelve weeks old.

BREEDING

Canaries are usually ready to breed in the early spring. The hen should be placed in the breeding cage at least two weeks before the expected time of pairing but separated from the cock by a partition. It is usual to pair a buff to a yellow bird, but which bird is female and which is male is largely irrelevant. It is particularly undesirable to repeatedly pair buff birds together. When the cock is singing

Border and Fife Canaries
1 Self Cinnamon Border
2 Cinnamon and White Variegated Border
3 Clear Yellow Border
4 Eye-, Wing-, and Tail-Marked Buff Border
5 Clear Yellow Fife

vigorously and the hen is restlessly flying from perch to perch carrying nesting material, the two can be put together. If the hen is ready, she will make a nest and begin to lay within a week. Usually she will lay one egg early each morning, laying four (occasionally five) in all. After each egg is laid, it must be removed carefully and stored and a dummy egg (which can be purchased) put in its place. When the fourth egg is laid, or just before, the dummy eggs must be removed and the original three returned to the nest. If the original eggs were left in the nest and not replaced by dummies, the last egg laid would not hatch until about four days afer the first, since the hen starts to sit after the first one is laid. Incubation takes thirteen to fourteen days and is done by the hen alone.

Canaries are not difficult to breed in aviaries, where it is usual to allow at least two or three hens to each cock to prevent too much squabbling. Nest pans and other suit-

Gloster Canaries
1 Wing-Marked Yellow Gloster Corona
2 Buff Gloster Consort

able receptacles can be fixed in sheltered, likely sites, and if bunches of twiggy branches are included, some hens will build natural nests like their wild ancestors.

A pair of canaries should not be expected to raise more than two broods a season.

CANARY BREEDS

Today there is a wide choice of canaries available. Most varieties conform to standard shapes, and these are generally known as type canaries. The different varieties are bred in a

Lizard Canaries
1 Clear-Capped Silver Lizard
2 Clear-Capped Gold Lizard

194

range of colors: yellow, white, fawn, cinnamon, red-orange, and various pastel shades. There are also green varieties, similar to the Wild Canary, and blue, although these colors are not as vivid as in other bird species. Canaries can be uniformly one color, or two or more that combine to form a pattern. Cock and hen canaries differ very little in appearance. Cocks are usually bolder in color and have a more jaunty carriage, but this is not an infallible guide. Normally, the only satisfactory distinction is the beautiful singing voice of the cock.

Border Fancy

This is probably the most popular canary and takes its name from the border countries between England and Scotland where it was developed.

Due to their hardiness, Borders are particularly suitable for beginners and make excellent pets. They are neat and compact with a bright alert manner. A good specimen should have a well-rounded appearance from all angles, and not exceed 14cm. (5.5in.) in length. Borders are free breeders that are bred for the purity and richness of their color.

Fife Fancy

This is a miniature version of the Border and was created in Scotland during the 1950s by people who believed that Borders had become too large. The length of the Fife should not exceed 11.5cm. (4.5in.).

Gloster Fancy

This is another popular and suitable bird for beginners. It is a comparatively new breed that was established less than fifty years ago. The Gloster is a lively, neat little bird whose length should not exceed 12cm. (4.75in.).

There are two kinds of Gloster, the **Corona,** which has a circular crest of long crown feathers radiating from a central point, and the **Consort,** which has a well-rounded uncrested head. Glosters are free breeders. A Corona should always be paired to a Consort regardless of which sex is which, otherwise the crest will either be too long and coarse or too small.

Lizard Canary

This is undoubtedly the oldest surviving variety. Being free breeders, Lizard Canaries are suitable for beginners. About 12.5cm. (5in.) in length, the Lizard is unique in being the only canary bred solely for the pattern of its plumage. Some Lizards have a distinct cap of light feathers which extend from the bill across the top of the head to the base of the skull. Such birds are known as clear-caps. Birds with dark feathers present in the cap are known as broken-caps, while those without a cap are known as noncaps. Lizard Canaries should have no light plumage about the body. They should have lines of small black markings on the back, known as spangling, and similar markings called rowings on the breast and flanks. The exhibition life of this canary is short as each time the bird molts the markings become less distinct. For breeding, a clear-cap Lizard should be paired to a broken-cap or noncap.

Norwich Canaries
1 Clear Buff
2 Clear Yellow
3 Heavily Variegated
4 Grizzle Crested Yellow
5 Variegated Crestbred

Norwich Canary

This breed has maintained its popularity longer than any other variety. Tradition has it that this canary was introduced into the area around Norwich in Norfolk, England, by the Flemish weavers who fled there during the sixteenth century. Today's birds measure 16–16.5cm. (6–6.25in.) in length. They are not as active as Borders but nevertheless are bold, attractive birds with a rounded and stocky appearance. The color, which together with feather quality is of utmost importance, must be as rich and even as possible.

The Norwich is what is known as a color-fed bird, which means that its natural color is enhanced by a coloring agent added to the food—a carotene or canthaxantin preparation available commercially. Compared with the previous varieties, more skill is needed in breeding Norwich Canaries, and it is best left to people with some experience.

Crested Canary

This bird is, in fact, a crested Norwich and the latter is therefore occasionally called the **Norwich Plainhead.** The Crested made its appearance during the eighteenth century and was at the height of its popularity during the nineteenth century. Crested Canaries are large birds and, as with all crested canaries, there are two kinds; the **Crested** which has a crest and the **Crest-bred** which is without a crest. A crested bird must always be paired to a noncrested although it does not matter which sex is which.

Cinnamon Canary

The present day Cinnamon Canary resembles the Norwich in shape. It used to be called the Dun and enjoyed its greatest popularity in the early part of the twentieth century. It is cinnamon brown in color with darker markings on the wings, flanks, and tail. The main objective with breeding this variety is true color. An unusual feature of the Cinnamon Canary is the pink eye color of the young which changes to a deep plum red when adult.

Yorkshire

This is a slim, elegant canary which stands very erect on its long legs. The Yorkshire is a large bird with an ideal length of 17cm. (6.75in.). Although Yorkshires have quite a pleasing song, they are kept and bred mainly for exhibition purposes in which case they are color-fed. Yorkshires are reasonably free breeders, but a buff should be paired to a yellow; otherwise the result is likely to be coarse-feathered unshapely offspring.

Frill

Formerly known as the **Dutch Canary**, this breed has now been developed in many countries so that today there are several strains including the **Dutch, Italian,** and **Parisian**

Mules
1 Goldfinch Mule
2 Greenfinch Mule

Frilled Canaries. The Japanese have produced a miniature type and extended it to the Red Factor. Frilled Canaries have curious plumage. Instead of lying close to the body, as is the case with other canaries, the soft feathers are long and curl outwards to give an extraordinary frilled effect. Frilled Canaries have an upright stance and are generally quite large; some birds exceed 20cm. (8in.) in length. A good Frill is very attractive, but a bad example can look monstrous. Frilled Canaries are fairly good breeders. Crossing a frilled with a nonfrilled bird will produce nonfrilled offspring.

Belgian Canary

The Belgian Canary enjoyed great popularity in its native country during the nineteenth century. Today, however, this breed with its rather deformed humpbacked appearance is largely out of vogue. It has never been a reliable breeder and foster parents are often needed to rear the young. It is a lively bird with a nervous temperament. Body length is difficult to measure accurately due to the bird's strange body shape but is approximately 17cm. (6.75in.). Color is unimportant.

Scotch Fancy

This variety resembles the Belgian Canary and has also suffered a decline in popularity. Interest in this bird has been concentrated mainly in Scotland and northern England. The head is small, compact, and slightly rounder than the Belgian. Again, color is unimportant.

Red Factor

The Red Factor is a breed developed in the twentieth century. In 1929 a German geneticist, Dr. Hans Duncker, published a theory on the possibility of producing a red canary. The breeding of true red canaries has proved more complicated than predicted and a really red specimen has yet to be bred. However, by crossing ordinary female canaries with male South American Hooded Siskins (*Spinus cucullatus*) and crossing any fertile offspring back to canaries, Red Factor Canaries which

are orange-red in color have been developed. Red Factors are suitable for breeding in cages and garden aviaries.

New Color Canary

From selective pairings of the Red Factor and the introduction of other colors, a wonderful range of bright and often delicate, extremely attractive colors are now available. Because they are a comparatively recent breed, and many new shades are still being produced, there is a marked lack of uniformity in the names used in different countries. Many of the New Color Canaries are best left to experienced breeders.

Roller

The Roller was developed in Germany and German-bred birds are sometimes known as **Hartz Mountain Rollers.** Rollers are unique in that they are the only canaries bred solely for the quality of their singing; their shape and color are considered unimportant. The song of the male Roller is exceptionally sweet and pure. Rollers sing a number of well-defined passages which are delivered in a continuous rolling manner—hence the bird's name. The passages, which are known as tours, are soft and melodious and produce a pleasing musical composition. Show or contest male Rollers must be trained to sing from an early age. They are hardy little birds that are similar to Borders but slightly shorter in length. Some birds are bred with a small crest on the head. Rollers breed freely in a cage or aviary and are suitable for a beginner. Choose birds of known song quality when selecting breeding pairs since they are more likely to produce offspring with good singing voices.

Mules

Hybrids are regularly bred from crossing canaries and finches, particularly European species which are reared in aviaries or those kept after injury in the wild. These offspring are known as Mules (the name being taken from the offspring of a horse and an ass), and they are usually sterile. Mules are often extremely attractive and unusually marked birds that are produced mainly for exhibition purposes. A few which lack show qualities are sold as pets. Cocks make particularly good pets and fine songsters. Though drab in color, Linnet Mules are outstanding songsters, while Goldfinch Mules are extremely popular and also good songsters. Hens have little value since they do not sing and cannot breed. However, they will frequently lay infertile eggs and can sometimes be used to foster orphan finches.

Mules can be bred in cages and aviaries much the same way as ordinary canaries. As a general rule it is easier to mate a cock finch to a hen canary, though with the Bullfinch the reverse is so. A small variety of canary such as a Border, Gloster, or even a Red Factor, should be paired with the smaller finches. If mules are wanted for exhibiting, however, a Norwich Canary should be used to produce offspring of a good size. Because finches are less tame than canaries, the nest site needs to be screened from view. Frequently canaries come into breeding condition earlier in the season than finches, so unless this can be regulated by keeping the canary on a plain diet for a little longer than normal, the first clutch may be infertile. If a finch can see or hear a member of the opposite sex of its own kind, it will probably be reluctant to mate with a canary. For young mules to be successfully reared, good quality soft food is essential.

Shell Parakeets

Shell parakeets, also called budgerigars or budgies, are the most popular of all cage and aviary birds and have an enormous worldwide following devoted to their keeping, breeding, and exhibiting. Shell parakeets are not only simple and inexpensive to keep in cages or aviaries, but are remarkably easy to breed. Young birds grow up to be splendid pets that frequently can be taught to repeat several words and even entire phrases. The average life span of a caged shell parakeet is about ten years.

The pet shell parakeet is descended from the small green parakeet or budgerigar (*Melopsitacus undulatus*) which is found in most parts of Australia. The first live birds were brought to Great Britain in 1840 by the renowned naturalist and artist John Gould. The first color mutation to be bred was light yellow, a color sometimes encountered in the wild. Toward the end of the nineteenth century, the first sky blue birds appeared. Their delicate colors caused a sensation and won shell parakeets many admirers. The first dark greens were bred in 1915, followed during the next ten years by the cobalts or powder blues and then the mauves. By 1925 the shell parakeet, or budgerigar, had become so popular in Great Britain that the first specialist organization was formed. First named the

Shell parakeets (budgerigars) are the most popular of all cage and aviary birds. When housed in an outdoor aviary (Top Center), *they form an active noisy community, yet individuals seem to thrive equally well indoors alone in a small cage* (Top Right).

Center Right. *This is the correct way to hold most adult cage and aviary birds. Tasks such as ringing (banding) and trimming overgrown claws and beaks can be easily and safely undertaken with a bird held in this way.*

Budgerigar Club, but later changed to the Budgerigar Society, it has become recognized as the world's parent body for the fanciers of these birds. About the time it was formed, or a little later, the first white shell parakeets were produced. In the period leading up to World War II a wide range of other new colors came into existence. As the demand increased for birds of known pedigree for the purpose of color breeding, breeding methods began to change; instead of mixed aviaries where pairing was largely uncontrolled, small flight aviaries, pens, and cages began to be widely used. From the late 1940s on, interest in shell parakeets increased and other new mutations appeared. One of the most interesting types created was the crested shell parakeet which is believed to have first appeared in North America. Today shell parakeets are found in a variety of shades and combinations of colors.

The ideal budgerigar nest box incorporates an inspection panel and removable base with a concave nesting depression which prevents the eggs from rolling about.

HOUSING

Indoors

Any of the popular all-wire cages is suitable for a pet that is kept indoors. Two or three well-placed perches are usually sufficient and, if there is enough space, a swing type perch will provide enjoyment. Shell parakeets also have a lot of fun playing with objects such as a small mirror, a ball, and plastic toys, though there should not be enough to clutter up the cage. The floor of the cage should be covered by a thin layer of clean sand or, better still, a sandsheet. A pet can be

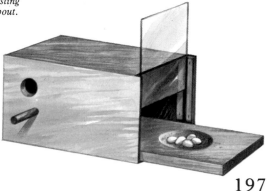

Red-Eyed Budgerigars
(1) Opaline Lacewing White
(2) Albino or Red-Eyed Clear White
(3) Lacewing Yellow
(4) Lutino or Red-Eyed Clear Yellow

Dominant or Dutch Pied Budgerigars
(1) Dominant Pied Opaline Dark Green
(2) Australian Dominant Banded Pied Gray (Blue)

housed satisfactorily in any room so long as the cage is in a position where the occupant gets plenty of daylight, yet is well away from drafts and windows. The cage should be covered by a dark cloth at about seven o'clock each evening.

Provided sensible precautions are taken such as closing windows and doors and covering open fireplaces, a tame shell parakeet can be allowed out regularly into a room. It will fly around and, after investigating the area, will invariably return to the cage on its own accord. Until a bird is familiar with a room, it is advisable to have the curtains drawn to prevent it from flying into a glassed window.

Outdoors

Shell parakeets generally thrive outdoors. Fit, healthy birds prove hardy and as long as they have a dry, draft-free aviary shelter for a retreat, they can remain outdoors all year round without artificial heating in a temper-

ate climate. Although shell parkeets can be housed with other small parrot-like birds, they are best kept on their own. The most attractive way of housing shell parakeets, if they are being kept purely for pleasure, is in a garden aviary. Several assorted pairs can be kept together and bred on the colony system. If this method is used, it is important to have an equal number of cocks and hens and to remove unmated birds. There must also be more than enough nest boxes to go round. Nesting arrangements are the main cause of quarrels which will invariably occur, so it helps to have all boxes of the same design and placed at roughly the same height. It is usual to fix the boxes close to the top of the aviary in a position where they are sheltered from direct sunlight and heavy rain. Avoid overcrowding which can reduce the chances of breeding, especially if the number of boxes is inadequate. So long as an aviary is not overcrowded and is reasonably large, most of the

area outside the shelter can be planted in grass or covered with a concrete floor. Shell parakeets will destroy growing bushes.

Breeding cages

The most common method of breeding shell parakeets in order to obtain superior birds for showing or high quality pets is in cages like the double breeder described for canaries, which is about 90cm. (36in.) long, 40cm. (16in.) high, or a little more and 30cm. (12in.) deep. Nest boxes vary in shape but a fairly typical example is rectangular and measures about 21.5cm. (8.5in.) long, 15cm. (6in.) high and 14cm. (5.5in.) deep, and it has a wooden concave block that fits snugly into the base. One end of the box is removable to facilitate examination and the entrance hole is about 5 cm. (2in.) in diameter. The nest box can either be fixed inside or to the outside of the cage in which case the interior can be examined more easily with less disturbance to the birds. Shell parakeets do not require any nesting material, just a little clean sawdust in the concave to prevent the eggs from rolling about and to help absorb moisture from the droppings.

FEEDING REQUIREMENTS

The most convenient method of feeding a pet shell parakeet is to give it a commercially prepared seed mixture. A millet spray should be offered at least once a week, along with a regular supply of fresh greenfood and a small piece of raw carrot or fruit such as apple. Pets tend to become overweight and should not be given high calorie foods such as bread, cake, or cookies. Fresh drinking water, grit, a piece of cuttlefish bone, and a commercially obtainable iodized vitamin block should be available at all times.

Birds kept in an aviary and breeding stock should be fed a seed mixture consisting of four parts canary seed, one and one-half parts white millet, and one-half part small yellow panicum millet, to which a few groats or clipped oats, linseed, and niger are added. Shell parakeets enjoy pecking the bark of fresh twigs from unsprayed fruit trees, and it helps maintain their beaks. As long as a variety of fresh greenfood is available, shell parakeets do not need special rearing foods when breeding although such foods do help in producing robust young. They can either be fed a proprietary rearing food or a little wholegrain bread moistened with milk or water. Such foods must be offered well before breeding begins so that the birds will have time to adjust to them. Uneaten rearing food must be removed at the end of each day and never allowed to become stale.

BREEDING

Shell parakeets should be paired in the early spring. Although they are able to breed at a few months of age, they should not be allowed to do so until they are at least eleven to twelve months old. If both birds are in breeding condition, mating will soon take place and the hen will lay within about ten days. Four to six white eggs are laid on alternate days. Eggs in excess of this number should be fostered to hens that have less. Incubation usually commences with the laying of the first or second egg. It is done entirely by the hen, although the cock may spend part of the day in the box with her. The incubation period is seventeen to eighteen days. Dummy eggs (necessary for breeding canaries) are not used for shell parakeets so there is often a difference of twelve days, or more, between the time when the first and last chicks hatch. Chicks are fed by both parents. The young leave the nest at four to five weeks of age. When they are about six weeks old and feeding themselves, they should be removed to another cage or aviary. Otherwise, the young may be attacked if the parents are preparing to nest in the box again. No pair should be permitted to raise more than about ten young a season, preferably in two broods.

While still in the nest, some young birds shed their flight and tail feathers which are weak and misshapen and often rotting at the base. This condition is known as French molt. It does not necessarily affect all the young in one nest or all the young produced by one particular pair. Some affected birds shed only a few feathers which eventually will grow again, but others are so badly affected that they are never able to fly. These birds are often known as runners, and the kindest course of action is to have them humanely destroyed. At present, although countless theories have been advanced, no cause of the ailment has conclusively been proved and it

Top Center. *Finches, such as these Green Finches, and other seedeaters make excellent cage and aviary birds as well as welcome visitors to our gardens.*

Top Right. *Shown are two styles of wicker nesting baskets suitable for small finches. Some finches prefer open-fronted wooden boxes.*

appears to be caused by a combination of factors.

TALKING BIRDS

Although both sexes will become delightfully tame and learn to talk, young cocks are the more gifted performers. Plumage has no bearing on talking ability. Many hens get extremely tame, but only a few become first-rate talkers.

The best time to start training a bird is when it is six to eight weeks old, soon after it has left the nest and is feeding itself. It can then be placed on its own in a room and, preferably, instructed by the same person (the higher toned voice of a female or child is better than a male's). Talk to it quietly, saying a phrase or name over and over again, or use a record or tape. At such an early age, even experienced breeders can have difficulty in recognizing young cocks with certainty. However, there are a number of indications, the best being the color of the bird's cere which is the small fleshy area at the top of the beak where the nostrils are located. A young cock usually has a pink or purplish-blue, rather prominent, cere while a young hen's is inclined to be whitish and flatter in shape. When fully adult a cock's cere is usually bright, deep blue or purple and the hen's is pale buff to deep chocolate. The plumage of both sexes is identical.

COLOR MUTATIONS

As well as the original **Light Green,** there are **Dark Green, Olive-green** and **Gray-green** varieties. The last two are similar, but the

Olive-green has a navy-blue tail and blue cheek patches, while the **Gray-green** has gray cheek patches and a black tail. Birds that have the same markings as the Light Green of the wild species are known as normals. Normal greens therefore have black and yellow markings. The basic colors of the Blue Series are sky blue, cobalt, mauve, and gray, and normals have blue and white markings. The mauve and gray are alike, only the mauve has a navy blue tail and blue cheek patches, and the gray has gray cheek patches and a black tail. Blues usually have a white face, but can also be bred with a yellow face and then are termed yellow-face blues or grays. Greens, blues, and grays can be bred with different colored wings, such as clearwings, graywings, or cinnamonwings. There are also **Pied Shell Parakeets, Fallows,** and various **Yellows** and **Whites,** including clear-colored birds such as **Lutinos** and **Albinos. Lutinos** are pure yellow and **Albinos** pure white, but both have red eyes. There are also dark eyed birds. Shell parakeets with the opaline factor have a different pattern of markings from the normal since barring of the head is less distinct and the color extends over the back into the V-shaped area between the wings, known as the mantle. The latter should be clear, but in practice very seldom is. Some shell parakeets have several colors in their makeup, one such bird being the aptly named **Rainbow Shell Parakeet.** The three types of **Crested Shell Parakeet** are the tufted half circular, and full circular. Just about the only colored shell parakeets not yet produced are black, brown, and red. There have been reports of red shell parakeets, though it is thought that this color can only be produced by crossing a shell parakeet with another parrot-like species. Apart from the challenge of producing a red shell parakeet there is still the possibility of breeding other new and exciting varieties. Exhibition birds must conform to strict standards and are specially bred for showing. They are larger than the ordinary pet birds or the wild shell parakeets and are generally bred indoors in long box-type cages like those used for breeding canaries. Many are also bred in controlled pens or flight aviaries, both indoors and outside. Flocks of shell parakeets are occasionally kept in fairly uncontrolled situations and homing strains have been developed.

Finches and Other Seedeaters

There are several fine songsters within this group of exotic cage and aviary birds, as well as gaily colored species with attractive or unusual markings. Some species have bright plumage or fancy long tail feathers especially for the breeding season. They are generally small birds, the size of a sparrow or smaller.

Most species are relatively easy to care for, the ideal beginner's birds being the Bengalese or Society Finch *(Lonchura striata),* which has long been domesticated, and the Zebra Finch *(Poephilia guttata).*

HOUSING

Most species indoors are happier in the box type of house than in the all-wire cage. The cage should be as roomy as possible to provide plenty of flying space. Standard perches can be replaced by smaller ones or by twiggy branches. In all cases the perches should be of the right thickness for the bird's claws to grip comfortably.

An outdoor aviary should be planted with grass, shrubs, or even small trees. Most species are good mixers and, as long as they are not overcrowded, different species of approximately the same size can be housed together. One pair of each species is usually the best number for a mixed aviary. Many seedeaters can be housed with canaries, occasionally with shell parakeets, and other small parrot-like species and softbills. Seedeaters should be thoroughly acclimatized before they are left outdoors all year in a temperate climate and, even then, they should have access to an aviary shelter. The shelter should be moderately heated at night during the winter for some exotic species, and artificially lit for the early part of long dark evenings.

FEEDING REQUIREMENTS

The main diet of seedeaters is millet and canary seed. Most species relish soaked or sprouting seeds and millet sprays. Seeding grasses and various wild and cultivated greenstuffs are also greatly enjoyed. A few species will eat berries and even a little fruit. All seedeaters require grit and cuttlefish bone. Clean water for drinking and, in most cases for bathing, should be constantly available. Other beneficial foods, especially at nesting time, include wholegrain bread moistened with milk, sponge cake moistened with honey water, canary rearing foods, and softbill or insectile mixtures. Small mealworms, maggots, and most varieties of tiny insects are appreciated and often essential to rearing the young successfully.

BREEDING REQUIREMENTS

Many seedeaters will breed in captivity. Natural nesting places and plenty of cover should be provided to encourage breeding. The chances of breeding are greater if a pair are housed by themselves. They will either choose a site of their own or build in a nesting receptacle using plant materials such as dried grasses. A choice of nest boxes should be offered. Spherical wicker nest baskets with an entrance hole in the side are especially popular with small species. Canary nest pans and boxes are also used. Many species favor square or rectangular boxes with the top half of the front open. Boxes with an entrance hole are less popular. The boxes should be placed at different heights, facing different directions, and should be sheltered from heavy rain and hot sun. A little soft hay placed in the bottom of each box and a screen of foliage will encourage nesting.

Waxbills
Waxbills are members of the genus *Estrilda* and are tiny, gaily colored birds so named because their bills have a waxy appearance. Waxbills are friendly little creatures and freely associate among themselves and with other peaceable small birds. Many species measure 9cm. (3in.) or less in length and these include the popular **Red-eared, Common** or **Black-rumped Waxbill** *(Estrilda troglodytes)* and the **Golden-breasted, Orange-breasted** or **Zebra Waxbill** *(E. subflava).*

Waxbills are almost entirely native to Africa, two of the few exceptions being the **Red Avadavat** *(Amandava amandava),* also known as the **Strawberry Finch, Tiger Finch,** and **Bombay Avadavat** and the **Green Avadavat** *(A. formosa).* The male Red Avadavat loses much of its white spotted, red plumage outside of the breeding season and takes on what is known as an eclipse, or nonbreeding, plumage. Except for retaining a red rump and perhaps a few body feathers

Waxbills
(1) Red-cheeked Cordon-Bleu
(2) Blue-capped Cordon-Bleu
(3) Peter's Twinspot
(4) Red-Headed Bluebill

200

Mannikins
(1) Indian Silverbill
(2) African Silverbill
(3) Tricolored Mannikin

and white spots, the male resembles the fawn-brown female at this time. (Males having nonbreeding plumage are referred to as "out of color" or O.O.C., as opposed to "in color" or I.C. at the time of breeding.) Before being exported from their country of origin, avadavats are sometimes dyed vivid colors which last until they molt. This process often kills the birds; dyed birds should be boycotted to discourage this inhumane practice.

Blue waxbills or cordon-bleus and the reddish-brown fire finches belong to the same family as the true waxbills and avadavats. Two well-known species are the **Red-cheeked Cordon-bleu** (*Uraeginthus bengalus*) and the **Red-billed, Common,** or **Senegal Firefinch** (*Lagonostica senegala*). Many other related birds may be available from pet shops, such as the **Green Twinspot** (*Mandigoa nitidula*), **Peter's Twinspot** (*Hypargos niveoguttatus*), **Red-headed Bluebill** (*Spermophaga rucicapilia*), **Quail finch** (*Ortygospiza atricollis*), and **Blue-capped Cordon-bleu** (*U. cyanocephalus*).

Waxbills can be housed in box cages or aviaries. The aviary should be fairly well planted and, if outdoors, in a sheltered but sunny position. Waxbills are not as robust or hardy as some other seedeaters. In a temperate climate they need to be acclimatized carefully and shut in a comfortable, preferably warm, aviary shelter each night during the winter or else brought indoors.

Feeding. The basic diet consists of a very small millet although other seeds are also acceptable. They should also be encouraged to eat other foods such as soft food, greenfood, and minute insect life which are beneficial when rearing the young. Mealworms and maggots are too tough unless cut up into small pieces.

Mannikins

Mannikins are members of the genus *Estrilda* and are especially suitable for beginners. They are sociable birds that adjust well to cage life and soon acclimatize to outdoor conditions where, provided there is comfortable shelter, they can live year round. Mannikins are usually black, brown, and white. The domesticated **Bengalese** or **Society Finch** (*Lonchura striata*) exists in a wide range of varieties and has its own specialist following. It is the easiest small seedeater to breed in captivity. Their breeding instinct is so strong that many breeders keep them to foster rare and unreliable species.

The **Black-headed Mannikin** (*L. atricapilla*), the **Tricolored Mannikin** (*L. malacca*), and the **Spice Bird** or **Nutmeg Finch** (*L. punctulata*) were formerly of the genus *Munia* and consequently are sometimes called munias or nuns. They are indigenous to Southeast Asia and, together with the **African Bronze-winged Mannikin** (*L. cucullata*), are popular species.

Grouped with them, although different in shape, are the longer-tailed silverbills, for example the **African Silverbill** (*L. cantans*), and **Indian Silverbill** (*L. malabarica*), and the slightly larger **Java Sparrow** (*Padda oryzivora*) which measures 12.5–14cm. (5–5.5 in.). The Java Sparrow is one of the most familiar exotic seedeaters. White and pied Java Sparrows have been developed and these are more free breeding than the wild type. Closely related to the Java Sparrow are two African species, the **Red-headed Finch** (*A. erythrocephala*) and the **Cut-throat** or **Ribbon Finch** (*A. fasciata*), so named because of the red band across the male's throat.

Feeding. The basic diet is a mixture of millet and canary seeds. Mannikins appreciate extras (greenfood, fruit, a turf of grass, seeding grasses, soaked seeds, insects) particularly when raising young.

Grassfinches

Australia is the home of many small seedeaters called grassfinches (family Estrildidae) but, because of an export ban, the demand for these birds exceeds the supply, the exception being the free breeding **Zebra Finch** (*Poephila guttata*) which is now considered to be domesticated. The original, or wild, type Zebra Finch is referred to as normal or gray, and the wide range of varieties include fawn, white, chestnut-flanked white, and the penguin. The **Long-tailed Grassfinch** (*P. acuticada*), the **Parson Finch** (*P. cineta*), and the **Diamond Sparrow** (*Zonaeginthus guttatus*) are popular, but the most sought after bird

Grassfinches
(1) Diamond Sparrow
(2) Parson Finch
(3) Long-Tailed Grassfinch

201

(Top) *Weavers*
(1) *Common Dioch*
(2) *Rufous-Necked Weaver*

(Center and Bottom) *Weaver Widow Birds*
(1) *Long-Tailed Widow Bird*
(2) *Red-Naped Widow Bird*
(3) *Crimson-Crowned Bishop*

among this group is the brilliantly colored **Gouldian Finch** (*Chloebia gouldiae*).

Parrot finches are closely related to the grass finches and are found in tropical Australia, some Pacific islands, and Southeast Asia. They are predominantly green, often with red and/or blue about the head. The **Pintailed Nonpareil** (*Erythrura prasina*) and **Blue-faced Parrotfinch** (*E. trichroa*) are perhaps the best known within this group.
Feeding. A mixture of millet and canary seeds should be offered. Some enjoy fruit and the Pintailed Nonpareil is fond of paddy rice (dry or soaked) and will accept clipped oats.
Weavers
These birds (family Ploceidae), also known as **bishop birds,** are named for their remarkable ability to weave extremely elaborate nests. There are about one hundred species in the Old World and most are indigenous to Africa. About the size of a sparrow or a little larger, these are robust birds with a strong bill. During the breeding season, most male weavers are brilliantly clad in striking combinations of yellow and black, or black with vivid splashes of red and/or orange. A few female weavers are brightly colored, but the majority are dull in appearance. Outside the breeding season most males lose their bright colors and closely resemble the females. It is difficult to identify weaver species accurately, especially the females and out of color males. The **Rufous-necked, Black-headed,** or **Village Weaver** (*Ploceus cucullatus*), the **Napoleon Weaver** (*Euplectes afra*), the **Red Bishop Weaver** (*E. orix*), and various masked weavers, such as the **Masked Weaver** (*Ploceus intermedius*), are often available. The **Red-Billed Weaver** or **Quelea,** also known as the **Common or Black-faced Dioch** (*Quelea quelea*) is the most common species within a small group which possess

predominantly brown streaky plumage that is sometimes relieved by red. Only the male has a black face. Most weavers are so lively and gregarious that they should be housed in groups in an aviary. Most species acclimatize well. They build their nests from lengths of grass that should be especially provided and from vegetation growing within the aviary. Nests are suspended from branches or the wire netting.
Feeding. The basic diet is a mixture of millet with some canary seed. During the breeding season they also require seeding grasses and soaked seeds but can manage without much live food.
Weaver Widow Birds
Widow birds (family Ploceidae), once considered separate and mostly in the genus *Coliuspasser*, are now classified with the weavers in the genus *Euplectes*. They are indigenous to Africa. In breeding condition the males taken on a velvety black plumage, frequently with brilliant patches of red, orange, yellow, and white on the upper part of the wings and, in a few instances, about the head, upper breast, and back, for example the **Red-naped Widow Bird** (*Euplectes laticauda*) and **Crimson-crowned Bishop** (*E. hordeacea*). Usually there is a ruff of feathers on the nape, and some species have long black tail feathers which play an important part in their extraordinary courtship flights and dances. The males lose their finery after the breeding season and resemble the short-tailed sparrow-like females which are smaller in size. Widow birds are greatly in demand by aviculturists due to their plumage and elaborate courtship rites, the most popular being the **Long-tailed** or **Giant Widow bird (Whydah)** (*E. progne*). Because of their long tails which, in the male, can reach 50cm. (20in.) long, whydahs require plenty of space and are best kept in an aviary.
Feeding. They require a mixture of millet and canary seed.
Whydahs and Combassous
These birds (family Ploceidae), belonging to the genus *Vidua*, are native to Africa. They are parasitic and rely on other species to raise their young. The males have a smart breeding plumage. The **Paradise Whydah** (*V. paradisaea*) and the **Broad-tailed Paradise Whydah** (*V. orientalis*) are predominantly black with areas of white and buff through to chestnut, and have two fancy, long tail feathers and another pair a third to a quarter as long. Three others the **Pintailed** (*V. macroura*), the **Queen** (*V. regia*), and **Fisher's Whydah** (*V. fischeri*) possess a red bill and a lot of black plumage. In the Pintailed, the black plumage is combined with white, in the Fisher's, with buff, and in the Queen Whydah's, with rufous-buff. All have four long narrow central tail feathers which are black in the Pintailed and Queen and buff in the Fisher's Whydah. The **Steel-blue Whydah** (*V. hypocherina*) is glossy black all over, including its long tail feathers.

The combassous or indigo birds are grouped with the parasitic whydahs. Formerly

Whydahs and Combassous
(1) Pin-Tailed Whydah
(2) Senegal Combassou

are, however, usually regarded as too dull and uninteresting to keep as cage and aviary birds. One exception is the **Golden** or **Yellow Sparrow** (*Passer luteus*) which is indigenous to Africa. It is a small, gaily colored bird measuring about 12.5 cm. (5in.) long. The Yellow Sparrow can be kept in an aviary with other seedeaters and will breed if several pairs are housed together. Although often called the **Golden Song Sparrow,** this bird does not have a fine singing voice. Sparrows should be housed in an aviary, and they do well in a colony.
Feeding. Sparrows are seed and grain eaters.

Local cheaper seeds can be added to their staple diet of millet and canary seed.
Finches★
Finches (family Fringillidae) are excellent cage and aviary birds that are relatively simple to keep. They are most attractive and often brightly colored, the males being more colorful than the females. There are about 120 species of finches, many indigenous to Africa, the most familiar being the **Green Singing Finch,** or **Yellow-fronted Canary** (*Serinus mozambicus*), and the **Gray Singing Finch** (*S. leucopygius*), which is especially esteemed for its singing ability. These birds

separated into the genus *Hypochera*, these birds are so similar that experts cannot agree on an exact number of species. The major species is the **Senegal Combassou** (*V. chalybeata*) which might have as many as a dozen races. Combassous are glossy black birds that do not have long tail feathers. Once male whydahs and combassous lose breeding condition, they resemble the sparrow-like females. Combassous and whydahs measure about 10–14cm. (4–5.5in.) in length.

The parasitic whydahs (sometimes also confusingly called widow birds) differ from the weaver widow birds in being smaller and having unusual nesting habits. The parasitic whydahs lay their eggs in other birds' nests and leave them to raise the young. The hosts are usually waxbills. Paradise Whydahs choose pytilias, the Pintailed Whydah chooses mainly the St. Helena and the Red-eared Waxbills, and combassous impose upon firefinches; occasionally the combassous, if housed in an aviary, will raise their own young. Most whydahs and combassous are regularly available and can be housed with waxbills and other small seedeaters. However, male whydahs, especially Pin-tailed Whydahs, can be spiteful.
Feeding. The basic diet is mixed millet and canary seed, greenfood, millet sprays, and a few live insects.
Sparrows★
Also members of the weaver family (Ploceidae) these birds are easy to care for. They

Finches
(1) Chaffinch
(2) Black-headed Canary
(3) Gray Singing Finch
(4) Siskin

Yellow Sparrow

make fine pets and can have long lives, although the average age is about seven years.

In Europe especially, a lot of attention is devoted to keeping, breeding, and exhibiting native finches. European species include the well-known **Chaffinch** (*Fringilla coelebs*) and the **Brambling** (*F. montifringilla*). These two birds, which are not always regarded as true finches, will cross breed with each other but not with the canary, despite many attempts by breeders to do so.

A number of fine songbirds are to be found among the serins; one of which, the **Wild**

*Many countries now place legal restrictions upon the kinds of wild birds which may be kept in captivity. Be certain to check these laws before keeping a sparrow.

*Many countries now place legal restrictions upon the kinds of wild birds which may be kept in captivity. Be certain to check these laws before keeping a finch.

Canary (*Serinus canarius*), was used to develop the present array of domesticated varieties. The **Serin** (*Serinus serinus*) is common over much of southern Europe.

The **Goldfinch** (*Carduelis carduelis*) has long been prized as a cage bird especially in Europe but unfortunately it is frequently confined in a tiny cage. The male Goldfinch has more red on its face than the female and has a fine singing voice. The Goldfinch has been introduced into parts of the eastern United States. Otherwise it is replaced by the similar **American Goldfinch** (*C. tristis*). The **Greenfinch** (*C. chloris*) is common in Europe, and color varieties of this species have been developed.

The **Siskin** (*C. spinus*) is another popular cage and aviary bird and is related to the **South American Red Hooded Siskin** (*C. cucullatus*) which is used to produce the Red Factor Canary.

The **Bullfinch** (*Pyrrhula pyrrhula*) is a traditional cage bird in Germany and is frequently hand reared and taught to whistle tunes. The Bullfinch is one of the most attractive finches; the male has a black cap and rosy-red underparts. The **Crossbill** (*Loxia curvirostra*) has, as the name implies, a bill that is crossed at the tips. The male of this species is almost entirely red. Hawfinches also possess a distinctive bill which in this case is exceptionally large. The most common species of hawfinch are the **Hawfinch** (*Coccothraustes coccothraustes*), the **Chinese, Japanese** or **Black-tailed Hawfinch** (*C. migratoria*), the **North American Evening Grosbeak** (*C. vespertina*), and the **Scarlet Grosbeak** (*Carpodacus erythrinus*). These are large, handsome birds measuring about 17.5–21.5cm (7–8.5in.). The **Linnet** (*Acanthis cannabina*) and the **Redpoll** (*A. flammea*) are brownish in color and usually have a patch or two of red.

Most finches do well in a roomy cage and are ideal aviary inhabitants. They are hardy birds although tropical species need a period of acclimatization before adjusting to the winter of a temperate climate.
Feeding. Finches, unlike most seedeaters, prefer a diet of canary seed rather than millet. Some of the larger finches will also accept sunflower seeds. All finches should be offered greenfood and fruit, especially wild berries. They should also be given seeding grasses, soaked seeds, and a variety of live food to help raise healthy young.
Buntings*
Buntings (family Emberizidae) are about the same size, shape and, often, color as sparrows and finches. The **Red-headed Bunting** (*Emberiza bruniceps*) is probably the most common species. Only the male has a red head which is actually a light chestnut. Many buntings from India, two species from Africa—the **Golden-breasted Bunting** (*E. flaviventris*) and the **Cinnamon-breasted Rock**

Bunting (*E. tahapisi*)—are often obtainable while European buntings are regularly kept and bred. Among the most popular European species are the **Yellow Bunting** or **Yellowhammer** (*E. citrinella*) and the **Reed Bunting** (*E. schoeniclus*). Buntings can be kept in a large cage, but undoubtedly do better in an outdoor aviary where much of the day is spent on or near the ground. Most species can be kept outdoors during the winter provided they have access to a comfortable aviary shelter.

Ranging from Panama into part of North America are six colorful species of American bunting. They are the **Lazuli** (*Passerina amoena*), the **Painted** (*P. ciris*), **Indigo** (*P. cyanea*), **Rainbow** or **Orange-breasted** (*P. leclancherii*), **Varied** (*P. versicolor*), and **Rose-bellied** (*P. rositae*) **Buntings.** They measure about 12.5–15cm. (5–6in.) and colors are confined to the males, some of whom are also good songsters. Single males, or pairs when they can be obtained (females are not in great demand and consequently are not exported in such large numbers) can be housed in a roomy cage or a planted aviary with other birds about their size. American buntings, especially the Varied, Rainbow, and Rose-bellied, need to be acclimatized carefully in a temperate climate before being left outdoors during the winter and even then these more still require a warm aviary shelter. The Indigo Bunting is one of the hardier species. Canary breeders have tried unsuccessfully to cross the male Indigo Bunting, which has an all blue breeding plumage (but loses most of this outside the breeding season) with a canary to produce a truly blue variety.
Feeding. The basic diet is a mixture of millet and canary seeds to which can be added some sunflower seeds. They should also be offered a supply of live food when rearing the young.

The Painted Bunting should be color-fed to retain its bright red underparts.
Seedeaters
Seedeaters, or **sporophilas** (family Emberizidae), are indigenous to Central and South America, although the name seedeater is sometimes used for some unrelated African species. They make good cage and aviary birds, but have little to distinguish them apart from, in some cases, a pleasant song. Sporophilas measure about 10cm. (4in.) in length and frequently have a large conical bill. There are approximately twenty-seven species making up this group, but few are regularly available. The best known is the **Lined Finch** or **Seedeater** (*Sporophila lineola*).
Feeding. As their name implies, they feed almost exclusively on seeds and show little interest in insects. Even when breeding it is rare for them to take live food although this should be offered.
Warbling Finches*
Warbling finches, **New World finches,** or **New World sparrows** (family Emberizidae) like the sporophilas, are difficult to acquire as pets. They are slightly larger with thinner bills than the sporophilas. Easiest species to

Buntings
(1) *Rainbow Bunting*
(2) *Red-Headed Bunting*
(3) *Black-Headed Bunting*
(4) *Yellow Hammer*

Seedeaters and Warbling Finches
(1) Lined Finch
(2) Crimson Finch

obtain are the **Crimson** or **Rhodospingus Finch** (*Rhodospingus cruentus*), the **Pileated Finch** (*Coryphospingus pileatus*), and the **Red-crested Finch** (*C. cristatus*).

Other examples among this large and anomalous group of New World finches and sparrows are the **grassquits.** Three are regularly kept: the **Melodious Grassquit** or **Cuban Finch** (*Tiaris canora*), the **Black-faced Grassquit** or **Jacarini Finch** (*T. bicolor*), and the **Yellow-faced Grassquit** or **Cuban Olive Finch** (*T. olivacea*). They are small, approximately 7.5cm. (3in.) long, lively, and attractive. They can be aggressive, especially when breeding.

Two other small American finches should also be mentioned: the **Black-crested Finch** or **Crested Bunting** (*Lophospingus pusillus*) which measures about 11.5cm. (4.5in.), and is highly insectivorous; and the bright orange-yellow **Saffron Finch** (*Sicalis haveola*) which is about the same size as the Black-crested Finch, aggressive, and also insectivorous. These finches must be acclimatized carefully.

Feeding. They all require considerable live food with their basic seed diet.

*Cardinals**

The South American cardinals (family Emberizidae) are large seedeaters, measuring 17.5–20cm. (6.5–8in.). The most typical, such as the **Pope** or **Dominican Cardinal** (*Paroaria dominicana*), the **Red-crested Cardinal** (*P. cucullata*), and the **Yellow-billed Cardinal** (*P. capitata*), have a red head, gray to black upperparts, and white underparts. The sexes are usually indistinguishable. The crested **Green Cardinal** (*Gubernatrix cristata*), however, is more soberly colored with olive-green upperparts, black crest, yellow cheeks and throat, and greenish-yellow underparts. The female is noticeably duller in appearance. The **Virginian Cardinal** (*Cardinalis cardinalis*) is a familiar visitor to yards in parts of North America. The male is a strikingly beautiful bird with a scarlet plumage, brownish-red wings, and black face,

chin, and base of the bill. The yellow-brown female, though not as brilliant in color, also has a distinct crest and the characteristic red bill.

Although cardinals can be kept in a large cage they are better housed in an outdoor aviary. They are not difficult to acclimatize and soon become hardy. Cardinals can be housed with other robust seedeaters, some parrot-like species, and softbills, for they are quite sociable, and not overly aggressive, in their behavior.

Feeding. The basic diet is a mixture of millet and canary seeds, to which can be added some sunflower seed. Cardinals need a variety of live foods, sprouting seeds, and seeding grains to raise their young successfully. Live food is also appreciated outside the breeding season. Unless the male Virginian Cardinal is color-fed the red plumage will fade to the same color as the female.

Cardinals
(1) Green Cardinal
(2) Pope Cardinal
(3) Yellow-Billed Cardinal
(4) Red-Crested Cardinal
(5) Virginian Cardinal

*Many countries now place legal restrictions upon the kinds of wild birds which may be kept in captivity. Be certain to check these laws before keeping a cardinal.

Softbills

Softbilled birds are fascinating to keep, can be successfully tamed, and make splendid pets. The Shama (*Copsychus malabaricus*) and several other softbills are superb songsters, while no other birds, not even parrots, learn to talk as well as many Hill Mynahs (*Gracula religiosa*).

The majority of softbills require considerably more attention than seedeaters and are not suitable subjects for a beginner.

HOUSING

A number of softbills, especially tame ones, settle happily in large box cages, but most species do better in aviaries that have grass and a variety of shrubs or even small trees. Some species eat young shoots, but generally softbills are less destructive to growing vegetation than seedeaters. In temperate countries, softbills from the tropics must be carefully acclimatized before they can be left outdoors during the winter and, even then, some need a heated aviary shelter. Several delicate species require tropical conditions and often do best in a greenhouse or conservatory-type aviary. During the winter such birds, especially the smaller ones, need some artificial lighting during the late afternoon and early evening.

Birds that will not use a dish of water for bathing and do not get wet when it rains must regularly be sprayed to keep their plumage from becoming sticky. Also, because of the nature of their food, softbills produce copious droppings. Their housing must therefore be cleaned frequently and perches regularly renewed or thoroughly washed along with other receptacles for food and water.

FEEDING REQUIREMENTS

Softbills need to be fed at least once a day and uneaten food must never be left to become stale. The more omnivorous and largely fruit-eating species are not as difficult to keep as the insectivorous and nectar-feeding softbills. Most softbills will eat all kinds of fruit and often like cooked vegetables and fresh greenfoods. Many will accept an insectile or softbill mixture, moistened poultry growers' pellets and dog biscuits. The more omnivorous softbills will often accept meat, shelled nuts, and sometimes seed and grain. It is essential that insectivorous species are fed a good quality insectile mixture—fine or coarse grade—depending on the species. Ingredients such as chopped hard-boiled egg, finely chopped lettuce, grated carrot or cheese, raw minced meat, or short strips of meat (in the case of the more carnivorous species) can be added to the mixture. (Details of breeding your own mealworms and fruit-flies is given in the chapters on **Reptiles and Amphibians,** and **Insects,** respectively.) Many of the insectivorous species enjoy nectar which should be given in moderation or occasionally as a tonic, but never to the exclusion of other foods. True nectar feeders should be given fruit, an insectile mixture, and a simple honey or sugar and water solution. A more nutritious solution is needed by species that feed on little else but nectar. Proprietary nectar is available but can also be made by mixing a tablespoon each of honey, condensed milk, malt, and baby food. Live food is essential for insectivorous softbills.

Drinking water and a large dish of shallow water for bathing should always be available.

BREEDING

Few softbills prove easy to breed. Unlike many seedeaters they rarely, if ever, nest in cages but must be housed where they have plenty of space and privacy. To have the best chance of success, pairs of softbills should be housed on their own. The majority of species construct some kind of nest and, provided with suitable materials, will often build in a nest box, basket, or other suitable site. Nearly all softbills, even fruit and nectar feeding species, must have large quantities of live food in order to raise healthy young.

Waxwings*

Waxwings (family Bombycillidae) are especially fine aviary birds that are easy to feed,

*Many countries now place legal restrictions upon the kinds of wild birds which may be kept in captivity. Be certain to check these laws before keeping a waxwing.

Softbill is a vague term applied to any small to medium bird which feeds on fruit, insects, and invertebrates. There is, therefore, a wide range of bird types found in this group, varying from the popular Hill Mynah (Top Left) and large-beaked hornbills (Top Middle) to the less well known but equally attractive Lilac Breasted Roller (Top Right).

hardy, and suitable companions even for quite small birds. The waxwing group consists of three species: the **Cedar Waxwing** (*Bombycilla cedrorum*) of North America; the **Bohemian Waxwing** (*B. garrulus*) of North America, Europe and Asia; and the **Japanese Waxwing** (*B. japonica*) of Japan and Asia. Waxwings are renowned for their beautiful, soft, silky, vinaceous brown to gray plumage which is invariably immaculate.

Feeding. Their staple food consists of berries and small fruits. During the breeding season, however, they will also accept insects.

Mousebirds

Mousebirds, or **colies** as they are often called, are unique to Africa and belong to the family Coliidae. They are unusual birds that make interesting cage and aviary subjects. All six species are crested and have a long thin tail attached to a sparrow-sized body. Some species have bright colors about the head: the Red-faced Mousebird (*Colius indicus*) is red cheeked; the **White-headed Mousebird** (*C. leucocephalus*) has a white head; and the **Blue-naped Mousebird** (*C. striatus*) has a blue nape. Apart from these colorings, mousebirds are uniformly brown to gray, and the sexes look alike. They are generally unaggressive and, in the wild, live in small sociable parties that creep somewhat like mice about bushes and trees.

Feeding. They feed mainly on fruit, sometimes the leaves of fruit-bearing plants, and occasionally on insects.

Barbets

As a general rule, barbets are not difficult to keep. They form a large family (Capitonidae) of mostly stocky birds, 9–30cm. (3.5–12in.) long, and are found in Africa, Southeast Asia with some in the New World tropics. The most regularly available are the Southeast Asian species. Several are adorned about the head and chest with vivid splashes of red,

206

Waxwings and Mousebirds (Top Left)
(1) Bohemian Waxwing
(2) Blue-Napped Mousebird

Top Right. *Fairy Bluebird*

blue, yellow, and white, while the rest of their plumage is often bright green. Barbets are so named because of the tufts of feathers some species have around the nostrils and the bristles growing by the base of the bill. The **Coppersmith Barbet** (*Megalaima haemacehala*) and some tiny African species called **tinkerbirds** get their name from their repetitive metallic-sounding calls. Other species available include the **Blue-throated Barbet** (*M. asiatica*) and the **Toucan Barbet** (*Semnornis ramphastinus*).

Some barbets settle down in large box cages, but are usually happier in aviaries. They tend not to be delicate, but few can withstand hard winter weather without access to a heated aviary shelter. Barbets like to have sections of rotten tree trunk to excavate and will also work on exposed aviary woodwork with their stout, sharp bills. Barbets can give a painful nip—a fact to keep in mind if there is a need to handle these birds. Throughout the year barbets like to nest in a hole they have excavated or a snug nest box. This applies to single birds as much as to pairs

which, when breeding time comes, may use the place to nest.

Feeding. The first choice of food is fruit, which should be mixed with an insectile or softbill mixture. They will, however, quickly snap up mealworms and other small live food.

Leafbirds

Members of this family (Chloropseidae) are unique to Asia and the Philippines and are closely related to the bulbuls (family Pycnonotidae). The most popular birds within this family are the leafbirds proper, consisting of eight species of bright colored birds, also frequently called **fruit suckers or chloropsis.** The species most commonly offered for sale is the **Golden-fronted Leafbird** or **Fruit Sucker** (*Chloropsis aurifrons*). Charming and often finger-tame, the male has a sweet song. Iı males are acquired as songbirds they should be kept on their own.

During recent years, the bigger starling-sized **Fairy Bluebird** (*Irena puella*) has become widely available, but both males and females can be aggressive to each other. The

male is a beautiful bird with ruby red eyes and shining light blue upperparts that form a startling contrast with his velvety black underparts. The female is almost completely dull greenish-blue.

Feeding. Sweet soft fruits, a few live mealworms, and a little insectivorous food make up their diet.

Crows*

Members of the crow family (Corvidae) are found throughout the world except for New Zealand and certain Pacific Islands. Crows and their allies—jays, magpies, and treepies—share many of the characteristics of starlings (Sturnidae). Members of this family are widely credited as being the most intelligent birds. If obtained as nestlings and hand reared, many, such as the **Eurasian Jay** (*Garrulus glandarius*), the **Common Magpie** (*Pica pica*), and the **Jackdaw** (*Corvus Monedula*), grow to be tame and make extremely good pets, able to perform simple tricks and even repeat a few words. Pet birds can sometimes be allowed to fly free and will generally return home, but are better not left at liberty all the time due to their mischievous ways. As a general rule, corvidas are best accommodated in large aviaries, where even tropical species quickly become acclimatized. Their great drawback as aviary birds, however, is their aggression which make most of them totally unsuitable companions for smaller birds. This is true of the **Red-billed Blue Magpie** (*Urocissa erythrorhynchus*), **Yellow-billed Magpie** (*U. flavirostris*), and **Azure-winged Magpie** (*Cyanopica cyanus*); but tree pies, for example the **Indian Treepie** (*Dendrocitta vagabunda*), are less spiteful and usually can be housed safely with smaller birds such as starlings.

The large jay thrushes or laughing

Barbets
(1) Coppersmith Barbet
(2) Blue-Throated Barbet
(3) Toucan Barbet

*Many countries now place legal restrictions upon the kinds of wild birds which may be kept in captivity. Be certain to check these laws before keeping a crow.

Crows
(1) *Lanceolated Jay*
(2) *Eurasian Jay*
(3) *Pileated Jay*
(4) *Mexican Green Jay*
(5) *Hunting Cissa*
(6) *Common Magpie*

thrushes are too big to confine in a cage. These birds quickly become hardy and thrive outdoors but possess an uncertain temper and must not be housed with smaller companions. Otherwise, jay thrushes are active and inquisitive creatures with a lot to commend them as pets except for being noisy. If you are a beginner in birdkeeping and want a pair of tough, long-lived softbills for a garden aviary, the **White-crested Laughing Thrush** (*Garrulus leucolophus*) and **Lanceolated Jay** (*G. lanceolatus*) are ideal. Less hardy are the **Pileated Jay** (*Cyanocorax affinis*) and the **Mexican Green Jay** (*C. yncas*). The **Silver-eared Mesia** (*Leiothrix argentauris*) has the advantage of being relatively easy to sex; males have red upper and under tail-coverts, while females have them orange to buff color.

The **Pekin Robin** (*L. lutea*), also known as the **Pekin Nightingale** or **Red-billed Leiothrix**, is also a popular softbill for beginners. It is colorful, sings well, and quickly adapts to life in a cage or aviary. Pekin Robins are sociable, and pairs can usually be housed in aviaries with small companions. The Silver-eared Mesia and the Pekin Robin soon acclimatize outdoors and are not too troubled by cold weather.

Feeding. Many crows, including jays, magpies, tree pies, and laughing thrushes, are scavengers by nature and will eat a variety of foodstuffs. The basis of their diet, however, should consist of some form of meat mixed with a coarse insectile food or moistened, crumbled dog biscuits or meal. They will also eat nuts, grain, or raw eggs, and many enjoy freshly killed mice or day-old chicks. They often eat their own eggs and even devour their young during the breeding season unless fed a high proportion of animal food.

The Silver-eared Mesia and the Pekin Robin require an insectile mixture with some fruit or berries added. They will also accept some seed such as canary seed and mixed millet. During the breeding season they should be offered live food.

New World Orioles*

Unique to the Americas, the New World orioles, or icterids (family Icteridae), are a remarkably diverse assemblage and include the true American orioles, which are often called hangnests and troupials—such as the **Troupial** or **Brazilian Hangnest** (*Icterus icterus*)—as well as American blackbirds and grackles, cowbirds, caciques, and oropendolas—such as the **Shiny Cowbird** (*Molothrus bonariensis*). The commonly kept **Red-breasted Blackbird** or **Marshbird** (*Leistes militaris*), although often known as the **Military Starling,** is not a starling. Icterids should not be confused with the Old World orioles (Oriolidae) which, although often similar in coloring, with black and yellow plumage, are not usually kept in aviaries. Apart from hangnests and troupials which are often tame and make good pets, the New World species are not well suited to cage life and should be kept in an aviary. Although hangnests and troupials can be spiteful in mixed company, most species are good mixers with other species their own size or a little bigger.

Feeding. Although caciques, oropendolas, hangnests, and troupials have a strong preference for fruit, most species are truly omnivorous and eat a wide variety of foods including seed. Unless a coloring agent, such as one of the canthexanthin or carotenoid compounds or even carrot juice is added to the softfood, the bright yellow, orange, or red feathering of many species will fade.

Flycatchers

Flycatchers (family Muscicapidae) are indigenous to the Old World, especially to tropical regions. The **Black-headed Sibia** (*Heterophasia capistrata*) resembles a small slim jay-thrush and is an attractive and common aviary bird. Species like the **Verditer Flycatcher** (*Stoparola melanops*) and the

*Many countries now place legal restrictions upon the kinds of wild birds which may be kept in captivity. Be certain to check these laws before keeping an oriole.

beautiful little **Rufous-bellied Niltava** (*Niltava sundara*) are not too difficult to keep. At first, they need to be housed in a box cage indoors and coddled. Later, when firmly established, they can be placed in a greenhouse, a conservatory-type aviary, or outdoors. An advantage of keeping flycatchers outdoors is that they can supplement their diet by catching insects. In northern countries and properly acclimatized, most flycatchers become hardy. It is, however, prudent to provide heated shelter or bring them indoors during the winter. The crested, little **Black-chinned Yuhina** (*Yuhina nigrimentum*) and the **Yellow-collared Ixulus** (*Ixulus flavicollis*) are only likely to prosper in a greenhouse or conservatory-type aviary.

Feeding. Their main diet is insects, houseflies and other suitable live food, and mealworms. The Black-chinned Yuhina and the Yellow-collared Ixulus require some fruit or berries added to their insectile mixture. They should be offered live food during the breeding season.

Turacos

Often known as **louries, go-away birds** and **plaintain-eaters,** turacos are unique to Africa. There are about twenty species making up the colorful turaco family (Musophagidae). Apart from having a crest and a slightly longer tail, all but one of the species—the **Great Blue Turaco** (*Corythaeola cristata*)—resemble a feral pigeon in size and shape. Both the male and the female of the species are alike in plumage. Popular for their bright colors and lively nature, the most commonly kept species are the mainly green turacos such as the **White-cheeked Turaco** (*Tauraco leucotis*) and the **Pink-crested Turaco** (*T. erythrolophus*). Also kept is **Hartlaub's** or the **Blue-crested Turaco** (*T. hartlaubi*).

Turacos are best appreciated in large

aviaries where they can run the length of long horizontal branches and where they have the space to take to the wing thereby revealing their striking red flight feathers. Once acclimatized, turacos often adapt remarkably well to cold weather.

Feeding. Fruit is the staple diet, but they will also eat buds and seeds, some insects, and invertebrates.

Pittas

Pittas (family Pittidae) are among the most beautiful birds in the world. Although unrelated to the thrush family (Turdidae), they are often called **jewel-thrushes.** There are twenty-three species.

The **Hooded** or **Green-breasted Pitta** (*Pitta sordida*) from Southeast Asia and the **Indian** or **Bengal Pitta** (*P. brachyura*) from India, China, and Japan are the only two species consistently available. Pittas are brightly colored, often combining irridescent blue, yellow, green, red, black, and white in their plumage. They are plump in appearance and have moderately long legs. Pittas seldom fly but live on and about the ground and move by hopping. They are best kept in a greenhouse or a conservatory-type aviary. Unless they are kept on a soft, moist surface such as peat, their tender feet become dry and sore. When resting, pittas like to sit on a stout branch or rock on the ground. Their accommodation must be spacious and have plenty of ground vegetation; otherwise it is rarely possible to keep more than one pitta.

Feeding. Pittas require an insectile mixture mixed with minced meat and live food such as worms and small snails.

Bulbuls

Bulbuls (family Pycnonotidae) are indigenous to Africa and Asia and the most readily available species are from India. They are usually not much larger than sparrows and are sometimes crested. Most bulbuls are gray, brown, dull green, or black with patches of bright red, yellow, or white about the head and vent area. If you are about to keep softbills for the first time, the recommended species are the **Red-eared** or **Red-whiskered Bulbul** (*Pycnonotus jocosus*), the **Red-vented Bulbul** (*P. cafer*), and the **White-cheeked Bulbul** (*P. leucogenys*). These birds have fine singing voices and usually become very tame. Although bulbuls will settle down to cage life, they are better kept in pairs in an outdoor aviary. Most of these birds acclimatize to cold weather and mix easily with other species. Related species requiring large planted aviaries include the **Golden-fronted Green Bulbul** (*Chlorepsis aurificas*) and **Hardwick's Green Bulbul** (*C. hardwickii*).

Feeding. Bulbuls should be fed a proportion of about 70 percent fruit and 30 percent insectile mixture, plus a few mealworms each day. Fruit can include some berries such as those of the barberry (*Berberis vulgaris*).

Toucans

There are approximately thirty-seven species belonging to the toucan family (Ramphastidae) and they are all indigenous to Central and South America. They are characterized by their huge, often brightly colored, bills. Their bills may serve several functions—to enable the bird to pluck fruits from the outer branches of trees, to serve as a defense weapon, or as a visual sign in display. Toucans range from the big **Toco Toucan** (*Ramphastos toco*) and **Sulfur-breasted Toucan** (*R. sulfuratus*) to the smaller species known as aracaris and toucanets, for example, the **Collared Aracari** (*Pteroglossus torquatus*). The sexes of most of the toucan family are alike in plumage, and can be distinguished only by the longer bill of the male. A notable exception is the Spot-billed Toucanet (*Selenidera maculirostris*). Toucans

Indian Pitta

are best kept in a planted aviary because they need plenty of exercise and produce copious droppings. Pairs of aracaris and especially toucanets can sometimes be housed safely with other birds provided they are no smaller than a starling. Unless the aviary is exceptionally spacious, pairs of toucans must be kept on their own. Toucans may sometimes live ten to fifteen years.

Feeding. Toucans are primarily fruit eaters but will also eat insects and other small creatures. In the wild, some may devour the eggs and nestlings of small birds. However, as a substitute, captive toucans will accept a few mealworms each day together with a coarse insectile mixture or moistened pellets. Occasionally, a few cubes of raw lean meat can also be added to their diet.

Starlings*

There are over one hundred species in the starling family (Sturnidae). They are found in tropical Africa, southern Asia and, to a

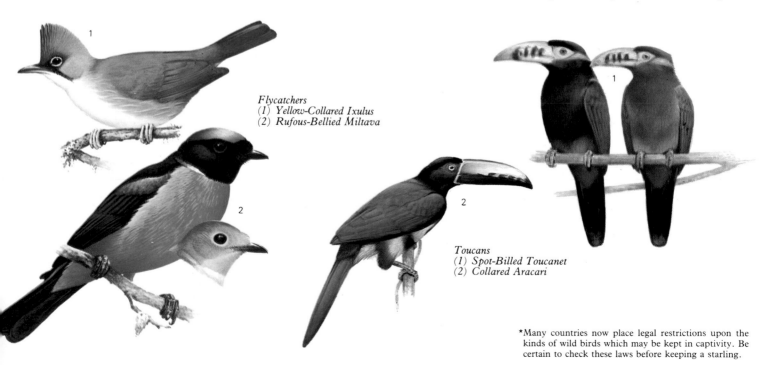

Flycatchers
(1) Yellow-Collared Ixulus
(2) Rufous-Bellied Miltava

Toucans
(1) Spot-Billed Toucanet
(2) Collared Aracari

*Many countries now place legal restrictions upon the kinds of wild birds which may be kept in captivity. Be certain to check these laws before keeping a starling.

lesser extent, in northern Asia and Europe. Starlings are adaptable, and the majority seem to enjoy cage or aviary life. Many young starlings become extremely tame and can be trained to talk.

Hill mynahs are sturdy, glossy, purplish-black birds indigenous to the forests of southeastern Asia. They are the least starling-like representatives of the family. Hill mynahs make good although messy pets—they often flick food about when feeding—and are famous for their unrivalled skill as talkers. There are several hill mynah species that vary in size and talking ability, the best talker being the **Greater Hill Mynah** (*Gracula religiosa intermedia*). Species such as the **Common** or **Indian Mynah** (*Acridotheres tristis*), **Bank Mynah** (*A. ginginianus*), and **Crested** or **Chinese Jungle Mynah** (*A. cristatellus*) are better as aviary birds than as pets. The most popular and widely kept aviary species are the African glossy starlings such as the **Superb Spreo** or **Superb Glossy Starling** (*Spreo superbus*), the **Golden-breasted Starling** (*Cosmopsarus regius*), the **Green Glossy Starling** (*Sturnus melanopterus*), and the **Rosy Purple Glossy Starling** (*L. purpureus*). African glossy starlings possess an attractive plumage which is colored in strong irridescent blues, greens and purples. They are relatively easy to look after. Other species available include **Rothschild's Starling** (*Leucospar rothschildi*), the **Black-winged Starling** (*Sturnus melanopterus*), and the **Rosy Pastor** or **Rose-colored Starling** (*St. roseus*). Most starlings quickly acclimatize to aviary life and are able to tolerate cold weather remarkably well. Starlings can be spiteful, however, and should be housed with birds their own size or a little bigger.

Feeding. Nearly all starlings enjoy an omnivorous diet which includes some raw minced meat and even canned dog meat. They should also be fed an insectile mixture, live insects, mealworms, and soft fruits. There is a commercially prepared food mixture in the form of pellets which is especially made to fit the dietary requirements of mynahs. Pellets are obtainable in many pet shops and can also be fed to other starlings.

Tanagers*

Tanagers are almost entirely confined to tropical and subtropical regions of the New World. There are over two hundred species belonging to the tanager family (Thraupidae) which is closely related to the Fringillidae (finches). Tanagers are among the world's most colorful birds; their plumage often contains several unusual and shimmering colors in dazzling combinations. The female is often as gaily clad as the male. Few softbills enjoy greater popularity than tanagers as aviary birds. They frequently head the list of softbill exhibits at bird shows and win many of the top awards. The best-known species is the **Blue-gray Tanager** (*Thraupis episcopus*). Other species such as **Mrs. Wilson's Tanager** (*Tangara larvata*), the **Blue-necked Tanager** (*T. cyanicollis*), the **Superb Tanager** (*T. fastuosa*), **Silver-throated Tanager** (*T. icterocephala*), and the **Spotted Emerald Tanager** (*T. gultata chrysophrys*) are more difficult to keep.

Most tanagers need to be housed indoors and coddled, especially when they are newly imported. After acclimatization they can be transferred to a planted aviary outdoors. However, without access to a heated shelter, few tanagers can withstand hard winter weather. Some species remain delicate and are best suited to hot humid conditions which can be provided by a greenhouse or conservatory-type aviary.

Feeding. Tanagers should be offered a variety of fruit mixed with a fine grade insectile mixture and some live food. Some small tanagers will accept nectar or sponge cake soaked with nectar.

Thrushes*

Members of this cosmopolitan family (Turdidae) are distributed throughout the world. The greater number of species are, however, found in Asia, Africa, and Europe. This family includes such birds as redstarts, rubythroats, robins, chats, and wheatears. Many species are outstanding songsters and are

*Many countries now place legal restrictions upon the kinds of wild birds which may be kept in captivity. Be certain to check these laws before keeping this bird.

highly regarded cage and aviary birds. The **Shama** (*Copsychus malabaricus*), the **Dhyal Bird** or **Magpie Robin** (*C. saularis*), and the **Orange-headed Ground Thrush** (*Zoothera citrina*) are extremely popular birds originating from Southeastern Asia. The males of these species are often bolder and more colorful than the females and are also good songsters. They frequently make good pets if housed singly in large box cages. However, these species are best kept in an outdoor aviary. In Europe and North America most native species do not require heated accommodation—nor, once acclimatized, do most other species. A few small migratory and tropical species do appreciate a heated aviary shelter during a hard winter.

Other species often kept in an aviary include the **Siberian Rubythroat** (*Luscinia calliope*), **Robin Chats** (*Cossypha* spp), the **European Redstart** (*Phoenicurus phoenicurus*), the **Song Thrush** (*Turdus philomelos*), and the **Blackbird** (*T. merula*).

Aviary companions must be carefully chosen since males, in particular, can be pugnacious. They often direct their aggression toward their mates so that, unless an aviary is spacious with a lot of dense foliage, it is sometimes impossible to keep pairs together other than briefly at breeding time.

Feeding. The basic diet for thrushes consists of an insectile mixture with a little minced meat and fruit added. In addition a wide variety of live food should be offered during the breeding season.

White-Eyes

These birds (family Zosteropidae), also known as **zosterops**, have silver eyes and appear to be wearing spectacles due to the white feathering around the eyes. They are ideal for someone starting to keep nectar-feeders because they have the least specialized dietary requirements. White-eyes possess a friendly disposition and can be housed satisfactorily with most small species, including waxbills. All white-eyes look remarkably alike—small and warbler-like with a relatively short pointed bill and generally yellowish-green to green plumage, sometimes with gray underparts.

Of the eighty-five or so different species living in the Old World, the most readily available is the **Oriental White-eye** (*Zosterops palpebrosa*) and **Chestnut-flanked White-eye** (*Z. erythropleura*).

Feeding. They should be offered a simple nectar solution and a choice of soft fruit mixed with a fine insectile mixture.

Sugarbirds

The **Yellow-winged Sugarbird** or **Red-legged Honeycreeper** (*Cyanerpes cyaneus*) and the **Purple Sugarbird** or **Yellow-legged Honeycreeper** (*C. caeruleus*) are the most commonly available species among this group (family Thraupidae).

They are indigenous to the West Indies and Central and South America, and they are quite distinct from the Hawaiian honeycreepers and true sugarbirds that are confined to southern Africa. Males are often gai-

Starlings
(1) Purple Glossy Starling
(2) Great Hill Mynah

Thrushes
(1) European Redstart
(2) Orange-Headed Ground Thrush
(3) Song Thrush

Hummingbirds*

There are over three hundred species of hummingbirds (family Trochilidae) which range from Alaska to Tierra del Fuego in the New World. They are often described as nature's living jewels. Hummingbirds range in size from the world's smallest bird, the **Bee Hummingbird** (*Mellisuga helenae*) of Cuba which has a total length of little more than 5cm. (2in.), to the **Giant Hummingbird** (*Patagona gigas*) with an overall length of about 21.5cm. (8.5in.). Only a few of the vast number of species ever become available, and these seldom do well in captivity. Those kept include the **Streamertail** (*Trochilus polytmus*), the **Sparkling Violetear** (*Colibri coruscans*), the **Ruby-topaz Hummingbird** (*Chrysolampis mosquitus*), and the **Heavenly Sylph** (*Aglaicereus kingi*). In most instances hummingbirds can only be satisfactorily maintained in a greenhouse or conservatory-type aviary.

Hummingbirds are solitary, aggressive birds with an even greater intolerance than sunbirds towards their own kind. They will intimidate any companions and drive them from the feeders. It is only possible to keep two or more together if they are housed in a large and heavily-planted enclosure amply supplied with many feeding sites and separate perches.

Feeding. It is imperative to provide a plentiful supply of *fruit flies*, along with a nectar that has a high protein content. Hummingbirds feed while on the wing, and nectar must be placed in special hummingbird feeders that can be suspended from branches or poles constructed for the purpose.

*Many countries now place legal restrictions upon the kinds of wild birds which may be kept in captivity. Be certain to check these laws before keeping a hummingbird.

ly clad in brilliant shades of deep blue, turquoise-blue, and blue-green, while females are more subdued and often predominantly greenish in color. Male Yellow-winged Sugarbirds usually lose their bright colors outside the breeding season and assume a plumage more like the female's. Although males are occasionally quarrelsome among themselves, pairs usually can be kept with other small species. Sugarbirds should not be expected to withstand hard winter weather and in temperate climates are best housed in a greenhouse or conservatory-type aviary, if possible.

Feeding. The basic diet is soft fruit and a simple nectar solution. They should also be offered a fine insectile mixture or fruit flies to supplement their basic diet.

Sunbirds

Sunbirds (family Nectariniidae) are in many respects the Old World's equivalent of the hummingbirds. There are just over one hundred species, the majority being indigenous to Africa although they are also found in southern Asia and one species reaches Australia. Best known species are the **Scarlet-chested Sunbird** (*Nectarinia senegalensis*), the **Tacazze Sunbird** (*N. tacazze*), the **Beautiful Sunbird** (*N. pulchella*), and the **Variable Sunbird** (*N. venusta*). Male sunbirds have brilliant, often irridescent feathering. Some species lose their colors outside the breeding season and resemble the females that are usually dull olive-green, yellow, and brown in color. In temperate climates, sunbirds prosper best in a greenhouse or conservatory-type aviary, although some species from the highlands of eastern Africa do exceptionally well outdoors. Great care must be exercised when mixing sunbirds as they are

notoriously quarrelsome. It is seldom possible to house two males together and even finding compatible pairs can be difficult.

Feeding. Few species show much interest in fruit or other such foods, but require a good supply of nectar and plenty of live food. Being small with slender bills (like most nectar-feeders) sunbirds are usually unable to tackle mealworms and require small soft bodied insects that can be collected around the house and garden, houseflies, and fruit flies (*Drosophila*).

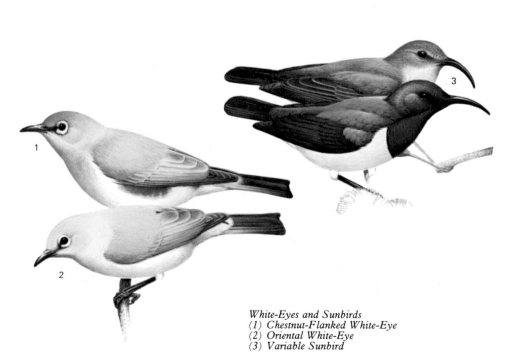

White-Eyes and Sunbirds
(1) Chestnut-Flanked White-Eye
(2) Oriental White-Eye
(3) Variable Sunbird

211

Hummingbirds
(1) Streamertail
(2) Sparkling Violetear
(3) Heavenly Sylph
(4) Ruby-Topaz Hummingbird

Parrots and Parakeets

The parrot family (Psittacidae) contains just over three hundred species and, although they are known by a variety of names (many species with long tails are called parakeets), all are easily recognized by their characteristic hooked beak and feet with two toes in front and two behind which are adapted for grasping. The shell parakeet (budgerigar) has been successfully domesticated and now forms a distinct group on its own.

If well housed and fed a good varied diet, parrot species are frequently long lived. Lovebirds and other small species usually have a lifespan of seven to ten years, though records of up to twenty years are common. Accurate records for many of the bigger spe-

212

cies are seldom available but a lifespan of forty to fifty years is normal.

Most psittacines adapt well to cage and aviary life, are extremely colorful, and can be affectionate and amusing pets, with a well-founded reputation for learning to talk and imitate sounds. Individuals of different species vary considerably in their talking ability, but few are as reliable as the African Gray Parrot (Psitticus eithacus). If any of the species is to be successfully trained to talk, it must be obtained when it is young.

HOUSING

Various cage designs are suitable for a parrot kept as a family pet. If the bird is tame enough, it can be allowed out into a room regularly and given an opportunity to exercise under supervision. Small species can be kept singly or in pairs in large all-wire parakeet cages while some of the larger species can be kept on T-shaped parrot stands. Psit-

tacines must be kept somewhere light and airy but draft-free. They should be sprayed at least once a week with a fine spray of tepid water to keep their plumage in good condition; otherwise it will become dry and brittle. Caged parrots sometimes pluck their feathers due to boredom or a dietary deficiency. Boredom can often be prevented by providing playthings such as wooden cotton reels. Fresh twigs from unsprayed fruit trees for nibbling and chewing are also beneficial.

Most parrot species do well in aviaries and should be housed in pairs. Even in a temperate climate most tropical species soon acclimatize and then, provided they have a dry, draft-free aviary shelter, they can live outdoors year round without artificial heating and lighting. Many species spend a lot of time climbing rather than flying, and they do not require particularly large aviaries, while those that like to fly are often happy in long narrow enclosures. Aviaries need to be strongly constructed since most species possess strong beaks and can be extremely destructive to wood and other soft materials. It is often advisable to have the aviary fitted with a metal framework, heavy-duty wire netting, and perches made of hardwood. Parrots must be handled with care since they can inflict a nasty bite.

FEEDING REQUIREMENTS

The basic diet of psittacines is seed—except for those that feed chiefly on nectar. Sunflower seed, canary seed, white millet, and spray millet are all suitable. Peanuts can be fed shelled or unshelled. A choice of greenfood and fruit should also be offered. Newly imported young birds are often unfamiliar with the usual hard seeds and should be offered soaked seed, boiled whole corn, greenfood, and fruit. They can be weaned gradually to hard seed. They can also be offered wholegrain bread mixed with ordinary or diluted condensed milk and baby food. Such foods are also invaluable for feeding sick birds and those rearing young. Most species enjoy nectar which can be given as an occasional treat or as a tonic to sick or newly imported birds. Grit, cuttlefish bone, and fresh drinking water must always be available.

BREEDING REQUIREMENTS

Psittacines usually nest in holes and can be persuaded to use various designs of nest boxes that have an entrance hole just big enough to admit them. They are more likely to breed in an aviary than in a cage and should be given a choice of at least two boxes fixed fairly high and sheltered from direct sun and heavy rain. An inverted piece of turf, peat, or decayed wood chippings in the bottom of the box is sufficient nesting material.

Cockatiel

The **Cockatiel** (Nymphicus hollandicus) is an ideal beginners' bird which, like the budgerigar, is indigenous to Australia and is now thoroughly domesticated and almost as free breeding. Taken from the nest and hand-reared, Cockatiels make enchanting pets. Some cocks are talented talkers that can also whistle tunes. Cockatiels are gentle and are one of the few parrots that can be trusted in mixed collections, even with birds such as finches. The Cockatiel is crested, long tailed, and about 32.5cm. (13in.) long. The male has a yellow crest and cheeks and an orange "ear" patch. There is a large area of white on the wings, otherwise the plumage is gray. The female has a paler crest and cheeks. The underside of her tail is striped yellow and gray whereas the male's tail is entirely gray. Aviary-bred color mutations have been developed.

Feeding. Cockatiels should be fed equal parts canary seed and white millet, together with a little hemp, oats, and sunflower seeds.

Lovebirds

True lovebirds come from Africa and Madagascar. None exceed 16.5cm. (6.5in.) long, and are short tailed, predominantly green birds, often with contrasting colors about the head. Species such as the **Peach** or **Rosy-faced Lovebird** (*Agapornis roseicollis*), **Fischer's Lovebird** (*A. fischeri*), and the **Masked Lovebird** (*A. personata*) are difficult to sex. There is an attractive blue mutation of

A number of parrots and parrot-like birds can be kept at full or semi-liberty, as is this macaw. However, this is possible only in rural areas where there are no neighbors likely to be troubled by the birds' inquisitive and mischievous ways.

the Masked Lovebird. Most lovebirds can be kept together and bred in cages or aviaries, although if species are mixed they may interbreed. They are unsuitable companions for small birds like finches, but in a large aviary, sometimes can be housed with parakeets. The **Abyssinian** or **Black-winged Lovebird** (*A. taranta*) is particularly suitable as a household pet.

Feeding. They should be fed equal parts of canary seed and white millet, together with sunflower seeds.

Parakeets

Australia is the home of many beautiful and eagerly sought parakeets. However, except in extraordinary circumstances, Australia bans the export of native animals, so that those available are usually aviary-bred. Among the most common parakeets are the **Red-rumped Parakeet** (*Psephotus haematonotus*), **Bourke's Parakeet** (*Neophema bourkii*), and the **Turquoisine Grass Parakeet** (*N. pulchella*). The Red-rumped Parakeet is about 35cm. (14in.) in length, and the male is mainly green and yellow with a red rump while the female is duller and lacks the red coloring. There is a yellow mutation of this species. The Red-rumped Parakeet can be a quarrelsome bird so pairs need an aviary to themselves where they are usually willing to breed, if given a nest box measuring 60cm. (24in.) high and about 25cm. (10in.) square. Bourke's, the Turquoisine, and other grass parakeets are attractive (females are usually duller than males), quiet, and inoffensive

Abyssinian Lovebird

birds. All do well in comparatively small aviaries, do not destroy vegetation, and can be safely housed with other small birds.

Other popular Australian parakeets include the **Prince of Wales** or **Queen Alexandra's Parakeet** (*Polytelis alexandrae*), the **Rock Pebbler Parakeet** (*P. anthopeplus*), **Barraband Parakeet** (*P. swainsonii*), the **Malga Parakeet** (*Psephetus varius*), and the **Crimson-winged Parakeet** (*Aprosmictus erythropterus*).

The **Indian Ringnecked Parakeet** (*Psittacula krameri*) and close relatives from Asia, like the bigger **Alexandrine Parakeet** (*P. eupatria*), make good single pets and aviary birds. The male Indian Ringnecked has a narrow band of pink and black feathers around the neck. The long tail accounts for about half of the total length which is approximately 38cm. (15in.). White, lutino, and blue mutations of the Ringneck also exist.

Feeding. Grass parakeets require equal parts of canary seed and white millet, and just a trace of hemp and sunflower seeds. Ringnecks and other large parakeets need equal parts of canary seed and white millet, half a part of sunflower seeds, and a few peanuts.

Rosellas

Rosellas are also native to Australia and enjoy great popularity because of their brilliant colors. They are essentially outdoor birds and require an aviary which allows plenty of flying space (more long than wide). Pairs are usually aggressive and will not tolerate the presence of other birds, especially their own kind. Three of the most popular species are the **Common Rosella** (*Platycerus eximius*), the **Golden-mantled Rosella** (*P.e. cecilae*), and **Pennant's Parakeet** or **Crimson Rosella**

accepted record is of a **Greater Sulphur-crested Cockatoo** (*C. galerita*) that lived fifty-six years. The largest is the **Palm Cockatoo** (*Prosciger aterrimus*) which makes a good pet but is rare. The **Roseate** (*Eolophus rosei capillus*) and **Leadbeater's** (*Cacatua leadbeateri*) **Cockatoos** make good aviary birds.

Feeding. They should be given equal parts of sunflower seeds, canary seed, peanuts (groundnuts), and white millet, plus a little hemp. They are also fond of sliced apple and carrots. It is generally true to say that they need a little more care with their diet than other parrots and appreciate a variety of tid-bits.

Parrots

The **Gray Parrot** (*Psittacus erithacus*), one of the few parrots to be found in Africa, is a talented mimic. It is essential to acquire a young bird for a pet since an untamed adult Gray Parrot is unsuitable and should only be

Parakeets
(1) Cockatiel
(2) Bourke's Parakeet
(3) Turquoisine Grass Parakeet

Cockatoos
(1) Great White Cockatoo
(2) Roseate Cockatoo
(3) Leadbeaters Cockatoo
(4) Greater Sulphur-Crested Cockatoo
(5) Palm Cockatoo

(*P. elegans*). The sexes of these species resemble each other although the female is usually a little duller in color and has a smaller head than the male.

Feeding. Rosellas require equal parts of canary seed and white millet, a little hemp, and sunflower seeds.

Cockatoos

The large crested cockatoos from the East Indies—New Guinea—Australia region are intelligent, amusing, and lovable pets if hand reared. They are mostly white, gray, or black with splashes of yellow or red. Although many birds learn to talk, they are seldom talented. Cockatoos delight in a lot of attention and can be kept indoors in a cage or on a stand if their raucous voices, powerful beaks, and generally destructive nature do not create problems. The most suitable household pet is the **Lesser Sulphur-crested Cockatoo** (*Cacatua sulpharea*) but the best known must be the **Great White Cockatoo** (*C. alba*).

Provided there are no neighbors living close enough to be disturbed by their screeching, cockatoos are fine aviary birds but they need an exceptionally strong, well-constructed enclosure. Although there are rumors of cockatoos living to be over one hundred years of age, the most widely

214

kept in an aviary. The young and adult birds can be distinguished since the young have gray eyes and the adult, yellow. Gray Parrots are intelligent, seldom noisy, and have a good temperament. Many develop astonishing vocabularies and learn to repeat whole nursery rhymes, whistle tunes, and sing songs. Frequently, the Gray Parrot's voice is indistinguishable from that of the person it is mimicking. These birds are also adept at imitating environmental sounds, such as squeaking doors and dripping taps. Unfortunately, they are often reluctant to perform in front of strangers, seldom enjoy being handled, and are prone to plucking their feathers. Gray Parrots are frequently long lived; a life expectancy of forty to fifty years is not unusual. Smaller African species such as **Meyer's Parrot** (*Poicephalus meyer*) and the **Senegal Parrot** (*P. sengalus*) also make good pets that occasionally learn to repeat a few words.

Amazon parrots are gaily colored birds from the tropical forests of Central and South America and the West Indies. The most common Amazon species are the **Yellow-fronted Amazon** (*Amazona ochrocephala*), the **Pangma Yellow-fronted Amazon** (*A.O. panamensis*), the **Orange-winged Amazon** (*A. amazonica*), and the **Blue-fronted Amazon** (*A. aestiva*), all of which can be good talkers.

Young Amazon parrots grow to be delightful pets that love to be fussed over and handled. They are highly intelligent and often become ridiculously tame and devoted to their owners. As they mature, however, their temperament sometimes changes and they may become spiteful. Due to their powerful beak, they are capable of inflicting a painful bite. Compared to Gray Parrots, Amazons talk more freely in front of onlookers, but seldom have large vocabularies or the ability to imitate voices with the same uncanny accuracy. They are also noisier and are frequently given to screeching. Most Amazons have predominantly green plumage, often with bright, contrasting colors about the head and, to a lesser degree, on the wings and tail. They are thickset birds that vary in size from 25–50cm. (10–20in.). The sexes are usually indistinguishable. As with Gray Parrots, Amazons can be kept indoors in a cage and regularly allowed out, or kept on a parrot stand. They also do well in strongly constructed outdoor aviaries. Species such as **Salvin's Amazon** (*A. autumnalis solivni*) are best suited to aviary life.

The **Blue-headed** or **Red-vented Parrot** (*Pionus menstruus*) possesses immense charm and makes a very good pet although it seldom learns to repeat more than a few words. Hand-reared young Blue-headed Parrots are particularly suitable for families with young children and for those who are a little wary of the larger species. They are gentle, quiet birds that measure about 27.5cm. (11in.) long. The **Red-capped Parrot** (*Pinopsilta pileata*) is also a good family pet since it rarely bites.

Parrots
(1) *Blue-Fronted Amazon*
(2) *Orange-Winged Amazon*
(3) *Salvin's Amazon*
(4) *Yellow-Fronted Amazon*
(5) *Panama Yellow-Fronted Amazon*

Feeding. Parrots should be fed equal parts canary seed, white millet, sunflower seeds, and peanuts.

Macaws

Among the most spectacular and gaily colored of all birds are the large macaws which, with their long tail, can measure as much as 95cm. (38in.). Despite their size and formidable looking beak, young macaws in particular make remarkably gentle and affectionate pets. They enjoy being handled and should be given plenty of attention. Unless this can be provided, keeping these birds is unfair. Also, before choosing one as a pet, it is important to realize that a macaw is one of the noisiest birds, particularly prone to screeching during the early hours of the morning. The **Blue and Yellow Macaw** (*Ara ararauna*) is the most popular macaw due to its attractive coloring, intelligence, playfulness, and mimicry. Much less frequently seen are the **Scarlet Macaw** (*A. macao*), the **Green-winged Macaw** (*A. Chloroptera*), the **Military Macaw** (*A. militoris*), and the **Hyacinthine Macaw** (*Anodorhynchus hyacinthinus*).

Large pet macaws are too big to cage and should be kept on a parrot stand and daily allowed to move about the house to exercise (under supervision). Macaws are fine aviary birds. A small aviary is suitable as they spend most of their time climbing and seldom bother to fly. Because of their huge destructive beak, the aviary must be exceptionally strong. An ideal way of keeping these birds is at full or partial liberty, but this is only possible in rural areas where there are no close neighbors to be troubled by their inquisitive and mischievous ways.

There are also a number of so-called dwarf macaws, such as the **Blue-winged Macaw** (*Ara maracana*) and **Chestnut-fronted Macaw** (*A. severa*), which make enchanting pets. Not only are they playful and affectionate, but they will often learn to repeat a few sen-

215

Macaws
(1) Hyacinth Macaw
(2) Blue-and-Yellow Macaw
(3) Scarlet Macaw

tences whereas the larger macaws rarely learn more than a few words. All macaws can be readily identified by the bare skin that surrounds the eyes and extends to the cheeks.
Feeding. The basic diet is equal parts of sunflower seeds, canary seed, peanuts, and white millet. Large macaws enjoy nuts such as Brazil nuts which they can easily crack with their powerful beaks.

Conures
Many New World parakeets, particularly those belonging to the genera *Aratinga* and *Pyrrhura*, are commonly known as conures. Birds of the genus *Aratinga* can be as large as 37.5cm. (15in.) and are mainly green with red, orange, light brown, or blue about the head. Those in the genus *Pyrrhura* measure 20–27.5cm. (8–11in.) and are mainly dark green, often with a scaly pattern on the throat, breast, and hind neck, and sometimes with a maroon tail. Members of *Pyrrhura* are not widely available whereas those belonging to *Aratinga*, especially the **Black-headed** or **Nanday Conure** (*A. nanday*) and the colorful **Jandaya** or **Yellow-headed Conure** (*A. jandaya*) are often seen in aviaries. **Petz's** or the **Halfmoon Conure** (*A. canicularis*) is popular in the United States and is commonly kept as a household pet. The young of this species are easily tamed and can be taught to talk and to do simple tricks.

It must be kept in mind, however, that conures can be very noisy and indulge in regular bouts of shrieking. They are inquisitive, mischievous birds that are often destructive.
Feeding. Conures should be offered equal parts canary seed, white millet, and sunflower seed, plus a little hemp and oats.

Parrotlets
Parrotlets bear some resemblance to the African lovebirds and are often regarded as their New World counterparts. Parrotlets are small, short-tailed birds that are green in color. The male is usually blue on the rump or wings. Parrotlets have much to commend them as they are neither noisy nor destructive and are often willing to nest. They can be kept in a cage but do better in a spacious indoor pen or an outdoor aviary. Despite their small size, parrotlets can be aggressive. If they are housed with other species, these should be larger than the parrotlets. The two species most often encountered are the **Celestial Parrotlet** (*Forpus coelestis*) and **Turquoise-Rumped Parrotlet** (*F. cyanopygius*).
Feeding. They should be offered equal parts canary seed and white millet, plus a little hemp and sunflower seeds.

Lories and Lorikeets
Unlike the previous birds, these parrots show little or no interest in seed, but feed largely on nectar. To facilitate this mode of feeding, the tip of the tongue has a brushy fringe. Lories and lorikeets are found throughout the East Indies, New Guinea, and Australia. They are delightful birds that are popular for their pleasing ways and often brilliant colors. The **Chattering Lory** (*Domicella garrula garrula*) and the **Yellow-backed Lory** (*D.g. flavopalliata*) are red with green wings and a varying amount of yellow on the back. The sexes of both these birds look alike and to confuse matters, two birds of the same sex often act like a true pair. The most frequently available lorikeets are the lovely **Rainbow Lorikeet** (*Trichoglossus haematodus*), the **Ornate Lorikeet** (*T. ornatus*), and **Swainson's Lorikeet** (*T. moluccanus*).

Although lories can be kept in a parrot cage, these birds thrive in an aviary. Being extremely messy, sticky feeders, they need extra attention to keep their accommodation scrupulously clean, and an outdoor flight exposed to the elements saves a lot of disagreeable work. Ample bathing facilities must be provided.
Feeding. They should be given nectar made from honey diluted with water, with the addition of malt, condensed milk, or baby food. Milk additives are nourishing, but great care must be exercised in their use in warm weather. Some species will eat canary seed, and many relish maggots and mealworms.

Conurine Parakeets
Conurine parakeets are closely related to conures but are smaller in size. Scarcely larger than a shell parakeet and usually green in color, these birds make good pets. The

Celestial Parrotlet

White-winged Parakeet (*Brotogeris versicolurus versicolurus*), the **Canary-winged Parakeet** (*B.v. chiriri*), the **Orange-Flanked Parakeet** (*B. pyrrhopterus*), the **Tui Parakeet** (*B. sanctithomae*), and the **Tovi Parakeet** (*B. jugularis*) are all regularly available. Young birds are easy to tame and grow to be inquisitive and mischievous. Some learn to repeat a few words, but are not talented mimics. The only fault is their harsh, noisy voices. A single bird can be housed in a large canary or parakeet cage, or even in a small parrot cage fitted with suitably thin perches. They are fond of bathing and often enjoy being sprayed.
Feeding. They should be offered a mixture of canary seed, white and yellow millets, plus a little hemp and sunflower seeds.

Pigeons

It is generally accepted that all domestic pigeons are descended from the wild **Rock Dove** (*Columba livia*) which inhabits the rocky coastlines of northern Europe and various parts of Asia and Africa. This bird is blue-gray in color with two black wing bars and a white rump. The feathers of the neck carry a greenish purple sheen and the eyes, legs, and feet are red. Modern varieties, however, have been created by the breeding of mutations. Once a variety has been established it is necessary to keep them separate from other varieties as cross breeding will result in reversion to the *Columba livia* type.

HOUSING

The variety of pigeon kept has some bearing on whether or not to house pigeons. Where pigeons are not permanently allowed their freedom, the accommodation provided must be adequately ventilated and not over-crowded especially when an outside aviary is not attached. The construction must be dampproof. As a rough guide, a building 180cm. long, 120cm. wide, and 180cm. high (6 x 4 x 6ft.) will accommodate four breeding pairs. The number of perches provided must exceed the number of birds. Box type perches are the most suitable for the flying varieties, and bracket or the inverted "V" type are more suitable for the fancy breeds. Nest boxes should be provided during the breeding season and, although expensive manufactured boxes are available, pigeons will nest quite happily in cheap wooden orange crates. More boxes than are necessary should be provided in order to reduce fighting for possession. A piece of board must be fastened across the bottom front of the box to prevent the youngsters from falling out, and a nest pan should be provided for each box.

Grit boxes, a bath, and somewhere to store the food to prevent contamination are also necessary. A good scraper for cleaning the housing is absolutely essential, cleanliness being one of the most important basic principles of pigeon keeping. Some form of trap will be necessary when racing homers and other flying varieties are kept to prevent them from escaping once they have entered the loft.

A dovecote is the most suitable housing for fancy pigeons. It should be placed at the end of a pole and be inaccessible to cats. The birds, of course, will be free flying and breeding will be indiscriminate; if a pedigree flock is joined by a stray of a different variety, cross-breeding will occur.

FEEDING REQUIREMENTS

Pigeons are grain eaters which swallow their food whole. If they must, pigeons can exist adequately on the widest possible food selection which includes bread, cakes, cooked vegetables, and all manner of scraps, as evidenced by the many pigeons inhabiting our cities. However, under controlled circumstances, the dietary needs of the domestic pigeon are normally met by a constant supply of such grains as beans, peas, corn (maize), wheat, and barley. The smaller pigeon varieties should not be given large grain.

The simplest way of feeding pigeons is to use one of the several types of manufactured pellets because these contain all the necessary nutrients. Any food given should not be contaminated by vermin or disease will ensue. It should be easy to tell whether corn is wholesome or not by smelling it.

Although methods of feeding vary, one feed early in the morning followed by another one in late afternoon is adequate. Appetites vary according to the breed, but generally the bird has had enough food when it stops eating to take a drink. One method of feeding is to throw the food onto the floor, a handful at a time, until the birds stop eating. A hopper system allows the birds access to food at all times and prevents it from becoming soiled.

To enable pigeons to digest grain, a good supply of mixed grit should be available at all times. Chicken eggshells, which have first been dried in an oven and then crushed into

Nearly everyone is familiar with the White Fantail Pigeon, which is the species most commonly kept in garden dovecotes.

small pieces, make a good substitute. Clean fresh water should be in constant supply, and the vessel used should be covered on top to prevent fouling. Pigeons drink in a manner which differs from all other birds. They plunge their beaks into the water and suck it up in one continuous draft. Other birds scoop it up in the lower mandible, and throw the head backwards allowing it to trickle down the throat.

BREEDING

Although pigeons will breed at an earlier age they should be at least six months old. Having selected the two pigeons you intend to pair, they should be placed in adjoining pens or in a box which has been divided with a wire partition so that the birds may see each other but not make physical contact. After a day or so, when the birds become used to each other, the partition may be removed and courting will usually commence. During this period the cock will drive the hen by cooing loudly, inflating its crop and advancing to-

Conurine Parakeets
(1) Tovi Parakeet
(2) Tui Parakeet
(3) Canary-Winged Parakeet

A basic loft for performing pigeons, like this one, should be raised on brick or concrete piers to guard against dampness and vermin.

217

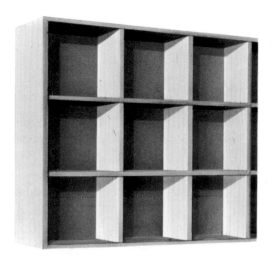

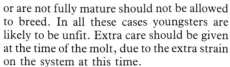

Pigeon perches: Box perches of the "pigeon hole" type (Left); inverted-V perches (Top Right); and simple bracket perches (Bottom Right).

wards her, sweeping his tail at the same time. Billing, or wringing of beaks, takes place and mating follows. They may then be returned to the loft as, having once paired, pigeons are monogamous. (Pigeons have short memories and once a pair has been broken up, they will usually accept a fresh mate after a week.) The first egg is laid within about one week of mating. There is a day's interval and the second egg is produced before incubation begins. The cock sits about seven to eight hours during the day and the hen the remainder of the twenty-four hour cycle. Incubation lasts about eighteen days and after hatching, the young, which are born naked, are fed with a liquid substance colloquially known as "pigeons' milk." This milk forms during the latter stages of incubation in the crops of the parent birds, and the young pigeon obtains it by putting its beak into the mouth of the adult where it is "pumped" up from the stomach. When the youngsters are about five days old, the milk starts to dry up and they

Nesting boxes for pigeons should have 6mm. (0.25in.) dowel bars spaced 40mm. (1.5in.) apart. When closed, the T-shaped, pivoting door provides a spare perch.

are then able to accept partially digested grain. Growth is now very rapid and pin feathers start to appear. After a few more days the young take regurgitated whole grain. Youngsters start to feed themselves around four weeks and begin to fly shortly afterwards. At this stage they should be placed in a loft which has been set aside for the purpose where they can be given special attention and allowed to develop without interference from the adults.

If the young are to be exhibited, they must be ringed with the official rings of the appropriate association when about seven days old. If ringing is not done at this time the feet will have grown so much that it will be impossible to get the ring on and the owner will be ineligible to fly or exhibit the pigeon in official competitions.

COMMON AILMENTS

Pigeons which have been well tended, given the correct food, and kept under clean conditions seldom suffer serious ailments. Birds which have suffered from serious illness, which did not develop normally when young,

or are not fully mature should not be allowed to breed. In all these cases youngsters are likely to be unfit. Extra care should be given at the time of the molt, due to the extra strain on the system at this time.

Pigeons, even those that are kept under ideal conditions, are subject to attack by lice, which either suck their blood or eat their feathers. Fortunately, these pests are easily eradicated by use of an insecticide produced especially for the purpose.

Pigeons suffer from minor ailments such as colds with symptoms similar to those of humans exhibited by runny eyes and nose and sneezing fits. One-eyed cold, as the name suggests, is diagnosed by the closing of the eye. The bird should be isolated, placed in a warm environment and treated with one of many commercially available products.

Unfortunately, clean and healthy pigeons sometimes come into contact with infections, when in race panniers or show pens at an exhibition. It is, therefore, advisable to examine carefully any pigeon which has returned from a race or show and to isolate it from other birds if there is any doubt.

PIGEON BREEDS

Domestic pigeons are roughly divided into three groups: Homers, Highfliers, and those described as "Fancy" varieties.

Homers
By careful selection of those birds which were able to fly faster than others, the modern **Racing Homer** pigeon emerged. Pigeons do not have to be trained to "home"—they do so by instinct—but with training they are likely to cover the distance in less time. (See **Training and Obedience.**) The Racing Homer is similar in appearance and hardiness to the wild Rock Dove. European and American Homers can be any color, the most common being dark checkers. The head should be full and the chest broad, but appearance is not as important as flying skill.

Highfliers
The Highfliers include the **Tipplers, Tumblers,** and **Rollers** which are the acrobats of the sky. Tipplers fly to great heights and, still within sight of their loft, are capable of sustained flight in excess of nineteen hours. Tipplers under normal circumstances would not fly for this length of time without training. These birds are usually flown in threes, known as a "kit." They are trained to remain in the sky until the owner calls them down by using a white pigeon, usually a Fantail, as a decoy on the roof of the loft. The decoy is called a dropper.

Tumblers probably derive their name from the ability to turn somersaults while in flight. These birds will often fly for as long as three or four hours and provide much entertainment for those watching.

The greatest performers of aerobatics are the Rollers. Their performance is made up of a series of short falls or rolls, which is accompanied by "twizzling," a sort of circling like a spinning plate. Good Rollers should roll in a straight line, the somersaults being so rapid that they cannot be counted. There are a great many Continental highflier breeds, including the **Danzigers, Koros, Berlin, Hanover, Vienna,** and **Cologne,** all of which are good performers.

Fancy Varieties

The fancy varieties which are bred for exhibition purposes are so remarkable and appear in such a diversity of shape, size, and color that it is sometimes difficult to believe that the Rock Dove was their common ancestor. The Longfaced varieties have the conventional pigeon beak while the Shortfaced varieties have such a short beak that it is unable to rear its own young. Shortfaces include such breeds as the **Turbits, Orientals, Frills,** and **Owls.**

There are clean legged varieties of pigeon, and there are varieties with feathers on their legs and feet so long that they give the appearance of an extra pair of wings. Heavily muffed or feathered leg breeds include the **Swallows, Shields, Spots, Monks, Priests,** and **Trumpeters.** The cooing or drumming of the Trumpeter is distinctive and needs to be heard to be appreciated. Trumpeters also have a crest at the back of the head and a circular crest or "rose" on the top. The "head" breeds, where the shape of the head with its various adornments is the special feature, include the **Carriers, Barbs,** and **Scanderoons. Pouters** which blow out their crop until it looks like a balloon come in many varieties. **Fantails** have tails spread out like a fan and, when displaying, hold their head back and down almost to the base of the fan. Fantails are also characterized by a curious shaking of the head when agitated. The Homers have their exhibition counterparts which are the **Genuine, Exhibition,** and **Show Homers.** Although the Tipplers and Rollers have also produced show types, the Tumbler has the most subvarieties for the exhibition field and these include **Longfaced, Shortfaced, Clean legged,** and **Muffed.**

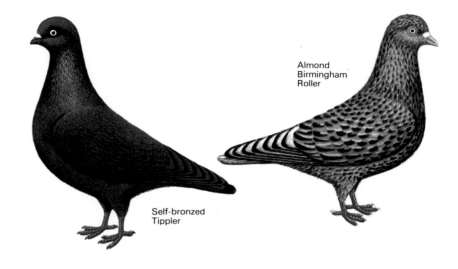

Almond Birmingham Roller

Self-bronzed Tippler

Domestic Poultry

Domestic poultry include those bird species and breeds that are kept mainly for eggs and meat. They include domestic fowl (hens, chickens, bantams), ducks, turkeys, and geese. Although not generally regarded as pets, poultry are often adopted as such. Some bantams are well suited to the role, being small and reasonably amenable to handling. The older breeds of bantams, such as **Rosecombs, Sebrights,** and **Perkins,** have been kept for generations purely for ornamental or exhibition purposes and do well as pets. Before keeping poultry in urban areas, however, it is wise to check on laws or other local prohibitions barring such pets.

HOUSING

Any weatherproof shelter free from drafts can be adapted for use. The houses should not be too warm. The best poultry houses are built specifically for the class of poultry intended to occupy them. Bantams require similar accommodation to large fowls but on a smaller scale. Ducks and geese have roughly the same needs except that perches are not necessary and nest boxes can be on floor level. Turkeys can be kept in the same type of house as large poultry, with a little more space.

The poultry house must be easy to keep clean and free from infestation by pests. It should be large enough to permit easy access by the owner or so constructed as to come apart for cleaning. Sectional type buildings are ideal.

A useful all-purpose house, 1.2m. (4ft.) long, 1.2m. (4ft.) wide, and 1.4m. (4.5ft.) high in front sloping to 1.2m. (4ft.) at the back, will sleep four to six large fowl or up to ten bantams. It should have a removable front or roof for cleaning purposes, perches fitted over a droppings board or shelf, out-

English Trumpeter

Satinette

Dark Checkered Racing Homer

Black Turbit

Red Tiger Swallow

Black
Carrier

Exhibition
Homer

Powdered
Silver Fantail

Black
Barb

droppings, a yearly coat of creosote, and periodic repairs will keep the house in good condition and the poultry healthy.

FEEDING REQUIREMENTS

A poultry mash or meal which is especially balanced to suit dietary requirements is commercially available for each class of poultry. There are those for free range layers, battery layers, intensive unit layers, broilers, growers, and young chicks. Turkeys, ducks, and pheasants in their different stages of development are catered to as well. The best method of feeding is by means of a trough or hopper. Household scraps can also be given as a supplement. Vegetable peelings and leftovers should be boiled, mixed with one of the meals to a drier consistency, and served warm. Poultry greatly appreciate this, especially in the winter months.

Even if the poultry are on grass, extra greenfood is always welcome, and if they are kept for intensive egg laying, it is essential to provide as much as they will eat. It can either be fed shredded or finely chopped for youngsters and bantams or fed whole from nets or racks. Cabbage, lettuce, and even rutabagas, and turnips are relished by poultry, and grass mowings may be used as long as they contain no long, stringy bits which can cause crop-binding and have not been treated with weedkillers. Uneaten greenfood should be cleared up before it begins to rot and smell.

A feeding of grain in the evening provides nourishment and warmth during the night. Wheat is the most suitable grain as it is a complete food. Corn (maize), barley, and oats—which are beneficial to growing stock—can also be given. All these are best used separately. If a mixed grain feed is pre-

side nest boxes, and a covered run or scratching shed. If the birds are to be confined to the house and have no outside run, reduce the number by about half. If ducks or geese are to occupy such a house, they must have access to more ground and a pond or stream if possible.

An alternative method of keeping poultry is to subdivide a large shed or outhouse into smaller units. In such a system it is a good idea to allow the birds out at liberty at convenient times. This system is popular with many keen exhibitors.

Poultry houses are best raised above ground level to discourage vermin. Also, if set on brick or stone piers about 30cm. (12in.) high, the floor will be free from ground dampness. The house must be secure against foxes and coyotes, all doors and windows should be securely fastened, and gaps or weak areas in walls, floors, or roofs must be repaired at first notice. Fresh air is essential to good health and adequate ventilation must be provided. However, all windows and ventilators must be covered with strong wire netting or metal bars set close enough so predators cannot get through.

The roof must be kept in good repair and be waterproof as poultry dislike damp, humid conditions. Perches should be adjusted for height according to breed or type; large heavy breeds cannot jump up to high roosts, whereas the lighter breeds and bantams prefer to perch as high as possible. Perches should preferably be made of planed

wood about 5cm. (2in.) square, with beveled corners or edges. Round perches are often blamed for crooked breastbones or breast blisters. Nest boxes should be provided, preferably accessible from outside the house, with a flap or lid to facilitate egg collection. Food and water vessels are best placed just above floor level on a shelf to prevent litter fouling them.

The house and run should always be clean and in neat order. Regular cleaning out of

Domestic poultry are best suited to large gardens or rural areas, such as this orchard where Muscovy Ducks and a few chickens are able to range free.

ferred, the grains should be purchased separately and then mixed. Mixed corn bought in pet stores sometimes consists of poor quality grain and cannot be recommended.

Feed poultry as much grain as they will eat; grain left lying around the floor indicates that the birds are being overfed. An approximate measure is a handful of grain per bird. Bantams need only about two handfuls for three or four birds, depending on whether they are the larger miniatures or small true bantams.

A very good food, to be used as a treat or conditioner, can be made from stale bread. The bread should be dried thoroughly in an oven and then broken into small pieces and soaked overnight in cold water. Before feeding it, the surplus water should be squeezed out and a little milk added. Most birds will eat this readily, either moist or mixed with a little dry meal.

Sprouted grain is another excellent food-stuff, especially in winter when other green-food may be scarce. It can be grown by filling a shallow dish or tray about 1.5cm. (0.5in.) deep with wheat or oats and covering the grain with cold water. The dish should be placed in a dark, warm place such as a cup-board and left there until the green shoots are 1.5–2.5cm. (0.5–1in.) high. The sprouting grain in the tray can then be fed to the fowls. Several trays can be started at intervals to keep a regular supply of this nutritious food to offer the birds.

Fowls should be given grit which is needed to grind up food and help make the eggshells. Mixed grit containing limestone for making shells, and harder chips for the grinding process are commercially obtainable. A water fountain will ensure access to clean water at all times.

Controlled breeding over the centuries has produced many breeds of poultry. The numerous types of bantam are ideal for the owner who wants fresh eggs but has a small garden.

DOMESTIC FOWL

All breeds of the domestic fowl are descended from the jungle fowl *(Gallus gallus)* which has been domesticated for some 4,000 years.

British and Northern European Breeds

Many of the British and North European breeds are especially suitable as pets or garden fowls. The majority have been bantamized for a long time and are especially well suited as pets for children. Their small size makes them easy to handle, and at least twice as many can be kept for the same cost in food and space as their larger equivalents.

Old English Game Fowl

Descended from the birds which were fought in the cockpits until about 150 years ago, the Game Fowl and its miniature have reached a very high standard of perfection, and may be thought of as the thoroughbred of the poultry world. Beauty of form, symmetry, and color are all attributes of this lovely old breed which is still bred in large numbers.

They are bred in many colors and have hard, close, and waxy plumage. They are great foragers and are ideal for those with large orchards, paddocks, or woodlots where they will find much of their own food. The bantams have similar form and feather and are bred in many colors. They tolerate confinements better than their large counter-parts and become very tame under such conditions. Both the bantam and fowl will hatch and rear their own chicks.

Cornish Game

The squat and scowling appearance of the Cornish Game has caused it to be compared to the Bulldog, although the bird is not always as fierce as it looks. This bird has a heavy cone-shaped body which is set on very short, thick shanks. It has a powerful neck, short broad head with overhung and fierce eyes, hooked beak, and a hard, close plumage. This breed is not for everyone. The bantams are exact miniature replicas.

Dorking

The Dorking is a heavily bodied bird with a rather low carriage; its special feature is the possession of a fifth toe. Mostly seen in **Darks** or **Silver-Grays,** both of which are single combed, there are **Cuckoos** which may have a rosecomb, and **Whites** which must have a rosecomb. This is a docile bird that makes a good garden pet. They are only rarely found in bantam forms.

Orpington

Orpingtons are of two types. The **Black and Blue** varieties, which are better left to the expert, and the **Buff.** The Black and Blue varieties have been compared to feather dusters with their masses of feather and fluff. The Buff is a much closer-feathered bird, more active, and better suited for free range than the Blacks and Blues. A **White** variety is sometimes seen and follows the Buff in type.

Sussex

The Sussex is similar in shape to the Dorking but has longer legs, four claws, and less tail. The **Light** variety is the most popular, but **Whites** and **Speckles** are common. Like the Buff Orpington they do well on free range or in fair-sized runs, but will also stand closer confinement. There are excellent **Sussex Bantams** in all varieties including a **Silver** variety seldom seen today in the large breed. They are ideal for beginners, being docile as well as good layers and sitters. Orpington Bantams are of a high standard.

Scots Dumpies

These resemble Dorkings with only four toes, and they are sometimes known as **Creepers.** The **Scots Gray** is more popular in Scotland than elsewhere. The bantam forms, which perhaps bear little relationship to the large breed, are charming little birds.

Hamburgh, Derbyshire Redcap and Old English Pheasant Fowl

This is a group of common origin. They all have rosecombs, fairly light bodies, and tight plumage. **Hamburghs** come in five color varieties: **Silver** and **Gold, Spangled, Silver Pencilled, Gold Pencilled,** and **Black.** The Derbyshire Redcap is bigger than the Hamburgh and has an extremely large, almost round rosecomb like a cap and reddish plumage marked with black half moons. It is very hardy. The Old English Pheasant Fowl is similar but has a smaller rosecomb, white earlobes, and a lighter ground color with black crescent shaped markings.

Rosecomb Bantam

This is a beautiful little bird with lustrous, beetle-green plumage which flows from head to tail in one long sweep. It has an attractive rosecomb and large white earlobes. It also has a jaunty proud carriage. A **White** variety is less common and is not quite so striking, lacking the contrast of the white lobes and black plumage. Like most old bantam breeds, they are friendly, easily tamed, and make good pets. Rosecomb bantams are best kept intensively and allowed out at liberty under supervision.

Sebright Bantam

Sebright bantams are perhaps even more

Silver Sebright · Nankin · Rosecombe Black · Buff Sussex · Dorking Dark · Redcap · Old English Game

beautiful than Rosecombs. Every feather is evenly laced all round with a black edging on either a white or buff ground. Those with predominantly white feathers are known as **Silvers,** and those with buff, as **Golds.** Males are henfeathered, which means that they have no pointed hackle feathers or sickles in their tails. Although fairly hardy as adults, Sebrights are delicate in early life and need great care in rearing. Sebrights are better kept intensively with access to lawns under supervision.

Nankin Bantam

These are true bantams with no large counterpart. Typical bantams in form and carriage, Nankins are deep buff or cinnamon in color and have large sweeping tails and usually single combs, although the rosecomb is standardized. They make charming pets and may be given full run of gardens or lawns.

Poland

Poland or Polish are not often seen in the large breed but are popular as bantams in the show world. Their chief feature is a very large crest and, in most varieties, whiskers and a beard. The **White-crested Blacks** and **Blues** lack beards, but the self colors and laced varieties are true to form. Because the crests sometimes obscure their sight, these nervous birds need careful handling.

Welsumer

The Welsumer, a brown egg breed originating in Holland, is of the natural black-red pattern and is attractive in color. Originally intended purely as a working fowl the standard was set to that end, and the breed still looks utilitarian. The Welsumer is single combed with yellow legs and flesh. Docile, yet active, this is an attractive garden bird. There is a bantamized version which, however, does not always lay brown eggs.

Barnevelder

The Barnevelder, also a brown egg breed from Holland, is larger and heavier than the Welsumer but is of a similar utility conformation. The plumage is dark brown with double black lacing on every feather. It is single combed and has yellow legs and flesh. Like the Welsumer, the Barnevelder is fairly docile though active and is an attractive garden bird. The bantam variety does not always lay brown eggs.

Old Dutch Bantam

This bird is like a small Old English Game Bantam in general appearance and color. Old Dutch Bantams have white lobes and single combs with larger, flowing tails than the Game Bantams. Like most old breeds of bantams they are ideal as children's pets.

Campine

The Campine, originating in Belgium, is bred in two varieties: the **Gold** and **Silver Pencilled.** Rather like a single-combed Hamburgh, this bird is flighty on free range and is better kept indoors. Campines have a proud and jaunty manner, the cocks always appearing to be about to crow. They are friendly, full of character, and can be recommended as pets.

Bearded Bantam

The Bearded Bantam from Belgium is bred in two forms and many colors. The **D'Ucle** is always single combed and feather legged while the **D'Anvers** must be rosecombed and have clean shanks. The most popular colors are **Millefluer, Quail, Porcelaine, Lavender, Cuckoo, Mottle, Black,** and **Blue.** The Bearded Bantam, like the Campine, has a proud and jaunty manner and is ideal as a pet.

Kriaenkoppe

This bird has a rather game-like character and an unusual walnut comb. The bantam

forms are becoming popular as showbirds and are perfect replicas of the large breed. Two colors are bred, the **Gold** and **Silver.**

Faverolle

The Faverolle is an attractive French breed that has a beard, slight legfeathers and, like the Dorking, five toes. There are several color varieties, most popular being the **Salmon** in which males are a mixture of red and black, and the females are red and pale buff. **Ermines** are like the Light Sussex in color, and there are also **White, Black,** and **Buff** varieties. This breed was fairly recently bantamized and, although still rather large, has proved quite popular.

La Fleche

This is a French breed which has a horn comb and two studs just in front of the beak. At one time fairly rare, this breed is being revived and should appeal to those who prefer an unusual type.

Mediterranean Breeds

The Mediterranean breeds were developed as egg producers and are of fairly light build and lack the broody instinct. Like most Light Breeds they are of a rather nervous disposition and are good fliers, so high fences are needed to restrain them if they are kept at liberty. They all adapt well to close quarters and under such conditions become quite tame.

Leghorn

Leghorns are bred in many colors and, although usually seen with large single combs, a rosecombed variety is standardized. They are active and smart in appearance, with flowing sickles, white lobes, and yellow legs. **Whites, Blues, Blacks,** and **Browns (Partridge)** are the most popular varieties. The miniature Leghorns are of excellent type and color and are popular with breeders.

Anconia

This breed is of similar ancestry to the Leghorn, and is bred mostly in the single comb type, although the rosecomb is sometimes available. Head size is less than in the Leghorn and only one color is bred—a beetle-green-black with triangular white tips to every feather. The legs are yellow with black spots. There is a bantam Anconia of high merit.

Minorca

This breed has a leg color that matches the plumage. **Blacks** are the most often seen, although **Blues** and **Whites** are standardized. Head points are a feature; the large single comb and white lobe are both of great importance in show birds. **Black Minorca Bantams** have reached a high standard, and **Blues** are being developed.

Andalusian

This breed is similar to the Minorca, which has been interbred with it. The general effect is of a blacklaced Blue Minorca, with leg color to match the blue ground color. The breed has a good following from experienced breeders who enjoy the challenge of difficult breeding problems. The Andalusian has been bantamized fairly recently, and the miniatures are of good type and color, although still a little oversized.

American Breeds

The American breeds resemble the British heavy types with the difference that they have yellow flesh and legs in contrast to the white of the British.

Rhode Island Reds

This breed has an oblong profile which has been compared to a brick with the corners knocked off. There is a rosecomb variety which is rarely seen, the single comb being usual. It is a rich chocolate-red in color, with some black in the (male's) tail and yellow or horn legs. They are excellent layers and are suitable for free range or more restricted conditions. The bantam forms are similar in all respects and are popular with fanciers.

New Hampshire Red.

This bird is deeper bodied than the Rhode Island Red and lighter in color. Otherwise they are similar in appearance. New Hampshire Reds are docile, good egg layers, and can be kept either free range or confined. They are not yet bantamized.

Plymouth Rock

These are active and workman-like fowls, well balanced with a rather upright stance. The **Barred** has a black and white pattern, the black bars being sharply defined. **Buffs** are an even shade of golden buff all over and are a good utility breed. **White, Black,** and **Partridge** varieties are also bred. **Rock Bantams** are popular in **Buffs** and **Barred,** the other varieties sometimes being seen.

Wyandottes

Wyandottes represent the American exhibition breed at its best, and they are bred in a large number of color varieties. The close fitting, helmet-shaped rosecomb is the hallmark of the breed and adds greatly to the overall appearance. Legs are of medium length and are a deep shade of yellow. Miniatures have been bred to an extremely high standard and probably achieve championship status more often than any other single breed.

Whites are the most popular in both large forms and bantams; **Blacks** are the second most popular in bantams but are not often seen in the large breed. **Partridge, Gold** and **Silver laced, Silver pencilled, Buff, Blue, Cuckoo,** and several other laced varieties are also bred and can usually be obtained from breeders. Docile and friendly yet quite active, the Wyandotte is a breed which will adapt to all conditions.

Asiatic and Australian Breeds

The importation of the Cochin and Brahma in the mid-nineteenth century from Asia laid the foundations of the modern poultry industry. Australia has one representative in the poultry world, the Australorp.

Cochin

This is a large, deep-bodied bird with a single comb and heavily feathered legs and feet. Several colors are bred, the chief ones being **Black, Blue, Buff, Partridge,** and **White.** A

Silver Wyandotte

Welsummer

Anconia

La Fleche

Plymouth

Campine Gold

Rhode Island Red

Leghorn Buff

Barnevelder

223

Phoenix
Black-Red

Silkie Buff

Brahma
Dark

Australorp

Sumatra Game

Croad
Langshan

Cochin Buff

Japanese
Black and
White
Longtailed

very tame and docile breed, Cochins are ideally suited as pets and may be kept at liberty or in restricted areas.

Brahma

This bird also has feathered shanks, but has tighter feathering than the Cochin and a triple or pea comb. There are three color varieties—**Dark, Light,** and **White**—the latter being scarce. In Europe and the United States a **Buff** is also bred. The male is mainly black with white lace hackles, and the female is gray with black pencilling. The Light Brahma is white with the same hackle and tail markings as the Dark. The breed has been bantamized for many years and is a good miniature reproduction of the originals. They are similar to the Cochins in temperament and may be kept under the same conditions.

Croad Langshan

The Croad Langshan is similar to the Cochin but with tighter plumage and less foot feather. An important feature of this bird is its high rising tail. **Blacks** are the most commonly seen and have lovely glossy plumage. They are suitable for both free-range or confined conditions. A **Modern Langshan** was once developed with a long neck and limbs but is seldom seen today. Croad Langshan bantams are sometimes available.

Sumatra Game

This is a glossy black fowl with a long tail carried low, a pea comb, dark red face, and double spurs on the legs. Many of the females of this breed also have double spurs. Although not very common, this breed is suitable for owners with a large garden or orchard.

Yokohama and Phoenix

These are the names by which **Japanese Longtailed Fowls** are known in the Western world. The Yokohama is walnut or pea combed and can be either **White** or **Red-saddled,** while the Phoenix is single combed and appears in **Duckwing** or **Black-red** varieties. The tail length of both types is usually 60–90cm. (2–3ft.), although in Japan birds with a tail of 9–10m. (30–33ft.) are not uncommon. Yokohamas and Phoenix are best kept on lawns and in orchards where they can be seen to advantage.

Cochin (Peking) Bantam

The Cochin, or Peking, Bantam is superficially like the Cochin, with its single comb, feather legs, and a mass of fluffy plumage. The general impression of the carriage, however, is much lower than in the Cochin and is like a ball. Bred in the same colors as Cochins, there are also the **Black, Blue Buff, Partridge,** and **White.** They are charming little birds that are easily tamed and highly recommended as pets. Reasonably hardy, they may be kept at liberty or indoors once they have attained full growth.

Japanese Bantam

The hallmark of a good Japanese, also known as a **Chabas Bantam,** is its very short shanks which give it the appearance of perpetually squatting down. The Japanese Bantam is a charming and unusual looking bird. The male has a single comb and towering, sword-shaped sickles, while the female has a normally shaped tail which is longer than usual and carried high. They are bred in **White, Black, Gray, Buff, Black-tailed White,** and also in silkie and frizzled feathered varieties. Like most old, true bantams they are good pets and popular with children.

Frizzles

Frizzles are not strictly Asiatic, being liable to occur in any breed of poultry. The **Frizzle Bantam** has been bred for many years as a separate breed or type and has regained popularity recently. It is single combed, rather like the Old English Game Bantam in type. Every feather must be well curled as if done with curling irons. Although they are quite hardy, they are better kept in well-sheltered runs. **Blue, Black, White,** and **Buff** varieties are the most common, but other colors are allowed.

Silkie Fowl

These are often regarded as bantams but are in fact standardized in Great Britain as a large breed. It is an ancient breed probably originating in the Orient, and it was known in Europe in the sixteenth century. Silkie fowls have several unusual features such as five toes, crests, a black skin, and a walnut comb. The plumage is soft, silky, and hair-like in texture. They are extremely docile and tame and make excellent sitters and mothers. The **White Silkie Fowl** is the most common, but **Black, Blue, Partridge,** and **Gold** varieties are also bred. These birds are highly recommended as garden pets.

Australorp

The name of this breed is an abbreviation for **Australian Orpington.** The original Black Orpingtons became very popular in Australia where they were developed as a dual purpose commercial fowl while retaining the original type. When the Black Orpington became purely an exhibition fowl in Great Britain, Australian Orpingtons were imported as commercial birds, and the present name was adopted. The breed has been successfully bantamized for many years now, and the miniature Australorps are among the most popular bantams. Both versions are active but fairly quiet birds, equally at home under confined or open conditions.

WATERFOWL

Waterfowl are best kept only where they have access to their natural element. They can be kept without having a stream or pond to swim in, but care must be taken to provide them with enough water in which they can completely submerge their heads. Plastic paddling pools which are commercially available are suitable, especially for the smaller ornamental ducks. If ornamental or wild ducks are to be kept, they are usually pinioned to prevent escape. Pinioning is best done by a skilled person soon after hatching. Another method is to cut short the primaries of one wing after each molt so that the bird is unbalanced in flight. Ducks can be messy creatures and small enclosures soon become fouled. Consequently they need a fairly large enclosure and access to running water if possible.

Geese make good guards and give a great deal of warning if strangers are near. They need plenty of space to meet their grazing requirements; six geese will eat as much grass as one sheep. They are hardy, but should be provided with a shelter to sleep in, allowing about 0.5m.^{2} (6 ft.^{2}) per bird. In the summer, good quality grass is often sufficient to meet their dietary requirements, but they should be provided with extra greenfood and grain in winter. Geese are not recommended for small gardens and are better suited to large orchards or paddocks with a natural water source. Nevertheless, it is not absolutely essential to provide swimming water.

Duck Breeds

Domestic ducks are all descended from wild species and often retain the same plumage pattern. The laying breeds are extremely productive, some being better layers than the modern hybrid hens.

Aylesbury, Pekin, and Rouen

Aylesbury ducks are massive white birds, bred mainly for their table properties. Pekins are similar but have a more upright carriage and a creamier colored plumage. Rouens are large table ducks with the Mallard plumage pattern.

Black East Indian and Cayuga

Black East Iindian Ducks may be regarded as the black sport of the Common Mallard. They are a lustrous black including bill and legs. The Cayuga is similar to the East Indian except that it is about four times bigger in size.

Indian Runner

This breed, originally from the East, is a good egg producer. Indian Runners are tall and slim and carry their bodies almost upright, having been compared to a bottle on legs. Several colors are bred; **Fawn, Fawn and White, Black, Chocolate,** and **White** are all standardized.

Campbell

This is also a laying duck and was developed

225

Brecon Buff · Toulouse · Buff · Beltsville White · Norfolk Black · Embden · Chinese

about the beginning of the twentieth century from a cross between the Runner and Common Mallard. The **Khaki Campbell** was named for its similarity in color to the British army uniform and was the original Campbell. A **White** variety exists, but it is uncommon.

Orpington

This is a dual-purpose breed, bred for both laying and table. In type it is similar to the Campbell, but the color is more of a buff with seal brown head and neck, both sexes being alike.

Muscovy

This is a distinct species (*Caizing moschata*) originating from South America. They are characterized by a caruncle on the face and over the base of the bill and a small crest, which is raised when the birds are excited. The drakes are twice the size of the ducks. These birds are popular as ornamental ducks around the garden or farm.

Crested

Crested ducks are like the Aylesburg in type but have large globular crests on the head. Once almost extinct they are now coming back into favor as ornamentals.

Silver Appleyard, Mandarin, and Carolina

The Silver Appleyard is a bantam duck quite often seen at shows. Being small it is suitable for the garden. The Mandarin and Carolina ducks are true wild species and are also suitable for the garden. The Mandarin is a beautiful bird that is chestnut, black, and white in color and has two "sails" which are raised over its back. The Carolina is related to the Mandarin and is similar in appearance

but lacks the sails. Both breed quite freely in suitable conditions.

Goose Breeds

Many of the wild geese can be kept under semidomestic conditions but some previous experience with farmyard geese is advisable.

Embden, Toulouse, and English

The Embden is a large white goose with blue eyes and a broad, thick, well-rounded body. The Toulouse, which originated in France, is a thickset goose with a characteristic gullet and paunch, and it comes in varying shades of gray. English Geese are rather like smaller variations of the Embden and Toulouse. They are bred in **White, Gray,** and **Gray-black.** English geese are hardy but poor layers.

Roman, Brecon Buff, and Sebastopol

Roman geese are active, graceful, and fairly docile white geese of medium size. The Brecan Buff goose resembles a buff Toulouse in color but English in type. Sebastopol geese are characterized by their long, curled plumage.

Chinese

The Chinese is sometimes known as a **Swangoose** because it is descended from the Asiatic wild goose of that name (*Anser cygnoides*). Besides the **White** there is a **Brown** variety which is of several shades of fawn.

TURKEYS

Turkeys have not been domesticated for nearly so long as domestic fowl and waterfowl, and they are consequently not as truly tame. Housing can be similar to that of

domestic fowls although turkeys need more space. They do well on free range and are good foragers, but otherwise should be fed on the special turkey rations which can be purchased from poultry feed merchants. Turkeys are suitable for owners with plenty of space, preferably a paddock or large orchard.

The turkey (*Meleagris gallopovo*) is indigenous to America and was raised by Indians. The modern domestic is thought to have descended from two differing wild subspecies—one in Mexico, the other in the United States. Vaccinations are imperative to ward off such diseases as Newcastle disease, air sac disease, and Marek's disease, and sanitation is extremely important.

Brooding and rearing of turkey chicks requires controlled temperatures which vary according to the age of the chicks and the surroundings. If more than one chick is being raised, debeaking (removal of part of the upper beak) may be desirable to reduce picking and cannibalistic traits. They do not require too much light for optimal growth, but a high-protein diet is necessary during rapid growth periods.

Turkey Breeds

As the turkey is now primarily kept by large operators as a commercial venture many of the old breeds most suitable for the individual owner are now becoming scarce.

Norfolk Black and The Bronze

The Norfolk Black is one of the oldest of the domestic turkey breeds and until recently was extremely common. It is a dense black all

Liberty peacocks provide a splendid sight in our parks and big gardens but are totally unsuitable in built-up areas because of their loud cries.

over with no admixture of any other color. The Bronze has been known by many names, including the **Cambridge** and **Cambridge Bronze,** but after being crossed with the American Mammoth Bronze the simple title of **Bronze** was finally adopted. It is a large bird, the male weighing up to 18kg. (40lb.), and it is a metallic bronze color with some black and white in the tail and wings.

Buff, White Holland, and Beltsville White The Buff is really of a copper hue rather than buff and is related to the White Holland or British White with which it shares the same standard for type. It is called the White Holland in the United States to distinguish it from the Beltsville White which has been developed from it as a commercial table breed.

Game Birds

A number of game birds, that is those which are frequently hunted in the wild for sport, have found their way into the domestic environment as ornamental garden and aviary birds. Some are recognized as the wild ancestors of our domestic poultry. This group includes the pheasants, jungle fowl, quail, and peafowl, all members of the family Phasianidae.

PHEASANTS AND JUNGLE FOWL

No other group of birds can claim to have made such an impact on the social and economic history of mankind. As sporting birds pheasants have been widely introduced throughout the Old and New Worlds. Their impact upon the economic scene has been even greater, since all breeds of domestic fowl are descended from one or more of the four species of jungle fowl.

Pheasants are hardy, fairly easy to rear, and make a colorful attraction in the garden or aviary. There are many beautiful varieties, but it is better for the beginner to start with the older, better known breeds. Pheasants are inclined to be quarrelsome with each other and are better kept in pairs or trios unless plenty of space is available. They mix well with other birds such as parakeets or doves, but the aviary must be designed to suit the pheasants, allowing them plenty of room. Although a hen pheasant makes a good mother, chicks can be reared by domestic fowls or bantams. The **Blacknecked** or **Common Pheasant** (*Phasianus colchicus*) is perhaps the most familiar bird. It is really native to parts of Asia but is now naturalized throughout Europe and North America where it has interbred with the **Chinese Ringnecked Pheasant** (another introduced

227

(1) Bobwhite Quail
(2) California Quail

parts with black and orange wings. Unlike other jungle fowl and domestic fowls, the Green Jungle Fowl has only one wattle—the fleshy tissue hanging from the neck. The **Gray Jungle Fowl** (*G. sonnerati*), also known as **Sonnerod's Fowl,** is perhaps the most beautiful of this group. The male has spotted feathers in brown, yellow, and white, rust-colored shoulders, and blue-gray underparts. Females are mostly brown with black-spotted wings.

PEAFOWL (PEACOCKS)

Peafowl are the most splendid members of the pheasant family. The male **Indian Peafowl** (*Pavo cristatus*)—the familiar **Peacock** which comes from India and Sri Lanka—is outstanding for its overall coloring and for its enormous spreading tail, which is of primary importance in courtship and a delight to the onlooker. The female (peahen) is much more dull in color and lacks the ornamental tail feathers. A closely related, but less common, species from Burma, Indochina, Malaysia, and Java is the **Green Peafowl** (*P. muticus*).

Over the centuries peafowl have been much admired for their beauty and hunted for their flesh, while in more recent times they have become a popular addition to parks and gardens. They may be kept at liberty on lawns or in spacious flights. If allowed to run at liberty, peafowl should be pinioned. They can be a nuisance in an ornamental garden, and their loud cries early in the morning are

variety of the same species). These birds are hardy, fairly easy to tame, and easily obtainable.

The male of the **Golden Pheasant** (*Chrysolophus pictus*) is a beautiful bird of bright golden plumage barred with black on the neck and a long tail of brown and chestnut. The male does not achieve full color until its second year. The female is dull brown in color. It is hardy, docile, and makes a good pet. Another prized ornamental pheasant is **Lady Amherst's** (*C. amherstiae*). This is a very elegant but hardy pheasant. Much like the Golden in build, the male has vivid green and blue wings, gray breast, and a gray tail which is marked with chestnut. The ruff is white, capped with scarlet. The female is a dull brown and hard to distinguish from the female Golden Pheasant. Full coloring of the male is reached in its second year.

In spite of their long lineage and importance, about one-third of the species of ornamental pheasants is now threatened with extinction. Fortunately bird lovers in both the United States and Great Britain are breeding some of these rare kinds, thus strengthening their numbers and in some cases sending eggs or birds back to their countries of origin for release in their native habitat.

Jungle fowl, as might be expected, do best when allowed full freedom. They can be kept in confinement with plenty of room and should be segregated into pairs or trios as the cocks are inveterate fighters. Management in general is the same as for bantams.

The **Red Jungle Fowl** (*Gallus gallus*) is almost certainly the main ancestor of all the modern breeds of domestic fowls. Somewhat between the Old English Game Fowl and the Old English Game Bantam in size, it is black-red in color, the females being partridge or brown with some yellow and black markings. The **Green Jungle Fowl** (*G. varius*) is heavier built than the Red Jungle and comes from Java. Males are mostly green on the upper

The art of falconry is an ancient sport that today, for the sake of the birds, should be restricted to a few experienced handlers. Shown here is a tame Lanner Falcon.

228

liable to upset neighbors. Although hardy and willing to roost outside even in bad weather, a shelter should be provided. Feeding requirements are the same as for turkeys. The Indian Peafowl is believed to be the least pugnacious of the peafowl and thus the best for beginners. The chicks tend to be delicate and prone to colds and must be kept clean and dry in a shelter or coop.

QUAIL

Quail are small, plump birds resembling fowls. There are two main groups: the New World and Old World quail. The most commonly kept New World species are the **California Quail** (*Lophortyx californicus*) and **Bobwhite Quail** (*Colinus virginianus*).

The Old World quail are considerably smaller; most males have striking markings on the head and throat, which in some species extend to the underparts. Otherwise, both sexes are cryptically colored so the birds blend with the grasslands and undergrowth where they live. Quail walk and run along the ground and only rarely take to the wing, although they can fly well. The **Japanese** or **Coturnix Quail** (*Coturnix japonica*) has been successfully domesticated by the Japanese. It is occasionally kept as an aviary bird, but is not as attractive as the **Chinese Painted Quail** (*C. chinensis*) which is often incorrectly known as the Button Quail.

Quails are not aggressive toward other types of bird, and pairs can be safely housed with many kinds, including some small softbills. They make an interesting contrast with the perching birds and utilize the floor space that is otherwise barely used. If they are kept in a cage it must be the box type and the floor area should be covered by a thick layer of sand or earth. Quail dislike damp conditions so a suitable outdoor aviary should be sited in a sunny position and have a well-drained, grass-covered floor with a patch of dry sand or earth for dust bathing. They should be brought indoors or shut in a shelter each night during the winter when frosts are likely.

If quails are startled, especially during the period immediately after being introduced to a new cage or aviary, they are inclined to fly upwards and may injure themselves. To minimize this risk, a small box with an open side or some form of shelter should be placed in a corner as a retreat.

Their basic diet consists of a seed mixture. Some appreciate greenfood, and most will quickly gobble up any small insects, including mealworms and maggots. If adults can be enticed to eat a canary rearing food, a softbill or insectile mixture, or even bread moistened with milk, it will be an advantage when they are raising young. This food can be mixed with finely chopped hard-boiled egg yolk, lettuce, and crushed chick starter crumbs or biscuit. Quail sometimes lay ten or more large eggs, which the females incubate for seventeen to twenty-one days. They nest on the ground and usually conceal their eggs

One of the most attractive of all owls is the Snowy Owl, which is frequently seen in bird collections of zoos and wildlife parks. They are native to the northern regions of Eurasia and America. Because of their size they are not suitable as pets.

beneath a clump of grass or undergrowth. If there is not a nesting place to their liking, females sometimes lay all over an area and ignore the eggs. If abandoned eggs are collected and placed in a shallow ditch in the ground, the hens will sometimes incubate them; otherwise they can be artificially hatched and reared.

Owls and Birds of Prey

Owls and birds of prey are, of course, undomesticated carnivores and as such they hardly make suitable pets. Of these two quite different kinds of birds, owls are the most frequently kept because of their quieter natures and apparent reserve; birds of prey by comparison are nervy and excitable. It is not unusual for orphaned owlets to be hand reared, whereupon many make charming pets while others never seem to lose their wildness and distrust of human beings.

With the current global pressures on wildlife, and the position of predatory birds at the head of a food chain (which means that even when "common" in an area their numbers are much less than that of seedeaters), no wild animal and certainly no healthy bird of prey should be taken from the wild. It is illegal in much of the world to keep a healthy bird of prey which has not been bred in captivity. The true birds of prey (falcons, hawks, eagles, etc.) are only suited to captivity in exceptional circumstances.

There are still some devoted enthusiasts of the art of falconry. This ancient practice calls for infinite patience in the trainer, who is apparently well rewarded by the resulting relationship. With the current protection of all birds of prey, falconry will be a limited sport.

Some birds of prey will, if hand reared, become tame and imprinted on their owner but most become either lethargic or excitable and neurotic. They demand special care and special accommodation if they are to prosper.

Birds of prey, including owls such as this young Tawny Owl, enter the pet environment when orphaned or injured. Healthy adult birds should not be taken from the wild, since many species are endangered.

Many of the training techniques are opposite to those we would consider correct for other birds.

Perhaps one of the major differences between birds of prey and owls in captivity is their manner of flight; the former's is rapid and direct while that of owls is slower and more deliberate. A falcon may "erupt" from a perch straight into the wire netting of its aviary and perhaps injure itself, but an owl will generally find another perch.

Handling birds so well equipped with talons and strong beaks is no easy matter; usually a gloved fist is necessary for even a tame bird to sit on. Birds of prey and especially owls give the impression of being more intelligent than other birds. They both greatly resent and remember rough treatment.

Keeping owls and birds of prey does have some advantages. They need to be fed only once a day and can readily withstand one or two days a week without food; indeed it is considered an essential part of their correct management. Their food does not as a rule require troublesome preparation. Day-old chicks, which may be obtained from a local hatchery, are a convenient complete food—providing the roughage essential to all carnivorous birds and also the vitamin-rich entrails and yolk sac.

Cage cleaning is another activity that can be reduced with birds of prey. Their droppings are high in ammonia and do not constitute a health hazard if left for a few weeks at a time. Their regurgitated pellets are simply fur, bone, and maybe the wingcases of insects. It is now almost a recognized part of their captive-breeding management that birds of prey are disturbed as little as possible. Owls in particular are well known for being highly dangerous when nesting.

FISH

Fish were probably first kept as a food source either in a garden pond or domestic vessel, but later they were kept because of their beauty and behavior. Keeping goldfish as pets dates back to the eleventh century in China, and the *Book of Vermillion Fish* written by Cheng Chi'en-te in 1596 describes the management of goldfish keeping. In 1665 Samuel Pepys in his famous diary describes fish kept in a glass of water.

The present-day hobbyist has a wide choice—the common cold-water fish, tropical freshwater fish, or marine tropical fish. Marine tropical fish are more expensive, and difficult to keep, so the aquarist must have the correct equipment and manage the tank carefully. There is enough variety, however, for everyone to have a choice. Fish have some advantages as pets: they do not need taking for walks, and they may be left for up to three weeks when their owner is on vacation. The well-kept community tank is an asset to the decor of any home.

The Tropical Freshwater Aquarium

Most tropical freshwater fish are easy to keep if the aquarist provides proper conditions. Many of the thousands of species of tropical freshwater fish are beautiful and with freshwater plants and some rockwork, they create a beautiful aquascape. In addition their breeding and raising of the young offer a great challenge and source of satisfaction to the fish keeper.

The tropical freshwater aquarium can vary from a simple tank with just one or two specimens to a complex habitat such as this one, featuring a school of Cardinal Tetras swimming among a variety of plants.

TANK EQUIPMENT

Types of Tank

There are several types of tank available for the tropical freshwater aquarist. The most popular of these is the all glass tank, made out of five sheets of glass sealed together with silicone rubber. Glass tanks are available in standard sizes: 45 x 30 x 30cm. (18 x 12 x 12in.), 60 x 30 x 30cm. (24 x 12 x 12in.), 90 x 30 x 30cm. (36 x 12 x 12in.) and 120 x 30 x 30cm. (48 x 12 x 12in.), although larger sizes can be obtained as special orders. One piece glass tanks are also available but only in smaller sizes up to 45 x 30 x 30cm. (18 x 12 x 12in). The best shaped tanks have a greater length than depth so that the surface area of the water is large in relation to depth thus allowing better exchange of gases between air and water.

The angle-iron frame tank, although

popular, has disadvantages. The iron frame on the tank's top rusts where the water condenses, and the products of corrosion may be toxic to fishes. These tanks can be prevented from rusting by treating in the following way: sand the surface of the metal to remove all paint and rust, paint with two coats of galvanizing paint, and then paint with two coats of a good enamel paint. Stainless steel frame tanks or plastic-coated angle-iron tanks avoid this problem.

Framed tanks will, if left dry for a period of time, tend to leak when refilled because the putty dries out and cracks. In this case the tank must be resealed with a silicone rubber sealant. Plastic tanks are usually only available in small sizes, are easily scratched, and may crack easily.

Every tank must have a lid to prevent evaporation, to keep the fish from jumping out, and to prevent dust from settling on the water surface. A sheet of glass makes an effective cover if a lid is not already provided with the tank. Special hoods are sold with many tanks. These are usually attractive and contain fittings for lights or spaces to fit lights; they have holes for the wires to pass through to the heater and thermostat. Many hoods also have an evaporation cover of transparent plastic or glass which prevents water condensing on the light fittings.

Heating

Most tropical fish live at a temperature of 22–27°C. (72–81°F.), which is also suitable for most aquarium plants.

The most common method of heating a tank is by means of an immersed heater and thermostat. These can be obtained separately (in which case they have to be wired together) or as a combined heater thermostat unit. The combined heater thermostat is completely submersible.

When the heater and thermostat are separate, the heater is always completely sub-

mersible, but the thermostat may be either submersible or designed so that the part with controls projects over the top of the tank. The partly submersible type can therefore be adjusted easily while the submersible type has to be removed from the tank to be adjusted. The heater should be placed at the bottom of the tank to give the most efficient heating since warm water rises. The thermostat should be placed as far from the heater as possible to ensure that the whole tank is heated. The manufacturer's instructions should be followed carefully when connecting heater and thermostat to the electricity supply.

A thermometer is necessary to check the water temperature in the tank. Mercury or alcohol column thermometers with the scale

The fascination of keeping fish attracts all ages. Many pet shops stock tropical fish. When buying fish from a pet shop or a dealer make sure the tanks are clean and appear disease-free.

marked on the glass are best. Some thermometers have a suction disc for attaching to the glass of the tank.

If there are many tanks in one room, it may be easier to heat the room to the required temperature rather than heat each tank individually. Alternately, tanks can be heated by means of hot pipes running underneath the tank.

Aeration and Filtration

Aeration and filtration are necessary when the tank contains many fish or a community

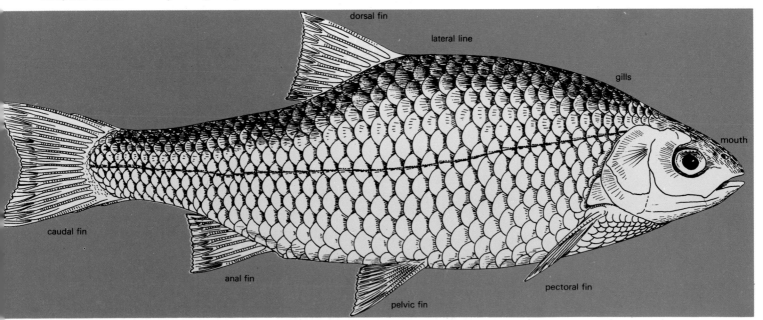

EQUIPMENT	DECORATION	FISH FOR SINGLE SPECIES TANK
Glass or Plastic Tank	Gravel	20 Neons
Tank hood	Plants (to choice)	or
Lighting	Rocks	20 Cardinal Tetras
Heater		plus
Thermostat		1 Sucking Loach
Thermometer		(for cleaning up algae)
Pump		
Filter (internal)		

In some tanks a filter may be required to clean as well as to aerate the water. There are several types of filters such as box filters inside the tank, filters fixed to the outside of the tank and through which the water is pumped, and under-gravel filters. Whatever type of filter is used, the principle remains basically the same: water is forced through the filter by means of a pump, and any suspended particles in the water are trapped in the filter material. Pumps and filters are available from most pet shops. A particular point to bear in mind is that the more expensive pumps are usually quieter and that internal filters usually need less attention than external filters. The manufacturer's instructions should be carefully read before the pump and filter are set up.

Lighting

Lighting is necessary for the growth of plants, as well as enhancing the fish. Some types of lighting exaggerate fish colors.

WATER

The health of aquarium fish depends greatly on the hardness of the water and the degree of acidity or alkalinity (pH).

The hardness of water is determined by the amount of calcium or magnesium in the water; the more calcium or magnesium the water contains, the greater the degree of hardness. The type of water depends on the rocks and soil through which the water passes before it is collected and piped into our water systems. If rain lands on limestone or chalk the water will pick up calcium. The calcium can combine with carbonate to form calcium carbonate, which will cause hardness. Hardness caused by calcium is temporary and can be removed by boiling the water and filtering

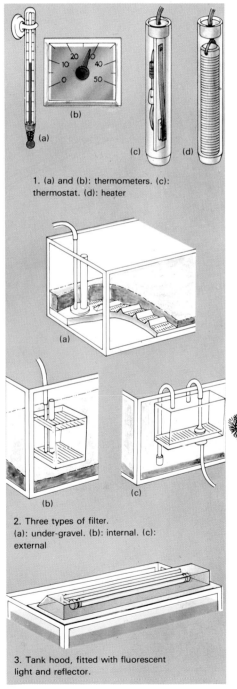

1. (a) and (b): thermometers. (c): thermostat. (d): heater

(a)

2. Three types of filter. (a): under-gravel. (b): internal. (c): external

3. Tank hood, fitted with fluorescent light and reflector.

of large fish. Aeration provides an air stream which agitates the water and helps the exchange of gases from the air to the water. Oxygen passes from the air to the water where some is dissolved. Because fish use up oxygen during respiration there has to be a continuous passage of oxygen from the air to the water. Fish produce carbon dioxide during respiration which also dissolves in water and becomes toxic if it builds up to high concentrations. This carbon dioxide diffuses from the water at the surface. If the water is agitated by means of an air stream so that it comes into greater contact with the air, the carbon dioxide diffuses out and oxygen is taken in. The air stream is provided by means of an air stone which is connected to a small electric pump, and several air stones can be connected to one pump.

Left. *Essential equipment for the tropical freshwater aquarium.*

Bottom. *Other aquarium equipment: (1) Catching net. (2) Tube cleaner. (3) Magnetic scraper used to clean algae from the glass. (4) Air stones used to diffuse air bubbles produced by a simple aerator.*

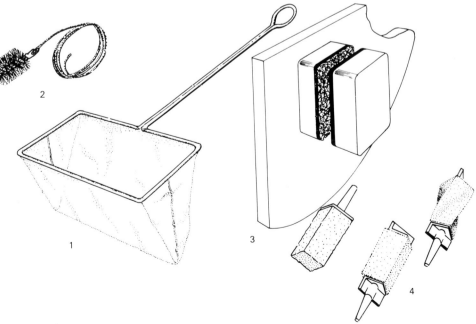

the precipitated calcium carbonate. Hard water can also be softened by use of ion-exchange resins (available in aquarist shops) which exchange calcium ions for "soft" sodium ions. Hardness caused by magnesium is permanent. Hard water does not lather well with soap whereas soft water does.

A good source of soft water is rainwater collected when the air is unpolluted because rain picks up chemicals in the air which may be toxic to fish. Rainwater can be collected by allowing rain to run into a plastic (to avoid contamination by metals) container. This water will be considerably softer than tap water and can be used for fish that prefer soft water. Rainwater is also preferable to tap water because it does not contain chlorine. Soft water can be hardened by adding rocks which contain lime to the tank gravel.

The acidity or alkalinity of the water is determined by the hydrogen ion concentration which is expressed in terms of pH. The pH of the water can be gauged by means of pH paper or Universal Indicator solution which turn a definite color for each level of pH. The range of pH suitable for fish keeping is pH6 (moderately acid) to pH9 (moderately alkaline); extremes of pH are not suitable. Soft water tends to be more acidic than hard water. If the water is too alkaline, previously boiled peat can be placed in the filter as a source of humic acid which passes to the water.

DECOR

Decoration in the form of gravel, rocks, and plants makes the tank attractive. The base of

the tank should be covered by gravel which are about 3mm. (0.1in.) to 5mm. (0.2in.) in diameter. If the gravel is too small the mulm (organic sediment) in the tank will lie on top

Top. *Bogwood, that is wood that has been preserved in peat bogs, can be used to build up terraces and give stepped background to a tank. It does not rot like ordinary wood.*

Bottom. *Common aquarium plants;* (1) Myriophyllum elatinoides. (2) Aponogeton undulatus. (3) Anubias congensis. (4) Egeria densa. (5) Riccia. (6) Hygrophila polysperma. (7) Salvinia auriculata. (8) Bacopa cardiniana. (9) Acorus gramineus. (10) Aponogeton fenestralis. (11) Vallisneria spiralis. (12) Pistia stratiotes. (13) Echinodorus paniculatus. (14) Cryptocoryne becketti. (15) Cabomba caroliana.

233

of it and look unsightly; if the gravel is too large pieces of uneaten food will fall between it and decay. Also, gravel of the size indicated provides an excellent medium for growing plants. Attractive rocks which can be bought or gathered from the seashore, streams, or rivers, add to the beauty of the tank. Limestone and marble should not be used because they harden the water.

TROPICAL FRESHWATER PLANTS

Plants are essential to an aquarium since they provide hiding places, shade, boundaries for territorial fish, places for fish eggs, and even food for vegetarian species. Physiologically, plants absorb respired carbon dioxide from the fish and use it for photosynthesis. They take up minerals through their roots, aerate the gravel, and finally release oxygen to the water as a by-product of photosynthesis.

Common Tropical Freshwater Plants

Anubias.
These are slow growing decorative plants with tough leaves and a creeping rhizome. *A. lanceolata*, which measures 30cm. (12in.), has lanceolate waxy leaves of a dark green color. The midrib and veins are distinctly visible. The petiole is reddish brown. *A. nana* and *A. afzelii* are also dark green but shorter, measuring 20cm. (8in.) in height, and have smaller leaves than *A. lanceolata*.

Aponogeton
These plants produce thin undulating leaves from a creeping tuber. *A. crispus* has long narrow lanceolate leaves, bright green in color with crinkled edges. Height is 25cm. (10in.). *A. ulvaceus* is a good centerpiece plant. It has pale green leaves which are translucent and spiraling with undulating margins. The leaves can reach 45cm. (18in.) in length. *A. natans* is similar to *A. ulvaceus* but has a long petiole. Leaf length is 20cm. (8in.). *A. undulatus* is translucent, pale green to bronze in color with lanceolate leaves that have a distinct midrib. The leaves have undulated margins. Height is 40cm. (16in.). *A. fenestralis*, commonly known as the **Madagascar Lace Plant,** is easily recognized by the skeleton-like appearance of its leaves, which are broad and oblong, reddish brown initially, becoming dark green when mature. Several strong veins parallel the midrib, and numerous cross veins produce the fenestrations. Although appearing fragile, they are hardy plants once established.

Cabomba
Also known as **fanworts,** cabombas have dichotomously branched leaves which are finely dissected and occur in pairs or whorls on the stem. The color varies from bright to brownish green. *C. caroliniana* has leaves measuring 2.5–5cm. (1–2in.) across, that are repeatedly divided into filiform segments. The floating leaves are 2cm. (0.75in.) long and entire. This plant will sometimes flower in a community tank. *C. aquatica* has paired leaves which are more finely divided while *C. piauhyensis* has reddish brown leaves.

Ceratopteris.
This is a genus of aquatic ferns. They have fronds (leaves) with divided pinnae. *C. thalictroides* (**Indian Fern**) has, when grown submerged, fronds of different lengths and shapes which are bright green in color. The margins of the pinnae produce small sprouts which can be propagated. When grown floating, the plant has branching roots with dense root hairs. The fronds lie flat on the surface forming a rosette. Young plants again form on the pinnae. *C. cornuta* (**Floating Fern**) has deep green, fleshy fronds which are shaped like an oak leaf. Each rosette produces dense roots. This plant is a fast grower which can be propagated.

Cryptocoryne
These plants can be as much as 50cm. (20in.) in height. There are fifty species in cultivation, displaying a variety of shapes and colors. They are delicate, slow-growing plants that can lose leaves when transplanted, but these soon develop again. *C. affinis* has lanceolate leaves with slight undulations. A brown-red petiole sets off the bluish green upper leaf surface and purple undersurface. The midrib is light green to white. Height is 30cm. (12in.). *C. beckettii* has lanceolate leaves which are green to reddish brown and brownish on the lower surface. They reach a height of 25cm. (10in.). *C. ciliata* has tapering pale green leaves, up to 5cm. (2in.) wide and 25cm. (10in.) long. The leaf edges are furled. Height is 35cm. (14in.). *C. cordata* is a highly decorative plant with dark green leaves that have purplish undersides. Height is 35cm. (14in.). *C. thawaitesii* has distinctive, finely serrated leaves with a roughened surface and leathery texture. The plant is dark green to yellowish brown and measures 15cm. (6in.). *C. willissii* has lanceolate deep green leaves up to 15cm. (6in.) long. The leaves often have purple or brown tinted veins. The petiole is reddish brown. Height is 25cm. (10in.).

Echinodorus
Also known as **swordplants,** members of the genus *Echinordus* have a bush-like appearance. They are ideal for center displays, but need good lighting. *E. paniculatus* (**Amazon

Swordplant)** grows up to 35cm. (14in.) long and has pale green lanceolate leaves with pointed tips. The plant has a rosette form. *E. brevipedicellatus* (**Junior Swordplant**) has lanceolate leaves up to 20cm. (8in.) long. *E. berteroi* (**Cellophane Plant**) produces a series of translucent lanceolate leaves with long petioles. These then develop by petiole and lamina growth into heart-shaped leaves. *E. grisebachii* is a smaller species, 15–20cm. (6–8in.) high with dark green, pointed elliptical leaves. It is easy to grow and produces chains of new plants.

Hygrophila
These are ideal plants for use as a screen or partition. *H. polysperma* is a branching plant which tends to be bushy. It has bright, pale green, entire leaves that develop in pairs and are lanceolate in shape. The thin round stem is sturdy. *H. difformis* has finely divided leaves.

Ludwigia
These are easy to propagate, especially from cuttings. *L. natans* is a strong plant producing roots at the lower nodes. The leaves are dark green, glossy above, and crimson-purple below when observed in good light. They are oval in shape, narrowing to a petiole the same length as the leaf blade. *L. arcuata* is less common. It has slender leaves, pale to bronze in color.

Myriophyllum
These plants have feather-like leaves, arranged in whorls of four to six. *M. brasiliense* (**Parrot's Feather**) has a weak stem that may grow out of water. The feathery leaves are yellow to blue-green and set in whorls. *M. heterophylum* and *M. elatinoides* are similar and grow well in aquaria.

Sagittaria
These are plants with erect leaves that are linear in shape, but have no distinction between the leaf and petiole. They form a central crown and can develop stolons bearing young plants. *S. latifolia* has long, fleshy linear leaves up to 45cm. (18in.) long and 2.5cm. (1in.) wide that are dark green in color. *S. subulata* is finer with long linear leaves. Although it is thicker, it resembles grass. Height is 35cm. (18in.).

Some plants suitable for tropical freshwater aquariums: Facing Page Center. Ceratopteris cornuta. Facing Page Right. Hygrophila difformis. Left. Ludwigia repens.

Vallisneria

Also known as **eel grass,** vallisnerias are favorite aquarium plants that need good lighting. The plants have elongated ribbon-like leaves arising from a basal crown. *V. spiralis* has narrow linear leaves which taper and twist spirally in some varieties. The leaves are 2cm. (0.15in.) wide and up to 30cm. (12in.) tall. The color varies from pale green to reddish brown. These plants produce runners in large numbers and are easily propagated. *V. gigantea* should be restricted to large aquaria. It has broad leaves 4cm. (1.5in.) across which can reach 1.2m. (48in.) in length. This plant prefers cooler temperatures.

Planting

Planting should take place after the water in the new tank has matured a day or two. The chief requirement for plant growth is light, which is best provided by top lighting from either fluorescent tubes or tungsten lamps of sufficient intensity. Usually, one 40 watt bulb per 900cm.^{2} (1ft.^{2}) of surface for a ten hour period is enough in the standard tank. Excessive light or direct sunlight will cause unsightly algal growth on the glass. Commercially available bulbs have been especially designed to aid plant growth.

The nature of the water does not affect the growth of plants too much as they are tolerant of a wider pH range than the fish. The rooting medium is important, and plants are normally embedded in fine sand or gravel. Soil makes the tank unsightly. For specimen plants, a thin layer of clay, 1cm. (0.4in.) deep, covered by gravel will assist growth. Large plants such as species of *Anubia, Cryptocoryne, Echinodorus,* and *Aponogeton* can be put into plant pots containing an equal mixture of coarse sand, peat, and garden soil covered with gravel. However, soil, sand, or peat under the gravel is not recommended for a community tank.

If cuttings are planted, the leaves should be removed from the lowest portion of the stem. Then the shoots can be put together, weighed down, and pressed into the gravel. Species of *Ludwigia, Miriophyllum, Hy-*

grophilia, and *Cabomba* can be planted in this way. If the plants are intact, the roots should simply be buried. With species of *Sagittaria, Ceratoperis,* and *Vallisneria,* the swollen bases should be exposed while with *Echinodorus, Cryptocoryne* and *Aponogeton,* the leaf bases should be just above the gravel. Planting is best done by hand because plant tissue is delicate. In a community tank, the larger plants should be arranged at the back.

Once set up and established, occasional gardening must be done. Growth and appearance are improved by removing old, deformed and yellowing leaves and pinching stem apexes to encourage branching and lateral leaf development. Submerged leaves will remain healthier and retain their color if floating leaves are cut back.

Propagation

The propagation of tropical freshwater plants can be achieved in various ways depending on the species. Many species can be propagated by taking cuttings from established stock, while with others, the root stocks can be divided and planted separately. Species of *Cryptocoryne* and *Vallisneria* produce stolons with small plantlets. Once these have rooted they can be cut off the parent plant. Propagation from seed is difficult. It can, however, be achieved by allowing the parent plant to flower so that pollination and fertilization may occur. In some species both male and female plants are required since not all plants are bisexual. If seeds form, they may not develop to maturity. If they do mature, the first sign will most likely be the growth of small plants from the gravel at the base of the parent.

SETTING UP THE TROPICAL FRESHWATER TANK

Choose a site where the tank will not be exposed to too much daylight or direct sunlight. The tank will need to be supported on a proper frame or strong table; a tank measuring 60 x 30 x 30cm. (24 x 12 x 12in.) weighs about 50kg. (110lb.). The gravel should be washed thoroughly (even though it may have been purchased as ready washed) as any dirt or color will pollute the tank. Place a layer of gravel in the tank about 8cm. (3in.) deep at the back sloping to 2.5cm. (1in.) at the front, and position a well-washed rock in the gravel. The water can now be added slowly by covering the gravel with a sheet of polyethylene and pouring the water onto it. This prevents disturbance of the gravel from a direct jet of water. The tank should be filled to within 2.5cm. (1in.) of the top. Finally, the heater and thermostat can be placed in the tank and regulated to heat the water.

The tank should be left for two or three days to ensure that there are no leaks and that the water temperature remains in the correct range. Plants can then be introduced into the tank. Each plant should be examined for snails or egg masses (transparent, often elongated, glutinous bodies) because the adults and young will eat the leaves.

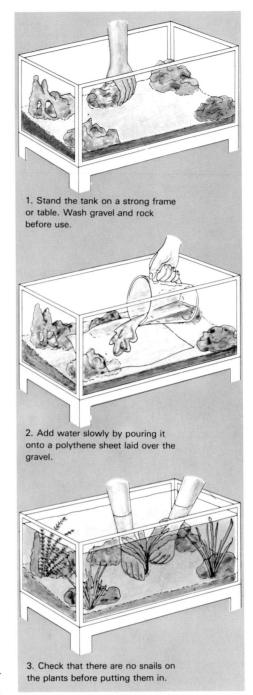

1. Stand the tank on a strong frame or table. Wash gravel and rock before use.

2. Add water slowly by pouring it onto a polythene sheet laid over the gravel.

3. Check that there are no snails on the plants before putting them in.

Stages in setting up a tropical freshwater tank.

Introducing the Fish

The tank should be left for another three days after planting before the fish are introduced. The number of fish in the tank depends upon the surface area of the water since this controls the amount of oxygen present. It is important that the tank not be overcrowded. Deep-bodied fish require a larger area than thinner species. An approximate guide is as follows.

Fish (length)	*Surface area allowed*
up to 5cm. (2in.)	30cm.^{2} (5in.^{2}) ea.
5–7.5cm. (2–3in.)	60cm.^{2} (10in.^{2}) ea.
7.5–10cm. (3–4in.)	120cm.^{2} (20in.^{2}) ea.
over 10cm. (over 4in.)	300cm.^{2} (50in.^{2}) ea.

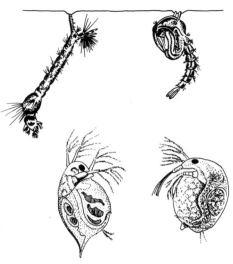

Introducing fish to a tank. Top Left. *The fish should be floated in their container and left in the mixture for half an hour. Then tank water should be added, and finally* (Top Middle) *the fish should be tipped into the tank.*

The fish should be allowed to acclimatize slowly to the temperature of the tank. The best method is to leave them in the plastic bag in which they were purchased and let it float on the surface of the tank water for about one hour. Then open the bag to admit some tank water. The fish should be left in the water mixture for half an hour. Finally, add some more tank water to the bag, and tip the fish gently out of the bag.

Fish for a Community Tank

As the name suggests a community tank contains several species of fish. At least two fish of each species should be put in the tank to promote their coloring and display to each other. Fish for this tank should be hardy, attractive, unaggressive, and without special requirements. Suitable species for a community tank are swordtails, platys and guppies, which are all attractive, brightly-colored fish. Neon tetras are small attractive fish which tend to swim in shoals; so, include at least six of them. Other tetras are also suitable for a community tank. Siamese fighting fish can also be included if there are one male and several females. These fish are not aggressive to other species, but the males will fight each other. Some species of gourami such as the Leerie Gourami are also suitable for a community tank. Finally, one or two catfish or similar fish should always be included to help keep the tank clean. The Sucking Loach is useful in reducing the amount of algae which grows on the plants and glass.

TANK MAINTENANCE

Once set up, the tank must be properly managed. It is important not to overfeed the fish because excess food in the tank sinks to the bottom, decays, and uses up oxygen. The tank should be cleaned frequently to remove any moldy food and dirt. Add water regularly to replace water lost by evaporation and to keep it fresh. The inside front glass should be cleaned with a razor blade cleaner or nylon scrubber to remove algal growth. Such mea-

sures will help keep fish healthy and give the tank a sparkling clean appearance.

FEEDING OF TROPICAL FRESHWATER FISH

Most fish are omnivorous. In the wild, they spend a large part of their time seeking out food and therefore their method of feeding is little but often. However, there are some totally carnivorous or piscivorous species which tend to gorge themselves while food is available and then spend a long time digesting it in a state of semi-stupor. Species that require a great deal of vegetable matter in their diet have much the same problem as landbased herbivores, that is, their diet is low in nutrient and they must spend much of their time actually feeding. When a fish is introduced into an aquarium, it is deprived of its natural food sources which contain the nutritional requirements. The aquarist must find out what the food requirements are and make sure that they are supplied or that suitable alternatives are found.

Fortunately, most fish show remarkable adaptability and present relatively few feeding problems. However, fish, like other animals, require a diet that includes proteins, carbohydrates, fats, vitamins, minerals, and a certain amount of fiber. It is always a good policy to vary the food given so that any nutrients missing from one food are made up in others.

The following is a guide to various types of live, commercial, and home-prepared foods that can be used for most aquarium and pond species. A combination of live, commercial, and home-prepared foods ensures that nutritional requirements are met.

Live Foods

Bloodworms, mosquito or gnat larvae, and glassworms are eaten voraciously by most fish and can be caught in ponds with a large, fine mesh net. Bloodworms are the larvae of midges (*Chironomus* sp). They are red in color and are found in still fresh water, usually inside their tunnel-like shelters which are constructed from small particles mixed with secretions produced by the animal. They can be as much as 3cm. (1.25in.) long but are generally smaller.

Food for fish: Top. *Mosquito larvae.* Below. *Daphnia.*

Mosquito or gnat larvae (*Culex*) are also found in ponds and other bodies of still water. Unlike bloodworms, they are more mobile and spend much of their time wriggling through the water or else lying just under the surface with their breathing tubes barely projecting. The pupae (which resemble a comma in shape) have breathing tubes on top of the head region.

Glassworms are the larvae of the Plumed Gnat (*Chaoborus* sp) and are found in the same type habitats as bloodworms and mosquito larvae. They are almost transparent and rest horizontally in the water. They are always found in large numbers.

Freshwater fleas, which are in fact crustaceans and not fleas, are the most popular live food. The most common species is *Daphnia pulex* found in vast numbers in ponds without fish, particularly during the warmer months. Since they are easily obtainable, it is hardly worth setting up cultures. Small species of fish sometimes find *Daphnia* too big to handle. However, they will often survive for a considerable time in the tank, sometimes producing broods of young which are quickly snapped up.

Mudworms, usually known by their scientific name *Tubifex* are also popular as food. They are thin, red worms found in waters containing a certain amount of organic matter. Even though most pet shops sell the clean specimens, they should be washed thoroughly for twenty-four hours or sterilized with one of the commercial preparations sold for this purpose. Unclean *Tubifex* can cause intestinal disorders which are hard to eradicate. Special feeders have small perforations through which the worms wriggle and are systematically picked off by the fish.

Whiteworms and Grindal Worms (*Enchytraeus albus* and *E. bucholtzi*) are a good live food. Grindal worms are smaller and require a higher temperature than whiteworms. *E. bucholtzi* reproduces well at 21°C. (70°F.) and

E. albus at 13°C. (56°F.). Culturing methods abound but most are similar to the following. Use a wooden box containing moist loam and place pieces of bread soaked in milk and water in small holes in the loam. The starter culture of worms is evenly divided among these pieces and a sheet of glass is laid on the surface of the loam. The culture is left for about four weeks at the required temperature before any worms are removed. Once this stage has been reached, the culture will continue to supply worms on a regular basis. It is also advisable to establish subcultures at regular intervals. The cultures for this food can be bothersome to maintain, and the worms tend to be fattening.

Maggots or Blowfly larvae (*Caliphora vomitoria*) can be obtained from any bait shop and can be fed whole to most large fish. For smaller fish, they can be either chopped or pulled apart with forceps. The pupae are quite easy to crush and are also relished by most fish.

Earthworms such as the Common Earthworm (*Lumbricus terrestris*) and the Long Worm (*Allolobophora longa*) are the most common species fed to fish. *A. longa* is the more convenient to use since it is smaller and can be fed to even small fish without being minced or chopped up into small pieces.

Snails which, from time to time, increase alarmingly in a tank, can be used as food. A reasonable number should be collected, crushed to a suitable size for the fish, and poured, shells and all, back into the tank. Some fish such as the Oscar (*Astronotus occellatus*) will eat whole snails and seem to enjoy cracking them open.

Many other live foods can be used but great care must be taken not to introduce possible predators. The Waterhog Louse (*Asellus* sp) and Freshwater Shrimp (*Gammarus* sp) are both suitable foods. Woodlice and slugs (preferably small species) are terrestrial invertebrates which are acceptable to fish. Small species and fish fry are sometimes used by aquarists to feed voracious species such as large cichlids.

Commercial Preparations

Commercial foods can now be found for almost any situation; there are, for example, staple foods, growth foods, conditioning foods, foods for live-bearers, and foods for characins prepared in a variety of flake sizes to suit different species. There are pellets for pond goldfish. Most of these foods are well balanced, containing all the basic food requirements.

Freeze-dried foods are highly nutritious. They consist of moisture-free foods which are often packaged in small "blocks." When pressed against the tank sides, they will adhere for a time. Freeze-dried *Tubifex*, shrimp, gnat larvae, and mosquito larvae are among the varieties available.

Small packets of deep-frozen foods are also available. Although relatively expensive, they have all the nutritional advantages of normal live foods.

Top Middle. *Young specimens of* Julidochromis ornatus *feed on brine shrimp eggs which are an ideal food for young fish.*

Top Right. *For herbivorous fish, such as this* Pterygoplichthys gibbiceps, *fresh lettuce leaves are an ideal food.*

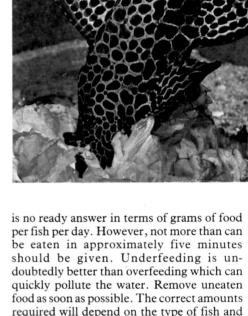

Home Prepared Foods

Liver (beef or lamb) is a favorite food but it clouds the tank because of its high blood content. This will not be a problem if the food is prepared as follows: the liver, sufficient dried breadcrumbs to absorb the blood, and one or two lightly boiled leaves of spinach or lettuce should be mixed in an electric blender. Put this mixture into a shallow container and place it in the freezing compartment of a refrigerator. Once frozen solid, the food "tablet" can be cut into slices of the required size and fed directly to the fish. If kept frozen, this food will last for months. Bran, oat flakes, or baby cereals can be substituted for the breadcrumbs.

Beef heart is another popular food. The heart is best minced and then finely chopped in a blender. Chopped spinach (one part of spinach to nine parts of heart) can be added and blended with the heart. This mixture is best frozen as ice cubes and kept in the freezer.

Cooked meats and fish are generally acceptable, provided they are not spiced. Canned salmon or shrimp may be used in an emergency. Even desiccated cake crumbs will do. If beaten egg is dribbled slowly into boiling water, it will coagulate into irregular, small pieces which many fish will take.

Practical Feeding

The fundamental questions with regard to feeding are how much and how often. There is no ready answer in terms of grams of food per fish per day. However, not more than can be eaten in approximately five minutes should be given. Underfeeding is undoubtedly better than overfeeding which can quickly pollute the water. Remove uneaten food as soon as possible. The correct amounts required will depend on the type of fish and can be ascertained only with experience.

Fish are capable of going without food for considerable periods, but if they are to be left for more than a week, it is advisable to arrange for someone, ideally an aquarist, to take over this duty.

Vacation food blocks which last for several weeks are now commercially produced along with automatic feeders, which dispense a measured amount of food at intervals. Some feeders can dispense food for periods in excess of a month.

Feeding Fry

When the fry are newly hatched they live for about twenty-four hours on the remains of the yolk sac. After this very small first foods must be supplied.

First foods for fry are available as commercial preparations, but homemade preparations and green water are also used. Commercial first foods are sold as emulsions in tubes, and drops of the food are added to the tank (the manufacturers' directions should be followed). The food consists of tiny particles which can be eaten by the fish, but

237

they also act as food for the tiny protozoans (infusoria) present in the tank. These infusorians multiply and are then eaten by the fish.

Homemade first foods can also be prepared. If a small piece 0.5cm. (0.25in.) in diameter of the yolk of a hard-boiled egg is rubbed gently between finger and thumb in the tank water it forms an emulsion of hundreds of tiny particles which can be eaten by the fish and also act as food for the infusoria.

Green water, which consists of cultures of green algae (*Euglena* and *Chlamydomonas*), can be found naturally in ponds (or even from old aquaria left in bright sunlight) and is a fine first food for fish. A jam jar full of the green water should be left to stand in the tank for twelve hours (so the temperatures become equal) and then slowly emptied into the tank. Add green water daily for a week by following this method.

After about a week of first foods the fry are ready for larger foods. Newborn live-bearers can be immediately fed these second foods. Newly hatched Brine Shrimp (*Artemia salina*) are a suitable food. Brine shrimp eggs are sold by pet shops and are hatched in twenty-four hours by incubation at 27°C. (80°F.) in a salt solution (four teaspoonfuls of salt per liter of water). The shrimp can be filtered off with a fine piece of cloth and *rinsed into the tank*.

Microworms (*Anguilluda silusia*) which are small white worms, 2–3mm. (0.08–0.12in.) long when full grown, also make a suitable second food for fry. A culture can be made by placing a small piece of moist bread into a plastic container measuring about 5–7cm. (2–3in.) in length and adding a starter culture of worms (available from a pet shop). The lid should be replaced, and the mixture incubated at 21–27°C. (70–80°F.).

Tropical Freshwater Fish

CHARACINS

Some of the most beautiful fish seen in the freshwater tropical aquarium come from the characin family (Characidae) and closely related families. It is one of the largest families and contains well over 1,000 species although only about 100 species are kept in the home aquarium since many are too large for confinement or relatively unattractive. Their native occurrence is limited to Africa and Central and South America. The majority of species come from the enormous Amazon basin, and new species are being discovered regularly with the development of that region.

If characins are to be seen at their best in the aquarium, its environment should match the conditions in their natural habitat. Most of the small species live in water which rarely receives any direct sunlight because the streams they inhabit are covered by the jungle canopy. Rainfall is heavy and continuous

Buenos Aires Tetra.

so that few salts are left in the soil and the water is very soft. Water temperature varies little and averages about 27°C. (80°F.). The aquarium therefore should match these conditions. It is not always possible to obtain sufficient soft water for aquariums, especially if a number of tanks are being used, but a mixture of hard tap water with rainwater is suitable. Plants will grow better in this mixture since very soft water lacks available nutrients.

Lighting should be provided by low wattage bulbs—no more than 25 watts per 1,000cm.^{2} (25 watts per ft.^{2}) of water surface. Although more expensive to start with, it is better to plant the tank with species that are slow growing, such as cryptocorynes which are more suitable for the subdued lighting. If standard gravel is used as a planting medium, the water will slowly increase in hardness so only soft water should be used for refilling to maintain the original salt level.

Characins come in all shapes and sizes. Some, like the Metynnis and piranhas, are deep-bodied fish while most of the tetras are slim and streamlined. Characins have teeth which, although not obvious in most species, can be seen very clearly in some of the piranhas. Characins are predominantly carnivorous and should therefore be fed as much live food as possible. They will, however, readily take most proprietary dried foods. Some, like the Metynnis, need a high proportion of vegetable matter in their diet and consequently devour any plants in the aquarium.

Breeding characins presents plenty of challenge; some are quite easy whereas some have never been known to breed in captivity. Most characins are egg scatterers. (See Breeding and rearing fish.) Water conditions are critical for breeding, and soft or very soft water is essential.

Most characins make ideal members of the community aquarium. The species listed below are the most likely to be seen in aquariums. They are indigenous to the Amazon region with the exception of the Congo Tetra which is native to the Congo Basin, and the Red Phantom Tetra and Emperor Tetra which are found in Colombia.

Cardinal Tetra (Cheirodon axelrodi)
Every community tank should have at least two of these brilliant-colored fish. The bottom half of the body is bright red topped by a blue-green line running from nose to adipose fin. The Cardinal Tetra is difficult to breed because it requires very soft water and the spawning, when successful, numbers no more than fifty.

Black Widow (Gymnocorymbus ternetzi)
This fish is a smoky gray color with two vertical black bars all over when young. A long-finned mutation has recently appeared. The Black Widow spawns easily. It grows to 6.5cm. (2.5in.) in length and has a peaceful disposition.

Buenos Aires Tetra (Hemigrammus caudovittatus)
The Buenos Aires Tetra is a large silver fish that grows up to 10cm. (4in.) in length. It has orange-red caudal and anal fins and a black bar in the caudal peduncle. Adults tend to be aggressive and nip the fins of other fish. They also nibble at the softer plants. This tetra prefers a lower temperature than most characins.

Glowlight Tetra (Hemigrammus gracilis)
This is a beautiful little fish with a red line running from nose to tail which glows if the fish is kept under correct conditions. Males are slimmer and smaller than females. Both sexes have white flashes on the fin tips.

Silver-Tipped Tetra (Hemigrammus nanus)
Also known as the **Copper Tetra,** male Silver-tipped Tetras are copper colored and the females are silver. Both have a black bar in

rear of the body. It is not as easily spawned as the Beacon Tetra.

Black Neon Tetra (*Hyphessobrycon herbertaxelrodi*)

Females of this species are larger than males, but their body patterns are the same. A thick black bar runs from gills to tail, above which is an iridescent line showing colors from yellow through green to blue. The Black Neon Tetra is ideal for the aquarium and easily spawned.

Neon Tetra (*Hyphessobrycon innesi*)

This fish is similar to the Cardinal Tetra although not as brilliantly colored nor as large. The Neon Tetra is usually available and should always be in the community aquarium. It is difficult for the amateur aquarist to get it to spawn in numbers.

Rosy Tetra

The fish that is known in the hobby by this name is in all probability *Hyphessobrycon ornatus*. The body and tail are suffused with red, and the dorsal fin is black. The male has a flowing dorsal fin and extended leading rays to the anal fin.

Bleeding Heart Tetra (*Hyphessobrycon rubrostigma*)

The Bleeding Heart Tetra is a beautiful fish which is similar to the Rosy Tetra. It does not like changes of water, and therefore is difficult to keep. Its common name is derived from the large red spot in the center of the body. The Bleeding Heart Tetra is not easily bred and, consequently, is expensive when available.

Serpae Tetra (*Hyphessobrycon serpae*)

The body color of this species is red, the dorsal fin black, while the anal fin has a black edging, and there is a black body spot just behind the gills. Sexing is difficult even in mature fish except that the female is much plumper. There are several subspecies in this group, but they all look much alike.

Black Phantom Tetra (*Megalamphodus megalopterus*)

Comparatively new to the hobby, the Black Phantom Tetra is similar in shape to the Rosy Tetra and Bleeding Heart Tetra, but its fins are proportionately larger. When in spawning condition the male's fins, which are larger than the female's, become jet black and the body dark gray. The female's color is not as intense and the ventral fins are red. Both sexes have a black shoulder spot.

Red Phantom Tetra (*Megalamphodus sweglesi*)

The Red Phantom Tetra is easily spawned and therefore more available than the Black Phantom. It has a body shape and fins similar to the latter but is colored like the Serpae Tetra, with a prominent black shoulder spot. The male's dorsal and anal fin is extended at sexual maturity, and the female has a yellow tip to the dorsal fin.

Congo Tetra (*Microlestes interruptus*)

This is one of the few African species that is seen regularly in the aquarium. The Congo Tetra needs a large tank as it grows to at least 10cm. (4in.). The scales are large and reflect iridescent colors which change with move-

Top. *Beacon Tetra*

Center. *Bleeding Heart Tetra*

Bottom. *Penguin Fish.*

the caudal peduncle and brilliant white tips to the dorsal, anal, and caudal fins. Always on the move, the Silver-tipped Tetra makes an ideal community fish.

Beacon Tetra (*Hemigrammus ocellifer*)

The Beacon Tetra is another ideal community fish deriving its common name from the golden spots above each eye and in the base of the tail. The Beacon Tetra is also referred to as the Head and Taillight Tetra. Males are smaller than females, and the species is easily spawned in normal characin manner.

Pretty Tetra (*Hemigrammus pulcher*)

This species is similar to the Beacon Tetra but is deeper bodied and has a black bar at the

Top Left. *Red Piranha.*
Top Right. *There-Banded Pencil Fish.*

ment. Mature males are easily recognized by the extended central rays of the tail and the long flowing dorsal fin.

Emperor Tetra (Nematobrycon palmeri)
The Emperor Tetra is one of the most beautiful fish seen in the aquarium if conditions are correct. A black line runs across the lower half of the body from eye to tail. Above this the body is suffused with blue. Males have extended dorsal, anal, and caudal fins making them easily identifiable. The Emperor Tetra is an ideal community fish, although it is expensive because it does not spawn a large number of eggs and the fry grow slowly.

Penguin Fish (Thayeria obliqua)
This is a common aquarium species which swims with a tail-down attitude. A black line runs from the gills down the lateral line into the lower lobe of the tail. It is a prolific spawner and a high speed swimmer.

Metynnis (Metynnis schreitmuelleri)
This species is not suitable for the normal community tank because it devours most of the plants quickly. It should therefore be provided with a high proportion of vegetable matter in its diet. Since it grows up to 18cm. (7in.) in length it is suitable only for large aquariums, but if several are kept, they make a most attractive display.

Red Piranha (Rooseveltiella nattereri)
The Red Piranha is *NOT* a fish for the community aquarium. It is vicious and in the wild hunts in shoals tearing victims quickly to pieces. It will even kill weaker members of its own species. A single specimen of this species can be maintained successfully in a large tank and fed on live fish and beef heart.

Marble Hatchetfish (Carnegiella strigata)
The most attractive of the hatchetfishes, the Marble Hatchetfish has dark brown bars diagonally across the body. The large pectoral fins and keel-shaped body enable it to glide just above the surface of the water when attacked. As the fish may try this form of locomotion in the aquarium, the cover should always be in place. A similar species is the Black-winged Hatchetfish (*C. marltiae*).

Golden Pencil Fish (Nannostomus beckfordi)
As its common name implies, the Golden Pencil Fish is a long slim fish with a black bar running from the mouth to the base of the tail that is bounded on both sides with gold. Males have red anal and caudal fins and more intense color than females. All the pencil fish have small mouths and need suitably sized food. Similar in appearance is the Dwarf Pencil Fish (*N. marginatus*).

Nannostomus (Nannostomus unifasciatus)
This pencil fish is similar in body shape to the previous species but is larger and less colorful. It swims at an oblique angle all the time as though it has a heavy tail. This could be because it feeds on small insects on the water surface. Again, it is important to feed this species small pieces of food.

CICHLIDS

Cichlids (family Cichlidae) are a fairly advanced group of fish closely related to the perch. They are found in most areas of Africa and in the tropical areas of North, South, and Central America. The only genus found elsewhere is *Etroplus* which comes from India where it is represented by two species. Most cichlids prefer to live in slowly moving water found naturally in lakes or quiet streams. Several varieties of cichlid choose rocky areas with small caves for protection.

Although cichlids vary tremendously in size and in body shape they can usually be identified by their large, well-developed dorsal fin, the front section of which is heavily rayed. These rays sometimes extend beyond the fin. Cichlids tend to be solidly built fish with well-developed heads and strong jaws. The lips are often pronounced, and the scales on the body are large and prominent. In most species the males can be easily distinguished by their bright coloration and often by their long pointed dorsal and caudal fins.

Cichlids are not shoal fish, several species being very quarrelsome; they are best kept on their own or with other similarly sized fish. They should be fed mainly live food and some dried food. The hardness of the tank

water is not too critical, but most species prefer temperatures around 27°C. (80°F.). Tanks should be set up with a thick layer of gravel since most species like to dig holes, and they should be provided with plenty of rocks, placed to form caves. Many cichlid species will not tolerate the presence of plants, especially at spawning time when they will uproot even large, well-established plants such as Amazon Swords and cryptocorynes.

The spawning procedures vary widely, but all species pair off following a courtship and they tend, more than other fish, to retain their partnerships. The parents guard their eggs and then their young and will defend them against enemies much larger than themselves. Because cichlids are longlived (some specimens have been kept in

Angelfish.

aquariums for longer than ten years), the young often take up to three years to mature sexually.

Angelfish (*Pterophyllum eimekei*)

The Angelfish is possibly the best known of all tropical fishes. It is indigenous to the Amazon Basin where it lives in quiet waters among reeds which provide camouflage. The Angelfish is a thin, flat fish that will grow up to 12.5cm. (5in.) long. Many color varieties of Angelfish, some with extended fins, have been developed.

Angelfish are mature enough to breed when they are 6.5cm. (2.5in.) long. Though they are difficult to sex they will pair naturally, and these pairs will often remain permanent mates. They lay their eggs on broad-leaved plants, smooth rocks, or even

Center. *Firemouth Cichlid.*
Bottom. *Discus Fish.*

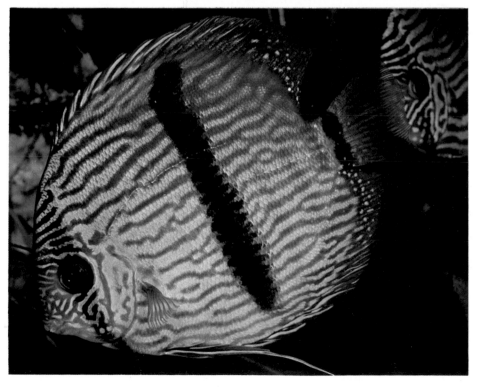

on the glass of the aquarium. Remove the eggs to a separate tank at the end of spawning because at the slightest provocation or alarm the pair will often eat them. The eggs will require gentle aeration to prevent fungus from developing. The eggs hatch within three days, and the fry remain attached to the leaves by a sticky thread for a further two days. They will then take very fine food. They grow rapidly and change to the characteristic "angel" shape after three weeks.

Discus Fish (*Symphysodon discus*)

Also known as the Pompadour Fish, the Discus is the king of tropical freshwater fish and comes from the Amazon Basin. It is disc-shaped, flat, and up to 20cm. (8in.) in diameter, with rounded fins. Though the colors vary with the individual, they are brilliant and especially intense about the head.

Discus live in slightly acid, soft water of a high temperature 27°C. (80°F.). They are delicate, difficult to keep, and prefer to live only with other Discus. They are not suitable for the amateur aquarist.

The Discus was not successfully bred until 1956; prior to this either all the eggs were eaten by the parents or the young died. In the same year it was scientifically proven that the parents secrete a mucus over their bodies on which the young feed. This mucus is essential to the fry, and no artificial substitute is known. The spawning of Discus is similar to that of the Angelfish.

Velvet Cichlid (*Astronotus ocellatus*)

This species, also known as the Oscar, comes from the Amazon Basin. It is large and can grow up to 30cm. (12in.) long. Dark brown in color its velvety textured appearance almost hides the scales. It has an eye spot at the base of the tail and blotchy dark markings on the body. Though not vicious it is a greedy fish and should be kept only with species of a similar size. The Velvet Cichlid is not easy to breed mainly because it needs such a large amount of space. Individuals can develop into great characters and often learn to recognize their owner and enjoy being hand fed. It is now possible to obtain a Red Velvet Cichlid with red markings.

Firemouth (*Cichlasoma meeki*)

The Firemouth comes from the Yucatan Peninsula. It grows up to 12.5cm. (5in.) long, with a brilliant red chin which gives it its common name. Normally a peaceful fish, it will spawn in a hollow in the sand or on a flat rock. Males of the species are easily distinguished by their elongated dorsal and anal fins.

Blue Acara (*Aequidens latifrons*)

Indigenous to Central America, this is a long, peaceful cichlid measuring up to 12.5cm. (5in.) long. It is green-blue in color with bright blue speckles on the body. The male has extended anal and dorsal fins. The Blue Acara digs holes in the sand in order to spawn on the base of the tank or else spawns on a flat rock. This species is easy to keep and to breed although it will uproot plants during the breeding season. The parents rarely eat their eggs and will protect their young.

Jack Dempsey (*Cichlasoma biocellatum*)

The Jack Dempsey is a large fish from the Amazon Basin, measuring up to 20cm. (8in.) long. It has a large head that bulges in old age. It is gray-blue in color with small green and red spots. Despite its name it is not pugnacious except at the time of spawning. After the eggs are laid this cichlid often attacks its mate.

Ramirezi (*Apistogramma ramirezi*)

This fish is a dwarf cichlid which only grows to 6cm. (2.5in.) long and is indigenous to Venezuela. It is a beautiful fish with a greenish pink body color and a brilliant blue sheen. The male has a dark extended ray on the dorsal fin. The Ramirezi is rather shy and is not an easy fish to breed. It likes to live at high temperatures, 27°C. (80°F). A Golden Ramirezi is now available.

Kribensis.

Egyptian Mouthbrooder (*Haplochromis multicolor*)

The Egyptian Mouthbrooder is a small peaceful fish, measuring 8cm. (3in.) long, that is found over a wide area of East and Northeast Africa. It can be kept in a community tank and will eat most foods. The breeding color of the male is dark brown with various metallic specks of gold, green, and blue. The fins are pale red with green bands, and edged with black. The females are pale brown with few markings. The Egyptian Mouthbrooder has particularly interesting breeding habits. The pairs spawn in shallow depressions in the sand where the female immediately gathers the eggs in her mouth and keeps them for ten days until they hatch. Then the female releases the fry to allow them to eat. At the first sign of danger, however, the fry will at once return to the safety of their mother's mouth. After another ten days the fry are considered able to fend for themselves and the female will eat for the first time since spawning.

Golden Lake Malawi Cichlid (*Pseudotropheus auratus*)

This is a beautiful cichlid from Lake Malawi whose coloring rivals that of marine fishes. The males are yellow, but at breeding time they become dark blue with longitudinal stripes. The females are striped in black and yellow. These fish, which grow to 10cm. (4in.) long, require a tank with numerous rocky caves and hard water. Being aggressive, they are best kept on their own. If plenty of cover is not available, the males may kill the females. The Golden Lake Malawi Cichlid is a mouthbrooder, and the female will incubate the eggs in her mouth for three weeks, after which approximately twenty fry, about 0.5cm. (0.25in.) in length, emerge.

The Golden Lake Malawi Cichlid is best kept by aquarists who specialize in cichlids as it is a difficult fish to keep and requires much care and attention.

Kribensis (*Pelmatochromis kribensis*)

The Kribensis is an African cichlid which comes from the Congo area. The males grow to 10cm. (4in.) long but the females are slightly smaller. The beauty of this cichlid is difficult to describe since the markings and hues change frequently depending on the mood of the fish. Basically, it is mauve with a bright red area on the belly. There are large dark spots on both the dorsal and caudal fins of the female. The male has a more pointed finnage.

The fish spawn best in upturned flowerpots. When the eggs are hatched, the young are moved to depressions in the gravel and protected by their parents for a further week.

CYPRINIDS

The cyprinids (family Cyprinidae), or carps and minnows as they are commonly called, are the largest known family of freshwater fish. They are found in all tropical continents with the exception of Australasia and South America.

Most species are found in clear, fast moving water where they feed mainly on small live foods which they obtain by grubbing along the bottom. For this reason most members of Cyprinidae are equipped with at least one pair of barbels, or hair-like appendages, on the lower (or sometimes upper) lip which are used to search out the food.

Keeping cyprinids is normally easy. They are tolerant of a fairly wide range of water temperature, and most species eat all usual aquarium foods. Well-aerated, soft water suits them best, and the first sign of any pollution in the tank is indicated by the fishes' loss of color and activity and by the fact that they gasp for air at the surface. If these symptoms occur, about one-third of the tank water should be changed immediately.

Cyprinids are egg layers and, with a few notable exceptions, tend to follow a similar breeding pattern. Spawning usually takes place in warm shallow water that has fairly dense vegetation. The female indicates the courtship by chasing the male; then the role is reversed, and the male becomes the aggressor. After a violent chase through the plants, several hundred small eggs are laid. Some species lay adhesive eggs which stick onto the plants whereas others lay nonadhesive eggs which fall down into the gravel. All species are avid egg eaters and adults must be removed after spawning. The eggs usually hatch in forty-eight hours and two days later

Rosy Barb.

the fry are free swimming. The fry should be fed on miscroscopic food for approximately ten days, after which they are large enough to eat small insects and fine dry food. Healthy growth of the young can be maintained by providing plenty of swimming space and frequent partial water changes.

The barbs are the most popular group of cyprinids kept in the aquarium. They come exclusively from the Old World and are found in Africa and Asia. There are over one hundred species known ranging in size from 3cm. (1.2in.) to 32.5cm. (13in.) in length. Danios are fast swimming fishes indigenous to India and Burma. They are prolific breeders and are tolerant of a wide range of water temperatures. Rasboras are found almost exclusively in Malaya. They are not as hardy as the barbs and danios and very few are bred successfully in the aquarium.

Rosy Barb (*Barbus conchonius*)

The Rosy Barb from India is a suitable fish for the beginner as it is extremely hardy and long-lived. The male exhibits the rosy hue from which the name derives, while the female is olive green with silver reflections. The Rosy Barb grows up to 9cm. (3.5in.) in length.

Black Ruby (*Barbus nigrofasciatus*)

This species from Sri Lanka grows to about 7cm. (2.75in.) long. The females are rather drab compared with the bright purple males. Several males can be kept in one tank so they will display their brilliant overall colors to each other.

Tiger Barb (*Barbus tetrazona*)

The Tiger Barb is a popular fish measuring 6.5cm. (2.5in.) long, which is indigenous to Sumatra. It has a yellow body color with four broad black vertical body bars, and orange fins and nose. An albino variety has recently been bred by aquarists.

Pearl Danio (*Brachydanio albolineatus*)

Slightly deeper bodied than the Zebra, the Pearl Danio grows to 5.5cm. (2.2in.) long. The pearl blue color of this fish is obvious in natural light.

Zebra (*Brachydanio rerio*)

This slim bodied danio is easily recognizable

by its alternating blue and silver horizontal stripes. The Zebra grows to about 4cm. (1.5in.) long, and is very active, moving continuously. It is a popular aquarium species.

Great Danio (*Danio malabaricus*)
The Great Danio comes from the Malabar coast of India and is the largest of the danio species, measuring 12.5cm. (5in.) in length. It is a silver fish with numerous alternating blue and yellow horizontal stripes, and the male has some red coloration in the fins. The Great Danio is a prolific breeder, which, unlike other members of its group, lays adhesive eggs.

Harlequin (*Rasbora heteromorphia*)
The Harlequin grows to 4.5cm. (1.75in.) long and has a distinctive orange-red body with a blue-black triangular marking toward the tail. It lays adhesive eggs on the underside of broad-leaved plants.

Spotted Rasbora (*Rasbora maculata*)
This fish is particularly small measuring 2.5cm. (1in.) long. In the wild, it lives in shoals. It is brick red in color and has two or three small black spots on the body and a large dark blue blotch behind the gills.

Scissortail (*Rasbora trilineata*).
This species can grow up to 17.5cm. (7in.) long in its native habitat but when kept in an aquarium will rarely exceed 7.5cm. (3in.). It is a transparent, silver-bodied fish with a narrow black line running the length of the body. It has a deeply forked tail with a black and white mark to each lobe.

White Cloud Mountain Minnow (*Tanichthys albonubes*)
This is a particularly beautiful small fish, 4cm. (1.6in.) long, which rivals the popular Neon Tetra in brilliance. It comes from the White Cloud Mountain region in China and, in its natural state, is found in low temperature areas. It is extremely easy to keep and breeds readily.

Red-Tail Black Shark (*Labeo bicolor*)
This species is not related in any way to the true shark, and it comes from Thailand and the Malay Peninsula. It often grows up to 17.5cm. (7in.) long and is the most popular of the "shark" species kept by aquarists. As the

Black Ruby.

name indicates, it has a jet black body and fins and a brilliant red tail. Red-tailed Black Sharks are relatively friendly with other fish but may fight among themselves; only one should be kept in a community tank.

Silver Shark (*Balantiocheilus melanopterus*)
The Silver Shark is also unrelated to the true shark and comes from Thailand, Sumatra, and Borneo. It has a large-scaled silver body with brilliant orange fins that are edged in

Top. *Zebra.*
Center. *Red-Tail Black Shark*

black. It is usually about 17.5cm. (7in.) long. It is an active fish that is apt to jump out of the water if the aquarium cover is not kept in place.

VIVIPAROUS TOOTHCARPS

The live-bearing toothcarps (family Poecilidae) are an extremely interesting group of fish which have developed to the point of producing live young. They are found only naturally in the New World, from the southern states of the United States down through the Caribbean and Central America, into South America. Most species live in densely vegetated streams in coastal areas while some are found at certain times of the year in estuarine conditions. With the exception of the Live-bearing Pike they are omnivorous. Breeding live-bearers is fairly uncomplicated and can be rewarding when the birth of the young is witnessed. Also, many interesting color varieties of the species can be developed by careful selection of the parent fishes. The broods of live-bearers vary in number from ten for some of the smaller varieties to over two hundred fry for some of the larger live-bearers.

In general, live-bearers accept all the usual

243

foods and most benefit from some added vegetable matter, such as spinach. They accept a wide range of tank temperatures varying from 21°–28°C. (70°F–82°F.).

Mollies are slightly less hardy than other live-bearers and unless fed a varied diet containing vegetable foods, may abort spontaneously, thereby proving difficult to breed. Mollies require slightly alkaline (salty) water so seasalt in the proportion of 1 teaspoon to 4 litres of water should be added to the tank.

Swordtail (Xiphophorus helleri)
This Mexican fish derives its name from the swordlike extension on the lower edge of the male's caudal fin. The Swordtail grows to about 12.5cm. (5in.) long and should be kept with other equally large fish. The Swordtail is easy to keep, eats all foods, and tolerates a wide temperature range. It is an active fish that is prone to jumping so that the tank should be covered with a close fitting lid. Numerous color varieties of this species have been produced, the most popular being the Green, Red, and Wagtail Swords. There is a variety with a large dorsal fin called the Hi Fin Swordtail, and another, which has all long fins, called the Lyretail Swordtail.

Platy (Xiphophorus maculatus)
This fish is a close relative of the Swordtail and is also indigenous to Mexico and neighboring Central America. It is a deeper-bodied fish than the Swordtail and has no tail extension. It is also of a quieter disposition than the Swordtail. The Platy grows to 5–7.5cm. (2–3in.). Again, many color varieties have been produced. The Platy and Swordtail can be crossbred. The Platy is an ideal fish for the beginner as it is attractive, hardy, and easy to breed. There is also a Hi Fin variety.

Variatus Platy (Xiphophorus variatus)
This fish is closely related to the Platy but is slimmer in shape. It is brightly colored with a combination of red, yellow, and blue markings.

Guppy (Poecilia reticulata)
The Guppy comes from the West Indies and Central America, and it is the most popular and well known of all tropical fishes. The male grows to 3cm. (1.25in.) whereas the female reaches 5.5cm. (2.2in.) long. In the wild the female is olive green in color, with a silver belly and clear fins. The male has color spots on the body and extensions to the fins. Many beautifully colored varieties have been developed that possess long flowing fins—even females have been created with colors on the body and larger, colored finnage.

Short-Finned Molly (Poecilia sphenops)
This small molly has a slim body shape and numerous color variations. It is from this species that the Perma Black or Midnight Molly has been artificially bred, and in recent years, mutations possessing lyre-shaped caudal fins have been produced.

Giant Sailfin Molly (Poecilia velifera)
This is the largest and most beautiful of the mollies and comes from the Yucatan Peninsula. It is an olive green fish that has many brilliant blue flecks and dark stripes on the body; it is characterized by a handsome, erect dorsal fin. Because the Giant Sailfin Molly grows to about 15cm. (6in.) long, it should be kept in a large well-planted aquarium together with other members of the family Poeciliidae.

Mosquito Fish (Heterandria formosa)
The Mosquito Fish derives its common name from its small size, not from the food it eats.

It comes from Florida and is possibly the smallest vertebrate known as the male grows only to 2cm. (0.8in.) long, and the female to 2.8cm. (1.1in.) long. The Mosquito is not one of the most brilliantly colored live-bearers. It is olive green with a dark brown line running the length of the body. The fins are a light yellow with black and red dots on the dorsal. It is a hardy, peaceful species that must, because of its size, be kept only with other small fish. The female Mosquito Fish produces her brood over a period of ten to fourteen days, while other live-bearing females produce their young over a period of two to three hours.

ANABANTIDS

Most anabantids come from Southeast Asia, while a few are found in tropical Africa. The true anabantids belong to the suborder Anabantoidea which includes four families, the Anabantidae, Belontiidae, Helostamidae, and Osphromenidae, all of which contain one or more interesting aquarium species.

These fishes have an accessory respiratory organ, the labyrinth, in the form of a modified first epibranchial bone. It is a highly folded vascular organ which lies on both sides of the gill chamber to which it is connected. Air taken in through the mouth at the surface of the water is forced into the labyrinth where gaseous exchange takes place between the atmospheric gases and the blood supply of the fish. Anabantids can therefore survive in waters with low oxygen concentrations, relying on the labyrinth organ for their respiratory requirements. This reliance has been evolved to such an extent that many anabantids will actually drown if prevented from periodically surfacing and gulping in air. With one exception, the Chocolate Gourami, all the anabantids described below are easy to keep, often surviving conditions which would kill other fish. They are suitable for the beginner and also have the added attraction of being beautiful, highly colored fish. Anabantids do best in water conditions of about 24–27°C. (75–80°F.).

Climbing Perch (Anabas testudineus)
This fish comes from Southeast Asia where it grows to 25cm. (10in.). It has remarkable powers of survival out of water because of its labyrinth organ. It is a dull-colored fish and even though a yellow (xanthistic) form exists, neither type is often seen in the aquarium. The Climbing Perch should be kept in a species tank with a well-fitting lid.

Gourami (Osphronemus goramy)
The Gourami is the only species of the family Osphromenidae. It is reared on a large scale in Southeast Asia as a food source. It can reach a size of 50cm. (20in.) and is therefore not suitable for the home aquarium. Nevertheless, young specimens are periodically available, and these can be kept for a con-

siderable time since growth tends to be limited by the close confines of the tank.

Kissing Gourami (*Helostoma temmincki*)
The only species of the family Helastomatidae, the Kissing Gourami is distributed throughout Thailand, the Malayan Archipelago, and Indonesia. This fish has become quite popular because of its unusual "kissing" habit which is more likely a form of aggression, as it is often observed between males disputing territories. The Kissing Gourami is largely vegetarian and the large, thick lips help the fish in this type of feeding. Two color variations are known: the wild or silvery-green type, which is rather unimpressive, and the Pink Gourami which is more common in aquariums. Fishes up to 30cm. (12in.) have been recorded in the wild.

Siamese Fighting Fish (*Betta splendens*)
This species belongs to Belontiidae, the largest family of anabantids. The Siamese Fighting Fish is well known and stories of its belligerence abound. Although these stories may be exaggerated, males are so aggressive toward each other that they have to be kept in separate tanks, otherwise their elegant fins are soon reduced to tattered shreds. Intensive breeding and selection has produced numerous color strains with greatly developed fins,

and the modern Siamese Fighting Fish looks different from the original wild stock. This fish measures about 6cm. (2.4in.). The female has shorter fins and looks drabber than the male. They are usually peaceful in the company of other species and make ideal and colorful additions for the community tank.

Like most anabantids, the Siamese Fighting Fish can tolerate a wide range of water conditions but seem to do best in clean, soft water between 24°–25.5°C. (75°–78°F.).

Dwarf Gourami (*Colisa lalia*)
The Dwarf Gourami is another attractive and easy species to keep which is indigenous to India and Bangladesh. Males are colorful even when not in breeding condition while the females are rather unimpressive. These fish are peaceful and do well in aquariums offering good cover. They like bushy vegetation which they incorporate into the neat, deep bubble nest under which the spawning embraces occur. General requirements are like those for the Siamese Fighting Fish, although a slightly higher temperature is preferred. Females are slightly smaller than males which measure 4cm. (1.5in.).

Thick-Lipped Gourami (*Colisa labiosa*)
This species is found in the Irrawaddy com-

plex in Burma and is isolated from the other *Colisa* species. It has a pattern of oblique, metallic blue lines and spots on the body, and an orange margin on the dorsal fin. It measures up to 8cm. (3.2in.).

Striped Gourami (*Colisa fasciata*)
Indigenous to the Indian subcontinent, the Striped Gourami is similar to the Thicklipped Gourami. It has a pattern of oblique, metallic blue lines and spots on the body with a whitish margin on the dorsal fin. The Striped Gourami can be bred with the Thicklipped Gourami, the resulting hybrids are fertile. However, hybrids resulting from a cross with the Dwarf Gourami are sterile.

Honey Gourami (*Colisa chuna*)
The Honey Gourami is a delightful little fish indigenous to India. It rarely exceeds 3cm. (1.2in.) in length. The female is more uniformly colored than the male which has a bright orange body color and black head and chest. This species is more timid than the Dwarf Gourami, but has the same requirements.

Three-Spot Gourami (*Trichogaster trichopterus*)
Also known as the Blue Gourami, Hairfin and Cantor's Gourami, this species is easy to keep and breed and is an ideal beginner's fish. A golden domesticated variety of this species exists as well as other varieties. Also, an amethyst-colored variety which resembles the Three-spot in the distribution of body

Center Left. *Siamese Fighting Fish.*
Center Right. *Lace Gourami.*
Bottom Left. *Three-Spot Gourami.*
Bottom Right. *Kissing Gourami.*

245

spots has recently been produced. The Three-spot Gourami measures up to 10cm. (4in.) and is even hardier than the above mentioned gourami species. Because of its larger size, it can be a problem when kept with smaller fish.

Lace Gourami (Trichogaster leeri)

The Lace, or Leeri, Gourami is a large species reaching 10cm. (4in.) in size but is more peaceful than the Three-spot Gourami. It is a striking fish and even the best color prints do not do it justice. The sides and fins are light brown in color broken by spots that have a mother-of-pearl sheen. The throat and chest is orange-red. Males in full breeding colors are among the most beautiful aquarium fish.

Paradise Fish (Macropodus opercularis)

Indigenous to East and Southeast Asia, the Paradise Fish is capable of withstanding low temperatures (reportedly down to freezing point) as well as temperatures of more than 21°C. (70°F.) and is, consequently, very hardy. It is attractive, having the metallic blue lines characteristic of most of the *Colisa* species. Males have longer, more pointed fins than females and, although rather pugnacious towards other species, are often gentle with females during spawning. Sizes up to 8cm. (3.2in.) are fairly common.

Chocolate Gourami (Sphaerichthys osphromenoides)

The Chocolate Gourami is difficult to keep and as such is not a fish for the beginner. It needs high temperatures 28°C. (82°F.) and soft acid water. The sexes can only be distinguished with difficulty and the fish, which is most difficult to breed, is a mouthbrooder.

KILLIFISH OR OVIPAROUS TOOTH CARPS

Killifish (family Cyprinodontidae) are closely related to the live-bearers and are distributed in every continent, except Australasia. Most species are from the tropics but some are found as far north as Canada and Europe and as far south as South Africa and Argentina.

In the wild they inhabit small areas of shallow water such as streams and pools that are well shaded by vegetation (both in and out of the water). Rainfall is usually heavy which means the water is soft with a temperature between 21°–24°C. (70°–75°F.).

Most species are long and slender with dorsal and anal fins set well back along the body which enables them to move at high speed over short distances. When frightened, they often leap out of the water. Their mouths are large and upturned as their natural diet is insects and mosquito larvae taken at or near the water surface.

Single eggs are laid at varying levels from near the surface to the debris on the pool bottom and take from three to eight weeks to hatch. The eggs are capable of withstanding short periods out of the water should the pond water evaporate and still hatch once the water returns. Some species which bury their eggs exist in areas where rainfall is concen-

Gardneri.

trated into a few months of the year, followed by a long dry period. Under these conditions, the pools which formed during the rainy season totally evaporate. Fish living in these pools deposit their eggs in the mud where they will withstand the drought for periods up to twenty weeks and hatch within hours of the returning rain.

Two or three nylon mops suspended from corks should be provided for those species that spawn near the surface. (See **Breeding and rearing of fish.**) For the egg-buryers add enough well-washed peat that has been boiled first to remove excess acidity to form a layer 1.5cm. (0.6in.) thick on the bottom. After the pair of fish have been placed in the tank, use a glass cover to prevent their jumping out.

Some killifish can be included in the community aquarium, but they do not show up too well as they are easily frightened and avoid bright lighting. It is much better to provide them with their own tank where, in the correct conditions, they are easy to keep.

Most of the smaller species do well in a tank 30 x 15 x 15cm. (12 x 6 x 6in.) which has the back, sides, and bottom painted to exclude light. The water should be soft with a hardness of no more than 75 parts per million.

Killifish should be fed as much live food as possible such as daphnia, *Tubifex*, whiteworms, and mosquito larvae.

Dageti (Epiplatys dageti)

Indigenous to West Africa, the Dageti is probably the best-known species belonging to the genus *Epiplatys*, which consists of small fish that spend their time just below the surface of the water. The Dageti male has a red-orange throat, vertical bars on the body and extended rays on the bottom of the tail. The female's coloration is duller and all her fins are rounder. Spawning is near the surface and eggs can be collected from floating mops.

Lyretail (Aphyosemion australe)

Some of the most brilliantly colored killifishes are found in the males of the genus *Aphysemion* to which this species belongs.

The Lyretail, a popular species, is so named because of the characteristic shape of the tail in the male. The male is reddish brown with red spots. The tail has orange edges and white tips to the points. The female, like all of those belonging to the genus *Aphyosemion*, is light brown with reddish brown spots. There is a golden variety of Lyretail, and both types measure about 6.5cm. (2.5in.) long. The Lyretail spawns at the top.

Gardneri (Asphysemion gardneri)

This fish is ideal for beginners since it is one of the hardiest and most easily bred species. The male has a greenish blue body color with red spots. There are two varieties of A. *gardneri*; one with yellow edges and the other with blue edges to the dorsal, anal, and tail fins. Both types measure 6.5cm. (2.6in.) long. A. *gardneri* is a top spawner.

Blue Gularis (Aphyosemion sjoestedti)

The Blue Gularis is one of the largest species requiring a bigger tank than normal as it grows to 12.5cm. (5in.) in length. The body color is light brown to yellow with dark brown spots. The anal and tail fins have either a bright orange or yellow-green patch above a pale blue area. The Blue Gularis is a bottom spawner and is easily bred. The offspring seem to be much stronger if the eggs are allowed to dry out before hatching.

Walkeri (Aphyosemion walkeri)

Measuring about 6.5cm. (2.6in.) the Walkeri is a suitable fish for the beginner. The body color is blue-green with red spots and the edges of the anal, dorsal, and tail fins are brilliant orange. The eggs of this fish do better if they are allowed to dry out.

Guentheri (Nothobranchius guentheri)

This fish is the most common species within the genus *Nothobranchius*, which is indigenous to East Africa. The overall body color of the male is blue-green. The scales are edged with red, and the tail is red-orange with a black border. The female is brown with paler undersides and clear fins.

All members of *Nothobranchius* live in annual pools and their eggs need to be stored dry for up to fourteen weeks before they will hatch. For breeding, two females should be used to one male. The Guentheri is not a suitable fish for the beginner.

Blue Gularis.

Palmquisti (*Nothobranchius palmquisti*)
This species is similar to the Guentheri, but' the body color is more distinctly blue and the tail is without the black border. Like the Guentheri, two females should be used for each male when breeding. The Palmquisti is unsuitable for the beginner.

Playfiari (*Pachypanchax playfiari*)
The Playfiari is a beautiful fish, the male having a lovely checkerboard pattern of red and pale brown along its flanks. The female is not so brightly colored and has a black spot on the dorsal fin. This species can be kept in a community tank and breeds easily before spawning at the top.

Dwarf Argentine Pearlfish (*Cynolebias nigripinis*)
This species is the best-known member of the genus *Cynolebias* and is found in South America. In shaded conditions the male is dark blue, with brilliant white spots and large dorsal and anal fins. The female is spotted brown overall. This species is only 4cm. (1.6in.) long. The Dwarf Argentine Pearlfish is an egg buryer, and the eggs require long drying out periods.

Whitei (*Cynolebias whitei*)
This species is larger than the Dwarf Argentine Pearlfish, growing to 10cm. (4in.) in length, and has large dorsal and anal fins, but it lacks the intense color of the latter. Whitei is an egg buryer requiring long drying out periods for the eggs.

Lineatus (*Aplocheilus lineatus*)
Found in Asia, the Lineatus is the most popular species belonging to the genus *Aplocheilus*. It resembles a pike in shape and grows to 9cm. (3.5in.) in length. It has a brown body covered with rows of red and white spots, long ventral fins, and large eyes. Lineatus is a top spawner.

CATFISH AND LOACHES

The catfish are one of the oldest and most primitive group of fish. They inhabit most tropical areas of the world and often live in conditions that would be intolerable for other fish. All catfish lack true scales, but several species have their bodies covered with numerous large plates that look like armor. Such species are commonly called mailed or armored catfish. A notable feature found in all catfish is the modification to the mouth. This can be in the form of feelers, like whiskers, that protrude from the upper and lower lips, or in the form of a sucker, in which case the whole mouth has been modified. The sucker enables the fish to pick up algal growth from rocks and plants which forms the main part of its diet. The feelers are extremely sensitive and are used to grub out food from the bottom of rivers and pools. Because of the low oxygen content of the water they inhabit, some species have a breathing mechanism which is adapted to take in gulps of air from the surface. Even in a well-kept, healthy aquarium, some catfish can be seen rushing to the surface of the water to take air.

Since their natural conditions are often fairly foul, and because their armor plating affords good protection against parasites and other predators, catfish are a very hardy group resistant to diseases.

The loaches are also scavengers living mainly on the bottom but, unlike the catfish, they inhabit clean water regions and are found mainly in rocky areas or among tree and plant roots. They also lack scales or any alternative protective coating, and so they are susceptible to disease. They eat most small foods and prefer warm, soft water at a temperature of 24°C. (75°F.). Most loaches are elongate and have small feelers on the mouth though some have the sucker modification for eating algae.

Bronze Catfish (*Corydoras aeneus*)
The Bronze Catfish is a popular fish which comes from Venezuela and Trinidad where it grows to about 6.5cm. (2.5in.) long. A shy, but long-lived, fish that soon settles down to aquarium life, this species has established itself as the most popular of all the catfish. It is basically a metallic golden-green color with pinkish, erect fins. Like other members of the family Callichthyidae, the Bronze Catfish is not easy to breed. Optimum results are obtained by using a large, well-planted tank containing four or five mature fish that have been well fed on *Tubifex*, whiteworms, daphnia, and chopped earthworms. The females soon fatten up on such a diet, at which time at least one-third of the water should be changed for cooler, freshly drawn tap water. This often triggers spawning; the females chase the males and then both sexes clean an area either on the glass of the tank or on flat leaves. The female then takes the milt from the male into her mouth and uses it to fertilize the eggs which she deposits in the cleared area by using her ventral fins.

This procedure is repeated until two to three hundred eggs are laid. These eggs hatch in about six days, and the young are then able to take microworms and newly hatched brine shrimp.

Leopard Catfish (*Corydoras julii*)
This species, indigenous to South America, is of a similar shape and size to the Bronze Catfish. It has, however, distinct body mark-

Bronze Catfish.

247

Peppered Catfish

ings consisting of numerous small black spots and bars on a basically silver body, which form a mosaic pattern. The dorsal fin has a large black spot at the top. This catfish is difficult to breed.

Peppered Catfish (Corydoras paleatus)
Also from South America, the Peppered Catfish is olive green in color with irregular dark brown patches on the body. The dorsal and caudal fins are scattered with fine dots. It is a hardy, long-lived species that breeds in the same way as the Bronze Catfish.

Bubble Nest Catfish (Callichthys callichthys)
This is a large, elongate catfish measuring 12.5cm. (5in.) long that is heavily armored, and has long whiskers. It comes from northeast South America and is dark brown-black in color. This fish builds a bubble nest at the surface of the water. Here the eggs are laid after a lengthy and noisy courtship. The fry fall to the bottom of the tank after hatching, and there they feed off small insects and worms.

Sucking Catfish (Plecostomus plecostomus)
As the name implies, this is a large suckermouth catfish, measuring 30cm. (12in.) long, that is indigenous to South America. It is sandy brown in color with numerous darker spots and blotches all over the body. The dorsal fin is large but is only occasionally held erect. This fish feeds almost exclusively on algae, so a plentiful supply of green food must be provided. As yet, the Sucking Catfish has not been bred in captivity.

Kuhli Loach (Acanthopthalmus kuhli)
This is a fascinating snake-like fish from the Malay Peninsula; it has an elongated and tubular body. There are numerous color varieties, or possibly even subspecies of the Kuhli Loach, but basically it has a pink-gray belly and dark brown and yellow bands along the length of the body. It has small fins that are almost colorless and short feelers at the mouth. In the wild the Kuhli Loach lives in small colonies so several species should be kept together in the tank. The breeding procedure is almost unknown, and aquarium success seems to have occurred more by accident than by design.

Clown Loach (Botia macreacantha)
The Clown Loach is the most beautiful of all the loaches and comes from Indonesia. It has a golden orange body with three broad black bands running vertically. Unfortunately, this fish is not only shy, but it is also prone to disease and is therefore difficult to keep. However, once the fish have been established in a well-planted tank they will eat most foods and can live for many years. As yet breeding of the Clown Loach has not been achieved in captivity.

ATHERNIDS

Although the rainbow family (Atherinidae) is largely made up of marine tropical fishes, there are a few freshwater species indigenous to Madagascar and Australia. Most rainbow species have two dorsal fins.

Madagascar Rainbow (Bedotia geayi)
This beautiful, elongate fish from Madagascar grows to about 10cm. (4in.) long (the females are slightly smaller). The basic body colors are green and blue, and the fins are orange, bordered with black. The tail is edged with red in the males, and both sexes have the characteristic two dorsal fins. It is an extremely active fish and a voracious eater taking any foods offered. The Madagascar Rainbow prefers hard, alkaline water kept at a temperature of about 24°C. (75°F.). Spawning these fish is fairly easy, the best results being obtained by using one male with two or three females. The eggs are laid in plant thickets over a period of up to a week. The parents do not eat their eggs so it is not necessary to remove the eggs each day. The eggs hatch after three or four days, and the young grow rapidly.

Australian Rainbow (Melanotaenia maccullochi)
This species, measuring 9cm. (3in.) long, is related to the Madagascar Rainbow but, as the name implies, is only found in Australia. It is a quieter species than the Madagascar Rainbow and is well suited to the community tank. The basic body color is a golden olive with numerous rows of broken brown horizontal strips while the finnage is reddish. Body and fin colors are brighter in the male than in the female. Spawning is similar to the Madagascar Rainbow, but the addition of a very small amount of salt to the water seems to be beneficial.

Celebes Rainbow (Telmatherian ladigesi)
The Celebes Rainbow is a beautiful but somewhat delicate fish from Celebes which is susceptible to changes of water. Ideally, the water should be fairly hard and slightly alkaline with a small amount of salt added. The Celebes Rainbow has a golden, translucent body with a pale blue line running from the middle of the body to the base of the tail. The fins are golden yellow, and the males have extensions to the filaments of the anal and dorsal fins.

These fish spawn over a period of three to four days when large clear eggs are laid in the plant thickets. The eggs adhere to the foliage by sticky threads and can easily be removed to a hatching tank to give the best breeding results.

CENTROPOMIDS

Species in the family Centropomidae are mainly salt and brackish water species and only a few have found their way into freshwater.

Glass Fish (Ambassis lala)
The Glass Fish is a truly transparent fish and comes from India and Thailand where it lives in hard, alkaline water which often has a slight salt content. Although the body is almost colorless, it has an overall faint gold tinge while the fins are a deeper tint of gold and have a bright blue edging. The fish spawn among floating plants where numerous small eggs are laid. The fry have small mouths and require extremely small food.

ARGUSFISH

This is a small group (family Scatophagidae) of coastal fish which also live in brackish and fresh water. They are indigenous to South-

Australian Rainbow.

east Asia, northern Australia, and parts of the Western Pacific.

Scat (Scatophagus argus)

The Scat is found in estuarine conditions in Indonesia, and in the wild it grows to 45cm. (18in.) long but aquarium specimens rarely exceed 20cm. (8in.). This fish has a round, laterally compressed body. The basic color is a golden, olive green with numerous large dark spots. Some varieties show red or brown colorations with the spots forming vertical broken lines. These color types are often called **Tiger** or **Ruby Scats**. Although Scats are greedy eaters, accepting most types of food including filamentous algae, they are peaceful fishes suitable for the community tank even when they are mixed with small fish. Sea salt should be added to the tank water. Scats have not bred in the aquarium.

FINGERFISH

This is a small Old World family (Monodactylidae) distributed in river mouths and coastal areas.

Malayan Angel (Monodactylus argenteus)

The Malayan Angel can be found in most coastal areas of Asia and can either be kept in water containing a small amount of salt or in a full marine aquarium. It is of typical angelfish shape with a silver body and two black vertical lines—one running down across the eye, and the other just behind the gill cover. The dorsal and anal fins are a brilliant orange, edged with black. The Malayan Angel will eat most foods and grows to about 22.5cm. (9in.) long. It is best kept in shoals at temperatures above 24°C. (75°F.). No records of tank spawnings have yet been obtained.

MORMYRIDS

This is a small family (Mormyridae) which is only found in the fresh waters of Africa. It is a particularly interesting group which has developed a characteristic, complex system of orientation. A series of electric organs can detect changes or obstacles in the individual's field and provide direction for moving and

Elephant Nose.

locating food. Mormyrids eat most foods.

Elephant Nose (Gnathonemus petersi)

The Elephant Nose is a fascinating fish found in the Congo area of Africa, where it inhabits slow moving streams with muddy bottoms. The long trunk-like appendage which extends from the nose is used to probe for food consisting mostly of small crustacea and worms. The fish has a dark brown-violet body with two irregular white vertical bars running between the anal and dorsal fins. The tail has dark, forked markings which accentuate its shape. Although the fish grows to 22.5cm. (9in.) long, it is peaceful and shy and can easily be kept in a community tank.

NANDIDS

Most of the species within this small family (Nandidae) are shy, showing predatory, and

Bottom Left. *Scat.*
Bottom Right. *Malayan Angel.*

Chameleon Fish.

often nocturnal, behavior. They are small fish that are found in South America, Africa, and Southeast Asia.

Chameleon Fish (Badis badis)

Found in most parts of India, the Chameleon Fish derives its common name from its ability to change color rapidly. Basically, it is a dark chocolate brown with darker bars. At various times red, green, or pink markings can be prominent, usually in a checkerboard pattern. It resembles a dwarf cichlid and is the only member of the family that is suitable for a community tank. However, Chameleon Fish tend to be vicious and ideally should be kept with similar species and fed mainly on live foods. The Chameleon Fish grows to 7cm. (2.75in.) long and spawns in a typical cichlid fashion, looking after the eggs and caring for the young.

The Marine Tropical Aquarium

Since saltwater fish live in a stable environment in large volumes of well-oxygenated moving water they are much less adaptable to variations in their habitat than their freshwater relatives. The aquarist has to control the environment in the tropical marine tank much more precisely than in the freshwater aquarium. On the other hand, there is the satisfaction of keeping fish which are rarely equaled in beauty by freshwater species.

TANK EQUIPMENT

The following equipment is necessary to set up and maintain a tropical marine tank.

The Tank

Seawater is a corrosive substance and will dissolve any metals with which it comes into contact. The best type available, therefore, is the all glass tank made by bonding five sheets of glass together with silicone rubber cement (as described in freshwater fishes). A suitable size is 75 x 37.5 x 37.5cm. (30 x 15 x 15in.), which holds 115 liters (30 gallons) when completely filled. It will weigh about 115kg. (250lb.) when filled and should be placed on a well-built, commercially available metal stand. The outside of the back glass of the tank should be painted either blue or green.

The hoods are usually made of aluminum and are bought already painted with heavy enamel. Any bare metal in the hood should be painted with primer and two coats of gloss paint to prevent corrosion by the saltwater. The evaporation cover is a piece of plain glass with smoothed edges which fits neatly on the top of the tank to prevent evaporation and the loss of fish by their jumping out.

Heating

To reduce the number of electrical connections, which are always a potential hazard near saltwater, the combined heater-thermostat is better for the marine aquarium. A wattage of 100 is satisfactory for the tank size recommended. A good glass mercury thermometer should be attached by a plastic clip to the front glass. Also, it is a good idea to check the temperature regularly by touching the front glass with the back of the hand.

Filtration

As with freshwater tanks the water must be filtered continuously if it is to remain clear and provide a suitable habitat for the fish. The filter should be under the gravel and fully cover the bottom of the tank. When this filter is covered with gravel and connected to an air pump, water is filtered by being drawn through the gravel. Ideally, the air pump should be the best vibrator pump on the market and possess two air outlets. Cheap air pumps tend to be noisy.

Coarse gravel about 0.5cm. (0.20in.) in diameter is used to cover the under-gravel filter to a depth of about 5cm. (2in.). This gravel is then covered with finer gravel, 0.3cm. (0.1in.) in diameter. These gravels form the filter medium in which various bacteria grow and which, together, form a zoogleal layer—a powerful living active filter medium. The color of the gravel used is a matter of personal choice.

External box filters are cheap plastic filters made up of an air lift and tubes which circulate the water between the aquarium and the filter. This filter should be driven by another air pump. The box should be filled with 5cm. (2in.) of nylon wool covered by 5cm. (2in.) of activated marine charcoal. This separate pump and filter system is a useful addition since it provides a backup device and the charcoal filter helps keep the seawater clear.

WATER

Seawater is a much more stable, but more complex, environment than fresh water. Marine fish are thus less able to withstand variations in aquaria and the aquarist is presented with a different set of problems if he is to maintain a suitable environment.

Synthetic Sea Salts

Natural seawater is too polluted or may contain pathogenic organisms unless it is collected from mid-ocean. Synthetic sea salts added to tap water provide a perfectly satisfactory substitute. For the size tank recommended, a pack of salt for 90 liters (24 gallons) is needed.

Hydrometer

A good quality marine hydrometer is an essential piece of control equipment. It is used to measure the specific gravity which is directly related to the salinity of the water. The specific gravity of the water must be kept within 1.018 to 1.022. The hydrometer should be already calibrated at 24°C. (75°F.) and must always be clean when used.

pH Kit

A pH kit is used to measure the pH of the saltwater which should register between 7.8 to 8.4, that is, slightly on the alkaline side.

FISH--Table 2

Tropical Marine Aquarium Equipment and Fish for the Beginner

EQUIPMENT	DECOR	FISH
All glass tank Hood Glass evaporation cover Lighting Heater and Thermostat Thermometer Undergravel filter External filter Two pumps Hydrometer pH test kit Nitrite test kit Synthetic sea salts Oodinium cure	Gravel Coral Shells Rocks	One specimen of each of 3 different species of Damsel Fish.

The marine tropical aquarium is more difficult to manage than its freshwater equivalent, but the extra trouble is worthwhile since marine fish are extremely colorful, as evidenced by these Moorish Idols, Long-Nose Butterfly Fish, and Angelfish.

FISH—Table 3
Nitrite Tolerant Fish

Malayan Angel	(*Monodactylus argeneus*)
Pretty Damsel Fish	(*Dascyllus marginatus*)
Domino Damsel Fish	(*Dascyllus trimaculatus*)
Electric Blue Damsel Fish	(*Pomacentrus coeruleus*)
Saffron Blue Damsel Fish	(*Pomacentrus melanochir*)
Sergeant Major	(*Abudefduf saxatilis*)
Royal Blue Trigger Fish	(*Odonus niger*)
Picasso Trigger Fish	(*Rhinecanthus aculeatus*)

Nitrite Test Kit

A nitrite test kit is essential, and the nitrite levels should be checked regularly. All organic matter in the tank, such as is found on dirty rocks, coral or gravel, or in the form of uneaten food, dead fish, urine and feces, is first broken down by bacteria (known as gelatine liquifiers) to ammonium compounds. These are toxic to fish and invertebrates. In the presence of oxygen another group of bacteria breaks these compounds down to nitrites which are also toxic. Another group of bacteria then oxidize the nitrites to the relatively harmless nitrates. These three groups of bacteria colonize the gravel and, with the movement of the highly aerated water through the gravel and undergravel filter, the efficient breakdown of the toxic compounds occurs.

DECOR

Coral, shells, and rocks are used for décoration and make useful hiding places for some of the more shy creatures. Corals, shells, and rocks should be placed in a bleach solution (available from pet shops) for three days, then washed under a running tap for one hour, and finally boiled for two hours in an enamel saucepan. The pieces are ready to add to the tank when they no longer smell of chlorine.

SETTING UP THE TROPICAL MARINE TANK

Points to bear in mind before deciding where to place the tank are: a sound floor, easy access to an electric outlet, and a site which is not exposed to direct sunlight. The tank should be placed on a piece of board on the stand and then filled with tap water for a few hours to test it for leaks. It should then be emptied, the undergravel filter placed in position, and the air tube connected to the air lifts. The filter should fill the bottom of the tank so that there are no areas of gravel through which water does not circulate. The previously well-washed coarse gravel should cover the filter and be packed well around the edges of the filter. The gravel should be about 8cm. (3in.) deep at the back and 4cm. (1.5in.) deep at the front so that any uneaten food is likely to fall to the front for easier removal. Now a layer about 1.5cm. (0.5in.) deep of the previously washed fine gravel should be added to cover the coarse gravel. Place a plastic sheet on top of the gravel to prevent disturbing it when the water is poured in. A clean plastic bucket containing a packet of synthetic sea salt should be placed on the plastic. Add water from the cold water tap, preferably via a hose to the bucket, using a spray to stir up the salts. Water from the hot faucet must never be used because it may contain minute amounts of copper which is toxic to the fish. The tank should be filled to within 10cm. (4in.) of the top, and the bucket and plastic sheet removed. Finally, the previously cleaned rocks, shells, and corals can be put in position. The quantity required and the positioning of these decorations is a matter of choice but taller items should be to the back, with a main feature off center. After adding the gravel and rockwork to the tank, the water level will be near the top.

The box filter should be fixed outside and at the back of the tank and input and output tubes connected. Now the airline can be connected to the first pump, and the air tubes from the undergravel filter to the air outlets of the other pump. The box filter should be filled with saltwater from the tank, the thermometer attached with a plastic suction disc to the front glass of the tank, and the evaporation cover placed in position. The manufacturer's instructions should be carefully followed when connecting the pumps and heater thermostat to the power supply. The lights in the hood can now be mounted and plugged in. The tank should be left for twenty-four hours to allow the seawater to mix and the temperature to rise to 24°C. (74°F.). If the water does not reach this temperature, the current should be switched off, the plug pulled out, and the thermostat adjusted. The specific gravity of the water can now be tested. If it is higher than 1.022, water should be added gradually, allowed to mix thoroughly, and the pH retested.

Maturation of the filter medium

The gravel filter must now be given time for the helpful bacteria to colonize the gravel. At this stage, a final decision must be made on whether the aquarium is to be a fish only tank or a fish and invertebrate tank. The advantage of keeping only fish is that the Oodinium treatment following water changes can be carried out in the tank. In an invertebrate and fish tank the invertebrates are poisoned by the Oodinium treatment so all fishes entering the aquarium have to be treated in a separate tank.

Fish-only Tank

No organic material enters the tank until after about three days when the filter system has developed the necessary colonies of bacteria. In the fish-only tank, up to 2.5cm. (1in.) of nitrite tolerant fish may be introduced at this point for every 19 liters (5gallons) of seawater; therefore, in the recommended size tank up to 12.5cm. (5in.) of fish can be introduced. A choice of nitrite tolerant fish can be made from the accompanying table.

251

Bearing in mind the size limitations in proportion to the amount of water, only one of each of the species should be selected from the above list as more than one of the same variety will establish territories and fight. At this stage it is much better to purchase two or three small fish to observe and use in maturing the tank rather than to fill the tank up to its limit and not leave room, for example, for a Butterfly Fish at a later stage. When the fish are brought home, turn off the light on the tank and float the plastic bags in the tank. Over the next hour increasing amounts of tank water should be introduced into the bags until the fish are eventually in pure tank water. They can be gently turned out of the bag.

The fish must now be given a treatment of commercial Oodinium cure to prevent their developing Oodinium. The tank lighting should be left off until the next day, and the fish should not be fed for two days, after which time they can be fed small amounts twice daily. All uneaten food must be siphoned off to keep the ammonium and nitrite levels from rising due to the decomposition of food particles and excreta. After three to ten weeks the nitrifying bacteria in the filters are sufficiently numerous to break down the nitrite into nitrates. At this stage the tank is mature. During the maturation period the nitrite levels must be tested daily; it should not reach more than 20 parts/million if feeding and removal of excess foods are carried out properly.

Even when the fish-only aquarium has matured, care must still be taken in adding new fish. A new fish must be introduced in the dark with a careful change from "bag" water to tank water. Then it should be placed gently into a perforated clear plastic box which is allowed to sink slowly to the aquarium floor. The fish should be left in its box for three days without food. The tank must be treated for Oodinium within one hour of the new fish's arrival in the tank. After three days, the fish can be released, preferably in the dark. If the established members of the tank have their territories staked out, it is wise to rearrange the positions of the major rockwork and corals to destroy existing territorial boundaries when the new fish is released.

Once the fish-only tank has been successfully managed for about six months, keeping the more difficult species may be attempted. Extreme care must be taken with the rarer

Young Brine Shrimp are excellent food for fish.

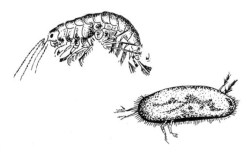

and more expensive marine coral fish to prevent the extermination of species which do not breed in captivity.

Invertebrate and Fish Tank

For the invertebrate and fish tank, the same procedure already described under setting up the tropical marine tank should be followed up to the point where the tank is ready to be matured. Maturation for this tank is achieved by adding nitrite tolerant invertebrates such as the anemone *Radianthus* or the One-banded Coral Shrimp. The nitrite level should be checked twice daily until the bacterial colonies in the filter bed are established. Coral fish may be added only after they have been given an Oodinium cure in a separate tank for ten days. Oodinium cures are poisonous to most invertebrates. Invertebrates, such as the octopus or the *Cerianthus anemone*, are not suitable for the community aquarium as they will kill small coral fishes.

FEEDING TROPICAL MARINE FISH

The principles of feeding marine fish are the same as for freshwater fish, but the hazard of overfeeding is considerably greater in the marine aquarium. All the foods used in the freshwater aquarium, such as whiteworm, earthworm, and *Tubifex*, are suitable. Daphnia are good but must be fed sparingly because they die rapidly in seawater. Chopped beef heart and spinach and, for a few well-adapted species, flake foods, are also suitable. Marine foods from a fish dealer are acceptable but potentially hazardous because of the risk of introducing infection. There are commercially available frozen and gamma ray sterilized fish foods, such as Mysis shrimp, mixed shell fish, squid, and some mollusks which are disease free. Live brine shrimp are suitable for the small fish or as special treats. As wide a variety of foods as the fish will accept should be given twice daily. Any uneaten food should be removed after ten minutes.

Tropical Marine Fish

There are thousands of marine tropical fish although some are rarely imported. This section deals with a carefully selected collection, the majority of which are suitable for the marine aquarium while including a few species of renowned beauty but which are difficult to keep.

ANGELFISH

Members of this family (Pomacanthidae) of very beautiful fish should not be kept until an owner has about six months' experience with easier to manage species. Angelfish appear flattened from side to side, and longer from nose to tail than from top to bottom. Their size varies from 2.5–45cm. (1–18in.). The species and individual fish within the same species vary as to their degree of aggression and diet. Only one should be kept in an aquarium to prevent fighting. They are midwater feeders and usually need protein food such as chopped earthworm, whiteworm, and seafoods (prawn, squid, or mussel meat). They can be weaned to chopped beef heart and, some species, to marine flake foods. Beginners should not raise these fish.

Coral Beauty Angelfish (Centropyge bispinosus)
This fish grows to 12.5cm. (5in.) and is widely distributed in the tropical Indian and Pacific Oceans. It is shy when first acquired but feeds well after a few days and is one of the easier angelfish to keep.

French Angelfish (Pomacanthus paru)
The French Angelfish comes from the Caribbean where it grows to 45cm. (18in.) long. It is most beautiful when about 5cm. (2in.) long and has brilliant yellow stripes on a black background. These stripes fade with age leaving a black fish with gold-edged scales. The French Angelfish can be difficult to feed initially.

Purple Moon Angelfish.

Whimple Fish

Yellow Long-Nose Butterfly Fish

Purple Fire Ball (*Centropyge fisheri*)

This species is another of the smaller angelfish from the Indian and Pacific Oceans where it grows to 6cm. (2.4in.) long. It is suitable for the beginner being easy to feed and hardy in the proper conditions.

Purple Moon Angelfish (*Pomacanthus maculosus*)

This larger angelfish grows to 35cm. (14in.) and is common in the Red Sea though it is also found along the east coast of Africa as far as Mozambique. In aquariums it is sometimes shy at first but soon settles down and can be persuaded to accept flake foods.

BATFISH

There are three species of batfish (family Platacidae) which are available from time to time. They have no special feeding requirements and have not been bred in captivity.

Common Batfish (*Platax orbicularis*)

This is the most common species and the smallest even though in the wild it grows to 75cm. (30in.). It is indigenous to the Red Sea, Indian Ocean, and western Pacific. It should not be kept in a tank smaller than 135 liters (36 gallons) because it always flees rapidly from any aggressor and, if confined to a small space, may be killed. The Common Batfish is nitrite tolerant, easy to feed, and grows well.

Graceful Batfish (*Platax pinnatus*)

Also known as the Redfaced Batfish, this species grows to 60cm. (24in.) in its natural habitat in the Indian and Pacific Oceans. It should have a large tank, preferably on its own, and must be given live foods.

Longfin Batfish (*Platax tiera*)

This species also comes from the Indian and Pacific Oceans where it grows to 75cm. (30in.). It should be given live foods.

BUTTERFLY FISH

There are over one hundred species of butterfly fish (family Chaetodontidae). They tend to be deeper in relation to length when compared with angelfish. Butterfly fish under about 5cm. (2in.) in size need to be fed on brine shrimp continuously during daylight hours and unless these feeding requirements can be met, fish of this size should not be purchased. Healthy specimens should feed well, swim with the pelvic fins extended, and be of good light coloration (dark coloration often suggests presence of disease).

Sunburst Butterfly Fish (*Chaetodon kleini*)

This beautiful yellow species comes from the Indian and Pacific Ocean where it grows to 15cm. (6in.). It is hardy, feeds well, and will accept dried flake foods.

Whimple Fish (*Heniochus acuminatus*)

This butterfly fish from the Indian and Pacific Oceans is not typical of the rest of the Chaetodontidae because of its unusual shape and the extended rays of its dorsal fin. It is sometimes mistaken for the Moorish Idol (*Zandus cornutus*). The Whimple Fish is one of the hardiest of the butterfly species and will eat most foods. When young it will peck at the body of other fish. Because this action is tolerated the Whimple Fish may be cleaning the other fish of external parasites.

Center. *Scissortail Sergeant.*
Bottom. *Clown Anemone Fish.*

Yellow Longnose Butterfly Fish (*Forcipiger longirostris*)

This species comes from the Indian and Pacific Oceans where it grows to 15cm. (6in.) in length. In spite of its specialized jaws, it usually accepts all protein foods and enjoys picking bits of food off rocks and coral. Although it is nonaggressive, it has formidable dorsal spines to warn off any potential aggressor.

CLOWN FISH

These fish (family Amphiprionidae) come from the coral reefs of the Indo-Pacific Ocean and swim with characteristic wriggling movements. Clown fish are also known as anemone fish due to the particular relationship they have with certain large tropical sea anemones. Both fish and anemone benefit from this symbiotic relationship; the fish cleans up the anemone from time to time and in return is protected from predators by swimming among the anemone's stinging tentacles from which it appears to be immune.

Common Clown Fish (*Amphiprion perrula*)

This is one of the best known marine tropical fish. It is sometimes known as the **Clown**

Anemone Fish because of its association in the wild with the Pacific Anemone (*Stoichactus* species). It is widely distributed in the Pacific and grows to 8cm. (3.25in.) long. The Common Clown Fish prefers fresh protein but will take dried foods. If *Stiochactus* anemones are not available, Clown Fish will associate with the more hardy anemone *Radianthus*. Clown Fish have been bred but not successfully raised in the aquarium.

DAMSELFISH

This group contains the nitrite tolerant species which are used to help mature the new marine aquarium. In addition, the fish themselves are colorful and interesting in their habits. All the species are territorial and will fight; two damselfish of the same species must not be kept together in the same tank.

Domino Damselfish (*Dascyllus trimaculatus*)

Sometimes called the **Threespotted Damselfish** because of the three white spots, two on the body and one on the forehead, the Domino Damselfish grows to 15cm. (6in.) in its natural habitat in the Indian and Pacific Oceans. It is aggressive in defending its territory, especially to members of the same species. Except in a large tank where there is enough space for each to have a separate territory, only one Domino Damselfish should be kept. It is nitrite tolerant and easy to keep. The fish has been bred but not reared in the aquarium. It also is capable of making a grunting noise.

Electric Blue Damselfish (*Pomacentrus caeruleus*)

This species comes from the central Pacific Ocean and, like all damselfish, is aggressive to its own species. It grows to 10cm. (4in.) long. This species is a great gravel digger, is easy to feed, and is nitrite tolerant.

Pretty Damselfish (*Dascyllus melanurus*)

This damselfish comes from the Red Sea and grows to 15cm. (6in.) long. It displays the typical damselfish behavior patterns but is active, hardy, easy to feed and keep. It is nitrite tolerant.

Sergeant Major (*Abudefduf sexatilis*)

The Sergeant Major is a widely distributed fish, ranging from the Indo-Pacific to the tropical Atlantic Ocean. In the wild it grows to 15cm. (6in.) long. It is pale green in color with four or five dark colored stripes running vertically on the body. It is an active hardy fish and will eat most foods. On the coral reef, the young fish live in large shoals. It is nitrite tolerant.

COWFISH

There are about ten species of cowfish (family Ostrociontidae) which are sold for the tanks of aquarists. The scales of these fish are fused together to form a rigid shell which encloses the body. Because of their odd body form they are slow swimmers. They are sometimes known as trunk fish because of their expanded snouts. They feed on small

shrimp and crabs in the wild by "squirting" away the sand and exposing their prey. Some species are reported to produce a poisonous mucus when frightened. They are easy to feed in the aquarium.

Long-Horned Cowfish (*Lactophrys cornutus*)

The Long-Horned Cowfish is an oddity of the sea and comes from the Indian and Pacific Oceans where it grows to 45cm. (18in.). Its common name is due to its long nose and the

Neon Goby.

set of protruding structures on its head. It also has another set of "horns" below the tail, and the body is covered with armor. It is inclined to jump if surprised, for example, by the aquarium lights being put on when the room is dark. Its eyesight is so poor that for the first few days in the aquarium, bits of earthworm or meat on the end of a thin knit-

Lion Fish.

254

ting needle may have to be placed under its nose.

GOBIES

Members of this very large family (Gobiidae) are common in rock pools around most coasts in temperate and tropical regions. They often have two dorsal fins and the pelvic fins are fused so as to act as a suction cap for holding the fish onto rocks. They are small, shy fish often hiding under the edge of rocks. The Neon Goby has spawned in the aquarium. They are hardy fish and have no special requirements for food.

Neon Goby (Gobiosoma oceanpos)
From the coral reefs of the tropical Atlantic, the Neon Goby is a peaceful, friendly fish which carries out cleaning behavior on other fish. This was the first marine tropical fish known to have spawned in the aquarium, and the young have been raised to the free swimming stage. Neon Gobies are egg placers, spawning similarly to the cichlids, and both parents protect the brood.

Scooter Goby (Bathygobius sp)
This fish comes from the Pacific around the Philippines; they grow to 8cm. (3in.).

LION FISH

The lion fish (family Scorpaenidae), sometimes called dragon, cobra, or scorpion fish, are so called because of the poisonous spines

in the spiny rays of the dorsal fin which are used as a defense weapon. Humans can be affected by these poisonous spines so the fish must be netted and handled with care. Lion fish are predators and, when first imported, must be fed with live fish such as appropriately sized guppies, or they can be conditioned to take pieces of meat. They are best kept on their own or with other fish of the same size. The tank should not have much in the way of decor which will provide hiding places for the living food.

Common Lion Fish (Pterosis volitans)
The Common Lion Fish comes from the Indian and Pacific Oceans and grows to 35cm. (14in.). It is the easiest lion fish to feed and can soon be trained to take pieces of meat or shrimp.

MONOS

These fish (family Monodactylidae) come from the river mouths and coastal areas of Africa, southern Asia, and Australia. It is essential to find out in what type of water (salt, brackish, or fresh) the dealer has kept them. If they have been in fresh or brackish water, adjustments to salt water should be made slowly.

Malayan Angel (Monodactylus argenteus)
This fish comes from the Malayan and African coasts where it is found in the sea and in the river mouths. It can be kept in fresh, brackish, or salt water. In its main habitat, the sea, it grows to 22.5cm. (9in.). It is easy to feed and nitrite tolerant.

Finger Fish (Monodactylus sebae)
The Finger Fish comes from the West African coast and grows to 20cm. (8in.). It is silvery yellow in color and has black stripes on its head. Coloration fades with age and size.

TRIGGER FISH

This is a large family (Balistidae) of colorful, hardy, and sometimes aggressive fish. They

Center Left. *Fingerfish.*
Center Right. *Sea Anemone* (Pseudactinia flagellifera).
Bottom Left. *Picasso Trigger Fish.*
Bottom Center. *Sea Horse.*
Bottom Right. *Starfish* (Oreaster nodosus)

are often shaped like an elongated diamond with a large head and eyes set high up and well back. The name *trigger fish* comes from the modification of the dorsal fin into a stiff spine which can be erected by the fish and then locked into place. This long spine is used by the fish to fix itself into holes or cracks when it is in its lair for the night or when taking refuge from danger. There are no problems with feeding. They have not been bred in the aquarium.

Royal Blue Trigger Fish (Odonus niger).
This species comes from the Indian Ocean around Sri Lanka and grows to 20cm. (8in.). It is hardy and although it prefers crabs and shrimp, it will adapt to all foods. It is nitrite tolerant.

Picasso Trigger Fish (Rhinecanthus aculeatus)
The Picasso comes from the Indian and Pacific Oceans where it grows to 30cm. (12in.). Young specimens are not aggressive and are hardy; they will accept all foods and are nitrite tolerant.

Moorish Idol (Zanclus canisceno)
The only member of the family Zanclidae, the Moorish Idol is a most beautiful fish from the Indian and Pacific Oceans. The Moorish Idol is difficult to keep since it will not accept food readily and is susceptible to disease. It also needs a large tank and, consequently, is not a fish for the inexperienced marine aquarist. The feeding requirements are typical for marine fish.

Curled Octopus (Eledone cirrhosa).

SEA HORSES

There are a number of different species of sea horse, the most popular being the Golden Sea Horse (*Hippocampus kuda*) from the Pacific where it grows to 60cm. (24in.), the *Hippocampus punctulatus*, and the Dwarf Sea Horse (*Hippocampus zosterae*). Sea horses can be green, yellow, brown, black, and white in color. They should have a piece of cured gorgonias coral on which to fasten themselves. They are difficult to keep since they will rarely eat anything other than live fish or brine shrimp. They are slow moving and must be kept separately so other faster moving fish will not eat their food. On importation they are often heavily parasitized. The breeding habits of the sea horse are fascinating since the male broods the eggs in his pouch.

MARINE INVERTEBRATES

Remember that there are certain difficulties in keeping fish and invertebrates in the same aquarium since many invertebrates are highly susceptible to Oodinium treatments. One should establish nitrite tolerant invertebrates first and then introduce the fish at a later stage after they have been Oodinium treated in a separate tank.

Anemones
These animals belong to the phylum Coelenterata and have a hollow body with tentacles at the mouth end and a "foot" at the other end. Some of the most hardy anemones belong to the genus *Stoichactis* (not nitrite tolerant) or the genus *Radianthus* (nitrite tolerant). They can be fed by dropping small pieces of meat or fish onto the tentacles.

Coral
Living coral belongs to the same phylum as do anemones. The coral polyp extracts salts from seawater and builds up the limestone external skeleton in which the animal lives.

Members of the genus *Goniopora* are the most suitable species to keep, but they are nitrite intolerant. The tiny tentacles of the coral polyp catch minute organisms or pieces of food drifting past. Live brine shrimp and small amounts of finely shredded mussel meat are suitable foodstuffs. Corals need good lighting.

Feather-Duster Worm (*Sabellastarte indica*)
This anelid makes a thin tube around its body. When feeding, the feathery tentacles emerge from the tube and catch microscopic particles in the water. It is nitrite intolerant.

Starfish
Starfish belong to the phylum Echinodermata and are often difficult to keep in the aquarium. *Protoreoster* species, however, will eat small pieces of prawn or meat and are nitrite tolerant.

Sea Urchins
These are echinoderms like starfish and tend to hide in the aquarium. The **Black-Spined Sea Urchin** (*Centrechinu* sp) is nitrite intolerant but is easy to feed, by dropping a small piece of food into the spines.

Shrimp and Crabs
The **Banded Coral Shrimp** (*Stenopus hispidus*), also known as the **Boxing Shrimp**, is nitrite tolerant and has been bred in the aquarium. Unless the tank is large and con-

tains many hiding places, only one specimen should be kept since they are exceptionally aggressive toward each other. They should be fed on small pieces of meat.

Hermit crabs of the genus *Clibanarius* are peaceful scavengers. Having no body shell of their own, they must find a disused mollusk shell. They should be fed with small pieces of meat or fish and are nitrite intolerant.

Octopuses
Octopuses are highly specialized mollusks and difficult to keep. They are highly intolerant of nitrites and even high levels of nitrates. They cannot be kept in the same tank as fish smaller than themselves or they will eat them. The tank should be prepared so that it has a small rock cave in which an octopus can hide, and the overall lighting should be subdued. The evaporation cover and tank cover should be substantial as there have been numerous instances of octopuses climbing out of tanks and dying. They should be fed fresh shrimp, crab, or prawn meat.

Keeping Cold-Water Fish

The range of temperature for cold-water fish is 10–18°C. (50–65°F.). Cold-water fish have a high rate of oxygen consumption. If the water temperature rises above 18°C. (65°F.), there is less oxygen in the water and the fish begin to suffer. The cold-water tank should be placed away from direct sunlight to prevent overheating. Overcrowding cold-water tanks will bring about a lack of oxygen and an excess of carbon dioxide, so these fish need more space than tropical species: 1cm. of fish for each 24cm² of water surface. The ordinary goldfish bowl is the worst possible shape in which to keep cold-water fish, since the water volume to surface area is at a minimum when it is filled.

There are now many cheap plastic small rectangular tanks available if only one pet goldfish is kept. It is far more satisfactory, however, to keep a community of plants and fish in a proper aquarium. As for the tropical aquarium, a wide range of tanks is available

Red Lion Head Veiltail Goldfish.

FISH—Table 4

Cold Freshwater Aquarium Equipment and Fish for the Beginner

EQUIPMENT	DECOR	FISH
All-glass Tank	Gravel	4 Common Goldfish
Hood	Plants	1 Veiltail
Lighting	Rocks	1 Moor
Pump		
Filter (internal)		

256

Top Left. *The common goldfish is the most popular of all fish for both indoors tanks and outdoor pools.* Top Right. *Goldfish are extremely easy to look after with little care. They are best housed in a small tank with water weeds. They serve as an ideal introduction to the hobby of fish-keeping.*

that vary in type and size. Obviously, the cold-water tank does not need a heater and thermostat but otherwise the principles and management are similar to those described for the Tropical Freshwater Aquarium. It also needs a degree of regular attention.

Many of the tropical freshwater plants such as *Vallisneria*, *Sagittaria*, *Myriophyllum*, and *Ludwigia* are also suitable for the cold-water aquarium. Additional cold-water species such as Canadian Pond Weed (*Elodea canadensis*), Hornwort (*Ceratophyllum* spp), Water Violet (*Hottonia palustris*), and Willow Moss (*Fontinalis antipyretica*) are also available. Waterlilies of the genus *Nuphar* grow from a rhizome and make a good centerpiece for the tank.

Food requirements for pond fish are the same as for tropical freshwater fish. Food pellets are available for larger pond fish and are satisfactory as part of a mixed diet.

Golden Orfe.

Cold-Water Fish

COMMON GOLDFISH (CARASSIUS AURATUS AURATUS)

The Common Goldfish is a domesticated subspecies of *C. auratus* and is a member of the carp, barp, and minnow family (Cyprinidae). By selective breeding over centuries various fancy varieties have been formed.

All the goldfish varieties spawn in the typical cyprinid fashion, scattering adhesive eggs over the plants or spawning medium. They can be spawned in the outdoor pond, and the pond weed with the eggs attached can then be placed in a bare indoor tank. Goldfish should be given a typical egg scatterer environment.

Young Common Goldfish are dark bronze but develop their gold and red color during their first year of life. Some fish retain the white, silver, or black patches of their juvenile coloring. They will eat all foods live or dried and a little vegetable food occasionally. Overfeeding rapidly leads to dirty, milky tanks. Females when mature have a plump rounded abdomen while males are slimmer

Golden Tench.

and some develop small tubercles on the gill covers and pectoral fins in the breeding season.

Many varieties of fancy goldfish have been artificially bred from the Common Goldfish. The behavior patterns of the fancy varieties are the same as for the Common Goldfish. However, as they have been bred to exaggerated eye or body shapes, they are more delicate than the Common Goldfish and do better in the relatively protected environment of the indoor aquarium rather than in the outdoor pond. The fancy varieties are better spawned indoors where the process can be more clearly observed.

Shubunkin
This variety is similar to the Common Goldfish but has a longer tail fin and is a calico variety. It has small transparent scales and is often wrongly described as being scaleless. The Bristol Shubunkin has larger fins and is better for the indoor tank while the London Shubunkin is better for the outdoor pool.

Comet
The Comet is similar in shape to the Common Goldfish but has a tail fin which is half the length of the body in size. It can be obtained in different colors and in both ordinary and calico varieties. The Comet does better in the garden pond than in the indoor aquarium.

Fantail
This attractive fish has a globular body and a double tail and anal fin. There are calico and scaled varieties—the latter is more suitable for the pond.

Veiltail
There are scaled and calico varieties of the Veiltail, which has a long flowing tail that is longer than the body length. It does better in an indoor tank but can be kept outside in the summer.

Moor
This fish has long fins and should be black without any yellow coloration. It has protruding "telescopic" eyes. This fish should be kept in an indoor aquarium.

A one-year-old butyl rubber pond clearly shows shelves below the water line.

Celestial

This variety has eyes which look upward and are even more protruding than the Moor's. The Celestial should be kept in an indoor aquarium.

Bubble-Eye

Similar to the Celestial, this fish has a lump under each eye. The Bubble-eye does better indoors.

Oranda

The head of this variety is covered with a wart-like growth. The Oranda should be kept indoors.

Lion Head

This variety has even more warts on the head (a little like a lion's mane) than the Oranda, and it does not possess a dorsal fin. It is not as hardy as the Oranda.

OTHER COLD-WATER FISH

The following cold water fish are frequently kept in aquaria and ponds.

The **Gold Orje** (*Leuciscus idus*) is a European species which makes a good pond fish. They grow quickly, reaching 75cm. (30in.) in length in the wild so that only young fish are suitable for the aquarium.

The **Golden Rudd** (*Scardinius erythrophthalmus*) is a golden variety of the Rudd and is a good pond fish. It is also an excellent tank fish when small.

The **Golden Tench** (*Tinca tinca*) is a peaceful bottom-feeding fish which can be kept in the aquarium when small or in a garden pond when large. The young fish is golden in color but often darkens with age. It prefers live foods.

The **North American Catfish** (*Ameirus nebulosus*) grows to 25cm. (10in.) long. It is nocturnal, and small specimens do well in the aquarium with fish of a similar size. It prefers live foods and is too delicate to survive a cold winter outdoors in a pond.

Also known as the **Koi** or **Nishiki-Koi,** the **Higai Carp** measures 45cm. (18in.) in length and was produced in Japan by crossing two species of carp, *Carassius carassius* and *C. auratus gibelio*. This has produced highly colored fish ranging from pure white to all black including red, white, gold, and black mixtures. It is a good pond fish and will eat all foods.

The **Stickleback** (*Gasterosteus aculeatus*) is a lively pugnacious fish from Europe, northern Asia, Japan, and North America. The male with its red belly during the breeding season is especially attractive. Sticklebacks prefer living on protein foods. They are best kept on their own, one male to three females. The male builds the nest and guards the young.

There are a number of other species of fish native to the United States which prefer temperatures of 7–18°C. (45–65°F.). Some of these are attractive but are inclined to be aggressive. They include *Red Shiner* (*Notropis lutrensis*), the **Yellowbelly Sunfish** (*Lepomis auritus*), and the **Bluegills** (*Lepomis macrochirus*). These fish are rarely available outside the United States.

The Garden Pond

Keeping fish in ponds or pools has been practiced for several thousand years. The ancient Egyptians and later the Romans used these pools, not so much for the pleasure of keeping fish as for the purpose of fattening them for eating.

Today ponds are popular and are found in yards of all sizes. Before building a pond, however, there are several important factors to be taken into consideration.

SITE

The best visual effects are obtained if the pond can be looked down upon and, ideally, it should be sited in the lowest part of the garden. Avoid siting a pond close to trees for not only is there the possibility of the underground roots damaging the pond, but the leaves of several species, such as laurel, holly, and laburnum, are toxic to fish.

DESIGN

It is possible to construct almost any size or shape of pond. Personal choice and situation of the pond will provide some of the guidelines that are required. The depth of the pond is important, and a fairly good-sized part of the total area should be more than 45cm. (18in.) deep to allow the fish to survive during extreme weather conditions when thick ice may form. Varying depths within the pond will allow for the growing of a wider range of aquatic plants even if the overall size of the pond is fairly small.

CONSTRUCTION

Present-day materials offer a wide choice of construction methods so the final choice will probably be dictated by the chosen size, shape and siting of the pond.

Puddled-clay

This is the oldest and in some ways the simplest form of pond. The shape is dug out of sticky clay and then puddled by using water and straw to work the surface into a malleable consistency. Ponds made by this method tend to be small and, due to climactic conditions, may spring leaks.

Prefabricated

This type of pond has a preformed shape and is usually constructed of fiberglass available in a variety of shapes, sizes, and colors. A hole corresponding in size and shape to the preformed pond should be dug out of the garden. This excavated area should then be lined with soft sand and the pond set into the hole. The prefabricated pond has the disadvantage of cracking with age and often of being too shallow.

Butyl Rubber Sheeting

This very strong modern material is ideal for making ponds, particularly those of an informal shape. The required shape should be dug out and layered with soft sand. The rubber sheeting should be loosely stretched out across the excavation and secured around the edges with either paving slabs or large rocks. The water can then be added, and the sheeting will shape itself to fill the contours of the pond. This type of construction is simple and long lasting.

Concrete

This is the most popular material and, if constructed correctly, produces the most

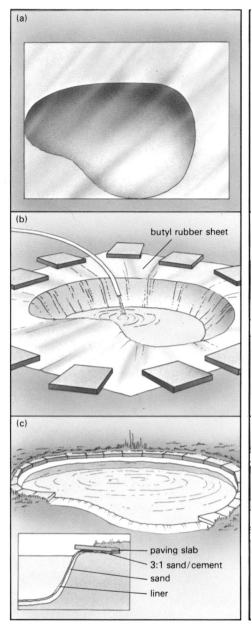

(a)

(b)
butyl rubber sheet

(c)
paving slab
3:1 sand/cement
sand
liner

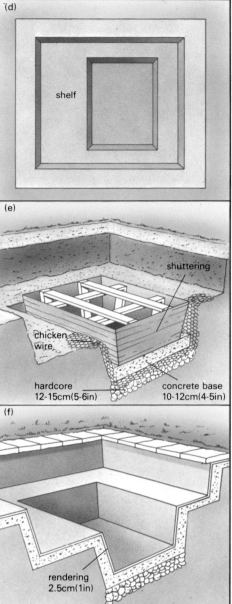

(d)
shelf

(e)
shuttering
chicken wire
hardcore 12-15cm(5-6in)
concrete base 10-12cm(4-5in)

(f)
rendering 2.5cm(1in)

The best way of locating water lilies is to plant them in a basket and submerge this in the pond. The plants are then easily removed when necessary.

rods during the construction of a large pond. Once the pond has been built the concrete has to be "cured" to remove the excess alkali that is harmful to fish. There is no simple way to cure a concrete pond: it entails three or four complete changes of water with at least a week's soaking between each change. Then, the surface should be scrubbed thoroughly with a stiff brush and sealed with a coating of sodium silicate (water glass) diluted with four times the volume of water. Proprietary solutions for coating the concrete are commercially available.

STOCKING THE POND

The best time for planting most aquatic plants is late spring. Some hardy submerged varieties such as Hornwort and Canadian Pond Weed can be introduced earlier since they will help establish a balance prior to stocking the pond with other aquatic life. Gold colored fish show up well in a pond.

Top Left. *The easiest way to make a pond is with butyl rubber sheeting as the lining (a–c). (a) First, dig a hole to the required shape and depth. (b) Line the hole with liner, pinning it around the margins with paving stones before adding the water. (c) Finally, trim off the surplus liner and bed down the paving stones. Concrete-lined ponds take longer to build but are the most durable (d–e). (d) Dig a hole large enough to take the foundation and concrete. (e) Firmly ram in the hardcore foundation, place chicken wire on top of this which should extend up the sides to the surface; lay the concrete base and erect wood shuttering before lining the walls with concrete. (f) When all the concrete is hard, apply a concrete rendering coat. (For curing, see text.)*

Bottom Right. *Tiny "boats" of male stamens floating towards a large half-submerged female flower of the Tape Grass.*

permanent type of pond. Considerable care must be taken to ensure that the correct thickness of concrete is maintained over the whole area of the pond to prevent lines of weakness that will eventually form cracks. It is advisable to incorporate reinforcing iron

Fish are best secured from a reputable dealer because those that are caught from the wild may have parasites or diseases. The pond should be stocked with small groups of fish of the same species rather than with single specimens of many different species. It is important not to overstock so allow a maximum of 2.5cm. (1in.) of fish to 60cm.^{2} (24in.^{2}) of pond surface. As most cold-water fish offered for sale are young, allow for space for growth. New fish should be introduced carefully into the pond.

POND MAINTENANCE

The problems of pond maintenance vary with the seasons of the year.

Summer

The two main problems in this season are heat and excess light. If the temperature of a shallow pond rises to over 21°C. (70°F.) it should be reduced by adding cold water. Too much sunlight will cause an overgrowth of algae and turn the pond green. Excess thread algae should be raked out and the pond surface shaded. The pond must be refilled regularly as water evaporates quickly in summer. Watch for such pests as herons, grass snakes, kingfishers, and cats, and remove any harmful water beetles and larvae with a net.

Fall

As the weather gets colder valuable fish should be removed from a pond that is shallower than 60cm. (24in.) and taken indoors. Fish must be fed well to build up body tissue before the winter months. A light net screen can be used to prevent leaves from falling into

The margin of a large pond shows a range of aquatic plants, including Flowering Rush (Left Center foreground), Water Hyacinth (Mid-Distance) and water lilies (Background.)

Top Left. *Floating and submerged Duckweed plants.*

A mature butyl rubber pond is ideal for cold-water fish. The plants have been allowed to develop to give a natural effect.

the pond; otherwise they should be skimmed off regularly. Aquatic plants should be tended about once a week.

Winter

During cold weather fish cease feeding and rest on the bottom of the pond. Consequently they do not need feeding except during warmer spells when they may become active and need small amounts of live foods. If the pond freezes over, the ice must be broken in several areas. This is best done by standing a metal can full of hot water on the surface of the ice.

Spring

Fish now start to become active and need conditioning by good feeding. They need to be checked carefully for fungal infections at this time of the year. Aquatic and marginal plants will need to be pruned, and any frogs removed from the pond.

POND PLANTS

Plants have many different functions, each of which is required to ensure a balance in the pond between a healthy environment for the fish and the visual beauty of the pond itself.

Most aquatic plants, especially the submerged varieties, serve to oxygenate the water thereby providing an essential element for the fish. Fish suitable for ponds usually make use of the plant cover provided as a spawning medium while the fry find protection from predators under the submerged leaves. Fish also use plant cover for protection and will shade themselves from strong sunlight by hiding under water lily leaves.

Plants are vital for aesthetic purposes. The green of pond plants enhances the colors of the fish, and careful selection of plants in regard to the flowers they produce will provide a variety of color around the pond.

Submerged Plants

The submerged pond plants are usually oxygenating plants and rarely flower.

Hornwort (Ceratophyllum demersum)
The Hornwort is a brittle plant of fir tree shape, dark green in color, and very fine leaved. It is a particularly good oxygenator and provides excellent cover for young fish. It has no true roots, and propagation takes place when small pieces of the plant break off and grow anew.

Canadian Pond Weed (Elodea canadensis)
This Canadian plant is dark green in color with many overlapping whorls of leaves along the complete length of the stem. Propagation of this plant is similar to that of the Hornwort.

Willow Moss (Fontinalis antipyretice)
This moss is a rich green color and grows attached to rocks. It is not a particularly good oxygenator but it serves well for decorative purposes, especially in areas of shallow water.

Tape Grass (Vallisneria spiralis)
Also known as **Eel Grass,** this southern European species is a tall, thin-leaved plant which can grow up to 45cm. (18in.) tall. It has roots and can propagate in two ways—by sending out runners which form new plants or by means of its flowers. The yellow and white flowers of the Tape Grass grow at the surface of the water and are attached to the plant by means of a thin spiral stalk.

Floating Plants

The main function of these plants is to provide the pond with shade from strong sunlight. However, they are apt to reproduce themselves rapidly and must be controlled to prevent the surface of the pond from becoming overgrown.

Bottom. *A bank of breeding tanks is placed above larger main tanks for adults. The individual breeding tanks have different water levels, depending on the stage of development of the young.*

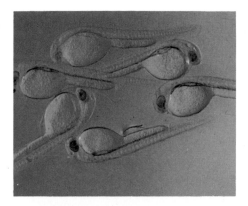

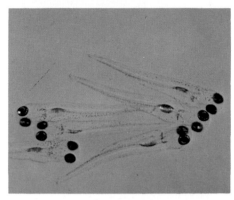

Top. *In freshly-hatched fry of the Sumatra Barb* (Barbus tetrazona) *the body is transparent and the swollen yolk sac is still present.* Center. *The same young at the final stage of embryonic development are free-swimming and have a swim bladder—the silver spots.* Lower. *These young* Rasbora daniconius *have well-filled stomachs.*

Duckweed (Lemna minor)
Duckweed is small and bright green in color. Some varieties of fish will eat it as part of their natural diet.

Water Hyacinth (Eichornia)
The Water Hyacinth comes from Africa, South America, and Australia and is not, therefore, hardy in a temperate climate. It should be removed from the pond for the winter and kept in an indoor aquarium. It has large, almost upright, leaves that grow out of water and long feathery roots that hang beneath the surface. Under ideal conditions this plant will produce delicate pale violet flowers.

Water Lilies
These are popular pond plants because of their extremely beautiful flowers. They are not strictly speaking floating plants since the roots rest on the bottom (or on a shelf) of the pond with the decorative part of the plant, the leaves and the flowers, floating on the surface of the water. Water lilies belong to two genera *Nymphaea* and *Nuphar*.

After an initial period requiring care and attention to become established, water lilies are fairly hardy. Although they produce seeds, lilies can be propagated either from cuttings or by splitting the crown of the plant. These cuttings should be placed in a water lily basket containing a rich soil which should remain in shallow water until the plant is established. It can then be lowered to a depth of about 45cm. (18in.), depending on the species. Water lilies are available in a variety of colors ranging from yellows, crimsons, and pinks, to white. Many of these varieties are hybrids produced by horticulturists. Patterns and colors of the leaves vary tremendously with the individual species.

Marginals

These plants, as their name suggests, grow in the shallow water parts of the pond, usually around the edges, the equivalent of the marshy areas of the rivers.

Yellow Flag (Iris pseudocorus)
This tall reedy plant can grow up to 60cm. (24in.) tall. It grows best if its roots are just under the water. It has a large yellow flower and is purely a decorative plant.

Marsh Marigold (Caltha palustris)
Aslo known as the Kingcup, this pretty plant with butter yellow flowers grows to about 25cm. (10in.) high. It is long flowering, producing flowers from early spring to early summer, and provides a lot of color around the edge of the pond.

Flowering Rush (Butomus umbellatus)
The Flowering Rush grows to 90–120cm. (36–48in.) tall and, because of its height, can be used to form an interesting variation among the marginal plants. It flowers during the summer producing rose-pink flowers.

Ferns

Ferns can be planted among the marginal plants to provide both color and leaf variation, though some species are too large for the smaller pond. Some ferns such as the *Osmunda regalis* can reach a height of over 180cm. (6ft.) tall, but others, such as the Maidenhair Fern (*Adiantum capillus-veneris*), grow only to about 45cm. (18in.) tall.

Carpeting Plants

Unless a more formal type of pond with a concrete or stonework surrounding area is preferred, carpeting plants are a useful means of blending the edge of the pond into the surrounding lawn. Some of these plants can grow in the water at the edge of the pond and provide color.

The Golden Saxifrage (*Chrysosplenium oppositifolium*) is a low creeping plant which provides a matted cover of pale leaves and yellow flowers.

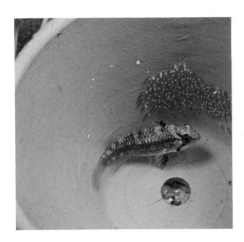

Species differ in the places in which they lay eggs. Left. Dwarf cichlids will lay their eggs in a flower pot, which can then be removed to a breeding tank. Middle. A male Leaf Fish (Monocirrhus polycanthus) guards eggs that have been placed on the underside of a leaf. Right. The glass walls of the tanks are a favorite spawning site with some species, as with this Ortmann's Dwarf Cichlid (Apistogramma ortmanni).

Baby's Tears (*Helxine soleriroli*) has tiny flowers and evergreen leaves that will actually grow at the edge of the water.

Breeding and Rearing of Fish

Fish follow the normal reproduction pattern of the Animal Kingdom in that the female produces ova which are fertilized by the male spermatozoa. However, because of their differing habitats, various methods of reproduction have evolved in the different families of fish. Basically, these differences can be categorized under two main headings, the Live-bearers and the Egg Layers.

THE LIVE-BEARERS (VIVIPARA)

In the live-bearing fish (Guppies, Platies, Swordtails) the anal fin of males changes its structure when they reach puberty and develops into a gonopodium. During normal swimming, this organ lies against the body pointing backwards, but during courtship and mating, it is pointed forwards and to one side so that the tip can be inserted into the female's vent. At the moment of contact the sperm are released and travel along a groove in the gonopodium thus entering the female. They proceed up the oviduct to fertilize the waiting ova. The eggs then develop, living off the yolk sac, but there is no placenta to form a connection between the egg and the mother as in mammals. More than one batch of young can develop from a single mating because the female is capable of storing sperm. The development period of the fry varies with the species and the water temperature but averages about four weeks. During this period, the female's body gradually becomes distended and a dark spot, known as the gravid spot, appears just in front of the anal

fin. When the fry are released by the female, they are completely developed requiring only to inflate their swim bladder before swimming off and looking for food.

The aquarist intending to breed any of the live-bearers needs to prepare an aquarium with suitable hiding places for the young fish, because most fish will make a meal of their offspring. The aquarium can be heavily planted especially near the surface, but the preferred method is to place a pair of adult fish in a breeding trap suspended inside the tank. Various types of garden netting are suitable using nylon line to lace the structure together. The mesh should be large enough for the fry to pass through but small enough to stop their parents from following. A 0.6mm. (0.25in.) mesh should be suitable for most species. Water conditions are not too important although hard water is preferable to soft.

Select a pair of fish that you wish to breed, and place them in the prepared aquarium. As the male is persistent in his attentions to the female, mating should take place within a week and the male can be removed. Feed the female well bearing in mind that if the trap method is used, any surplus that falls to the bottom must be removed to prevent pollution. When the young are born they will be able to swim through the mesh and will require separate food. Any of the commercial first foods for fry are suitable but live foods, such as microworm and brine shrimp, are much better. As they grow, larger foods like sieved daphnia, cyclops, and chopped or shredded *Tubifex* can be included. If young adults are used for breeding, the first batch of youngsters may be small in number but subsequently the number per batch will increase to between seventy-five to one hundred. As soon as the young fish are sexually mature, they will mate; if planned breeding is contemplated, the sexes should be separated as soon as they can be differentiated.

THE EGG LAYERS (OVIPARA)

The vast majority of the fish of the world fall into this category. The methods of spawning differ, being determined to a great extent by the conditions under which the fish live.

There are six categories of egg layers:

Top spawners	
Bottom spawners	best seen in the killifish
Egg buriers	fish
Egg placers	most cichlids
Nest builders	many anabantids but others such as the Stickleback
Egg scatterers	the most common method in characins, barbs, and minnows and most coldwater fish.

The first three types—top spawners, bottom spawners, and egg buriers—are seen in a popular group of aquarium fish, the killifish or egg laying toothcarps. Although most of these fish breed easily, they are not a fish for the beginner. They prefer soft acid water and do not like bright light. They can be bred in small tanks 30 x 20 x 20cm. (12 x 8 x 8in.). Like their close relatives, the live-bearers, the males are continuously trying to mate with the females so it is better to use at least two females with each male. Soft, slightly acid water should be provided. If your tap water is not soft, collect rainwater or mix tap water with deionized water to give a hardness of about 50 parts per million of dissolved salts. The temperature should be 70–75°F. (21–24°C.), and the aquarium should only receive a small amount of light.

The above conditions are basic for keeping killifish, but special conditions must be given for each of the three breeding categories.

Top Spawners

Under natural conditions, these fish would lay their eggs on any floating plants. In the aquarium, it is much easier to use mops made from nylon knitting yarn. Wind a dozen loops of wool around the hand and then cut the wool in half. Attach and suspend them from a cork so that the fish can wriggle in among the strands to lay their eggs. After the fish have been in the aquarium for a week, take the mop out, gently squeeze the water from it, and check for eggs. Any that are found should be carefully removed and placed in a hatching box which contains about 4cm. (1.5in.) of water from the original tank. Numerous types of plastic containers are available for hatching boxes, but the most suitable one is made of clear plastic and measures about 15–20cm. (6–8in.) long by 8–10cm. (3–4in.) wide. Little fish can be seen developing within the eggs. Infertile eggs turn white and should be removed although they do not seem to affect the others. After about three weeks, the fish will hatch. Sometimes the fish are deterred from hatching by a lowered oxygen content of the water due to little or no movement of the plastic container. The simple remedy is to place the lid on the box and give the whole box a vigorous shaking. Usually the desired effect is seen within a few hours. Very soon after hatching, the fry will need feeding. Most species will be large enough to take freshly hatched brine shrimp and microworm, but some of the smaller ones require first foods for fry. If the eggs do not hatch at the same time, the aquarist is faced with a problem because it is inadvisable to feed in a container which still has unhatched eggs. Any dead uneaten food will decompose creating adverse hatching conditions. Remove either the young fish or the unhatched eggs bearing in mind that the new container should contain water from the original tank.

Growth is fairly rapid and early transfer to a larger accommodation has to be arranged. Once again water conditions should be as much the same as possible in both containers. Make the transfer by floating the smaller container in the larger and allowing the water to mix slowly before releasing the fish from one to the other. As the fish grow, larger types of live food can be introduced.

Bottom Spawners

In their native habitat these fish lay their eggs on or near the bottom of the pond or stream. In the aquarium one of two methods can be employed—either the use of the nylon yarn mops or the placing of a layer of peat on the bottom. Different species prefer different

The Stickleback is a classic nest builder. Left. *The male first builds a nest of plant material and debris.* Middle. *He then attracts a female and courts her until she lays her eggs, which he then fertilizes.* Right. *The female is chased away by the male who collects up the eggs and places them in the nest, which he guards until they hatch.*

A female Jack Dempsey (Cichlasoma biocellatum) *guards the eggs she has placed on a rock.*

methods and trial and error or past experience has to be utilized.

Use the mops without a cork attached so that when waterlogged they will sink. Use more than one mop because the fish do not care for the bare glass on the bottom of the tank.

If the peat layer method is used, the type of peat is a matter of choice for the aquarist. Boil the selected type in soft water to remove excess acid and then wash it under running water so that only the coarser particles are left. The finer pieces tend to have a density close to that of water and will cause the water to be cloudy nearly all the time. Squeeze excess tap water from the remaining peat and then place it on the bottom of the tank to a depth of approximately 1.5cm. (0.5in.). Collection of eggs using the peat method can be a time consuming occupation because finding the eggs among the peat is difficult. The simplest way is to remove the peat with a net, squeeze out as much water as possible and store it in an airtight container. Record date and species details on the container.

The eggs of these fish are able to develop whether stored in water or moist peat. The length of storage time does not appear to vary with the method, and for the bottom spawners it is from six to nine weeks depending on species. After hatching, the water-stored eggs should be reared as top spawners. "Dry-stored" eggs and the peat should be emptied into a small tank after the required period has elapsed and covered with fresh soft water at about 24°C. (75°F.). If the timing is correct, the fish will hatch during the next twenty-four hours and should be reared in the usual way.

Egg Buriers

These fish are the true annual fish living in ponds where the water evaporates completely during the dry season. To enable the species to survive from year to year the eggs are buried in the mud where they develop while withstanding quite high levels of dehydration around them. The egg hatches with the re-

turn of the rain, very often within an hour or two. Development is rapid; the fish become sexually mature early and from about eight weeks old spawning is continuous until their lives end with the drying up of the pond.

Reproduction for egg buriers in the aquarium is a simple matter. The aquarium should be prepared as for bottom spawners with a layer of peat on the bottom. Increase the depth—about 3cm. (1in.) for the smaller species and 4cm. (1.5in.) for the larger. If possible, use two or three females to one male.

After the adult fish have been in the aquarium for two weeks, remove the peat, squeeze out the water, and store in an airtight container. The storage time for this group is the longest required by the killifish and can be anything from twelve to twenty weeks. Hatching the eggs and rearing the young follows the same procedure as the bottom spawners.

Egg Placers

Although most fish show no care for either their eggs or offspring the cichlids are different. Most species pair off and establish for themselves a territory into which no other members of the species are permitted. Then the pair will select a site for spawning. Some species prefer a smooth rock; others choose the stiff leaf of a plant; others like to make a depression in the gravel; and others find small caves. Once a suitable site has been selected the fish proceed to clean it with their mouths before starting to spawn. The female passes over the site depositing a row of eggs which are fertilized by the male following closely behind. They continue this process crisscrossing the site until the female is spent. From the time they are laid the eggs are continually fanned and guarded by one or other of the parents. This fanning, done by rapidly moving the pectoral fins, removes any sediment and ensures a supply of fresh water over the eggs. The parents also pick up the eggs in their mouths to clean them and then replace them among the rest.

The eggs hatch in from two to four days, but the small fish are not fully developed and the parents continue to care for them. Each fry is picked up as it hatches, washed in the parents' mouth, and then placed in a previously prepared depression in the sand near the spawning site. Parental care is continuous, and at no time are the fry left unguarded. They are moved a number of times to clean depressions during the first five to eight days, after which the little fish are fully developed and free swimming.

At first the fry swim together in a tight shoal closely guarded by the parents. Any one that strays from the fold is quickly caught by one parent and returned. As they grow larger, the youngsters become bolder, foraging farther afield for food until after about nine weeks the parents no longer have any interest in them and prepare to spawn again.

Reproduction in the aquarium presents a few problems. Because of their territorial behavior plenty of space is required. If adult pairs of fish are not available a group of youngsters, up to a dozen, should be purchased and grown to maturity. During this time, they will pair off and select a territory. Select the best pair and remove the others.

The breeding aquarium should be set up allowing plenty of space with rocks and at least 5cm. (2in.) of gravel. Do not include plants, because most species will tear them up. Maintain temperatures in the range 24–28°C. (75–83°F.) and introduce the selected pair. Keep a careful watch to be sure that both fish are ready to spawn. If not, place a glass partition between them until both fish exhibit heightened colors and display for each other through the glass. When both fish are ready to spawn, they will move most of the gravel from one place to another in their urge to find the correct site. Once the selection is made spawning proceeds as previously explained.

During their stay in the breeding aquarium the adults should be fed well. As soon as the fry are free swimming feed them brine shrimp followed by larger foods as they grow.

The sight of a shoal of young fish being cared for by the parents is rewarding, but the prudent aquarist may wish to remove the adults because frightened parents are liable to devour their young. The fry are quite capable of fending for themselves.

In some species of cichlids, known as the mouthbrooders, parental care is taken a stage further. One of the parents, usually the female, takes the eggs into her mouth and stores them until they hatch. During this time, usually about ten days, she is unable to feed and the male should be removed from the aquarium to give her some peace.

When the fry hatch, they are released but swim around close to the female's head and at the slightest alarm they return quickly to the safety of her mouth. The female feeds for short periods at first because the fry are not released for long. Since she has not eaten during the incubation period, plenty of food should be provided so she will not be tempted to eat her own fry. The fry should be fed on brine shrimp as a first food followed by the usual larger foods when appropriate.

Nest Builders

Another group of fish that look after their eggs are the bubblenest builders. The bubblenest builders belong to the anabantid family and have the ability to take in air at the water surface and expel it again in small bubbles which they use to build a nest. The bubbles are covered with a secretion to keep

---

FISH—Table 5

Freshwater Fish Disease Chart

DISEASE	SYMPTOMS	CURE
Fin Rot	The fins get very ragged and appear to be disintegrating.	First try a commercial white spot cure. If this does not work use 250mg. of aureomycin per 25 liters of water.
Fungus	*Saprolegnia*—cottony tufts growing from site of injury. Sometimes seen on mouth.	Gently net fish from water and add methylene blue from a dropper until fungus turns blue. Return fish to tank. Repeat twice daily until cured.
Flukes	Found on gills or skin. Gill cover slimy and filaments are pale. Small spots of blood can be seen on skin and gills. (1mm. long).	Put fish in a separate small container full of tank water. Add 1 percent methylene blue (1ml. to 5 liters). Leave for one week. Watch other fish in tank for symptoms.
Pop Eye	Eye swells and stands out; the cornea may go cloudy.	Gently net fish, remove from water and put two drops of 1 percent methylene blue on the eye. Repeat twice daily. Methylene blue may damage plants so do not give treatment over the aquarium.
Velvet	Very small yellowish spots as if dusted with pollen grains. Fish scratch against rocks and must be examined carefully.	Use a commercial velvet disease cure, according to instructions. Raise water temperature as in White Spot.
White Spot	Pinpoint white spots appear anywhere on body, usually best seen on fins. Fish scratch against rocks.	Buy a commercial white spot cure from your pet shop and use according to instructions. Raise temperature gradually to 28°C. (82°F.) as this speeds up the life cycle of the parasite.

them from breaking up too quickly. Most species spawn at the surface although some place their bubbles and eggs under the curve of a large plant leaf just below the surface.

Spawning is a fascinating process of display, courtship, and mating. The male selects an area at the surface usually in among floating plants and proceeds to build a nest of numerous bubbles reinforced by pieces of plant. During this time, he rushes off to display to his selected mate and drive her in the direction of the nest he is building. When she is ready to spawn, she needs only a little persuading and follows her mate directly up beneath the nest. The male wraps his body around the female so that their vents are close together. They slowly roll over in this embrace, and the eggs are released and fertilized. The fish sink gradually and break apart after about ten seconds. The male immediately collects the eggs in his mouth and propels them up into the nest to mix with the bubbles.

Meanwhile, the female has recovered and is ready to lay more eggs so the same procedure is repeated until she is spent. At this stage, the male will chase her away and stand guard under the nest to catch and replace any eggs that fall. In some species, the egg contains a minute amount of oil so that it floats all the time.

The eggs are small and numerous, up to 5,000 in a spawning with some of the larger species. They hatch in about thirty-six hours, and the fry are free swimming about two days later when they need copious supplies of minute food.

Breeding in the aquarium is quite easy.

This Cardinal Tetra (Cheirodon axelrodi) *suffers from white spot disease, which is easily cured with commercial remedies.*

Use a 45 x 25 x 25cm. (18 x 10 x 10in.) tank and fill with old water. On the surface there should be some floating plants preferably Indian Fern (*Ceratopteris thaliotroides*). A temperature of between 24–27°C. (75–80°F.) should be maintained. Introduce the pair of fish; the female should be bulging with roe. Almost immediately, the male will start his nest construction and spawning should take place within two or three days. Remove the female as soon as spawning has finished because the male will drive her away and possibly kill her. When the fry have become free swimming, remove the male fish and feed the fry. Keep the tank covered with a glass sheet to maintain a warm humid atmosphere for the young while their labyrinth organ develops. Remember that you will have many more fry than you see and feed accordingly.

Egg Scatterers

The last group of fish with a common method of spawning are the egg scatterers which in all probability includes more species than all the others put together. The characins, barbs, danios, and many cold-water fish are all in this group.

Males court the females by displaying before them and when suitably excited they come together side by side either among, or just above, some plants. Eggs and milt are released, and the fish spring apart scattering eggs in all directions. Most species have eggs which are slightly adhesive and stick to the plants where they remain hidden from their hungry parents. They hatch quite quickly (from twenty-four to forty-eight hours) and the fry hide while they develop, living off the yolksac. When free swimming they are shy and hide wherever they can. Obviously, their lives are in great danger from other adult fish foraging for food.

A standard arrangement can be used to breed most of these fish. For the smaller species a 45 x 25 x 25cm. (18 x 10 x 10in.) tank is adequate. Hard tap water can be used in some cases, but it is much better to use soft. Instinct tells the adults not to spawn in bright light where all can see, so paint the back and sides black to exclude light. Water to a depth of 15cm. (6in.) should be sufficient at a temperature of about 27°C. (80°F.). Place on the bottom either small pebbles (lime free) or glass marbles that have been thoroughly washed and on top of that some nylon mops, as used for killifish, or boiled coconut fiber. Put the selected pair of fish in the tank in the evening, and cover the top glass and front with newspaper to exclude light. Next morning, with luck, the fish will have spawned. The female will look much slimmer, and her fins may look ragged from the attentions of the male. If spawning has not taken place, leave them for three or four days; then if nothing has happened, remove them and try again later.

Leave the tank covered until the eggs have hatched. If the covers are removed after dark and a light is shone into the tank the little fish can be seen diving for shelter. When the fry become free swimming either first foods or brine shrimp and microworm should be fed depending on the size of the fry. If in doubt, feed a variety of foods as the mouth is generally large in proportion to body size. Continue feeding various foods, increasing in size as they grow. As there may be two hundred and fifty or more in the spawning, remember to transfer them to larger tanks periodically so none will become stunted.

Fish Ailments

Fish like all other animals suffer from ailments. These may be classified as toxic diseases, infections, cancers, degenerative diseases, congenital diseases, and injuries. However, a number of these are peculiar to fish due to their aquatic habitat.

AILMENTS OF TROPICAL FRESHWATER FISH

Toxic diseases are those caused by poisonous substances in the water, the most common one being due to the toxic products of left-over food. This is usually associated with lack of oxygen, the available oxygen being used by the millions of bacteria involved in the decomposition of the leftover food. As with many diseases prevention is better than cure, so fish should only be given as much food as they can eat in ten minutes. If the water becomes cloudy and foul because of over-feeding, one-third of the water should be changed immediately. Siphon off any rotting food and use an air stone and air pump to aerate the water. Other rare sources of toxins are rockwork such as limestone which dissolves in the water, turning it milky and alkaline, or immature pieces of wood put in the aquarium for decoration.

Infectious diseases are the most important problem in the aquarium because the disease may be transmitted from an ill fish to all the other fish in the tank. The other problem is that these diseases in the early stages may be difficult to recognize.

Cancers occur in fish as they do in other animals, and there is no effective treatment other than surgery.

Degenerative conditions of old age usually seen in fish are either the development of a humpy back or marked loss of weight in spite of an apparent good appetite. There is no treatment.

This Firemouth (Cichlasoma meeki) suffers from mouth fungus.

FISH—Table 6
Marine Fish Disease Chart

DISEASE	SYMPTOMS	CURE
Benedenia	Poor appetite. Small white/gray triangular flukes on body particularly near the eye. Point of triangle towards tail.	Use commercial *Oodinium* cure. Carefully follow manufacturers instructions for *Oodinium*.
Body Rot Fin Rot	White/gray areas around wounds or fins appear to rot away.	Put fish in bare treatment tank and add one of the tetracycline antibiotics 250mg. per 25 liters of water. Remove to established tank if fish shows signs of distress. Never add antibiotics to established tank—they kill nitrifying bacteria. Treat for one week.
Fungal Disease	Cottony tufts of fungus at site of damaged scales.	Remove fish from tank, add drop of 1 percent methylene blue to fungus until it turns blue. Put fish in a small bare container of sea water for a few minutes to remove excess methylene blue before netting and returning to tank. Repeat twice daily.
Fish Lice	Obvious flat parasite up to 5mm. long.	Remove parasite with tweezers or use commercial cures as instructed.
Itch	Caused by parasitic crustacea. Fish scratch on rocks and corals and minute white spots are sometimes seen on body.	Apply commercial itch cure as directed.
Lymphocystis	Whitish cauliflower lumps appear on the body.	Can only be removed surgically and wound must be sterilized with acriflavine.
Oodinium	Lack of appetite, listless, scratching on rocks and corals. Swims near surface, distressed and has rapid respiration (100 plus gill beats per minute) due to infection on gills. In late stages body appears dusted with pollen.	Use commercial *Oodinium* cure as directed. It is possible to use homemade cures using freshly prepared copper sulfate solutions but a commercial preparation is much more convenient to use. *Oodinium* cures are very toxic to marine invertebrates.
Pop Eye	Eye swells and stands out.	Gently net the fish and remove from tank. Put two drops of 1 percent methylene blue on the affected eye. Then put fish in a bare container of sea water to remove excess methylene blue. Then net and return to tank. Repeat twice daily.
White Spot	Pinhead size spots appear over fins and body. Fish appears to have an itch.	Use a commercial white spot cure.

Aggressive fish should be removed from the aquarium or plenty of hiding places provided for the smaller fish.

Prevention is better than cure, therefore:

1. Buy healthy fish from a reputable dealer.
2. Do not buy fish from a tank containing ill or dead fish.
3. Do not buy fish which swim oddly, appear to have an itch, have spots, torn fins, or missing gill covers.
4. If possible, put any new fish in a tank of their own for four weeks before putting them in a community tank.

AILMENTS OF TROPICAL MARINE FISH

Toxic diseases may occur more frequently in the saltwater aquarium because it is a more finely balanced habitat and seawater is a more corrosive medium than fresh water. Exposure of metals in the tank hood or in the frame of angle iron tanks results in corrosion and poisoning of the fish by metal ions. Overfeeding can rapidly lead to the buildup of poisonous ammonium compounds and nitrites which may either kill the fish or predispose them to infections. Disease is always relatively more serious in the marine tank because the fish are usually more expensive, perhaps cannot be replaced at the dealers as easily and cannot be bred in the aquarist's tank. On the coral reef the oxygen content of the water is high, and the proportion of fish to water volume (estimated at 2.5cm. [1in.] of fish to 4,500 liters [1,000 gallons] of water) is very low. Low oxygen tension due to poor aeration, overcrowding, or overfeeding can easily lead to poisoning of marine tropical fish or predispose them to infection.

AMPHIBIANS & REPTILES

There are about 8,500 known living species of reptiles and amphibians, but very few are bred commercially. Almost all specimens offered for sale have been taken from the wild population and as a result some species are in danger of extinction. Purchasing one of these animals may encourage this trade. On the other hand, although even reptiles and amphibians indigenous to the locality are not easy to breed in captivity, it is certainly possible to provide habitats and food for the smaller indigenous species within suitable gardens. Such provision is a positive step towards conservation, which provides the most exciting and challenging aspect of keeping these animals. (See **Wild Animals as Visitors and Pets** for the capture and keeping of indigenous animals.)

Reptiles are not the fastest-selling pets. Be suspicious if you are offered a large lethargic, seemingly docile lizard, monitor, or snake and told that it is "tame." This may be true, but the animal is more likely to be in bad condition and may regain its former vigor with care together with a wild creature's fierce reactions to being handled. One of the best indications of good health is appetite. Choose a specimen you have seen feeding, or at least one that looks well nourished.

Amphibians

Almost all of the 2,500 species of amphibians live both in fresh water and on land, but a few are entirely aquatic. Amphibians are cold-blooded vertebrates. Most lack scales and lay and fertilize their shell-less eggs in water or damp places; a few species give birth to active young. The emerging larvae usually breathe with gills at first. Most species later develop lungs, although some, such as the lungless salamanders, take up oxygen entirely through the lining of their mouths and their soft skin. The larval stages are often vegetarian, or partially so, unlike the adults which are wholly carnivorous.

Those species of amphibians alive today are divided into three orders: the Apoda (caecilians), the Urodela (salamanders and newts, tailed) and the Salientia (frogs, toads, and close relatives). Only the Urodela and Salientia normally furnish pets. The worm-like, burrowing caecilians are tropical and seldom available.

Amphibian pets are generally easier to keep and breed than reptiles. Some, especially the newts and salamanders, require little space out of the breeding season. Nevertheless they must not be overcrowded, as they are particularly susceptible when crowded to a number of highly infectious, fatal diseases. Many species, especially the toads, are easily tamed if approached quietly

Top. *The best known of all reptile pets is the tortoise. However, tortoises are not as easy to look after as they may seem. Millions of tortoises are exported annually from their native lands, but only ten percent survive more than one year.*

Bottom. *The handler is demonstrating the correct way to hold a snake by grasping it firmly behind the head. Once the snake is tame, these precautions are unnecessary with nonpoisonous snakes, but care must always be taken with unknown species.*

and carefully. Treated in this way they will soon accept your presence without fear and may feed from your hand.

Handling, Catching, and Collecting

Your hands are as good as any tool for catching most reptiles except snakes. Smaller lizards can often be caught by a noose made of very fine wire, thread, or angler's catgut on the end of a long thin pole (an old fishing rod would be ideal); maneuver this around the animal's neck and quickly jerk it into the air. When captured it may turn like a snake and bite, so hold it closely behind the head; grip the body and legs; never hold the tail, for many lizards will shed their tail to escape.

The more aquatic amphibians and small-to medium-sized terrapins can be captured in a long-handled, deep fishing net, with mesh not more than about 6mm. (0.25in.). A finer net is needed for tadpoles. Once caught, a large frog or toad should be held firmly but gently around its waist with its legs held together under the body. When holding a middle- to large-sized terrapin, keep the hands well away from its head. Some, such as the American snappers, can inflict painful and serious wounds.

To catch snakes you need a snake stick. This looks much like a golf putter and can be easily adapted from one by filing down the metal end. The stick is made from a light L-shaped metal rod fixed at right angles to a long wooden handle. Gently pin the snake just behind its head. Never pick a snake up unless you can positively identify it as a harmless species; then grasp it firmly, but without squeezing, behind the head so that it cannot turn and bite. Support its weight with your other hand.

In looking for these animals, you will need to turn over logs and stones, look under abandoned sheets of corrugated iron, old boards, and so forth. Always replace such objects, for you may be disturbing a whole miniature ecology. Use a strong, short rake rather than your hands in areas where there are poisonous snakes.

Once caught, reptiles should be put into loosely woven collecting bags made in a long rectangular shape so the open end can be knotted. Amphibians must be kept wet by putting plenty of moss and damp paper in with them. Most reptiles need only slightly dampened material.

Avoid direct sunlight on the bag and any extremes of temperature. Snakes and lizards should always first be put in a bag and the bag placed in a stout box. Cans, partially filled with damp moss or paper and with ventilation holes punched from the inside, can be used to carry most smaller reptiles.

Do not put small and large animals in the same container, and make sure that you do not risk mixing predators with prey. Some species, such as the Fire-bellied Toad and Pickerel Frog, give off secretions which can be toxic to other creatures.

Housing Requirements

OUTDOORS

The best place to keep reptiles which are accustomed to climatic conditions in your area is an outdoor vivarium. You need an area not less than 2.5 x 2m. (8 x 6ft.). The sun should shine directly on a part of the inside for most of the day. Frogs and toads need broken sunlight (many like to bask in the sun near or in water) while newts and salamanders prefer shade.

Outdoor enclosures allow greater space, some direct sunlight and rain, and better conditions for growing plants within the enclosure. Seasonal changes will be felt and reptiles from temperate climates will be able to hibernate almost as in nature. The chance of successful breeding will be increased, and the animals can be observed under more natural conditions.

A simple outdoor vivarium can be constructed using a metal frame. Cover the top with fine nylon or plastic mesh instead of glass (which will concentrate the sun's rays

Outdoor vivariums are the best places to keep reptiles and amphibians from the local countryside or from parts of the world with similar climates. Top. A vivarium suitable for keeping amphibians. Center. An adopted frame for larger reptiles, which can be put outside on hot days—note the plastic mesh top which keeps the vivarium cool.

and intensify the heat). Lizards and snakes generally need some dry area so a third of the cover should be glazed at one end. A wooden frame covered with wire mesh fitted over the top and held in place by bricks keeps out potential predators (cats, dogs, or birds), or a stronger and more permanent structure can be built of brick with an overhang to prevent escape.

Lizards, snakes, and tortoises usually need warm dry conditions; drainage should be excellent, especially in winter, when reptiles can easily drown while hibernating. Sand, rock, or gravel make good surface materials along with plants which simulate the natural habitat. All reptiles need an old sink or a plastic container filled with water and set into the ground, mainly for drinking purposes. For amphibians keep a pool filled which takes up half the enclosed area. For a larger pond a sheet of tough plastic can be used to line an excavated hollow. Even if shallow, this should have stones lining the sides so that small specimens will not fall in and drown. For amphibians the pool should be at least 20cm. (8in.) deep in the middle with shallow shelves and aquatic plants at the edges to help them climb out more easily.

Hibernation Quarters

Frogs often hibernate in underwater mud and debris, and this requires a depth of at least 45cm. (18in.), but a damp hibernating chamber alongside the pool is often better.

Hibernating chambers for all reptiles and most hibernating amphibians should be excavated near the center of the enclosure, about

60cm. (2ft.) square, dug below the frost level. The hole should be filled with logs, flat pieces of wood, sandy soil, bracken, straw, and similar materials or, in the case of amphibians, with damp sphagnum moss and half rotted logs on a floor of soft damp crumbly earth. Entrance tunnels can be made from old drainage pipes 7–10cm. (3–4in.) in diameter which can be sealed with a wooden plug to keep out frost. The chamber can be roofed with a large flat stone or a sheet of corrugated metal and a mound of earth at least 60cm. (2ft.) high which can be covered with rough stumps of wood, bricks, and stones to provide summer basking places. For amphibians, spaces and entrance holes should be left open and the whole area covered with damp soil and leaf mold to a depth of at least 45cm. (18in.) to ensure that frost is excluded. Here the occupants can safely remain through the winter and find places to hide during the summer. The rest of the enclosure should be surfaced with sand, rocks, gravel or whatever will simulate the natural habitat, and should be suitably planted.

Warning: If animals come out from hibernation during a warm spell in winter they must be replaced deep in the ground to prevent freezing to death when frost returns.

INDOORS

An indoor vivarium should either suggest the natural habitat, complete with plants, or follow laboratory practice, with an emphasis on hygiene. The difference will probably be more apparent to you than to the reptiles themselves. In some cases, there is a real advantage in choosing the simpler approach, especially for bigger snakes and monitors, when large amounts of fecal matter and uneaten food have to be removed regularly and the animals may be difficult to handle.

Laboratory housing is often made from polystyrene plant propagators or aquariums but, whatever is used, the interior is usually plain and simple.

A ready-made vivarium can be purchased, but it is often expensive and sometimes less suitable than a cage adapted from an aquarium. The size should not be smaller than 45 x 25 x 25cm. (18 x 10 x 10in.), with a top of strong plastic, nylon mesh, or perforated zinc firmly fixed to a 2.5 x 2.5cm. (1 x 1in.) wooden frame that fits tightly around the top. A secondhand aquarium that has begun to leak will be satisfactory for non-aquatic subjects, such as snakes and lizards.

Housing for snakes and lizards, which like dry conditions, can be made from wood. Wooden cages will be lighter, warmer, and better ventilated but not so easy to disinfect against disease or rid of pests such as mites.

Heating and light require sockets for tungsten bulbs fitted either into the wooden back or a reinforced section inside the roofing. If the creatures are small and will not damage the socket, bulbs may be suspended in one corner a little off the floor. Animals must be able to escape from the light and heat into

This ready-made indoor vivarium has been set out to replicate as much as possible the natural habitat of the amphibians kept in it.

cover; a lamp with too much wattage can inflict severe burns. In a heated room bulbs of 25, 40, or 60 watts will be sufficient, but large monitors may need 100–150 watts.

Desert Vivariums

Careful management of temperature and humidity is absolutely essential for desert-dwelling creatures. Clean drinking water must always be available in a small shallow dish. A square-shaped container set in a wooden frame is best. Some lizards need to have their cage, plants, and rocks sprinkled with water instead. There should be enough to drink without causing humid conditions to develop.

Strangely, some desert creatures like to immerse themselves in water from time to time: this can be important in helping them to shed their skins. Provide larger containers, every few days, and this observation will soon show what size is needed. Make sure that the water cannot splash over to dampen the floor covering.

Aim at a temperature of 30°C. (86°F.) by day and 20°C. (68°F.) at night for most desert creatures.

Moist, Shady Terrarium

Cages suitable for the European Common Frog, American Wood Frog, European Common Toad, American Toad, newts and salamanders, small burrowing skinks, and the American Five-lined Skink should be made from a watertight aquarium or a commercial vivarium with a sliding glass front which slopes backwards at about 45° to its base. If an aquarium is used, the lid must fit tight and should be covered with nylon mesh for ventilation.

The floor should be covered by three layers—gravel, charcoal, and compost—to ensure conditions which are moist but not waterlogged. A planted terrarium will provide shelter; ferns and other damp-loving plants collected from the natural environment should be put in pots standing on the first layer of gravel. Alternatively, house plants of the kind grown in bottle gardens may be used; plants which may have been treated with insecticides must be carefully wiped with damp cotton. Feed these plants only with organic liquid manure.

The correct humidity can be produced by adding just enough water to keep the first gravel layer saturated. The soil above should be only slightly moist. It is best to use rainwater or water from a healthy pond, but if tapwater is used, it should stand for a couple of days before being introduced into the area. Amphibians need a dish large enough to cover a third of the floor area and deep enough for submerging themselves. Clean the dish out regularly and keep it filled with fresh water.

The temperature should be about 21°C. (70°F.) by day, falling to 16°C. (60°F.) at night, so normal living room temperature will suffice.

Semiaquatic Vivarium

Most frogs, toads, and newts require more water during the breeding season. A permanent semiaquatic vivarium suits the Yellow- and Fire-bellied Toads, Edible Pickerel Frogs, and the Pleurodele and Japanese Newt. Divide the vivarium in half with bricks or flat stones to a height of 15cm. (6in.). One end should be filled with layers of gravel, charcoal, and compost (as above), the other covered with 4 cm. (1.5in.) of aquarium gravel (in which aquatic plants should be rooted) and filled with water. An alternative is to make the pool from plastic sheeting. Do *not* feed plants with liquid manure since it could pollute the water.

The same precautions pertaining to water should be observed as for moist terrariums.

Breeding and Supplying Live Food

Providing the essential fresh, varied and, often, living food for reptiles and amphibians is usually the most difficult part of keeping these animals successfully. If you want to keep any of the insect-eating species (such as frogs, toads, lizards, and chameleons), you will find it necessary to breed the insects yourself. Some of them require more care than others, but all need frequent attention.

LOCUSTS

The most useful insect for feeding purposes is undoubtedly the African Migratory Locust (*Locusta migratoria migratoriodes*). During its development it ranges in size from 8mm. (0.3in.) when a nymph to roughly 7.5cm. (3in.) when fully adult, so that the different stages will suit small or juvenile, larger or adult insectivorous species.

Locusts can be bred throughout the year. The smallest breeding case is basically a strong well-made box, 60cm. (2ft.) high by 50cm. (20in.) square, with a sliding glass front. It must have a false floor of perforated zinc or hardboard, secured 10–13cm. (4–5in.) above the base. Cut holes in this to accommodate three or four glass jam jars, their tops flush with the false floor. Fill the jars with clean, damp, coarse sand in which the females can lay their egg pods. Locusts need to be kept at a temperature of around 34°C. (94°F.) during the day and 28°C. (83°F.) at night. About half a dozen pairs of adult locusts can be put in such a cage.

Locusts must be fed daily on fresh grass standing in a pot of water and on a dish of dry wheat bran. If grass is not available, use wheat, grown in a shallow dish of water, with an occasional unsprayed cabbage leaf, chopped raw carrot, and tomatoes. The cage should be cleaned daily.

After mating, the females will deposit pods containing thirty to one hundred eggs in the damp sand, about one pod every six days. The eggs take about eleven days to hatch. Rear the nymphs separately by removing the sand jars containing the eggs to another similar warm case, where they will emerge as nymphs. They will go through five "instars," or stages, before reaching the adult size in about a month. Feed them on grass and bran, and provide some rough sticks to aid molting.

EARTHWORMS

These are another important food. It is best to use the common species, *Lumbricus* and *Allobophora*. Avoid any with an unpleasant smell. Earthworms can, of course, be dug up in good quantities or obtained commercially, but in winter or long dry spells in summer it is advisable to have your own continuous supply.

To breed or store the worms, place them in large well-drained wooden tubs, boxes, or big earthenware pots, raised on wooden blocks and with perforated zinc lids, filled with three parts dry, light sandy soil to five parts peat moss. A further addition of hydrated lime may be needed if the soil is acid; a pH reading of about seven (neutral) is ideal. Keep the containers at about 15°C. (60°F.), and feed the worms on dung and unsprayed vegetable leaves, or a thick paste mix of twenty-five parts (volume) finely ground whole grain flour to one part potato pancake mix, and a spoonful or so of powdered milk, spread on top of the soil and covered with sacking. Avoid overfeeding—it leads to fungal growths and infections. Kept in this way earthworms will breed throughout the year.

MEALWORMS

The yellow mealworm, the larva of the small beetle *Tenebrio molitor*, is bred commercially on a large scale for sale in pet shops. Although used primarily for birds, it also serves for insectivorous mammals, reptiles, amphibians, and fish. Mealworms are expensive to buy and often in short supply but they are not difficult to breed. They can be reared in wooden boxes lined with zinc about 45 x 50 x 30cm. tall (18 x 20 x 12in.), in plastic buckets or square tin boxes. The sides must be smooth to prevent escape, and the lids should be made of perforated zinc.

The container should be three-fourths filled with alternate layers of the following ingredients: first, a mixture of wheat bran, with a few handfuls of flour and a couple of tablespoons of yeast, to a depth of 5–8cm. (2–3in.), then covered with sacking or tissue paper to help the larvae change their skins. Continue layering the food mixture and sacking. Fresh wholegrained bread, a few apple peelings (unpolluted by pesticides), and lettuce leaves should be added regularly to the top of the culture.

Put two hundred or so larvae in the containers. In time, they will pupate and then emerge as dark brown beetles. They will mate and lay their eggs in the sacking. The life cycle takes four to six months. A temperature of around 21–27°C. (70–80°F.) should be maintained, and the culture should be disturbed as little as possible.

The larval stage is definitely the most valuable for food. Spare pupae are only suitable for terrapins, and the beetles are of little use for feeding purposes. The newly molted larvae—easily recognized by their white soft skin—are better for feeding small reptiles or amphibians.

HOUSEFLIES AND BLOWFLIES

These insects are a main part of the diet of chameleons, anole lizards, and tree frogs. Although most people prefer to buy maggots from angling shops, where they are sold as bait, it is possible to breed them. Place the maggots in a large tin box kept in a warm place (25–30°C. or 77–86°F.) and feed them raw or cooked, unsalted meat. The maggots will pupate in a few days. The pupae are best put directly into the vivarium, where the flies will emerge. Maggots are too tough to give directly to vivarium creatures. Adult flies should be fed with a mixture of brown sugar and milk on a cotton ball in a small dish which is changed daily. You can store flies and pupae for several months in any area with a temperature of 5°C. (41°F.). It is easy to keep a supply in the warmer months. Just put pieces of meat or liver out of doors and you will have all the flies, eggs, and maggots you could want. In addition, a fly trap can be made out of a glass bowl with a cone-shaped paper funnel leading inward at an angle and a bait of raw meat at the bottom. Or you can make a smaller version using a jam jar with a small hole in its lid.

SWEEP NETTING

One of the best ways of catching a wide variety of live insects and spiders from the countryside for vivarium animals is by using a sweep net. This is a long, very tough cloth bag fixed to a strong metal frame of a triangular shape squared off where it attaches to the short handle. The technique is to sweep the net continuously from side to side fairly quickly with a regular arm movement describing roughly a figure eight. Brush through meadow grass, through groups of wild plants such as nettles, along sunlit edges of fence rows and other places where insects congregate. When you feel you have collected enough, fold the bag over to keep the insects inside until you can tip them into the vivarium. Leave the animals to consume the insects and spiders that they find palatable, and after a day or so release those they reject.

Newts and Salamanders

Newts and salamanders include the simplest amphibians to keep, so long as it is remembered that many lead "double lives," becoming aquatic animals at certain times. Most urodeles spend the greater part of the year hidden away in cool, dark, damp places, such as crevices in walls and underneath logs and stones. In the breeding season they usually become aquatic. Here the word *newt* is used for all members of the salamander family (Salamandridae), except for the Fire Salamander, whose common name is well established. The term *salamander* applies to all the other, generally terrestrial and often larger, urodeles. Newts generally require more water area than salamanders, though the adult European Salamander (a newt) needs only shallow water in which to produce its gilled larvae, while the Axolotl (a salamander) is usually totally aquatic.

If you intend keeping newts and salamanders permanently in one vivarium, it must be either the indoor semiaquatic or the outdoor woodland frame type with pool. If you have a choice, the outdoor arrangement is better.

Newts. Top Left. *Female and male Common or Smooth Newts, the male in breeding dress. Note the well-planted aquarium essential for breeding.* Top Right. *Female and male Great Crested Newts, the male in breeding dress—particularly prominent are the crests on the back and tail.* Center Left. *Larva of the Great Crested Newt showing the prominent, feathery external gills.* Center Right. *Spanish Ribbed Newts courting, the male swimming by his back legs while his front legs are hooked over those of the female.*

For salamanders, water depth should be about 10cm. (4in.) only, with stones near the edge to allow them to leave the water easily. They need a cool environment without direct sunshine—about 18°C. (65°F.) to a maximum of 21°C. (70°F.) during the summer.

All stages of urodeles are carnivorous. For captive adults the main food is the earthworm, plus small slugs, smooth caterpillars, and other soft-skinned insects. When natural food is short, offer tiny fragments of canned dog food or small lean strips of beef or liver, which may have to be waggled in front of the pet to stimulate its interest. Remove uneaten food within a day.

Breeding

Newts and salamanders kept indoors should first be allowed to hibernate fully in a cool, dark, frostproof place (a cellar is ideal), at a temperature range of 2–7°C. (35–45°F.). They must be in good condition, for they will be drawing upon stored reserves rather than feeding at these temperatures.

In spring, when the crests and breeding colors develop, not more than two pairs of newts of one species should be put in an aquarium no smaller than 60 x 30 x 30cm. (24 x 12 x 12in.) full of cold water. The surface should be covered with about 8cm. (3in.) of aquarium gravel and thickly planted with submerged aquatics; the species of *Elodea*, *Potamogeton*, or *Chara* are suitable. Following an elaborate courtship display the male deposits a tiny sperm-filled capsule (spermatophore) in front of the female, so she will take it up into her vent. The eggs, which are inside her, can then be fertilized. Some commonly available species, such as the Crested, Marbled, Smooth, Palmated, and Spotted Newts, then lay their eggs singly, sticking them carefully on the leaves of submerged

waterweeds; others lay them in a haphazard fashion. After laying has ended, all adults should immediately be moved to another tank provided with an island, as they gradually resume their terrestrial stage. They should then be returned to a vivarium.

On hatching, the tiny larvae have external gills which are slowly absorbed. It is essential that the water in the aquarium is cool and well oxygenated; an aquarium oxygenator is a great help. At first the carnivorous larvae should be fed on infusorians and other microscopic pond organisms. As they grow they can progress to larger prey, such as daphnia (water fleas), *Cyclops*, *Tubifex* worms, and mosquito larvae. The time taken for metamorphosis to be completed depends on conditions such as temperature and food, as well as on individual species, but is not less than three to four months and is often much longer. As they mature the larvae should also be provided with an island, and when they lose their gills they should be transferred to a special rearing tank divided so there are dry and wet ends. The tiny newts will have to be given a frequent supply of pieces of small

earthworms, baby slugs, and greenfly. It is best to attempt rearing only a few newts at a time; if the species is indigenous the remainder should be released as soon as possible in reasonably mild weather in a flourishing pond. If the young newts have metamorphosed and appear to be well nourished, they may be hibernated like adults.

NEWTS

The following species are suitable subjects for vivariums.

The **Californian Newt** (*Taricha torosa*) grows up to 9cm. (3.5in.) long and is plain brown on its back with a yellowish or orange belly. This newt has an aquatic breeding period from December to May when the male's tough skin becomes smooth, his tail flattens, and the vent region swells. It is found in the western United States.

The **Red Spotted Newt** (*Triturus viridiscens*) is bright orange or red in the terrestrial eft (young newt) stage which lasts up to three years. The adult, 8–10cm. (3–4in.) long, is olive or brown with a black-spotted yellow belly. The eastern United States is home to most of these creatures. In late spring, the breeding male develops a high tail fin and black excrescences on the legs and during courtship climbs on the female's back.

The **Smooth Newt** (*Triturus vulgaris*), up to 8cm. (3in.) in length, is dull brown with rows of dark spots on back and sides and an orange-yellow belly with dark spots. It breeds in early spring when the skin becomes glossy smooth, and the male grows a tall undulating vertebral crest. Colors intensify greatly then. Great Britain, Europe, and Asia Minor are where most of them are found.

The **Great Crested Newt** or **Triton** (*Triturus cristatus*) is up to 10–15cm. (4–6in.) long, with skin moist and warty all year. Its back and sides are dark purplish brown or grayish with darker spots, and its belly is bright orange with dark blotches. In spring the breeding male has a tall serrated crest along the back and tail; the female has a crest on the tail only. This species is widespread in Europe, but becoming scarce in Great Britain where it should *not* be collected.

The **Marbled Newt** (*Tritus m. marmoratus*), up to 10–15cm. (4–6in.) long, is similar to the Crested Newt (with which they can interbreed) but are green marbled with black, and grayish undersides. Females have a thin vertebral orange stripe. The breeding male (early spring) has an unserrated crest. It is found predominantly in France, Spain, and Portugal.

The **Palmated Newt** (*Triturus helveticus*), up to 8–9cm. (3–3.5in.) in length, has colors similar to those of the Smooth Newt (an orange belly), but the throat is seldom spotted; its hind feet are fully webbed. The breeding male develops in early spring a short spiky filament at the end of its tail. It is widespread throughout the British Isles and central and southern Europe.

The **Alpine Newt** (*Triturus alpestris*) grows up to 8–11cm. (3–5in.) long, with upper parts grayish black or dark brown with unspotted orange-red belly. In early spring the breeding male develops a low yellow dorsal crest covered with small spots; his upper parts brighten to blue-gray. Neoteny (see Mexican Salamander, below) may occur at high altitudes in the natural range. It prefers the mountainous regions of central Europe.

The following are almost entirely aquatic and may be kept all year round in a fully planted aquarium with a small island, such as a rough-barked log.

The **Japanese Newt** (*Cynops pyrrhogaster*) is up to 10cm. (4in.) in length, brown, olive or blackish above and bright carmine or orange beneath with dark blotches. For breeding, keep the newts in a temperature of 3°C. (37°F.) without food for eight weeks during winter to bring them into condition. Males have a larger cloacal region. These newts are found in Japan and China.

The **Spanish Ribbed** or **Waltl Newt** (*Pleurodeles waltlii*), up to 15cm. (6in.) in length, is gray-green or brownish gray above

with dark spots, with a grayish belly with black spots and a strange flattened head. The ribs have sharp points which may protrude from warts along its side. It is voracious and large. Never mix it with smaller companions. It probably breeds throughout the year. The Iberian peninsula and Morocco are the two areas where this species is found.

SALAMANDERS

The following are the species most available and most suitable for captivity.

The **European** or **Fire Salamander** (*Salamandra salamandra*) averages 15–18cm. (6–7in.) in length. It is shiny black with brilliant yellow or orange stripes or spots on back and sides which is a warning coloration to deter predators: it can secrete toxic fluid from the parotid gland. Its tail is cylindrical. Although almost entirely terrestrial, this species likes damp conditions. Male and female are alike, but the male has a large cloacal region. Mating on land occurs throughout the active months; the female gives birth to up to fifty living, gilled young which metamorphose at about three months. Remove the adults, and rear the larvae as newts. It is found in central

The Axolotl is a species of salamander that rarely "grows up," that is it stays in the larval form and even breeds in this stage. Center. The larval form of the Axolotl showing its prominent gills. Bottom. A metamorphosed (or adult) form of the Axolotl, this stage has to be artificially induced.

and southern Europe, but not in Great Britain.

The **Spotted Salamander** (*Ambystoma maculatum*) averages 15–18cm. (6–7in.) in length and is dull black with round yellowish spots along each side, and a slate gray belly. It breeds during early spring in water where clumps of eggs are laid. The northeastern United States and Canada have this species.

Two species less commonly available are both from the eastern United States. The **Marbled Salamander** (*Ambystoma opacum*) is 9–10cm. (3.5–4in.) long, black with silvery white (male) or gray (female) irregular bands across its back, breeding in the fall. The **Eastern Tiger Salamander** (*Ambystoma tigrinum*) is 18–33cm. (7–13in.) long and is the largest salamander in the United States. Black or brown above with irregular yellow or brown blotches, it is neotenic (see next species) in some areas and breeds in early spring.

The **Mexican Salamander** or **Axolotl** (*Ambystoma [Siredon] mexicanum*) is neotenic (breeds from its larval form, which it normally retains for life). It is hardy, easy to feed, and all those commercially available have been bred in captivity. Young specimens (larvae) may occasionally be induced to metamorphose by gradually reducing the water level and by liberal feeding. To provide adequate space for a pair fill an aquarium to about 25cm. (10in.) with cold tap water, but allow it to stand for several days to remove

The Fire Salamander is the most widely kept of salamanders; its vividly contrasting black and yellow colors make it a strikingly colorful species.

the chlorine. Hiding places, small tunnels or caves, must be provided. Feed with earthworms and raw lean meat (e.g., beef heart) twice a week and clean out fecal matter regularly. Mixed sizes should never be kept together. The Axolotl is about 25cm. (10in.) long when fully grown. The permanent aquatic (neotenic) stage is dark velvety brown or gray with dark spots or is albino. Metamorphosed specimens lose their large gills and are dark gray with yellow spots; they have the typical tail, round in cross section, of a terrestrial salamander, and are poor swimmers. Breeding males have a swollen cloaca. For spawning, plant the tank thickly with clumps of waterweed such as willow moss, among which the several hundred eggs may be laid. Rear the larvae as newts and avoid overcrowding. They should grow rapidly, maturing in eighteen months, and they have been known to live up to twenty-five years.

Frogs and Toads

All the 2,600 species of the Order Anura (the tailless amphibians) are correctly known as frogs, but the term *toad* is commonly used to designate those species, as in the family Bufonidae, that have dryish warty skins, relatively short legs, and external parotid glands, one behind each eye, which produce bitter secretions used to deter enemies. In contrast, the frogs in the family Ranidae have moist shiny skins, longer more powerful hind legs, more fully-webbed feet, and live in closer association with water.

All adults are carnivorous and will only take moving prey, from mice for the largest bullfrogs down to fruitflies for the little cricket frogs. Never mix disparate sizes of frogs, as many species are cannibalistic.

In captivity, the frogs' accommodation will vary with the size and nature of the species. The frogs must always have enough clean water to submerge themselves and

absorb the moisture so vital to them. Serious diseases are frequently caused by microscopic organisms that flourish in cramped dirty conditions, so keep the frogs clean and change water regularly.

Feed about twice a week with a varied diet: earthworms, slugs, snails, crickets, locusts, flies, beetles, mealworms, caterpillars, moths, and other insects. If natural food is not available some frogs will eat small strips of raw lean beef wiggled before them on a loose thread of cotton. In suitable climates healthy members of the temperate species should be allowed to hibernate in an outside enclosure if you want them to breed. Alternatively frogs can hibernate in a cold (3–10°C; 37–50°F.), dark, frost-free place in an aquarium containing damp moss, soil, and peat. Otherwise the frogs must be kept at normal room temperature and fed as usual with earthworms and homebred supplies of insects.

Breeding

There is often no striking difference between male and female frogs, though females tend to be larger. However, in the breeding season the males of some species develop pronounced nuptial pads—rough patches on their forelimbs which help them grasp the generally larger females during mating (amplexus). Male frogs are more vocal and some have highly developed vocal sacs. For successful mating, most temperate frogs need an outdoor pool of natural pond water with plenty of aquatic plants. Some toads lay long chains of spawn (up to 35,000 eggs in the Marine Toad) entwined with water weeds; some frogs lay large masses of spawn; while others produce separate eggs at random. As the female is laying her eggs, the male ejects sperm directly into the water, fertilizing the eggs immediately.

The following method of rearing the spawn of the European Common Frog (*Rana temporaria*) applies to most temperate species. A small amount of spawn should be placed in fresh pond water about 15–30cm.

The Edible Frog is mainly aquatic and prefers to be kept in a sunny garden pool.

(6–12in.) deep, in the largest pool or tank available, planted well with freshwater weeds, and kept at a constant outdoor temperature. On hatching, the gilled tadpoles attach themselves to the plants and will not need feeding for two or three days, after which their natural diet (algae) is best supplemented by small amounts of finely flaked commercial tropical fish food and small pieces of lettuce leaves or spinach. As the tadpoles grow they absorb their gills and become carnivorous, requiring tiny pieces of finely chopped earthworm or raw lean beef. Remove any uneaten fragments after a few hours to avoid pollution of the water.

As the tadpoles develop, their hind legs appear first, followed by the fore limbs, before the tail is eventually absorbed. At this stage the tadpoles must have a rock or log island on which to rest or they will drown. They will only feed on minute insects which are difficult to obtain. If the froglets are indigenous, it is best to release them among undergrowth on the edge of an unpolluted pond without obvious predators such as ducks, moorhens, or grebe. Place the froglets you wish to keep in an outdoor enclosure and feed them large numbers of greenfly, whiteworms, minute earthworms, fruitflies, and other small insects. Do not try to keep too many; it can be difficult to feed even half a dozen.

Temperate Frogs and Toads

The following are best kept in suitable climates in an outdoor vivarium or, less successfully, in a moist, shady terrarium which, in the case of frogs, should have a pond covering half its total area.

The **European Common Frog** (*Rana temporaria*) is up to 10cm. (4in.) long and variable in color: yellow, reddish to blackish brown, textured with darker blotches and a dark patch on either side of the head from nose to tympanum; the hind legs have dark bands; the belly is cream or yellowish with darker spots. Largely terrestrial, it has been known to live for twelve years in captivity. This frog can be found from Europe to Japan.

Females of the **Edible Frog** (*Rana esculenta*) may reach 12cm. (5in.). The

Top. *The correct way to hold large frogs so that they are not injured.*

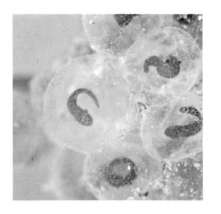

One of the most satisfactory achievements is to breed amphibians. The Common Frog is a typical example. Top Right. The spawn is laid in masses in water at the beginning of the spring. Center Left. The embryo begins to develop inside the egg and feeds on the jelly until it has reached a stage when it can hatch and swim free. Center Middle. *The free-swimming tadpole gradually grows legs, the hind ones first; then (Center Right) the fore limbs emerge and the tail is absorbed. The young frog is now ready to leave the water and will develop into an adult (Bottom).*

upperside is mainly green, with black blotches particularly in males, and a pale dorsal stripe, often yellow. Males have large round vocal sacs behind the mouth. Voracious, cannibalistic and mainly aquatic, they are best kept in a sunny garden pool and will breed freely in good conditions. They are found in northern and central Europe, Italy, North Africa, and Asia.

The **Leopard Frog** (*Rana pipiens*) is the most common frog in the United States and averages 5–8cm. (2–3in.) in length. Color is variable, usually bright green or brown with two or three rows of round pale-bordered spots between the dorsolateral ridges and white underparts. If kept indoors, this very active species should have a large terrarium. Only the northern race (*Rana p. pipiens*) should be hibernated outside in the colder temperate regions.

The **Pickerel Frog** (*Rana palustris*) is similar to the Leopard Frog but yellowish brown with two rows of square spots on the back, and the inner sides of its legs are bright yellow. The male has vocal pouches. Skin glands secrete toxins which deter predators.

Top Left. *A Yellow-Bellied Toad with only its eyes above water.* Top Middle. *A male Midwife Toad with eggs wound around his back legs.*

Eastern North America is where most of them are found.

The **Green Frog** (*Rana clamitans*) is up to 9cm. (3.5in.) long. Color variable, bright green (especially the head) or brown with dark brown blotches above. There are pronounced dorsolateral folds and white undersides with some mottling; males have bright yellow throats. Found in or near water in Canada and the eastern United States, the Green Frog has a short hibernation period and has lived ten years in captivity.

The **American Bullfrog** (*Rana catesbeiana*) is a huge frog with females up to 20cm. (8in.). It is green above or green with brown markings; the underside is white with dark spots and there is no dorsolateral ridge. Males often have yellowish throats. It is aquatic and voracious (diet as for large tropical frogs), and it has been known to live up to sixteen years in captivity. Tadpoles (to 15cm.) take three years to metamorphose. Most of them are found in the northern United States east of the Rockies, but they have been introduced elsewhere.

The **European Common Toad** (*Bufo bufo*) grows to 8–12cm. (3–5in.). Coloring is variable: olive, reddish, or yellow brown with underside grayish, usually with brownish spots. Sexually mature at four years, it breeds in the spring and can live for forty years or more. It is indigenous to most of Europe and temperate Asia.

The **Green Toad** (*Bufo vitidis*) grows to 9cm. (3.5in.), although females up to 20cm. (8in.) occur. The rather shiny, pale gray back is patterned with green blotches, often with red warts, and the underparts are whitish. Color varies according to surroundings. Its natural habitat is coastal and sandy areas, especially in central and southern Europe and southwestern Asia. An active toad, it is best to bring it indoors during the winter.

The **American Toad** (*Bufo americanus*) is 5–9cm. (2–3.5in.) long and of variable coloring, plain brown, olive or reddish, sometimes

with buff or yellow blotches; there may be a middorsal stripe. Its undersides are light, but often darkly spotted. Males have a dark throat and a large vocal sac. It has lived for thirty years in captivity. It is widespread in the northeastern United States.

The **Western Toad** (*Bufo boreas*) is the most common toad in the western United States. It is some 9cm. (3.5in.) long, greenish or gray with dark blotches and a light dorsal stripe. It does not hibernate in captivity.

The two spadefoot toads (family Pelobatidae) described below are chiefly terrestrial; they have a horny "spade" on the side of each hindfoot for burrowing; they have vertical pupils and rather smooth skins. They should be provided with slightly damp soil and should not be hibernated away from their native areas. The **European** or **Common Spadefoot** (*Pelobates fuscus*) indigenous from temperate Europe to Asia grows up to 8cm. (3in.) long. Color varies from pale gray or brown with olive or brown markings, and a pale gray underside. The male has an oval gland on each foreleg. The **Eastern Spadefoot** (*Scaphiopus holbrooki*) of the eastern United States is about 5cm. (2in.) long, brownish with two yellowish lines down the back and black "spades." Western species include *S. hammondi* and *S. couchi*.

Two toads of the family Discoglossidae are available as pets: the **Fire-bellied Toad** (*Bombina bombina*) of northern Europe and the **Yellow-bellied Toad** (*Bombina variegata*) of central and southern Europe. These two small toads grow to 3–5cm. (1.5–2in.) and are a light or dark olive-gray above with darker spots. They do well in an indoor semiaquatic vivarium and will breed in captivity.

The **Midwife Toad** (*Alytes obstetricans*) common in western Europe excluding Great Britain is about 5cm. (2in.) long, pale gray or brown above with darker blotches and a very pale underside. After mating the male winds eggs around his legs and remains on land; when the tadpoles are due to emerge he enters the water. The male has a bell-like call.

Tropical Frogs

Tropical frogs need a temperature of not more than 21–27°C. (70–80°F.) and fairly dim

illumination (a 40 watt bulb). Plants should not be put in with the larger frogs. The vivarium for the giant species can be made from an aquarium which is at least 90 x 45 x 30cm. (36 x 18 x 12in.). Make a removable top of plastic mesh stretched over a wooden frame. The interior should be simply arranged, with several inches of clean soil or slightly damp peat moss on the floor, and a cork bark hiding place. Provide a large bowl of clean water in which the creatures can submerge. A mixed diet of large earthworms, small mice, locusts, and mealworms will suit all larger tropical amphibians.

The **Giant Marine Toad** (*Bufo marinus*) found from Texas to Patagonia can grow to 23cm. (9in.), and a full-grown specimen can easily devour a young rat. If alarmed, it can emit toxic juices from the parotid glands behind its eyes which cause great discomfort to cuts or eyes. This toad does well in captivity, and often becomes remarkably tame. It is known as the Cane Toad in Australia, where it has been introduced (as in Puerto Rico, Haiti, and Hawaii) to combat beetles which attack sugarcane crops.

Among other large species occasionally imported are the **South African Bullfrog** (*Pyxi cephalus adspersus*), which spends much of its time in water, and the **Indian Bullfrog** (*Rana tigrina*), a very active species with long legs requiring a very tall vivarium.

The **Leopard** or **Square-marked Toad** (*Bufo regularis*) of Africa and Saudi Arabia grows to 15cm. (6in.). Color varies from reddish brown to olive with dark blotches on a light background. The floor of its vivarium should be covered with dry sandy soil. It feeds on small insects and earthworms.

The grotesque South American horned frogs (*Ceratophrys* species) require a diet mainly of mice, smaller frogs and even small snakes, need damp sphagnum moss in which to hide, and can inflict a painful bite. They include the **Colombian Horned Frog** (*C. ornata*) and the **Escuerzo** (*C. dorsata*), both of which have large broad heads with small soft triangular "horns" above their eyes.

Tree Frogs

Tree frogs (family Hylidae) are well adapted to arboreal lives; special adhesive disks on the end of their toes and an extra bone in each finger and toe help them cling to leaves and stems or climb a vertical sheet of glass. They can partially change color, and the males have inflatable vocal sacs. Cages covered with soft, durable mesh material are necessary to prevent tree frogs from damaging their heads as they leap about after insects. (The largest nylon drum, about 45cm. tall and 40cm. in diameter, sold for breeding butterflies is ideal.) Tree frogs like sunlight, and cages should be placed outdoors in suitable weather. Indoors a 25 watt bulb should be suspended above a basking area. Tropical and subtropical species should be kept at 21–24°C. (70–75°F.) and be fed throughout the year. Place one or two broad-leaved potted plants in the cage and sprinkle them with

The Giant Marine Toad is one of the largest toad species and survives well in captivity.

water daily, or use branches of laurel pushed through a small hole in the lid of a jam jar filled with water. Provide a deep bowl of clean water for bathing. The cage is also suitable for chameleons, who mix well with frogs, provided the relative sizes are not too disparate.

Finding enough food is the main problem in keeping tree frogs: they need a generous supply of soft-bodied insects, flies, moths, locusts, and crickets. Some species will accept occasional earthworms.

If a tree frog is injured on the snout, the resulting wound heals readily when treated with antibiotic ointment obtainable from a veterinarian.

The beautiful **European Tree Frog** (*Hyla arborea*) has now become rare in central Europe due to pollution and use of pesticides. From 4–5cm. (1.5–2in.) long, it has smooth bright green-gray or brown skin above, with a narrow dark stripe from nostril to groin.

The **Spring Peeper** (*Hyla crucifer*) indige-

Bottom Middle. *The European Tree Frog is becoming rare in its native regions. Bottom Right. All tree frogs, such as this Gray Tree Frog climbing glass, have special adhesive discs on each digit of their feet.*

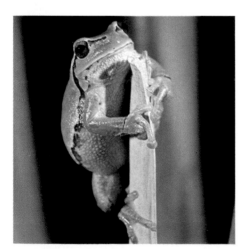

nous to the United States is a tiny species about 2.5cm. (1in.) long. The voice is a repeated whistle. Usually brownish, it has a dark cross on its back. Its food consists of greenfly, small worms, mosquitoes, and fruitflies.

The **Common** or **Gray Tree Frog** (*Hyla versicolor*) found in the United States is about 4–5cm. (1.5–2in.) long. It is gray, brown or green, with orange on the hind legs. It trills loudly.

The **Green Tree Frog** (*Hyla cinerea*) of Florida, Cuba, and the West Indies is usually bright green, often with little golden spots, and has a light stripe along its sides. Some 13–15cm. (5–6in.) in length, it is voracious and may attack smaller species.

Wholly Aquatic Frogs

The **Clawed Frog** (*Xenopus laevis* and other species) of Africa is an ideal pet, simple to keep, lives up to fifteen years in captivity and, best of all, it is bred in captivity for marketing as pets. They are rather strange looking, about 10cm. (4in.) in length, with round bodies and small pointed heads covered with a green and brown pattern above, grayish undersides, and tiny lidless eyes staring upward. The hind feet are webbed with small black claws on the first three toes. Males make a call underwater which sounds like a watch being wound; the females respond with a thumping noise. *X. laevis* is also known as the "pregnancy" frog; an unmated female toad will lay eggs if injected with urine from a pregnant woman.

A pair should be kept in an aquarium filled with 10–15cm. (4–6in.) of pure rainwater or dechlorinated tap water and covered with plastic mesh to prevent their leaping out. They need no special heating. Twice weekly offer earthworms or strips of raw lean beef which they will take from your hand. If you are lucky and your frogs mate, put the eggs in another medium–sized aquarium and raise the water temperature to 21°C. (70°F.). When the tadpoles are free-swimming, they should be transferred to another tank and fed two or three times a week on nettle powder, obtainable from health food stores. Change the water once a week, keep the temperature constant, and be careful not to overcrowd

them. The tadpoles can gradually be given larger food such as *Daphnia, Tubifex,* and mosquito larvae until they are big enough to take earthworms or other similar foods.

Reptiles

Modern reptiles are divided into four orders: Chelonia or Testudinata (tortoises and turtles), Crocodilia (alligators and crocodiles), Squamata (lizards and snakes), and Rhynchocephalia (with only one surviving species—the strictly protected New Zealand tuatara). Most reptiles have become adapted to terrestrial life and lay their eggs or produce their young on land. They have dry skins covered with scales or horny plates and, except for snakes, have claws on their four feet. They are cold-blooded animals whose body heat, behavior, and egg hatching are regulated by general environmental temperature, a vital factor in their well-being. During the colder months, those that live in temperate regions must hibernate to survive.

Tortoises, Terrapins, And Turtles

This group of about 210 species of reptiles is known collectively as *chelonians.* The group's survival is due in large measure to the bony armor which covers much, or all, of the animal. The rigid top part (carapace) is formed by a fusion of the backbone and the ribs which have become greatly flattened and widened to form bony plates. The lower part (plastron) is usually joined to the carapace by a bony bridge on either side. The whole shell is generally covered with a symmetrical pattern of broad, horny shields. Chelonians cannot expand or contract their chests so they have developed their belly muscles to widen and contract the body cavity to pump air in and out. They have no teeth, but their jaws are covered by a strong, horny beak. Although lacking external ears, they can hear and are sensitive to vibrations through ground or water. They lay their eggs on land.

TORTOISES

Of the millions of tortoises exported for pets each year from their native lands, less than 10 percent survive more than a year. Their continued collection from the wild for sale as pets is threatening their extinction and condemns countless numbers to death on their way to the pet shops. Pet shop specimens frequently suffer from "soft shell," a condition caused by lack of calcium in the diet. A healthy tortoise should feel heavy. A shell length of 19cm. (7.5in.) should, for example, give a weight of about 1.5kg. (3.5lb.). The tropical species are particularly difficult and expensive to maintain in colder climates.

Mediterranean species are best kept outdoors during the drier, warmer months as they use direct sunlight for bone deposition. They need a large, dry area and should never be kept in humid conditions, regardless of the temperature. If your garden is enclosed they will enjoy its freedom, but they may eat some of your plants—they particularly seem to favor flowers with yellow petals. For a fixed site, you can surround a warm dry area at least 4 x 2m. (13 x 8 ft.) with walls 30cm. (12in.) high. Half the area should be sandy with a shallow container of clean water sunk in one corner, large enough for them to sit in and deep enough for them to immerse their heads while drinking. A low hutch, filled with straw, with a waterproof roof, raised floor to ensure dryness, and a ramp for access, is essential. An infrared lamp suspended 60cm. (24in.) from the ground will provide warmth during colder weather and encourage the tortoises to feed. If a fixed site is not possible, a wooden frame some 2 x 1.3m. (6 x 4ft.) can be moved at least every other day over dry, level land where clover, dandelions, and plantains grow. Tortoises will, however, always need additional food.

Tropical species can only be put outdoors on warm summer days but should be brought in at night. Indoors these species do best in a heated room of their own at not less than 20–30°C. (70–85°F.) with eight hours of artificial light daily. They need a wooden enclosure about 2 x 1m. (6 x 3ft.) with 50cm. (20in.) walls raised on legs to escape floor drafts.

Tortoises need a great amount and variety of fruits, vegetables and wild plants: dandelions, plantain, goose grass, alkanet, clover, chickweed, bindweed, buttercup, cabbage, lettuce, cucumber, pea and bean leaves, strawberries, bananas, tomatoes, apples, and pears will all be acceptable as daily diet. They must be free of chemical sprays. Once weekly, protein should be given in the form of raw strips of lean beef, hard-boiled eggs (with their shells crushed), earthworms, sprats, shrimp, canned dog food, and—especially if roughage is lacking—offer moist puppy food once or twice a week. A vitamin supplement can be dusted on fruit and other food two or three times a week. Cuttlefish bone will supply essential extra calcium.

Larger tropical tortoises can eat a great deal; an adult Leopard Tortoise can get through three or four lettuce heads and 0.5kg. (1lb.) of bananas or tomatoes in a day *and* continue to eat at that rate all year round!

Preparing for Hibernation

In the fall in temperate countries tortoises stop feeding, become sluggish, and start to dig themselves into the ground. Individuals which are underweight for their size or under 10cm. (4in.) long must be kept active at 27°C. (80°F.) and fed throughout the winter—as must all tropical species. Hibernators in good condition should be put in a large, strong wooden box 60cm. (24in.) square, with a tightly fitting, perforated zinc lid (to keep out rodents), filled with dry straw, hay, or leaves. If several are to be hibernated, place each in

Tortoises do not breed very often in captivity, but occasionally females lay eggs, as with this Hermann's Tortoise (Top Middle) that has scraped out a depression in the soil. Top Right. The young hatch in a fully developed form after ten to twelve weeks.

Center Right. *This newly-hatched tortoise has been turned on its back to reveal the remains of the yolk sac that will be gradually absorbed.*

its own separate cardboard box in the center of the larger wooden box to prevent their disturbing each other. Put the large box, well covered with sacking, in a cold but *frost proof* cellar or shed. The tortoises should not be disturbed, or allowed to get warm, until the following spring. A temperature range of about 3–8°C. (38–47°F.) is ideal. When the weather improves, about April or May in northern temperate conditions, and the surrounding temperature has risen to about 16°C. (60°F.), it is time to bring them out into the sun again. First their heads may need gentle washing with water, then they should be given a drink of tepid water. Tempting food should be offered, although they may not eat for several days. Until the danger of cold or wet weather is over they should go back into their boxes after a few hours in the sun. The awakening process must be done gradually and carefully because the animals are vulnerable following their long fast.

Breeding

Male tortoises have concave plastrons and larger tails than the females, who have flat plastrons. Prior to mating the males butt the females and bite at their feet. Occasionally tortoises lay eggs in captivity, although they are seldom fertile. Eggs may hatch if you bury them carefully, without turning them over, in a box of fine dry sand about 8cm. (3in.) deep which is kept undisturbed at a temperature of 27–29°C. (80–85°F.). After about ten to twelve weeks, a hatchling may emerge. At first it will probably only want water but should be offered a variety of finely chopped soft items from the adult diet. Keep the temperature at about 27°C. (80°F.) until the hatchling is 10cm. (4in.) long; then gradually treat it as an adult.

Diseases

Tortoises may be infested with ticks, round gray parasites that suck blood. Never try to remove them without first putting a drop or two of heated wax or lighter fluid on them with a brush to make them loosen their grip. Blowflies may lay eggs on tortoise's skin, especially if it is dirty around the tail. Keep your tortoises clean, but if maggots do appear, seek expert advice. Consult your veterinarian if your tortoises appear to have internal worms or eye infections. Minor wounds can be treated with a weak solution of disinfectant, but serious injuries or ailments may need antibiotics, to which many reptiles respond rapidly. If your tortoise develops a cold, take it indoors, keep it dry and very warm—about 27°C. (80°F.). If the cold does not clear up in a few days, take the tortoise to the veterinarian.

Mediterranean Tortoises

The **Spur-Thighed** or **Algerian Tortoise** (*Testudo graeca*) is one of the two species most frequently sold in Europe. It has a prominent conical spur on each thigh and comes mainly from semidesert areas in North Africa. It is prone to colds and other fatal diseases in captivity. **Hermann's** or the **Greek Tortoise** (*Testudo hermanni*), the other frequently sold species, is hardier and comes from the Balkans. It has a horny tip on the end of its tail.

Horsfield's or the **Four-toed Tortoise** (*Testudo horsfieldii*) is native to the Caspian shores and northwest India. It can be easily distinguished from the preceding species as it has only four claws on each limb. It is not hardy.

The **Marginated** or **Margined Tortoise** (*Testudo marginata*), from rocky and mountainous regions of Greece, is as hardy as Hermann's Tortoise.

Tropical Tortoises

The following tropical species are sometimes available for purchase. The **Angulated Tortoise** (*Testudo angulata*) from South Africa has a carapace up to 25cm. (10in.) long, strikingly marked with black and dull yellow.

The **Leopard Tortoise** (*Testudo pardalis*), a large African species up to 70cm. (27in.) long, has a highly domed carapace decorated with hundreds of black irregular spots against a dull yellow. It is entirely vegetarian and eats quantities of grass.

Bell's Ringed-Back Tortoise (*Kinixys belliana*) is an unusual, medium-sized African species, apt to be shy in captivity. The rear part of the carapace is hinged and can be lowered as a defense mechanism. Diet consists of earthworms, meat, hard-boiled egg, and the normal vegetarian diet.

The **South American Red-footed Tortoise** (*Testudo carbonaria*) grows up to 50cm. (20in.) long and has a dark brown carapace and orange scales on its legs. It drinks more water and likes more meat than other tortoises.

The **Indian Starred** or **Star Tortoise** (*Testudo elegans*), 25cm. (10in.) long, has a highly domed carapace and a yellow star pattern on each shield.

Gopher Tortoises

The three gopher tortoises are the only tortoises native to the United States. The **Desert Tortoise** (*Gopherus p. agassi zii*), **Berlandier's Tortoise** (*Gopherus p. berlandieri*), and the **Gopher Tortoise** (*Gopherus p. polyphemus*) do not thrive away from their special desert climatic conditions. They are officially protected in the United States as an endangered species.

TERRAPINS AND TURTLES

Terrapins or freshwater turtles have broad webbed feet and a streamlined shell. The great marine chelonians (which are wholly unsuitable as pets) are always known as turtles, but the freshwater species are often known outside the United States as terrapins. In this chapter the term *turtle* is used for American freshwater species and *terrapin* for those which come from other parts of the world. None provides suitable pets for young children, because their proper care and maintenance is too difficult. There is also the risk of infection (salmonellosis) to humans unless strict hygiene is observed. Importing and selling some species is now banned in the United States for this reason. Be sure to disinfect your hands after handling terrapins in addition to keeping them and their aquarium very clean. The species commonly sold as juveniles are listed below. Avoid buying any with a shell under 5cm. (2in.) in length. A few species, such as the **Snapping Turtle**

This pool, made from plastic sheeting and loose bricks inside a greenhouse where the temperature can be controlled, makes a fine home for terrapins but they can easily climb its low walls which would have to be much higher if it were used as warm weather accommodation outdoors.

(*Chelydra serpentina*) from North America, are very aggressive and should not be put in a pool with other turtles. At their full size of up to 45cm. (18in.) shell-length, they can be quite formidable to people too!

In temperate climates all juveniles of 8cm. (3in.) or less must be kept indoors and only be taken outside in hot summer sunshine. *Never* cramp them or keep them in bowls. Even the smallest specimens need an aquarium at least 60 x 25 x 25cm. (24 x 10 x 10in.) with a dry basking platform of cork, bark, or half a log, supported by bricks or stones incorporating a hiding place below water level. A 60 watt light suspended about 10cm. (4in.) above the platform should be turned on for eight hours a day. The water should be at least 8cm. (3in.) deep and kept at 24–29°C. (75–85°F.) by a thermostatically controlled fish tank heater. Terrapins soon die if overheated. Adult tropical terrapins can be kept indoors in larger aquariums in the same way, or preferably in a heated greenhouse pool.

Outdoors an inflatable children's wading pool or a washtub (set on a platform and under shelter) will make a suitable home for baby terrapins and turtles on hot summer days. When over 10cm. (4in.) long they can be safely put into a garden pool, about 30cm. (12in.) deep and fenced with netting with an overhang of 20cm. (8in.) pointing inward at an angle of 45°. In temperate climates they should only be kept there during the very warmest months, and a 150 watt pond heater should be installed for use on colder days.

Only the adults of larger European pond terrapins, Spanish, Chinese, or Reeve's Terrapins and other species from temperate areas can safely live outdoors for most of the year in the cooler parts of the world. If these species are in really good condition, they can be successfully hibernated under water with the pond heater to provide a warm local area on the bottom of the pond which will not freeze in the coldest weather. The heater must be in a part of the pond at least 60cm.

The Hermann's Tortoise is one of the most widely kept tortoises and survives reasonably well in temperate climates if properly looked after. It can live up to 100 years.

Some of the other tortoise species that have been kept as pets: Top Left. *Spur-Thighed Tortoise.* Top Right. *Leopard Tortoise.* Center Left. *Star Tortoise.* Center Right. *Desert Tortoise. (*Both these species are now in danger of extinction and should no longer be kept in captivity.)*

(24in.) deep, and there must be an island for summer basking.

Another method of hibernating the hardier species is simply a "damp" version of the method used for tortoises. Place the terrapin in a large box filled with moist soil and leaves at least 30cm. (12in.) deep. Cover the box

A number of turtles and terrapins are kept as pets. Shown here are (Bottom Left) *the Spanish Terrapin,* (Bottom Middle) *the Soft-shelled Turtle,* and (Bottom Right) *the Florida Box Turtle.*

with some perforated metal to keep out rats.

Feeding. All terrapins and turtles must have a variety of food rich in calcium: raw herring with skin, sprats, shrimp, water snails, earthworms, and small pieces of cuttlefish bone. Medicinal bone flour and a vitamin supplement such as halibut liver oil should be rubbed into small pieces of raw meat and offered several times a week before other food. Also provide waterweeds, lettuce, watercress, soft fruit, and hard-boiled egg fragments. Dried commercial turtle food is not recommended. Some species tend to change to a vegetarian diet as they mature.

Diseases. Eye ailments can be caused by malnutrition or dirty water. Direct sunlight

can help, but if the trouble does not clear up consult the veterinarian.

Breeding. If a captive terrapin lays eggs, handle them carefully, keeping the same end up as when laid. Bury them in a mixture of damp, clean sand, keep them at 29°C. (85°F.) and, if you are extremely lucky, a hatchling will appear in three to five months.

Tropical and Subtropical Species

The **Red-eared Turtle** (*Pseudemys scripta elegans*), the species most commonly available in pet shops, comes from the United States. It has a finely patterned green shell and a red stripe on each side of its head and grows up to 28cm. (11in.). The **Slider Turtle** (*Pseudemys scripta scripta*), a subspecies similar to the Red-eared Turtle, has yellow stripes on its head. It grows up to 27cm. (10.5in.).

The **Painted Turtle** (*Chrysemys picta*) is not literally painted (a turtle's shell never should be), although the brilliant red edge of the olive-brown carapace and bridge gives this shy turtle its name. Rather prone to shell infections in captivity, it is less suitable as a pet than the two preceding species. It grows to 18–25cm. (7–9in.).

Temperate Species

The **European Pond Tortoise** (*Emys orbicularis*), sadly becoming much scarcer in its native habitat, has a black shell streaked with lemon yellow, yellow spots on its head, and a long tail. It grows to 25cm. (9in.).

The **Spanish Terrapin** (*Clemmys caspica leprosa*) has an olive-brown carapace with irregular orange patterns and orange-yellow stripes on its gray-green head and neck. As with all terrapins these colors become dimmed with age.

Soft-shelled Turtles

The tropical and subtropical soft-shelled turtles from North America, Africa, and Asia have lost the outside horny scales and retain only a loose bony structure beneath the leathery skin of the carapace and plastron. They are best kept by themselves in a large tank with sand at the bottom. In general they should be treated as other carnivorous turtles although they are less robust. The **Florida Soft-shelled Turtle** (*Trionyx ferox*) reaches up to 18kg. or 40lbs. They tend to bite and scratch when picked up. Specimens are

rarely available and are not suitable for beginners.

North American Box Turtles
So named because they have a hinged plastron which closes tightly against the carapace at both ends, making the shell into a sealed box, these turtles are basically terrestrial. In their own areas they are best kept outside in a large pen in a shrubby shady area with piles of loose leaves and soil. They need a shallow pool and are excellent climbers; their fencing needs an 18cm. (7in.) overhang. In summer box turtles like a temperature of about 21°C. (70°F.). In colder months they should be hibernated, except for *Terrapene carolina bauri*, which likes more humidity and is best kept in a greenhouse for most of the year.

Box turtles eat the same diet as other turtles, plus blackberries, fungi, slugs, crushed snail, and melon. With good care they live a long time; individuals have been known to exceed a century. There are two species which come from the United States.

The **Common Box Turtle** (*Terrapene carolina carolina*, one of several subspecies, differently marked) has a high, arched, dark brown shell with orange patterns, and orange spots on its dark brown head and forelimbs. Males usually have red eyes, and females have brown. The plastron is less decorated than the following species. Length is about 14cm. (5.5in.).

The **Ornate Box Turtle** (*Terrapene ornata ornata*) has a flat top to its carapace, a highly patterned plastron with light stripes on a dark background. It enjoys living in drier, warmer environments.

Crocodilians

Most of the world's Crocodilians (alligators and crocodiles) are seriously endangered and many are nearing the point of extinction. They are both difficult and expensive to keep and in no way suited as a pet. A healthy baby caiman, for example, will increase its weight by eight times and add 35cm. (14in.) to its length in its first year; the broad-nosed and black caimans grow to 3.6–4m. (12–13ft.) in length. They can also inflict painful and dangerous wounds. Crocodilians have a place only in those zoological collections which can provide for them properly.

Snakes and Lizards

Snakes and lizards belong to the same order Squamata, the scaly reptiles. There are two suborders: Serpentes, the snakes (10 families, approximately 2,700 species); and Lacertilia, the lizards (17 families, approximately 3,200 species).

Snakes and lizards share some anatomical features; a particularly interesting common feature is known as Jacobson's organ, two special sensory cavities in the roof of the mouth. Snakes and some lizards (such as the monitors) use their forked tongues to pick up minute particles of scent and carry them back into this sensitive smelling device to indicate the presence of prey, mates, or danger.

Limbless species of lizards, such as the Slowworm and the various species of "glass snakes," look more like snakes proper. Most lizards, however, have externally visible eardrums, while snakes do not; most lizards have moveable eyelids while all snakes have a transparent fused scale or "spectacle" over their eyes which they cannot blink or close. The snake's jaw is much more highly specialized; each side of the lower jaw can move independently as it is connected to the skull by an elastic ligament which enables it to swallow prey much larger than its normal mouth size. Lizards chew their plant or animal food, but all snakes are carnivorous and swallow their prey whole.

Top Right. *Most of the world's Crocodylians are endangered species, and for this reason alone they should not be kept as pets. Even the relatively small Brown Caiman shown here requires a large pool if it is to survive.*

SNAKES

Few snakes are dangerous to man, but many people have an irrational fear of *all* snakes. If you are considering keeping snakes, remember that other members of your household or neighbors may live in fear of your snake's possible escape. Snakes are brilliant escapologists and sooner or later you are almost certain to lose one which may be killed on sight by someone who is afraid of them.

Poisonous species (which should always be kept in padlocked vivariums) are totally unsuitable for the nonprofessional herpetologist, and it is illegal to keep them in many countries without a special license. *Before* deciding to keep a snake, consider its feeding requirements, which may be specialized. Another vital point to bear in mind is the fully grown size and temperament. Some of the adult pythons, for example, can become 10m. (33ft.) long and weigh over 70kg. (150lb.). They can inflict very severe wounds and are obviously unsuitable pets for normal households. On the other hand, some species, such as the American garter snakes, rarely exceed 1m. (3ft.), are relatively easy to care for, and are certainly best for the beginning snake keeper.

Housing

Species from cool temperate countries may be kept in the outdoor enclosures described above provided the ambient temperatures are suitable. Generally, however, snakes are best kept indoors in a simple cage which is easy to clean. A modified aquarium is most suitable for smaller species, with a *secure* homemade cover which allows for good ventilation. At least half of the top should be covered with perforated metal or strong plastic mesh (never wire) on a wooden frame which fits tightly around the top of the aquarium and is weighted so that the snake cannot push it open. A

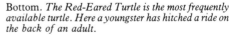

Bottom. *The Red-Eared Turtle is the most frequently available turtle. Here a youngster has hitched a ride on the back of an adult.*

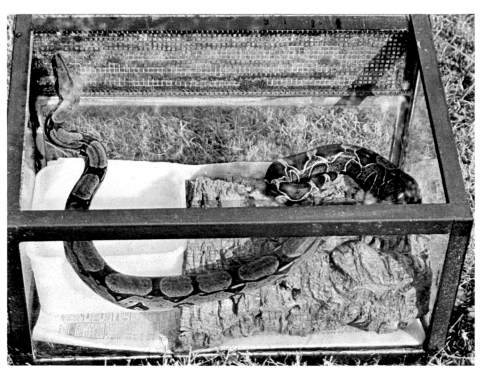

Top Left. *Most snakes will get used to being handled given time, but all are individuals and some will always be nervous. Tame young boas, such as the Emperor Boa, can be handled quite safely by children, but large ones can inflict nasty bites.*

light bulb socket may be mounted on the wooden end of the top for a low wattage bulb (not more than 40 watt).

As a general rule for most snakes, the length of the cage need be only about half the extended length of the snake it accommodates because reptiles spend so much of their time coiled up. The floor of the cage should be covered with absorbent paper towel or newspaper and perhaps a shallow covering of medium-sized round shingle. A few dried leaves can be added to give a more natural effect. Most snakes like to climb, so include a few branches that are substantial enough to support them.

Some dealers supply ready-made glass vivariums for snakes, but these are not always well designed and you may prefer to make your own from a wooden box. Make sure that you include ample ventilation and that there are no rough surfaces on which the snake may rub its nose raw. The disadvantage of wooden cages is that they are much more difficult to disinfect and clean than those made from glass, although they are warmer and lighter. The cage should contain a box with a small opening into which the snake can retire; a piece of cork bark will do for smaller species. Rough pieces of bark or stones which are not easily dislodged are needed as an aid to sloughing.

The temperature range will vary to suit the individual species, but aim at a daytime temperature of about 22°C. (72°F.) for those from temperate zones and around 26–30°C. (78–85°F.) for the most tropical specimens; the temperature can be allowed to drop about

Top Center. *This simple vivarium provides all that a young boa constrictor needs and is easy to clean and keep disease-free, although the snake must be allowed out for exercise. This specimen is growing fast and is due for a larger cage.*

10°C. at night. To be sure of the temperature, install a thermometer inside the cage where you can easily read it from outside. Although snakes will tolerate periods when the temperature falls below these levels, their digestive processes are highly dependent on temperature. When the surrounding temperature is too low, their food may be only partially digested or even putrify within the reptile with disastrous consequences. If the room is not warm enough for species kept indoors, place heating pads or tubular metal heaters controlled with a thermostat under the cage—never inside it. The bottom of the cage must be raised an inch or two above the heater. Start with the lowest setting and gradually raise the temperature to the required level.

Of species from temperate zones only the hardy snakes may be hibernated, so long as they are in really good condition and their temperature does not fall below 5°C. (41°F.), even during the most severe frosts. Reptiles from warmer temperate countries are safer brought indoors and kept active.

Feeding

Snakes should be offered food about once a week or every ten days. Adult specimens can survive *voluntarily* without food for long periods if they have access to clean drinking water. The water container should be large enough for the snakes to submerge in it from time to time, especially when they are about to slough, but the water should not overflow to cause damp, unhealthy conditions. It is absolutely essential, even for water snakes,

that completely dry areas be available in the cage or vivarium.

Although all snakes under natural conditions eat living prey (with the exception of the egg eaters), this is not necessary or desirable in captivity. Feeding live creatures is often a cruel (and in some countries an illegal) practice, and it is also possible for a rat or mouse to severely injure a snake. It is usually easy to persuade a hungry snake to take freshly killed prey or frozen prey that has been carefully warmed up.

Recently acquired snakes may take some time to settle down before they start to feed. If a healthy snake fasts it is probably the conditions that are at fault. Try presenting different types of suitable food, raising the surrounding temperature, making sure it has an adequate den, or try feeding at night. Sometimes a warm bath is helpful. As a last resort, force feeding may have to be employed, but this process is not recommended for amateurs without expert advice from a veterinarian.

Snakes should not be disturbed while eating or for at least forty-eight hours after a meal. Stress often causes a snake to vomit its prey.

Sloughing

Snakes shed their outer skins at fairly regular intervals. During these times they need a large water container to keep their skins damp. The snake becomes temporarily blind and will usually refuse food. About a week before sloughing the eyes become opaque and the skin becomes dull due to an oil secretion between the old and the new skin. The old skin first loosens around the mouth and the snake rubs against rough objects and crawls out, leaving the old layer behind. *Never* attempt to help a snake slough its skin.

281

All snakes periodically shed their skins. Shown here is the head section of the sloughed skin of a Grass Snake.

Breeding

Snakes which are kept under unusually good conditions may sometimes mate in captivity. If the snake is a live-bearer the resulting young should be kept under similar conditions but at a slightly warmer temperature. Those that eat warm-blooded creatures should be given young pink mice. Those that eat fish or amphibians will usually take tadpoles, guppies, or other tiny fish from a shallow dish of water; some will eat earthworms. As with most reptiles, variety in diet is important.

Hatching snake eggs depends on finding them at once and keeping them with the same end up as when found. Keep them in a small open jar surrounded with slightly damp paper towels or cotton balls. Stand this jar within a larger container with a lid and put 5–8cm. (2–3in.) of water in it before closing the lid. Keep the eggs undisturbed in a warm place, such as cabinet or cupboard, until they hatch a few days to several months later.

Do not hibernate baby snakes in their first year but keep them warm and feeding indoors.

Handling Snakes

Many snakes will get used to being gently handled though great care must be taken with nervous individuals.

Grasp the snake firmly but very gently directly behind the head while supporting the rest of its body with the other hand. Be certain that the snake feels secure and is never in danger of falling. Move slowly and deliberately. By degrees there should be no need to restrain the snake behind the head and it may be allowed to climb over your arms at will without your fearing its escape.

There are about eleven families of snakes but two families are the most frequent providers of pets—the Boidae (boas and pythons) and the Colubridae (colubrids). The boas and pythons come from the tropics and include the world's largest snakes, though not all are large. Boas are mainly found in the New World while pythons are confined to the Old. Boas are live-bearers but all pythons lay eggs. All the Boidae are constrictors—they suffocate their prey in their coils until the heartbeat has ceased.

Over two-thirds of all snakes are contained in the family of "typical snakes," the Colubridae. Most colubrids are nonpoisonous and either swallow their prey alive or constrict. A minority kill their prey with poisonous bites of the small grooved fangs at the rear of their upper jaws. Although these are rarely serious to human beings, except in some snakes including the Boomslang (*Dispholidus typus*), rear-fanged snakes are not recommended as pets. Colubrids kept as pets include the garter snakes, water snakes, rat snakes, king snakes, racers, whip snakes, green snakes, indigo snakes, and mole snakes.

Boas and Pythons

Given the right conditions some species can do well in captivity; the common Boa Constrictor and the African Rock Python have lived for many years in zoos. Some tame and feed easily while others always remain difficult. It is wise to wear gloves when handling newcomers; large boids of 2m. (6ft.) or more can inflict vicious wounds and are unsuitable for a young or inexperienced keeper. Young boids may quickly outgrow their vivariums; they will also need meals of progressively larger prey, such as birds and rodents, which may be difficult to obtain.

For adults the temperature should be 22–27°C. (72–80°F.) by day and 20°C. (68°F.) at night, though their young need a more constant temperature of about 26°C. (78°F.). Boas and pythons like to bathe in warm water.

The boids most commonly kept include the **African Rock Python** or **African Python** (*Python sebae*), the largest of the African snakes which grows to about 6m. (20ft.), and the **Royal** or **Ball Python** (*P. regius*), a smaller—up to 2m. (6ft.)—though heavily built species from West Africa which coils up when frightened.

The huge, handsomely marked **Reticulated Python** (*P. reticulatus*) from Southeast Asia to the East Indies grows to 10m. (33ft.) and is probably the most aggressive of the pythons. The **Indian** or **Asiatic Rock Python** (*P. molurus*) is becoming uncommon; only captive-bred specimens should be considered. It is tree loving like the Reticulated Python and occurs in a pale form in India and a larger, darker form in Sri Lanka, Burma, and Indonesia. It grows to 6m. (20ft.).

From the New World, the **Boa Constrictor** (*Constrictor constrictor*), widely distributed in Central and tropical South America, up to 5.5m. (18ft.), is the most commonly kept boid. The Anaconda (*Eunectes murinus*) from South America, up to 11.5m. (37ft.) long and 1100kg. (half a ton) in weight, is chiefly aquatic.

Sand boas seldom exceed 1m. (3ft.) in length. They are found in North Africa and western Asia and have wedge-shaped heads, small eyes, tiny nostrils to keep out the sand, and abruptly tapering tails. In the wild they feed on small rodents and lizards. They give birth to living young. Species kept include the **Javelin Sand Boa** (*Eryx jaculus*), a docile species from southern Europe and Asia Minor which seldom bites, the **Theban Sand Boa** (*E. colubrina*) from North Africa which defends itself by repeated slashing bites, **John's Sand Boa** (*E. johni*) from India, and **Russell's Sand Boa** (*E. conicus*) from western Asia. All need some 10cm. (4in.) at least of clean dry sand and gravel, some cork bark or similar material for hiding, and a small bowl of drinking water.

Garter Snakes

Garter snakes (*Thamnophis* species) are perhaps best for beginners. They are the most common and among the more colorful snakes of North America. They are attractive, easily kept, and readily available as pets. Most of the twelve or more species are dark with two or three vivid yellow or orange stripes and measure 50–75cm. (20–30in.). Most but not all eat earthworms or strips of raw fish. They may also take frogs and toads, slugs, insects, and small mice, birds, and lizards. If not tamed, they may strike and emit a foul smelling secretion from the cloaca, but young specimens (which are born live in broods of fifty or more) will tame easily and may live ten years in captivity. The **Common Garter Snake** (*Thamnophis sirtalis*), of

Center. The African Python is the largest African Snake. Bottom. Sand Boas, such as this Russell's Sand Boa, are the smallest of boas.

Garter Snakes, such as the Common Garter, are the best snakes for beginners and can be kept in an outdoor vivarium.

the northwestern United States, with three stripes is commonly available. Two subspecies, the **Red-Spotted Garter Snake** (*T. s. concinnus*) and the **Californian Red-Sided Garter Snake** (*T. s. infernalis*), are particularly attractive. Often available, but less suitable, are the slender **Ribbon Snake** (*T. sauritus*), from the eastern United States which prefers wetter places but may not eat fish or earthworms, and the **Western Garter Snake** (*T. elegans*).

Water Snakes
Popular both in the United States and Europe, water snakes are closely allied to the Garter Snakes and need similar treatment. They live near or in water, are excellent swimmers, and love to bask in sunlight. They may be hibernated from October to April according to the climatic conditions.

The **Northern** or **Common Water Snake** (*Natrix sipedon*) is a heavy-bodied species from the United States, the adults reaching 60–120cm. (2–4ft.). Unlike the European water snakes, it does not lay eggs but bears alive up to ninety young. The American wa-

Bottom Left. *A Common Water Snake devouring a frog considerably larger than itself.* Bottom Center. *The European Grass Snake, showing the characteristic yellow collar around its neck.*

ter snakes (some twelve species, and the different races of *N. sipedon*) tend to be bad tempered, biting and discharging foul smelling fluid from the anal glands if disturbed; they do not tame easily but will accept almost any kind of raw fish whole or cut into pieces about twice the size of the snake's head.

The **European Grass Snake** (*N. natrix*) is found throughout most of Europe. It attains a length of 70–150cm. (27–60in.) and seldom bites but defends itself when seized with offensive smelling secretion and by going limp and feigning death. The staple food is the common frog, but some will take small fish or newts. The **Dice Snake** (*N. tessdata*) from southeast Europe to central Asia looks similar but lacks the yellow collar, is smaller, and has a dark V-mark on the nape and square patches along the body. The **Viperine Snake** (*N. maura*) from southwest Europe has a dark zigzag along the back like the poisonous Common Viper or Adder but also has eyespots along the sides. It eats earthworms.

Rat Snakes
These include some of the most popular pet snakes. All of the fifty species, from the Americas, Europe, and Asia, are constrictors, and many are good climbers. They feed on small mammals, birds, and eggs. Young rat snakes (which hatch from eggs) include lizards and amphibians in their diet, and their markings often differ from those of adults. When threatened many rat snakes strike, hiss fiercely, and vibrate their tails; some discharge foul smelling fluid. The following species settle down well and thrive in captivity.

The **Corn** or **Spotted** or **Red Rat Snake** (*Elaphe guttata* from the southern and eastern United States) averages 90–120cm. (3–4ft.) in length. Strikingly marked above and on its sides with terra-cotta blotches on a yellowish background, it is usually docile. Captive specimens have lived up to twenty years. The **Fox Snake** (*E. vulpina*), similar in size, has a more northerly range and is more heavily built. It is boldly marked with brown or blackish blotches on yellow or light brown. The **Black Rat Snake** (*E. obsoleta obsoleta*), **Yellow Rat Snake** (*E. o. quadrivittata*), and

The Red Rat Snake can live up to twenty years in captivity.

Gray Rat Snake (*E. o. spiloides*) are races of the same species, which occurs in gradually changing colors from one range to another.

The **Four-lined Snake** (*E. quatuorlineata*), which occurs from southeast Europe to western Asia, is one of Europe's largest snakes, occasionally reaching 2.5m. (8ft.). Adults take mice, rats, birds, and eggs while the young feed mainly on lizards. Some individuals become remarkably tame, but all snakes should be treated with some caution.

Other Colubrids
The following colubrids are less common or less easy to keep.

Hog-nosed snakes (*Heterodon* species) from North America feed almost exclusively on toads. They are relatively fat, short (0.5–1m.), and harmless. If the intimidation display (spreading the neck like a cobra and hissing loudly) fails, they feign death. Most often available is the **Eastern Hog-nosed Snake** (*H. platyrhinos*).

There are many species and subspecies of king snakes (*Lampropeltis*), which are medium-sized constrictors ranging from Canada to Ecuador. They eat small mammals, birds, eggs, reptiles, even poisonous snakes. The **Eastern King Snake** (*L.g. getulus*) can exceed 180cm. (6ft.), while the little **Scarlet King** or **Milk Snake** (*L. diolata*), which includes fish and earthworms in its diet, is some 45cm. (18in.) long. The latter, like the **Red King** or **Eastern Milk Snake** (*L. d. triangulum*), eats mice, not milk!

The slender, fast-moving, tree-dwelling racers and whipsnakes (*Coluber* and *Masticophis*) are restless and aggressive in captivity. They include the North American **Black Racer** (*C. constrictus*), the European **Whip Snake** or **Angry Snake** (*C. vividi-flavus*), which is slightly larger at 1.8m. (6ft.) and the even thinner American coachwhip or whip snakes. The **Eastern Coachwhip** (*M. flagellum*) may exceed 2.5m. (8.25ft.).

Much more heavily built are the pine and bull snakes (*Pituophis*) from the United States and Mexico. They have relatively small, pointed heads for burrowing and aver-

An extremely tame Four-Lined Snake.

The Mole Snake.

age around 2m. (6ft.) in length. Among those kept are the **Northern Pine Snake** (*P. m. melanolencus*), the **Bull Snake** from the Midwest (e.g., *P. m. sayi*), and the **Gopher Snake** from the West (e.g., *P. melanoleucus*).

The American green snakes (*Opheodrys*) are small, delicate insect eaters. They include the tree-dwelling **Rough Green Snake** (*O. aestivus*) and the **Smooth Green Snake** (*O. vernalis*). Although often available they do not feed well in captivity.

The indigo snakes, from the warmer states of the United States, are large, attractive, and easy to tame, but they are restless, may not feed well, and require large vivariums. They are not recommended for the amateur. The **Eastern Indigo Snake** (*Drymarchon corais couperi*) has attained 2.7m. (9ft.).

The **Mole Snake** (*Pseudaspis canna*) from southern Africa grows to some 2m. (7ft.) and will usually thrive in captivity on a diet of rodents, lizards, and eggs.

LIZARDS

Lizards, the most abundant and diverse modern reptiles, are found in almost every part of the world except polar regions. They range in size from the colossal Komodo Dragon which reaches 3m. (10ft.) in length

to a tiny gecko of less than 2cm. (0.75in.). There are tropical lizards that can glide, marine iguanas that feed on seaweed, a poisonous species that lives in the desert, and others which live underground, lack limbs, and are almost blind. Most lizards are carnivorous and feed on invertebrates; some are vegetarian; and others are omnivorous. Some larger species eat rodents and eggs. Lizards do not slough their skins like snakes but molt more gradually, shedding their skins in separate pieces. Do not attempt to help a lizard rid itself of its shedding skin because you may harm it.

Lacertids

The two hundred species of this family (Lacertilia) are widely distributed across Europe, Africa, and Asia. One, the Viviparous Lizard, is found within the Arctic Circle. All have well-developed limbs and long pointed tails. They lack dorsal crests or dewlaps, and do not change their color to match their surroundings. They can discard their tails readily. Almost all lay eggs, and most feed entirely or mainly on small invertebrates. Most of the six species below can usually be found in pet shops in Europe, although in recent years their numbers have declined drastically in many of their former haunts. In North America, they are less often available. They can all be kept under similar conditions, but specimens of disparate size must never be kept together. Males tend to be territorial, and it is best to have only one in an average-sized vivarium. An ideal size is about 90 x 30 x 30cm. (3 x 1 x 1ft.) or bigger for the largest eyed lizards. The interior can be arranged as a sort of blend between the desert and woodland vivarium kept at warm room temperature. Set up a basking platform at one end which is reached by sunlight, and include a shallow dish of drinking water in a surface of stones, cork bark, logs, and dry moss. These lizards also do well in suitable climates in an outdoor frame-type vivarium. Food must include as large a variety as possible of small soft-bodied invertebrates, such as crickets, locusts, spiders, earthworms, white or gray slugs, and small pieces of sweet,

soft fruit. Most lizards appreciate a drink of diluted fruit juice sweetened with a little glucose once a week. The eyed lizards must also be given small rodents or strips of raw beef. Some will even accept raw herring.

The **Viviparous Lizard** (*Lacerta vivipara*), from northern and central Europe and northern Asia, grows to 10–18cm. (4–7in.). Both sexes are brown above with dark spots or streaks on the back. Males have orange bellies speckled with black; in females the bellies are a plain shade of yellow. The five to twelve young are born alive. Viviparous lizards prefer damp areas and cannot stand high temperatures. They are best kept outdoors.

The **Sand Lizard** (*L. agilis*) from northern Europe is rare and totally protected in some countries. The male is greenish, particularly during the breeding season, the female brown or purplish grey, both with brown markings running down the back and on the sides. The males have greenish undersides usually spotted with black while the females have cream-colored undersides and lay five to twelve eggs in the ground. They are 15–25cm. (5–10in.) long and prefer heath and warm sandy areas. They hibernate from October to April.

The **Wall Lizard** (*L. muralis*) from Europe (excluding Great Britain) to Asia Minor, has extremely variable coloring and pattern, but the back is usually a shade of brown or green; males often have a network pattern or many dark spots on the back and females a line of spots down the center of the back and a row of spots with a whitish line above and below on their sides. They grow to about 20cm. (8in.) and live in dry, warm, stony places, even in populated areas. The hibernation period is short.

The Viviparous Lizard of Europe and Asia, which bears live young.

Green Lizard.

Eyed Lizard.

The **Ruin Lizard** (*L. sicula*), 20–30cm. (8–12in.) long, is mainly found in Italy, Sicily, Corsica, and the western Balkans. It looks like a larger Wall Lizard, inhabits the same type of terrain, and is equally variable in coloration and markings, but usually some shade of gray, blue-green, or yellow, with longitudinal rows of dark spots and a blue spot behind the shoulder. Males often have blue spots along the body.

The **Green Lizard** (*L. viridis*), 30–40cm. (12–15in.) long, from the Channel Islands, central and southern Europe, is predominantly green with pale yellow undersides. In males the throat is often blue in the breeding season. Females usually have a brown irregular pattern on back and sides and several whitish longitudinal stripes. It inhabits dry, warm areas with scrub or heath and hibernates (only in cold areas) up to five or six months.

Sand Skink.

African Five-Lined Skink.

The **Eyed Lizard** (*L. lepida*), at 50–60cm. (20–24in.), the largest of European lizards and occurs in southern and western Europe and northwest Africa. It is predominantly green with blue-black markings resembling eyes on the sides. Mature males have a distinctive massive head, are heavily built, and have a powerful bite. They are chiefly terrestrial and inhabit rocky and woodland areas.

Skinks

The skinks form a large family (Scincidae) of over six hundred species of small- to medium-sized lizards with almost worldwide distribution. Many are burrowers with specially adapted conical heads, smooth shiny scales, and cylindrical bodies. Some even have special transparent "windows" in their eyelids so that they can still see when their eyelids are closed. Many also have small earholes. Some skinks have well-developed legs and are extremely fast; others have no external limbs and move like snakes. Most skinks are shy and furtive and need sand for burrowing and ample hiding places in the form of logs and cork bark. A basking area should be provided, and most species need a shallow water dish. Apart from the two North American skinks, the species described are suited to a desert vivarium.

The **Sand Skink** or **Sand Swimmer** (*Scincus scincus*) is a desert skink from North Africa that reaches about 20 cm. (8in.) long. It is smooth, with a wedge-shaped head, short legs and tail, and able to close both its nostrils and earholes. Its toes have special fringes to help it move in fine sand, and the coloration is sandy or light brown with purplish brown crossbands. It is insectivorous.

The **Eyed Skink** (*Chalcides ocellatus*), from North Africa to northern India, is about 25cm. (10in.) long. It has smooth, shiny scales and, though its legs are small, it can move quickly. Coloring is generally gray or yellowish brown with white spots edged with black. It is insectivorous.

The **African Five-lined Skink** (*Mabuya quinquetaeniata*) is a tremendously speedy and shy skink but does well in a desert vivarium with ample hiding places. It has well-developed legs, a long tail, and attains some

25cm. (10in.). Males are brown with a metallic sheen while the females and young are dark brown with five longitudinal stripes and bright blue tails. Like most skinks it loves to bask and is insectivorous.

The following skinks may be kept in a woodland/desert vivarium that is somewhat dry.

The **American Five-Lined Skink** (*Eumeces fasciatus*), about 20cm. (7.5in.) long, from woodland areas and the **American Broad-headed Skink** (*E. laticeps*), up to 30cm. (12in.), are both from the southeastern United States. They may be kept in a rather dry combination of the woodland and the desert vivarium with a floor covering of some 7–10cm. of mixed sand and soil, the usual logs, and a few branches for climbing. Adult male Five-lined Skinks are olive-brown with traces of the juvenile stripes. The females always retain the stripes. In addition the juveniles have bright blue tails. Three to six eggs are laid usually in rotting wood; the females guard the clutch for about six weeks until they hatch. The Broad-headed Skink looks similar though larger; the males are orange-brown with large orange heads. They eat insects and spiders; some will take earthworms and strips of raw lean meat.

Geckos

Geckos (family Gekkonidae) are found in most warmer areas of the world. Mainly nocturnal, they have large, often lidless, eyes with vertical pupils behind a transparent membrane. Climbing geckos are tremendously agile; they can escape in a flash and run up walls, sheets of glass, even ceilings, using the numerous microscopic hair-like hooks beneath their enlarged toes. For climbers, cages should be tightly closed with access for hands through a small hinged opening in the top. All geckos are delicately made and should be handled very gently if at all. Most lay eggs, which should be removed and incubated separately. Smaller geckos may be harassed or eaten by larger ones; any that are aggressive should be kept separately. All but the desert species require a light spray of water on their foliage daily for drinking and humidity. Spraying one corner is sufficient for the desert species which must be kept very dry.

Pea gravel is the best floor covering for small- and medium-sized lizards except for burrowing species which prefer sand. The diurnal geckos need one or two 40 watt light bulbs within their cage. All geckos like to hide, and cork bark provides ideal shelter, either fixed to the back of the cage for climbing species or placed on the floor for ground-dwellers. Geckos eat a wide selection of invertebrates including crickets, cockroaches, locusts, and spiders; some eat earthworms, too. Most (especially day geckos) like a piece of banana and appreciate a drink of fruit juice sweetened with honey.

If well cared for, the following species do well in captivity:

Banded Geckos (*Coleonyx* species) are small nocturnal terrestrial lizards with slen-

Indian Fat-Tailed or Leopard Gecko.

Turkish Gecko.

der toes, coming from dry stony areas of the southwestern United States. They average 10–13cm. (4–5in.) in length and are patterned with chocolate-brown bands on yellow. They tame easily and can be kept in a large goldfish bowl without a top.

The **Turkish Gecko** (*Hemidactylus turcicus*), a dull-colored but agile nocturnal species some 10cm. (4in.) long, comes from Mediterranean countries. It has also come to Florida and other southern states.

The **Tokay Gecko** (*Gekko gecko*), from southeast Asia, grows up to 28cm. (11in.) long. It is agile, can inflict a sharp nip, and is vociferous, especially at night, repeating the sound "to-kay." Food may include small mice, and small pieces of chalk should be added to the diet.

The **Indian Fat-tailed** or **Leopard Gecko** (*Eublepharis macularius*) is a ground-dwelling Asian species about 18cm. (7in.) long that does particularly well in captivity in dry conditions. Although gentle as a pet, it may be hostile with its own kind, especially if specimens of the same sex are kept together. It stores fat in its tail as an extra food supply.

Glass Snakes and Slowworms

This family (Anguidae) includes both four-legged and snake-like lizards. Most are medium-sized and terrestrial, although some burrow and a few are arboreal.

The glass snakes (*Ophisaurus*) have special fracture points at which the tail can break off, enabling a captured animal to escape; they should therefore be handled carefully. There are several shiny glass snake lizard species in the United States. **Pallas's Glass Snake** or the **Scheltopusik** (*O. apodus*), from southern Europe to western Asia, has a distinctive fold

along both sides of the body and minute vestigial hind limbs.

More recommended as a pet is the **European Slowworm** or **Blindworm** (*Anguis fragilis*) which is a small, gentle lizard, also limbless, usually gray or brown, the males sometimes with blue spots. Females have dark longitudinal stripes and are ovoviviparous. The dozen or so young are born in late summer and can be fed on tiny pieces of slug or earthworm, which the adults will eat whole. They hibernate in the ground from October to April and do best in an outdoor vivarium. They like to alternate between basking and hiding under logs.

Alligator lizards (*Gerrhonotus*) from Central and North America, have short limbs, stout bodies, squarish scales, and longitudinal folds. Although usually small—to 25cm. (10in.)—they inflict painful bites.

Iguanids

Almost all the seven hundred species of iguanid lizards (family Iguanidae) are from the New World. They have well developed limbs, most have long tails, are carnivorous and oviparous, and all share the ability to replace lost or damaged teeth.

The **Common Iguana** (*Iguana iguana*) grows to 2m. (6ft.) and is the largest iguana. Hundreds of thousands are taken as babies from South American tropical forests for pets, but few survive. Before buying one you *must* be sure you can provide adequate space, food, and heat. Although not normally aggressive, these iguanas can inflict nasty bites, severe scratches, and whiplash blows with their long tails. For an adult the vivarium needs to be some 2.5m. (8ft.) long and 2m. (6ft.) high, maintained at 29–38°C. (85–100°F.) with only a slight decrease at night. Keep well ventilated and dry and use a light spray two or three times a week. Add one or two 60 watt bulbs and also stout branches. In very warm weather iguanas benefit from being outside in direct sunlight (with access to a substantial shady area) in an escapeproof frame with plastic mesh top. Iguanas are omnivorous with a vegetarian bias; young ones especially enjoy a mixture of raw grated fruit and vegetables. They should have a sprinkling of calcium and balanced vitamin supplements twice a week, a small bowl of grit (as for chickens), and a permanent dish of clean drinking water. The diet should include as many as possible of the following: dandelion, clover, narsturtium, hibiscus flowers and leaves, rose petals, cabbage, lettuce, plantain, alkanet, grated carrot, avocado, cooked marrow, beans and peas, cucumber, tomato, melon, banana, blackberries, and most sweet fruits. Provide once a week some raw lean beef occasionally mixed with raw egg or dog food. Iguanas also need to eat locusts, crickets, mealworms, and earthworms; some adults take young mice.

The **Common Anole**, or American Chameleon, (*Anolis carolinensis*) is also commonly sold and is known for its color changes through green, yellow, brown, and dark

gray. This native of the southeastern United States averages 15cm. (6in.). It should be kept at warm room temperature in a woodland vivarium, brightly lit, and with branches, potted plants and cork bark, sprinkled lightly each day with water. The males, with pink dewlaps, are territorial, so it is best to keep only one. Females usually lay two eggs in damp debris. Their food is flies, caterpillars, other soft-bodied insects, and spiders.

Also kept are the voracious **Collared Lizard** (*Crotaphytus collaris*), to 30cm. (12in.), from desert areas of the southwestern United States, and the smaller **swifts** or **fence lizards** (*Sceloporus* species) widely distributed in North America. Both are active and require relatively large vivariums.

The **Horned Lizards** (*Phrynosoma* species) and the **Desert Iguana** (*Dipsosaurus dorsalis*) from Mexico and the southwestern United States are not recommended for the amateur. The former are now protected species and require a large number of ants in their diet; the latter feed on cactus flowers and other desert plants.

Agamids

In many ways the three hundred agamid lizard species of the Old World resemble the iguanids of the New. Typically they have a short broad head, sometimes a dewlap and skin outgrowths on the back. The limbs are well developed, and the tail does not easily break off. Most are terrestrial, and all are oviparous. The following active species need large vivariums and are difficult to keep.

The colorful **Margouillat Lizard** (*Agama agama*) from central Africa is insectivorous and needs a rocky desert vivarium, as does the **Starred Agama** (*A. stellis*) which is insectivorous and herbivorous and found from southeastern Europe to Saudia Arabia. The **Indian Bloodsucker** (*Calotes versicolor*), a tree lizard from southeast Asia, eats insects, not blood, and is reddish brown.

Spiny-tailed agamas or **Mastigures** (*Uromastix* species) are herbivorous. Among those available are **Bell's Dabb-Lizard** (*U. acanthinurus*) from North Africa and **Hardwicke's Dabb-Lizard** (*U. hardwickii*) from India and Pakistan.

Chameleons

There are about ninety species of these fascinating Old World lizards perfectly adapted to arboreal life. Their strange eyes can move independently or focus together on prey, which the lizard may catch by shooting out its long tongue to a distance almost equal to the body's length. The feet grip like fingers—the toes fused into two opposing "bunches"—and in most species the tail is prehensile. Chameleons change color—generally through greens, browns, yellows and grays—according to factors such as light, humidity, and mood.

Owners must provide a constant daily supply of live insects—locusts, crickets spiders, flies—and chameleons do best given the run of a room at 24°C. (75°F.) with a

Top Right. *The Common Chameleon showing its prehensile tail and bunches of toes which are both used to grip twigs.* Top Left. *Flap-Necked Chameleon shedding its skin.*

windowsill of potted plants sprayed with water daily. (Chameleons are thirsty creatures.) Chameleons are best kept alone.

The "**Common**" or **Mediterranean Chameleon** (*Chamaeleo chamaeleon*), which occurs across India and Sri Lanka, is actually becoming scarce, but the similar **Flap-necked Chameleon** (*C. dilepsis*) from southern Africa (to 30cm., 12in.), with white markings on the side, is reputedly hardier. Also occasionally available are the small **Two-lined Chameleon** (*C. bitaeniatus*) from mountainous East Africa and the large **Jackson's Chameleon** (*C. jacksonii*) from the African highlands, the male of which has three large horns, the female a single, small one.

Girdle-tailed Lizards

Only a few species from this small family (Cordylidae) are usually kept as pets. They have spiny scales on the tail which can be curled across the soft belly for protection. They are found in dry savannah south of the Sahara and are live-bearers. They like a pile of flat rocks to hide in and a basking platform beneath a light, on a floor covering of sand, with a shallow drinking dish.

Lord Derby's Girdled Lizard or the **Giant Zonure** (*Cordylus giganteus*) is the largest, growing to 40cm. (16in.); it eats insects, small rodents, and birds. The **Armadillo Lizard** (*C. cataphractus*), about half the size, is similarly covered with spiny armor; if threatened, a wild specimen curls up, grasping its tail in its mouth. The aptly named **Flat Lizards** (*Platysaurus* species) have smooth scales but keeled tails. If pursued they wedge their bodies in crevices and inflate themselves. Some males are brilliantly colored.

Teiid Lizards

Very few of this New World family (Teiidae) of two hundred species are sold as pets. Many resemble the Lacertids. The whiptails and racerunners (*Cnemidophorus* species), from the United States to South America, are very active and streamlined, up to 25cm. (10in.) long. They need a large desert vivarium and eat insects, small snails, and occasionally chopped beef with raw egg. Probably the best known is the **Six-lined Race Runner** (*C. sexlineatus*). The **Banded** or **Black Tegu** (*Tupinambis texuicin*) is perhaps the largest of a genus of powerful South American Lizards, up to 140cm. (4-5 ft.) long. Like the moni-

The Common Iguana is the best known of all iguanid lizards, but few bought as pets survive more than a few months.

The brightly-colored Margouillat Lizard must be kept in a desert vivarium.

287

The long-tailed Collared Lizard is a voracious eater and requires a large vivarium in which to live.

Monitors are large lizards totally unsuitable as pets. Shown here is a Nile Monitor which can reach 2cm. (7ft.) in length.

tors, tegus are not suitable pets for amateurs.

Monitors

Monitors are tropical lizards from Australia, Africa, and Asia, the majority of which are over 1m. (3ft.) long. The **Nile Monitor** (*Varanus niloticus*) grows to 2m. (7ft.), the **Two-banded Monitor** (*V. salvator*) to over 2.5m. (8ft.) and, largest of all, the **Komodo Dragon** (*V. komodoensis*) from Indonesia, can exceed 3m. (10ft.) and weigh 150kg. (330lb.). Monitors are not suitable as pets for the amateur; even "tame" young specimens are likely to become intractable, even aggressive, when adult. The backward-curving teeth and the claws can be dangerous. Monitors require strongly constructed cages at least four times the animal's body length, with large bathing tanks. They are entirely carnivorous.

The European Slow Worm or Glass Snake may look like a snake, but is in fact a legless lizard.

INSECTS

Insects, together with their close allies the spiders and scorpions, have an external skeleton of hard plates of chitin joined by flexible membranes. True insects (butterflies, moths, ants, wasps, etc.) have a body divided into three distinct regions: the head, thorax, and abdomen, with the thorax bearing three pairs of legs. In arachnids (spiders, scorpions, etc.) the head and thorax are fused into one unit which bears four pairs of legs. Many people think of spiders and scorpions, together with other small creeping animals, as true insects. Technically this is not so, but the spiders and scorpions will be considered in this section along with the true insects.

Most insects survive for less than a year, and some for a very short time indeed so owners are unlikely to become as attached to individuals as they would to other types of pets. Insects are not companion pets, but they can be fascinating creatures to study due to their great diversity, strange life patterns, peculiar shapes, and remarkable camouflage. The beauty of their wings is most appealing and results in greater interest in butterflies and moths than in other insect forms.

Many people mistakenly believe that insects need little or no attention. Many of them need daily feeding and cleaning of their cages. Some require very specialized diets and food plants may have to be grown for them. The water-living insects will need an aquarium, but others will prey on other insects or feed on bran and sugar. Most insects can be kept in a very small space and, if properly cared for, seldom make any smell or mess. Locate their home on any shelf or table where you can watch them for long periods.

If you keep insects not native to your area, take care that they do not escape and upset the local ecology. This is a greater risk with insects than with most other animals and confusing to local naturalists. Some insects can do serious harm; locusts, if accidentally released in a warm climate, could easily become a plague, although in temperate regions they are not able to breed and may have difficulty surviving. Many people are breeding butterflies to increase the local butterfly population. Little is yet known of the precise conditions butterflies need to establish themselves successfully, and it is advisable to breed a fairly common local species which will not upset the local fauna.

Collecting Insects

One of the best ways of collecting a variety of insects from the wild is by "beating." Lay a sheet of cloth or hold an umbrella beneath a branch and beat or shake the branch so the falling insects will be caught in the receptacle

The best way to catch insects in grassland is to use a long-handled, wide-necked sweep net.

below. Another way is to look under stones and search hedges and ground vegetation. These methods are best since, in most cases, the insects are found in their natural habitat and on a natural food source. Recognizing the food plant and making positive identification of the insect is important at this point. Great care must be taken when collecting insects from an area where poisonous species are to be found. It may be better to obtain eggs or larvae from an insect breeder.

Housing and Food Supply

Food plants can be gathered from the countryside and fed either in plastic boxes or standing in a jar of water in a cage. They must be very fresh, unpolluted, and free of insecti-

cide or other chemicals from nearby cropland. They must also be dry. Ideally plants should be grown specially so you can have a constant and uncontaminated supply. Potted plants stay fresh and do not need frequent changing, and if you have garden space you can "sleeve" caterpillars in netting bags slipped over branches or shrubs and tied at both ends. Then there is little cleaning out or food-changing to be done. Remember that domestic fly sprays and vaporizing chemicals will kill "pet" insects.

Butterflies and Moths

Of the many thousands of butterflies and moths (order Lepidoptera) a great number can be reared. Common local species can be collected as eggs or caterpillars and raised to adults. The listing of species given here is only a small fraction of those which can be reared, and many are available from butterfly breeders. These have been chosen because of their suitability for breeding and because of their particular interest or beauty.

There is no clear distinction between butterflies and moths. Indeed some languages have no provision for such a distinction. Many moths, contrary to popular belief, are brightly colored and beautiful.

Greenhouses give all-weather protection to butterflies and moths from many parts of the world.

289

Butterflies and moths live an average of four to six weeks. Their eggs take up to a month to hatch and the larval stage (caterpillar) lasts from one to three months. The pupa sometimes develops in a few days, more usually in about a month, and often lasts several months when it commonly encompasses a diapause, or resting, stage. Most moth and butterfly eggs can be hatched in a small transparent plastic box. When the larvae have eaten their way out of the eggs, they can be housed in a larger plastic box (sandwich-box size). Line the box with paper and sprigs of the appropriate food plant and transfer the baby caterpillars on the tip of a watercolor brush. Renew the lining and contents daily replacing the larvae after cutting around the sections of plant on which they are resting. Place the fresh food over them since larvae like to crawl upward. All food must be clean and dry.

When the larvae have grown to about 2cm. (0.8in.) they can be transferred to a glass-sided or netting cage which contains their food plant either growing in a pot or standing in a jar of water. The top of the jar should be plugged with cotton to keep the larvae out of it. Replace cut shoots before they show signs of wilting. Some moth larvae need a layer of soil or peat about 10cm. (4in.) deep in the bottom of their cage in which they pupate. Others spin a cocoon and attach it to the twigs or leaves of the food plant which must then be left undisturbed until they emerge. If the new adults are left together in the cage, they will probably mate and lay without any further attention and the life cycle begins again. Some will lay directly on the food plant and others all over the cage, where the eggs can be left to hatch. Although the adults are relatively short-lived and some do not feed, many butterflies and moths should be provided with fresh, nectar-rich flowers or pads soaked in a sugar solution from which to feed.

SWALLOWTAILS

Members of the swallowtail family (Papilionidae) are found on every continent and include the largest and most handsome of all butterflies—the birdwings which are found in Indo-Australia. A typical papilionid is the *Papilio machaon*, known as the Swallowtail in Europe and with subspecies or close allies on every continent. Papilios like this can be bred once some experience with butterflies has been gained and can even be hand paired (a technique for achieving mating by holding the two butterflies in close contact). The larvae of most members of this family feed on leguminous plants, but many tropical species feed on various creeping vines of the family Aristolochiaceae. A characteristic feature of the larva is the forked structure, called an osmaterium. This structure is found immediately behind the head of the butterfly and emits a strong odor that smells much like rotting fruit when the larva is disturbed.

Wild Plants that Attract Butterflies (in order of flowering through the year)	
Primrose	*Primula vulgaris*
Pussy Willow	*Salix caprea*
Dandelion	*Taraxacum* species
Pink Campion	*Silene dioica*
Garlic Mustard	*Alliaria petiolata*
Clovers	*Trifolium* species
Hawkweed	*Hieracium* species
Lucerne	*Medicago sativa*
Moon Daisy	*Leucanthemum vulgare*
Hemp Agrimony	*Eupatorium cannabinum*
Thistle	*Carduus, Cirsium & Silybum* species
Bramble	*Rubus fruticosus*
Marjoram	*Origanum vulgare*
Scabious	*Scabiosa* and *Succisa* species
Knap weed	*Centaurea* species

Note: Most *Compositae* (dandelion, daisy family) and most species of *Cruciferae* (cabbages and cresses) are very attractive to butterflies

Cultivated Plants that Attract Butterflies (in order of flowering through the year)	
Polyanthus	*Primula vulgaris* varieties
Alyssum	*Alyssum* species
Aubrieta	*Aubrieta* species
Wallflower	*Cheiranthus* species
Thrift	*Armeria* species
Honesty	*Lunaria annua*
Sweet Rocket	*Hesperis matronalis*
Valerian	*Kentranthus ruber*
Sweet William	*Dianthus* species
Viper's buglos	*Echium* species
Lavender	*Lavandula* species
Catmint	*Nepeta* species
Phlox	*Phlox* species
Heliotrope	*Heliotropium* species
Buddleia	*Buddleia davidii, B. globosa* and others
Aster	*Aster* species
Golden Rod	*Solidago* species
Michaelmas Daisy	*Aster nova-belgii*
Ice Plant	*Sedum spectabile* (not cultivars)

PEACOCKS AND TORTOISESHELLS

Peacocks, tortoiseshells, and their allies are members of the largest butterfly family (Nymphalidae), all members of which are characterized by the fact that the front pair of the six legs are degenerate. As well as the peacocks and tortoiseshells of Europe the family is represented in the tropics by the robust *Charaxes, Agrias,* and a multitude of **leaf butterflies** (*Kallima, Zaretes, Anaea, Dolleschallia*). Most adults feed from liquid exudation such as sap, dung, fruit, or carrion, as well as nectar. They fly swiftly and have great strength. They are difficult to pair in captivity although their larvae, often spiny, are usually quite easy to rear. The larvae of the **Peacock** and **Small Tortoiseshell** feed on nettle (*Urtica dioica*) and a number of other species.

WHITES AND BRIMSTONES

Cabbage whites, brimstones, orange tips, and **clouded yellows** are found throughout the world and all belong to the family Pieridae. The bright colors of this family are based on black and white or bright yellow, often decorated with red or orange. Some of the tropical species resemble enlarged versions of

Adult females and eggs of the Orchard Swallowtail (Papilio aegeus).

Caterpillar of the Scarce Swallowtail (Papilio podalirus).

290

Peacock Butterfly (Inachis io).

those found in Europe; for example members of the genus *Delias* from Asia are particularly striking for their color and infinite variety of form. Many pierid larvae, particularly those found in Europe, feed on members of the cabbage family (Cruciferae). In the tropics the pierids favor plants of the pea family (Leguminosae). The butterflies are not easy to pair in captivity, but when they do breed the result is often a swarm.

COPPERS AND BLUES

Represented throughout the world by the **Coppers, Hairstreaks,** and **Blues,** members of the family Lycaenidae are all small butterflies, often colored with the brilliance of jewels. Many form an association with ants in their larval stage, and some actually eat the larvae of ants instead of vegetation. Lycaenid larvae taper at the head and tail, rather like the shape of a woodlouse; leguminous plants are their usual food. Most lycaenids are not easy to breed, but if you can obtain eggs or larvae they are not difficult to rear, especially on potted food plants.

MILKWEED BUTTERFLY

The **Milkweed Butterfly** (*Danaus plexippus*) is the most famous representative of the fam-

The Common Jezabell Butterfly (Delias eucharis).

Caterpillar of the Two-Tailed Pasha (Charaxes jasius).

ily Danaidae, a family found almost exclusively in the tropics. The Milkweed migrates over long distances, even from the United States to Europe. They are one of the easiest butterflies to breed and many of their larvae feed on *Asclepias* (milkweed). The pupae are rounded, often gilded or silvered. The butterfly, caterpillar, and pupa are distasteful and poisonous to predators. Even after being crushed, the butterfly has remarkable powers of recovery and is often able to fly again after an hour or so. The black butterflies of the tropics, known as crows, belong to this family and many larvae can be fed on *Nerium* (oleander).

BROWNS

With practically no exceptions the larvae of the family Satyridae feed on grasses. Some breed easily in captivity and produce eggs in amazing quantity. Temperate species often hibernate in the larval stage and are best kept outside on growing potted grass for the winter. Some species let their eggs fall on the ground as they fly; others attach the eggs to the foliage as is normal. The general coloration is a combination of browns or grays in most attractive and subtle patterning. The largest species, found in the tropics, can measure up to 8cm. (3in.) across.

Pupa of the Black-Veined White (Aporia crataegi).

Right-hand Column. *Stages in the emergence of a Milkweed or Monarch Butterfly* (Danius plexippus) *from its pupa.*

SILKMOTHS

These moths (family Saturniidae) include the largest of all lepidoptera. Examples of the **Giant Atlas Moth** have been known to measure up to 30cm. (12in.) across and even those reared in captivity are commonly 29cm. (10in.) across. The larvae of most saturniids spin a silken cocoon, and some produce silk that is used commercially. This family is particularly recommended for breeding in captivity, and the results are spectacular. Substitute food plants are often accepted in temperate countries by the tropical species. The moths have only rudimentary mouthparts and do not need to be fed, although in dry conditions they will sometimes sip at drops of water.

Silkworms are the caterpillars of the moth *Bombyx mori.* They originated in China, but the species no longer exists in the wild. The only satisfactory food plant is mulberry. Eggs need to be refrigerated—1–4°C. (34–39°F.)—until mulberry (Morus) leaves are out in the early spring. As soon as the eggs hatch, they should be treated as other larvae previously described. When they are larger, they do not need a cage; just provide an open tray and they will not crawl away. Pick the mulberry leaves without stems, and lay them flat. Feed the silkworms at least twice a day. If conditions in the tray are not too moist, it will not need cleaning out and a layer of harmless dried leaves will build up beneath the larvae. In the fifth month place straw or fine wood shavings around the edge of the tray and here the silkworms will spin their cocoons of real silk. The moths emerge after about five weeks. They cannot fly so they can be kept on trays also. Line the tray with paper, on which the eggs will be laid. Then you can fold the paper and store the eggs in a box for the winter in a cool place ready for the next season. The culture of silkworms is called sericulture. Although each cocoon provides approximately one-half mile of silk thread, many are required to produce cloth. The cocoon is formed by the larva's manufacturing a substance known as fibroin, mixing that with wax, and hardening.

HAWKMOTHS

Hawkmoths (family Sphingidae) are famous for their streamlined shape, very fast flight, and for their larvae which are an impressive size and characterized by a hook or spike at the tail. Most are quite easy to breed. Some adults are without a proboscis and therefore need no feeding, but others must be provided with nectar-bearing flowers. The **Death's Head Hawk** is particularly famous as a rare migrant to Europe and because of its skull-

Keeping silkworms allows you to oversee production of your own silk. (See text for details of looking after the silkworms.)

Commercially, the silk is wound off after boiling the cocoons to kill the pupa inside. This is done because the moth naturally breaks the silk as it pushes its way out of the cocoon. The cocoons are then floated in water and the thread from each is fed through a tunnel and onto a reeling machine.

However, you can reel your own silk at home with very simple apparatus. It is not even essential to boil the cocoons although a dip in warm water helps to loosen the thread. First, remove the fluff surrounding the cocoon and eventually, only one thread will come loose. Take the thread from 20 to 50 cocoons and draw them through a hole in a cardboard box. Attach one end of the threads to a crochet needle and the other end to a cotton reel. When you spin the reel, all the threads will be twisted into one. Then wind the single thread of silk onto the reel and keep drawing more threads from the box of cocoons. Repeat the process until you have a fine reel of your own home produced silk.

like markings on the thorax. The moth even squeaks loudly when agitated. It is common in Africa and related species are found in Asia. In size the hawks are second only to the silkmoths.

TIGER MOTHS

Many of the tiger moths (family Arctiidae) are very brightly colored and some fly during the day. Several South American species have iridescent coloring as bright as the most exotic butterfly. The caterpillars of tiger moths are known as woolly bears. The larvae are mostly polyphagous, favoring low-growing plants, and are no trouble to rear. The moths usually breed quite easily, some feeding on nectar.

OTHER MOTHS

There are many thousands of moth species. Those which are most satisfactory to keep include members of the Lymantriidae (**Tussock Moths**) whose hairy larvae are exceptionally colorful and rewarding to keep but can give a nasty skin rash; the **stick caterpillars** of the family Geometridae, which can sometimes be found by "beating"; members of the Notodontidae which includes the **Puss Moth** with its strange tailed caterpillar and a number of other **Prominent Moths** which are also noted for their strangely shaped and colored larvae. Many "**looper**" caterpillars are worth keeping. Known also as **inchworms** in the United States because of their gauged method of walking, these also belong to the Geometridae, like the stick caterpillars. A very large family that should not go unmentioned is the Noctuidae. The larvae are not usually spectacular, although some species are striking both in the larval and adult stages. Many of them are serious crop pests and must not be allowed to escape.

Locusts and Their Allies

The order Orthoptera comprises locusts, crickets, grasshoppers, praying mantids, and leaf insects. Cockroaches are treated here as well, although strictly speaking they fall under the order Dictyoptera.

LOCUSTS, CRICKETS, AND GRASSHOPPERS

These can all be kept in similar cages, about 50 x 30cm. (20 x 12in.) and 30cm. (12 in.)

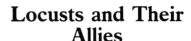

high. The cage should be constructed with solid sides, sliding glass at the back and front, a solid roof with a ventilated door about 15cm. (6in.) square for feeding and a floor of perforated hardboard. This gives ventilation through the bottom and the top, especially if the cage is raised on short legs. A light bulb should be fitted to hang from the roof. Blades of coarse grass or cut grass standing in jars of water will be an adequate food source. Beakers of moist sand, preferably set into the base of the cage, provide adult females with a medium for egg laying. Young hatch after about five weeks.

Field crickets, house crickets, and other scavengers will feed upon vegetable material such as lettuce, apple, and carrot. They also need bran and moist cotton in a saucer. They like to hide in rolled up corrugated paper or any similar material with crevices.

Cockroaches can be kept in the same way. They are not disease carriers, nor are they dirty. They do have a bad reputation because they establish themselves in warm kitchens and reproduce so quickly that they become a pest. A giant species from Madagascar is sometimes available. Their breeding should be carefully controlled. (See also **Amphibians and Reptiles** for the breeding of locusts.)

Bottom Left. *Female Praying Mantis.*
Bottom Middle. *A pair of locusts showing their large wings.*

Top Left. *A cylindrical case set-up for leaf and stick insects*. Top Middle. *Nymph of a stick insect* (Clemacantha *sp*). Center. *Female Leaf Insect* (Phyllium bioculatum).

PRAYING MANTIDS

Praying mantids (*singular:* mantis) or their egg masses are often found in warmer countries, and they can also be bought from dealers. The eggs hatch simultaneously, and there are usually more young than can easily be handled. Mantids live on insects—even their own kind. Keep them in a netting cage with twigs for climbing, and feed them on tiny flies. Some of the mantids will grow more rapidly than others, and these will then feed on the less vigorous of their kind. These strongest individuals should be kept singly in an aquarium tank or plastic rearing container. Fruit flies (*Drosophila*) are suitable food for mantids. If you keep locusts, the young hoppers are ideal as food for larger mantids. They need to be fed every few days, and the prey must be alive, although they can be tempted to take small pieces of meat offered with forceps.

STICK AND LEAF INSECTS

Stick insects are long stick-like creatures with six prominent legs and are remarkably well camouflaged. They must not be confused with the caterpillars of some of the family Geometridae (Lepidoptera) which are also stick-like and walk with a looping motion, but lack long legs.

Young stick insects can be reared either in plastic containers or in netting cages. All species appreciate warmth, and certain tropical species do not do well at less than 20°C. (68°F.). The **Indian** or **Laboratory Stick Insect** (*Carausius morosus*) is the best known but there are at least half a dozen other species that can be obtained and reared quite easily.

The newly hatched nymph is a miniature of the adult; there is no larval stage. The nymph grows and changes its skin regularly but it does not have wings. Those species which have winged adults do not get their wings until the final change into the adult stage. An almost universal food for stick insects is bramble (*Rubus fruticosus*).

Two outstanding giant species come from Queensland, Australia. *Acrophylla wulfingi* has a tiny egg, but the winged female grows to a length of well over 25cm. (10in.). The male is smaller, slender, and winged. *Extatosoma tiaratum* starts life looking and moving like a large wood ant. When larger its curled tail makes it resemble a scorpion, but it is harmless. The female is fat and one of the heaviest of all insects. Her legs are flattened and somewhat like those of a leaf insect. Her wings are rudimentary, but those of the rather slight male are well developed and he will often fly round the room if given the chance!

Leaf insects are closely related to the stick insects. The species that is sometimes available is *Phyllium bioculatum* from Java. It is not difficult to hatch the eggs, if they are laid out on moist sand, kept at about 25°C. (77°F.), but the young nymphs need a lot of coaxing in their eating. They will feed on oak leaves, including evergreen oak which is particularly good, and bramble as well. The adult female looks like a bunch of walking green leaves—they are incredible creatures and well worth the effort if you are interested in the extremes of nature's adaptability.

Beetles and Their Allies

The common name *beetle* is applied to all insects of the order Coleoptera whose members have one pair of wings modified to form wing cases.

BEETLES

Most kinds of beetle are unsuitable for breeding in captivity. It is, however, possible to keep beetles alive for many months as "pets." They are seldom available to buy but can be found by searching the countryside. A glass aquarium tank or plastic rearing container provides a suitable environment. A layer of soil should be put in the bottom with moss, pieces of bark, and stones upon it. This is not only the most suitable habitat for beetles but makes an attractive setting. Some beetles have specific food and living requirements but most will feed and live happily from a mixture of raw vegetables, bran, and sugar solution soaked into sponge or cotton.

LADYBUGS

Ladybug (known in some countries as ladybirds) larvae are easy to keep, and watching them develop into pupae and, eventually, into adult ladybugs brings great satisfaction. Both larvae and adults feed on aphids.

Bugs

Certain plant bugs (order Hemiptera) resemble beetles, and many tropical species are incredibly beautiful. These can be kept in conditions similar to those for beetles. If they do not take to the food described for beetles, try whole or potted plants as these insects live by probing stems with a sharp proboscis and drawing the sap.

Ants, Bees, and Wasps

All these insects belong to the order Hymenoptera, a group in which the hind and forewings are held together and function as one.

A pair of Stag Beetles (Lucanus cervus).

ANTS

Before starting to keep ants it is best to get some information, as there are many kinds and some of the tropical species are rather vicious. It is possible to buy ant farms. These usually contain the **Yellow Ant** (*Lasius flavus*), which makes hillocks and is an ideal species to keep. One way of making your own farm is to tape two panes of glass together with a thin layer (2mm.) of soil trapped between. Keep this in a fitted wooden box. The ants will make tunnels in the soil which can be seen when the lid is removed. The lid must normally be closed since ants live in the dark. To make a feeding chamber, break the seal in one place and force some cotton between the glass. Soak this every day with sugar solution using a suction tube or dropper. Finding a

A colony of Red Ants housed between two sheets of glass so that the tunnels of the colony can be seen.

Yellow Ant queen is hard to do, so breeding is difficult. It is best to release the ants after a season and to collect more the next year.

Red ants (*Myrmica* spp) can be kept in a number of ways. One is to farm them outdoors. They can be gathered from the countryside, together with brood and queen, using a spoon or trowel and brought to the yard or garden in a plastic box. A shallow depression should be hollowed out in the soil, the contents tipped from the box, and a large flat stone used to cover the ants, which then usually settle down if there is a brood to look after. The nests are made below ground, and

A beekeeper tends his hives. Note that even an experienced handler wears fully-protective clothing.

the ants only come to the surface on warm days, so they cannot be observed in such detail as when kept indoors.

There are several ways of keeping red ants indoors. One way is to provide a nest without soil in which the ants live under a piece of red glass in a plastic basin. (Ants cannot see through red glass and are thus not disturbed.) However, in these conditions it is difficult to keep them at the correct humidity. Another method is to put some soil into a bowl to a depth of 4cm. (1.5in.) and to cover the soil with a solid turf of grass. Place the ants beneath the turf. They need a shallow container of sugar solution available for feeding with a dead insect added daily to provide a protein source. The ants usually do not stray, but for extra protection the bowl can be floated on a pan of water. Ants sting, especially when they are being gathered. A suction device, known as a pooter, can be used to collect them, but it is a slow process so a tablespoon is the best practical approach.

With enough space it is possible to keep **Wood Ants** (*Formica rufa*) which build mounds of pine needles into a nest. However, this ant has a powerful sting, and it is a species best left to the more experienced ant enthusiast.

BEES

The honeybee is of the genus Apis. The honeybee is a social insect that can survive only in a community known as a colony, nest, or hive. There are three castes—the queen, the worker, and the drone. The queen is the only sexually normal female in the community and the mother of all drones and workers, laying as many as 1500 eggs a day. She can sting repeatedly if provoked. Her average life span is one to three years. The worker secretes wax, builds the honeycomb, gathers nectar, pollen and water, and converts the nectar into honey as well as cleaning and guarding the hive. The drone is stingless and defenseless, and his sole function is to mate with the queen after which he dies.

The method of raising bees varies depending upon the locale, and honeybee hobbyists usually obtain information on raising bees from county agricultural agents and beekeeping associations in their areas. A great deal of knowledge is required to keep bees in a hive either for honey production or simply for study. Raising bees can prove to be dangerous, especially for people with allergic reactions to them.

A modern bee hive consists of a flat base, supporting a box-like wooden section about 20cm. (8in.) high, in which flat comb sections are suspended vertically like files in a cabinet. The combs are flat but patterned with the typical hexagonal pattern of the honeycomb which gives the bees the foundation for an organized arrangement of comb and encourages maximum honey production. The nucleus of queen and workers should be bought from a supplier and introduced into the hive. Put a top over the first section of

295

Biting spiders, such as Bird-Eating Spiders (Top Left), and poisonous arachnids, such as the Scorpion (Hadogenes troglodytes) (Top Middle), can only be kept if their housing is escape-proof. They must be handled with tongs.

hive until they have settled, built a comb, and started to produce a brood. Once the brood chamber is established, a second one may be added. Later other hive sections, in which honey will be stored by the bees, are added above the brood chamber with a queen excluder between the sections so she cannot get up into them and use them for raising a brood. In order to inspect the hive or remove honeycombs it is necessary to wear a hat and veil over the face, gloves, and a long coat to minimize the risk of being stung. A smoke gun is normally used to quieten the bees when the hive is being handled.

Arachnids

SPIDERS

Large house spiders are quite harmless and interesting to keep by using a glass tank filled with stones and some sort of hiding place. Flies or moths are the best food, which are caught by the spider in a funnel-shaped web. The familiar trellis webs that you see outside are made by many garden spiders. In Europe *Araneus diadematus* is the most familiar garden species and is recognized by a white cross marking on its abdomen. It is important to be careful of spiders that you do not recognize, especially in hotter countries where many species are venomous and dangerous. It is wise to consider any strange species as venomous and not to actually handle it. The **Black Widow Spider** (*Latrodectus mactans*) is quite small and dangerous but could well be mistaken for a harmless garden species. Younger individuals are indistinguishable from domestic spiders and pose a greater risk.

It is quite possible to keep the giant bird-eating spiders and tarantulas. They will survive satisfactorily in a glass aquarium fitted with a firm lid. They should be fed larger insects. These spiders can bite, but they can be kept without risk if they are only handled with tongs.

Some spiders will breed in captivity, and it is interesting to watch their development. Water spiders can be bred in the correct aquatic conditions such as those required for insects. (See Aquatic Insects below.)

The courtship of spiders is often protracted and fascinating to observe. The female lays a large quantity of eggs, often in a round ball of silk. These may hatch quite quickly or lie dormant for several months. The young spiders usually hatch simultaneously and often live in a cluster. Some cling to the mother like the young of a scorpion.

SCORPIONS

Scorpions are more dangerous to keep than spiders, but if handled only with tongs and kept in a covered glass tank few problems should arise. The stinger is in the tail which is usually carried crooked up over the scorpion's back. They require a sand habitat with a number of stones for hiding. They eat in-

Water Insects. Center Middle. Water Spider (Argyroneta aquatica) with air bubble around abdomen. Center Right. Lesser Water Boatman (Corixa punctata). Bottom Middle. Great Diving Beetle (Dytiscus marginalis). Bottom Right. Water Scorpion (Nepa cinerea).

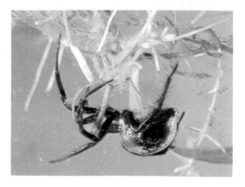

sects such as moths, locusts, mealworms, flies, beetles, and cockroaches, which should be provided every few days.

Aquatic Insects

Quite a number of insects live in water and can be housed in a simple aquarium. This should be set up as for cold water fish, with gravel and water plants. It is a good idea to collect and keep snails, fish, and other pond creatures with the insects. **Water boatmen,** such as *Corixa punctata*, resemble beetles and are adapted with "oars" for swimming. They make a fascinating start to collecting water insects. The **caddis fly** larvae conceal themselves by living in a tube covered with shells or water weed, stones or debris. **Mayfly** larvae or the ferocious **dragonfly** larvae, which will eat many of the other creatures, can also be collected from the wild. There are many types of **water beetle**; both they and their larvae are possible to keep but they are carnivores. Other curiosities are the **water scorpions** (*Nepa* species) whose tail is actually harmless.

The aquarium should be largely self supporting as long as you have oxygenating plants and scavenging insects and snails. A small amount of fish food put in every few days may be useful to some of the inhabitants. Whether or not they take it will depend on what you have in the aquarium. Water spiders gather a bubble of air from the surface of the water, drag the bubble down, and create a clearly visible silvery diving bell in which they can live and bring up their family. The larvae of a few moths live under water, but no butterflies do. Such an aquarium can be instructional for young children by providing them a host of ceatures to observe.

ZOO ANIMALS

Nearly every week zoos get telephone calls from people asking advice on keeping zoo animals as pets. Someone wants to buy a special present, or a friend of theirs is thinking of keeping an animal which is a bit *different*. The answer is always the same: "Don't."

Since August, 1975, the London Zoo has received between four and six telephone calls each week, asking advice on how to keep lions, either from prospective owners or, in a more desperate tone, from those who have already bought their cubs. More disturbing is that the same lions keep being mentioned by different callers; each time the cub is a little older and the new unsuspecting owner a little more worried.

There is a mistaken belief that this type of pet will combine companionship with the excitement of keeping in captivity an animal of great size, exotic origin, or even potential danger. In fact, of course, none of these animals is "suited" to captivity, even with expert care and the simulation of their native habitats offered by range zoos, safari parks, or game farms. (Other chapters in this book deal with reptiles and small mammals kept as pets, and there is a separate chapter on those wild animals which from time to time visit our gardens.)

Apart from the problems of expense, food, space, and security measures required for zoo animals, you must be constantly aware that these animals may suddenly jump at your throat or bite you. When you choose an established pet like a cat or dog whose ancestors have been domesticated for centuries, you are letting your ancestors do the dirty work for you; whereas if you choose an exotic pet you have to do it all yourself. If you attempt to raise a domestic cat alongside a European Wild Cat, this point will become painfully clear.

One further point to be considered is that international, national, state and local laws and regulations govern the capture, keeping, transportation, import, export, and quarantine measures of many, if not all, of these animals. A careful check with the local office of the humane or animal protection society should precede any decisions on acquiring any animal more exotic than the domesticated species.

There are many popular animals one might now see in a zoo or wildlife park. At times over the years they have been kept as pets, but not one of them is a suitable pet. Some of the specific reasons against keeping each animal are mentioned in order to further discourage anyone who might consider keeping one as a pet. Legal restrictions, the animal's size and temperament, or difficulty in properly meeting the animal's needs are just a few of these reasons.

Apes and Monkeys

Apes and monkeys (for smaller primates and prosimians see **Small Mammals**) are closely related to each other and for someone looking for companionship in a pet, or for a surrogate child, they would seem to be an obvious choice. However, as pets primates have many disadvantages, one of the most important being that it is not possible to housetrain them satisfactorily. Some people have put their pet primates into diapers and some have even been known to dress them as miniature human beings—even shaving their faces! This unnatural and undignified treatment is repellent. A monkey or an ape is a monkey or an ape, not a subnormal human. Another disadvantage is that when monkeys and, particularly, apes reach maturity they become much more fierce and intractable: a two-year-old chimpanzee is charming to look at and clinging and child-like in its habits; a six-year-old chimpanzee is ferocious and surprisingly strong. The owner of an adult chimpanzee therefore has two alternatives—both unsatisfactory: either he must have a large, strong escape-proof cage constructed, in which the chimp can spend the rest of its life (which may be thirty years) or the animal must be killed. Furthermore, the prospective owner should consider the number of diseases and parasites which monkeys and apes share with human beings and which may be caught by the pet owner or his family. These include the common cold, tuberculosis, pseudotuberculosis (which can cause lymphadenitis in children), measles, salmonella poisoning and a variety of viral infections which can prove fatal to humans.

Finally, apes and monkeys, however tame, may in moments of stress or fear inflict very nasty bites. In all likelihood the victim will not be the owner, but a stranger. Children, with their shrill voices, quick, abrupt movements and lack of caution, are particularly at risk. The large apes are quite capable of killing a man, let alone a child.

There are four kinds of apes: the Chimpanzee *(Pan troglodytes);* the Gorilla *(Gorilla gorilla)*, which is the giant of the family weighing 250kg. (600lb.); the Orangutan *(Pongo pygmaeus)*, which is gentler by nature

Monkeys and apes are not as easy to keep as is often supposed—they have specialized diets, suffer from many diseases, and may have uncertain tempers. Left. This young Patas Monkey could weigh up to 14kg (30lb.) when adult. Right. Most popular of all apes are young Chimpanzees whose antics have delighted children for generations, but adult chimps are suitable only for zoos.

Looking after big cats requires specialized knowledge and care and must be left to zoos and other professional establishments. Top Left. *This tiger cub will develop a special relationship with his handler that will allow the sort of play seen with this huge adult* (Middle) *who could kill with a blow from one paw if he wished.*

than the previous two, but extremely rare and jealously protected; and the Gibbon (*Hylobates* species), which is very much smaller and is the acrobat of the ape family, extremely beautiful to watch in motion as it swings from the branches by its long arms, but dangerous because of its temper.

Monkeys can be distinguished from apes by the tails that most of them have (apes do not) and by their much shorter arms. The New World monkeys from South America (Cebidae) have rather human-like faces and, usually, prehensile tails which they use in climbing; the Old World monkeys (Cercopithecidae) from Africa and Asia have more of a snout and a straight tail used only for balance. The New World monkeys include the woolly and spider monkeys (*Lagothrix* and *Ateles*), the capuchins or organgrinders' monkeys (*Cebus*) and the brightly colored Squirrel Monkey (*Saimiri sciurea*). Many South American species have been brought to near-extinction by the pet trade, and for each monkey offered for sale many others will have died in capture and during transportation. If you buy a bedraggled monkey because you feel sorry for it, you are not doing the monkeys in general a favor, but merely endorsing this unfortunate trade. These South American monkeys are less fierce when adult than the Old World species such as the baboons (*Papio*), macaques, including the Rhesus Monkey (*Macaca mulatta*), and guenon monkeys, including the Green or Grass Monkey or Vervet (*Cercopithecus aethiops*), but have the disadvantage of being susceptible to respiratory infections.

Cats

Cats comprise the family Felidae of the order Carnivora—the meat-eaters. Their natural

distribution is fairly worldwide but excludes Australia and New Zealand. The cats are often divided roughly into the Big Cats, which include the Lion, Tiger, Leopard, Snow Leopard, Clouded Leopard, Jaguar (all *Panthera* or *Felis*) and Cheetah (*Acinonyx jubata*), and the Small Cats (all *Felis*), of which there are twenty-eight different species, ranging from the Puma (*Felis concolor*) to the domestic cat (*F. catus*). The Big Cats can roar but purr intermittently, whereas, due to a different arrangement of parts of the throat, the Small Cats do not roar but purr almost continuously and also have proportionately larger heads than most Big Cats. Many cats have beautifully striped or spotted coats which help to camouflage these mostly forest dwellers in scenery of patterned light and shade. Unfortunately for them, this has made them uncomfortably popular with humans, who kill them for their fur.

Wolves are the probable ancestors of the Domestic Dog, and although they can become relatively tame they are too large and aggressive to be kept safely as pets.

BIG CATS

Because of their great strength, their fierce nature and their enormous appetite, Big Cats do not make suitable pets. Nevertheless, quite large numbers of them are kept, particularly in Europe. Zoos and wildlife parks have become enormously successful at breeding Big Cats, especially lions, and have been blamed for the release of cubs onto the open market. Advertisements appear in newspapers advertising lion cubs as "cuddly," "house- and car-trained" and "good with other pets and children." Many of these animals have been acquired by people with a lack of facilities and knowledge. Big Cats have been kept in a bathroom or in the owner's van or automobile. Often they escape and innocent neighbors or passersby are terrorized or injured. The animal must then be shot if it cannot easily be recaptured. Indeed when zoos are telephoned for help by Big Cat cub owners, they often recommend that the cub should be put down. By the time a "tame" cub reaches sexual maturity it will be capable of killing its owner at any time. Furthermore, it will normally be difficult to sell or give away a lion, for example, to a zoo or wildlife park—they have more than enough of their own. As the life span of a lion could be about twenty-five years, an owner could be stuck with it for a long time.

SMALL CATS

Apart from the Puma (also called the Mountain Cat, Cougar, Catamount, Painter or Panther) from the New World, Small Cats sometimes include the Lynx (*Felis lynx*, Old and New Worlds), Bobcat (*F. rufa*, New World), Caracal (*F. caracal*, Old World) and the attractively marked Ocelot (*F. pardalis*) and Margay (*F. wiedi*), both from the New World.

More than half of the Small Cat species are on the list of animals endangered by trade,

Camels and llamas have been domesticated for thousands of years, but this has done little to sweeten their tempers. They are best kept in large enclosures. Top Left. This camel has a thick winter coat. Top Middle. Llamas can be kept in small groups and breed fairly well, which is an added attraction at zoos and wildlife parks.

and this includes practically all the South American Small Cats. Export from the countries of origin is now strictly controlled, and other countries have import restrictions.

Small Cats are graceful movers and this, together with the beauty of their coats, makes them a pleasure to watch. However, they do not make good pets. As a rule they are extremely shy and fierce, and you are unlikely to tame them. Even the kittens can be surprisingly fierce and intractable with those who have reared them.

Wolves

Wolves have been much maligned by folk legends and fairy tales. They do not, as is popularly believed, hunt in enormous, murderous packs—in fact, during spring and summer, when the cubs are being born and reared, the wolf hunts singly; later the cubs join the parents to hunt in a pack of about five individuals. Only in very hard winters when food is scarce do small packs tend to join forces, but a pack of over thirty is rare.

Wolves are near relatives, and probable ancestors, of the Domestic Dog, the first animal to be domesticated by mankind. Wolves cannot be recommended as pets for they are large and heavy and certain laws govern their capture. The adult Timber Wolf or Gray Wolf (*Canis lupus*), best known of the three species, weighs about 45kg. (100lb.), and is capable of killing a man. Although an escaped wolf is more likely to be terrified than aggressive, it may well kill domestic animals in order to eat and, if frightened or cornered, it will probably attack its would-be captors. Even if it does neither of these things in all likelihood, it will have to be shot.

Elephants

If elephants were one quarter of their actual size they would make charming pets. Intelligent and affectionate, their lifespan is about seventy years.

The Indian Elephant (*Elephas maximus*) has been kept in semi-domestication for centuries and is still used by men for working in the teak forests (See **Working Animals**). It is a more tractable animal than its African cousin (*Loxodonta africana*), slightly smaller with an arched back and domed head and much smaller ears. In the Indian species only the males sprout tusks, whereas both male and female African elephants have them.

Elephants are the most popular of all zoo animals. They are easily trained, intelligent, and affectionate. The only drawback is their size!

In spite of their enormous size unfortunately elephants have been kept as pets. London Zoo's famous "Diksie" started life in East Africa as a pet. On one occasion, for a bet, her owner persuaded her to climb the stairs into his bedroom. The young elephant, finding herself in such a strange situation, panicked and refused to come down again, reacting in fear.

Camels and Llamas

Camels and llamas belong to the same family, and both have been domesticated for thousands of years. There are two species of camel, the Bactrian Camel (*Camelus bactrianus*) with two humps and the one-humped Arabian Camel or Dromedary (*C. dromedarius*). The Bactrian Camel is very hardy, growing a thick winter coat which originally protected it from the freezing temperatures in the cold deserts of Central Asia. During the spring and summer this coat is shed giving the beast an unkempt appearance. There are very few wild camels today and the wild ancestors of the llama were probably extinct by the time the conquistadors invaded South America, although some people think that the Llama (*Lama glama*) is a domesticated form of the Guanaco still living in the Andes.

Camels and llamas were used chiefly as beasts of burden although originally also a source of meat and wool. (See **Working Animals**.) The llama has bare glandular patches on its back legs and camels, from birth, have bare protective callosities on the chest and leg-joints which take the weight when the beast is at rest.

All three animals breed well in captivity, although the male llama will not tolerate the presence of his sons for very long. During the mating season male camels and llamas may

become very belligerent; in camels the soft palate enlarges and may protrude from the mouth and the glands at the back of the head produce an evil-smelling secretion.

Camels and llamas have bad tempers, and both will attack by kicking, biting, and spitting (during which not only the copious saliva but the contents of the stomach too may be ejected with some force at the offending person). Biting can be really dangerous because the animals possess large, sharp, well separated teeth which can inflict an extremely serious wound.

Deer and Antelopes

Deer and antelopes, together with camels, pigs, cattle, and goats, are even-toed ungulates or Artiodactyls. Like most Artiodactyls they are ruminants—they chew the cud. Antelopes and male deer, with the exception of the Musk Deer (*Moschus*) and Chinese Water Deer (*Hydropotes inermis*), have bony outgrowths from their heads. Deer have antlers which are shed yearly, while antelopes have permanent horns. Both these groups comprise a large number of species.

There are about forty species of deer, varying in size from the huge Moose or Elk (*Alcesalces*) which stands 2m. (6.5 ft.) high, to the tiny mouse deer, or chevrotains (*Tragulus*, not a true deer) of Asian forests, which only reaches 30cm. (1ft.) in height. The antlers are used for courtship fights only (rutting), deer attacking in other circumstances with their legs and hooves. The females, other than Reindeer and Caribou, lack antlers and the males shed theirs annually after the mating season. When the new antlers sprout they are covered in soft furred skin or "velvet," but this wears off before rutting starts. The small size of some deer and their dainty form and movement can be misleading. Deer in the mating season (usually the autumn) will attack men, and

Deer and antelope are best kept in groups within large enclosures with high fences, since some species, such as this Impala, can jump 3m. (10ft.) high.

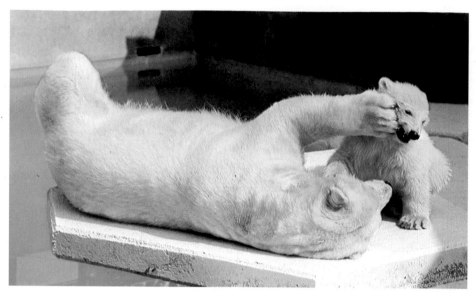

Top. *A major attraction at zoos, the Polar Bear requires a large pool and has the most unpredictable temper of all bears.*

Top Right. *Otters are playful animals that can make interesting pets. Kept in pairs, as are these Small-Clawed Otters, they are charming to watch. However, some species are endangered and should only be kept where the facilities allow breeding.*

their timid appearance and often slow or even "playful" approach make them all the more dangerous.

Antelope species are even more numerous and diverse than the deer. The most appealing of these are the small, delicate Gazelles (chiefly *Gazellu*).

Bears

Bears are solitary, irritable animals which are totally unsuitable as pets, despite the number of tame and performing beasts which have been kept. In the wild they avoid each other, especially the old males which are quite likely to kill any other bear they may happen to encounter. In a study of Brown or Grizzly Bears in Alaska it was found that in areas where hunting was permitted the number of bears actually *increased*, and this was thought to be because hunters killed the old males, which made the best trophies.

Bears are said to be treacherous and poker-faced—which means that the danger signals shown by most animals before they attack and which are easily read as in wolves or domestic dogs are not as easily discerned in bears. They attack seemingly without reason and without warning and, because of their great size and strength, they are lethal. One of the axioms of zoo-keepers is that no man should ever go into a bear's cage.

Bear cubs are born in the winter months during the so-called hibernation of the mother, and are small, being the size of a rat, and very helpless. The cubs do not leave the den for several months but when they do finally appear they are playful and charming. In a few more months, however, they become too strong and fierce to be handled.

Kangaroos and Wallabies

Kangaroos and wallabies are natives of Australia and New Guinea. Like most Australian mammals they are marsupials, which means that they do not bear fully formed young as most mammals do, but give birth to their young at a very early stage of development. These tiny (1.5g. in the Red Kangaroo) babies then crawl into their mothers' pouches where they attach themselves to the nipple and remain for some months to grow and complete their development. For some time after the baby has first left the pouch it will return for warmth and protection.

Kangaroos are the largest of the marsupials. A male Red Kangaroo (*Macropus rufus*) may be over 2m. (6.5ft.) tall and have enormously powerful back legs with which they can cover a distance of 8m. (25ft.) at one bound. They also use their hind legs to kill their enemies. If cornered, a kangaroo will rear up on its tail and kick out with these formidable limbs. Apart from the Red Kangaroo, the Eastern Gray Kangaroo (*M. giganteus*), the Western Gray Kangaroo (*M. fuliginosus*), and the Hill Kangaroo or Wallaroo (*Osphranter* species) are the best known of the larger members of the family.

The thirty or so species of wallaby are smaller than kangaroos, but very much like them in appearance and habits. Many will breed well in captivity, but they do not make good pets. Their intelligence is limited, and the males become aggressive as they mature.

Otters

Otters are distributed throughout the world except for Australia and Madagascar. They are carnivores and aquatic members of the weasel family. One of the most widely distributed species is the **European Otter** (*Lutra lutra*) which is not in fact confined to Europe but extends from the British Isles across Russia to Japan and is also found in North Africa. It is closely related to the **Canadian Otter** (*Lutra canadensis*) but like the **North American Sea Otter** (*Enhydra lutris*) it enjoys a certain amount of protection in some countries where it is illegal for individuals to capture them.

Dolphins

Dolphins are in reality small toothed whales, related to the killer whales. There are over thirty different species of dolphin, but the two species which are most likely to be encountered are the Common Dolphin (*Delphinus delphis*), often seen at sea playing in the bow-wave of a ship, and the Bottlenosed Dolphin (*Tursiops truncatus*—often called "Common Porpoise" in North America), which is the one most frequently seen in dolphinariums. (In North America and some other parts of the world dolphins are often mistakenly called "porpoises" a name correctly

Kangaroos settle reasonably well in captivity but do not make good pets. Wild specimens are exported from Australia but only to zoos and wildlife parks.

Dolphins are extremely intelligent mammals. The Bottle Nosed Dolphin is the species most frequently seen in dolphinariums.

applied to smaller, blunt-nosed whales of another family, Phocaenidae. The Dolphin Fish or Dorado, *Coryphaena hipparus*, is a large, fast-swimming game fish, not a mammal.)

Dolphins are extremely intelligent animals. Their brains are large and convoluted as are those of humans. This enables them to learn and perform the tricks one sees in dolphinariums. In addition, they seem to like the company of humans, and there are well documented stories of friendships between dolphins and human beings—especially children. If a dolphin has been receiving human attention in a dolphin show or experimental program and it is then neglected it will mope about and probably start to refuse its food. Some dolphins have been known to "pine" to death.

The dolphin has a powerful tail, a very hard snout and a mouthful of sharp pointed teeth all of which can be used in fighting, but they never seem to use these against humans.

Dolphins are mammals, which means that unlike most fish they breathe air and give birth to live young. They are also warm-blooded. Immediately after birth the baby is pushed to the surface by the mother so that it may breathe, which it does through the single nostril or blow-hole at the top of its head.

To sum up the reasons why "zoo animals" should not be kept as pets: they will be expensive and difficult to keep in a manner that is safe for humans. They may endanger human life if they escape or, if they escape and establish themselves in the wild, they could endanger indigenous animals or damage the environment as has happened with escaped mink, coypu, and rabbits. They may, more insidiously, endanger human or animal life by being a reservoir of disease.

With every animal that we remove from the wild we deplete the numbers of that species, and in some cases the pet trade has contributed significantly to near extinction of a species. Few wild animals will breed in captivity so that the process of domestication cannot continue: with each animal the process of taming starts anew. Finally, many exotic pets are kept in conditions amounting to cruelty—not because the owners mean to be cruel (indeed, they would probably consider themselves as animal lovers) but because they lack sufficient facilities or knowledge. Many such animals in captivity suffer from malnutrition due either to ignorance or the difficulty of obtaining suitable food. Even those which are kept satisfactorily will usually lead a restricted and unnatural life.

Zoo animals should *not* be kept as pets. Leave them to the zoos and wildlife parks which will come nearer having the facilities and the experience to do the job properly.

WILD ANIMALS AS VISITORS & PETS

In this chapter we deal with two quite distinct groups of animals that are native to the temperate regions of North America and western Europe. In the first section we discuss the capture and keeping of native wild mammals which includes an account of those species most likely to be kept as pets, while in the second section we deal with the subject of encouraging native bird species to visit our yards and creating the best possible habitat for a wide range of species.

Keeping Wild Mammals

GENERAL CONSIDERATIONS AND THE LAW

It can be very gratifying to have a pet which is different from all others in the neighborhood. It must be for this reason that zoos are bombarded with requests for suggestions of wild animals which make good and unusual pets. To this question there is no simple answer. All of the kinds of animals which are known to make good pets are already being kept as pets. Occasionally a new kind of good pet is discovered and rapidly becomes popular. For example, the Golden Hamster was discovered less than fifty years ago, and all the pet Golden Hamsters of today are derived from one small group. Gerbils have become popular much more recently, and already millions of people have kept them. (See **Small Mammals.**) The hard fact is that there are no unusual pets that are easy to keep. Animals which are not normally kept as pets have this status because they are, in one way or another, difficult to keep. It follows that only those who have been very successful with a wide variety of the commonly kept pets should consider tackling an unusual species. This is particularly true if the animal concerned is one which normally lives wild in Europe or North America, where most of the wild animals have been killed by mankind, and where most of the surviving animals are inconspicuous, shy, or in danger of extinction.

To keep such animals successfully requires great understanding and considerable commitment. Mere curiosity or a casual whim are not sufficient justification.

Some kinds of animals are virtually impossible to keep satisfactorily in any case. Most kinds of deer, for example, are too large and bears are too dangerous. Wild rats are too risky because of the disease that they may carry. Burrowers such as moles have needs

which cannot adequately be satisfied in captivity. Wild rabbits, hares, and wildcats are very shy and virtually impossible to tame. If confined they are likely to injure themselves in their frenzied efforts to escape. For some of these animals there are closely related species which are much easier to keep, such as domesticated white rats, rabbits, and cats. (See **Small Mammals; Cats.**)

Top. *Few people would consider keeping a wild bear as a pet or encouraging one in a garden. But in places like the Yellowstone National Park, it is possible to see wild bears, although it is illegal to feed them—a precaution for the good of both animals and visitors.*

Bottom. *For many people there is much more satisfaction and pleasure in seeing wild animals in the garden rather than in keeping them as caged pets. Indeed, it is illegal to keep the Gray Squirrel in captivity in some regions where it is regarded as a pest.*

Another consideration before deciding to keep wild mammals is the prevailing law. For example, in Great Britain the European Otter (*Lutra lutra*) is protected by law, and in western North America the Sea Otter (*Enhydra lutris*) has the same protection. This is because these animals are rare. It goes without saying that animals in this category should be left alone. So too should animals which are the subject of legal controls for other reasons. For example, Gray Squirrels (*Sciurus carolinensis*) can only be kept in Great Britain by those authorized by the Ministry of Agriculture, and in practice this permission is never given to private individuals because these animals are regarded as pests. Since changes in the law occur from time to time, and since laws vary widely in different countries and from one state to another in the United States it is impossible to give detailed guidance. If in doubt ask a zoological garden, the biology department of your closest university, or the state conservation departments in the United States.

OBTAINING WILD PETS

The availability of wild animals from dealers varies from country to country. In Great Britain only very rarely will a dealer have indigenous local mammals for sale, but in North America animals such as coyotes and skunks are often available. New laws are constantly being introduced in the United States to protect native wildlife and these laws generally forbid commerce of any kind. If you are ever offered an animal for sale, intelligent observation can save a great deal of trouble. Never buy unhealthy animals out of pity. They tend to die with ungrateful speed and you will not get your money back. Healthy mammals are lively and have clear eyes, dry noses, and sleek coats. Evidence that they have been feeding is valuable. Their droppings should never be runny.

Intelligent observations about the state of health should be made on any wild animal that you catch. Healthy wild animals try to avoid capture and any that you come by too easily should be regarded with suspicion. Certainly they should be quarantined, and for a period kept well away from all animals that you already have. Acquiring wild animals by chance can pose other problems too. You are not likely to have housing ready and all young mammals which have not been weaned can be a source of great worry and disappointment. (See **Breeding and Rearing**.) They will need regular feeding with milk throughout the day and night, and probably regular rubbing in the anal region with cotton moistened with warm water, so as to resemble the touch of the mother's tongue, which may be necessary to stimulate bowel movements. To raise them to weaning requires very strong motivation. However, mammals which have just been weaned are the ideal subjects with which to begin. They will adapt to captivity much better than older specimens.

For small mammals such as shrews and mice, which make regular use of the same tracks, the simplest traps to use are glass jars, which can be carefully sited as pitfalls sunk into the ground. Any animal falling into such a trap will need some shelter, such as dry grass, and food until you visit the trap. Traps of all kinds need to be visited every few hours at least, and jars should be removed so that other animals will not fall in and starve to death. When not "set" they should at the very least be inverted so that animals can pass over them in safety. A variety of special live traps can be purchased. Some made from aluminum or stainless steel are resistant to corrosion. They are very sensitive and suitable for catching shrews, mice, and voles. Bait for traps is not essential, since some mammals seem to enter them out of curiosity. However, once trapped the mammal will need some food and nesting material for shelter, especially in cold weather. At any time of year all traps should be visited regularly and frequently.

Traps should be sited inconspicuously among undergrowth. This is the most likely place to find small mammals, and it provides some concealment for expensive traps that might be stolen or vandalized. The odds are against any one trap's being sprung during the course of a few hours so that time and effort are saved if a number of traps are set at the same time. If one location proves unsuccessful, move on to another after a couple of days. When a catch is made, the trap should be opened inside a large, transparent plastic bag, and the animal then can easily be caught and transferred to a temporary metal container, which has small air holes for ventilation.

HANDLING WILD MAMMALS

Wild animals should be handled as little as possible. For the smallest species gloves are not necessary or desirable, since they interfere with the firm but gentle touch that is essential. For speedy transfer from one container to another shrews and small rodents can be picked up by the base of the tail.

A Longworth live trap suitable for catching most small mammals.

Moles do not make good pets since they spend much of their lives underground and require a constant supply of worms and insects.

Larger mammals must be held by the shoulders with the hand kept well away from the animal's teeth. Gloves may be essential to prevent scratching from claws. Be calm, approach slowly, and talk quietly whenever you handle a wild animal. If you make a habit of handling wild animals, sooner or later you will get bitten and be in some danger of more than mere pain. In some parts of the world, many mammals are carriers of rabies. Many rodents can infect humans with leptospiral jaundice. From any deep bite there is always a risk of tetanus. When you are bitten you have no choice but to see a doctor as soon as possible. In any event, after handling animals you should always wash your hands thoroughly.

DIETS

Obviously herbivores require hay and vegetables or perhaps seeds, such as corn or fruit, and carnivores require meat. However, it is not quite as simple to provide a satisfactory diet as it may appear.

Problems arise in providing a satisfactory diet for wild animals for a number of reasons. Most kinds of wild animals have not had their diets studied in great detail and little is known about essential vitamins or minerals. It is therefore wise to offer as varied and natural a diet as possible. Carnivores such as weasels should be offered the whole carcasses of freshly killed small birds or mammals, rather than minced butcher's meat, since the gut contents and internal organs may provide the carnivore with essential substances, and even the fur or feathers and bones may provide essential roughage. Most carnivores also like some plant food as part of their diet, as in the case of raccoons.

Gathering a completely natural diet for a wild animal is often impossible. Instead you must make partial use of purchased items of food. For a shrew that eats at least its own weight of insects and other invertebrates every day this can be very expensive, since blow-fly maggots (gentles) cost more per pound than steak. (See **Amphibians and Reptiles** for details of producing your own maggots.) Some shrews are willing to eat some canned dog food. Since plant material may form part of their diet in the wild, some rolled oats can be mixed into the meat. Worms, small snails, and insects gathered from the wild should also form at least part of the daily diet.

Some wild rodents drink very little, and some of those from semidesert areas normally obtain all of the water that they need from their food. However, it is a sound principle to see that all animals have constant access to clean drinking water, which should be in a stabilized container. Drinking bottles suitable for such laboratory animals as white rats can be purchased and are often the best solution.

CAGING

The conventional cage for small mammals, often on sale in pet shops, has a solid top, bottom, back and sides, and wire mesh at the front. It may have mesh at both front and top. Where wire or bars are used, the spaces between the elements should be narrower than you may at first think desirable. Small shrews, for example, can squeeze through a gap .10mm. (0.4in.) wide, and small species of bats can pass through an opening no larger than a wedding ring. If cages with open tops are used, their sides should be vertical, smooth, and higher than the occupant of the cage can possibly jump. All cages should be kept in a secure area so that any escaping animal cannot get far.

For mammals with powerful teeth, such as rodents, the cage should not have exposed corners which the animals can gnaw. Many rodents can easily bite through metals such as aluminum. The wood required for exercising their teeth should take the form of branches provided specially for the purpose, rather than parts of the cage itself. Aquariums with suitably ventilated lids offer advantages as cages for small mammals. If the center of an aquarium is filled with bricks, and the space between them is packed with peat, bulb fiber, or some similar material, small rodents will construct burrows which allow for visibility.

Peat, dry soil, or sand are also suitable materials to use at the bottom of more open cages. The cage should be furnished with materials appropriate to its occupant such as branches for climbers and cover for undergrowth dwellers. Droppings should be removed every day, as should surplus food. However, surplus plant food is psychologically important to rodents and should not be removed. Clinical cleanliness within the cage is not important. It is certainly not necessary to disinfect the cage of a healthy animal each

day. Some smell is normal and inevitable with many kinds of mammals. Shrews or members of the weasel family, for example, have scent glands with which they mark their surroundings.

If keeping mammals in cages sounds troublesome, remember that with some mammals there is a much better alternative. In North America chipmunks will stay in your yard if you provide food for them and especially if you have a wooden verandah beneath which they can live. In Great Britain it is equally easy to encourage the hedgehogs and squirrels which are common even in many suburban gardens.

BREEDING

Many kinds of wild mammals, especially small ones, tend to lead rather solitary lives. It is not always easy to persuade two of them to share the same cage. If you do try to introduce a pair, use the largest possible cage, and furnish it so one can escape from the vicinity of the other. After making the introduction, watch to see that fighting does not follow. If it does and the loser cannot escape, then murder may be done. This is the real tyranny of the cage, and you must do all you can to overcome it.

Most male wild mammals play no active part in the care of their young and should be removed from the cage after mating. At the end of the gestation period make sure that the female has a nest and absolute peace and quiet.

DISEASE

If keen observation and common sense indicate you have a sick animal keep it well away from others of its kind and consult a veterinarian. Since most veterinarians are concerned with common domesticated animals there may not be much help available. However, in an emergency any veterinarian can painlessly destroy animals which are beyond recovery.

WILD MAMMALS AS PETS

The following are examples of native wild mammals which might be kept as pets either in Europe or North America:

OPOSSUMS

Opossums are North and South American marsupials, and the newborn young live in a pouch on the mother's abdomen. The only North American species is the **Virginian Opossum** (*Didelphis marsupialis virginiana*). Opossums are active mainly at night. They need a cage at least 1.5m. (5ft.) square. Chicken wire makes a suitable covering, but it needs to be extended beneath the ground to prevent the animal's digging its way out. Branches for climbing are essential. Opossums are omnivorous and easy to feed. They will take table scraps, meat, fish, worms,

Virginian Opossum.

insect larvae, fruit, bread and almost anything else. They also like to drink milk. They rarely become tame except when caught very young.

SHREWS

These mammals are common but inconspicuous in the wild, since they spend much of their lives in undergrowth or under the litter layer on top of the soil. Various species occur throughout the world mainly in the Northern Hemisphere, such as the **European Shrew** (*Sorex araneus*) and the **Short-tailed Shrew** (*Blarina brevicauda*). Although tiny, they are as fierce as tigers. They require relatively large amounts of food, such as canned dog food containing some raw rolled oats. Some insects, worms, or woodlice are also highly desirable. Aluminum pans make a cheap cage, but something larger is much better. Unless you have a huge cage, individual shrews must be kept separately.

HEDGEHOGS

The **Common Hedgehog** (*Erinaceus europaeus*) occurs throughout temperate Europe and Asia. They are poor climbers but good diggers. They feed on slugs, earthworms, insects, and a limited amount of plant material such as berries and acorns. If kept outdoors in temperate and cold regions they will hibernate between about December and March. For this purpose they need a sheltered place to build a nest of moss, leaves, and grass. They are mainly nocturnal and are frequent visitors even to urban gardens. They can be encouraged to visit with a regularly placed bowl of bread and milk.

ARMADILLOS

In the wild, nine-banded armadillos (*Dasypus* species) are found in southern North America. Armadillos are exceedingly powerful diggers, but poor climbers, although they can climb low wire fences. In captivity they can be fed on raw or cooked eggs, raw meat, fruit, bread, and table scraps. They also eat insects and worms.

TREE SQUIRRELS

Tree-living squirrels of the gray species are native to North America, although they have also been introduced to parts of Europe, where the indigenous **Red Squirrel** (*Sciurus vulgaris*) has now disappeared from many areas. (See **Small Mammals** for further details.) Squirrels provide an excellent example of animals which are more attractive if left free in the yard rather than being caged, provided you can tolerate damage to garden plants and the "theft" of bird food.

FLYING SQUIRRELS

Two flying squirrel species, *Glaucomys sabrinus* and *G. volans*, occur in North America. These small squirrels are really gliders rather than fliers, using webs of skin between the fore and hind limbs as wings and the tail as a combination rudder and parachute. They are social animals and normally live in groups. They are nocturnal but can become somewhat tame if you spend some of the hours after dark with them. Their diet consists of seeds, cereals, fruits, and nuts. As with other rodents, some hard food is essential to keep their teeth in good condition.

WOODCHUCKS AND PRAIRIE DOGS

These North American short-tailed, burrowing rodents of the squirrel family live in burrows and can best be caught by digging them out, although it requires considerable effort. It is difficult to provide adequate opportunities for burrowing in cages. The cages must certainly be very large, with wire extending several feet below the surface of the ground. **Woodchucks** (*Marmota monax*) hibernate in

Nine-Banded Armadillo (Dasypus novemcinctus)

The common Hedgehog is a frequent visitor to suburban and rural gardens in England. It will return regularly to a dish of food left overnight. The hedgehog is a prime example of an animal best left in the wild which nonetheless gives great pleasure by its presence in the garden.

the winter; if they are kept outdoors, they must have good shelter and nesting material. They eat vegetables and fruit of all kinds and some meat including bones and cereals. **Prairie Dogs** (*Cynomys* species) do not hibernate, but remain in their burrows for days on end during extremely hot or cold weather. They eat grass, hay, cereals, fruits, vegetables, and they will gnaw at bark and tree roots. They are social animals and should be kept in groups. The European equivalent of these animals is the **Marmot** (*M. marmota*) which occurs in mountainous regions. It also hibernates in winter.

CHIPMUNKS

The chipmunks of North America belong to the squirrel family, and are often sold in pet shops in many parts of the world. (See **Small Mammals**.) They are good examples of animals that can be much better enjoyed if left at liberty and encouraged to visit yards and parks.

CRICETID MICE

North American mice of various species, including deer mice (*Peromyscus* species), jumping mice (*Zapus* species), pocket mice (*Microdipodops* species), and grasshopper mice (*Oncychomys* species) belong to the same family (Cricetidae) as the bank voles (*Clethrionomys* species) and field voles (*Microtus* species) of western Europe. The **European Water Vole** or Water Rat (*Arvicola terrestris*) also belongs to this group, but unlike the others should not be kept in captivity since it is impossible to provide it with an adequate environment. The members of this group have slightly varied feeding requirements, but should be offered predominantly plant food including green vegetables, fruits including rosehips, nuts, chopped vege-

305

A number of ground-living members of the squirrel family can be kept as pets. Shown here are (Top Left) a Woodchuck and (Top Middle) a pair of Black-Tailed Prairie Dogs.

tables, and cereals. Up to one-third of the diet may consist of insects and other invertebrates. Any species you select should be offered a wide choice from among these alternatives, and the diet should be adjusted to suit the preferences observed. They all need some cover and nest boxes. If possible they should have the opportunity to construct burrows.

Some wild mice can be captured from the wild and kept as pets. Examples are: (1) The European Common Field Mouse, (2) the Bank Vole and (3) Harvest Mice.

MURID MICE

These are the long-tailed mice of the ubiquitous family Muridae to which the **House Mouse** (*Mus musculus*) belongs. The **European Common Field Mouse, Wood Mouse** or **Long-tailed Mouse** (*Apodememus sylvaticus*) belongs to the same group. They feed mainly on plant material, such as seeds and hazel nuts, with some fruit, berries, and green stuff. They also eat insects and spiders. Sometimes they breed in captivity, but they never become truly tame. If they are picked up by any part of the tail except the base, the skin peels away, and eventually the tail is lost. (See also **Small Mammals** for the domesticated mouse.)

HARVEST MICE

These tiny European mice (*Micromys minutus*) also belong to the murid group, but deserve special mention because of their charm. They climb among cornstalks, in which they build their nests in summer and, if caged, will use climbing facilities. Since they spend the winter in burrows, they should also be provided with a sheltered nest box. They feed on cereals, fruits, green vegetables, and some insects.

COMMON DORMOUSE

At one time this small but rather squirrel-like European rodent (*Muscardinus avellanarius*) was much more common than it is today and was much more commonly kept as a pet. It climbs well and needs a nest of dry grass and bark within which to rest. It is most active at night and hibernates during the winter. It feeds on beech mast, hazel nuts, chestnuts, and other seeds of trees including conifers and young shoots and bark.

EDIBLE DORMOUSE

This European rodent (*Glis glis*) was introduced to England in 1902, and now lives wild in parts of Buckinghamshire, Bedfordshire, and Hertfordshire. It is larger than the Common Dormouse, but smaller than the Gray Squirrel and is nocturnal in habit; it needs a secluded nest in which to hide during the day. It climbs well and is one of the rodents

1

2

3

Top Left. *The Coyote or Prairie Wolf.*
Top Right. *Foxes, such as this Red Fox, are increasingly moving into the suburbs to scavenge on the waste of human society. This activity should not be encouraged, since these animals carry many diseases, most notably rabies.*

that does not store food. It eats all kinds of fruit, nuts, willow and plum bark, and some insects. Although not eaten by human beings today, it is said to have been kept and fattened for the table by the Romans. It hibernates from about October to April.

FOXES

Distributed throughout the Northern Hemisphere the **Red Fox** (*Vulpes vulpes*) is found in Europe, Asia, Africa, and North America, although in the latter it is sometimes considered a separate species *V. fulva*. Other North American species include the **Kit Fox** (*V. macrotis*), the **Swift Fox** (*V. velox*), and the **Gray Fox** (*Urocyon* species). Being a member of the dog family a pet fox should be inoculated against hard pad, distemper, and rabies. As with any carnivore, only young, preferably newly weaned animals can ever make acceptable pets, and even then foxes may grow to be destructive and kill other animals. Foxes can climb better than other dogs, so an ordinary wire run may not be adequate to contain one. If they are kept indoors the scent of their musk glands can be offensive. Pet foxes are often neutered by veterinarians which reduces their musky odor and moderates their more aggressive behavior. It is almost impossible to tame a fox. They never cease trying to escape into the wild. Food used for a domestic dog is suitable. Foxes are increasingly becoming scavengers of our urban environment, but this activity should not be encouraged since they are carriers of rabies and other diseases. In some areas organizations have been started to return foxes to a more "wild" environment where they may hunt as natural predators.

COYOTES

The **Coyote** or **Prairie Wolf** (*Canis latrans*) is native to the North American grasslands and is a close relative of the wolf and the domestic dog. Accordingly, it should be vaccinated against hard pad, distemper, and rabies. It can be kept outdoors in a large run with a fence at least 2m. (7ft.) high, and furnished with a draft-proof kennel. Most kinds of food given to domestic dogs are suitable. If caught very young a coyote may become tame enough to be taken out on a leash. However, as with all wild animals, it will never become as trustworthy as a docile domesticated animal.

RACCOONS

These North American members (*Procyon lotor*) of the order Carnivora can become quite tame, if they are caught young enough. However, their insatiable curiosity and mischievous behavior mean they can never be allowed freedom inside a home. A raccoon needs a spacious, sunny, outdoor cage covered with strong wire mesh at the sides and at the top since they are natural climbers. Due to their strong teeth, wood alone should not be used. A large rubber ball makes a good toy for a raccoon. The diet consists of all kinds of

Raccoons can make charming and inquisitive pets, but they are natural climbers and require strong cages.

meat, including fish, and such invertebrates as crayfish, fruit of all kinds, and cereals, such as sweet corn.

WEASELS AND THEIR ALLIES

Members of the weasel family are voracious hunters. They have very sharp teeth and should always be handled with care. If caught

extent. Exceptional badgers will learn to walk on a leash. Their jaws are very powerful, and a bite from a badger can be quite serious.

PORCUPINES

These large spiny rodents belong to two quite distinct families, one confined to the Americas (Erithizontidae) and the other to the tropics of the Old World (Hystricidae). Only one species, the **North American Porcupine** (*Erithizon dorsatum*), occurs in North America. This rodent of cool evergreen American forests is an expert climber and in the wild the bark of trees makes up a large part of its food. In captivity it will eat almost any vegetable food, including dog biscuits, bread, root and green vegetables, sweet potatoes, and sweet corn. It needs salt in the diet. In an outdoor enclosure it requires something to climb on. The cage should either be enclosed at the top or should have smooth inwardly sloping wooden walls at least 1.2m. (4ft.) high. A sheltered den comparable to the hollow logs favored by wild porcupines should also be provided. This species does not hibernate in winter. (See **Insects; Amphibians and Reptiles.**)

Wild Birds As Visitors

By judicious feeding, selective cultivation of any available outdoor area, and the thoughtful erection of nest boxes and feeders it is

Few free wild birds will become hand tame, but the European Robin is a particularly tame species in Great Britain, although shy and retiring elsewhere. (In some areas keeping wild birds as pets is illegal.)

BADGERS

These are more heavily built and more omnivorous than other members of the weasel family. The **European Badger** (*Meles meles*) inhabits woodlands of much of Europe and northern Asia, and the slightly smaller **American Badger** (*Taxidea taxus*) inhabits sandy, more open country. Badgers are powerful diggers, and will only be contained by a cage with a solid concrete floor and strong wire sides. Being nocturnal they require a solidly built dark den. They can be fed on any kind of meat, especially young rabbits, with the addition of almost any kind of plant food, including some dog biscuits. Those caught young can be tamed to some

Top Left. *Badgers are shy, nocturnal animals which only make reasonable pets if hand raised. In a few instances wild cubs have become hand tame.* Center Left. *North American Porcupine.*

young the **European** or **American Weasel** (*Mustela nivalis*) can become remarkably tame. The larger **Stoat** (*M. erminea*), **Mink Mink** (*M. vison* and *M. lutreola*), and the arboreal **martens** (*Martes* species) can never be trusted to such an extent. A more easily obtained alternative as a pet is the ferret, which is a domesticated form of the **European polecat.** (See **Small Mammals.**) These animals need a secluded nest box and a secure but spacious outer enclosure. The most satisfactory diet for them is freshly killed animals such as rats, mice, and other meat including rabbit and chicken. The smaller kinds of food animals should be fed whole.

SKUNKS

These American members of the weasel family are sometimes available from pet shops as well as from the wild and make quite good pets. If you get a skunk from the wild, be careful to avoid its bite until a veterinarian has checked it. (See **Small Mammals.**)

possible to acquire a constantly changing mixed flock of wild birds. In just the same way that unrestrained shell parakeets depend on their home base, so wild birds come to depend on any regular feeding station. You can, therefore, enjoy the birds in your yard while allowing them to retain their freedom.

The addition of more unusual neighborhood birds and even the possibility of unexpected rarities, passage migrants, and seasonal visitors can provide an interesting collection that amply makes up for the absence of pet or aviary birds.

ATTRACTING BIRDS

Birds are attracted to the average yard by a variety of means. Apart from birds such as robins, thrushes, starlings, finches, and tits which occur as part of the natural ecology, many other kinds can be lured from the surrounding area by the sheer diversity of habitat which different people produce in their own yards or gardens. Even in isolation, the

Birds will visit all gardens, but for the real enthusiast there are a number of ways to encourage a wider range of species. Shown below is a plan for an "idealized" bird garden, together with a table giving the favored nesting sites of some garden birds.

average garden with its separate spots of monoculture fortuitously creates the varied world that will attract many birds—from small insectivores and nectivores to the larger woodpeckers and magpies.

Wild birds can virtually be summoned at will. It is astonishing how quickly they locate foods such as peanuts, fat, soaked bread, fruit, and seeds and learn to appear at regular feeding times. In scientific circles this is called a conditioned response. This *regular* feeding is the most valuable and rewarding approach, but it brings with it added responsibilities. Even by distributing a small amount of food, you are encouraging the wild creatures that visit your home to behave in an unnatural way, and your responsibility is increased with the "service" you offer, especially in the winter. Birds come to rely on you, and a greater number will be attracted to the area than it can naturally support; so, if regular feeding is begun it must be either continued or phased out gradually. A sudden break of several days might cause an imbalance to the lives of the birds. They will be forced to compete for the natural food available, and aggression is bound to increase. The stronger birds will drive away the weaker; and if the surrounding territories are

already fully exploited, young birds will be the losers.

Winter is a time of great hardship and anxiety to all wild animals. In offering additional food to birds at this time of year remember that birds need to drink regularly and that fresh water is just as important as food. A shallow dish (a trash can lid is ideal) replenished regularly in icy weather with warm water will attract a host of wild birds.

The summer is a different matter altogether, and although birds still need to drink just as much, wild food is more abundant and much better for birds and their young than anything we can supply. At this time of the year we can offer help by erecting nest boxes, keeping an area quiet and peaceful, deterring cats, and making a mud pool to help swifts and swallows build their nests. Many of the birds will be different from the ones we watched in the winter.

The smallest yard in suburbia is important, not only to regular town birds like sparrows, starlings, pigeons, and small crows but also to birds like finches, insectivores, and small fruit-eaters from the nearby countryside which are always on the lookout for the chance to extend their ranges. Even the backyard and windowsills have their parts to play

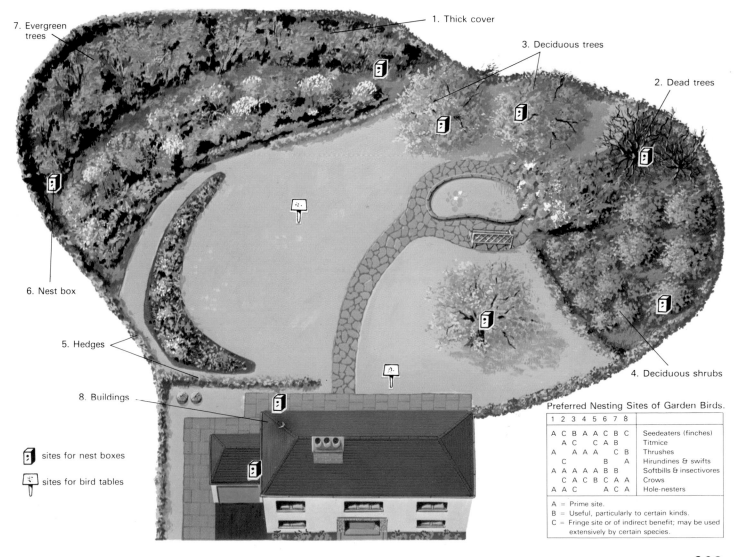

7. Evergreen trees

1. Thick cover

3. Deciduous trees

2. Dead trees

6. Nest box

5. Hedges

8. Buildings

4. Deciduous shrubs

🗋 sites for nest boxes

🗋 sites for bird tables

Preferred Nesting Sites of Garden Birds.

1	2	3	4	5	6	7	8	
A	C	B	A	A	C	B	C	Seedeaters (finches)
	A	C		C	A	B		Titmice
A		A	A	A		C	B	Thrushes
	C			B			A	Hirundines & swifts
A	A	A	A	A	A	B	B	Softbills & insectivores
	C	A	C	B	C	A	A	Crows
A	A	C			A	C	A	Hole-nesters

A = Prime site.
B = Useful, particularly to certain kinds.
C = Fringe site or of indirect benefit; may be used extensively by certain species.

in providing a retreat from the noise and danger of towns.

Anyway sparrows have as much right to be there as the eagles in the mountains, and they and their friends will assuredly be supplemented by birds of passage and occasional visitors. Ornithologists must forever be on their guard against elitism, and the worship of rarity for rarities sake. The omnipresent chance that something completely unexpected like a roving hawk or owl or tired migrant will appear, literally out of the blue, produces sufficient spice to make the simple pleasure of being a part of the lives of ordinarly humble creatures exciting enough. Without belaboring the point, even the window-box is a world in its own right to the organisms that live there and can be of absorbing interest to us. (Robert Stroud in Alcatraz did not let his lack of facilities prevent him from becoming one of the greatest of all birdmen.)

DESIGN OF "BIRDGARDENS"

Obviously each garden has its limits, which will vary in accordance with the owners' interests. A few are content with nothing short of a miniature nature reserve—a garden of wild plants such as briars, nettles, thistles, dandelions, and willow herbs in which nature is only minimally directed. An alternative to this ideal is to leave a corner untended. Here the wild plants and, indeed, a complete little ecosystem can flourish, attracting warblers, flycatchers and other small insect eaters. In an increasingly urbanized world where the countryside is under enormous pressure from agriculture and industry, those odd corners can be the salvation for much of our everyday wildlife.

In the more conventional small formal

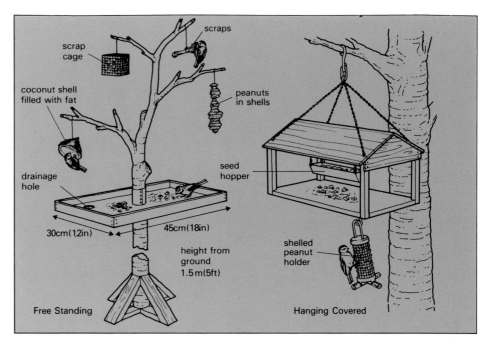

An ideal way to encourage birds to a garden is to provide a bird table on which food is placed and hung—and the best models are designed and built by amateurs! Shown here are two simple designs that can be made easily at home.

yard, owners can help in other ways. Closely cropped lawns are a happy hunting ground for birds like wagtails and thrushes. Because of the absence of nearby cover which could conceal a predator, they feel safe to feed on the insects, worms, and other invertebrates in the short grass. Flower and herbaceous borders, shrubberies, hedges, and fruit trees are all great attractions. Direct supplements of extra food, drinking and bathing water, and various kinds of artifacts are the bonuses

that many wary or strange birds find impossible to resist. Planting shrubs, especially those like elder, hawthorn, and holly, which bear and retain their berries until the winter and are ornamental in the bargain, is an obvious starting point.

FEEDING STATIONS

Bird feeders can be both decorative and useful. They dispose of household scraps such as bacon bits—which should be firmly tied together with string and hung so as to swing free—fat, and the residue from saucepans. Carefully positioned near a window, they can provide entertainment during mealtimes or

Guide to the Food Preferences of Garden Birds

SHELLED NUTS	PEANUTS	OTHER WHOLE NUTS	SEEDS/GRAINS	VEGETABLES	FRUIT	SOAKED BREAD	FAT/MEAT/BONE MARROW	GENERAL SCRAPS	
A	A		A	B	A	C		B	Small Finches
A	A	B	A	B	A	B		B	Large Finches (and other seedeaters)
					A	B	A	A	Thrushes
A	B				A	C	A	A	Other Insectivores
				A	B	A	A	A	Starlings
B	B	C		A	C	A	A	A	Crows
B	B	B			C		A	C	Woodpeckers
					C		A	A	Gulls

A = Major item
B = Usually of secondary importance but variable within the type.
C = Fringe item, possibly important to some kinds.
NB Prepare to be flexible

Plants that Attract Birds to the Garden

FRUIT TREES	CONIFERS	BERRY-BEARING SHRUBS	ROUGH GRASSES	THICK COVER	MOWN GRASSLAND	PLANTS ATTRACTIVE TO INSECTS	
A	A	B	A			B	Finches
A	A	A	A	B		B	Other Seedeaters
B	B			A		A	Tits
A		A	B	B	A		Thrushes
A	B	A	A	A	A	A	Other softbills & Insectivores

A = Direct benefit
B = Secondary or indirect benefit
NB The absence of a symbol does not necessarily indicate no benefit

Top Left. *Providing nest boxes is another way to encourage birds into a garden.*
Top Right.*Two types of nest box that are quite easy to build. They can be constructed from single planks of wood.*

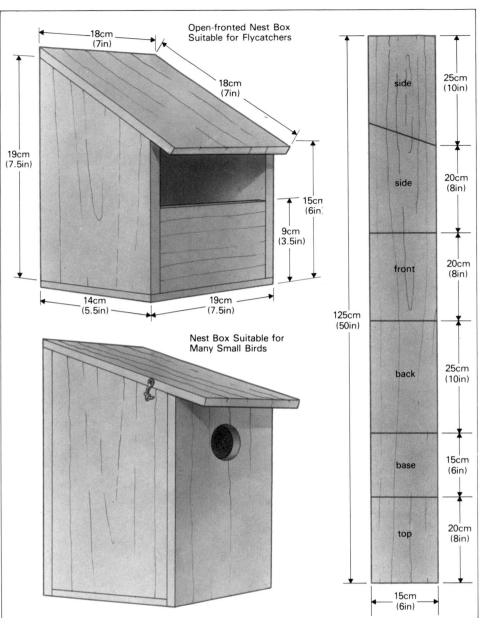

duties at the kitchen sink. Some feeders may be very decorative, but the bird's welfare should have priority over the architectural appeal. Birds do not care about the style of the feeder providing it is kept clean and free of disease.

An ordinary flat shelf on top of a smooth pole is probably the best style of feeder. Although birds do not feed in heavy rain and roofs are probably unnecessary they have some advantages in protecting certain foods. If the feeder has good drainage, heavy rain helps to clean it. Having the feeder on a high smooth pole protects the birds from cats, rats, and other injurious influences. Quite a number of birds do not readily feed under cover and the sort of semienclosed feeder that hangs from tree branches may attract the attention of scavengers and predators. Cats are a constant problem for birds. However, one resident cat will often keep out large numbers of neighboring cats which pose an even greater threat.

A windowsill is a convenient alternative to a feeder, but many timid birds will not venture that close to a house. There are all manner of devices and accessories for the provision of different kinds of foods. All are usually acceptable but avoid using any which have sharp edges or small holes that could trap a claw, foot, or head. One of the simplest and most successful ways of offering a highly nutritious food is to pour liquid fat into half a coconut shell; once solidified, it can be inverted and suspended from a branch or the feeding stand itself. The smaller more agile birds like tits can gain access to this feeder while the larger, more omnivorous species

such as starlings, gulls, and doves are precluded.

Apart from cats some robust birds like the omnivores mentioned above and some rodents and mustelids can be troublesome if they take over the facilities intended for smaller birds. Each situation varies so keen observation and a considerable amount of resourcefulness are required to make coexistence possible.

BIRDHOUSES

As with feeders, there are many different sorts of birdhouses or nesting boxes; the most useful are illustrated. Of crucial importance is the diameter of the entrance hole; if it is too small nothing will be able to get in, a centimeter too large and everything will. Since bird varieties and sizes vary from district to district, it is generally advisable to start with a hole of about 8cm. (1in.) in diameter. If larger birds or sparrows seem to be taking

over, reduce the size of the hole by simply tacking a strip of wood across the bottom.

Another type of birdhouse is the open front sort used by many flycatchers. Regardless of the type, position or height, all birdhouses should face away from direct sunshine and prevailing winds and preferably have some shelter from torrential rain.

Once erected and in use, they should be cleaned out each autumn but not taken down since many small birds will roost in them in severe weather. Thick trees, hedges, and ivy-clad stone walls provide the other essential nesting grounds and the roosting sites that birds need every night. If trees are sparse, a tall song post or two will attract some males in the spring (and therefore possibly a family).

In conclusion, the best way to encourage wild birds to stay and breed in your yard is to provide peace, safety, and a wilderness area which will, incidentally, engender its own supply of wild rearing food. We must try to live with nature, not dominate it.

311

The Healthy & Sick Pet
YOUR PET'S BODY & SENSES

The aim of this chapter is to describe in simple terms how the animal body works. To this end it will also serve as an introduction to the following chapters—**Care of the Sick and Injured Pet; Dictionary of Ailments**—because a knowledge of how the healthy body functions is essential for understanding the symptoms of illness.

General Characteristics of the Body

The body of any large animal is made up of millions of cells. When living tissue is examined under a powerful microscope, the units which contribute to its structure appear almost like bricks in a wall. However, cells differ from simple building blocks in many respects, the most important of which is that each is alive and performs some function. Cells need oxygen and nutrients to function which, as we will see later, are supplied by the blood and lymph. Although the duty performed by each cell is minute in itself the result is significant when all the myriad cells of that tissue act in unison. Each muscle cell, for instance, has the capacity to contract due to tiny fibers *(myofibrils)* within its structure and the simultaneous contraction of a great many cells produces the muscle power which lifts a horse over a gate or sends a greyhound hurtling around a race track.

All cells have in common the general processes required to sustain the life of each cell, but the appearance and function of cells differ markedly from one tissue to another. For instance the cells in the liver produce bile and those in the pancreas insulin—together with other substances. Such cells are of importance to the body because of the enzymes and hormones they produce. However, in some cells it is the structure of the cell that is of primary importance and here one thinks of the bone cells which become calcified and contribute to the formation of the skeleton.

Cells can be thought of as having senses because they respond to stimuli. For instance their function can be regulated by body temperature and hormonal and nerve stimuli. The cells of the sense organs also respond

to external stimuli such as light, sound, and smell. Such stimuli are converted into impulses by the sense organs, and these impulses are transmitted to the brain by the nerves. The brain then coordinates the response to these external stimuli.

The brain is comprised of highly specialized cells which directly or indirectly control all the others in the body. If the brain is

damaged, the rest of the body is able to live (provided it is supplied with oxygen and nutrients) but it does so in a completely uncoordinated fashion. Muscles can be made to contract by stimulating them individually, but the unconscious animal cannot be made to stand because this action requires coordination of several muscle groups as well as the cooperation of the balancing organ in the

The responsibility for the general care of pet animals lies with their owners, but when pets become ill the services of a trained veterinarian are often essential. Indeed, it may be illegal for anyone other then a veterinarian to administer certain treatments. A responsible owner will acquaint himself with the local veterinarian before treatment is needed.

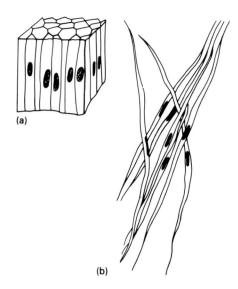

(a)

(b)

All cells perform the same basic functions necessary to their own "life," but their forms vary from tissue to tissue. Shown here are (a) from the lining of the small intestine, the brick-like columnar cells which secrete the enzymes necessary for digestion and (b) from the stomach wall, elongated, isolated muscle cells which in the muscle tissue collectively bring about involuntary contractions of the stomach.

middle ear. This coordination is brought about via the brain.

Nerves are the main communication system in the body, and they carry impulses almost instantaneously between the brain and outlying parts of the body. Each nerve fiber conveys messages in one direction only. The *efferent* fibers carry impulses from the brain to the tissues, and the *afferent* fibers carry them in the opposite direction. Many nerve bundles, however, carry information in both directions, and when severed the animal loses the capacity both to feel and

Cross-section of the exoskeleton of an insect showing its layers: (1) Bristle. (2) Epicuticle. (3) Exocuticle. (4) Endocuticle. (5) Epidermis. (6) Basement membrane. (7) Gland. (8) Socket-forming cell. (9) Bristle-forming cell.

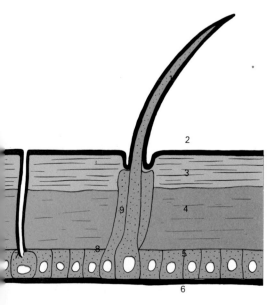

move the area supplied. Such nerve bundles contain both afferent and efferent fibers.

The blood and lymph are the body's most important transport systems. They carry oxygen from the lungs, gills or skin and nutrients from the intestine to the tissues. Utilization of these nutrients provides the animal with its bodybuilding protein and energy. Nutrients that are not used immediately are stored in the form of sugars and fats which can be converted to energy later. The blood also carries other substances such as waste products to the organs of excretion and hormones which control the long term function of the different parts of the body. These will be discussed later.

The Animal Kingdom

The animal kingdom is divided into many groups and subgroups, only some of which are of interest to the pet owner. At the broadest level it is divided into *vertebrates* and *invertebrates*, that is, those with and without a backbone. All mammals, birds, fish, amphibians, and reptiles are vertebrates while insects and spiders are invertebrates.

Mammals suckle their young and, in most, reproduction is by live birth. Two interesting exceptions are the Duckbilled Platypus and Spiney Anteater. Both these Australian species, which belong to the group known as the monotremes, lay eggs. To a greater or lesser extent mammals have bodies that are covered by fur which helps them maintain their body temperature.

Mammals are warm-blooded (*homoiothermic*) which means they are able to keep their body temperature constant to within a few degrees. However, in cold periods some mammals still have to hibernate or go into torpor, as do hedgehogs, marmots, squirrels, bats, bears, and some badgers, and in these the body temperature drops precipitously during the winter. In this state little energy is required so little or no food is eaten, and the heartbeat and other bodily functions slow down.

Birds are warm-blooded and have bodies covered with feathers. Most can fly and even those which cannot (such as ostriches and penguins) have forelimbs modified into wing-like appendages. Characteristic features of birds are the lightness of their bones relative to the weight of their bodies, the absence of teeth and the presence of a beak, which varies greatly in form depending on the feeding habits of each species. The pelican's beak, for instance, is adapted for shoveling in fish, that of the parrot for opening seeds, and that of the hummingbird for taking nectar delicately from a flower.

Reptiles are mostly land-dwelling and cold-blooded (*poikilothermic*) animals so that their body temperature fluctuates with that of their surroundings. Most have scales and many hibernate in cold weather. Members of this group, which includes snakes, lizards, and turtles, either give birth to live young or

lay eggs with leathery shells. All reptiles breathe through lungs although some also have the capacity to take in oxygen through their skin.

Amphibians are also cold-blooded. Their life cycle includes an aquatic larval stage during which time they obtain oxygen via the gills. Later they undergo a change in form (metamorphosis) from aquatic larva to basically land-living adults which breathe mainly through lungs, but also through the skin. In some (as in the Axolotl) the aquatic larval stage can persist for the whole life span. Typical examples of amphibians are frogs, salamanders, and caecilians (earthworm-like creatures).

Fish are cold-blooded, live in fresh and saltwater, and have upright tail fins. Their bodies are covered with scales. All have gills although some need to gulp oxygen from the atmosphere and will drown if they do not have access to the surface of the water. Fish can be either egg layers or live-bearers.

Insects are removed in structure from the previous groups. These primitive animals have an external skeleton of armored plates; air is taken in through openings in the body wall; nervous, circulatory and digestive systems are simple in form; they lay eggs; and, in most cases, the young undergo metamorphosis. Insects have six legs and usually wings. Examples include butterflies, moths, ants, locusts, and bees.

Arachnids, such as spiders, are similar in some respects to insects but differ in that they have eight legs and no wings.

The Skeleton, Muscles, and Movement

TYPES OF SKELETON

The skeleton has a number of functions. It acts as a framework which supports the organs of the body, prevents the organs from damaging each other, and maintains the shape of the body. It protects the most delicate organs encasing them either in a solid structure, for example the skull enclosing the brain, or in a rigid framework of bones, for example the rib cage protecting the lungs and heart. The bones of a skeleton with their associated muscles are vitally important in bringing about movement and locomotion.

Broadly speaking there are two types of skeleton found in the animal world—exoskeletons and endoskeletons. Insects and spiders have an exoskeleton which comprises a system of external plates of a hard substance known as sclerotin. This skeleton, or cuticle as it is sometimes known, forms a complete external covering to the body. To allow movement the plates are joined by flexible chitin membranes, and the muscles are attached to the inner surface of the skeleton.

Endoskeletons comprise a system of bony structures inside the body which are surrounded by the soft tissues; the whole body surface has a complete external covering of

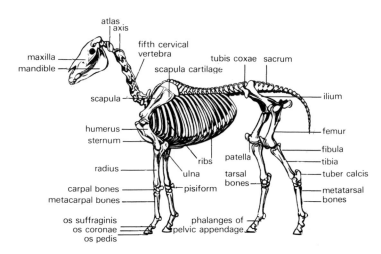

Skeleton of the horse.

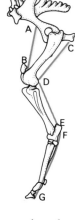

The schematic diagram of the hind limb of a horse shows the importance of the site of insertion of the muscles in controlling the limb. For instance, contraction of AB draws the limb forward and that of CD draws it backward; contraction of DE pushes the animal forward by straightening the lower limb, while contraction of FG flexes the toe.

skin. Muscles are attached to the external surfaces of the bones. Endoskeletons are found in vertebrates, that is reptiles, amphibians, fish, birds, and mammals.

STRUCTURE OF BONES

The bones which make up an endoskeleton are composed largely of calcium salts. They are hinged together at joints which are held together by tough fibrous bands—the ligaments. Many of the joints are enclosed in leathery sacs, the joint capsules which contain an oily lubricating fluid, the synovia. In order to minimize jarring, the ends of the bones are covered with a layer of cartilage and, in the case of some joints, a pad of cartilage is interposed between the two surfaces. In the case of the knee these cartilages are called *menisci* and in the spine the *discs*. In

Bone and joint structure. (a) Dog's femur during growth. (b) Cross section of metacarpal bone of horse showing the fine structure. (c) Section of knee joint showing meniscus (cartilage). (d) Lumbar vertebra showing disc (cartilage).

some fish, such as sharks, the skeleton is made entirely of cartilage tissue.

The flat bones of the head are generally made up of flat sheets of bone. Each is comprised of a double layer of dense *compact* bone, and the intervening space is filled with a mass of finer reinforcing plates running in various directions (spongy or cancellous bone). This makes for a strong arrangement, suited to protecting the most sensitive organ, the brain.

The long bones, such as in the limbs, consist of cylinders of compact bone and a central space filled with marrow. At the ends of the bone the central cavity is filled with cancellous bone. The outer surface of all bones is covered with a fine membrane, the periosteum, which has a good supply of nerves and blood vessels and is sensitive to pain. At each end of the long bone where the shaft (*diaphysis*) joins the enlarged ends (*epiphysis*) there is an area known as the growth plate (*metaphysis*). In young animals this is formed of cartilage and it is in this area that the bone cells multiply to produce growth in length of the

bones. At puberty multiplication of the cells slows down, and the growth plates start to calcify. Once the epiphyses and diaphyses have fused no further growth in length can occur.

Contrary to what one might expect from its appearance, bone is built of living tissue as is the rest of the body. The bone cells are encased in a rigid calcified matrix, but this is penetrated by a network of vessels which bring nutrients to the cells. When compact bone is cut transversely and examined microscopically its structure becomes evident. Blood vessels run down the length of the bones in fine canals (*Haversian canals*), and these are surrounded by concentric layers of bone cells (*osteoblasts*), each in a pocket of bone (the *lacunae*). Smaller canals (*canaliculi*) run in a radial fashion to connect the lacunae to one another and to the Haversian canals.

When bones are fractured, healing is a complex process. The space between the broken ends is first filled with clotted blood which is later replaced by cartilagenous tissue. Finally osteoblasts grow into the cartilage, reform their concentric patterns around the blood vessels, and the new bone becomes calcified. Calcification, however, is dependent on the bones being immobilized and, if there is any movement between the fractured ends, an unstable cartilagenous union results.

LOCOMOTION IN VERTEBRATES

Movement and locomotion of limbs, organs, and the complete body is brought about by a coordinated interaction between the expansion and relaxation of muscles and the consequent reaction on the bones of the skeleton. Stimulated muscles become short and tense, and upon relaxation they return to their original length. It is easy to see how such contractions move the limbs in one direction, but how the movements of limbs are coordinated, for instance in kicking, is more difficult to understand. Here a closer look at the anatomical structure is required. In a limb there are twenty or more separate muscles, each attached at their ends to different bones and at different positions on these bones. Each muscle contraction achieves a specific movement by virtue of the position of its

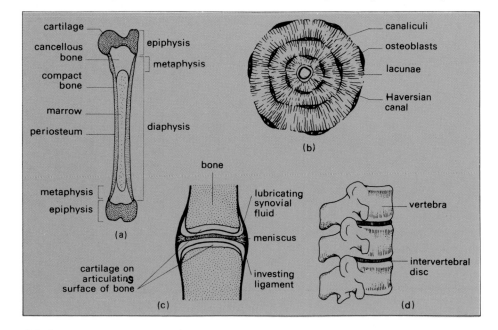

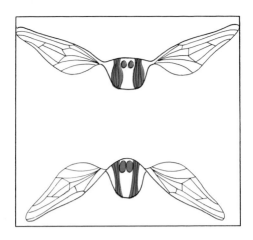

Wing movement in insects works upon a principle quite different from that operating in birds' wings. The muscles are not attached to the wings but to the body wall. When the vertical muscles contract, the upper part of the exoskeleton (tergum) flattens and the wings snap upwards; when the longitudinal muscles contract, the tergum arches and the wings snap downwards.

attachments. The accompanying figure demonstrates how a hind limb can be precisely controlled by the contraction of certain muscles and the relaxation of others. Each muscle is supplied by a nerve, and most muscle contractions and extensions are consciously controlled from the brain by these nerves. Balance, however, is maintained automatically by a stream of stimuli passing down the nerves which tense the flexors and extensors simultaneously and produce rigidity of the limbs.

In addition to the *voluntary muscles* (those consciously controlled from the brain via nerve impulses) there are muscles which contract and relax without conscious control. Some, such as the heart muscle (*myocard*) and muscles of the intestinal wall, contract rhythmically of their own accord. Others, such as the muscles of the blood vessels, may contract and dilate as a result of biochemical effects. The hormone adrenalin, for instance, which is released in the body in emergency situations produces dilation of the blood vessels in the muscles where blood is most needed. Although the heartbeat throbs of its own accord, it can also be influenced by nerve impulses and biochemical influences; hence the beat quickens as a result of fright or excitement.

LOCOMOTION IN INSECTS

In animals with exoskeletons (e.g., insects), the methods of locomotion differ although a coordinated system of muscles and skeleton is still of primary importance. Most frequently, legs are used to propel the insect on land or in water and the legs are moved by the pull of muscles attached to the inside of the rigid cuticular skeleton. Where the rigid skeleton is not present, as in the soft bodied larvae and caterpillars, the muscles act against a hydrostatic skeleton provided by the pressure of the body fluids (hemolymph) to produce crawling movements.

FLIGHT

Flight is a highly specialized form of locomotion, and only birds, insects, and bats have achieved true mastery of the air. In simple terms the wings of birds are highly modified forelimbs. In general, the forelimb of a bird has changed from a flexible limb moving mainly forward and backward to a structure which moves mainly up and down. The whole body of a bird is geared to achieving flight. Flight requires a great deal of energy so the heart is large, the lungs are efficient, and the body temperature is high for rapid "fuel" usage. To save weight, the bones are strong but light, the teeth have been lost, the head is reduced in size (compared to mammals), and the reproductive organs almost disappear outside the breeding season. The flight muscles need a strong anchor for resistance. This is provided by the large breastbone, or sternum, which has a keel to increase the surface area for muscle attachment.

For powered flight two forces are generated by a bird's flapping wings: lift keeps the bird in the air and thrust propels it forward. The two forces are complex and vary among species. For a strong flier, such as a pigeon or duck, in straight and level flight, the wing can be considered as two units. The inner part, bearing the secondary flight feathers, moves in a mainly vertical plane and generates most of the lift. On the downstroke the broad surface of the inner wing forces air down and pushes the bird up. It also acts as an aerofoil on both up and down strokes, lift being generated as the air flows over its surface. The outer wing with the primary flight feathers provides most of the thrust to push the bird forwards.

The principles of flight in insects are much the same as in birds although there are clearly several structural differences. Most insects have two pairs of membranous wings. In some insects (e.g., beetles), the forewings are modified to form protective wing covers. Although most insects have two pairs of wings, these pairs do not act independently in flight. By various means (overlapping edges, bristles, hooks,) the fore and hind wings are linked so that effectively a "two-winged" condition is achieved. Another difference is that the muscles that bring about wing movement are not directly attached to the wings themselves but are attached to the exoskeleton of the thorax. By contracting they modify the shape of the wingbearing thorax segments, and this in turn produces vibration of the wings.

SWIMMING

Locomotion in fish presents a unique problem since water is about 800 times as dense as air. Typically fish are streamlined to a tapering cigar shape. Their movement through the water is achieved by fin vibrations and undulations running the length of the body. These undulations result from the action of muscles on the vertebrae of the backbone. The tail or caudal fin plays an important role in forward propulsion. The vertical fins—the one or more dorsal and anal fins—serve to stabilize the body against rolling, reduce water turbulence, and play a part in guiding the fish. The paired pectoral and pelvic fins control the pitch of the fish enabling it to swim up or down. The pectorals can also be used in turning and braking. Although the drive force of most fish comes from undulations of the body culminating in lateral sweeps of the tail and tail fin, the other fins may also be used in propulsion, particularly in the slower moving fish.

Fish are denser than water and unless they keep moving they will sink. For sharks and their allies there is no alternative—if they stop swimming they drop to the bottom. But the bony fish possesses a long air-filled bladder (*swim bladder*) running below the spinal column. The swim bladder gives fish buoyancy so that they do not sink when they stop swimming.

Teeth

Teeth occur in all vertebrate groups except birds. The simplest forms are found in fish and the most complicated in mammals. Many shapes and forms of teeth adapt to the specialized diets and feeding habits of the various animal species.

Where teeth serve only one purpose, as with fish where they serve to hold the prey, no variation occurs within each individual. However, in mammals there are four specialized forms of teeth. In these animals teeth can be categorized according to their shape and position: *incisors* (front cutting teeth), *canines* (fangs or eyeteeth), *premolars* (those behind the fangs) and *molars* (grinding cheek teeth). The number of each kind varies from one species to another. It is customary to indicate the dental arrangement in a *dental formula*. For instance $\frac{3123}{3123}$ indicates that the species has three incisors, one canine, two premolars, and three molars on each side of the upper and lower jaws.

Mammals produce two sets of teeth. The milk, or deciduous, teeth break through during infancy, and these are replaced by the permanent teeth during adolescence. In the dog and cat this replacement occurs at about five to seven months of age.

Many herbivores and all rodents lack canines and have a gap (*diastema*) between the incisors and cheek teeth. Some cloven-footed animals (sheep and goats for instance) also lack upper incisors and instead have a hard pad of gum (*dental pad*) which serves as a chopping block for the lower incisors. (See **Feeding your Pet** for diagrams of different mammalian dentition.)

Another important specialization in herbivores is the continual growth of the teeth from their bases. In rodents that are prevented from gnawing, the teeth will continue to grow in length until they curve backward

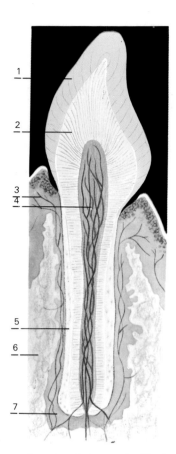

Cross-section of an incisor tooth. (1) Enamel. (2) Dentine. (3) Gum. (4) Pulp. (5) Cement. (6) Socket. (7) Root.

into the mouth which may lead to starvation. The lower incisors of the cavie (Guinea Pig) are reported to grow about 26cm. (10in.) a year! All pet rodents should therefore be provided with some material for gnawing in order to maintain their dental health.

The teeth of venomous snakes have a groove or central canal which carries poison from glands situated at their roots. These teeth are often able to fold back when not in

A horse's teeth grow out continously from the gum and wear down from the crown. An estimate can be made of the animal's age from an examination of its teeth. This is fairly accurate in the first six or seven years of life and sometimes after that time. The accompanying diagrams show the appearance of the horse's teeth at various ages from two and one-half to thirty years of age. The deciduous teeth, which are all present at two years, can be recognized by their shape (they have constricted bases) and by the heavy grooves on their front surface. At two and one-half years the central milk teeth are shed and replaced by permanents. These come into wear at three years. At three and one-half years the teeth second from the center (the laterals) are shed and replaced by permanents and these in turn come into wear at four years. At four and one-half years the incisors third from the center (the corner teeth) are replaced so that by five years all the incisors are permanent and in wear. At six years all the incisors show signs of wear and at seven years the corners develop a "hook" (a), that is a protruding point at their outer chewing surface. In horses older than this, the age can be estimated from the appearance of the chewing surface, the shape of the teeth and their angle. At about ten years a groove (Galvayne's Groove) appears in the corner teeth and progressively works its way down the teeth during the next twenty years. With increased age the teeth progressively jut forwards.

use. The teeth of certain lizards (e.g., the Cainian) are peg-like and suitable for cracking the shells of snails, which form the main item of their diet. Some fish, like the South American Piranha, have a formidable set of teeth which can inflict a painful wound on a human finger.

On the other hand when teeth are unused they tend to degenerate, as do the other tissues of the body, and in the case of Butterfly Fish (Chaetodontidae) the teeth are scarcely more than bristles.

Some animals have structures which, although not teeth in the strictest sense, serve to cut, grind, or break the food. The snapping turtle has no teeth, but it has a sharp horny rim around the mouth suited to biting. The egg-eating snake (*Dasypeltis*) has projections which protrude from the lower surface of the neck vertebrae onto the esophagus. Eggs, which are swallowed whole, are broken against these projections so the contents can be swallowed and the shells regurgitated.

STRUCTURE OF TEETH

The teeth of mammals have a quite complex structure. They are covered with a thin layer of *enamel* which is made of calcium salts and is the hardest substance in the body. Beneath this is the dentine which contains tiny canals (*dentinal tubules*). A fiber in each tubule transmits pain and makes the tooth sensitive. Finally there is a *pulp cavity* in the center of

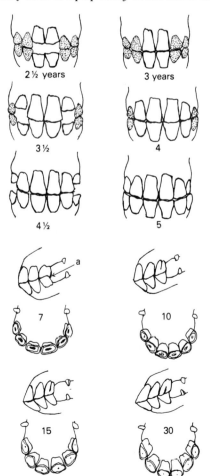

each tooth which contains blood vessels and nerves. Enamel is only present on the external faces of the teeth but is represented by the cement in the rooting portion.

CARE OF THE TEETH

The teeth of dogs and cats over seven years old should be inspected periodically to check on the buildup of tartar. If neglected this produces gum inflammation (*gingivitis*) and loose teeth. Tartar builds up at different rates in individual animals, but the teeth of dogs and cats commonly need scaling when they are nine years or older. This should be done by a veterinarian and usually requires some form of sedation.

Older horses may need to have their cheek teeth rasped periodically because uneven wear produces jagged surfaces and inefficient mastication.

SKIN AND EPIDERMIS

The epidermis is the outer layer of the body of animals. In some aquatic invertebrates it consists of no more than a single layer of cells (*epithelium*), but in all vertebrates it is many layered (*stratified epithelium*). This is either periodically molted, as in reptiles, or continually lost at its surface and replaced by cell division at its base, as in mammals. In vertebrates the epidermis itself rests upon a bed of connective tissue (*dermis*), the two together forming the skin.

The epidermis performs a number of important protective functions. In land vertebrates, for example, it controls loss of water by evaporation and also prevents the penetration of harmful ultraviolet radiation. Derivatives of the epidermis, such as feathers and hairs, are important as insulating materials to prevent heat loss. Epidermal glands of various kinds may be concerned with such functions as mucus production (fish and amphibians), poison manufacture (some amphibians), temperature regulation (in mammals), or the production of chemical substances which act as markers of territory or sex attractants. In some amphibians oxygen is absorbed through the skin and carbon dioxide released.

In the mammalian superficial epidermis, cell division is largely confined to the basal layer of cells—the *stratum germinativum*. As the cells get pushed outward they build up within them an insoluble fibrous protein called *keratin*. As the cells move outward they form successively the *stratum granulosum* (or *granular layer*) and the *stratum corneum*. Ultimately, in the top layer the cells have no nuclei and contain only dead keratin.

The hair follicles may be regarded as tubular inserts of epidermis. The hair—a tough cylinder of keratin—is formed by division of cells at the base of the follicle in a region known as the matrix. Follicles do not produce hair continuously. Hairs are periodically shed and replaced by new ones, either in a pattern as in animal molting, or in a continuous process as in the human scalp, which loses fifty to one hundred hairs a day. Molting of mammals, like reproduction, is controlled through the hormonal system by seasonal changes in the environment. Attached to each hair follicle is a sebaceous gland, which secretes the waxy sebum. The activity of sebaceous glands is under control of hormones. Primates including humans also possess sweat glands which are separate from the hair follicle; they function to help control body temperature by evaporation.

The Digestive (Alimentary) System

Most raw materials for energy and body building requirements are taken in by eating and drinking. In all but infant animals food materials can only be absorbed through the intestinal wall after they have been broken down into simple chemical substances. This breakdown process, known as digestion, is achieved by the action of digestive juices (enzymes) and, in some cases, by the fermentation of food in the gut by bacteria.

Digestive enzymes may be produced by glands in the stomach and intestinal wall or by more distant glands (salivary glands, pancreas, liver). In the latter cases the enzymes reach the alimentary tract by means of ducts. After digestion the nutrients are absorbed and transported by the blood to the liver

A cross-section of mammalian skin shows the important anatomical features. The outer layer of the epidermis is composed of two layers, the stratum corneum (1) and the stratum granulosum or pigmented layer (2). Below this is the dermis (3) and the subcuticle layer (4). Organs contained within these layers are blood vessels (5), nerves (6), sense organs (7), hairs (8), sebaceous or oil glands (9), hair muscles (10), and sweat glands (11) that open onto the surface through pores (12).

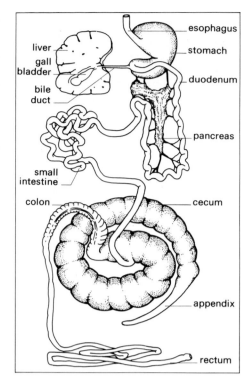

The diagram of the digestive system of the rabbit shows the main regions of the alimentary canal and associated organs.

where they are processed and sometimes stored. Eventually they are carried to the part where they are needed and either incorporated into the body as protein, carbohydrates, or fats or broken down further to provide energy for the body processes.

Let us follow the passage of food down the digestive tract of a carnivorous animal. Meat is torn from the bones by the canine teeth and chewed. This mastication serves mainly to impregnate the food with saliva, and in most animals the food is swallowed in lumps. The

saliva not only lubricates its passage down the gullet (esophagus) but also contains the enzyme *ptyalin* which converts starch into soluble sugars.

The food passes into the stomach where it is mixed with hydrochloric acid and the enzymes pepsin, rennin, and lipase, each of which has a specific function. Pepsin, for instance, breaks proteins down to peptones, that is, groups of amino acids. Amino acids, the basic constituents of proteins, can be absorbed through the intestinal wall whereas peptones cannot. Consequently the peptones formed in the stomach require further digestion in the intestine. Hydrochloric acid also breaks down proteins while rennin and lipase act on milk and fats, respectively.

After four to six hours in the stomach the food passes through the pyloris (constriction at the lower end of the stomach) into the duodenum, which is the first part of the intestine. Enzymes in this part of the gut come from three sources.

First the intestinal wall secretes *peptidase* and *enterokinase* (which act on proteins), *maltase, sucrase,* and *lactase* (which act on sugars) and *lipase* and *amylase* (which act on fats and starches, respectively).

Second the bile duct brings *bile salts* from the liver. These render the fats soluble and facilitate their absorption. Bile also contains waste products from the liver (*bilirubin* and *cholesterol*) which are to be excreted in the feces.

Third the pancreatic duct brings *trypsin, pancreatic lipase,* and *amylase* into the intestine and these enzymes act on proteins, fats, and starches, respectively.

At this stage the intestinal content is watery. As the food traverses the rest of the small and large intestine (*colon* and *rectum*) much of the fluid containing nutrients in digested form is absorbed. Eventually the undigested waste which remains is excreted as the feces.

The food is moved along as a result of continuous wave-like contractions (*peristalsis*) in the muscles of the gut wall. If for any reason (inflammation or irritation) the peristaltic rate is increased, inadequate resorption of the fluid occurs and diarrhea results.

The processes described above are modified in herbivorous animals. The carbohydrate cellulose is one of the chief constituents of the plants these animals eat but they do not produce digestive enzymes that are capable of breaking this substance down into absorbable units. Instead, herbivores have a number of compartments along the digestive tract where the materials containing cellulose are fermented by bacteria. The bacteria, now containing the break down products of cellulose, are then digested as they pass farther down the intestinal tract. Thus bacteria are not always causes of disease, and they are in fact, absolutely essential to the health of herbivores. Fermentation occurs in the fore-stomachs (the *rumen, reticulum,* and *omasum*) in sheep, goats, cattle, and deer while in horses it occurs mainly in the cecum.

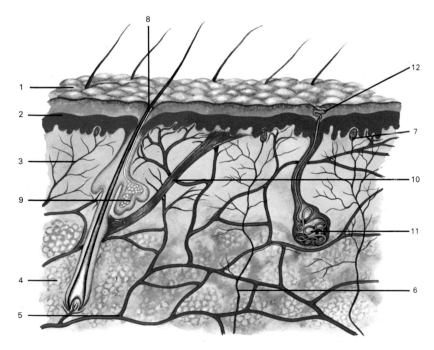

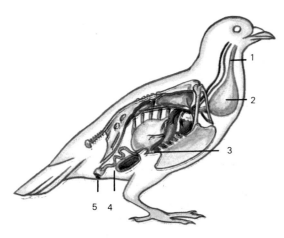

Digestive system of a bird viewed from the side: From the mouth the digestive system starts with the esophagus (1) which leads to the crop (2) and then into the stomach (3) that comprises two chambers—the proventriculus and gizzard. The intestine (4) runs to the cloaca (5) which serves as the point of exit for the waste products.

In birds the reservoir (the *crop*) where fermentation occurs is a dilatation of the esophagus situated at the chest entrance. The digestive tract of birds differs further from that of mammals in that the stomach is divided into muscular and glandular chambers—the *proventriculus* and *gizzard*, respectively. The gizzard generally contains a few pebbles which serve to grind the food to a pulp before it passes on to the true stomach for further digestion. Birds also have a double cecum, the function of which is not satisfactorily explained and a cloaca which is a common opening for both the digestive and urogenital canals.

Fish may be herbivorous or carnivorous and have a diversity of digestive mechanisms equivalent to their terrestrial counterparts. Some have a muscular gizzard-like stomach containing sharp sand particles for grinding vegetable material. Most have long coiled intestines where bacterial fermentation takes place. Many marine animals feed on plankton, the minute animals which grow like scum on the surface of the sea. These animals filter the plankton out of the water by means of specially adapted "gill rakers" at the side of their mouths, which act as a sieve. Although the plankton are individually minute they grow in such profusion as to appease the appetite of some whales and of the mighty basking shark which grows to 30ft. (9m.) in length.

The gut of insects is similar in many respects to that of other animals. It is divided into three regions, the foregut, midgut, and hindgut. The foregut is lined with cuticle which prevents secretion of enzymes and absorption of food. The foregut is therefore more a storage area and may be much enlarged for this purpose. Some digestion may occur here due to the enzymes added to food with the saliva or regurgitated from the midgut behind. Many insects digest their food outside the body by disgorging some of the gut contents containing the enzymes and

then sucking up the digested fluids. This technique is used by houseflies, plant bugs, and the larvae of aquatic *Dytiscus* beetles. The midgut, in which most of the digestion and absorption occurs, does not have a cuticuler lining. The hindgut is again lined with a cuticle, but it is thinner and more permeable than in the foregut so that some absorption, particularly of water, can occur. An equivalent to the bacterial fermentation of herbivores is found in wood eating termites where protozoan flagellates in the gut digest the cellulose in the diet.

DIET

Because food is broken down into basic elements before absorption it is not possible to say that one diet is any more healthy than another. However, any animal must have a varied diet which contains the whole range of its requirements. Some essential substances occur only in some foods, and it is especially important that the diet contain these foods. An animal receiving an adequate diet would not become any more healthy by eating an overabundance of any one item but the absence of certain foods can cause ill health. Take care not to feed pets too much because obesity can also cause severe health problems. (See **Feeding Your Pet.**)

Structure of mammalian lungs. The trachea or windpipe (1) divides into two bronchi (2), one to each lung. These branch repeatedly into bronchioles (3) each ending in a blind sac or alveolus (4) where capillary arteries (5) and veins (7) meet in a network (6). At this point oxygen is taken from the inspired air, and carbon dioxide is passed into the bronchioles to be expelled to the outside. The inset shows a detail of the capillary network.

Respiration

The term *respiration* is used to describe two biologically related systems. At the cellular level all living cells respire—whether they are unicellular plants or animals, or just one of the millions that make up a multicellular plant or animal. This respiration is the chemical process by which oxygen and sugars are burned in the cells to create the energy that is needed by all the body processes. Another result of this life giving process is the creation of carbon dioxide as a waste product. In higher animals the term *respiration* is used to describe the processes by which oxygen enters the body and carbon dioxide is removed; it is thus synonymous with "breathing." In this section we are concerned with this latter meaning.

Respiration (breathing) is thus the process of exchanging oxygen for carbon dioxide. It occurs in two parts. Oxygen is first absorbed from the air through the lungs, or in the case of most fish, from the water via the gills. The dissolved oxygen is transported by the blood to the tissues where the oxygen is released to individual cells and carbon dioxide is picked up. This carbon dioxide is then transported back to the lungs or gills where it is released.

The respiratory system as it occurs in most terrestrial vertebrates is comprised of the nasal passages, trachea, bronchi, and lungs. The lungs are composed of elastic tissue and lie in the oracic cavity bounded by the ribs and diaphragm. The diaphragm is a dome-shaped sheet of muscle stretching across the lower end of the rib cage. It divides the trunk into thoracic and abdominal sections.

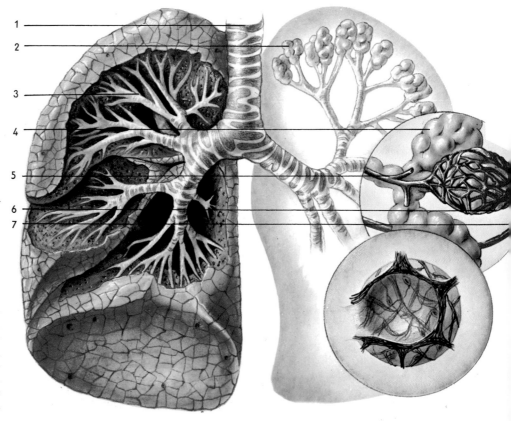

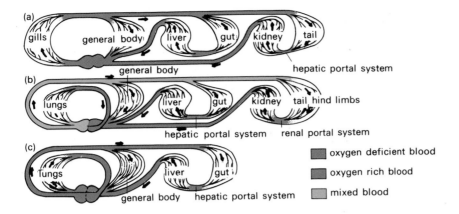

(a)
gills general body liver gut kidney tail
general body
hepatic portal system

(b)
lungs liver gut kidney tail hind limbs
hepatic portal system renal portal system

(c)
lungs liver gut
general body hepatic portal system

oxygen deficient blood
oxygen rich blood
mixed blood

These diagrams illustrate the blood circulatory systems in (a) a fish, (b) a terrestrial amphibian or reptile, and (c) a mammal or bird. In fish the heart has just two chambers, the auricle and ventricle, whereas in reptiles and amphibians the auricle is divided into two chambers. In amphibians there is only one ventricle so that oxygen-rich and oxygen-deficient blood mix together. In reptiles the ventricle is partially divided into two in an attempt to keep the two types of blood separate. In mammals and birds there are two separate ventricles.

At inspiration the ribs are raised and the diaphragm straightened. This serves to enlarge the thorax and, consequently, the lungs expand to fill the chest cavity. The result is that air rushes in at the nose, travels down the trachea, and eventually fills the millions of small sacs (*alveoli*) which make up the lung tissue. The walls of the alveoli are well supplied with small blood vessels (capillaries), and here the blood gives up its carbon dioxide and absorbs oxygen from the air.

Expiration follows next. The muscles of the rib cage and diaphragm relax, and the chest cavity becomes smaller. The lungs return to their original size and the contents, now heavily laden with carbon dioxide, are expelled into the atmosphere.

The gills of fish are paired narrow openings, usually five in number, between the mouth cavity and the outside of the body. The openings are covered by a gill plate which enables the gills to be opened and closed. The gill slits themselves are lined with folds of tissue (gill filaments) well supplied with capillaries. Respiration is accomplished by the fish taking one mouthful of water after another and pumping it through the gill slits. As the water flows over the filaments, dissolved oxygen is absorbed and replaced by waste carbon dioxide. So although different in detail, the fundamental principles of respiration are the same for aquatic and terrestrial animals.

In some fish (tunas, some sharks, and mackerel) there is no pumping action but the water flows continuously into the mouth and out of the gills by virtue of the fish swimming forward. These fish have to keep moving in order to remain alive. Some fish also need to breathe air from the atmosphere and if prevented from doing so (perhaps by a film of oil on the surface) they suffocate.

The process of respiration described for mammals is basically the same in reptiles and amphibians, but it is not particularly efficient in either of these groups. In birds, on the other hand, the lungs are extended to form a series of eleven interlinking air sacs in the abdomen, thorax, and long bones, and the air is led from one to the other on a continuous circular route before it passes back to the lungs proper to be expelled. This greatly increases the efficiency of gaseous exchange and also reduces the body weight. As we have already seen, flight consumes a great deal of energy for which a high level of oxygen in the blood is required.

Transport of oxygen to the tissue is accomplished in vertebrates by hemoglobin, the substance which imparts the red coloration to blood. (See also Blood below.) This substance forms a loose link with oxygen and consequently combines with it when the oxygen concentration is high (in the lungs) and releases it when the oxygen concentration is low (in the tissues). In many amphibians oxygen also enters the blood through the highly vascularized skin, which must be wet for the oxygen to dissolve. The quantity of oxygen absorbed in this way is low and, although it is enough to sustain life, it is not sufficient to allow much activity. Some amphibians remain aquatic all their lives and retain their gills, although gills only occur in the larval stages for most amphibians.

Insects are not dependent on the blood for carrying oxygen to the tissues. Instead they have a branching system of air tubules (trachea) which carry air directly to the cells which need them. The respiratory system may occupy half the body volume, and each tubule ends in an air sac where the interchange of gases between the atmosphere and tissues takes place. There is one pair of air openings (spiracles) per segment, each covered by a flap which opens and closes as the insect breathes. Air enters the system either by diffusion or by expansion and contraction of the segments.

Blood

The main functions of the blood are to transport oxygen and carbon dioxide to and from the lungs, to carry nutrients to the tissues and waste products to the organs of excretion, to transport hormones to the cells whose function they regulate to combat disease by conveying white blood cells and antibodies, and to control the body temperature in warm-blooded animals.

CIRCULATION

Blood is the body's most important transportation system. The blood runs in a network of arteries, veins and capillaries and is kept flowing by the pumping action of the heart, an oval muscular organ which contracts rhythmically. A series of valves in the heart and veins ensure that the blood flows in one direction only. The blood transports red and white cells to the parts where they are needed and also many dissolved substances which include nutrients, hormones and antibodies (proteins which combat infection).

In terrestrial animals the blood flows in two loops. First, it flows to the lungs where it loses carbon dioxide and picks up oxygen and then goes back to the heart (the *pulmonary circulation*). Then it is pumped to the rest of the body tissues where it loses oxygen and picks up carbon dioxide and again goes back to the heart (the *systemic circulation*).

In mammals the heart has four chambers, two of which (the auricles) receive blood from the pulmonary and systemic circulations and two of which (ventricles) pump the blood out. A system of one-way valves keeps the blood flowing in a figure eight course, first on its loop to the lungs where it loses its carbon dioxide and picks up fresh oxygen and then on its loop around the other tissues where it loses oxygen and picks up waste carbon dioxide.

The pulmonary artery carries blood from the heart to the lungs, and the pulmonary vein brings it back. The aorta is the main artery from the heart in the systemic circulation; it branches again and again until at the extreme reaches of the body the vessels are as fine as hairs when they are known as capillaries. The capillary walls are only one cell thick and here the blood and tissues exchange gases and nutrients.

The capillaries now join and rejoin one another to form the veins which lead the blood back to the heart. This branching into capillaries *generally* takes place only once in any one circuit. For instance, the vessels to the muscles split into capillaries on their way out and join up to form veins on their return. However, the circulation to the digestive tract is exceptional in that the vessels branch into capillaries first in the gut walls where they collect nutrients. They then join up to form veins which lead to the liver where they again branch into capillaries to give up some of their nutrients for processing and storage. This double branching arrangement is known as the *hepatic portal system*.

Amphibians, reptiles, and fish have an extra branching arrangement known as the *renal portal system*. Here the blood vessels break into capillaries twice during their circuit to the hindquarters and kidneys.

Fish have a simple circulatory system. The blood does not return to the heart for re-pumping after it has traversed the gills. It continues on its way to supply the tissues with oxygen before returning to the heart. This obviates the need for a complex four-chamber heart and in fish the heart is a simple S-bend muscular pouch.

COMPOSITION OF BLOOD

Blood appears to be a thick red, sticky fluid which clots on exposure to air. Analysis, however, shows that it is comprised of a clear yellow fluid called plasma containing many millions of red blood cells (*erythrocytes*) which impart the red color. Blood also carries white cells (*leucocytes*) which combat infection and *platelets* which play a role in the clotting mechanisms.

The red cells are profuse and in the horse, dog, and cat number about eight million per cubic milliliter of blood. Each is a disc-shaped sac containing hemoglobin, the red substance mainly responsible for the trans-port of gases.

The white blood cells of which there are several varieties (*neutrophiles, lymphocytes, eosinophiles, basophiles*) protect the body from disease. The neutrophiles, for instance, wrap themselves around invading germs and eli-minate them; this process is known as *pha-gocytosis.* The lymphocytes attack invading germs directly and produce antibodies (see below) while eosinophiles and basophiles probably play a role in allergic conditions. (Increased numbers of eosinophiles are generally found in the vicinity of worm and other parasitic infestations.)

The blood is confined to the blood vessels and does not come into direct contact with the tissue cells. However, a clear fluid, the lymph, which is formed from the blood plas-ma bathes the cells, and it is through this fluid that nutrients are transferred from blood to tissues. After serving this purpose the lymph flows along thin-walled transpa-rent vessels which join together to form the thoracic duct in the chest. This is the main lymphatic vessel, and it enters the circulatory system just before the great veins enter the heart. The lymphatic ducts pass through the lymph nodes on their passage to the heart and in so doing transport lymphocytes from these glands into the general blood circulation.

Clotting is a complex process initiated by substances liberated from damaged blood vessel walls and from the fragile platelets. These substances combine with one of the blood proteins (*fibrinogen*) to form *fibrin*, the jellylike clot material.

Antibodies

It is necessary to understand a little about protein chemistry in order to appreciate the way in which antibodies protect animals from some of the damaging effects of infection. Proteins are complex substances made up of hundreds of thousands of amino acids which are relatively simple molecules present in the body in about twenty forms. The sequence in which the amino acids are linked to form a protein and the resulting branching and fold-ing of the protein are characteristic for each protein. Antibodies are a type of protein (*im-munoglobulin*) which form in the body in re-sponse to some foreign invading proteins and their amino acid sequence of branching and folding duplicates that of the invader. The result is that these "tailor-made" proteins can combine with the invaders and inactivate them efficiently.

Antibody production takes a week or more to develop, and in the case of the more viru-lent disease an animal may die before the antibodies are formed. *Vaccination*, de-veloped by Louis Pasteur in the latter part of the nineteenth century, involves exposing the animal to weak or killed germs (or mod-ified poisons) which stimulate antibody production but do not themselves produce serious illness. If at a future time the animal is exposed to the virulent agent, it already has antibodies fully formed to provide protec-tion. Antibodies subside within a variable time (often six months to one year) so it is necessary to have periodic booster vaccina-tions against the more dangerous illnesses.

BLOOD IN INSECTS

Insects have what is termed an open blood system in which the blood is not confined to vessels but circulates among the organs. The blood is propelled around the body by the heart—the only blood vessel in the body—which is a tube situated above the gut extend-ing through the thorax and abdomen.

The blood, or hemolymph, consists of a fluid plasma in which cells are suspended. It is usually yellowish or greenish and, as in the blood of higher animals, it is also involved in protection of the body against disease.

Excretion

Waste products of the body are excreted in various forms through the lungs and skin, in the feces and urine. The lungs (or gills) get rid of gaseous waste (carbon dioxide mainly) while in vertebrates (especially the horse) urea is excreted through the skin. The feces and urine are more important excretory pro-ducts.

Feces consist mainly of the food residue from the action of the digestive juices, but additional waste substances are also excreted into the bowel. The bile, for instance, con-tains unwanted products formed in the liver, which include cholesterol and bile pigments, the latter derived mainly from the break-down of hemoglobin and myoglobin. The feces also contain other waste substances (in-dole and skatole) which are excreted by the wall of the large intestine in addition to numerous bacteria, many of which are dead.

The feces of herbivorous animals contain a fairly high proportion of undigested food as only 50 to 70 percent of the vegetable intake is digested. This inefficient digestive system means that these animals spend the major part of their lives in eating.

THE KIDNEYS

Urine is the product of the kidneys and con-sists of waste products derived from the cleansing of the blood.

On cutting a kidney transversely one sees that it is composed of outer and inner zones called the cortex and medulla, respectively. A central open area (*renal pelvis*) with an outlet tube (*ureter*) leads urine into the blad-der, and the bladder in turn has an outlet (*urethra*) which takes the urine out of the body.

Microscopic examination reveals that the kidney is comprised of numerous units (nephrons) packed closely together. An understanding of the kidney as a whole can be obtained by examining the function of these nephrons individually. Blood is sup-plied to the kidney through the renal artery which, after branching many times, breaks into a tuft of capillaries, the *glomerulus.* There is a glomerulus at the upper end of each nephron surrounded by a structure called the *Bowman's capsule* which has a filtering func-tion.

This filtration apparatus leads to a series of tubules, some convoluted and some straight, which lead in turn to collecting tubules and ultimately into the renal pelvis.

The glomeruli and the convoluted tubules are found in the cortex of the kidney, while the straight sections of the tubules (*Henle's loop*) are packed side by side, with many veins, in the medulla.

As blood passes through the glomerular capillaries its fluid components filter through the capillary walls and glomerular capsule. This fluid contains most of the blood plasma constituents other than proteins. As the fluid passes down the renal tubules the substances which are needed by the body are resorbed into the bloodstream, and the waste products become more and more concentrated. The lining cells of the tubules also excrete addi-tional waste products, and the fluid in the tubules assumes the character of urine. The tubules also regulate the quantity of fluid retained in the body. For instance, when an animal is deprived of fluid the urine is sparse and the waste products which it contains are highly concentrated. On the other hand if fluid intake is high, the urine is copious and dilute.

The quantity of urine formed may also be influenced by hormones from the anterior pituitary gland or pancreas. (See the Endoc-rine Systems later.) Occasionally urination may be more frequent but no more copious; this is generally due to the presence of in-flammatory conditions of the lower urinary tracts (bladder and urethra).

In birds and snakes the urine and feces are passed together since the urinary and

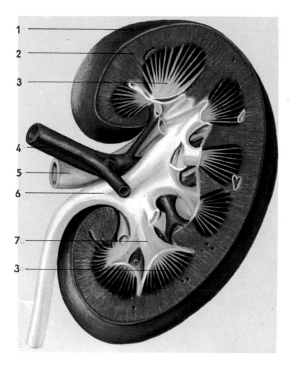

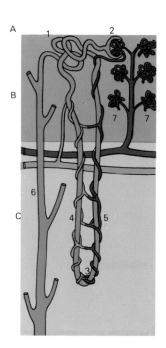

Top Left. *Vertical section of a mammalian kidney:*
(1) Outer membrane. (2) Cortex. (3) Medulla. (4)
Renal artery. (5) Renal vein. (6) Renal pelvis. (7)
Ureter. Top Right. Diagram showing a nephron and
its associated structures: (A) Outer membrane; (B)
Cortex; (C) Medulla. (1) Convoluted tubule. (2)
Bowman's capsule. (3) Henle's loop. (4 and 5)
Ascending and descending limbs of Henle's loop. (6)
Collecting tubule. (7) Glomerulus Arteries and arte-
rioles red; veins and venous capillaries blue.

alimentary tracts have a common outlet, the
cloaca. The urine of birds is a thick, cream-
colored semisolid mass which is passed
together with the darkly colored feces.

Insects lack kidneys but instead have
structures called Malpighian tubules, which
are not unlike nephrons. These long, narrow
tubules have one end bathed in the blood
contained in the body cavity and the other
opens into the front of the hind gut. They
absorb water, salts, and excretory products
and discharge them through the rectum
along with undigested food material.

The Senses

Perception of the surrounding world is all
important for animal survival. Species, as
well as individuals, often depend on the
sharpness of their senses to avoid predators,
to find food, and to find a mate. On the other
hand senses which are not required tend to
degenerate over thousands of generations.
Creatures which spend the major part of their
lives in darkness (moles or cave-dwelling
characin fish to name two) have poor eyesight
or no eyes at all.

Describing the anatomy of the sensory
organs—eyes, the ear, nose, mouth, and
skin—is relatively simple but it is less easy to
determine just what others can see, hear,
smell, taste, and feel.

Furthermore animals sometimes possess
senses which have no human counterpart,
which make them more difficult to understand. For instance, birds and fish have an
uncanny sense of direction and are able to
find their way across hundreds of miles of
unknown land or sea to reach some predetermined spot.

The senses of animals are sometimes similar to those of humans but many times more
acute. Snakes are able to feel vibrations that
are produced by the movements of other
animals through their forked tongues; insects
are able to establish the presence of others of
their species more than a mile away by virtue

The diagram shows how an image is transmitted to the
brain via the eye. A picture of the objects in view passes
through the transparent window (cornea) at the front of
the eye and through an aperture (pupil) in the colored
section (iris). This picture is focused by the lens onto a
sensitive membrane at the back of the eyeball (retina),
which acts as a screen from which the optic nerve
transmits the picture to the brain. The cornea is covered
by a transparent membrane (conjunctiva) and pro-
tected by the lids. The iris acts as a curtain to control the
amount of light entering the pupil, contracting in bright
light and dilating in dim light.

of their smell, and bats flying in total darkness can avoid objects by listening for the
echoes of the chirping sounds they emit.

SIGHT

Eyes are the main organs of sight in all animals, but their form varies from the compound eyes of insects to the pair of eyes in
vertebrates. The structure of the mammalian
eye is shown in the accompanying figure.

An image, produced by the reflection of
light from an object, enters the transparent
section at the front of the eyeball (*cornea*).
This is focused both by the lens and the thick
gelatinous substance (*vitreous humour*) onto
the retina, which is a sheet of light-sensitive
cells at the rear of the eyeball. The retina
translates the light image into impulses
which are transmitted along the optic nerve
to the brain.

In most mammals the lens is able to
accommodate, that is, change its shape in
order to focus the image onto the retina. The
amount of light reaching the retina is regulated by the *iris*, a circular membrane positioned in front of the lens. It has a central
aperture (*pupil*) which dilates in dim surroundings to admit maximum light and contracts in bright surroundings to protect the
retina from glare.

The light which reaches us from the sun is
comprised of rays of different wave lengths.
The rays with shortest wavelength are called
"ultraviolet" and those with longest, "infrared," neither of which can be perceived by
the human eye. The rays with intermediate
wavelengths give rise to a sensation of color in
the retina, each wavelength appearing as a
different color. When light is reflected from
an object before entering the eye, that object
appears to be the color of the reflected light.
In other words the color of any image depends on which wave lengths are absorbed
and which are reflected. Objects which
absorb all wavelengths appear black and
those which reflect all appear white. Only
one particular group of cells in the retina, the
cones, are responsible for the perception of
colored light.

The truly nocturnal species have enormous eyes capable of receiving sufficient
light. Nocturnal vision is short range

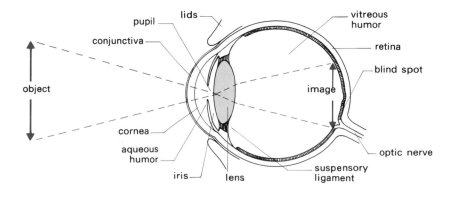

(myopic) which is why owls hunt close to the ground. The retinas of nocturnals are poorly endowed with cones, which provide acuteness of sight, but well supplied with rods, which provide sensitivity to light intensity. Diurnal birds have few rods and are almost helpless in the dark. Changes occur on rods and cones when light falls on them so that most nocturnals can see fairly well in daylight if allowed to get accustomed slowly to the light.

Color plays an important part in nature, indicating, for instance, desirable or poisonous foods, dangerous or friendly animals, and sexually available individuals.

The sight of birds is well developed, especially in predators (hawks and buzzards). The acuteness of vision is thought to be related to number of cells per unit area of the retina and in some birds these cells are eight times as dense as in human beings. Accommodation (focusing of the image on the retina) is accomplished in birds (and some reptiles) largely by changing the convexity of the cornea. Another feature common to birds and reptiles is the presence of a nictitating membrane or third eyelid, which is almost transparent and is extended over the eye periodically to clean and protect it.

In many birds and mammals, objects which lie ahead can be seen by both eyes simultaneously. This gives a three-dimensional (stereoscopic) effect and enables them to judge distance with accuracy.

Most reptiles and fish have spherical lenses which focus by moving the whole lens forward or backward within the eyeball. Cones in the snakes' retina are plentiful suggesting that they have good color vision. Some burrowing snakes which spend their lives underground have no eyes at all.

Light plays an important part in regulating the sexual cycle of reptiles and birds. It also regulates egg laying and the migratory urge. The Japanese practice of *yogai* consists of stimulating the song of cagebirds during winter by the use of candlelight.

Some reptiles and amphibians have light-sensitive skins or special receptor organs at the top of their heads for the purpose of perceiving light. In frogs this appears as a small colorless spot between the eyes.

Insects also have light-sensitive skins, and certain cockroaches avoid light even when decapitated. The compound eyes of insects are formed of numerous units of vision packed closely together, each with a lens and visual nerve. Insects also have other sensitive organs (the *dorsal ocellum* and *stemmata*) which enable them to discern light and darkness.

HEARING AND BALANCE

The most sophisticated organ for perceiving sound is the typical mammalian ear as shown in the accompanying figure. Sound waves are guided into the auditory canal by the outer ear (*pinna*), which in many mammals can be moved to face the source of the sound. When the sound waves reach the eardrum (*tympanum*), they set up vibrations in the *ossicles*—three small bones (*hammer, anvil and foot plate*) situated in the middle ear. These are connected one to the other and transmit vibrations from the far side of the drum to the *cochlea* in the inner ear. The cochlea is a spirally-shaped apparatus with nerve endings which translate the vibrations into nerve impulses and transmit them to the brain.

In mammals the eardrum is at the bottom of the auditory canal which serves both to protect it and to channel the sound waves. In many reptiles, birds, and amphibians the eardrum is superficial.

Bats, dolphins, and probably many other animals negotiate by echo location. They emit a continuous stream of sound (clicks and whistles) and use the echoes of these to locate obstacles in their path. Bats, for instance, can avoid a series of wires strung across a room in complete darkness, but when their ears are temporarily plugged they blunder. This echo-location mechanism is so sensitive that it enables bats to catch small insects.

Animal species hear a different range of sounds from those descernible to humans. Dogs, for instance, react to a whistle which is too high in pitch for our own ears. Birds also appear sensitive to a wider range of sound than we are. Hearing is particularly acute in nocturnal hunting birds such as the owl.

Fish have acute hearing, and sound waves carry well in water. The sounds are picked up and magnified in their swim bladders and are passed to the inner ear by a series of interconnected small bones, much the same as the ossicles of terrestrial animals.

Water pressure and turbulence are registered by an additional sensory mechanism present in fish only. This is the lateral line

Structure of the mammalian ear: (1) Outer ear. (2) Malleus (hammer). (3) Semicircular canals. (4) Incus (anvil). (5) Stapes (foot plate). (6) Cochlea. (7) Eustachian tube. (8) Eardrum (tympanum). (9) External auditory canal.

The inner ear is the organ of balance. In cats this sense is particularly acute—a cat can right itself while falling and make a remarkable landing on four feet, as this photo shows.

system, which comprises a strip of cells running down the head and body, connected to nerve endings.

Hearing appears to be less important than other senses in the reptiles, although they are able to pick up ground vibrations through the lower jaw and tongue.

Insects detect sound through vibrations set up in the hairs of their bodies. Caterpillars, for instance, become insensitive to soundwaves if their body hairs are removed. Male mosquitoes recognize the sound of the females' wings by vibrations set up in their own antennae.

The organ of balance in higher vertebrates, the laborynth, is situated in the middle ear and consists of three hollow *semicircular canals* at right angles to one another which contain fluid and granules. Within the canals

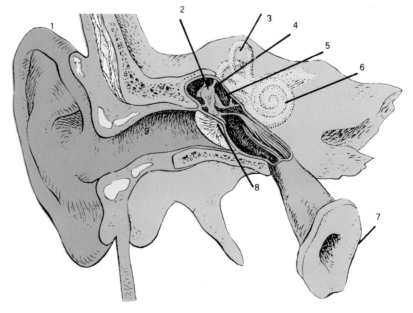

are nerve endings which indicate to the animal where the granules have come to rest, and hence the direction of the gravitational pull. The animal bases its sense of balance on these signals. If the granules are disturbed by spinning the animal around, the laborynths send a confused message to the brain and dizziness results. In the healthy animal the keeping of balance is an automatic process and only when some disorder of the middle ear occurs do we fully appreciate the importance of this function.

SMELL

Smell is the sensation produced by the presence of minute chemical particles in inspired air which stimulate the olfactory area of the nasal membrane of the nose. This is an area situated toward the back of the nose and is, not surprisingly, largest in animals with the best sense of smell. By sniffing, the air coming in contact with this area is changed repeatedly and so the stimulus is increased. Nerve endings in the olfactory area send the information to the olfactory lobe of the brain.

It is well known that many pet animals have a more acute sense of smell than their owners. In fish, smell is used as a means of communication. Frightened fish secrete pheromones which put other fish on the alert. When water from a tank containing an injured fish is added to another tank, it causes the fish in the second tank to scatter in panic.

Some fish have olfactory pits situated as are the nostrils in terrestrial animals. Some fish have olfactory pits at the corners of the mouth while others (the Lake Gourami and Catfish for example) have areas used for taste or smell on the fins and barbels (whiskers).

Smell is developed fairly well in reptiles, less so in amphibians, and poorly in birds.

TASTE

Taste buds consist of groups of sensitive cells on the tongue and other parts of the mouth in mammals. They appear as small red pimples on the mouth and tongue and are able to discern only sweet, sour, bitter and salt tastes. The buds in different areas are devoted to receiving one taste only. Sweetness is detected at the tip of the tongue, bitterness at the back, and saltiness and sourness mainly at the edges of the tongue.

COORDINATION

Although the parts of the body and their functions are described separately, they invariably act in a highly integrated fashion which is essential if there is to be a coordination of bodily functions. In even the simplest of actions several parts of the body cooperate to achieve their objective. The eye, middle ear, brain, and muscles cooperate to achieve balance, and at feeding time the brain, eye, nose, mouth, and stomach cooperate to produce a flow of saliva, secretion of stomach digestive juices and increased stomach mobility. Much of this cooperation is achieved through the action of the nerves and brain, and it has been said that the body acts as an orchestra with the brain as conductor.

Stimuli travel along the nerves almost instantaneously. To appreciate this, one has only to think of the speed at which blinking occurs in response to some flying object.

However, the body has another regulatory system, the endocrine system, which controls those functions with slower and longer lasting action. They influence body growth, temperament, sexuality, urinary output, milk secretion, and birth contractions. The endocrine system is comprised of a set of glands in various parts of the body which liberate substances known as hormones into the bloodstream. These hormones either regulate a bodily function directly or else the function of some other endocrine gland.

The main endocrine glands, the hormones they produce, and their functions are shown in the table on the next page.

Reproductive Organs

The male and female gonads, the testes and the ovaries, are the primary reproductive organs of any species showing sexual reproduction. In the male or the male component of an hermaphrodite, the testes produce the male gametes, the spermatozoa, while in the female the ovary is responsible for the female gametes or ova. In addition the gonads synthesize and secrete the male or female sex hormones which are responsible for embryonic differentiation of the accessory sex organs, the sexuality of the adult animal, and the maintenance of full sexual functions.

In the simpler animal forms in which ova and sperm are shed into water to achieve fertilization the reproductive structures can be quite simple; an opening to the exterior is all that is needed. Water supports the eggs so that shells or similar materials are unnecessary.

With increased complexity in reproduction, particularly with land dwelling forms, more specialized systems are found. The gonads come to lie in the peritoneal cavity. The ovary passes the ova into the peritoneal cavity from whence they can be extruded outside the body. But such an arrangement is not suitable for eggs requiring a shell or other special treatment. Hence a funnel-ended collecting duct, the oviduct, is formed along with the various specializations needed, not only for oviparity (egg laying) but also for viviparity (live bearing).

In the great majority of animals there is no connection between the ovary and oviduct. The ovum must cross some of the peritoneal cavity after ovulation.

Among the cartilaginous fishes, reptiles, and birds, eggs are laid with an albuminous covering and some form of shell. In these animals a special zone of the oviduct acts as a nidamental gland; the upper part secretes the

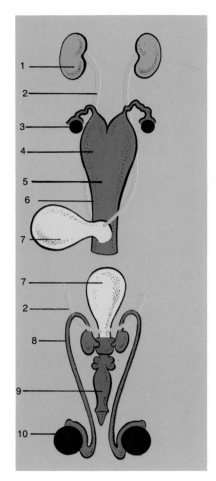

Reproductive organs of mammal: Top. *Female.* Bottom. *Male.* (1) *Kidney.* (2) *Ureter.* (3) *Ovary.* (4) *Uterus.* (5) *Vagina.* (6) *Birth canal.* (7) *Bladder.* (8) *Vas deferens.* (9) *Penis.* (10) *Testis.*

albuminous covering and the lower the shell. For reptiles and birds the names of mammalian anatomy are used so we say the upper nidamental secretions occur in the uterine tube and the shell is supplied in the uterus. Thus in these forms, as well as in the mammals, fertilization must take place high in the uterine tube. Birds are remarkable in that they are unilateral and only the left ovary and oviducal system remain. The oviduct or ducts then open into the cloaca.

Viviparity requires an adequate chamber for embryo development, and this function is adopted by the uterus. In the simplest form of viviparous animal, the developing ova is nourished by uterine secretions, but with formal placentation the embryonic membranes become intimately linked with the uterine wall so that exchange of material can take place between embryonic and maternal blood streams.

In most mammals the two uteri remain separate, joining together to open into a common vagina, the other end of the system specialized for reception of the penis in mating. In others a lower common uterus is found, while in the human female union of the two uteri is complete with the uterine tubes opening into the single chamber. This in turn opens by a muscular cervix into the vagina.

GLAND	HORMONE SECRETED	ACTION
Pituitary (Anterior)	Adrenocorticotrophic	Growth and function of adrenal gland.
	Thyrotrophic	Growth and function of thyroid.
	Growth	Growth and function of the body.
	Follicle stimulating	Growth and function of the body.
	Lutenizing	Growth and function of the corpus luteum of the ovaries.
	Prolactin	Maintenance of lactation.
		Maintenance of corpus luteum.
		Development of sperm in males.
Pituitary (posterior)	Vasopressin	Raises the blood pressure.
		Reduces urine flow.
		Controls bleeding in the womb.
	Oxytocin	Causes contractions of the womb at time of parturition.
Adrenal (Cortex)	Corticosterone	Maintains muscular efficiency and blood glucose levels.
		Maintains water and salts at correct levels in the body.
		Maintains body temperature.
		Regulates secretions from sexual organs.
Adrenal medulla	Adrenalin	Prepares the body for action, as in controlling blood pressure, heart rate, and heart output. Relaxes stomach and intestine muscles.
		Increases bloodflow to muscles.
		Dilates pupils.
		Causes sweating.
		Increases blood sugar.
Thyroid	Thyroxine	Controls the rate of bodily functions (the metabolism).
Parathyroid	Parathyroid hormone	Regulates calcium levels in blood and bones.
Pancreas	Insulin	Regulates blood sugar levels.
Ovaries	Estrogen	Increases sexual receptiveness (secreted by ovarian follicle).
Ovaries	Progesterone	Prevents heat periods and contractions of the uterus while the animal is pregnant.
		Makes the walls of the womb receptive for implantation of the fetus.
Testicle	Testosterone	Regulates sexual desire in males. Causes development of sexual features such as the comb of roosters.
Thymus	Thymic hormones	Regulates development of certain immune mechanisms.
Pineal	Unknown	Unknown. Thought to play a part in sexual development.

The mammalian vagina is separate from the anus and the urethra.

The testes provide large numbers of sperm which require an effective duct system to be carried from the gonads to the outside in all except a few species. Unlike the ovary, where individual ova are shed from the surface, the testes of higher vertebrates are made up of a complicated system of sperm-producing tubules with the hormone secreting cells lying between them. The spermatozoa are therefore already contained in a seminiferous tubule-system which is eventually collected into a single vas deferens (or efferens) from each testis. In some lower forms, however, the spermatozoa are produced in rounded ampullae which are individually discharged as a sperm packet.

In the majority of vertebrates the testes remain on the posterior body wall close to the kidney with the vasa opening into the cloaca. In many mammals, however, they are carried outside the abdomen in scrotal sacs, to which location they descend during puberty.

When the spermatozoa of higher vertebrates are first formed in the testes, they are still not mature; the maturation process takes place in a convoluted tubule, the epididymis, which also secretes a small amount of the fluid component of the seminal fluid which carries the spermatozoa. In mammals other glands contribute to this fluid, the prostrate, seminal vesicles and bulbo-urethral glands.

In certain groups a penis (hemipenes in snakes and lizards) presents the sperm into the vagina of the female while many fish have claspers for the same purpose.

THE MAMMALIAN FEMALE CYCLE

Females undergo a sexual cycle during which the eggs mature, develop and are expelled, and this cycle corresponds with behavioral changes leading to copulation when the eggs are ripe.

At puberty, which varies in time of onset from one species to another, the anterior pituitary secretes hormones that cause a follicle (containing the egg) to develop in the ovary, ripen and burst. (The word *egg* is used here to indicate the female cell capable of forming an embryo, present both in animals which lay eggs as well as in those which do not.)

As the follicle develops it produces hormones called estrogens which influence the female's behavior and also make her attractive to the male. When the female is willing to copulate, she is said to be in estrus or "on heat."

After the follicle releases the egg it develops into a yellow nodule called the corpus luteum which has a most important function. It secretes the hormone *progesterone* which prepares the uterus for implantation of the fertilized egg or fetus.

If copulation has occurred the ovum may be fertilized by the sperm as it passes down the fallopian tube and, on reaching the uterus, embeds itself in the wall. Progesterone from the corpus luteum generally stops the anterior pituitary from producing more follicle stimulating hormone so that the sexual cycle comes to a standstill during pregnancy.

The connection between the embryonic bloodvessels and the uterus is known as the placenta, and in the later stages of pregnancy the placenta also produces progesterone.

THE MAMMALIAN MALE

At puberty the male sex organs or testes develop under influence of hormones from the anterior pituitary. Hormones produced by the testes (testosterone) cause development of the secondary male characteristic such as muscular build, aggressive temperament, and sexual drive.

After copulation the sperm travels with remarkable speed up the female genital tract. Sperm can be found in the fallopian tubes of female rats less than a minute after copulation.

Pregnancy and Birth

The accompanying table shows the length of pregnancy (gestation period) and the duration of heat in different animals.

The mechanism which initiates birth (parturition) is still not fully understood. Oxytocin, the hormone from the posterior pituitary, does indeed produce uterine contractions but this hormone is only effective when the uterine muscles are in a state of readiness. Earlier injections of oxytocin have no effect. One theory is that the fetus itself produces the substances which cause the initial sensitivity of the uterine muscles.

As the time of parturition approaches, the corpus luteum regresses, the uterine muscles contract rhythmically, and the cervix, a narrow cartilaginous canal at the mouth of the uterus, dilates. The contractions expel the fetus and the blood vessels which join the fetus to the mother tear, the newly born individual then draws its first breath. (See also **Breeding and Rearing,** and for details of the breeding and rearing of individual pets see **Dogs, Cats, Horses, Small Mammals, Birds, Fish, Reptiles and Amphibians, Insects.**)

CARE OF THE SICK & INJURED PET

This section of the encyclopedia will help you to give first aid and to treat routine conditions. It will help you to recognize when your animal is sick and veterinary help is needed and will aid your understanding of the prescribed treatment. Nevertheless the owner should note any changes in behavior or condition because these changes will frequently be the only means of knowing that something is wrong. All too often illness goes unnoticed until it is so advanced that successful treatment is endangered. Experienced and observant owners learn to sense when an animal is sick. When grooming or feeding your pet or cleaning out its accommodations, you should automatically check for signs of parasites, digestive disorders, and unusual conditions.

Keeping a record of your pet's history, medical and otherwise, is an invaluable aid. Date of birth, vaccinations, if and when neutered, dates of season, worming, mating etc. should be carefully noted; add your veterinarian's name, address, telephone number, and emergency times.

The Medicine Cabinet

To avoid confusion with human medications keep animal supplies apart from your domestic medicine cabinet, and keep them locked up safely out of the reach of children. Some human medication is quite suitable for animal use, but strengths and doses vary so enormously that if a medication has not been specifically prepared for an animal, it should be avoided. Drugs that are harmless to one species may be dangerous to another and if you compare the size of the average adult with that of a small dog or a mouse it is easy to understand that many human preparations would be far too strong; similarly they would have to be used in far too big a quantity to be practicable for a horse. Do not keep or use old drugs. Their efficacy may have diminished, or they could actually promote extra infection since they may no longer be sterile.

Your medicine box might include bandages, dressings of various sizes, cotton swabs or sticks, a mild liquid antiseptic, blunt end and curved scissors useful for trimming away fur, antiseptic for sterilizing scissors and other equipment, antiseptic dusting powder or cream, antiparasitic dusting powder or shampoo, a mild laxative, absorbent agents (such as kaolin), and worming pills (carefully matched to the age and size of the animal).

Care of the Sick Pet

NURSING

Most sick animals need quiet and solitude. If normally kept with a number of their fellows, it is better to remove them to a separate area, cage, or tank.

Many species instinctively turn upon ailing members of their community and destroy them, which makes their separation imperative. It is clearly necessary when an infectious condition is diagnosed or suspected.

Feed and tend healthy animals before attending sick ones to avoid carrying disease. Always wash and disinfect your hands after handling sick animals. A coverup over your clothes to reduce the risk of carrying infection is a sensible precaution.

An ill or injured animal should be protected from the elements and made comfortable. Check conditions on the floor or around the bedding area to be sure there is no draft. Dim lighting will usually encourage an animal to rest. Bedding should preferably be disposable or covered with some impervious or washable sheeting. Soiled or wet bedding should be changed immediately. Most heat is lost through the floor of the animal's bed and, although a pet may be covered with hair, it can lose a great deal of heat if it is immobile or wet. Some form of cover, if it will be tolerated by the animal, is a good idea.

Normal facilities should be provided for defecation and urination. Housebroken animals used to going outside will find it very distressing if unable to do so and may need to be carried outside for the purpose at their regular times. If this is impossible, encourage their use of newspaper or a litter tray. Severely incapacitated pets may need to be supported while they perform these functions and in certain cases require manual help as well—your veterinarian will show you how.

FEEDING OF THE SICK PET

The sick animal must be nourished with its normal food and water if possible, although if the head and/or mouth has been injured very soft or liquid food may be necessary. Baby foods and invalid mixes will often prove acceptable and sometimes the normal diet processed through a blender will be suitable. In all cases the diet should be matched to the normal balance of carbohydrate, proteins, and other nutrients. (See **Feeding your Pet**.) Water should be changed frequently. After an operation and certain other treatments food may have to be temporarily withheld. Always carefully follow any dietary instructions your veterinarian may give, but discuss a range of alternative foodstuffs if you find the one suggested difficult to obtain. An animal which has been vomiting should not be given free access to water. Supply a little at a time or an ice cube which can be slowly licked.

ADMINISTERING DRUGS

Injections

The quickest way to getting a drug to where it is needed is by injection through a hypodermic needle. Some drugs are only available in this form and sometimes an animal's condition may mean that this is the only way in which drugs can be administered. There are three main ways of giving injections: subcutaneously (into the connective tissue between the skin and muscle), into the muscle, and directly into a vein. Subcutaneous injections are gradually absorbed into the bloodstream at a steady rate so that only one injection daily may be necessary. Some drugs are irritants if given subcutaneously but cause no problem if injected into the muscle. Since muscle has a better blood supply the drug is absorbed more quickly. Intravenous injections go straight into the blood stream.

Pills, Medicines, and Ointments

Most drugs to be administered at home will be in the form of powder, pills, liquid medicine, or ointment. Powders can be mixed in with food, if this does not make the animal reject it, and sometimes pills can be inserted into meat or other foodstuffs. Apart from the possibility of rejection by the animal, mixing a drug with food makes it difficult to tell whether or not it has actually been taken, or in what quantity, if not all the food has been consumed. If more than one animal has access to the food, there is the possibility of some of the drug going to the wrong recipient. The same problems apply when medication is added to drinking water. However, with some animals, this is the most practical method for the pet keeper and for most animals it is a satisfactory way to give dietary supplements or conditioning treatments which do not have to be regulated exactly and which will not harm other animals.

Pills can be given to dogs, cats, and small mammals by holding the mouth open and placing the pill on the back of the tongue. (Large tablets may have to be given in several pieces if the animal cannot swallow them

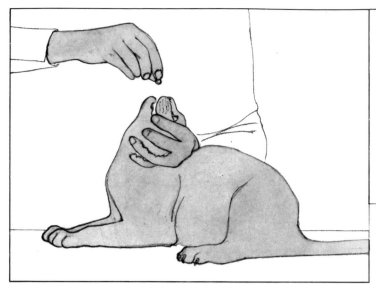

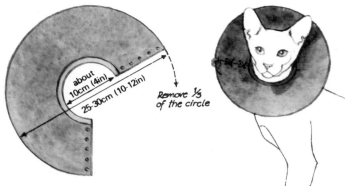

Top Left. *The technique used to administer a pill to a reluctant patient: Move the head upwards and backwards, squeezing gently on either side of the mouth with the fingers. Press the lower jaw down by gently pressing on the gum and slip the pill onto the back of the tongue. Hold the mouth shut and stroke the throat until you are sure the cat has swallowed the pill.*

Top Right. *An "Elizabethan" collar made of cardboard wil prevent a cat from licking wounds or scratching sore eyes or ears.*

whole.) Hold the mouth closed and stroke the throat to encourage swallowing until you are certain that the pill has gone down. Some animals, cats particularly, will pretend to have swallowed a pill and then spit it out as soon as you are not looking. Large animals such as horses and sheep are usually given pills by blowing them down a tube into their throat. Liquids can be poured into the pocket formed by pulling out the lower lip of some animals. When the mouth is too small for that method, it is easier to give medicine through a syringe or a dropper. In either case liquids should be given in small quantities so there is no risk of choking the animal.

Ointments are easier to apply but will be licked off by many pets. If they need to be applied to the eyes, the eye will have to be held open since most animals will blink as the tube nozzle gets near. Ear drops, used particularly for the treatment of mite infection in dogs, cats, and rabbits, are easily applied by dropper but it will help to hold the animal so the drops run down deep into the ear.

Always follow your veterinarian's and the manufacturer's instructions when giving medicines and do not exceed the dose prescribed.

Treating External Parasites

Some pets never seem to pick up a single flea while others suffer from heavy infestation. The tell-tale indication is usually the tiny specks of the parasite's excreta on the animal's fur. Then you may see the fleas themselves on the base of the tail or around the eyes. Regular inspection when grooming will usually catch an infestation in its early stages. Treatment with a dusting powder suitable to the animal is simple and effective. Pyrethrum-based powders are safe with cats and dogs.

Not only mammals suffer from external parasites—birds can play host to mites and lice. Scabs around a bird's vent usually indicate infection by the northern mite. Scaly-leg is caused by a tiny mite which attacks feather-shanked birds. Fish also have their own para-

sites. (Detailed information and illustrations of parasites are given in the **Dictionary of Ailments** and the Fish Ailments Charts in the **Fish** Chapter.)

Treating Internal Parasites

Animals can frequently play host to internal parasites without any apparent debilitation but dogs, cats, horses, apes and monkeys should nevertheless be treated if they are suspected of being infected, and in many cases should be regularly wormed. This is almost standard practice with puppies, kittens, and stabled horses.

Digestive Disorders

Vomiting, looseness, and constipation may all be symptoms of more serious disorders. However, members of the cat family regularly bring up balls of fur they have swallowed during washing, and birds of prey regurgitate the indigestible remains of foodstuff while others actually may vomit objects accidentally swallowed. Only in horses is this perilous; they are not anatomically able to regurgitate and may die. If the vomit contains no indication of why it has been brought up, look for other symptoms, including the presence of worm segments.

Looseness and constipation may be due to dietary changes or to unsuitable food; if you discover your pet has licked out a bowl of cooking fat do not be surprised if its body reacts accordingly. In nervous dogs looseness can be brought about by stress due to such situations as change of ownership or strict obedience training. Occasional imbalances are no cause for concern in most animals but if they persist for more than twenty-four hours they may be a sign of serious disorder.

Blood passed in the motions or in urine, or bloody vomit may indicate internal hemorrhage, especially if accompanied by loss of color from lips and gums. It is dangerous to attempt any medication until the cause is known which may be infection, poisoning,

injuries, or foreign bodies. Confine the animal in comfortable surroundings allowing water (except in the case of continual vomiting) and no food. In cases of poisoning, infection, or injury anything given by mouth is likely to add to the problem. The cause may be as simple as an injured tooth or a spicule of bone caught in the gums or rectum. If you can see it, remove it but do not attempt cautery or dressings.

Do not take your pet to the veterinarian and simply say it has been sick or has diarrhea. Take along a sample of the vomit or feces. Scoop it up into a clean container to avoid extraneous germs being included. It will aid diagnosis more than any description you can give.

Urine samples are a little more difficult to collect. If your pet uses a litter tray scoop up some from the puddle before it has had time to soak into the litter or place the tray on a slight slope and fix a board across the lower end to keep the litter clear. With other animals you will have to be ready to move into action when they do and catch what you can! Don't forget to wash your hands afterwards.

The Older Pet

Old age is relative to species and may range from hours in some insects to much longer than the human life span. For those animals with short life expectation there will be little need for geriatric care but in many companion pets, such as cats and dogs, there will be a fall in vitality in their later years and a tendency to minor physical malfunction and geriatric illness as in humans. Working animals should be allowed to enjoy a relaxed retirement. Remember that the elderly animal will be more susceptible to temperature changes, less able to cope with long walks and strenuous exercise, and may develop rheumatism or arthritis (quite common in dogs), digestive disorders and occasional incontinence, loss of vision and all the other effects of old age that humans suffer. Aging animals may also lose their teeth and require specially prepared food. They may not be able to manage stairs and need to be carried.

Accidents and Injuries

Whatever the accident or injury that befalls a pet, the owner or the person finding the animal must first decide how serious the injury is. It may be something that the owner can deal with alone depending on previous experience. The animal may be able to wait for treatment until the next surgery time at the veterinary clinic; it may need temporary first aid to ease pain and prevent worsening of its condition, or it may demand immediate professional attention. Whatever the circumstances, the rule should always be "If in doubt contact your veterinarian." You may be able to get immediate advice by telephone on how to help the animal before getting it to the veterinarian.

ACCIDENTS IN THE HOME

Doors and Windows

Cats and dogs are liable to get their tails caught in doors and windows, and as anyone who has shut his finger in a door knows this injury is *very* painful.

A crushed tail is invariably bruised, frequently cut, and possibly broken. There are three main things to remember; first your pet will be shocked and may scratch and bite if you try to examine the injured tail; second a waving cut tail can distribute blood over a surprisingly large area of floors, walls and ceilings; and finally (this is probably a job for your veterinarian) it may need stitches, bandages, or even amputation.

Occasionally an animal will attempt to run straight through a pane of glass. Thick glass and a small animal will probably result in a stunned animal, but it might be as serious as a fractured skull. The signs of this are vomiting and bleeding from the ears which requires veterinary attention as soon as possible. Epistaxis (nosebleed) can also be a serious and messy problem, since animals will try hard to breathe through their noses and the continual coughing and sneezing makes it difficult for a clot to form. Again veterinary advice should be sought if the bleeding continues for any length of time.

The combination of thin glass and a heavy or fast-moving pet can have far more dramatic and bloody results demanding immediate veterinary attention. This type of injury may result in rapid death if an artery is severed, so first aid may be of vital importance. It is possible for a bird to break its neck by flying into a window, so cage bird owners should curtain the windows before releasing their pets to fly indoors.

Electricity

Electricity is another hazard, although it leads to injury less often than might be expected. The most common cause is chewing through electric wiring which may result in burns, unconsciousness, or immediate death. Turn off the power before approaching the animal. If this is impossible make sure that you do not touch the animal, or anything in contact with the current. Many animals urinate with shock; do not stand in the puddle because urine, like water, conducts electricity. If the animal is unconscious but still breathing, call the veterinarian and keep it in a warm, quiet area until he or she arrives. If breathing has stopped the animal may need artificial respiration and perhaps heart massage. Do not attempt to deal with burns until you are certain the animal is alive.

Fires

Danger to life in the case of fire can come in two ways: first by burning and heat, and second from suffocation by smoke and fumes. It is the latter case which claims a surprisingly large number of animal victims. This is most noticeable in cage birds, for instance in the case of smoldering foam-filled furniture which can produce toxic fumes that are extremely dangerous to them. Moving pets to the open air away from smoke and fumes is particularly important with horses, when injuries are most often caused by panic. Examine them for any burning of the skin, as distinct from singed hair, and be sure to check the pads of their feet which can sometimes sustain severe burns. Burns may result from animals accidentally getting too close to fires and heaters in the home, and these are sometimes slow to heal. Blisters from burns may not be apparent through the fur for about a week after the accident.

Gas

The first step in dealing with a gas leak is to turn off the source and to open doors and windows. Birds are particularly susceptible to gas. Remember that there are many harmful vapors other than cooking and heating gas, and take great care not to use cleaning solvents and chemical aerosols near pets.

OUTDOOR RISKS

Outdoors an animal is exposed to a wide range of poisonous plants and the many chemicals which are used on private gardens, in agriculture, and as pesticides. There is more likelihood of encountering pollen and other substances to which an individual pet may be allergic and a much greater chance of risk from thorns, splinters, broken glass, cans, barbed wire, and even deliberately set traps. Free-ranging dogs and cats may also get involved in fights, and any animal in the open could be attacked by predators.

Walks in the woods, especially in areas where there are sheep, may expose a dog to ticks. Sheep ticks vary in size from about 5–15mm. (0.2–0.6in.) when engorged with blood and can cause considerable irritation to dogs. Be careful in removing ticks that the mouth parts do not separate and stay on the body to develop an unpleasant sore. A drop of alcohol on the tick will usually make it release its hold and come off easier. (Do not forget to destroy the ticks.) Grass seeds, particularly of the barley type, can also be an unexpected hazard for dogs. They can penetrate the skin of the feet and cause painful septic foci which track under the skin. They cause an even greater problem if they get into an animal's ears where the irritation is maddening. If a dog shows a sudden onset of head shaking and ear scratching after a walk in the country, suspect a grass seed in the ear. Your veterinarian may give the dog a general anesthetic before trying to find the seed in the depths of the ear. Always check a dog's coat and ears (especially those of Cocker and Springer Spaniels) when returning from a walk at the time of year when grass is seeding.

Drowning is relatively rare in animals since most (including cats) swim well. Problems usually arise only when the exit from the water is up a steep slippery bank and the animal becomes exhausted, or when it has tried to swim too great a distance and perhaps begins to panic as it tires. If the animal shows any sign of survival when it is removed from the water, try to drain water from its lungs and administer artificial respiration before drying and warming the animal.

Fish and fully aquatic reptiles can often survive for quite long periods out of water, and fish may jump out of a pond and some distance away. They should be returned to water as soon as possible but be carefully watched for the development of any fungal or other infection on wounds or scratches. This will obviously be easier in an inspection tank.

Heat stroke may affect any animal but is particularly seen in dogs in two distinct sets of circumstances. The first is the result of overexertion in the hot sun from such activities as chasing a ball on a beach or in a park. The animal gets so hot that eventually the body thermostat can no longer function and its temperature goes up until the brain function is impaired and the animal loses consciousness. This seizure has to be distinguished by your veterinarian from a heart attack or an epileptic fit. Fortunately most animals make a good recovery after being sprayed with cold water and then placed in a cool, dark room. The other main cause of heat stroke is all too frequently seen and is the result of simple neglect or stupidity on the part of the owners who leave animals in locked automobiles in hot sunshine or in other confined quarters without sufficient ventilation. The animals first start panting before they pass out. They may die from the heat or from suffocation, or from a combination of both. Submerge or spray the animal in cold water, or surround it with ice packs. Artificial respiration may be required.

CAT AND DOG FIGHTS

Stopping a fight is often difficult and dangerous, although a pail of water or a blanket thrown over the contestants may prove effective. Do *not* attempt to separate two fighting animals with your bare hands.

There are three possible kinds of injury from cat fights—scratching, biting, and injuries resulting from falls during a chase. Cat scratches generally seem to heal well unless the eyes are concerned; if you suspect your cat has an eye injury seek veterinary advice; if you wish to clean the eye area, sponge gently with clean water or a dilute (1 in a 100) salt solution. Do not attempt to put any medication into the eye unless instructed to do so by your veterinarian. Cat bites are generally more serious and frequently become infected and develop into abscesses. These are very painful and debilitating, and although they eventually burst on their own they can cause considerable distress to your cat. It is important to have your cat examined by your veterinarian, since it will need treatment to combat the infection.

Dog fights vary considerably in the degree of injury to participants. It may well be true that the damage inflicted is often inversely related to the amount of noise. If the dogs are of similar size and build, the injury is likely to be evenly divided, but when different breeds are involved it becomes obvious that some fight better than others. Whereas cat bites tend to be septic puncture wounds, dog bites are often more in the nature of open slashes or crushed tissue. The open slash type of wound may need stitching along with some treatment to control infection. The crushing type of bite is most frequent and, although bleeding may be slight, bruising will be considerable. There may be bone fractures which will only show up on x-ray examination. This last type of bite is often inflicted by dogs on cats, while a cat is more likely to scratch than bite a dog. Again the scratches likely to prove most serious are those on the face, particularly around the eyes. If you suspect this kind of injury, have your veterinarian check for scratches on the cornea of the eye, which can develop into ulcers and result in blindness.

TRAFFIC ACCIDENTS

Traffic accidents involving pets are distressing for several reasons. No responsible pet owner will allow an animal to roam on any public highway or traffic area both for its own good and because it could be responsible for an accident causing injury to others, in which case the owner may be liable. In such accidents the first responsibility is to check for human casualties and if necessary to telephone for police and ambulance. Someone must warn and direct traffic to prevent other accidents or injury to those giving aid. If an animal is injured and recumbent a veterinarian should be contacted, and the owner informed as soon as possible. Both these contacts can be done by the police.

To clear the road for other traffic it will probably be necessary to move the injured animal which must be approached carefully. It will strongly resent any interference and

may even bite its owner. Gently maneuver the animal onto a sack, rug, or coat which can be used as a stretcher to carry the animal to a safer and more comfortable place. If an injured dog is inside a vehicle it may also try to defend its territory. Open doors with caution and have a noose ready to restrain it. If farm stock are involved and there is a danger of fire, open doors and ramps and let them escape—they can be rounded up later. At night it will help the veterinarian's initial examination if the animal's stretcher is placed near a light source such as an automobile's headlights.

Should it be necessary or practical to take the animal to a veterinarian, lay the animal on its stretcher on a level surface in a vehicle, and have someone to hold it gently but firmly during the drive. Small animals, like cats, should be put in carrying baskets that close securely. Call ahead or ask police about the nearest veterinarian on duty so you will not waste time going to a clinic that is closed.

Horses involved in road accidents are most likely to be injured on the legs, which are susceptible to damage. Remember that a frightened horse on the ground will desperately try to regain its feet so it will then feel more secure. Recumbency is best maintained by keeping the horse's neck extended with pressure applied to the poll while attempting to achieve maximum calm and quiet. Some form of head harness or bridle should be fitted. When the animal rises it may need lateral support at first to prevent another fall, and control of the head is essential. The standing animal should be kept quiet and gentled until veterinary help arrives.

First Aid Treatment

FRACTURES

The signs of fracture are usually obvious; there will be indication of pain, the animal will not want to move, the shape of the area affected will probably change, there will be a swelling and—in the case of compound fracture—the skin will be damaged and the bone may even project. But there are occasions when the animal will give little indication that anything is wrong. Splinting a bone in an amateur way can do a great deal of harm. In most cases treatment of the shattered bone does *not* constitute an emergency and is better left until the animal can be taken to a veterinarian.

CUTS

Commonly caused by glass or sharp metal, cuts can result in severe bleeding. Before a pressure bandage is used, try to remove pieces of glass or metal from the wound. A tourniquet may be more effective if the flow is fast and the wound is in a suitable place.

Blood loss from an artery is more rapid than from a vein and has more pressure behind it. Venous bleeding is more commonly

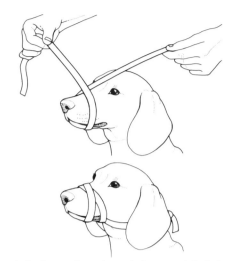

A simple muzzle can be made from a necktie, belt, or leash.

seen and less serious. The blood is darkish red and flows evenly; arterial blood is bright red and spurts in time with the heart beat. If a large artery is cut an animal can bleed to death in a few minutes. Some wounds may require stitches.

CRUSHING WOUNDS

Road accidents, slamming doors and, in the case of small animals, being stepped upon are typical causes of crushing wounds to pets. In addition to cuts they will almost certainly involve severe bruising and possibly broken bones as well. Because of the possible complications great care and restraint must be exercised in dealing with this type of injury. First aid treatment must be aimed at preventing severe bleeding, preventing the pet from aggravating the injury by trying to move, and preventing infection in the wound. All three tasks may be complicated by the possibility of broken bones.

Because of the associated damage around the wound a tourniquet, placed well away from the wound, may be more suitable than a pressure bandage. Fortunately the majority of this type of wound do not bleed too severely, and the gentle application of a pad of clean cotton with a piece of sterile gauze over the wound, *lightly* held in place with a bandage, will often arrest the bleeding; after a short time natural clotting of the blood will seal the wound. Gentle washing with warm water and a little soap may help to clean the wound and reduce the risk of infection, but it may also promote further bleeding. In such cases it is better to cover the wound with a dry clean cloth until the veterinarian can examine it.

ABRASIONS

Abrasions can be extremely painful and are particularly susceptible to infection. In terms of immediate danger to your pet they are less serious than other wounds but they may take a long time to heal. The bleeding from these wounds is often not serious and consists of a slow ooze from the damaged area. The best course is to cover the area with a clean cloth or piece of gauze, after washing with salt water and dusting with an antiseptic powder to dry up the wound, and to bandage the dressing firmly in place. If the graze is particularly dirty it might require cleaning by a veterinarian and possibly the use of antibiotics to prevent infection.

CONTROLLING BLEEDING

Pets are liable to all sorts of injuries which result in external hemorrhage. Most bleeding can be controlled with common sense home treatment. In the case of small animals and birds where even a small loss of blood represents a large proportion of their total supply, bleeding is a very serious condition. If there is substantial bleeding from a wound in a large animal, the bleeding will have made the wound relatively clean so that stopping the blood loss is more important than cleaning and disinfecting the area. Then get the animal to a veterinarian who will take steps to control infection.

Pressure Bandages

A pad of cloth secured by bandaging will control bleeding when the blood flow is not excessive. Wounds on limbs are the easiest to treat. First hold a piece of cloth (a handkerchief or even a packet of paper tissues will do) over the wound with as much pressure as possible and then bind it tightly with a bandage or strips of cloth wound round the limb. For body wounds wind the bandaging right around the trunk. With head wounds be careful not to obstruct breathing. For wounds to the ear place a pad tightly on either side of the ear and then bandage flat against the head. Bleeding in or around the eye can often be controlled by pressing a moistened pad against it and holding it there while you get the animal to a veterinarian. If the animal can see through the other eye, it will be less likely to panic.

Scrotum wounds are more difficult. Place a pressure pad over the scrotum and keep it firmly in place with bandages crisscrossed over the back and around the hips. For penis wounds keep the pad in place with bandaging around the body. Bandage the whole tail for tail wounds. If the wound is near the base of the tail, start the bandage half way up the tail and work toward the body. Anchor the bandage to the hair on the back of the spine with adhesive tape. In a serious fight the neck is the main area for attack and is the place where many predators make their killing bite. If the jugular vein or carotid artery is severed, death comes too quickly for aid to help. In other cases a pressure bandage can save life.

The most common sort of injury on the feet is a corn or cracked claw or hoof or a puncture wound into the pad itself. Usually there is so little bleeding that there is no need to control it, except in the case of small birds where the proportional blood loss may be

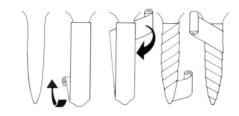

Bandaging the tail.

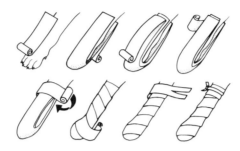

Bandaging the foot.

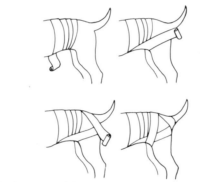

Bandaging the abdomen.

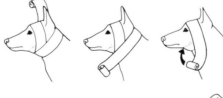

Above. *Bandaging the head.*

Below. *Bandaging the elbow.*

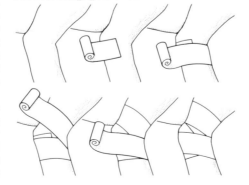

great and must be stopped rapidly. Potassium permanganate applied to the broken tip will often stop the flow of blood; a styptic pencil or stick commonly found in homes may do as well.

Bleeding from a pad can usually be controlled by a pressure bandage. Place bits of cotton between the toes. Then place two or three ample pieces of gauze or a couple of handkerchiefs over the entire foot. Wrap all with appropriately sized bandages or strips of cloth. Go well above the foot, and keep the bandages flat. Do not twist or tighten at any particular point lest you cut off circulation. Then encase it all with elastic or plastic tape. Often an animal can be distracted from the main dressing by a few strips of bandage or tape around the unaffected limbs.

Tourniquets

Tourniquets are only necessary where there is so much bleeding that one cannot see the point of injury or where blood is being lost very rapidly. Accidents of this kind are those in which an animal's foot becomes caught in an escalator, an electric fan, barbed wire, a lawn mower, or a farm machine.

Find an appropriately sized piece of strong fabric. A man's necktie, for example, would make an adequate tourniquet to control bleeding in the foot of a cat or all but the largest breeds of dogs. A scarf would do for a pony, an average-sized horse, or a cow. Do not choose wool or any material with too much "give" in it. A length of nylon or cotton clothesline can be used to construct a tourniquet. One must be careful in applying the pressure not to cut the skin, bruise the muscles or, in smaller creatures, to snap a bone. One may use a combination of any materials at hand (a sweater, straw, or even newspapers and a nylon cord). Place the material under the cord to distribute the pressure and lessen the chances of tissue damage.

Position the material around the narrow part of the leg above the ankle. Tie it firmly, but not too tightly. Put two or three knots in it. It does not really matter what sort of knot is used so long as it holds. Then place a piece of wood or metal into the knot. A pencil might be sufficiently strong to twist the tourniquet on a cat or a rabbit. A piece of broomstick would be necessary to tighten the tourniquet on a pony. A wooden matchstick and a piece of half inch gauze would be adequate for a gerbil.

Tighten the tourniquet by simply turning the wooden handle around and around. When the tourniquet is sufficiently tight, anchor the handle by tying some of the bandage around it or have someone hold it. Within a few seconds the bleeding should lessen or stop. Then wash or wipe off the blood and try to determine the location of the injury. Apply a pressure bandage to the whole foot, then release the tourniquet. If the bandage immediately becomes saturated with blood tighten the tourniquet again and repeat the procedure after about ten minutes. If the bandage still oozes blood you will have

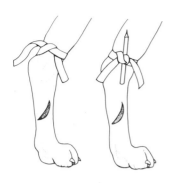

Left. *A simple tourniquet tied tightly above a bleeding wound.* Right. *A less tightly tied tourniquet in which a piece of wood, such as a pencil, is used to adjust pressure.*

to tighten the tourniquet and redo the whole procedure. If, however, there is but a slight seepage of blood into the bandage it is generally better to leave it in place. After a few moments the bleeding will gradually stop.

WARNING: No tourniquet should be left on tightly for more than twenty minutes. It is a technique used not as a cure but as an aid to a cure. Bandages properly applied are safe. Tourniquets are safe as a temporary measure, but may cause permanent damage if left on too long.

BURNS

Burns on pets are complicated by the presence of hair. Often the hair may serve to protect the skin but, if the burn is bad, healing can be complicated by the presence of burnt hair. Hair may also disguise the severity of the burn so that the owner may not be aware of it until several days have elapsed when the blisters start to burst. The most common burns are on an animal's pads caused by its running through hot embers or jumping on a hot surface. If the skin is unbroken, cover with a dry clean pad and bandage. Use a soothing ointment if the skin is broken. The veterinarian will give more detailed treatment. Do not attempt to remove burnt hair or tissue from the damaged area but cover the area with a clean piece of gauze and attach it lightly with adhesive tape.

Scalds may result from hot water or hot fat, as can happen when cats and dogs get under your feet in the kitchen. A wide range of caustic liquids and other substances can also cause serious burns. If an animal is known to have been in contact with paints, paint solvents, and gasoline (petroleum) as well as the more obvious burning acids and alkalis, bleaches, or scouring cleansers, it should be washed in plenty of soap and water and very thoroughly rinsed. (Take care not to get soap, or contaminated liquid, into the animal's mouth or eyes.) Even if such substances do not penetrate the fur and reach the skin, the animal will probably lick them and may burn its lips and tongue.

Burns are normally classified into three degrees: first degree burns sear only the outer layer of skin; second degree burns kill the outer layer and cause blisters which break and weep; third degree burns destroy all the layers of skin and often the underlying tissue as well. First degree burns can be treated by a suitable burn remedy for human use—even a sunburn ointment can be used, or the area could be washed in a strong solution of tea, which is a useful first aid for all burns. Second and third degree burns require professional treatment and in the case of third degree burns the animal is likely to suffer from shock which may make a blood plasma transfusion necessary.

FOREIGN BODIES IN THE SKIN

Thorns and splinters become embedded in the paws more frequently than elsewhere and may be the cause of a limping pet with a swollen pad. If the foreign body and the path of its entry can be clearly seen, or if it still protrudes from the surface of the skin, then apply gentle pressure to push it out and grip the end with a pair of tweezers. Be careful that you do not get injured by the pet in the process.

INGESTED FOREIGN BODIES

Some animals will try to eat almost anything—toys, balls, bones, stones, needles, pieces of wood, string. Very serious problems can result for cows, and other farm animals from eating pieces of plastic bags.

If you see an animal eat something it should not or have seen it playing with an object that then disappears you can guess the nature of the problem when loss of appetite, apparent constipation, or just general discomfort show that something is wrong.

Needles or pieces of bone may get wedged in the throat or mouth. Sometimes they are there for days before anyone realizes it. If on inspection you can see something wedged in the throat, a pull or a sharp tug may dislodge it—a pair of pliers will help you avoid bitten fingers and will probably get a firmer hold. If you are in any doubt about being successful, take the animal to your veterinarian.

If your pet has swallowed a piece of thread or a shoelace and you see it hanging from the rectum, do not try to pull it out. You may pull the rectum lining with it. A *little* gentle easing may help to free it but if there is any resistance give up and trim it off as close to the animal's anus as you can. This will keep the animal from pulling it and doing worse damage. Use sharp scissors to avoid an accidental tug.

POISONS

If you regularly use known poisons, such as weed killers, it would be sensible to discover their antidote and keep a supply in case of accident. A standby "universal antidote" can be made by your druggist to combat a wide range of poisons or in an emergency can be made from: milk of magnesia, burnt toast, and strong tea. This mixture can absorb as much as fifteen times its own weight of coal tar poison and more than one hundred times its own weight of strychnine.

As a last resort—but *never* with horses, or in the case of poisons which are corrosive or petroleum based—induce vomiting to remove the poison by administering a weak solution of hydrogen peroxide (1:12 parts water). Give a cat or dog about 200ml. (½pt.) of mustard in water mixed to the consistency of milk. This will not necessarily bring up all the poison but will give the pet a fighting chance if done quickly, and your veterinarian can take over from there.

If you know that poisons are being used in the neighborhood, find out exactly what they are and what the antidotes are. Your local health officer should be able to supply information. In the United States the Public Health Service operates a clearing house for information on all new toxic hazards and disseminates data to local centers. In Great Britain poison centers have been established for many years.

ARTIFICIAL RESPIRATION

When artificial respiration is applied to drowned animals the pet's body should be placed with the head hanging lower than the body so that gravity will help expel the water. With most animals artificial respiration is easier to apply if the animal is also laid on its side. Always make sure that the tongue is not blocking the air passage and clear what fluid or mucus you can from the nasal passages. Gentle but firm pressure on the chest should be applied rhythmically and released with about four seconds between each movement for cats and dogs and somewhat more quickly for smaller animals. If the animal is not large enough to require the use of both hands on the chest, one can be placed over the diaphragm to exert equal pressure there which will increase both the expulsion of air and the consequent inspiration. With cats, smaller dogs and young puppies, and other animals where the mouth can be completely covered by your own, mouth-to-mouth resuscitation is often to be preferred to avoid risk of damage to the ribs. The rescuer should breathe into the animal's mouth while keeping the nose pinched shut, removing the mouth after each breath to enable the air to leave the patient's lungs. Frequency should be according to the animal's size—about every four seconds for a cat or small dog. Manual resuscitation may be used if the rescuer is not confident about giving mouth-to-mouth.

Taking an Animal's Temperature

Checking body temperature is easily done with a specially thickened thermometer which is inserted into the animal's rectum, while a helper holds the animal. Generally a rising temperature is a sign of infection. With the use of modern antibiotics many infections are easily controlled.

DICTIONARY OF AILMENTS

The aim of the following dictionary of ailments is to give the pet owner some insight into the wide range of complaints that can affect pet animals. It has been compiled by a team of veterinarians, several of whom are specialists in particular branches of veterinary medicine. However, this dictionary is *not* intended to be a substitute for the professional services of the veterinarian; it would be actually dangerous for the layman to undertake most of the treatments. The information includes details of history, symptoms, diagnosis, and treatment of the common ailments of our pet animals as a background which will help the owner to realize that a pet is not well and to be alert to the range of possible symptoms. It will also aid the owner in understanding why particular treatments are being given by his veterinarian and what precautions can be taken to prevent illness.

A system has been introduced which uses SMALL CAPITALS to act as signposts for entries with further information.

ABSCESS
An accumulation of pus in a previously non-existent tissue space. It is caused by the introduction of bacteria into the deeper tissues, and this may come from a source outside the body (for example, bite wounds) or an inside source (for example, blood borne from an infection elsewhere in the body). Abscesses occur in most domestic pets but cats are especially susceptible. The pus in an abscess contains protein-digesting enzymes so that abscesses tend to break through to the body surface. Once this happens and the pus escapes the condition generally resolves itself. Experience is often needed to differentiate between an abscess and other swellings. Treatment consists of lancing the abscess and then administering antibiotics.

ACARIASIS
Infestation of a pet with parasites of the group Acarina (TICKS and MITES). Tick infestations occur on many pet animals including snakes and tortoises in warmer climates. Ticks are only 1–3mm. (0.04–0.12in.) long when they first invade the animal but swell to become bluish–gray blisters about 6mm. (0.24in.) long after sucking blood.

Mites are smaller and may be barely visible to the naked eye. They cause MANGE and ear irritation in many pet animals.

ACHLORHYDRIA
Lack of acid secreted by the stomach wall resulting in INDIGESTION.

ACHONDROPLASIA
(Chondrodystrophia)
A hereditary abnormality of cartilage growth during fetal development which occurs as a result of selective breeding. Certain dog breeds with pug noses (Boxers, Boston Bull Terriers, Bulldogs, King Charles Spaniels, Pekingese, Pugs) and short twisted legs (Basset Hounds, Dachshunds) are known as achondroplastic breeds. Achondroplasia may occur occasionally as an abnormality in other dog breeds and other species (cattle, sheep, mice, tortoises).

Achondroplastic breeds are dwarfed, the bones of the limbs short, thick, and twisted with enlarged ends. The cranium is dome-shaped, the nose short and compressed, and the lower jaw protrusive (Bulldog head). The spine is short, the ribs widely sprung, and the tail short and twisted.

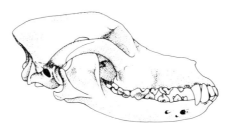

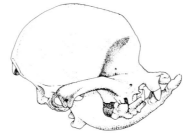

Top. *Normal skull.* Below. *Achondroplasic skull.*

ALLERGY
A reaction to substances previously experienced to which the animal has become sensitive (sensitized). It occurs in all domestic animals and runs in families. Among dogs, Boxers and Poodles are especially susceptible; cats are often afflicted and horses and cattle only occasionally. A wide range of substances act as sensitizing agents (allergens) including medicinal substances given by injection or mouth (antibiotics, sulfonamides, vaccines), foods, the bites of fleas or other insects and substances inhaled or absorbed through the skin.

Immediate allergy reactions occur shortly after exposure to the allergen and are characterized by skin itchiness and sometimes respiratory or digestive signs. In some cases the itch is localized, as in the irritation on the abdomen of spaniels and other retrievers after contact with long grass. The animal makes frenzied efforts to scratch, shakes its ears, and rubs its body vigorously against rough objects. Blotchy swellings develop on the face, especially around the eyes and lips, and sometimes on the body.

A respiratory form similar to asthma in humans is a prominent type of allergy in guinea pigs, cattle, and sheep. The animal breathes fast, coughs, gasps, and froths at the mouth. In severe cases animals may collapse and die, but most animals recover after two or three hours. A digestive form, characterized by sudden bloody diarrhea, is uncommon but can have serious consequences.

In the delayed type of allergic reaction, symptoms usually appear two to six days after contact with the allergen which makes identification of the responsible factor difficult. The signs of delayed reactions are generally constant itching and/or a scabby skin on various parts of the body.

In cases of allergy a veterinarian should be consulted to prescribe corticosteroids which are often effective. Antihistamines are also used but may give disappointing results. Additional treatment is required for the different forms of illness; antidiarrheals and fluid injected into the bloodstream may be needed to counteract dehydration in the gastrointestinal form. Aerosol inhalants (disodium cromoglycate) used in human asthma may offer relief in the respiratory form.

ALOPECIA (Baldness)
Hair loss without sign of irritation is generally caused by hormonal factors. Bare patches appear symmetrically over each rump and the underlying skin appears smooth and thin. A tendency to OBESITY suggests thyroid deficiency while gynomastia (prominent teats in males) and pendulous prepuce suggests imbalance of sex hormones. Thyroid deficiency can be corrected with tablets while baldness in older males may be cured by castration and hormone replacement.

ANAL SAC INFECTION
The anal sacs are membranous pockets about 1.5cm. (0.5in.) long which lie beneath the skin on either side of the anus. The lining of these sacs exudes a waxy material that emerges from ducts near the anus and has a lubricating action. Overfilling and infection of the sacs occurs frequently in dogs and occasionally in cats and other species.

Discomfort occurs in the anal region, the tail is held low and the animal drags its bottom along the ground or bites at the area. As the infection increases, the color of the discharge changes from brown to yellow-green. An abscess may develop, accompanied by severe pain. The condition can be treated by a veterinarian who will empty the sacs and prescribe antibiotics.

ANAL ADENOMAS. See TUMORS.

ANEMIA
Decreased concentration of hemoglobin (the oxygen-carrying substance in the blood) usually coincides with a reduction in the number of red cells (erythrocytes). Hemoglobin, contained within the erythrocytes, combines with oxygen in the lungs and releases it in the tissues. Old erythrocytes are continously replaced with new ones so anemia may occur as a result of excessive erythrocyte loss or deficient replacement.

The common signs of anemia are pale membranes, thready pulse, panting, general weakness, and watery blood. The main causes of anemia are noted here.

External hemorrhage, such as from a severe cut, may require a blood transfusion to restore the red blood cell level.

Internal hemorrhaging can be brought about by bruising, warfarin (rat poison), or purpura praemorrhagica (an allergic condition in horses, dogs, cattle, and pigs). Vitamin K is administered for warfarin poisoning and corticosteroids and antibiotics for purpura.

Parasites, such as LICE, TICKS and HOOKWORM, for which many home treatments are available, but veterinary help is advised.

Bloodborne parasites. *Babesia* and *Anaplasma* are single cell organisms which are carried by ticks in tropical and subtropical areas. The parasites invade the blood and destroy the red blood cells, causing biliary fever in dogs and red water and gall sickness in cattle. These conditions are common in Africa and also occur in some parts of Europe and the United States. Treatment is with Berenil or Phenamedine for red water, and Epsom salts and iron injections for gall sickness.

Sphaerochaetes. *Leptospira* germs cause anemia in dogs, cattle, and other animals. Infection enters through intact skin, often after contamination with infected urine. Antibiotics can be used to treat the infection while a vaccine is available to protect dogs.

Defective diet. Deficiencies of minerals (iron, copper, cobalt), vitamins (B_2, B_6, B_{12}, C) and protein impair the body's ability to replace erythrocytes. This is especially severe in young animals, particularly piglets. Supplements to the diet, especially iron, should correct the symptoms.

ANESTRUS
The time in the reproductive cycle in female animals when they are not in estrus, (also called "heat" or "season"). Sometimes, due to abnormalities in the endocrine glands, females remain in permanent anestrus and require treatment with drugs such as prostaglandin to reestablish the estrus cycle.

ANOREXIA
Lack of appetite. A symptom of illness often associated with FEVER. However, fussy eaters and old animals may ignore food for minor reasons. Also, some animals feed sporadically or hibernate during some months.

ANTHRAX
A highly infectious disease affecting humans and other animals particularly cattle, horses, sheep, goats, and pigs. It is usually rapid in onset and frequently fatal if not treated early. It is caused by a virulent bacterium, *Bacillus anthracis*, which is highly resistant and may survive in the environment for up to forty years. Infection may take place if these bacteria are swallowed, inhaled, or if they enter through cuts or abrasions on the skin. The bacteria multiply rapidly in the blood causing septicemia. Humans, horses, and swine are more resistant than cattle, sheep, goats, and other herbivores.

Immediate veterinary attention is essential and with prompt diagnosis the disease responds well to penicillin; otherwise it is fatal.
Prevention: vaccination is available in areas where the disease is frequent. In many countries cases of anthrax have to be reported to the government veterinary authorities, and there are strict regulations pertaining to hygiene measures.

ARTHRITIS
Inflammation of the joints. A number of specific arthritic conditions are recognized.
Traumatic Arthritis. This includes sprains, wrenches and twists, and results from the application of force. It is frequent in horses, especially those which are unfit or suffer conformation defects (upright pasterns). This form of arthritis and many other injuries also result from abnormal conditions imposed by humans on jumpers and polo ponies. Dogs are occasionally afflicted. (See SPRAINS.)
Septic Arthritis. Infection of a joint, which results from penetration (as result of a cat bite, for instance) or spread from elsewhere in the body. The latter occurs in newly born animals after navel infection and is known as JOINT ILL.

Antibiotics are administered either by injection or orally.
Osteoarthritis. The symptoms are chronically enlarged painful joints in older animals, especially dogs and horses. In horses, osteoarthritis of the hock (spavin), foot joint (ringbone), and navicular (navicular disease) are frequent. (See LAMENESS.) In dogs, the stifle is sometimes affected, and arthritis of the spine is common in old age. In most cases the cause is unknown but longstanding strain seems important. Dogs of large breeds are most prone, and afflicted animals are often overweight.

Palliative rather than curative treatment is given since the arthritic changes in the joints are permanent. Painkillers and anti inflammatory substances are useful but should be prescribed by a veterinarian. Rest should be enforced as much as possible.
Rheumatoid Arthritis. Often simply called arthritis as its relationship with rheumatoid arthritis in humans has not been established, it occurs occasionally in dogs. Symptoms include sudden onset of pain in one or more limb joints with or without fever. If more than one limb is affected, the animal may

remain in its bed shivering, uninterested in food, and unwilling to stand. Corticosteroids, rest, and warmth are the recommended treatment.
Arthritis of the spine in cats. This occurs at a relatively early age (sometimes as early as one to two years) and is associated with an excess consumption of vitamin A, often the result of overzealous dosing with cod liver oil. Weight reduction and lowering of vitamin A intake will relieve the condition.
Warning: Painkillers such as aspirin should not be given to cats and to other animals only at low dosage.

ASCARIDS
Parasitic roundworms (nematodes) that inhabit the small intestine of many species including dogs, cats, horses, wild carnivores, aquatic mammals, birds, and reptiles. The worms are white or pink in color, up to 50cm. (24in.) in length (depending on the size of the host) and are most common in young animals. Infection is usually by mouth, the worm eggs having been ingested. In dogs, however, infection often occurs before birth with the larvae invading the puppies while they are still in the womb of the bitch. Dogs can also be infected by eating prey which have ingested the eggs.

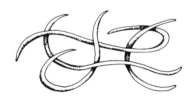

Toxocara round worms.

Ascarids are usually harmless in moderate numbers, but due to their large size, heavy infections can cause serious obstruction of the intestine, sometimes with fatal consequences. This sometimes occurs in ornamental fowl which have been kept for long periods in crowded pens where the ground has become heavily contaminated with worm eggs. Such pens remain infective for a year after the fowl have been removed.

Symptoms include enlargement of the abdomen and failure to thrive. Whole worms are vomited or passed in the feces. Puppies with worms sometimes eat gravel or sand. Treatment involves use of anthelmintics, of which the most widely used are the piperazine compounds. Periodic repeat dosing three or four times a year is advisable as is the worming of pregnant bitches.
Prevention. Since the eggs adhere to the coat, special attention should be paid to grooming along with the ordinary hygienic regime for quarters and disposal of bedding. In lactating animals, the skin on and around the mammary glands should be sponged daily to remove eggs which would otherwise be ingested by the young.

ASCITES
An accumulation of free fluid in the abdomen

which generally produces distension. (Other conditions producing abdominal distension include bladder blockage, pregnancy and gas accumulation due to twisted gut of stomach). Ascites, also known as dropsy, may result from several ailments.

Heart weakness. This is common in old dogs and is often accompanied by coughing and lethargy. Treatment with heart stimulants (such as digitalis) may prolong life, but ascites often persists.

Liver or kidney damage. This results in low blood protein concentrations which can lead to escape of fluid from the blood vessels. Drugs which increase urine output (diuretics) and high protein diet supplemented with glucose may help.

Starvation. This produces decreased blood protein concentrations with the same result as above.

In all conditions the abdominal fluid may be drained off although it is only temporary.

ASPERGILLOSIS
A fungal infection of a bird's lungs and air sacs through inhalation of the spores of *Aspergillus fumigatus*, which can be present in any decaying vegetation. This disease is usually fatal. There is no known cure, but preventive measures include adding potassium iodide at the rate of 5.5 grams per liter (0.1 ounces per pint) to drinking water.

ASTHMA. See ALLERGY.

ATRESIA ANI
A condition in which piglets, pups, and calves are born with no anus. The intestine ends blindly some distance from where the anus should be, or opens into the vagina. An operation can sometimes stitch the intestine to an artificial opening.

ATROPHY
Wasting of some part of the body due to disuse or pressure. For example, the shoulder muscles waste in horses, dogs, and cats when the radial nerve is paralyzed (often caused by an accident) and in dogs the hindquarters waste after damage to the spinal nerves from the distemper virus. Efforts to exercise unused muscles by bending and stretching have been recommended but are seldom effective.

AUTUMN FLY
A nonbiting fly (*Musca autumnalis*), especially common on cattle. The female resembles the housefly, but the male can be distinguished by its orange-yellow abdomen with a black longitudinal stripe. This fly feeds on the secretions from the eyes, nose, and mouth and pesters animals in the pastures. Dusting powders for use around the eyes are widely available.

AZOTURIA
A disease of horses characterized by a stiffness of one or both hind legs. This disease occurs most often in the well fed, stabled horse when it is taken out for exercise after a period of rest. The muscles over the loins become hard to the touch, and the urine may show a dark wine color.

Treatment involves resting the horse immediately. Cover the loins with rugs and summon veterinary assistance. Treatment with intravenous corticosteroids and antihistamines is the current method. It may be necessary to pass a catheter into the bladder if the by-products of the illness cause retention of urine.

BENEDENIA
An ailment caused in fish by a small white-gray fluke of triangular shape which can be seen pointing toward the tail. Loss of appetite is the usual symptom. A commercial Oodinium cure usually clears up the disease. (See **Fish**).

BLADDER STONES
Bladder stones (urolithiasis or calculi) occur in many species including dogs, cattle, sheep, horses, rabbits, hamsters, and tortoises. The signs of illness are usually those of CYSTITIS (frequent passage of small quantities of bloody urine). In males, however, the stones may obstruct the penis causing a distended abdomen and continuous efforts to urinate with the passage of little or no urine.

If the obstruction is not removed the animal's system becomes poisoned with waste products which produce depression, coma, convulsions, and finally death. (See uremia described under NEPHRITIS, CHRONIC.)

BLEPHARITIS
Inflammation of the inner membranes of the eyelids usually as an extension of CONJUNCTIVITIS. It is common in cats with flu or in allergic reactions. The membrane inside the lids protrudes to form a pink rim around the eyes. Treatment is as for conjunctivitis.

BLINDNESS. See PROGRESSIVE RETINAL ATROPHY.

BLISTER
An accumulation of clear fluid (transudate, lymph) in the superficial layers of the skin or membranes. A blister is rarely seen in animals other than as the manifestation of a specific disease, as in foot-and-mouth disease.

Burns and scalds which commonly cause blisters in humans do not usually do so in animals, because of their fur covering. However when blisters do occur, they can be serious since they may not be seen until they burst. (See **Care of the Sick and Injured Pet**.) Salivary cysts under the tongues of dogs and cats which may be mistaken for blisters are in fact the result of blockage of the salivary ducts. Fluctuating swellings on the earflaps of dogs and cats are blood blisters rather than true blisters and result from excessive head shaking. (See also HEMATOMA.)

Blister is also the name given to strong liniments (for example biniodide of mercury) sometimes used to treat inflammation of the tendons and other conditions of horses.

BODY ROT. See FIN ROT AND BODY ROT.

BOTS
Larvae of a furry, bee-like fly, *Gasterophilus*, that become attached to the stomach wall of the horse and donkey during the fall and winter. When they are ready to pupate they separate from the stomach, are passed in the feces, and crawl into the ground. Bot pupae can be seen in horse dung during the spring and summer. They are brownish red barrel-shaped organisms, about 1cm. (0.75in.) long. The larvae in the stomach are usually harmless, although in large quantities they may cause a dry bristly coat and overall loss of condition. The adult flies lay their eggs on the coat and especially the legs, of the horse or donkey, and the buzzing noise they make often panics the animal. If the condition of the animal is impaired the larvae can be washed off with a mixture consisting of two tablespoons of medicinal turpentine and 0.5 liter (1 pint) of linseed oil.

BROKEN WIND
Common term for emphysema of the lungs involving the breakdown of the air sacs to form cavities. Horses particularly become afflicted as a sequel to certain infectious diseases such as STRANGLES, but the main cause is probably fungal toxins carried on spores in stable dust or a simple spore allergy.

An afflicted horse must live outside stables for the rest of its life, and its hay must be dampened before feeding. If secondary infection occurs, antibiotics should be given.

BRONCHITIS
Inflammation of the airways (bronchi) caused by infection. Symptoms include rattling breath, persistent cough, listlessness, and variable appetite. Treatment is usually by antibiotics and cough mixtures. In older animals a chronic form occurs which is resistant to treatment.

BURSITIS
Inflammation of a bursa, a membrane that separates adjacent structures and facilitates

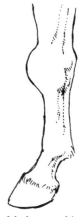

Bursitis (hygroma) of the knee resulting from bruising.

motion between them. Following injury these membranes become thickened and secrete abnormal amounts of fluid, giving rise to large soft swellings over the area concerned. In the horse the most common sites are the knee (called "hygroma"), the points of the elbow and the hock ("capped elbow" and "capped hock"), and the withers and upper surface of the spine. In all cases the inflammation is due to injury or chronic irritation, such as an ill-fitting saddle.

In simple cases treatment is by drainage and injections of corticosteroids combined with a pressure dressing if possible. Severe cases may require surgical removal.

CALCULI
Stones that block the urinary tract. (See BLADDER STONES.)

CANCER. See TUMORS.

CANINE HARDPAD. See DISTEMPER.

CANINE LEPTOSPIROSIS. See LEPTOSPIROSIS.

CANKER OF EARS
Long-standing infection of the ears. Dogs with long earflaps and small hairy earholes (e.g., poodles and spaniels) are especially susceptible, but cats, rabbits, and donkeys may also succumb. The initial source of irritation is often unknown but may be infestation with EAR MITES or the penetration of a grass seed. Symptoms include repeated head shaking, scratching (which can cause additional damage), acute pain, and unpleasant smell. The folds inside the ears become thickened, inflamed, and sometimes covered with pus. Insecticide eardrops will rid the ear of mites. Cleaning the ear with antibiotic, antifungal, and antiinflammatory (corticosteroid) ointments should be done by a veterinarian who may also prescribe antibiotics and corticosteroids administered by mouth or an injection. Tranquilizers decrease the scratching and bandaging the earflaps back allows better aeration. Treatment must be diligently pursued because recurrence is common.

CANKER IN BIRDS
An infection of poultry and other birds characterized by accumulations of yellow cheesy pus in the throat and sinuses. If not treated, it sometimes kills the bird. Symptoms include gaping and ruffled body feathers. Cheesy pus can be seen in the throat when the beak is opened. A remedy is commercially available.

CAPILLARIASIS
Infection of the intestinal wall with the small hair-like roundworms, *Capillaria*. Though it occurs in many species of animals, it is commonly a disease of birds. Affected individuals generally waste away and die although occasionally these parasites may cause sudden death. Some species of *Capillaria* spread directly from one bird to another, but other species need an intermediate host (the earthworm). Symptoms include diarrhea (some-

times bloody), anemia, and emaciation. Anthelmintics added to the drinking water prevent the occurrence of this disease.

CARDIAC INCOMPETENCE
Weakened heartbeat which produces accumulation of fluid in the chest and abdomen. (See ASCITES.) It is fairly common in old dogs and sometimes occurs in younger ones also; the symptoms include persistent cough (generally worse at night), lethargy, a swollen abdomen, and labored breathing. The dog may fall over and become unconscious. Horses also occasionally suffer from heart defects which produce incompetence. Drugs can be administered to strengthen the heart beat, and diuretics will increase the urine output which sometimes diminishes the fluid accumulated in the abdomen.

CATARACTS
Opacity of the lens of the eye. In dogs cataracts may be due to inherited factors which either cause cataracts at the time of birth or result in their slow development at any time between one and six years. Dogs older than this may develop cataracts due to DIABETES MELLITIS or GLAUCOMA. Some haziness of the lens often develops, for unknown reasons, in aged pets but causes little incapacity. Horses are occasionally afflicted, as are tortoises and fish. In afflicted animals the pupils are dilated and appear gray or dull white instead of black.

The lenses can be removed by operation, but vision will remain permanently blurred.

Dog with one eye affected by cataracts.

CAT FLU
A highly contagious respiratory disease of cats caused by a number of viruses, and complicated by secondary bacterial infection. Two viruses, feline viral rhinotracheitis (FVR) and feline calici virus (FCV) are responsible for about 80 to 90 percent of cases. Neither disease has a high mortality rate.

Both viruses cause nonspecific signs such as high temperature, vomiting, sneezing, sniffles, and loss of appetite. However, the affinity of each virus for different tissues allows clinical recognition of each type of infection. FVR is typified by CONJUNCTIVITIS, discharge from the eyes and nose, and sneezing. FCV causes minimal changes in the upper respiratory tract and the conjunctivae, but most FCV strains cause ulcerative lesions

on the upper surface of the tongue and the nasal septum.

Natural infection does not produce a lasting and strong protection against reinfection and this is especially the case with FVR infection. With both infections recovered cats may be carriers even though they have circulating antibodies in the blood and show no signs of disease. Recently vaccines have been developed to protect against the disease, but their efficacy has yet to be proven.

"CHOKE"
An obstruction in the pharynx, larynx, or esophagus caused by ingested food material in a horse. The horse is a fussy eater and rarely swallows apples or root vegetables without first chewing. However, these cubes when damp after chewing may reform as a bolus in the back of the throat. The horse suddenly appears distressed when eating and may cough violently and salivate profusely.

The condition frequently resolves itself but a veterinarian should be called immediately to clear the obstruction.

CHONDRODYSTROPHIA. See ACHONDROPLASIA.

CLEFT PALATE AND HARELIP
A fairly common hereditary disease in dogs (especially bulldogs and Pekingese), cats, mice, and cattle in which the palate, or roof of the mouth, fails to close in development so that the mouth is directly connected to the nasal cavity. This deformity is often accompanied by a hairlip. Victims usually die in infancy due to their inability to suckle. When afflicted calves are offered milk in a bucket, they submerge the nostrils as well as mouth and this enables them to suck the milk up.

COCCIDIOSIS
An intestinal infection which causes severe diarrhea in a variety of mammal, bird, and reptile species. In birds coccidiosis causes bloodstained droppings while in rabbits the infection damages the liver; in both cases the disease is usually fatal. Animals contract the illness when their feed is contaminated with infected droppings. Treatment with sulfonamides added to the drinking water may be successful, and droppings must be cleaned away thoroughly at least once a day.

COLIC
Abdominal pain in any species, but particularly referring to acute horse diseases. The pain may be associated with any abdominal organ (for example, renal colic is the name for kidney pain), but colic usually originates in the digestive tract. There are many varieties of this condition including **impaction colic** (blockage of the large intestine with food or sand), **tympanitic colic** (accumulations of gas), **volvulus** (twisted gut), or **spasmodic colic**. Inflammations (enteritis) and diarrhea may also cause the signs of abdominal pain. Worm infestations sometimes cause blockage of the blood vessels supplying the gut causing

verminous colic. Horses are the only animals to suffer commonly from this condition.

Treatment is aimed at controlling pain, maintaining body fluids, and restoring normal bowel movements. The animal must be placed in a grassy paddock or padded box to avoid injury while tranquilizers and pain-killers will help to calm it. Laxatives (Epsom salts, liquid paraffin) are given for impaction. Veterinarians should always be summoned.

CONJUNCTIVITIS

Inflammation of the transparent membrane (conjunctiva) covering the eyeball. Conjunctivitis may occur as a sign of generalized infection (DISTEMPER in dogs, INFLUENZA in horses) and is then accompanied by poor appetite, cough, and other signs.

It may be contagious in horses and cattle (pink eye, New Forest disease) or caused by local factors (injury, infection, ALLERGY, ulcer, ENTROPION, DISTRICHIASIS) in these and other species. Symptoms include blood-shot eyes with an overflow of tears or an accumulation of pus at the corners. The eyelids may be swollen and half closed, and the pink membrane (third eyelid or nictitating membrane) may protrude across the eyeball.

Objects such as grass seeds must be removed and ulcers, ENTROPION, and DISTRICHIASIS treated. Infectious conditions often respond to antibiotics.

CONSTIPATION

A condition occurring infrequently in most pet species but is somewhat common in male cats. In old male dogs it may be due to perineal hernia or enlarged prostate gland. Symptoms include straining and producing small quantities of dry feces which are sometimes covered in mucus or blood.

Laxatives such as liquid paraffin for dogs and cats, Epsom salts for horses and cattle, may be tried but in persistent cases a veterinarian should be consulted. Perineal hernias are sometimes operable.

CONVULSIONS. See FITS.

CORNEAL ULCER

A condition in which the corneal surface of the eye becomes eroded and the ulcer may be surrounded by blood vessels. It is common in dogs with protruding eyes (Pekingese especially), although unusual in other breeds. The cause is unknown but inadequate lubrication may be a factor. This condition sometimes occurs during long-standing irritations, for instance with ENTROPION or DISTRICHIASIS.

Antibiotic ointments often cure the ulcer but sometimes cautery is required. In stubborn cases stitching the eyelids closed for one or two weeks helps.

CORNEAL WOUNDS

Injury to the cornea of the eye is rare since blinking is so fast. Cat scratches generally heal quickly with only a slight blemish, but horn injuries may cause blindness in cattle. Corneal wounds caused by sharp objects or flying glass can be stitched, but in order to produce a minimal scar the edges of the wound must be carefully matched. However, other structures such as the iris and lens are often damaged at the same time.

"CRIB BITING" AND "WINDSUCKING"

Some neurotic vices seen in horses. They both involve gulping air into the stomach, but in crib biting the horse takes in air while grasping a fixed object in the mouth. They tend to cause loss of body condition due to chronic indigestion, and in some cases bring on frequent bouts of COLIC.

Various straps which cause pain when the neck is arched can be applied, or a hollow bit which prevents the formation of the necessary air pressure in the mouth can be fitted. Surgical operations have been devised ranging from partial removal of some of the throat muscles to the creation of a permanent opening into the mouth through the skin of the cheeks. The perfect remedy has yet to be found. (See also ROARING AND WHISTLING.)

CYSTIC OVARIES

Large fluid-filled cavities in the ovaries. They sometimes appear and produce striking changes in behavior and appearance. (See NYMPHOMANIA.)

CYSTITIS

Inflammation of the bladder common in dogs, especially females. The signs are frequent efforts to urinate with the passage of only small quantities of urine, sometimes bloodtinged. Vomiting and loss of appetite may also occur. In severe cases the gait is straddled and male dogs may squat like bitches during urination. Cystitis is caused by infection and/or bladder stones.

Infections respond to antibiotics and urinary disinfectants. If bladder stones are the cause, these must be removed to effect cure. (See BLADDER STONES.)

CYSTS. See INTERDIGITAL CYSTS; ABSCESS; NYMPHOMANIA.

DANDRUFF

The small flakes of skin sometimes found on the coats of animals. They usually occur in association with chronic skin disease.

DEAFNESS

Dogs and cats are sometimes born deaf. Deafness may be linked to the color of the animal's coat. White Bull Terriers, merle Collies (marbled black and white), harlequin Great Danes (three or more colors), and white cats with blue eyes are more often deaf than breeds of other colors. Inborn deafness is also to be found in Pekingese, Fox Terriers, and Fox Hounds. For the good of future generations, animals with this (or any other) hereditary defect should not be allowed to breed. Dogs sometimes go deaf with age presumably due to degeneration of the nerves. Certain drugs and antibiotics, such as streptomycin, may damage the hearing of pets as they do in humans. Treatment is not undertaken. Temporary deafness or partial loss of hearing may be a symptom of other ear conditions such as HEMATOMA, EAR MITES, FOREIGN BODIES, and MIDDLE EAR INFECTION.

DEPLUMING ITCH. See MANGE.

DIABETES INSIPIDUS

Condition caused by deficiency of the anti-diuretic hormone, which limits the production of urine and is produced in the pituitary gland. This tiny gland is situated above the roof of the mouth and if its function is impaired, for example by inflammation or tumor, hormone imbalance and excessive urination follow. Excessive urination and thirst are the main features of this condition.

One effect is that the urine remains consistently thin and copious. This symptom is used as a diagnostic test. The animal is deprived of water for eight hours and the urine concentration measured. If it remains thin and watery (and signs of other illnesses are absent) diabetes insipidus is likely. Periodic injections or oral doses of posterior pituitary hormones relieve the condition.

DIABETES MELLITIS

A disease of middle-aged dogs, cats, and possibly other pets which is caused by deficiency of insulin (the hormone produced by the pancreas). Insulin normally acts to keep blood sugar low. The main signs of this illness are excessive thirst and urination and increased levels of sugar in the blood and urine. Scurfy skin, cataract (opacity of the lenses of the eyes), and wasting may develop later. Diabetes mellitis can be distinguished from other conditions which also cause thirst (DIABETES INSIPIDUS, chronic NEPHRITIS, PYOMETRA) by testing the urine for sugar.

Tablets which lower the blood sugar levels are helpful in some cases only. More severely affected animals need periodic insulin injections which must be regulated for each case separately because individual requirements vary and excess insulin may be dangerous. Carbohydrates should be reduced, and items rich in sugar eliminated from the diet.

DIARRHEA

A common condition in pets which usually signifies inflammation of the intestine. It is most often due to minor dietary upsets which can be cured by a day's fasting, but may also be due to serious illnesses such as PANLEUCOPENIA (in cats), DISTEMPER (in dogs), Johne's disease (in cattle), transmissible gastroenteritis (in pigs), or COCCIDIOSIS (in birds and snakes). Worms are often the cause in sheep. Irritants and poisons may also be to blame. In dogs nonspecific intestinal infections are most commonly responsible.

Sulfonamides and antibiotics are the most effective treatment when given by mouth and mixtures of kaolin and chlorodyne also help. Atropine injections are often effective and fluids in large volumes can be administered directly into the bloodstream when dehydration is severe. (Fluid by mouth may promote vomiting.) Food should be withheld for twenty-four hours.

DISLOCATION
Luxation, Out of Joint
The displacement of a bone from its socket at a joint. The condition is usually caused by some forceful incident (a fall or an automobile collision), although in cases where a joint is inherently badly formed (hip displasia, for instance) luxation may be caused by a minor event. The dislocation may be complete or incomplete (also known as total luxation and subluxation), and there is often severe stretching or tearing of the joint capsule and ligaments.

Dislocations are most common in the hip joint and lameness is the main sign.

In elbow dislocations the joint is locked in an abnormal position while in dislocations of the jaw the mouth cannot be closed. The knee cap is quite often dislocated in horses and in small breeds of dogs. (See STIFLE CONDITIONS.)

The dislocation should be corrected (reduced) as soon as possible to avoid unnecessary stretching of the joint capsule. A general anesthetic is often needed to relax the powerful ligaments surrounding the joint and replacement can then be accomplished by manipulation so that the displaced bone "clicks" back into place. In horses (and cattle) a block and tackle may be needed in order to exert the necessary traction on the limb. An operation may be needed to remedy recurring dislocations of the knee cap.

Replacement of a dislocation should be followed by rest, and, where possible, supportive bandaging.

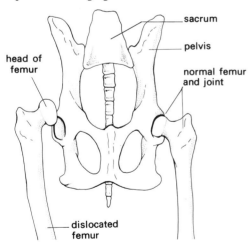

Dislocated femur.

head of femur —
sacrum —
pelvis —
normal femur and joint —
dislocated femur —

DISTEMPER (Canine Hard Pad)
A serious virus disease of dogs, wolves, foxes, dingoes, coyotes, jackals, skunks, mink, ferrets, badgers, weasels, and raccoons. The virus attacks the nervous system and often leaves survivors suffering from fits, paralysis, or weakness of the hind legs and muscular twitches (chorea). Further complications can be thickening of the skin on the nose and foot pads, and brown and pitted discoloration of the teeth. Distemper is fre-

quently accompanied by simultaneous infection by other organisms which produce BRONCHITIS, PNEUMONIA, and DIARRHEA. The mortality rate is often high but this depends on the strain of the virus involved.

Symptoms include a thick yellow or green discharge from the eyes and nose, cough, and diarrhea. Temperature may be increased to 39.4–40°F. (103–104°C.), and the appetite may be normal, increased, or absent. Nervous twitching of the facial muscles, fits, and weakness of the hind legs develop later.

No treatment is effective against the causative virus itself. However, antibiotics alleviate secondary bacterial infection, and sedatives may ease nervous problems.
Prevention: Vaccination is effective and should be administered at twelve weeks of age.

Immunity to distemper should be reinforced by booster vaccinations at regular intervals.

DISTEMPER, FELINE. See PANLEUCOPENIA

DISTRICHIASIS TRICHIASIS
A row of abnormal eyelashes that irritates the eyeball. In districhiasis, an extra row grows along the margin of the eyelids while in trichiasis, the normal quota of lashes is present but some grow in the wrong direction. The abnormal hairs are often very fine and difficult to detect. Symptoms include frequent blinking and a watery discharge. In neglected cases the surface of the eyeball becomes clouded and ulceration of the cornea may develop.

The abnormal lashes are removed by cauterizing their roots. An operation is also possible to remove the part of the lid containing the unwanted lashes. (See also CONJUNCTIVITIS; PROGRESSIVE RETINAL ATROPHY; CATARACT; POP EYE; GLAUCOMA.)

DROPSY. See ASCITES.

DYSPHAGIA
Inability to eat or drink which may be due to a painful condition in the mouth, bad teeth, a damaged tongue, or tumors. The animal may come to its bowl when food is offered but backs away after attempting a mouthful. Drooling of saliva and food falling from the mouth are additional signs. Dysphagia may be a sign of paralysis of the throat muscles as in RABIES.

EARFLAP WOUNDS
Cuts on the earflaps are common in dogs and often result from fight wounds or catching the earflaps on sharp objects. Although not serious these wounds are alarming because head shaking produces profuse bleeding which is difficult to suppress. Stitches are often necessary. As a first aid measure the earflap should be bandaged back flat on the head. (See **Care of the Sick and Injured Pet.**)

EAR MITES
Tiny parasites barely visible to the naked eye which infest the ear canals of cats, dogs, rab-

bits, donkeys, and other pets. Some animals show little sign of discomfort but in others there is itching, thickening of the skin inside the ear, waxy discharge, and scab formation. There is often a characteristic musty smell. Constant scratching and secondary bacterial infection may lead to CANKER.

The parasite spreads from one species to another so when one animal in the household is infested all should be treated whether they show signs or not. After cleaning eardrops containing insecticide are instilled into the ears followed by antibiotic drops.

ECTROPION
A deformity where the eyelids sag outward to reveal the pink pouch beneath the eyeball. This may give rise to repeated bouts of CONJUNCTIVITIS. It is common in Bloodhounds, spaniels, and St Bernards. It may also develop in old age. Treatment involves removal of a wedge of skin to tighten up the lid. (See also ENTROPION.)

ECZEMA
The symptoms, such as redness, thickening, and oozing, of the skin caused by skin inflammation. Several factors may be responsible although ALLERGY is probably the underlying cause.

Antibiotic and cortisone injections are the standard treatment. The inflamed area may be shaved while the animal is under sedation, then washed, dried, and treated with corticosteroid cream.

EGG BINDING
A fairly common complaint of female cage and aviary birds and poultry when they are unable to lay the eggs formed within them. The condition is indicated when a hen sits miserably straining, often on the floor of the cage, with feathers fluffed and anal area swelled. She should be immediately brought into a temperature of about 30°C. (86°F.). If this and anointing the vent with an enema of liquid paraffin or glycine does not free the egg, expert advice must be sought.

Egg binding is most likely to occur with first egg of the season and in cold weather. It results either from an oviduct that is too small or a broken egg. A good balanced diet with cod-liver oil added to seed in the breeding season and sensible management greatly reduce its incidence.

ENDOMENTRITIS
An inflammation of the lining membrane of the womb in horses. It usually results from infection introduced at, or soon after, foaling. Failure to expel the afterbirth normally is another common cause. Endomentritis may occur in the acute form with severe illness, or in a form so mild that no symptoms are seen until it is diagnosed when the mare is unable to conceive.

The acute form must be treated with antibiotics given by injection and by direct infusion into the uterus. If complications such as laminitis occur, the outlook for complete recovery is not good. (See LAMENESS.)

336

ENTERITIS. See GASTRITIS AND ENTERITIS.

ENTROPION
In this condition the edges of the eyelids fold inward so that the lashes irritate the eyeball. It is common in dogs, especially the Chow Chow, and may be either inborn or appear at a later age when the skin of the face becomes loose. Affected animals blink frequently and have a watery discharge. In severe cases the surface of the eye becomes hazy and CORNEAL ULCERS develop.

An operation involving the removal of a thin strip of skin below the lid is carried out. When the edges of this wound are stitched together, the eyelid is tensed and the lashes drawn away from the eyeball. (See also ECTROPION.)

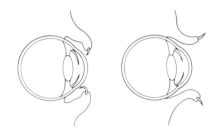

Left. *Entropion*. Right. *Ectropion*.

EPIPHORA
Overflow of tears. A common, but not serious, condition of dogs, especially poodles, which may be caused by CONJUNCTIVITIS or blocked tear ducts. (These ducts run from the corners of the eyes into the nose and allow the drainage of tears.) In pug-nosed dogs, especially Pekingese, hair on the facial skin folds may irritate the surface of the eyes and cause watering.

Conjunctivitis, if present, must be treated. Blocked tear ducts can be cleared by passing a nylon thread down them and instilling cortisone and antibiotic drops into the eyes. Hair on the face which irritates the cornea should be trimmed away periodically.

EQUINE INFLUENZA. See INFLUENZA.

EPISTAXIS
Bleeding from the nostrils. It occurs in horses in three forms:
(a) Bleeding following an injury such as a kick; this is usually of short duration and stops without treatment.
(b) Sudden bleeding during a period of exertion, as in a race. This probably arises from the lungs and is a sequel to a previous infection. This type tends to recur after exercise and prevention requires long periods of rest.
(c) Severe bleeding which may be fatal occurs as a sequel to GUTTURAL POUCH INFECTION.

ERYSIPELAS
An infectious disease, rare in most pets, but commonly affecting pigs. It is caused by infection of superficial wounds by the bacterium, *Erysipelothrix rhusiopathiae*, which is capable of surviving for long periods in water, soil, pasture, decaying organic matter, and carcasses. Treatment involves high dosages of antiserum and penicillin, and an effective vaccine is available.

EYEBALL PROLAPSE
A condition in which the protruding eyes of Pekingese, pugs, and similar breeds are dislodged from their sockets. This may occur during dog fights or when the animal is lifted by the scruff of the neck. The eyeball can be replaced by lubricating with liquid paraffin and pressing it back into place with a pad of moist cotton. If treatment is prompt there are no ill effects, but if delayed, blindness may result. First aid by the owner until the animal can be seen by a veterinarian may include applying pads of cotton soaked in warm salt water or liquid paraffin. The veterinarian will almost always stitch the eyelids together to keep the eyeball in place.

EYE WORMS
Slender worms (*Thelazia*) up to 2cm. (0.75in.) long, which live under the eyelids and in the tear ducts of animals (mainly of cattle), in certain parts of the United States. They also occur occasionally in horses, dogs, cats, and rarely humans. They are transmitted from animal to animal by flies which are attracted to the tears and to any inflammatory discharge. Symptoms include irritation, CONJUNCTIVITIS, and excessive secretion of tears. Treatment involves manual removal.

FEATHER PLUCKING
A habit among cage birds and poultry of plucking at their own feathers as the result of some disorder. Parrot-like birds are especially vulnerable. The main causes are unbalanced diets (particularly a deficiency of vitamins A and D), environmental stress, and unhygienic living quarters, which encourage ectoparasites. These can be killed with an insecticide, such as louse powder, and diets can easily be improved. Nervous conditions induced by restricted cages, boredom, or overcrowding are the most common cause. In such circumstances feather plucking can quickly become a persistent habit.

FELINE INFECTIOUS ENTERITIS.
See PANLEUCOPENIA.

FELINE INFECTIOUS PERITONITIS.
See PERITONITIS.

FELINE INFLUENZA. See CAT FLU.

FELINE LEUKEMIA
A serious and invariably fatal disease of cats. The virus which is now known to be the cause of feline leukemia (FeLV) was only identified in Glasgow in 1964. Even more recently it has been discovered that the infectious agent can be transmitted by direct contact, and feline leukemia is now recognized as a contagious disease of cats.

Feline leukemia is characterized by leuke-mia (abnormal increase in the number of white blood cells), and the presence of tumors (lymphosarcoma) of two main types. In the "alimentary" form the tumors are found in the mesenteric lymph nodes and the alimentary tract; in the "multicentric" form of the disease they are generalized throughout the body. Occasionally a "thymic" form is seen (the principle lesion is in the thymus gland) especially in Siamese cats and in young animals with infection.

The major signs shown by affected cats are lethargy, weakness, and lack of appetite, followed by progressive wasting and terminal anemia. If the lesion involves the thymus and the lymph glands in the chest, breathlessness due to the presence of fluid in the thoracic cavity may be the main symptom. Diagnosis depends on carrying out laboratory tests.

Unfortunately the disease is invariably fatal, and there is no logical or effective treatment available.

FEVER
Elevation of the body temperature above the normal range. It is generally an indication of infectious disease and as a rule is accompanied by rapid pulse, loss of appetite, listlessness and sometimes shivering. Fever may result from bacterial or viral infections, and low grade fever may also occur for a few days after surgery even in absence of infection.

FIN ROT AND BODY ROT
A bacterial disease of fish causing white or gray areas around wounds and fins which appear ragged and eventually rot away. Marine and freshwater fish should be transfered to a tank devoid of plants with 250mg. tetracycline added per 25 liters of water (fresh or salt as appropriate) and kept under treatment for one week. The treatment should be discontinued if the fish show signs of distress. Freshwater fish can sometimes be cured by adding a white spot remedy (commercially available) to their home tank in the dose recommended by the manufacturer.
Note: Antibiotics to the home tank can destroy nutrifying bacteria.

FISH LICE
An infestation of small crustaceans often referred to as fish lice, but are unrelated to true LICE. These flat parasites 5mm. (0.25in.) long can be removed from the fish with tweezers or with a commercial remedy.

FISTULOUS WITHER
A condition affecting horses in which there is an open wound in the region of the withers which exudes pus and fails to heal. It is usually found in association with the roundworm *Onchocerca* which lives in the large ligaments of the neck and is transmitted by midges. However, the true cause may be bacterial. An operation usually involves the removal of all diseased tissue and the drainage of pus.

FITS
Fits or convulsions may be seen in dogs and

cats but in the case of the former species they are much less common since canine distemper, one of the major causes, has been largely controlled by widespread vaccination. Fits may be mild or severe. In mild cases the only signs shown are shaking of the head, twitching of the facial muscles, salivation, and champing of the jaws.

Severe fits begin as described above but are followed by loss of consciousness and collapse. While unconscious, violent muscle contractions occur, and the animal will paddle violently. There is usually copious frothy salivation, and involuntary passage of urine and feces often occurs. This state can last from a few minutes to several hours and may lead to death from asphxiation or exhaustion.

There are many causes of fits in animals, some of which are listed below, but it is important to realize that the fits shown in each instance are indistinguishable, and diagnosis requires professional help. Among the principal causes of fits in dogs and cats are: canine DISTEMPER, DIABETES, kidney disease, MILK FEVER, neoplasia, poisoning (particularly with lead, strychnine, and certain plant poisons), RABIES, teething, TETANUS, TRAUMA, vitamin deficiencies, and worm infestations.

FLEAS

Parasites that feed on warm-blooded animals. They can survive without food for long periods and may live for many months in vacant premises. Although they have host preferences, fleas will feed on a wide variety of animals including wild creatures brought into the home. Fleas carry the larvae of the common TAPEWORMS of dogs, cats, rats, and mice but fleas have to be swallowed before the pet develops tapeworm. Fleas may also transmit MYXAMATOSIS of rabbits and bubonic plague of rats (and human beings).

Common fleas usually cause little harm beyond irritation, although repeated injection of saliva into the pet's skin can lead to allergic sensitization and ECZEMA.

Fleas are sometimes difficult to detect but their presence is indicated by their droppings, visible as dark brown spots deep in the hair or feathers.

Insecticide should be applied not only to the animal but also to its usual resting places and bedding. Flea eggs which may contaminate bedding are unaffected by insecticide so treatment should be repeated two or three times at weekly intervals to kill new larvae. *Note:* Cats, birds, and exotic pets are susceptible to poisoning by some insecticides.

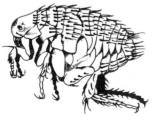

Dog flea (Ctenocephalides canis)

FLU. See INFLUENZA.

FLUKE, GILL

A small parasite (*Dactylogyrus*) 0.5cm. (0.2in.) long causing gill disease in many species of freshwater fish. They feed on the cells of the gills, possibly also on blood, causing much tissue destruction and anemia. The damaged gills may be swollen and show as woolly masses outside the gill covering. The gills become pale, and the fish shows exaggerated breathing movements.

The fish should be placed on its own in a tank containing 1 percent methylene blue (1ml. to 5 liters of water) and left for a week. Other fish should be inspected for signs of infection. (See also BENEDENIA; FLUKE, SKIN.)

FLUKE, LIVER

The most common liver fluke is *Fasciola*—a flat leaf-shaped worm up to 5cm. (2in.) long found in the liver of sheep, cattle, and less commonly in horses, rabbits, and humans. Liver flukes cause severe wasting. The animal is infected by swallowing the young stages of the fluke with food. Serious outbreaks of acute and fatal disease occur in sheep.

The liver fluke *Dicroelium*, 1cm. (0.4in.) long, is less harmful. It does not burrow through the liver but travels to it up the bile ducts from the intestine. After excretion with the feces the young stages of the worm are eaten by ants which are then eaten along with vegetation by the main host animals.

FLUKE, SKIN

A parasite of fish somewhat similar to the gill fluke (See FLUKE, GILL.) in which the scales become slimy and spots of blood are visible. Treatment is as for the gill fluke.

FLY WORRY AND FLY BITE REACTION

Horses are particularly attractive to flies, and the summer is a time of constant head shaking and tail swishing for many horses. Constantly settling around the eyes, the flies cause excessive watering and sometimes CONJUNCTIVITIS, with sores forming at the inner canthus. The bite of the HORSEFLY and the gadfly are painful and may produce a marked swelling. Other flies may cause an allergic rash to appear all over the body.

Providing shelters or trees for shade reduces the worry of flies and a fly fringe on the head collar discourages the head flies, but a long-lasting repellant which does not irritate the horse has yet to be found.

FOREIGN BODIES

Foreign objects such as grass blades often become lodged in the ears or embedded in the skin between the toes of dogs. Occasionally they may also lodge in the eyes. Pieces of wood or bone sometimes wedge themselves between the teeth of dogs in spite of their frantic efforts to dislodge them. Foreign objects such as pieces of rubber, balls, or pieces of bone may be swallowed by dogs and become lodged in the throat, at the entrance to the chest, or in the bowel. Anesthesia and surgical removal is most often needed although sometimes dogs may be made to vomit back smooth objects. (See also **Care of the Sick and Injured Pet.**)

FOWL PEST

A serious and often fatal disease of poultry, but not often encountered in domestic flocks. Symptoms include diarrhea, loss of vitality, and the tendency to gather in a corner of the run. In a less acute form there is only a watery discharge from the nose and eyes. Cure in acute cases is not common, but it is possible to vaccinate poultry against this disease.

FRACTURES. See chapter **Care of the Sick and Injured Pet.**

FRENCH MOLT

A condition in shell parakeets (budgerigars) in which the first-formed feathers, particularly those in the wings and tail, are malformed. It is all too familiar to budgerigar enthusiasts. Feather disorders, particularly of the wings and tail of juveniles, are usually attributable to this condition—the causes of which are still not definitely known.

Many juvenile birds lose these abnormal feathers at the first molt (in the autumn for spring-hatched chicks) when they are replaced by normal feathers. However, in some cases the condition persists throughout life.

FUNGAL DISEASES OF FISH

These cause the development of furry tufts of fungus at the site of damaged scales. The fish should be removed from the tank and drops of 1 percent methylene blue should be added to the fungus until it turns blue. The fish should then be rinsed in a separate tank of clean water for a few minutes and returned to the home tank. Administer twice a day.

FUNGAL DISEASES OF MAMMALS

The role of fungi as a cause of disease has only recently been realized. Most fungi are harmless to animals, but those which are pathogenic cause disease in three ways.

(a) By growing in animal tissues, e.g., ASPERGILLOSIS.

(b) By growing on the surface of the body, e.g., RINGWORM.

(c) By growing in food or water where they produce toxins which are ingested causing mycotoxicosis, e.g., AFLATOXICOSIS.

The signs shown depend on the organs affected and treatment will vary according to the site of infection.

FUR BALL

Fur licked from the coat of cats (especially long-haired breeds) that is swallowed and forms a ball or diffuse plug in the intestine. This produces vomiting. Fur and feathers from eaten prey can also produce similar trouble. Liquid paraffin administered frequently facilitates the passage of the obstruction and weekly dosing prevents recurrence.

GADFLY. See HORSEFLY.

GAPES
A disease of domestic chickens, turkeys, grouse, bantams, pheasants, partridge, quail, and guinea fowl caused by the worm *Syngamus trachea* (Gapeworm) which lives in the trachea. The male and female of this worm live in permanent copulation. Birds become infected by ingesting the eggs of the worm from the ground or by eating earthworms which carry the eggs. The birds gasp for air with gaping beaks (hence the name), lose condition, and may die.

GASTRIC TORSION
Twisted stomach sometimes occurs in dogs, producing occlusion of the inlet and outlet and accumulation of gas. The abdomen becomes swollen and resilient. Abdominal pain and restlessness, whimpering, drooling of saliva, and heaving are followed by depression and coldness. An immediate operation is essential to correct the stomach position. However, shock is generally severe and in many cases the animal dies.

GASTRITIS AND ENTERITIS
Inflammation of the stomach and intestine. This condition is frequent in pets and causes vomiting and DIARRHEA. Dietary upsets and infections are the most frequent causes in dogs. Cats are especially prone after licking substances such as medications and paint that have contaminated their coats. Virus infections, such as FELINE ENTERITIS (in cats), DISTEMPER (in dogs), swine fever (in pigs), and rinderpest (in cattle), and bacterial infections, such as *Salmonella* and *Escherichia coli* (in calves) all cause enteritis. Germs in the gut which normally cause no trouble may become harmful when the animal's resistance is weakened. COCCIDIOSIS is frequently the cause in birds, while worms cause it in sheep.

The cause of the inflammation must be established. Specific remedies are available for worms and coccidiosis, and there are antidotes for some poisons. (See chapter **Care of the Sick and Injured Pet.**) Food should be withheld for twenty-four hours. The drug chlorodyne soothes the intestine and kaolin absorbs excess moisture. Atropine relaxes spasms and dries out the gut. Antibiotics such as neomycin and sulfonamides are especially suitable when given orally. Commercial antidiarrheal remedies often contain a mixture of these beneficial agents. Body fluid should be replaced by injection when severe diarrhea and vomiting have produced dehydration.

GILL DISEASE. See FLUKE, GILL.

GINGIVITIS
An inflammation of the gum which is common in older dogs and cats and is generally the result of dental incrustations (TARTAR). These encrustations damage the gums and expose them to infection. The main signs are bad breath and red swollen gums above the tooth margin. Cats salivate, paw at their mouths, and have difficulty with chewing. Although interested in food they quit eating after a few mouthfuls. In untreated cases the teeth become loosened.

Tartar should be removed (scaled) periodically by a veterinarian and loose teeth extracted. Infected gums can be treated with antibiotics or antifungal remedies. Vitamin C tablets may also help.

In horses gingivitis occurs as a red swollen area of gum behind the front teeth in young animals (**lampus**). The cause is unknown, but the condition often clears up in two to three weeks.

GLANDERS
A contagious bacterial disease of horses which is usually fatal. It affects other members of the horse family but also can be fatal in humans and other animals. In horses, glanders, (or **farcy**) may be sudden and severe or, more frequently, long lasting. In donkeys it is always sudden. The incubation period is about two weeks, followed by severe fever and pus secreted from the nose. Nodules containing pus form in the nasal chambers, lungs, and skin, and ulcers and scars form on the legs and face. An immunological skin test (Mallein test) aids diagnosis. No treatment is available. In view of the danger to humans all affected animals must be destroyed and the disease reported to health authorities. Control of the spread of glanders depends on quarantine, strict hygiene, and vigorous disinfection of infected premises. These measures have been effective, and the disease is rare in most parts of the world.

GLAUCOMA
An eye condition of dogs and other species characterized by increased tension within the eyeball and bulging eyes which usually lead to blindness. The aqueous humor (fluid within the eyeball) is formed in one part of the eye and leaves at another and the increased tension is due to blockage at the point of outflow. Hereditary factors are suspected of being responsible for some cases. Among dogs, Cocker Spaniels and Basset Hounds are most prone. Glaucoma can also be caused by displacement of the lens, inflammation within the eye, and adhesions of the iris to the cornea (anterior senechiae) after a cataract operation. In severe cases increased tension can be felt by placing the fingertips over the closed lids; in less obvious cases tension in the eyeball can be measured with a special instrument (tonometer).

Treatment involves using miotic eyedrops (causing pupil dilation) and substances to slow the formation of aqueous humor (carbonic anhydrase inhibitors).

GOITER
An enlargment of the thyroid gland associated with low levels of thyroid hormone in the blood (hypothyroidism). (See chapter on **Your Pet's Body and Senses.**) The thyroid is situated beside the windpipe at the throat of animals or just inside the chest in birds. Goiter occurs occasionally in dogs and produces obesity, lethargy, and hairless patches over the rumps. In cage birds there is breathing difficulty, a squeak with each breath, ruffled feathers, and eggs that fail to hatch. When affected infant birds usually die.

The condition may be due to a diet deficient in iodine (an essential constituent of thyroid hormone). Goiter occurs often in cage birds fed on iodine-deficient seed.

For mammals, thyroid tablets and iodine diet supplements are given and part of the thyroid gland is sometimes removed. For birds cod-liver oil is administered.

GRASS SICKNESS
A serious disease of horses that is usually seen in the summer months shortly after turning out to grass, although cases have been recorded in stabled horses. An acute form involves signs of nervousness combined with severe colic followed by death within twenty-four hours of the onset. However, the most common variety is the chronic form, which can last up to six months. Symptoms in these cases are lethargy, loss of appetite with wasting, salivation, and difficulty in swallowing. In addition, the characteristic sign of muscle twitching is seen.

The cause is still not known for certain, but it is likely that either a transmissible agent, such as a virus, or a toxin of plant or bacterial origin, attacks the nervous system.

No specific treatment is known and the majority of animals affected die.

GUTTURAL POUCH INFECTION
The guttural pouches are situated on either side of the pharynx. In the horse they may be invaded by a membrane which becomes ulcerated with eventual invasion of associated arteries and consequent hemorrhage. On occasions it can be massive and fatal. Treatment involves specialized surgery to isolate and ligate the branch of the artery (usually the internal carotid) concerned.

HABRONEMA. See SUMMER SORES.

HAIRLIP. See CLEFT PALATE.

HALITOSIS (Bad Breath)
GINGIVITIS associated with the accumulation of TARTAR on the teeth is the most common cause of halitosis in dogs and cats. Occasionally it may also result from digestive disturbances. In horses, impacted food material between the teeth may be the cause. Dental decay in animals is rare. In horses the mouth should be searched for retained hay boluses between the molar teeth and the cheeks. Sharp teeth, due to uneven wear, sometimes produce mouth ulcers, infection, and unpleasant odor. Sharp and uneven teeth should be rasped.

HARD PAD. See DISTEMPER.

HEART DISEASE
Animals suffer from heart disease, but the

incidence is much less than that in humans, principally because diseases of the coronary arteries are not a problem. However, congenital deformities (e.g., defects in the wall between the right and left sides of the heart or patent ductus arteriosus), valvular disease (e.g., stenosis or incompetence of the heart valves), pericarditis, myocarditis, and endocarditis all occur, especially in dogs.

In general, heart disease can be classified into acute or chronic types. In the latter, animals show signs of exercise intolerance, attacks of coughing, or accumulation of fluid in the abdomen or thorax, depending on the type of lesion present. Acute heart attacks most commonly result in the animal's fainting but occasionally cramp may be a feature.

Although heart disease is serious, in many cases treatment is possible and the animal is capable of leading a comparatively normal life. Daily medication is usually necessary.

HEARTWORM
A slender roundworm (*Dirofilaria imitis*) 20–30cm. (8–12 in.) long which lives in the right side chambers of the heart and pulmonary artery of dogs, cats, wolves, foxes, and bears. Heartworm is found in tropical and subtropical countries, and the larvae are transmitted by the bites of mosquitoes and probably fleas. Heartworm can be tolerated in small numbers by dogs which do not undertake strenuous activities. However, moderate infection may cause incompetence in old and working dogs, and heavy infections are often fatal.

HEAT STROKE AND EXHAUSTION
Occurs in many animals and especially in dogs under humid conditions. The signs are collapse and frenzied panting. Body temperature may rise to 43°C. (110°F.). Imbalance of salts is an added complication since much is lost through sweating. Treatment involves spraying the animal with cold water and applying ice around the head. An electric fan directed toward the patient helps. Intravenous injections of salt solutions are sometimes required. (See also chapter **Care of the Sick and Injured Pet**.)

HEMATOMA
Painless fluctuating swellings under the skin caused by a burst blood vessel. The condition occurs commonly in the earflaps of the dogs and cats due to vigorous headshaking or ear scratching. Hematomas may also occur elsewhere on the body due to some forceful incident (bite or kick). If untreated, the blood in the swelling may be resorbed, but in the earflaps there is often distortion and an ugly "cauliflower ear" results. The hematoma can be opened by a veterinarian with a bold S-shaped cut, the contents evacuated, and the skin layers of the blister stitched together.

HEPATITIS
Inflammation of the liver, which may be brought about by infectious and noninfectious causes. Noninfectious hepatitis results from the ingestion of certain poisonous substances such as arsenicals or phosphorous. Some plants also contain substances which damage the liver.

Ragwort, for instance, contains an alkaloid causing chronic liver damage (cirrhosis). The liver may also be damaged by viruses (infectious canine hepatitis, duck virus hepatitis), bacteria (LEPTOSPIROSIS in dogs and calves, black disease of sheep), protozoa (toxoplasmosis in mammals and birds, histomoniasis in turkeys, COCCIDIOSIS in rabbits) and worm and fluke infestations in many animals.

HEPATITIS, INFECTIOUS CANINE
A virus disease of dogs which is often fatal. Young dogs are particularly susceptible. Symptoms include a high temperature, abdominal pain, vomiting, and diarrhea. The membranes of the eyes and mouth become pale or yellowish, indicating liver damage. The dog becomes depressed and does not eat.

There is no treatment for the disease itself, but antibiotics prevent secondary infection and diet supplements may hasten recovery.

Vaccination against this disease is normally combined with a distemper vaccine.

Note: After clinical recovery the virus may be excreted in the urine for many weeks. During this time the recovered dog remains a source of infection to others.

HEREDITARY DEFECTS
Hereditary defects are transmitted from one generation to another as a result of defective genes. The abnormalities may or may not be congenital (present at time of birth).

The factors transmitted from one generation to another, for example coat color, shape of ears, or temperament, are controlled by minute elements known as *genes* which are strung together on microscopic threads, the chromosomes. These are packed into the heart of the sperm and egg of the father and mother, respectively. At fertilization the sperm and egg fuse and the chromosomes align themselves in pairs, one from each parent, so that the corresponding genes are adjacent. Each feature of the new individual is thus under command of a pair of genes. If both genes are normal the feature controlled will be normal and if both are defective the feature will be abnormal.

If, however, the gene from one parent is normal and that from the other is defective, the result depends on the mode of transmission for that defect. At its simplest, in *dominant conditions*, the defective gene overrules the normal one and the offspring shows the abnormality, while in *recessive conditions* the undesirable gene is overruled and the offspring appears normal. *Codominant conditions* also occur where both genes exert an influence and the defect occurs to some intermediate extent, while in *multifactorial inheritance* defects occur as a result of a number of gene pairs. A knowledge of the mode of inheritance enables one to predict the chances for normalcy in the offspring and also the chances of effectively reducing the incidence of defects with selective breeding schemes.

In dominant conditions about half the offspring from a defective and normal mating are afflicted. Selective breeding from normal animals only can be employed to reduce the incidence of the abnormality rapidly because those with the dominant defective gene are usually afflicted and can be singled out.

In recessive conditions, an animal may carry the defective gene but appear normal. Here selective breeding schemes would be very slow in reducing the frequency of defects because the apparently healthy carriers of the defect are not identifiable and these far outnumber the afflicted animals. In recessive conditions affliction occurs only when a defect is inherited from both parents, and the risk of this is increased when the parents are closely related to one another.

Only those conditions of special interest will be described here. Hereditary defects encompass not only obvious physical and temperamental maladies but also conditions like susceptibility to disease.

Overshot and undershot jaws. The upper jaw is longer or shorter than the lower one. These are recessive conditions seen in dogs, cattle, sheep, and pigs.

Strabismus (squint). A condition common in collie dogs and Siamese cats. Cattle which are born with apparently normal vision sometimes develop squint during the first year of life as a result of recessive genes.

Microphthalmia/anophthalmia (small eyes or absence of eyes). This occurs in dogs (Chow Chow and collies), cattle and pigs, often together with other defects.

Polydactylis. Extra toes such as double dewclaws which are fairly common in dogs and cats.

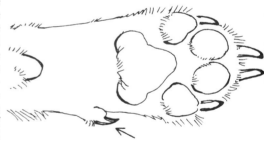

Dew claw on foot of a dog.

Short or absent tail. This sometimes occurs in dogs and if this (dominant) defect is inherited from both parents the pups are stillborn. Consequently the short-tailed survivors have one healthy and one defective gene and should not be mated to one another.

Hip dysplasia. Shallow hip joints are common in many large dog breeds. The mode of inheritance is unknown but may be multifactorial. Severity varies and it is often difficult to establish whether hips are faulty even with X-rays. Most afflicted animals show no sign of disability although arthritis and lameness may develop later. In severe cases the hips become dislocated repeatedly.

Albinism. Absence of pigment (usually recessive) which occurs in many species. White mice and rats are albino strains. White cats with pink or blue eyes and some white Bull Terriers, collies, and Pekingese are deaf. Such association of two characteristics (albinism and deafness) suggests that the genes controlling these features are linked on the same chromosome and inherited as a unit.

Merle/harlequin factor. A pigmentation characteristic linked with the blind-deaf defect. Collies, Great Danes, dachshunds, and Dunkerhounds are sometimes colored gray with black mottling. When two such animals are interbred about a quarter of the litter are blind and deaf. The blind-deaf defect has the characteristics of recessive inheritance.

Hernias. Defects which occur in the muscle wall, often at the navel (UMBILICAL HERNIA) or scrotum (inguinal hernia). A loop of gut or other tissue protrudes to form a lump under the skin. Common in all species, it is inherited multifactorially and can be repaired with an operation.

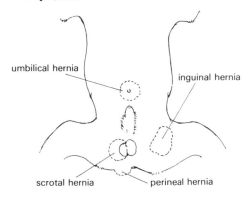

Common sites of hernias.

Cryptorchidism. A condition where the testicles are retained within the abdomen instead of descending to the scrotum. This is common in horses, pigs, and dogs. Cryptorchidism is dominant in horses but recessive in other species. The animals are fertile if only one testicle is retained but often sterile if both are affected.

Epilepsy (fits) and temperament difficulties. Nervous conditions tend to run in families but the mode of transmission is generally unknown. Poodles are sometimes excessively excitable and certain strains of Alsation (German Shepherd) extremely timid.

Hemophilia. A rare condition of dogs and other species in which the blood fails to clot. Afflicted animals may bleed to death from a small cut. The condition is *sex linked* (the defective gene lies on the chromosome governing sex) and occurs almost exclusively in males. (See also CATARACTS; DISTRICHIASIS; PROGRESSIVE RETINAL ATROPHY.)

HERNIA. See ABSCESS, HEREDITY DEFECTS, UMBILICAL HERNIA.

HOOKWORM

Fine thread-like roundworms 1–2cm. (0.4–0.8in.) long which infest the small intestines of mammals, especially dogs and humans. Animals become infected by ingestion of larvae, or else the larvae penetrate intact skin. In the dog family the two prevalent hook-

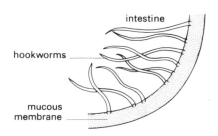

Hookworms embedded in the intestine wall.

worms are *Uncinaria* and *Ancylostoma*. Most wild foxes carry *Uncinaria*, but this worm, also called **northern hookworm** from its distribution in cool temperate and cold countries, does very little harm and is common in kenneled dogs. *Ancylostoma*, however, is a vicious bloodsucker which occurs in all tropical and many temperate countries and can kill whole litters of pups wihin a few weeks. Heavy infections will remove about a third of a pup's blood volume in a single day. One species of *Ancylostoma* occurs in cats, but infestations are generally light.

Aside from the bloodsucking, hookworms also cause a form of dermatitis resulting from invasion of the skin by larvae (both *Uncinaria* and *Ancylostoma*).

Intestinal worms produce severe anemia, pallor of the membranes, and weakness. Signs of skin infestation appear on the feet. The skin between the toes is reddened and itchy, and the footpads become thick and soft. Lameness occurs sometimes. Several commercial remedies are effective.

Prevention: Hookworm infestation is encouraged by unhygienic, cramped quarters. Feces and bedding material should be disposed of regularly, and floors kept clean and dry. Raised beds are best.

HORMONE DEFICIENCY AND IMBALANCE

Hormones, the secretions from the endocrine glands, are instrumental in controlling many of the body functions and their levels in the blood stream are delicately balanced against one another. (See chapter **Your Pet's Body and Senses.**) In certain individuals, however, this balance is disturbed and a variety of signs indicate the imbalance, depending on the hormones involved. These signs include hair loss, OBESITY, NYMPHOMANIA, PYOMETRA, DIABETES MELLITIS, DIABETES INSIPIDUS, and many others.

Modern techniques using radioactive substances are extremely sensitive and make it possible to measure the very low concentrations of hormones normally present in the blood. In some cases deficient levels can be supplemented.

HORNFLY

A bloodsucker common in cattle. The Horn Fly's (*Lyperosia irritans*, also known as *Haematobia irritans*) name is derived from its habit of lighting on the base of cattle horns for warmth in cool weather. It is especially prevalent in the southern United States.

HORSEFLY

Same species of this large brown fly (*Tabanus*) have spots or stripes on the abdomen. It is a bloodsucker that flies with a loud droning sound which horses soon come to associate with the very painful bite. Once the fly has made its slashing bite there appears to be no further pain, and horses will often stand quietly while it feeds. (See also FLY WORRY AND FLY BITE REACTION.)

HYPHEMA

Bleeding within the eyeball which is usually caused by a blow. Blood can be seen through the cornea which hides the iris pupil and produces blindness. Treatment involves a surgical opening in the cornea through which the blood is rinsed out.

INCONTINENCE

Uncontrolled urination. Spayed bitches sometimes leak small quantities of urine, apparently unknowingly. This is due to hormone imbalance and can be remedied with estrogen tablets. Inability to hold the urine overnight may be due to CYSTITIS (small quantities are voided) or POLYURIA (increased quantities of urine). (See also CALCULI, DIABETES INSIPIDUS, DIABETES MELLITIS, NEPHRITIS, CYSTITIS.)

INDIGESTION

Failure to digest food often due to a deficiency of digestive juices. This condition is little known in animals other than dogs. It may result from a deficiency of intestinal juices (malabsorption syndrome) or lack of the acid secreted by the stomach wall (achlorydia). Presence of partially digested food in the feces, loss of condition, and diarrhea are the most obvious symptoms.

Laboratory tests arc used to establish which digestive juice is lacking and this can sometimes be supplemented in tablet form.

INFLUENZA

True influenza is caused by viruses classified as myxoviruses. Influenza in humans and in horses fall into this category. However, a number of conditions with similar symptoms in humans, cattle, sheep, and dogs are caused by related viruses of the parainfluenza group. Feline influenza (CAT FLU) is caused by completely unrelated viruses.

Influenza viruses in humans are subdivided into types A, B, and C. The influenza A viruses affect animals and include Influenza A/swine, causing influenza and pneumonia in domestic pigs, influenza A/equine (substrains 1 and 2) affecting horses and a virus affecting poultry and ducks.

Equine respiratory disease, attributable to influenza A virus, has an incubation period of one to five days. There is fever followed by a dry cough which persists for several weeks and a watery or thick yellow discharge from the nose. The virus may affect the heart and liver and cause swelling of the legs. Pneumonia sometimes occurs especially with influenza A/equine subtype 2.

In a stable an outbreak spreads rapidly. Following infection and recovery a horse may be resistant to reinfection with the same virus for about one year.

Herpes, rhino and adenoviruses may also cause respiratory disease and coughing in horses. Prevention by vaccination is possible. Due to the lack of crossimmunity it is necessary to include both subtypes in the vaccine. Within each subtype it is important to select the strain of virus appropriate to the current situation because of the tendency of field strains to change their characteristics.

Existing equine influenza vaccines provoke fairly severe reactions in some animals so horses should be rested for at least a week after vaccination.

INTERDIGITAL CYSTS

Cysts in the skin between the toes. These are commonly seen in dogs, particularly in the terrier breeds. These cysts have a tendency to recur and are often a problem to the patient, the veterinarian, and the owner. Occasionally ingrowing hairs may be the cause of cyst formation but more commonly they result from infection in hair folicles which are stopped up with sebaceous material.

Surgical excision or cautery is the treatment of choice usually preceded by the administration of antiinflammatory steroids and antibiotics to control the excessive inflammation and bacterial infection.

INTUSUSSEPTION

Invagination of one part of the intestine into another which is frequently the result of intestinal irritation (usually worms) in pups and piglets. Symptoms include bloody diarrhea and straining. Diagnosis is confirmed by X-ray examination. An operation is necessary to cure the condition.

ITCH

An ailment among saltwater fish caused by minute parasites which infest the scales. The infected fish will scratch itself on rocks and corals, and minute white spots can sometimes be seen on the body. Commercial itch cures are available.

ITCHY LEG. See MITES.

JAUNDICE

The discoloration of tissues and body fluids with bile pigment. Jaundice (or **icterus**) itself is not a disease but a symptom which can be the result of a number of disease entities. Jaundice is often classified into three types: hemolytic, toxic, and obstructive.

Hemolytic jaundice results from excessive breakdown of red blood cells with the release of hemoglobin which leads to an increased production of bile pigment. Among the originating causes are bacterial infections, parasitic infestations, and certain poisons. In toxic jaundice bile pigments accumulate because liver cells damaged by toxic chemicals or bacterial toxins are not able to process and excrete the pigments normally. Obstructive jaundice results from the fact that bile is prevented from escaping from the liver and is consequently reabsorbed into the blood.

In the typical jaundice case the skin and mucus membranes show a yellow discoloration and the urine is much darker than normal. Affected animals usually refuse to eat and vomiting is frequently a sign.

Treatment will obviously depend on the cause and specialized attention should be sought without delay. This rapid attention is especially necessary with dogs since jaundice is most frequently associated with leptospiral infections which can be transmitted to humans. The availability of modern drugs, intravenous infusions, and concentrated vitamin injections now make it possible to cure all but the most acute and chronic cases.

JOINT ILL

Painful swollen joints which occur in calves, foals, and lambs as a result of bacteria from an infected navel. Most cases occur in the first ten days of life. The animal becomes dull, lies down a lot, and refuses to suckle. Respiration is rapid, and the temperature rises. The affected joints (hock, knee, stifle, elbow and/or fetlock) are enlarged, hot, and tense. The navel too is usually swollen and, when handled, exudes pus. In absence of treatment about half of the affected animals will die. Antibiotic injections are usually effective.

KENNEL COUGH

A highly infectious and contagious respiratory disease commonly affecting dogs which have been in kennels. The main symptom is a persistent dry cough. The cause has not yet been definitely established although a virus is probably responsible. The condition spreads quickly and is usually introduced into premises by symptomless carriers. The fact that dogs may suffer from kennel cough more than once after a short interval suggests that immunity is weak or that different viruses or strains are responsible.

The dry cough may persist for two weeks or longer and is aggravated by excitement or exercise. Other than this the appetite and general health are unaffected. However, respiratory complications may result in death.

No treatment is effective although antibiotics are sometimes given to prevent secondary invaders. Cough mixtures may soothe inflammation in the upper respiratory tract. **Prevention:** A vaccine is available in the United States.

KERATITIS

An inflammation of the cornea of the eye. It can be the result of injury or of generalized illnesses (HEPATITIS in dogs). The surface of the eye becomes hazy blue. The disease usually responds well to antibiotic and corticosteroid eye ointments.

KIDNEY STONES. See

NEPHROLITHIASIS.

KIDNEY WORMS

Kidney worms (*Stephanurus* and *Dioctophyma*) occur in the kidney or its vicinity in mammals. *Stephanurus* usually lives in the fat near the kidneys in pigs. *Dioctophyma* is found in dogs and is one of the longest known parasitic roundworms. The female sometimes attains a length of 1m. (3.3ft.) and the entire substance of the kidney is often destroyed. Dogs become infected by swallowing aquatic worms carrying the young stages of the parasite or by eating frogs and small fish which have themselves swallowed the young stages. It is thought that the dog may be only accidentally affected and that mink are the true hosts.

Symptoms include blood in the urine and severe wasting. There is no known medicinal treatment. Surgical removal may be a solution if only one kidney is affected.

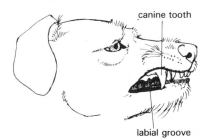

Site of the labial groove in the dog.

LABIAL GROOVE INFECTION
(Labial Dermatitis)

In dogs a fold of skin at the sides of the lower lip sometimes becomes infected. This gives rise to an unpleasant smell and some irritation. The condition is most common in the loose-lipped dogs such as spaniels, setters, and boxers which are also inclined to slobber. The animal shows signs of the inflammation by pawing or rubbing at its mouth. On closer examination, the hair around the fold is found to be moist and discolored.

The condition develops because the labial groove makes an ideal site for the multiplication of bacteria and the area is constantly moistened with saliva.

Treatment usually consists of clipping or shaving the hair in the groove and the administration of antibiotics both locally and topically. Antiinflammatory drugs such as the corticosteroids may also be helpful.

LAMINITIS. See LAMENESS.

LAMENESS

Lameness can occur for many reasons in pets (e.g., injury or rheumatism) but the horse is the most commonly afflicted. In horses the majority of cases involve the structures below the knee or the hock and derive, in part, from the stresses imposed by the change from the pentadactyl (five fingers or claws) limb to the single line of bones in the modern horse. Selective breeding over the last few hundred years has complicated the problem with its specialized purposes such as racing or show jumping, in addition to the stress of carrying a person's weight. Along with the general

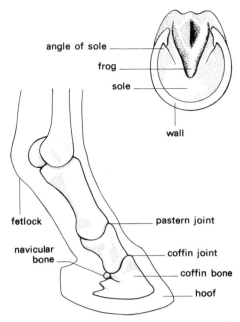

A horse is only as good as its feet. Shown here is the detailed structure of a horse's hoof.

root causes many of the disease conditions listed below result directly from inherited faults in conformation, that is, deviations from the normal anatomy of the part concerned. Lameness results either as a consequence of pain in the limb, or mechanically due to malfunction of a particular part without pain necessarily being involved.

The following conditions of horse lameness are listed from the foot upward, with diseases special to the hind limb inserted at the end.

Seedy toe. A separation of the wall or the sole of the hoof from the soft tissues below. This produces a cavity which often contains flaky horn material. The cause is thought to be pressure from faulty shoeing but the ailment is sometimes associated with chronic laminitis. Treatment involves removal of the overlying horn, scraping out the foreign material, and disinfecting the cavity. Protection, in the form of a dressing and special shoe, will be required until the new wall or sole has grown.

Dropped sole. The normal sole is slightly concave. Following certain foot diseases, notably chronic laminitis, the sole may drop and assume a convex shape. Little or no treatment is possible, but special shoes with protective pads may be applied.

Bruised sole and corns. These are different varieties of the same condition. Pressure from contact with sharp objects on the ground can bruise the sole at any point, but corns are usually a result of bad shoeing or delay in replacing worn shoes. They occur at the "seat of corn," that is between the wall and the bars of the frog at the heels. To relieve the condition the shoe is removed and the overlying sole pared away. Simple cases will recover spontaneously but suppurating corns, due to secondary infection, will require total exposure, poulticing, and disinfection of the diseased area.

Penetrating wounds of the sole. Nails are the most frequent cause of this common injury which usually results in severe pain and pus formation. Drainage is vital and antibiotics may be necessary.

Thrush. A degenerative condition of the central cleft of the frog involving the deep sensitive area and characterized by a foul odor and discharge. The causes are unsanitary stable conditions often combined with overgrown heels which obstruct proper frog pressure with the ground.

Treatment involves trimming away the affected horn and then soaking the foot in disinfectant or iodine solutions. Cleanse and spray the affected area daily with antibiotic sprays.

Canker of the hoof. A degenerative condition of all the outer structure of the foot of the horse. The horn slowly crumbles away, and a moist discharge is evident. The skin above the heels may be inflamed and exude serum. The cause is poor hygiene in the stables and involves wet bedding. Although formerly common, particularly in draft horses, it is rare nowadays. Treatment requires removal of all the diseased tissue and cleansing with iodine solutions. Injections of broad spectrum antibiotics are essential in severe cases. The stable and bedding must be kept dry.

Laminitis. Laminitis or "fever of the feet" is a common condition, particularly seen in overweight ponies. It also occurs in cattle. The sensitive laminae become inflamed and swollen and give rise to intense pain and lameness. Usually all four feet are involved, but sometimes only the forefeet are affected. The acute form is often seen in early summer when the lush grass appears and again during the autumn flush of grass. This form may progress to the chronic form when the typical cautious gait is noticeable to some degree all the time. As the disease progresses the pedal bone inside the hoof rotates downwards, and in advanced cases, may penetrate the sole. Acute cases are also seen in connection with other conditions, notably infections of the womb after foaling. The cause of the disease is still not completely understood.

Treatment requires use of corticosteroids and antihistamines and, in severe cases, pain relieving drugs should be given. Relief may be obtained by standing the horse in cold water if he is able to move. In advanced cases where pain is constant and uncontrollable, humane destruction is advised.

Sidebones. Ossification (hardening) of the lateral cartilages. These cartilages are present at the side of the foot toward the heel and can be felt as springy structures when pressed just above the coronary band. Inflammation may occur following direct injury or as a result of constant concussion on a hard surface, which causes the cartilages to gradually become ossified and hard to the touch. Lameness is usually only present in the active inflammatory stage. Sidebones are often wrongly diagnosed as the seat of lameness when, most often, they are a symptom of other diseases in the foot. Sidebones also tend to occur naturally in old age and as a direct consequence of poor conformation such as contracted heels. If poor conformation is the cause, then grooving of the walls at the heel may relieve the condition.

Quittor. A condition in which breaks at the coronary band discharge pus, arising from infections of the lateral cartilages. These may follow direct injury in the area or the upward tracking of infection from the foot as in corns or penetrating foreign bodies. Irrigation of the sinuses with antibiotic solutions, poulticing, and antibiotics given orally or by injection cure the condition.

Grass crack. A split in the outer wall of the hoof, beginning at the sole and progressing up toward the coronet. The condition is common and frequently arises from inadequate trimming at the toes, particularly when the horse is unshod in summer.

To treat this condition a deep transverse groove is cut, either by knife or by hot iron, at the uppermost point of the crack and the wall is trimmed back at the origin of the crack.

Sand crack. A more serious split arising from the coronet and proceeding down toward the sole. This occurs due to a defect in the horn-growing part of the coronary band, and the split is often deep enough to expose the soft tissues below with resulting fluid and pus discharges. If not treated, the hoof may completely separate.

Searing or grooving as for a grass crack may be adequate for sand cracks but transverse nailing or stapling of the split may be necessary after treatment of any infection.

Navicular disease. A common and progressive cause of chronic lameness in the forefeet of horses. The most likely cause is repeated concussion, and it is probably seen only in the forefeet since the hind limbs are used mainly for propulsion. The disease is characterized by poor blood supply to the navicular bone following the formation of blood clots in the small vessels that supply the bone. Gradually the bone becomes porous and may, in extreme cases, fracture.

Symptoms include lameness of fluctuating severity, often improving after rest. The horse tends to point the affected toe when stationary and, if both feet are affected, alternate pointing is often seen. At the trot the horse will present the toe to the ground and is more reluctant to go downhill since this necessitates taking more weight on the heels.

Successful treatment has recently been achieved by giving daily doses of Warfarin, an anticoagulant, but the dosage must be constantly monitored to prevent hemorrhages in other parts of the body.

Pedal Osteitis. Weakening of the third phalanx (pedal bone) caused by chronic inflammation from a number of different causes such as concussion, bruising or penetrating foreign bodies. The lameness is progressive and difficult to control with drugs. No satisfactory long term treatment is yet possible and partial cutting of nerves is used to relieve the pain caused by the disease.

Ringbone. A term that embraces all types of new bone outgrowths occurring on any of the

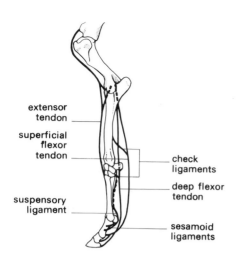

Diagram showing the main tendons supporting the leg of a horse.

extensor tendon
superficial flexor tendon
suspensory ligament
check ligaments
deep flexor tendon
sesamoid ligaments

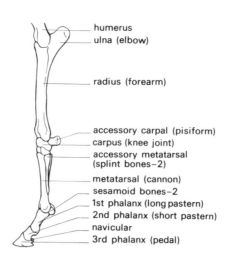

Bones of the foreleg of the horse.

humerus
ulna (elbow)
radius (forearm)
accessory carpal (pisiform)
carpus (knee joint)
accessory metatarsal (splint bones—2)
metatarsal (cannon)
sesamoid bones—2
1st phalanx (long pastern)
2nd phalanx (short pastern)
navicular
3rd phalanx (pedal)

three major bones below the fetlock. They can happen around the joint between the first and second phalanx (high ringbone) or between the second and third phalanx (low ringbone). Additionally, they may be found on the shafts of the first and second phalanx not involving the joint, and these are usually painless. Pain and consequent lameness occur when the joint surfaces are involved. Concussion or direct injury to the bone are the main causes and the condition is more common in the fore feet. Young horses and thoroughbreds are relatively immune.

Horses may recover from cases diagnosed early if the site is injected with corticosteroids and then the foot encased in plaster for four weeks, followed by stall rest for a few more weeks. However, established cases are extremely difficult to treat. Surgery to fuse the joint permanently or neurectomy (severing the nerve supply to the area to eliminate all sensation) is occasionally performed.

Sprain of joints. Stretching or tearing of the components of joint capsules. Swelling, and sometimes hemorrhage, occur at the site, and the condition is very painful. Cold water bandages or ice packs and rest are usually sufficient to produce full recovery.

Windgalls. Soft swellings at the back and above the fetlock joint which may result from a minor strain of the associated tendon. More frequently, they are of a hereditary nature, commonly seen in ponies and draft breeds. By themselves they do not cause lameness and merely constitute a blemish.

"Splints." Bony swellings along the shaft of the splint bones. They are hot and painful when they first appear but become cold and, unless they impinge on adjacent structures such as the flexor tendons, are merely a blemish.

Cold bandages with corticosteroid applications relieve the condition when it is in the active inflammatory stage. If the splint bone is fractured, then surgical removal of the lower portion is carried out.

Sesamoiditis. Inflammation of the two sesamoid bones which are situated at the back of the fetlock joints. The cause is an injury to

the union of the suspensory ligaments at the attachment to the sesamoids. It is most commonly seen in racehorses and show jumpers due to overextension of the fetlock joint. Simple strains are accompanied by pain and swelling and will recover completely after treatment. In some cases chronic lameness is the outcome.

Applications of alternate hot and cold poultices in the early stages with immobilization of the joint by a plaster cast will assist recovery in most cases. The chronic form is unlikely to improve sufficiently to allow normal work.

Sesamoid fracture. Spontaneous fractures of the sesamoid bones occur usually in racehorses when fatigued at the end of a race. Surgery may be performed to remove small displaced bone particles or to pin the fracture with compression screws. Alternately, plaster casting of the joint for several weeks may be sufficient to promote healing.

Split pastern. Longitudinal line fractures of the first phalanx are common and frequently occur at the gallop without any direct injury to the bone. Transverse screws are inserted if there is separation of the fragments. Simple plastering may be adequate if the bone is only cracked and not split.

Sore shins. Inflammation of the periosteum (the membranes covering the shaft of the cannon bones), is commonly seen in immature thoroughbreds particularly after galloping on hard ground. The shins are warm and painful to the touch. Severe cases that may involve hairline fractures on the surface of the bone often become permanently callused and are then known as "bucked shins."

Immediate rest for at least one month, combined with applications of corticosteroids dissolved in a solvent that has the capability of penetrating intact skin, will resolve the condition.

Tendinitis. Inflammation of a tendon. The most common seat of this ailment is the flexor tendons of the forelegs situated at the back of the leg between the knee and the fetlock joint. The tendons are hot, swollen, and painful throughout their length. This gallop-

ing or jumping injury is a warning that further exercise may lead on to sprained or ruptured tendons.

Rest in a stable is required with cold water bandages followed by strapping or plastering to immobilize the area. Corticosteroids may be used to shorten the recovery period.

Sprain of tendons. Rupture of some of the fibers that comprise the tendon. A hot, painful swelling appears at the site, accompanied by a degree of swelling in the rest of the tendon. In serious cases the fetlock joint shows a marked drop toward the ground.

Prolonged rest (up to six months), immobilization with plaster casts followed by bandaging will promote healing. However, tendon fibers do not heal directly, but are joined with scar tissue which is not as strong as the original tendon. Even after apparent recovery and a long rest further breakdowns often happen. Surgical techniques such as tendon splitting to increase the blood supply to the fibers, or carbon fiber implants are sometimes used. Complete rupture of the tendons requires extensive surgical repair and the prognosis is unfavorable.

Check ligaments. These two ligaments form part of the complicated stay apparatus that supports the limb and prevents excessive extension of the fetlock joint. Both are subject to sprains, particularly in jumpers, and are frequently the cause of recurrent lameness despite long periods of rest.

Accessory carpal (pisiform) fracture. This bone protrudes at the back of the knee, and while it does not directly bear weight, it func-

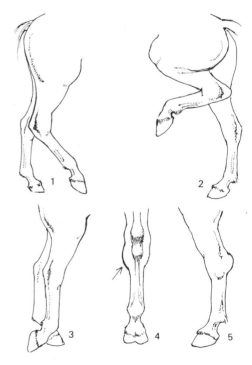

(1) Typical action with a sprained Achilles tendon.
(2) Typical action in a case of stringhalt.
(3) Typical attitude of a leg in which the patella is dislocated.
(4) Spavin formation on the right hock as seen from behind.
(5) Capped hock.

tions as a tendon attachment that flexes the knee joint. Fractures of this bone are quite common and occur, in most cases, spontaneously without any direct injury. Pain and lameness are marked but not too severe.

Surgical removal of fragments torn away by the pull of the flexor tendons combined with compression screwing of the major fragments is usually performed. This is a difficult technique so that conservative treatment involving knee bandaging combined with at least six months stall rest may be preferable. Many animals recover completely but a percentage will never be able to flex the knee joint properly.

Lymphangitis. Inflammation of the lymph vessels draining the limbs. The condition was formerly common in heavy draft horses and was frequently seen after a day's rest. The leg swells producing a painful lameness because of the inability to bend the joints. The probable cause relates to high energy diets with interrupted work patterns. Another form is of infectious origin.

The condition responds to corticosteroid and antihistamine treatment in the dietary form. Infectious lymphangitis requires long programs of antibiotic therapy.

Shoulder lameness. Although frequently suspected by the layman, true shoulder lameness is rare. Cases that do occur are mostly traumatic injuries resulting in bruising and muscle inflammation. Occasionally arthritis of the shoulder joint is seen, and paralysis of the radial nerve producing a dropped elbow joint is another uncommon cause.

Invariably rest is the only required therapy, but in cases where muscle damage or wastage occurs, Faradism (electrical stimulation of the relevant muscle) may be useful. Injections of corticosteroids into and around the shoulder joint are given when indicated.

Myositis. Inflammation of muscles. In the horse this syndrome is most often seen in the muscles lying over and underneath the vertebral column in the lower back region. The condition happens after severe exertion and is characterized by marked stiffness in the hind limbs. The condition may be a sequel to azoturia or occur independantly. (See also AZOTURIA, SLIPPED DISC.)

Corticosteroids and varying periods of rest, depending on the severity of the attack, relieve the condition. Sometimes injections of vitamin E and selenium are given.

Thrombosis. The aorta is the main artery supplying the hindquarters and lies underneath the spine; at the lower end it branches to each limb in the iliac arteries. Thrombosis (clot) formation usually occurs around this bifurcation. This impedes the blood supply and causes a characteristic lameness which disappears with rest and appears at exercise, causing sweating, and other signs of severe pain. The cause is damage to the lining walls of the arteries by migrating redworm larvae. If the clot grows sufficiently large, then total paralysis and collapse are seen.

Treatment is usually only attempted in mild cases. Successful cures using in-travenous calcium solutions combined with anticoagulants have been reported, but the prevention of suffering is crucial.

Stringhalt and shivering. Both these ailments probably involve disease of the spinal cord. Stringhalt is an involuntary upward jerk of one or both hocks seen intermittently but more pronounced when turning or backing. Shivering is a curious lifting of the hind limb with the tail; the limb shakes for a short time before returning to normal without any apparent pain being involved.

Shivering is incurable at this time but stringhalt can be relieved by tenotomy—an operation to sever a small tendon on the outer aspect of the hock joint.

Spavin. This is the common term for osteoarthritis involving the lower inner aspect of the hock joint. It is mainly a disease of old age and poor conformation. Many treatments are attempted but the condition rarely responds.

Dislocated patella or subluxation. The patella, or knee cap, commonly becomes fixed in a high position on the inner edge of the femur. It is not a true dislocation and shows a tendency to occur in both hind limbs. The leg locks out backwards with the toe pointed so that the horse struggles to maintain its balance. Often the patella will regain its normal position unaided, but it may be necessary to pull the leg forward with a rope while pushing the kneecap down.

Since this condition can recur at any time surgical treatment should be considered.

Capped hock. A soft swelling containing fluid over the point of the hock. The same condition occurs over the elbow joint when it is called capped elbow; both are forms of BURSITIS. The cause is invariably an injury, often self-inflicted on walls, mangers, or other objects. Pain and consequent lameness arise in the initial stages.

Treatment involves drainage of the fluid and injections of corticosteroids into the bursa combined with careful pressure bandaging. Some horses will not tolerate a tight bandage over the hock. In such cases repeated drainage and injections may be necessary.

Articular thoroughpin. Also called "bog spavin," this condition involves soft swellings on the front inner aspect of the hock joint. There is some lameness when they first appear but they are of little long-term consequence. Essentially they denote weakness in the conformation of the hock and occur most often in animals with straight hocks.

Curb. A swelling exactly in the midline at the lower rear extremity of the hock joint. Curbs are caused by a sprain of the joint ligament and are most commonly seen in sickle hocked horses. Although painful when they first appear they subside after a period of rest, leaving only a blemish. Hard swellings at this site *not* in the midline are false curbs and are of no consequence.

Cellulitis. Diffuse swelling of the limb caused by infections and associated with lymphangitis. Surface ulceration with purulent discharge may appear, and lameness is se-vere. The cause is said to be abrasions which occur during the grooming or the spread of infection from the feet. Protracted courses of broad spectrum antibiotics are necessary.

LAMPUS. See GINGIVITIS.

LEECHES
Bloodsucking worm-like parasites which are free-living except when feeding. They are most common in tropical regions. They generally attach themselves to parts covered by membranes (mouth, nose, or eyes) and drop off the body of their hosts once they are fully engorged with blood. Many species prefer a water environment and attack fish, aquatic fowl, and wading mammals indiscriminately. In aquatic fowl, leeches attached to the eyes may produce blindness.

LEPTOSPIROSIS
A bacterial disease caused by *Leptospira* which affects a wide variety of species including dogs, cats, horses, rodents, farm animals, and humans. Dogs with leptospirosis warrant attention not only because it is severe in this pet species, but because they may be a source of infection to humans.

Also known as Stuttgart disease, infectious jaundice and canine typhus, canine leptospirosis is caused by two bacteria—*Leptospira ioterohaemorrhagiae* and *L. canicola*. Dogs usually become infected from contact with infected urine. The main symptom is kidney inflammation. (See NEPHRITIS.)

LEUKEMIA. See TUMORS.

LICE
Small, slow-moving parasites which infest the skin of most warm-blooded pets. They are usually dark brown or pale yellow, though sometimes bluish in color, and do not spread from one species to another. Their entire life cycle is usually spent on one animal. Biting lice feed on hair, feathers, and skin debris and are found on mammals and

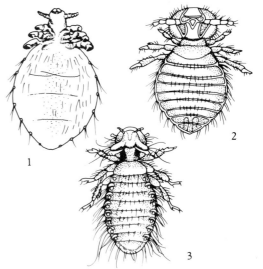

(1) *Dog louse* (Linognathus setosus).
(2) *Sheep louse* (Trichodectes canis).
(3) *Feather louse* (Menopan gallinae).

345

birds. They cause marked itching and are also the carriers of the common tapeworms of dogs and cats. Sucking lice feed on blood and tissue fluids and are found on mammals only. Spread of infection is usually by contact and by grooming equipment, harnasses, clothing, and bedding. Sucking lice are generally more harmful than biting lice and cause anemia and even death if infestation is severe. Louse infestations are often secondary to wasting illnesses and malnutrition, since lice proliferate when animals cease to groom themselves. Insecticide treatment is effective but it cannot kill the eggs. Two treatments with a two week interval are required to kill the newly hatched young stages. In long-haired animals clipping may be necessary for the insecticide to reach the lice which cannot live away from the animal for more than a few hours. Birds should be treated only with an approved insecticide. (See also FISH LICE.)

LIGAMENT DAMAGE. See SPRAINS.

LIVER FLUKE. See FLUKE, LIVER.

LUNG CANCER. See TUMORS.

LUNGWORMS
Round worms which inhabit the respiratory system in many species. The most important lungworm of dogs, *Filaroides*, lives in wart-like nodules at the base of the trachea and provokes rasping breathing and coughing. These signs are more serious in active rather than sedentary dogs. A less common dog lungworm (*Angiostrongylus*) lives in the blood vessels of the lung and may also cause distress during exercise. The cat lungworm, *Aulorostrongylus*, is harmless and *Dictyocaulus*, which infects equines, provokes coughing in horses, but no symptoms in donkeys. No treatment is known for dogs and cats. Tetramisol, methyridine, and diethylcarbamazine are used in cattle and cyanacethydrazide in pigs.

LYMPHANGITIS. See LAMENESS.

LYMPHOCYSTIS
A disease of marine fish which causes white cauliflower-like lumps to appear on the body. The cause is unknown, but may be viral. Surgical removal and wound sterilization with acriflavine is the usual treatment.

MALNUTRITION
Inadequate feeding and diet can result in general loss of condition. For details of specific feeding requirements for your pet see the chapter dealing with that animal, and for general information see the chapter **Feeding Your Pet.**

MAMMARY TUMORS. See TUMORS.

MANGE
Skin infections caused by MITES which lie permanently in or on the skin. Mange mites are the most harmful and are divided into burrowing and nonburrowing types. Bur-rowing mites are responsible for the type of mange known as scabies in mammals. The mites tunnel into the skin and cause irritation, redness, loss of hair, crust formation, and thickening of the skin. The burrowing mite, *Sarcoptes*, is mainly a problem in dogs; it has, however, many varieties occurring in nearly all mammals and can cross infect from pets to humans. **Sarcoptic mange** in horses is a disease requiring notification of health authorities in some countries. Sarcoptic mange usually begins at the head and can infect the whole body. Another burrowing mite in mammals is *Notoedres*, which has a preference for the ears, head, neck, and extremities. *Notoedres* is common in cats, rabbits, and occasionally rodents, causing irritation and discharge within the ear followed by crust formation.

The burrowing mite *Demodex* is common in dogs, cattle, and wild carnivores and occurs occasionally in horses and goats. In dogs it usually attacks the short-haired breeds. The most frequent route of infection is probably the transfer from the skin of the dam to the pup during suckling; hence it occurs most commonly in young dogs and on the muzzle, ears, and paws. In the early stages there is loss of hair on these areas, then thickening of the skin, and exudation of pus.

The burrowing mite *Cnemidocoptes* in birds causes mange known as **scaly face, scaly leg, tassel foot,** and **depluming itch,** especially in psittacines, particularly the budgerigar. The mites are first active on the head, in the skin at the base of the beak causing a whitish crustlike growth. They then extend to the cere, eyelids, and horny part of the beak which may become thickened, porous, and deformed. On other non-feathered parts, the skin becomes scaly and thick, and on the feet the outgrowths may extend into tassel form. This type of mange is seen even in singly kept birds which have been infected as nestlings, since mites can remain more than a year on birds without causing harm, until resistence is lowered by privation or disease.

Nonburrowing mites occur on most mammals and birds. Their effects are not as severe, much of the damage being self-inflicted when the animal scratches and rubs itself. Such mange is generalized or localized to specific areas from where it extends. The

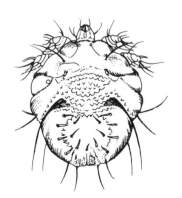

Mange mite (Sarcoptes scabei).

mite *Psoroptes* is the most common and in this case cross infection does not occur. However, **psoroptic mange** is a notifiable disease in some countries; in horses and sheep it is called sheep scab. Localized mange in cattle is caused by *Chorioptes* and found mainly at the base of the tail. In horses *Chorioptes* causes **heel mange** or **itchy leg** and is found usually below the hocks causing scab formation and itching, especially in animals with feathering on the fetlocks. The irritation makes horses stamp and kick, especially at night. A localized form of mange also occurs in the ears of cats and rabbits. In these cases, the effects are mild, but irritation causes head shaking and scratching. In rare, severe cases the ear may be blocked.

Many remedies are available for the treatment of mange although some types are fairly difficult to cure.

MASTITIS
Inflammation of the mammary glands or udder. It usually affects animals that are producing milk but may occur at other times. Summer mastitis sometimes occurs in dry cows. Mastitis can result from either trauma caused by mechanical injury (cuts, bruises or chills) or by clinical means, but by far the most common cause is bacterial infection. In cattle, diet may also play a part in the causation of the disease.

In the typical case the glands become hot, swollen, and painful, and the milk secretion is different in consistency. In severe cases the animal may show systemic signs of illness, a raised temperature, and lack of appetite. If untreated death may result from toxemia.

In cattle, sheep, and goats the condition is usually treated by local "infusion" of antibiotics into the udder via the teat canal. In other species, particularly bitches and queens, systemic treatment with antibiotics is mostly given. In advanced cases where abscesses are forming lancing and drainage may be needed.

MEGAESOPHAGUS
An inherited condition of dogs characterized by an abnormally wide esophagus or one with a pouch resulting from a muscular weakness in the wall. Although inborn, the signs (vomiting after meals) are first apparent at six to eight weeks when the pup starts taking solids. X-rays show the esophagus bulging with food.

The underlying cause of the condition may be a defective nerve supply which causes the esophagus to lose tone. An alternate cause may be spasm at the cardia (esophagus-stomach junction) which prevents the passage of food.

Frequent small meals of broths or meat extracts may help if started before the esophagus is stretched. An operation to dilate the cardia can be undertaken.

METRITIS
Inflammation of the uterus or womb. As a general rule the condition occurs following

parturition and results from bacterial infection particularly if the fetal membranes (afterbirth) have been retained.

In the typical case the affected animal has a raised temperature and there is a thick, bloodstained, foul-smelling discharge from the vulva, which may be very persistent. Frequently infected untreated animals will die from toxemia. Sometimes the infection persists in a chronic "subclinical" form which often results in infertility, abortion, or death of the newborn.

Metritis is usually treated by the administration of antibiotics by injection or by mouth and, in large animals especially, by the local application of antiseptics as pessaries or lavages. Since infection with some bacterial organisms may be transmitted venerally, treatment of the male may be required.

MIDDLE EAR INFECTION
(Otitis Media)
Cats, dogs, and rabbits sometimes suffer infection of the middle ear which causes loss of balance and disorientation. The pathogen usually enters the inner ear via a broken eardrum but occasionally by way of the Eustachian tube which connects the throat and ear. Symptoms include the head held sideways or upside down and the animal walking with a swaying gait and falling over when it shakes it head or sneezes. The eyes often show a spasmodic side to side movement and the pupils are of unequal size. CANKER may be present.

Injections, tablets, and ear ointments or antibiotics and corticosteroids are normally given. If these are unsuccessful an operation involving the drainage of pus from the middle ear can be performed.

MIDGES
Small biting insects (*Culicoides*) which appear in great numbers during warm, overcast weather. Their bites cause intense itching and can result in SWEET ITCH, an allergic skin condition in horses. They also carry the larvae of *Onchocerca*, a filarial worm in the horse involved in poll evil and fistulous withers. (See LAMENESS.)

MILK FEVER
Milk Fever, also called **eclampsia, peverperal tetany, post parturient tetany,** or **hypocalcemia,** occurs occasionally in female animals of most species soon after giving birth. It is caused by lower than normal levels of calcium in the bloodstream resulting from the greatly increased requirement for this mineral in milk production.

In ruminants the disease is characterized by a staggering gait, recumbency, bloat, and eventually death. Bitches and queens become restless, excitable, and pant excessively, they lose coordination, and finally collapse. A small number of untreated cases recover spontaneously, but in most cases death is preceded by paralysis and coma.

Fortunately few animals die from the disease because of injections of calcium salts.

MITES
Small eight-legged parasites, the majority barely visible to the naked eye. They have three preferred locations:

(a) Superficially, on the hair or feathers, or on the ground with occasional visits to the skin. Though association with the animal is essential to the survival of the mites, it is not as dependent as other types of parasites.

(b) Permanently in or on the skin. This type of infection is called MANGE.

(c) The respiratory mites, a minor group, occur in the air passages of some animals.

Superficial mites include *Cheyletiella*, red mites (*Dermanyssus*), and harvest mites (*Trombicula*). *Cheyletiella* occur on many animals (including humans) and are especially common in rabbits. They inhabit the coat and skin where they cause dermatitis and dandruff. This mite is easily eliminated by weekly soap and water baths and/or insecticides. Red mites are parasitic on birds. When unfed they are whitish, but assumes red color after engorging on blood. They settle on birds at night and cause irritation, ruffled feathers, and severe anemia which can be fatal. The related northern fowl mite (*Ornithonyssus*) is also common and causes thickened skin and soiled feathers. Harvest mites are parasitic in their young stages on grazing animals and dogs.

Respiratory mites occur in the air passages of birds, monkeys, aquatic mammals, and reptiles. Nearly all macaques seem to be infected. The mites are well tolerated in mammals, and in monkeys the only sign of infection is a slight cough. In cage birds in South Africa, the United States, and Latin America, mites in the lungs and air sacs, especially of the finch group cause breathlessness and, sometimes, pneumonia.

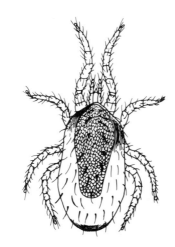

Poultry mite (Dermanyssus gallinae).

MYXOMATOSIS
A viral disease of rabbits. In Brazil and Australia, it is spread by mosquitoes and in the United States and Europe by fleas. Direct infection from one rabbit to another is also possible, but requires close and prolonged contact. Most infected rabbits die, but the occasional survivors become permanently immune although they may be infertile. Myxomatosis can flare up from latent infection in an apparently recovered colony.

First symptoms are a rise in temperature followed by severe discharge from the eyes. The eyelids become thickened and sealed by pus. There is generally inflammation of the testes or vulva, rapid emaciation, and death. No treatment is available, although a vaccine provides immunity for six to nine months.

NASAL FLY/NASAL WORM
A parasite (*Oestrus ovis*) of sheep in which the larva (worm) inhabits the nasal cavity and causes sneezing and nasal discharge. The Nasal Fly lays its eggs on the nostrils, and the larvae which hatch crawl into the nasal passages and sinuses where they cause irritation. Eventually the larvae are sneezed out, pupate on the ground, and the adult fly emerges from the pupa. These buzzing flies harass sheep and cause loss of condition. No treatment is available.

NASAL WORM
A large parasitic worm (*Linguatula serrata*) which infects the nasal passages of dogs and causes sneezing, nasal discharge, and loss of condition. The worm may be up to 15cm. (6in.) long and usually invades one nostril.

The life cycle of the worm is largely unknown but it does involve the formation of a cyst in the lymph nodes of rabbits, sheep, and cattle. The dog becomes infected when it eats uncooked tissues from these animals.

No treatment is available although nose drops containing anthelminthics may help.

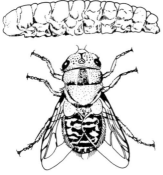

Nasal fly (Oestrus ovis). Top. *Mature larva.* Below. *Adult fly.*

NAVICULAR DISEASE. See LAMENESS.

NEMATODES. See ASCARIDS.

NEPHRITIS
Inflammation of the kidneys which is usually due to a thread-like germ, *Leptospira*. In the past this condition was frequent in dogs and cats but recently the incidence has declined in some areas. This may be due to the increasing use of vaccination and a decline in the population of rats which carry the infection. Leptospira germs, which abound in infected urine, are able to penetrate unbroken skin and the canine habit of sniffing urine contrib-

utes to the spread of illness from dog to dog. (Humans are susceptible so gloves should be worn when contamination is possible.)

Acute nephritis occurs as a sudden illness in young dogs. There is raised temperature, loss of appetite, listlessness, excessive thirst, and vomiting. The eyes and mouth may be jaundiced (yellow). The back is arched, and the dog moves stiffly suggesting a painful back. The coat is dry and the skin tense. Urine is scanty, strong smelling and dark yellow, while analysis reveals abnormal constituents (protein, bilirubin, blood, and cell debris).

Antibiotics are effective against the germs if given early. However, death may occur if the kidneys are severely damaged.

Leptospirosis and distemper vaccines are injected when dogs are twelve weeks old and repeated annually.

Chronic nephritis is fairly common in older dogs and cats, generally the result of earlier leptospirosis damage. The condition develops gradually with occasional bouts of ill health, loss of appetite, and vomiting which become more frequent with time. The signs are weight loss, excessive thirst, bad breath, and dry, scaly skin. These signs are often attributed to old age. The urine is copious and watery, and abnormal conditions may be detected on laboratory examination. Eventually the kidneys are unable to cope and wastes accumulate in the blood (uremia). The appetite fails, vomiting becomes severe, and the animal becomes listless and dies.

The kidneys are usually severely damaged by the time signs are evident, but nonetheless life may be prolonged for some years. Antibiotics and urine disinfectants should be given whenever the dog is off color. Provide a low protein diet and plenty of fluid.

Warning: Dogs which have recovered from leptospirosis and those which have experienced mild or inapparent infection may shed the bacteria in the urine for a considerable time, thus becoming a source of infection to both humans and other dogs.

NEPHROLITHIASIS
Disease resulting from particles of kidney stones which break off and block the ducts (ureters). The affected kidney is generally severely damaged by pressure from the stone or from obstructed urine by the time the condition is discovered. A single kidney is able to cope adequately with the body wastes so nephrolithiasis in one side may cause only pain and elevated blood pressure. The affected kidney should be removed. (See also BLADDER STONES.)

NICTITATING MEMBRANE, Disease of
The nictitating membrane or "third eyelid" is a membrane-covered cartilage which nestles in the inner corner of the eye in many pet species including dogs, cats, horses, birds, and some reptiles. If the pet is in good health this structure remains unseen, but inflammatory conditions cause it to protrude prominently. This may be due to local in-flammations (CONJUNCTIVITIS or inflammation of the gland on the inner surface of the membrane) or to generalized illnesses (for example CAT FLU). Protrusion of the third eyelid may also be due to spasm and serve as an early sign of TETANUS. By far the most common condition affecting the third eyelid, however, is simple protrusion, sometimes called "haws." It is usually a sign of general debility and often occurs after a severe systemic illness such as DISTEMPER.

In most cases the membrane returns to its inconspicuous position when the primary condition subsides. Occasionally the gland of the nictitating membrane remains enlarged and inflamed and needs to be cauterized or cut out. If this fails to resolve the condition, or in cases of rolled cartilage, the whole structure can be removed under local anesthesia.

NYMPHOMANIA
Normal female animals come on heat for a few days or weeks while the ovaries are ripe. Animals with nymphomania, however, remain on heat far longer due to hormonal upsets and the development of cystic ovaries. Affected animals are sometimes vicious and either mount others or stand for mating. There is often a vaginal discharge, and the animals fail to conceive.

For bitches hormone injections (luteinizing hormone) can be tried but removing the ovaries is more effective. If a mare is not to be used for breeding, surgical removal of the ovaries is an alternative.

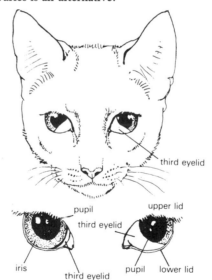

Top. *Cat with haws.* Bottom Left. *Normal eye.* Bottom Right. *Eye with third eyelid (nictitating membrane) protruding.*

OBESITY
Obesity is frequently encountered in pet dogs and cats and is most common in female and neutered animals. It gives rise to locomotor difficulties, heat intolerance, and lethargy. It is especially troublesome in middle-aged animals suffering from ARTHRITIS because joint pain limits exercise. This lack of activity promotes obesity which in turn aggravates the stress placed on the joints.

The first step in any weight reduction program is to convince everyone associated with the animal of the necessity for it to lose weight. Subsequently a low calorie diet should be fed (calorie intake must be less than that expended) or the animal hospitalized and completely fasted. Where possible, exercise should be increased.

OODINIUM
Infestation of marine fish with *Oodinium ocellatum,* a pinpoint-sized flagellate parasite which invades the gills and skin in large numbers. Main symptoms are lack of appetite and listlessness. The fish scratch on rocks and coral and swim near the surface showing distress. There is rapid respiration (100 or more gill movements per minute) due to infection of the gills and the body appears as if dusted with pollen.

Commercially prepared Oodinium cure should be used.

OSTEOARTHRITIS. See ARTHRITIS.

OSTEOSARCOMAS. See TUMORS.

OTITIS MEDIA. See MIDDLE EAR INFECTION.

OVERGROWN BEAK AND CLAWS
These conditions may arise if cage and aviary birds are poorly cared for. Caged birds living on slim, machine-doweled perches most frequently have this minor problem which requires attention from a veterinarian to trim back excess growth. Severe bleeding may occur if the cut is not made beyond the vein. The vein becomes apparent if the claw is held up to the light and it is better to leave claws on the long side rather than endanger the blood vessel. A pair of sharp nail clippers is preferable to scissors.

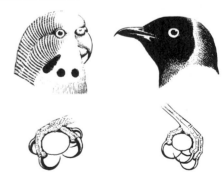

Overgrown beaks and claws need veterinary attention.

PANLEUCOPENIA
A highly contagious and often fatal virus disease of the cat family and of members of the racoon family when kept in captivity. It is also known as **feline enteritis, feline agranulocytosis, cat plague,** and formerly **feline distemper.** Of the domestic cats, the oriental breeds (Siamese, Burmese) are the most susceptible. Crowded housing conditions as in badly run pet shops and boarding catterys,

inevitably favor the spread of the disease. Precautionary vaccination at least two weeks before putting a cat in a boarding establishment is strongly recommended. Chief symptoms are high temperature 40–40.6°C. (104–105°F.), vomiting, painful abdomen, arched back, listlessness, lack of appetite, rapid weak pulse, and bad odor from mouth. Dehydration is severe, and the animal will lie with its forelegs tucked under its chest and its head drooping over the water bowl apparently wanting water but not drinking any. In the later stages vomiting becomes less frequent but more painful and the cat brings up green or brownish fluid indicative of bile or feces.

There is no treatment for the virus itself, but antibiotics prevent secondary bacterial invaders. Dehydration can be treated by injections of fluid under the skin while substances like kaolin and bismuth by mouth soothe the stomach and intestine. After the vomiting has stopped, the animal should be given a little glucose water and egg white every three or four hours. Convalescence may take four to six weeks, during which time the cat should be confined indoors.
Prevention: Vaccination should be administered at eight to twelve weeks and repeated every two years.
Note: A new cat should not be introduced into previously infected premises sooner than four months after the infection has been cleared.

PANSTEATITIS (Yellow fat disease)
In cats an inflammation of the subcutaneous fat with concurrent deposition of a mustard-colored pigment. It is caused by diets rich in unsaturated fatty acids and deficient in vitamin E. Symptoms include generalized soreness when handled and loss of agility, while the lightest touch can cause pain. Vitamin E supplementation and discontinuation of the harmful diet is the usual treatment.

PARATYPHOID. See TYPHOID.

PERITONITIS
Inflammation of the peritoneum (membrane lining the abdominal cavity), caused by microbial or irritant agents. Bacterial peritonitis may be caused by the contamination of the peritoneum following perforation of the stomach, uterus, or intestine, or after perforation of the abdominal wall. Occasionally it is caused by rupture of an abscess in the abdominal cavity. Cats also suffer from a serious form of peritonitis (**feline infectious peritonitis**) caused by a virus.

As the condition progresses the abdomen becomes distended with fluid and sometimes gas. So much fluid may be lost from the bloodstream that circulatory collapse occurs, often followed by shock and death. The animal is reluctant to move, resents abdominal examination, has an elevated temperature, and loses its appetite.

Antibiotic injections and fluid injections under the skin are effective. There is no cure for feline infectious peritonitis, but recovery is possible.

PHARYNGITIS
Inflammation of the throat, which often occurs as a symptom of generalized illness and is sometimes transmissable to humans. Symptoms are a cough, retching, swallowing movements, poor appetite, and enlarged lymph glands under the jaw. Antibiotics are administered by injection or by mouth.

PLEURISY
Inflammation of the membranes covering the lungs and inner walls of the chest. Caused by infection, the condition is most common in cats where it is usually chronic and is caused by virus infection. It is rather unusual in other pet species. Symptoms include heavy breathing, cough, poor condition, and sometimes fever. The chest becomes filled with pus, and the animal refuses to lie on its side. (In an upright position the fluid in the chest causes less interference with breathing.)

The pus can be drained from the chest and antibiotics injected. However, this treatment usually produces only temporary relief.

PNEUMONIA
Inflammation of the lungs. This illness may be caused by bacterial, viral, or fungal infections or by foreign substances introduced accidentally into the lungs. In normal circumstances the entrance to the trachea is automatically closed at the throat during swallowing, and this mechanism prevents fluid and other foreign materials from getting into the lungs. However, substances given too quickly may enter the trachea. LUNGWORMS also cause pneumonia in some species. Bacterial pneumonia may occur as a secondary effect in animals weakened by other illness or those kept in unsuitable conditions (such as captive wild animals). Fungal infections (for example, ASPERGILLOSIS) may cause pneumonia in birds and may also do so as secondary invaders in mammals.

Lungworms can be eradicated with special remedies. (See LUNGWORM.) Antibiotics should be injected for other forms of pneumonia.

POLYDIPSIA
Increased thirst which commonly occurs in chronic NEPHRITIS, DIABETES MELLITIS, DIABETES INSIPIDUS, and PYOMETRA. It is also a side effect of cortisone treatments.

POLYPS. See TUMORS; CANKER.

POLYURIA
An increased volume of urine which may be associated with chronic NEPHRITIS, DIABETES MELLITIS, and DIABETES INSIPIDUS. Polyuria is usually accompanied by polydipsia (increased thirst). Certain drugs which promote polyuria (diuretics) are useful treatments for conditions where fluid accumulates in the body (dropsy, false pregnancy, and others).

POP EYE
Bacterial infection of fish in which the eye swells and stands out and the cornea becomes cloudy. Infected fish should be removed from the tank and treated with 1 percent methylene blue eyedrops twice a day. The dye is harmful to plants so on each occasion the fish should be rinsed in a container of seawater before being returned to its tank.

PROGRESSIVE RETINAL ATROPHY (PRA)
An inherited condition of dogs, and some other animals, which leads to blindness. It sets in at any age from one to eight years and is most common in pedigree inbred animals. The eyes appear normal, but vision fails. At first the dog has difficulty in seeing at night or sees moving objects more easily than stationary ones. The condition progresses at a variable rate but generally ends in total blindness after a few years. PRA is caused by retinal degeneration and is predetermined at birth by genes inherited from both parents.

PSOROPTIC MANGE. See MANGE.

PSEUDORABIES
A virus disease of pigs, cattle, sheep and rats, which may be transmitted to cats and dogs and more rarely horses. It is also known as **mad itch, Aujesky's disease,** and **infectious bulber paralysis.** The disease is most prevalent in the United States, where it is a major problem in pigs. It is thought that cats and dogs become infected by contact with afflicted pigs or rats.

Pseudorabies causes a change in the normal behavior pattern. The animal becomes lethargic and seeks seclusion; affected cats may mew as if in pain. They refuse to eat and drool saliva due to paralysis of the pharynx. There is usually localized and intense itching, and the animal will rub, bite, and scratch at the area. Pseudorabies can be distinguished from true rabies by the itching, by the fact that affected animals do not attack others, and by absence of progressive paralysis. There is no available treatment. The animal should be destroyed by a veterinarian after confirmation of the disease.
Prevention: Eradication of rats and avoidance of contact with infected swine is advised. Pigs may be vaccinated.

PSITTACOSIS ORNITHOSIS
An infectious disease of birds which is transmissible to humans and other animals. Birds of the parrot family (parrots, budgies, cockatoos) are particularly prone although others (canaries, finches, pigeons, fowls, turkeys, mynahs) are all susceptible.

The symptoms are variable. Some strains of the germ kill most victims, but others produce few symptoms. The usual picture is a ruffled, sleepy, depressed bird with diarrhea and no appetite. Laboratory examination of a blood sample is necessary to make sure of the diagnosis.

In humans psittacosis causes respiratory infection with bronchopneumonia, cough,

349

fever, vomiting, and headache as the main symptoms. Prior to the advent of antibiotics the illness killed some 20 percent of human cases and even now a few older patients die.

Psittacosis infection in cats is quite common and produces symptoms similar to those of flu (sneezing, poor appetite, running eyes and nose). The animals usually recover.

Antibiotics (tetracyclines) are effective and can be given to birds in their drinking water or seed. Cats and other animals also respond well to this antibiotic (injection or tablets).

PYOMETRA
A very severe condition seen commonly in bitches and occasionally queens shortly after they have been in estrus. The uterus becomes filled with a large amount of fluid which may or may not contain bacteria.

Toxemia resulting from absorption of this fluid gives rise to the characteristic signs of the condition, particularly excessive thirst—sometimes animals may drink several pints of water in the course of a day—vomiting, poor appetite, and a raised temperature.

Animals in which the cervix remains closed invariably die unless prompt treatment is given. Death is preceded by coma, a subnormal temperature, and other signs of shock. Consequently it is important to seek veterinary advice without delay if a bitch starts to drink excessively a few weeks after she has been on heat.

Cases in which the cervix remains open are characterized by a putrid, foul-smelling vaginal discharge and, although not so serious, still require veterinary attention. Open cases may respond to antibacterial medication but are likely to recur following the next heat. Closed cases require surgical removal of the uterus and ovaries.

QUITTOR. See LAMENESS.

RABIES
A disease caused by a virus which is transmitted through the saliva of affected animals. It is one of the most terrifying of all diseases because of its dreadful symptoms, transmissibility to humans, and its almost invariably fatal result. The disease is initiated when infective saliva enters a wound and may occur from the bite of a rabid animal or when the saliva contaminates a skin abrasion.

After infection of the salivary glands, the virus goes to the brain where damage to nerve cells causes characteristic symptoms and death after a few days.

In the early stages of illness subtle changes of behavior occur, but these may not be noticed except in the dog and cat. Dogs appear restless and uneasy. Most seek solitude and hide, but others, especially puppies, become excessively affectionate. Observers suggest that the animals appear to feel insecure. The body temperature does not alter, but the animals refuse to eat and drink. Drooling of saliva may commence at this stage due to paralysis of throat muscles.

After the early stage, rabies can take two courses, namely the furious form or the para-

lytic form. In the furious form, which is most common in the cat family, the animal becomes vicious and attacks any moving object regardless of its size. Dogs and cats may inflict severe bite wounds upon themselves. Dogs often have a depraved appetite and consume feces, sticks, straw, stones, and other foreign objects. Cats are particularly dangerous to people as they attack suddenly without warning. Foxes, skunks, and mongooses may also show a furious stage and attack humans, cattle, and horses.

The first sign of rabies in horses is usually irritation at the site of the infected bite or wound, which they rub and chew until it is severely damaged. At this stage the animals often go berserk and charge about, damaging themselves, and their surroundings to a horrifying extent. As the furious stage of the disease progresses signs of incoordination and convulsions appear in all species followed by general paralysis.

Some animals enter the paralytic stage directly without passing through a furious stage. The signs in these cases may be misleading. The inability to swallow and drooling suggests that something is stuck in the throat, but a close examination of the mouth contaminates the hands with saliva.

When an animal has been bitten by another suspected of rabies, immediate veterinary attention must be sought. If the animal has been vaccinated regularly, it may only require a booster dose. However, once the disease has been diagnosed, the animal must be caged and then destroyed. In most countries, rabies is a notifiable disease.

Prevention: Countries with no land frontiers usually demand a quarantine period of six months before an animal is permitted entry although the incubation period of rabies may be six months or even longer. Most countries, however, depend on vaccination.

RAIN RASH
A condition seem frequently in horses kept at grass. The hair over the back and quarters becomes caked and when pulled away leaves bare areas underneath. It is caused by frequent wetting which mixes with the dirt trapped in the coat to deposit a thin layer of mud at the roots of the hairs. This in turn creates a rash which may erupt and secrete serum to matt the hairs and cause the crust.

Treatment involves removal of the caked areas with an iodine and detergent wash. Rinse and dry and repeat on three consecutive days. New hair will then quickly grow.

RECTAL PROLAPSE
A condition in which the rectum turns inside out and protrudes through the anus. The cause is generally severe irritation and diarrhea. This is sometimes produced by worm infestation in pups and piglets.

It is essential that a veterinarian return the prolapsed part to its correct position.

REDWORMS
Roundworms of the large intestine of horses.

They can be divided into small redworms and large redworms. The latter cause serious anemia. Most horses become infected with these worms during grazing, but periodic treatment with piparazine and thiabendazole will keep the infestation at tolerable levels.

RESPIRATORY INFECTIONS
These may be viral, bacterial or fungal and combined infections are frequent. Virus infections of the respiratory system are common in dogs (DISTEMPER, KENNEL COUGH), cats (CAT FLU), guinea pigs (virus pneumonia), and mink (distemper). Bacterial infections occur in horses (STRANGLES) and rabbits (SNUFFLES) and in all species when resistance is low. Fungi may also cause pneumonia in birds (ASPER-GILLOSIS) and in mammals generally in conjunction with other forms of infection.

Sneezing, cough, nasal discharge, difficult breathing, listlessness, fever, and poor appetite are the main symptoms.

Antibiotics and other antibacterials (sulfonamides) are effective against bacterial but not viral infections. These remedies are, however, used in most respiratory illnesses because infections are generally mixed. (See also BRONCHITIS, PHARYNGITIS, PLEURISY, PNEUMONIA, RHINITIS, ROARING, SINUSITIS, TONSILITIS.)

RHEUMATISM
A condition causing pain and lameness. Rheumatism sometimes occurs in one leg and sometimes in another; it is thought to occur in many species. The condition is prevalent in old dogs especially in cold, damp weather. Lameness is usually worse in the mornings but eases after exercise. The cause is unknown. A variety of drugs (phenylbutazone, aspirin, corticosteroids, leucotropin) relieve the pain but none produce permanent cure. (See also LAMENESS.)

RHINITIS
Inflammation in the nose, usually accompanied by nasal discharge and sneezing. The presence of additional symptoms (poor appetite) suggests general respiratory infection. Other causes include foreign objects (grass seeds), sinusitis, bone infections, nasal worms, or fungus infections. In horses the inside of the nose can be seen with special instruments, but in small animals the position and size of the nostrils hamper investigations. X-rays and laboratory examination of the discharge may help. Treatment is often unsatisfactory because of the difficulty of establishing the cause. Antibiotics are used for bacterial infections, and some are also available to treat fungi; foreign objects may work their way out in time.

RHINOTRACHEITIS
Inflammation of the nose and windpipe which affects several species and is usually caused by virus infections. In cattle the contagious virus illness (infectious bovine rhinotracheitis) produces widespread illness, abortions, and milk loss. In cats rhino-

tracheitis is caused by a variety of viruses (referred to collectively as CAT FLU) which produce sneezing, cough, and loss of appetite. In dogs respiratory infections which cause coughing are produced by the DISTEMPER and KENNEL COUGH viruses. Both bacterial and viral illnesses (STRANGLES, equine INFLUENZA, viral rhinopneumonitis) may infect the upper respiratory tract of horses and produce similar signs.

Certain respiratory infections (e.g., distemper, equine influenza) can be prevented by vaccination. Antibiotics are usually effective against bacterial conditions but are also given in viral illnesses to prevent secondary bacterial invasion.

RICKETS
Poor bone formation resulting from inadequate calcification. Rickets and its counterpart in adults (osteomalacia) was once an important disease in all young, fast-growing animals, but now it is rather rare in developed countries. Rickets is caused by an imbalance of vitamin D, calcium and/or phosphorus.

An adequate dietary intake of vitamin D is essential for daily growth. Most commercially available diets contain sufficient vitamin D for the animal's requirements. Any diet supplements must be supplied in balanced quantities. Oversupplementation, such as excess cod-liver oil, can lead to disorders. Calcium and phosphorus can be given in the correct ratio by adding a little bonemeal to the food.

RINGBONE. See LAMENESS.

RINGWORM
A fungal skin disease of many pets caused by *Microsporon* and *Trichophyton*. Bald, dry, scaly patches develop on the skin of most mammalian pets. Itching is not severe. Ringworm is transmissible from one animal to another and also to humans, so suspected cases should be handled carefully. In cattle and horses ringworm produces dry, chalky white areas 2cm. (0.8in.) or more across, often covered with scabs. The head and neck are common sites of infection.

A prolonged course of griseofluvin tablets is usually effective together with local applications of iodine tincture or zinc undeconate ointment. Some animals with ringworm show no indications so it is best to regard all contact animals as infected. In cattle and horses scabs should be removed with warm water and soap and affected areas sprayed with dichlorophen aerosol.

ROARING AND WHISTLING
Abnormal rasping, breathing noises which occur in horses after exertion. The conditions are caused by paralysis of the vocal cords which then hang permanently across the airways. This causes interference with the flow of air and produces abnormal sounds. Unfitness also results.

A surgical operation (known as Hobday's operation) to attach the cords to the laryngeal

walls is the usual form of treatment. Alternatively the horse may be "tubed" which involves inserting a metal tube into the windpipe below the larynx in order to permit air to flow freely into the lungs. This, however, must be regarded as an unsatisfactory and temporary procedure.

RODENT ULCER
An inflammatory lesion predominantly found on the lips of adult cats. The lesion usually starts as a shallow concave ulcerated area which develops into a tumorous swelling which is often eroded. As the lesion enlarges it becomes typically brown and scaly, and its edges roll over. Often there is secondary bacterial involvement, and there may be swelling of the local lymph glands. In severe cases, the lesions may be spread by licking to other locations, such as the skin on the inner surface of the thigh or abdomen.

Cat with rodent ulcers.

Treatment of advanced cases may prove extremely difficult, and veterinary advice should be sought without delay. The oral administration of the antiinflammatory corticosteroids or the synthetic derivatives of the sex hormone progesterone sometimes produces spectacular results. Many cases are treated successfully by surgical removal or by radiation therapy. The cause of rodent ulcer (**eosinophilic granuloma**) is not known.

ROUNDWORMS
Familiar name for a group of worms also known as nematodes. The worms are elongated, more or less round in cross section, and are not segmented. This shape is opposed to the cestodes (also known as TAPEWORMS) which are elongated, flat, and divided into segments, and the trematodes (FLUKES) which are flat, unsegmented and leaf shaped.

SALMONELLOSIS. See TYPHOID.

SARCOPTIC MANGE. See MANGE.

SCABIES. See MANGE.

SCALY FACE AND LEG. See MITES.

SEEDY TOE. See LAMENESS.

SIDE BONES. See LAMENESS.

SINUS INFECTION; SINUSITIS
Sinuses are narrow hollow cavities in the facial bones of the skull which frequently become infected as a sequel to nose and throat infections (e.g., "STRANGLES"), via a diseased molar, or following a violent injury to the face. The nostril on the affected side has a chronic muco-purulent discharge, occasionally the face bulges over the affected area, and the animal resents tapping with the fingers on the overlying bone.

Antibiotic treatment alone is rarely completely successful without draining the sinus, either by cutting the skull or removal of the tooth in question.

SKIN TUMORS. See TUMORS.

SLIPPED DISC
**(Intervertebral Disc Lesions/
Disc Protrusion)**
A condition especially common in long-backed dogs such as dachshunds, spaniels, and the Basset Hound. It is rarely seen in animals other than dogs. The discs which are present between each vertebral junction are firmly attached to the vertebrae and consist of a fibrous outer edge (anulus fibrosus) and a softer central part (nucleus pulposus).

The function of the intervertebral discs is to absorb shock and concussion to the spine. With increasing age the discs tend to degenerate, and their outer fibrous rims become more pliable. The result is that the central nucleus may protrude and press on the spinal cord which lies immediately above the discs. The signs which develop depend on the disc affected and the degree of protrusion. If the discs of the neck are severely affected, the animal may become paralyzed in all four legs, whereas a partial protrusion of a disc near the hindquarters may only cause an intermittent lameness of one back leg.

About 70 percent of dogs get better after three or four days treatment with corticosteroid or painkilling tablets. For those which do not improve an operation may be per-

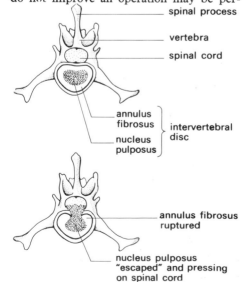

Top. *Normal vertebra with disc in correct position.* Below. *Vertebra with disc "slipped" and pressing on the spinal cord.*

formed, but it is painful and often unsuccessful. Euthanasia is probably a wiser choice.

Disc protrusion sometimes causes pain and stiffness of the hind legs in horses. This can be treated by rest, corticosteroids, and painkillers. Most disc protrusions, however, cause weakness and temporary paralysis of both back legs. Pain is sometimes acute for a day or so in the early stages but subsequently subsides and the animal shows no sensitivity.

SPAVIN. See LAMENESS.

SPRAINS
Damage to ligaments which are fibrous thickenings that strengthen joint capsules. They are attached to the bones and cartilage which make up joints and closely adhere to the joint capsule itself. The inelasticity of ligaments adds stability to joints but also makes them relatively easy to damage by forcible overextension or flexion. A sprain is said to have occurred when the ligaments and other tissues surrounding a joint are stretched or torn as a result of violent exercise. Such an injury is characterized by heat, pain, swelling, and loss of function in the joint concerned. Diagnosis of sprains is not always easy and an X-ray examination may be needed to rule out the possibility that a fracture has occurred.

Treatment mainly consists of rest, possibly with splints. Cold compresses and pressure bandages are good first aid treatments since the limitation of swelling promotes healing.

SQUINT
An inturning of the eyes. This condition (strabismus) may be inherited, as in Siamese cats and in some lines of Jersey or shorthorn cattle, or it may result from damage to the eye muscles or head trauma. Strabismus is often a sign seen in rabid dogs.

STABLE FLY
A bloodsucking fly (*Stomoxys calcitrans*) closely resembling the common housefly, which feeds on most animals, especially horses and cattle. Its bite, a sharp prick, causes restlessness in horses and a drop in milk production in cows.
Prevention: It breeds in moist dung and straw so numbers can be limited by keeping stable bedding clean and dry and by regularly turning over the dung heap. Pyrethrum fly sprays are also effective.

STRANGLES
An acute, highly contagious disease of horses caused by *Streptococcus equi*. First signs are inappetance, lethargy, and a high temperature quickly followed by a profuse nasal discharge and enlargement of the submaxillary and/or parotid glands which eventually burst and discharge pus. If inadequately treated, complications such as arthritis, pneumonia, or abscessed abdominal glands may occur.

Some antibiotics (penicillin, ampicillin, or tetracyclines) given as a series of injections over several days usually cure the disease.

STRINGHALT AND SHIVERING. See LAMENESS.

STROKE. See HEAT STROKE AND EXHAUSTION.

STIFLE CONDITIONS
The stifle joint is the meeting place of the femur and tibia. The patella (kneecap) covers the front of the joint at rest but moves up a groove in the femur as the joint moves. Common malfunctions are: dislocated patella, torn cruciate ligaments, and torn cartilage.
Dislocated patella. When this occurs in dogs (small breeds especially), the animal runs normally for a few paces, skips a few carrying the leg, and then resumes normal gait. On examination the patella can be felt slipping inward off its groove as the leg is bent and righting itself as the leg is straightened. The cause may be shallow trochlear groove or poor alignment of the femur and tibia. An operation is usually carried out to realign the patella ligament and make the trochlear groove deeper.

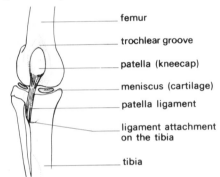

femur
trochlear groove
patella (kneecap)
meniscus (cartilage)
patella ligament
ligament attachment on the tibia
tibia

Poor alignment between the ligament attachment and the trochlear groove encourages patella dislocation.

Torn cruciate ligaments. These ligaments which bind the tibia and femur together are sometimes torn in dogs and cats. The signs are lameness and looseness of the joint. (The femur can easily be pushed from its seating on the tibia.) A nylon substitute ligament is usually inserted to remedy the condition.
Torn cartilage (meniscus). This condition occurs in dogs as a result of forceful twisting. It causes lameness and pain on pressure at the inside of the stifle. The condition may be relieved by removing the cartilage.

SUMMER SORES
A condition of the skin of horses and donkeys caused when larvae of the horse stomach worm *Habronema* are deposited in open wounds. They cause a reaction in the form of large growths of raw tissue. The condition occurs in warm countries during the summer months when flies are rampant. Most adult *Habronema* produce no ill effects although one variety causes fairly large nodules in the stomach wall. The growths are surgically removed or cauterized followed by insecticide dressings. Frequent use of fly sprays in the stable, hygienic conditions, and early disposal of manure are recommended as preventive measures.

SWALLOWED OBJECTS
Animals commonly swallow objects although the majority of them pass through without causing obstruction. In birds, grit or pebbles are commonly found in the grinding stomach, where they help break up food. Each species has a predilection for swallowing certain types of objects; kittens swallow needles as a result of playing with the attached thread, or fishbones which lodge in the throat. Pups infested with worms eat earth, while others swallow rubber or plastic toys during play. Greedy feeders often bolt down bones such as ribs which stick in the throat or esophagus. However, most objects swallowed by dogs lodge in the intestine.

Symptoms vary according to the circumstances. Objects in the throat of dogs and cats produce retching and distress, but those in the intestine cause little indisposition other than vomiting. If the obstruction is complete, vomiting is frequent and causes dehydration and the accumulation of wastes.

In small animals the object can sometimes be felt through the stomach wall. X-rays are often helpful. In cattle metallic objects can sometimes be detected with a mine detector apparatus. An operation is generally required to remove the obstruction.

SWEET ITCH
An allergic skin condition of horses due to the bites of midges. It affects chiefly the mane and tail regions causing intense itching. The animal damages the skin by rubbing it raw.

Prevention is important. Insect repellant should be used and, in severely endemic areas, horses should be stabled during the most active period of the day for midges—late afternoon and evening in the summer. Corticosteroids (injections and ointments) alleviate the irritation.

TAPEWORMS (Cestodes)
Flat ribbon-like worms, usually composed of many segments and of variable length, which often live in the intestines of animals. In mammals, the tapeworm is often harmless. The common dog and cat tapeworms are acquired in different ways. *Taenia* has its young stages in various locations such as muscles, abdominal cavity, and brain of sheep and rabbits, while dogs are infected when these tissues are eaten raw. *Dipylidium* develops in fleas and lice, and the dog and cat are infected by swallowing these parasites. *Taenia* of cats is carried in the liver of rats, mice, and squirrels, and the cat is infected when its preys on these animals. Infection of horses by *Ano-*

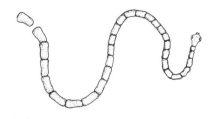

A typical tapeworm.

plocephala and of sheep by *Monezia* occurs from swallowing mites during grazing. Rats, mice, and hamsters are infected by *Hymenolepis* which are carried by grain beetles and fleas, but there are rarely any signs of infection. Direct infection from one mouse to the other is also possible. Monkeys, apes, and humans are infected by *Bertialla* after swallowing forage mites which infest grain. In birds, tapeworms sometimes cause considerable harm in the form of occlusion of the gut, causing enteritis and death.

Segments of tapeworms are sometimes seen emerging from the anus, in the feces or contaminating the coats of dogs and cats. Dogs sometimes rub the anus along the ground to alleviate itching. Anal gland infections may be initiated by the tapeworm.

Commercial preparations are available which rid the animal of tapeworms but unless an attempt is made to control the acquisition of the intermediate host, reinfection should be expected.

TARTAR (Dental Calculus)
As they get older the teeth of dogs and cats become encrusted with deposits of solid material called dental calculus or tartar. Animals living in the wild state have little problem with dental calculus, but it occurs in most dogs and cats over five years of age fed a diet comprised mainly of soft foods.

Dental calculus can lead to infection of the gums and loosening of the teeth. Finally it may necessitate tooth extractions.

Tartar should be periodically removed from the teeth of dogs and cats by a veterinarian. Under a light anesthetic the deposit is scraped off—a procedure called scaling. Giving the dog bones to chew may help to prevent the formation of calculus.

TASSEL FOOT. See MANGE.

TENDINITIS. See LAMENESS.

TENDON DAMAGE
Tendons are the fibrous ends of muscles which act as the chains anchoring the muscles to bones. The sudden wrenching of a limb can result in the stretching or tearing of a muscle and the tendon attached to it. The resultant injury is called a **strain** and is characterized by lameness, tenderness, and some

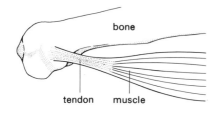

Diagram showing muscle attachment to a bone via the tendon.

swelling of the affected area. In severe cases the tendons may be ruptured.

First aid treatment consists of limiting swelling with cold compresses and pressure bandages. Apply splints to the limb to minimize any gap in the tendon and to provide complete rest.

TETANUS
An acute infectious disease of animals and humans, arising from infection of wounds by the bacterium *Clostridium tetani*. Tetanus bacteria are present in most cultivated soils, especially those which receive dressings of farmyard manure. The horse is most susceptible, although cattle, sheep, goats, and pigs can be affected and, less frequently, cats and dogs. Young animals are more prone than adults. The germ multiplies in airless conditions so that deep penetrating wounds are most dangerous.

Infection produces excess sensitivity of the nerves; consequently all the muscles contract at the slightest provocation. The lips are drawn back into a grin, the face is set in an anxious expression, ears erect and the nictitating membranes of the eyes protrude. In later stages the legs stiffen and slight noises send the animal into severe generalized spasms which are very painful. In the terminal stages, the animal is unable to stand and lies on its side with the head, tail, and limbs in rigid extension. Death follows paralysis of the respiratory muscles.

Any infected wounds should be cleaned with disinfectant and the animal placed in a dark, quiet place. In the early stages specific tetanus antitoxin and massive doses of penicillin may help. The animal has to be kept under sedation for a protracted period, fed by injection, and carefully nursed. Sometimes treatment is ineffectual.
Prevention: All horses should be regularly vaccinated. Wounds should receive prompt attention and antitetanus injections given.

THIRD EYELID INFLAMMATION. See NICTITATING MEMBRANE, DISEASES OF.

THRUSH
An infection of the mouth with the fungus *Candida albicans*. This may or may not occur in presence of tooth encrustations (TARTAR) and GINGIVITIS. The signs are fetid breath, red gums, and white slimy deposits on the membranes of the mouth. The teeth should be cleaned and antifungal tablets administered (metronidazol).

Thrush is also a disease of the frog in the horse's foot. (See LAMENESS.)

THYROID DISORDERS
Thyroxin, the hormone from the thyroid gland, controls the rate of the body processes (metabolism). (See chapter **Your Pet's Body and Senses.**) Animals with plentiful thyroxin have a high metabolic rate, that is, they are energetic, highly strung and eat well but remain thin. The heart rate and pulse are quick. On the other hand animals with low thyroxin output tend to be calm, lethargic, and plump.

Hypothyroidism (low thyroxin level) is fairly common in dogs, and the main signs are obesity and bald patches which occur symmetrically on both sides of the body. The skin under these patches is smooth and darkly colored. Occasionally there may be enlargement of the thyroid gland in the neck (goiter). Such animals can be treated with thyroid tablets.

Caged birds, especially shell parakeets (budgerigars), may suffer from hypothyroidism since bird seed is often iodine deficient. The main signs are poor hatchability of eggs and sometimes death of the baby birds. Adding a piece of cuttle fish to the diet makes up the deficiency and in some countries birdseed with vitamins and minerals is available.

TICKS
Eight-legged, blood sucking parasites which attach themselves to many mammal, bird, and reptile species. When first they infest their host they are generally no more than 3mm. (0.1in.) in length. However, they anchor their mouths into the skin and as they engorge with blood they swell to two or three times that size. At this stage they may be blue-gray, brown, or multicolored, smooth, and shiny. Ticks occur mainly in warm regions where they carry a variety of illnesses (biliary fever in dogs and horses, redwater, anaplasmosis and sweating sickness in cattle and Q-fever and Rocky Mountain spotted fever in humans). Eventually ticks drop off their hosts and lay eggs on the ground. The larvae hatch in warm weather and climb on grassblades to await a new host.

In poultry one group of ticks (Argasidae) produces severe anemia. These ticks differ from those usually found on mammals in that they attack the birds only at night and remain hidden in woodwork during the day.

Individual ticks can be removed with care to avoid leaving the mouth parts embedded in the skin. Heavy infestations are best treated by saturating the coat of the animal in insecticide. This is advisable at regular intervals where ticks are a recurring problem. Poultry can be treated with dusting powders and their roosts fumigated. (See ACARIASIS.)

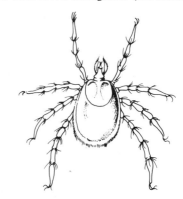

Sheep tick (Ixodes ricinus).

TONGUE WORMS
Parasites of the air passages occurring mainly in reptiles, although one species, *Linguatula* occurs in the nasal passages of dogs. Dogs are infected by eating the young stages which develop in the offal of sheep, cattle, goats,

and rabbits. Symptoms include sneezing and heavy discharge from the nostrils (generally one side only). No treatment is available.

TONSILLITIS

A condition involving inflamed tonsils which often occurs in dogs and occasionally cats. The cause and treatment are similar to PHARYNGITIS. The tonsils are removed only if infection occurs repeatedly. The animal affected may be uninterested in food, with coughing and retching as if there is a bone in the throat. (See also PHARYNGITIS.)

TOXOCARA. See ASCARIDS.

TOXOPLASMA

A protozoan infection which occurs in all mammals and birds. It has two forms. The more important occurs in all tissues of the body in the form of small cysts invisible to the naked eye and is generally transmitted by eating undercooked or raw meat. In pregnant animals the cysts may be transferred by the bloodstream to the fetus in the uterus. Infection may also be possible by droplets emitted during sneezing and coughing. The second form of this infection occurs in cats as cysts which are harbored in the intestine and passed in the droppings from which they are a source of infection for other animals.

A variety of symptoms are possible depending on where the cysts occur. Muscle pains and stiffness are occasionally apparent. Brain disorders and balancing difficulties have also been ascribed to these cysts in the nerve tissues. No treatment is known.

TRAUMA

The damaging of tissues by a violent injury. The consequences are invariably swelling and pain, and if the skin is broken, infection. Fractures are not common in connection with trauma. Treatment of simple bruising consists of alternate applications of heat and cold, but rest is usually the best medicine. (See **Care of the Sick and Injured Pet.**)

TRAVEL SICKNESS

Dogs, cats and occasionally pigs can become sick during road, sea, or air travel. The motion of the vehicle affects the organ of balance in the ear and centers in the brain. Salivation and vomiting are the main signs. Some cats also become alarmed during their first trips, jump around, and yowl continuously.

Food and water should be withheld for three hours before traveling, but froth and bile may still be vomited. Animals can be given motion sickness tablets (chlorpromazine, for example) about thirty minutes before journeys. These tablets, which are available on veterinary prescription, prevent vomiting and have a tranquilizing action. In addition they reduce salivation. Animals that travel frequently may soon adapt to the motion and no longer need medication.

TRICHIASIS. See DISTRICHIASIS.

TUBERCULOSIS

An infection caused by a bacterium (*Mycobacterium tuberculosis*) characterized by the formation of calcified cheesy nodules (tubercles) in the tissues and by wasting. This is no longer a common disease in many countries due to control measures, but it is discussed here since transmission may occur between animals and humans. There are human, bovine, and avian varieties of the tuberculosis organism which may infect a wide variety of species. The host range of the human type is the most limited as it seldom causes progressive tuberculosis in animals other than monkeys and apes, and rarely in dogs and parrots. The avian type is the only important one in birds, but it also affects cattle, sheep, pigs, deer, and zoo animals. The bovine type affects the widest ranges of species which, apart from cattle, includes horses, sheep, goats, deer, pigs, dogs, cats, and humans.

Tubercle bacteria usually enter the body by inhalation or ingestion. The disease commonly affects the lungs in mammals and causes coughing which spreads the bacteria in droplets to other animals nearby. Alternatively, infection can take place by swallowing bacteria, and cats may be infected when eating meat or drinking milk.

Symptoms vary according to the extent and site of the infection. Small tubercles may produce no sign of illness. Progressive weakness, chronic wasting, low grade fever, loss of appetite, and an intermittent hacking cough are the usual symptoms. Cows with tuberculous udders are especially dangerous as the milk becomes heavily contaminated with bacteria. Infected animals are best destroyed because of the danger to humans.

Prevention: Cattle infected with tuberculosis may be detected by a skin test. Milk should be pasteurized before being consumed by humans or pets. This process, which involves heating the milk, does not impair its flavor and destroys tuberculosis bacilli. Vaccination (BCG) is used in humans.

TUMORS

Growths occur in the tissue of all species due to excessive multiplication of cells. Tumors may be benign or malignant.

Benign tumors, warts for example, grow slowly, are neatly rounded or on stalks, and do not spread from one part of the body to another (do not metastasize).

Malignant tumors (cancers) generally grow rapidly, are irregular in shape, infiltrate the surrounding tissues, and often metastasize. There are however many degrees of malignancy: some tumors grow very rapidly and kill in a few weeks while in others growth is hardly more rapid than benign growths.

Signs of Illness. Tumors may occur in any tissue of the body and are, themselves, painless. However, they often cause pain by pressing on or stretching some sensitive tissue. The signs of illness vary greatly according to where the tumor occurs. For example, tumors of the spine may cause paralysis, those in a limb lameness, in the nose bleeding, and in the gut vomiting.

Causes. A number of causes have been identified of which virus infections are probably most important. However, tumor viruses are widespread in nature, and additional factors are often necessary to render the animals susceptible. Although tumors are most prevalent in older animals, infection may occur early in life (even before birth).

Contact with certain chemicals (carcinogens) may also promote tumor growth. Such substances usually require time to act but even a single exposure to inhaled substances may result in carcinogenic particles remaining in the lungs for some years.

Infestation of the windpipe or esophagus with the worm *Spirocerca lupi* may also be a predisposing factor. Hormonal factors may influence the growth of tumors in both sexes.

Certain families and breeds appear to be particularly prone to malignancy although it is difficult to be sure whether this is due to hereditary factors or some other factor transmitted from one animal to another during close contact. Some 7–10 percent of dogs and 3–5 percent of cats develop tumors.

Treatment of tumors. Surgical removal is generally the first consideration. This may be effective if the tumor is benign or slow growing and diagnosed early. However, removal must be thorough because regrowth can occur from minute remnants. Spread to other parts (metastasis) often follows surgery suggesting either that malignant cells, disturbed during the operation, may be carried away by the bloodstream to take root elsewhere, or that regrowth occurs more easily in individuals weakened by surgery.

Much research is devoted to preventing growths by immunological methods. Efforts have been directed toward finding the essential difference between malignant and normal cells in the hope that the body defenses could be stimulated by a vaccine containing the tumor-specific substances. Most encouraging is the eminently successful virus vaccine to prevent leukemia in poultry.

The following are the main forms of tumor found in pets.

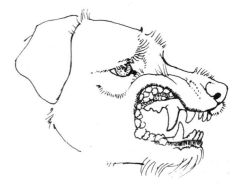

Dog with warts on lips.

Skin Tumors. The skin is the most frequent site for tumors in animals. Benign growths (**warts** in dogs, **sarcoids** in horses) are common and usually require no treatment. They can, however, be removed if prominent or worrisome. A rash of warts sometimes appears suddenly in the mouths of pups and is due to virus infection. Almost overnight the tongue, gums, and inside of the lips become covered with hundreds of warts. Although alarming to the owners, the animal does not appear to have much discomfort and about three weeks later the warts vanish as suddenly as they appeared. **Polyps** are benign tumors on stalks which grow in the ears and nose. Ear polyps are especially common in cats and the accumulation of wax in the crevices around their base often leads to infection and CANKER. The polyps have to be surgically removed in order to clean and treat the ear.

Boxer dogs are prone to mast cell tumors which are gray or black button-like growths on the skin, usually 1–2cm (0.2–0.4in.) in diameter. Although malignant, these tumors grow slowly and surgical removal is often successful.

Tumors in the mouth. Carcinoma (malignant tumors of the superficial cells) are especially common in the mouth and throats of old cats. These are fast growing and afflicted animals are best destroyed to avoid suffering.

Tumors around the anus: anal adenomas. These occur in the glandular tissue round the anus of old male dogs and appear as knobby growths under the skin. Sometimes the skin surface breaks open and bleeding results. The tumors can be reduced in size by castrating the dog and injecting estrogens (female sex hormones). If the tumors are especially large they can be surgically removed.

Mammary tumors. These are frequent in middle-aged bitches and less so in queens. In dogs a minor proportion are malignant, but in cats most are. Dog mammary tumors grow to a large size and are best removed when they become a nuisance. Spaying (removal of the ovaries) is recommended but appears to confer little benefit when performed on adults. In the cat, mammary tumors often recur after removal, and there is evidence that they are caused by virus infection.

Venereal tumors. These are fast-growing tumors which occur in the vagina of bitches and on the surface of the penis of dogs. They do not spread to other tissues and are transmitted sexually. If not too extensive, the tumors can be removed surgically.

Leukemia. Cancerous growth of the white cells in the blood and lymph which occurs in many domestic species (dogs, cats, mice, fowls, cattle, pigs, horses). In dogs the lymph glands become much enlarged and the animal looks like a child with mumps. Dogs become lackluster, lose weight, and sometimes the number of white cells in the blood is greatly increased. In cats (particularly Siamese) and fowls the internal tissues are more often affected and the liver, kidneys, and membranes become riddled with the excessive lymphoid tissue. The condition is caused by virus infection, and in poultry flocks a high proportion of birds may be affected. In poultry the ailment is known as Marek's disease. An excellent vaccine is available for prevention in birds. Leukemia sometimes kills

quickly but at other times the victim may survive in fairly good condition for a year or more. Cortisone appears to prolong life in some cases, as do the antimetabolite drugs used in human cancers. (See also FELINE LEUKEMIA.)

Lung cancer. The lung is the most common site for secondary cancers (those which have spread from elsewhere in the body). Primary cancers (new growths) are less common in the lung though there have been reports recently that this is increasing. The signs are dry, persistent coughing, and diagnosis can be confirmed by X-rays. Treatment is generally futile.

Bone tumors (osteosarcomas). These are malignant tumors generally occurring in limb bones which cause swelling, pain, and lameness. (Sarcoma is the general name for malignant growths of the connective tissues such as bone, muscle, and tendons.) Osteosarcomas are most common in middle-aged dogs of the heavy breeds (St Bernard, Great Dane). If the condition is diagnosed early, amputation may cure, but in most cases secondary spread to the lungs occurs shortly after the operation.

Amputation, especially of a hind leg in dogs and cats, causes little disability.

TYPHOID

Typhoid fever is the most severe of the enteric fevers of human beings, which collectively are caused by bacteria belonging to the genus *Salmonella*. *Salmonella typhi*, the cause of typhoid fever, is pathogenic only in humans. An effective vaccine incorporating killed bacteria is widely used, especially for people traveling abroad.

PARATYPHOID (salmonellosis) of animals can be caused by numerous types of *Salmonella*, many of which are also associated with food poisoning in humans. Fowl typhoid, caused by *S. gallinarum*, is only one of several important *Salmonella* infections of poultry. Anemia, diarrhea, and wasting are typical signs.

UMBILICAL HERNIA

In some animals there is a small gap in the abdominal muscles at the navel which permits a loop of gut, or some other abdominal tissue to protrude and form a pronounced lump just beneath the skin.

This condition is inborn, common in many species, and usually causes no ill effects. Occasionally, however, the hernia may become strangulated, that is, the blood supply to the protruding part becomes occluded, and this produces dangerous complications.

Umbilical hernias can be repaired by returning the protruding tissues to the abdominal cavity and sewing up the defect.

UROLITHIASIS. See BLADDER STONES.

URTICARIA

Sometimes called **nettle-rash**, urticaria is a skin condition which is allergic in origin and denoted by a series of small or large circular raised swellings. A large number of allergens

can cause the condition ranging from the common nettle and the bites of certain flies to various foodstuffs, usually protein in nature. When the swellings first appear they may itch, but after a short time they can be handled without bothering the animal.

Often the swellings disappear as quickly as they come without any treatment, but in cases that persist or frequently reappear, antihistamines and corticosteroids may have to be given.

VACCINES

Vaccines are used to confer an artificial active immunity against disease. Basically, there are two types of vaccine available—those containing live antigens and those containing inactivated antigens. With the former, usually only a single dose is required to establish a lasting immunity. It is necessary to give two doses of an inactivated vaccine, usually at an interval of four to six weeks, for primary immunization and booster injections are generally required annually to maintain protection. Inactivated vaccines have the advantage of safety and indeed in the case of some diseases which can be transmitted to humans (zoonoses) live vaccines are not approved. In young animals where maternally derived passive antibodies may be present, multiple, usually double, vaccination regimes are required if active protection needs to be established early in life. In the case of some diseases it is possible to vaccinate the dam so that she is able to pass passive protection to her offspring via the colostrom (early milk). Consult your veterinarian about the specific vaccines your pet needs.

VELVET

A common protozoan disease of freshwater fishes caused by a dinoflagellate, *Oodinium limneticum*. This parasite lives on the skin of the fish where it forms a cyst within which hundreds of daughter cells develop. They then leave the cyst and swim about until they find a new host, although they can survive for a considerable time in a free-living state.

Infected fish scratch against rocks, and small yellow spots like pollen dust can be seen on their scales. A commercial velvet cure should be used. Raising the water temperature slowly to 28°C. (82°F.) will accelerate the life cycle of the parasite.

VENEREAL DISEASES

Those diseases transmissible by coitus only. Monkeys are susceptible to syphilis and gonorrhea, which produce sores and discharge from the genitalia. Cattle suffer from infectious vaginitis. This produces small translucent nodules in the vulval mucosa and occasionally on the penis.

Dogs are susceptible to transmissible canine venereal tumor. These are red cauliflower-like tumors which grow rapidly and are found on the penis and the prepuce of males, and vulva and vagina of females. Persistent dripping of reddish discharge from the prepuce or vulva is a common clinical finding. Surgical removal is often recommended, although in most cases the tumor regresses spontaneously if left alone. **Dourine** is a venereal infection in horses which is caused by a protozoan parasite. *Trypanosoma equiperdum.* First symptoms of this disease are swelling and edema of the external genitalia followed by a mucropurulent discharge. Later, characteristic skin plaques develop on the head and neck. Months or years later emaciation and paralysis set in. Dourine is usually fatal.

WARBLE FLY

Flies (*Hypoderma*) which are closely related to BOT and NASAL flies. They lay their eggs on the coat of cattle, the larvae hatch and burrow through the skin, then migrate through the body, and eventually form large cysts under the skin of the back. They make a hole in the skin through which they eventually emerge and pupate on the ground. Remedies, such as larvaemisol, applied to the back kill the larvae before they encyst.

WARTS. See TUMORS.

WHIPWORMS

Roundworms (*Trichuris*) 5 or 6cm. (2–2.4in.) long which infest the lower bowel (cecum and colon) of many animals, especially dogs in warm climates. Heavy infestations produce diarrhea which may be blood tinged. Anemia rarely occurs. The worm eggs are hardy, and premises may remain infective for a year or more. These worms are difficult to eradicate since the adults bury their heads deeply in the intestinal wall. Dichlorofos may be administered in capsule form or in the food.

WHISTLING. See ROARING.

WHITE PATCH

Disease in which patches of the black coloration appear to peel off in marine Angelfish. The disease clears up in a few days if the fish is isolated in a one gallon plastic container to which is added 50 mg. of sulfonamide.

WHITE SPOT

Disease of fish caused by a single-celled parasite *Ichthyophthirius multifiliis.* This parasite grows in the skin of the fish for a few days then drops off to form a free-living cyst within which hundreds of "swarmers" develop. These swarmers break out of the cyst and swim about looking for a new host. If they fail to find a new host, they die within a week. Pinpoint white spots on the body and fins are the first symptoms to appear. The fish then scratch themselves against rocks.

Commercial white spot cure is available. The water temperature should be raised gradually to 28°C. (82°F.) as this will speed up the life cycle of the parasite and expose the swarmers to the remedy.

Note: Water containing the living cysts is infective, and the disease may be transmitted from one tank to another by equipment.

WINDGALLS. See LAMENESS.

WINDSUCKING. See CRIB BITING AND WINDSUCKING.

WOLF TEETH

Small shallow-rooted teeth frequently seen immediately in front of the upper premolars in horses. They are easily removed if they cause trouble with the bit.

WORMS. See FLUKES; ROUNDWORMS; TAPEWORMS.

Vaccines Available for Pet and Farm Animals

SPECIES	DISEASE	TYPE OF ANTIGEN IN VACCINE	PRIMARY VACCINATION AGE AND DOSAGE SCHEDULES	NEED FOR BOOSTER DOSES	COMMENTS
DOG	CANINE DISTEMPER	1. Live attenuated canine distemper virus.	(a) A single dose at 12 weeks. (b) For early protection 2 doses, the first at 6-8 weeks and the second at 12 weeks.	Usually every 2 years but will depend on local incidence of the disease.	A single dose is effective in puppies devoid of maternally derived antibodies. For puppies less than 12 weeks of age which are at risk, the double dose schedule is commonly used.
		2. Live attenuated measles virus.	From 6 weeks of age.	This heterotypic vaccine does not provide lasting or complete protection; therefore a dose of conventional canine distemper vaccine must be given subsequently, usually at 14 weeks of age.	The efficacy of this heterotypic vaccine is not adversely affected by the presence of maternally derived passive antibodies. A combined vaccine containing canine distemper and measles viruses is available.
	INFECTIOUS CANINE HEPATITIS	1. Live attenuated ICH virus.	12 weeks.	Not required.	This vaccine promotes higher antibody levels and longer protection but may cause side effects.
		2. Killed ICH virus.	2 doses (6–8 weeks plus 12 weeks).	Single injection annually.	Killed vaccines give shorter protection but are free of side effects.
	LEPTOSPIROSIS	Killed *Leptospira icterohaemorrhagia* and *L. canicola* antigens.	Puppies: 2 doses (6–8 weeks and 12 weeks). Adults: 2 doses at an interval of at least 2 and not more than 6 weeks.	Single injection annually.	Vaccination is important because *L. icterohaemorrhagia* is the cause of Weils disease in humans and anicola fever results from infection with *L. canicola.*
	RABIES	1. Inactivated virus.	2 doses at 2–3 week interval.	Annually where required and permissible.	Vaccination against rabies is controlled by local regulations in most countries. In the United States both live and inactivated vaccines are available. In Great Britain only inactivated vaccine is permitted.
		2. Modified live virus.	A single dose at 3–4 months of age.	A single dose at 1 year of age, thereafter every 2–3 years.	
CAT	FELINE INFECTIOUS ENTERITIS	1. Live attenuated FIE virus.	(a) Cats over 12 weeks of age—a single dose. (b) Kittens 2 doses at 7 and 12 weeks.	A single dose every 2 years is commonly recommended up to 6 years of age. However less frequent boosting may be recommended as FIE virus is a good antigen and natural boosting probably occurs relatively often.	Not recommended for use in pregnant queens.
		2. Inactivated strains of FIE virus grown in tissue culture.	Adult animals a single dose. Kittens with maternally derived passive antibody (i.e. less than 10–12 weeks) 2 doses at an interval of 2–4 weeks.	A single dose annually is commonly given, but dependent on local circumstances boosting may be less frequent.	May be used in pregnant queens and other felines.

SPECIES	DISEASE	TYPE OF ANTIGEN IN VACCINE	PRIMARY VACCINATION AGE AND DOSAGE SCHEDULES	NEED FOR BOOSTER DOSES	COMMENTS
	CAT FLU (feline rhinotracheitis/ feline calici virus infection)	1. Modified live feline rhinotracheitis and calici viruses.	2 doses, 9 and 12 weeks for early protection. After 12 weeks, 2 doses 3–4 weeks apart or a single dose (intranasal vaccines).	A single dose annually.	Some makes of vaccine are given by intramuscular injection, others by intranasal instillation.
		2. Inactivated FVR vaccine.	2 doses, 10 and 13 weeks. For early protection 3 doses 7, 10 and 13 weeks.	A single dose annually.	Given by intramuscular injection.
	RABIES	1. Inactive virus.	Similar to that described under the dog.	Booster doses required.	Rabies vaccination is governed by local regulations in most countries.
		2. Modified live virus.			
MINK, FERRETS, FOXES and EXOTIC ZOO SPECIES	CANINE DISTEMPER	Live attenuated canine distemper virus.	2 doses in young animals if maternally derived antibodies are present. A single dose in adults.	As natural boosting of immunity is unlikely to occur, annual booster injections are advisable.	Some canine distemper vaccines prepared for use in dogs can safely be used in these species, but others are not safe. Some manufacturers recommend a reduced dosage.
	FELINE INFECTIOUS ENTERITIS	Modified live and inactivated strains of FIE virus.	Vaccination at 2–4 week intervals between 8 and 16 weeks.	A booster dose is recommended at 6 months, 1 year and then annually.	FIE vaccine is used to protect Mink against the closely related disease mink enteritis.
RABBITS	MYXOMATOSIS	Suspension of tissue containing the virus of Shope fibroma.	Single dose.	Annually or in areas of high risk, 3 monthly.	Antibiotics must not be used with vaccination. Pregnant animals must not be vaccinated.
MONKEYS	TUBERCULOSIS		Single dose.		Not commonly used.
RUMI- NANTS CATTLE SHEEP GOATS	ANTHRAX	Suspension of living spores of an uncapsulated avirulent strain of *B. anthracis*.	Single dose at any age.		
	BRUCELLOSIS	1. Heat killed 45/20 strain of *B. abortus*.	Animals over 6 months of age are vaccinated with 2 doses at 6–12 week interval.	Annually.	45/20 vaccine may be used in pregnant animals. Vaccination against brucellosis is controlled by law in some countries.
		2. Living culture of *B. abortus*, strain 19.	The vaccine is usually given to animals 6–18 months of age. Single dose.		
	CLOSTRIDIAL DISEASES (Blackleg, Braxy, Lamb Dysentery, Pulpy Kidney, Struck, Tetanus)	Adjuvanted formalin cultures or formol toxoids of the relevant organisms.	2 injections at an interval of 3–6 weeks. Vaccination is timed to give maximum protection before a period of increased risk.	For continuous protection revaccination every 6 months is needed. However, annual booster doses are usually advised to ensure maximum protection.	Single and multivalent vaccines are available so that animals need to receive the minimum number of injections commensurate with the protection required. Vaccination of pregnant animals is practiced.
	ERYSIPELAS in Lambs	Killed strains of *Erysipelothrix rhusiopathiae*.	2 doses at an interval of 4–6 weeks.		Vaccination is carried out a few weeks before season of maximum disease incidence.
	FOOT ROT in sheep	Formalin treated strains of *Fusiformis nodosus*.	2 doses at an interval of 8 weeks to be completed shortly before disease is expected to spread.	Single dose annually.	Vaccination of ewes late in pregnancy is not recommended.
	HUSK (Bovine Parasitic Bronchitis)	3rd stage infective larvae of *Dictyocaulus viviparus* partially inactivated by ionizing radiation.	2 doses at an interval of 4 weeks to calves over 2 months of age and in good general health.		This vaccine is given by mouth.
	LOUPING ILL	Inactivated antigen from tissue culture.	Single dose.	Sheep are revaccinated at 2 yearly intervals.	For use in sheep, cattle and goats.
SWINE	PIGLET ENTERITIS	Polyvalent–killed cultures of selected strains of *E. coli*.	Sows—2 doses, 6 and 3 weeks before farrowing. Boars and Store pigs 2 doses at an interval of 2 weeks. Piglets 2 doses at an interval of 2 weeks. First dose at birth (or 10 days).	—	Sows are vaccinated in order to protect the piglets.
	SALMONEL- LOSIS	Living avirulent strain of *Salmonella cholerae suis*.	Single dose between 2–4 weeks of age.	—	Piglets less than 2 weeks should not be vaccinated.
	SWINE ERYSIPELAS	Killed strains of *E. rhusiopathiae* adjuvanted.	2 doses at an interval of 4–6 weeks.	In the second half of pregnancy or annually.	—
HORSES PONIES DONKEYS	ANTHRAX	As described under ruminants.	—	—	—
	INFLUENZA	Inactivated strains of A/equi 1 and A/equi 2 viruses.	Two doses at an interval of 6 weeks.	Annual. Pregnant mares may be boosted.	Initial vaccination not advised for foals under 3 months or in pregnant animals.
	TETANUS	Purified toxoid of *Clostridium tetani*.	2 doses at an interval of 4–6 weeks.	Annual.	This vaccine may be used to protect all species using a similar dosage regime.

357

SPECIES	DISEASE	TYPE OF ANTIGEN IN VACCINE	PRIMARY VACCINATION AGE AND DOSAGE SCHEDULES	NEED FOR BOOSTER DOSES	COMMENTS
POULTRY: CHICKENS TURKEYS GEESE DUCKS	AVIAN ENCEPHALO-MYELITIS (Epidemic Tremor)	Live virus administered by the drinking water.	Dosage schedules are planned to suit individual circumstances and will be affected by age and type of birds kept, the disease incidence and the need to protect against other diseases.	Possibly—but depending on type of stock kept. The vaccine should not be used in a breeding or laying house where there is a risk of transmitting disease to nonimmunized stock.	The vaccine should not be allowed to come into contact with the eyes of human attendants. There are a number of restrictions on the use of this vaccine. It must not be given within 14 days before or 3 weeks after other live vaccine.
	ERYSIPELAS in turkeys	Killed strains of *E. rhusiopathiae* adjuvanted.	3 doses at 3 weeks, 9 weeks and point of lay.	Breeding adults between laying.	May be used in the event of a clinical outbreak of disease.
	FOWL CHOLERA (Pasteurellosis)	Inactivated *Pasteurella multocida* serotypes.	6–9 weeks of age repeated 4–5 weeks later, by subcutaneous administration.	—	—
	FOWL POX	Living attenuated fowl pox virus.	—	—	Not for use in pigeons.
	INFECTIOUS BRONCHITIS	1. Living Massachusetts type ML virus strain. 2. Living 1B H52 virus strain. 3. Living 1B H120 virus strain.	Dosage schedule needs to be designed to suit individual circumstances.	Following a primary immunization course a booster may be given at point of lay to provide immunity lasting throughout the laying period.	The vaccines are mostly given by the drinking water and some may be used by spray techniques or administered as eye or nose drops.
	MAREK'S DISEASE	Living turkey herpes virus.	Preferably at day old, but may be given up to 3 weeks of age.		Given by intramuscular injection.
	NEWCASTLE DISEASE (Fowl Pest)	1. Living Hitchner B1 Newcastle disease virus. 2. Living Lasota strain of Newcastle disease virus. 3. Inactivated strains of Newcastle disease virus with oil adjuvant.	Dosage schedules are designed to meet particular needs, especially in respect of early protection. Programs involving the use of live and dead vaccines are often used.	Yes	The live vaccines are usually given by the drinking water. Spray techniques or administration by eye or nose drops is used in some cases. The inactivated vaccine does not present a danger to other animals or wildlife and is probably the most effective vaccine to use.
PIGEONS	PIGEON POX	Live virus.	Single dose.	The disease tends to have a seasonal incidence; vaccination is given when the likelihood of infection is high.	Administered by skin scarification. Not often used.

No vaccines are available for most pet small mammals (mice, rats, cavies, hamsters, bats, chipmunks, jerboas, squirrels, skunks, bush babies, mongooses and gerbils) and cage and aviary birds (budgerigars, canaries, finches, parrots, and softbills).

Diagnosis of Ailments

The following charts give a guide to the diagnosis of the most common ailments of dogs, cats, and horses. They do not cover all illnesses nor are they a shortcut to being a veterinarian. To use the chart follow this procedure:

(a) Note the most prominent sign of illness and its locality according to the number or letter in the relevant figure. Find the corresponding number in the first column of the chart.

(b) Find the appropriate sign of illness in the second column of the chart. Possible additional signs or clues are shown in the third column.

(c) The fourth column shows the various diagnostic possibilities. In the majority of cases, further information about the ailment can be found either in the **Dictionary of Ailments** or in other parts of the book as indicated.

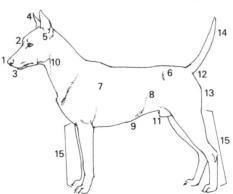

Key diagram to cat diagnosis chart.

Key diagram to dog diagnosis chart.

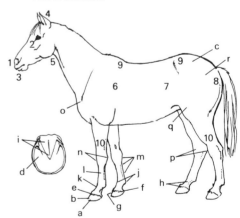

Key diagram to horse diagnosis chart.

Diagnosis Chart for Common Ailments of Cats

LOCATION	MAIN SYMPTOM	ADDITIONAL SYMPTOMS (Sometimes Present)	POSSIBLE AILMENT
(1) NOSE	Discharge from one nostril. Discharge from both nostrils. Sneezing.	Discharge with pus and sneezing. Discharge watery. Sneezing. Protruding third eyelid. Generally off color. Erosions on tongue.	Foreign body. Cat flu. Cat flu.
(2) EYES	Discharge from both or one eye. Discharge from one eye. Redness inside eyeball at pupil or iris. One eye only. Bluish/gray haze on surface of eyeball. One eye only.	Discharge greenish. Kittens one to two weeks old. Discharge greenish/yellow. History of a blow. Often occurs with other eye conditions.	Conjunctivitis (purulent). Foreign body. Hyphema. Keratitis. Corneal ulcer. Entropion. Corneal wound.

LOCATION	MAIN SYMPTOM	ADDITIONAL SYMPTOMS (Sometimes Present)	POSSIBLE AILMENT
	Keeps one eye half closed and blinks frequently.	Crater-like defect 1–2mm. in diameter.	Corneal ulcer.
	Protruding membranes at corner of eyes.	Generally off color and sneezing. Eyes bloodshot.	Cat flu. Conjunctivitis.
(3) MOUTH	Sore on lip.		Rodent ulcer.
	Difficulty with eating.	Salivates and paws at mouth. Often in old cat.	Tartar.
	Salivation.	During journey.	Travel sickness.
		After medicinal applications or contamination of coat.	Licked poison.
		Reddened gums.	Gingivitis.
	Vomiting.	Severe diarrhea and wasting, particularly young cats.	Feline enteritis.
			Gastritis. Foreign body. Fur ball.
	Retching.		Pharyngitis. Foreign body.
	Yellowing of membranes.		Poisoning. Tumor of liver.
	No appetite.	Lethargy.	Fever.
	Excessive thirst.	Old cats losing condition.	Nephritis. Diabetes mellitis.
(4) EAR FLAPS	Blister on one ear.	Scratches at ear. Shakes head.	Hematoma.
(5) INNER EAR	Shakes head to one side. Scratches ear.		Otitis media. Polyps. Mites. Canker.
(6) BACK	Pain.	Puncture wounds. Matted hair.	Common site for infected cat bites.
(7) LUNGS	Heavy breathing.	Long-standing loss of condition. Noisy breathing.	Pleurisy.
(8) ABDOMEN	Distension.		Pregnancy. (See chapter **Cats**.)
			Peritonitis.
		Straining but no urine passed.	Bladder stones.
(9) LOWER ABDOMEN	Lump.		Umbilical hernia. Cysts.
(10) THROAT	Cough retching.		Foreign body. Pharyngitis. Tonsilitis.
(11), (12), & (13). BLADDER	Increased need to urinate.	Loss of condition.	Nephritis. Diabetes mellitis.
	Increased efforts to urinate (males only).	No urine passed or only a few blood-tinged drops. Painful yowling.	Bladder stones.
(14) LIMBS	Lameness.		Fracture. Dislocation.
		Swelling of paw.	Infected bite.
(15) SKIN	Small scabs.		Eczema. Allergy.
	Itching.	Bare patches.	Mange. Fleas. Lice.
	Bare patches.	Extensive circumscribed patches.	Ringworm. Hormonal deficiency or imbalance.

Diagnosis Chart for Common Ailments of Dogs

LOCATION	MAIN SYMPTON	ADDITIONAL SYMPTOMS (Sometimes Present)	POSSIBLE AILMENT
(1) NOSE	Discharge on both sides.	Greenish discharge at corners of eyes. Young dog. Cough.	Distemper.
	Discharge on one side.	Sneezing.	Foreign body. Fungus infection. Nasal worm.
	Sneezing.	Watery or yellow/green discharge.	Allergy. Foreign body. Nasal worm. Fungus infection.
(2) EYES	Discharge from one eye.	Discharge yellowish/green.	Foreign body.
	Discharge from both eyes.	Discharge yellowish/green. Cough. Young dog. Nasal discharge in young dog.	Distemper.
	Discharge from one or both eyes.	Bloodshot eyes. Watery or yellowish matter in the eye corners.	Allergy. Conjunctivitis.
		Watery marks down face (poodles often).	Epiphora. Blocked tearduct.
		Watery discharge. Frequent blinking.	Blepharitis. Entropion. Ectropion. Trichiasis. Districhiasis.
	Redness inside eyeball at pupil or iris.	History of a violent accident or blow.	Hyphema.
	Grayness at pupil in one or both eyes.		Diabetes. Cataract.
	Bluish-gray haze on surface of eyeballs.	Often occurs together with other eye conditions (ulcer, trichiasis, districhiasis).	Keratitis.
	Bluish-gray haze on surface of eyeball of both eyes.		Hepatitis.
	Yellowing of membranes.		Jaundice. Hepatitis. Leptospirosis.
	Crater-like defect on eyeball.	Blinking. Bluish surround.	Ulcer.
	Protruding membrane at corners of one or both eyes.		Nictitating membrane disease.
	Abnormal protrusion of one or both eyes.		Dislocated eyeball. Glaucoma.
	Blindness in both eyes.		Progressive retinal atrophy.
	Blindness in one or both eyes.		Glaucoma.
	Blindness in one eye.		Corneal cuts or damage. Ulceration.
(3) MOUTH	Unpleasant smell.	Discolored teeth.	Halitosis. Tartar.
		Reddened gums.	Gingivitis. Indigestion. Labial groove infection.
	Salivation.	Car/other journey.	Travel sickness.
		Pawing at the mouth.	Foreign body.
		Unpleasant smell (often spaniels).	Labial groove infection.
		Tries to eat but cannot. Discolored teeth.	Tartar.
		Reddened gums.	Gingivitis.
		Reddened or ulcerated tongue.	Poisoning. (Irritant)
		White slimy film on gums.	Thrush.
		Depression, bad temper, or abnormal behavior.	Rabies.
	Vomiting.	Brings up food or yellowish/brown slime. Eats grass.	Gastritis. Foreign Body. Poisoning. Travel sickness.
	Retching.		Foreign body. Pharyngitis. Tonsilitis.
	Yellowing of membranes.		Jaundice. Hepatitis. Leptospirosis.

LOCATION	MAIN SYMPTON	ADDITIONAL SYMPTOMS (Sometimes Present)	POSSIBLE AILMENT
	No appetite. Excessive thirst.	Lethargy. Vaginal discharge. Loss of condition.	Fever. Pyometra. Nephritis. Diabetes mellitus. Diabetes insipidus.
(4) EAR FLAPS	Blister.	Scratches at ear or shakes head vigorously.	Hematoma.
(5) INNER EAR	Shakes head/scratches ear.	Smell and discharge.	Middle ear infection. Ear mites. Canker. Polyps. Foreign body.
(6) BACK	Pain.	Arching of back. No appetite. Loss of condition. Weakness of hind legs.	Nephritis. Slipped disc.
(7) LUNGS	Panting/Fast breathing.	Humid weather. Old dog with cough and distended abdomen. Cough. No appetite.	Heat stroke. Heart disease. Tumor (Lung). Respiratory infection.
(8) ABDOMEN	Distension.		Obesity. Ascites. Pregnancy. Pyometra. Heart.
	Pain/discomfort.	Older dogs cough. Sudden onset. Severe depression. Only a few drops or no urine passed at all.	Torsion of stomach. Calculi. Gastric torsion. Gastritis. Calculi. Poisoning. Slipped disc.
(9) LOWER ABDOMEN	Lump.		Umbilical hernia. Cyst.
(10) THROAT	Cough.		Distemper. Kennel cough. Respiratory infection. Heart disease. Foreign body. Pharyngitis. Tonsilitis.
(11), (12), & (13) BLADDER & SEX ORGANS	Excessive urination.	Increased quantity of urine. Vaginal discharge. Loss of condition. Frequent efforts to urinate but in small quantities.	Diabetes mellitus. Diabetes insipidus. Pyometra. Nephritis. Cystitis. Calculi.
(14) TAIL	Tail kept down.		Anal gland infection. Injury.
(15) LIMBS	General lameness on one side.		Sprain. Rheumatism. Arthritis. Dislocation. Fracture. Tendon damage.
	Weakness both sides. Lameness at stifle joint.	Swaying gait. Unable to jump. Paralysis. Looseness and pain on manipulating stifle joint.	Slipped disc. Stifle condition.
(16) SKIN	Itching. Loss of hair.	Circumscribed patches only. Leg and face often. Back. Patches equally arranged on both sides of the body. Parasites visible.	Eczema. Mange. Allergy. Fleas. Ringworm. Mange. Eczema. Hormonal deficiency. Thyroid. Fleas. Lice.

Diagnosis Chart for Common Ailments of Horses and Ponies

LOCATION	MAIN SYMPTOM	ADDITIONAL SYMPTOMS (Sometimes Present)	POSSIBLE AILMENT
(1) NOSE	Clear discharge from one or both nostrils.	Often seen normally, especially after exercise. Sneezing. Watery eyes.	Allergy.
	Mucous or purulent discharge from one or both nostrils.	Cough, watery, or purulent discharge from eyes. Inappetence, depression. Sometimes foul odor. Swollen glands under jaw or throat.	Equine influenza. Rhinotracheitis. Sinus infection. "Strangles." Tumors. "Choke."
	Bleeding.	Sudden onset, often profuse during exercise. Pain and swelling frontal bones area.	Epistaxis. Guttural pouch infection. Fractures / Trauma. Tumors. Bronchitis.
(2) EYES	Discharge from both eyes.	Discharge mucopurulent.	Foreign body. Conjunctivitis. Fly reaction. Trauma.
	Discharge from one eye only. Redness in front chamber of eye with red bruise on white part of eye.	Watery swollen lids. Watery discharge from nose. Pain on palpation of area.	Allergy. Trauma.
	Gray pupils. Bluish haze on surface. Severe yellowing of membranes. Swelling in inner corner of eye. Ulcer on skin close to inner corner.	Pupils dilated. NB Pale yellow is often seen normally.	Cataracts. Keratitis. Corneal ulcer. Jaundice. Hepatitis. Nictitating membrane disease. Fly reaction.
(3) MOUTH	Unpleasant smell.	Tartar around base of teeth. Blood at corners of mouth. Difficulty in eating. Abnormal sensitivity to bite.	Halitosis. Tartar. Guttural pouch infection. Impacted food material. Wolf teeth. Cheek wounds from irregular teeth or severe bit. Infected ulcers.
	Salivation.	Difficulty in eating. Attempts at vomiting. Unpleasant odor.	Foreign body. "Choke." Tongue injury. Gingivitis.
	Retching. *Severe* yellowing of membranes. No appetite.	NB Pale yellow is often seen normally. Depression. Occasionally looks at flanks and paws ground. Rolls on ground and sweats.	Foreign body. Jaundice. Hepatitis. Fever. Colic.
	Excessive thirst. Sucking air into stomach.	Loss of condition. Usually seizes solid object with teeth at same time.	Nephritis. Crib biting. Windsucking. Colic.
(4) EARS	Shakes head. Flicks ears.	Scaly material inside ear flap. Spots on outside of ear flap.	Fungus infection. Fly bite reaction.
(5) THROAT	Swollen and/or discharging glands.	Nasal and/or eye discharge.	"Strangles." Equine influenza. Rhinotracheitis.

LOCATION	MAIN SYMPTOM	ADDITIONAL SYMPTOMS (Sometimes Present)	POSSIBLE AILMENT
	Abnormal noise on inspiration at exercise.	Poor performance during strenuous exercise.	"Roaring." "Whistling." "Tongue swallowing."
	Cough.	Nasal and/or eye discharge.	Equine influenza. Rhinotracheitis. "Strangles."
		Double "lift" seen in flanks on inspiration.	"Broken Wind." Allergy.
		Cough dry and of long duration.	Lungworm.
		Sudden onset, difficulty on inspiration. Rapid breathing.	Asthma. Allergy.
		High temperature, depression, accelerated shallow breathing.	Pneumonia. Respiratory infection.
(6) LUNGS	Fast breathing.		"Broken Wind." Asthma. Pneumonia. Respiratory infections. Allergy.
(7) ABDOMEN	Pain.	Looking at flanks. Pawing the ground. Rolling. Sweating.	Colic. Enteritis. Impaction. Flatulence. Calculi. Gastric torsion. Worms.
(8) URINARY TRACT & SEX ORGANS	Vaginal discharge. Prolonged estrus cycle. No estrus exhibited. Urine dark wine color. Frequent urination.	Failure to conceive. Stiffness in muscles over loins occurring suddenly during exercise. Pain on passing urine, excessive thirst, and loss of condition.	Endometritis. Cystic ovaries. Anestrus. Azoturia. Cystitis. Nephritis.
(9) BACK	Back pain. Itching back.	Stiffness, particularly when turning. Unwilling to jump. Sudden stiffness during exercise. Swellings over spine. Mane and tail rubbed, mainly in summer.	Slipped disc. Dislocation. Arthritis. Bursitis. Azoturia. Warble fly larvae. Bursitis. "Sweet itch." Allergy. Lice.
(10) LIMBS	Lameness. Lameness in all four legs or both forelegs. Lameness in both hind legs. Lameness—usually in single leg.	Soles yield on pressure. Both forelegs spread out while resting on heels. Hoof hot to touch. Mainly fat ponies in spring and summer—rarely thoroughbreds. Moves with very short steps. Progressive increasing weakness of hind limbs at exercise. May lead to paralysis. Painful. Legs cold to touch. Worse over stony ground than grass. Heat in foot. Pain gets progressively worse. Discharge at coronary band sometimes. Mild chronic lameness fluctuating in degree from day to day. Lameness at the trot sometimes both forelegs. Points toe when at rest. Split in hoof, arising from sole, not extending to coronet. Split in hoof arising from coronary band and extending to sole. Pain on palpation in front just above coronary band. Hard swelling 25–50mm. (1–2m.) above coronary. Smell from frog, usually not lame. Smell and moist area around coronet with separation and lameness. Swollen fetlock joint. Swelling at back of fetlock joint. Diffuse swelling of pastern. Sudden onset at exercise. Tenderness at front of cannon bone. Diffuse swelling without "bowing" of back tendons. Hard lump on inside of cannon bones. Prominent swelling in particular area of tendon with pain. Severe swelling with fetlock dropping towards ground. Swelling and pain just below rear of knee. Soft swelling and pain at front of knee. Swelling of knee joint. Swelling of knee, severe pain on flexion, and on palpation of back of knee. Leg swings from shoulder when walking. Resents putting leg forward. Stumbles as foot is not lifted clear of ground. Hard swelling on inside at bottom of hock. Lameness more pronounced when leg lifted up for 30 seconds and then trotted immediately. Soft swellings on point of hock. Soft swelling on front and inside of hock joint. Swelling exactly in midline at rear lower hock. Hard swelling slightly to side of midline rear of hock. Leg locks straight out backwards. Intermittent hind leg lameness of short duration. Pain over point of hip. Whole leg swelling, sometimes with multiple discharging openings. Involuntary spasmodic lifting of hind leg. Diffuse swelling on any part of leg. Sometimes swelling leaves dent when pressed with finger.	Seedy toe. Dropped sole. Laminitis. Thrombosis. Pelvic or spinal injury. Iliac thrombosis. Bruised sole. Corns. Penetrating wound of sole. Quittor. Sidebones. Pedal Osteitis. Navicular disease. Navicular disease. Grass Crack. Sand Crack. Low Ringbone. High Ringbone. Thrush. Canker. Sprain. Arthritis. Windgalls. Sesamoid fracture. Sesamoiditis. Split pastern. "Sore shins." Tendinitis. Splint. Sprain. Sprain and rupture of flexor. Tendons. Check ligament. Bursitis. Sprain. Arthritis. Accessory carpal (pisiform) fracture. Shoulder lameness. Myositis. Spavin. Capped hock. Articular thoroughpin. "Bog" Spavin. Curb. Arthritis. False curb. Dislocated patella. Chronic subluxation. Patella. Arthritis. Lymphangitis. Stringhalt. Cellulitis. Trauma.
(11) SKIN	Dry scaly patches, usually circumscribed. Bumps over large areas. Bare itchy areas along mane and at root of tail. Multiple sores under girth and saddle. Dry, caked areas along back. Minute eggs firmly adhering to hairs on inside of forelegs. Itching.		Ringworm. Urticaria. Allergy. Fly bite reaction. "Sweet itch." Allergy. Lice. Infection. Girth galls. Rain rash. Bot fly eggs.

Bibliography

Anderson, R.S. *Pet Animals and Society*. British Small Animals Veterinary Association, 1974.

Austin, Oliver L. and Singer, A. *Birds of the World*. London: Hamlyn, 1965.

Austin, Oliver L., Jr. *Families of Birds*. Jamestown, Ohio: Western Publishers, 1971.

Axelrod, Herbert R., et al. *Axelrod's Tropical Fish Book*. New York: Arco, 1964.

Bates, Henry and Busenbark, R. *Finches and Softbilled Birds*. Neptune, New Jersey: TFH Publications, 1970.

Breen, John F. *Encyclopedia of Reptiles and Amphibians*. Neptune, New Jersey: TFH Publications, 1974.

Browne, A. *The Hamlyn Guide to Dogs*. London: Hamlyn, 1974.

Burger, Carl. *All About Cats*. New York: Random House, 1966.

Campbell, Bruce. *Birds in Color*. New York: Sterling, 1974.

De Schauensee, Rodolphe M. *A Guide to the Birds of South America*. Wynnewood, Pennsylvania: Livingston, 1970.

Forshaw, J.M. and Cooper, W.T. *Parrots of the World*. Garden City, New York: Doubleday, 1973.

Fox, Michael W. *Understanding Your Dog*. New York: Coward, 1972.

Frank, E.R. *Veterinary Surgery*. Minneapolis, Minnesota: Burgess Publishing Co., 1953.

Glasier, Philip. *Falconry and Hawking*. Watertown, Massachusetts: Branford, 1979.

Gooden, Robert. *All Color Book of Butterflies*. New York: Crown, 1974.

Gooden, Robert. *Wonderful World of Butterflies and Moths*. London: Hamlyn, 1977.

Harmar, Hilary. *Dogs and How to Breed Them*. Neptune, New Jersey: TFH Publications, 1975.

Henderson, G.N. and Coffey, D.J. *Cats and Cat Care*. North Pomfret, Vermont: David and Charles, 1973.

Henderson, G. N., et al., eds. *The International Encyclopedia of Cats*. New York: McGraw, 1973.

Hickman, John and Walker, R.G. *Atlas of Veterinary Surgery*. New York: Lippincott, 1973.

Hickman, John. *Veterinary Orthopaedics*. Edinburgh and London: Oliver and Boyd, 1964.

Hoskins, H.P., Lacroix, J.V., and Mayer, K. *Canine Medicine*. Santa Barbara, California: American Veterinary Publications, Inc., 1962.

Knight, Maxwell. *British Amphibians, Reptiles, and Pond Dwellers*. New York: State Mutual Book and Periodical Service, 1978.

Knight, Maxwell, Ball, D., and Norris Wood, J. *Tortoises and How to Keep Them*. Leicester, England: Brockhampton Press, 1964.

Leutscher, Alfred. *Keeping Reptiles and Amphibians*. North Pomfret, Vermont: David and Charles, 1978.

Loxton, Howard. *Guide to the Cats of the World*. New York: Two Continents, 1975.

Lynch, G. *Canaries in Color*. New York: Sterling, 1976.

McKeown, D.B. and Strimple, E.O. *Your Pet's Health from A to Z*. Bethesda, Maryland: Luce, 1973.

McNeillie, A. *Guide to the Pigeons of the World*. New York: Two Continents, 1976.

Matthews, L. Harrison and Knight, Maxwell. *Senses of Animals*. New York: Philosophical Library, 1974.

Mayland, Hans J. *The Complete Home Aquarium*. New York: Grossett and Dunlap, 1976.

O'Connor, J.J. *Dollars Veterinary Surgery*. London: Bailliere, Tindall, and Cox, 1952.

Parsons, D. *Do Your Own Horse*. London: J.A. Allen, 1977.

Ramshorst, J.D., van. *The Complete Aquarium Encyclopedia*. Oxford: Elsevier-Phaidon, 1978.

Restall, R.L. *Finches and other Seedeating Birds*. Bridgeport, Connecticut: Merrimack Book Service, 1975.

Robbins, Chandler, et al. *Birds of North America*. New York: Golden Press, 1966.

Rogers, Cyril H. *Budgerigars*. St. Petersburg, Florida: Palmetto Publishers, 1973.

Rogers, Cyril H. *Cage and Aviary Birds*. Val Clear, ed. New York: Macmillan, 1975.

Rogers, Cyril H. *Foreign Birds*. New York: Arco, 1976.

Roots, C. *Softbilled Birds*. London: John Gifford, 1970.

Sandys-Winsch, G. *Animal Law*. London: Shaw and Sons, 1978.

Silver, Caroline. *Guide to the Horses of the World*. New York: Two Continents, 1977.

Simon, Seymour. *Tropical Saltwater Aquariums*. New York: Viking Press, 1976.

Singer, Andrew. *The Backyard Poultry Book*. New York: Arco, 1979.

Soper, T. *New Bird Table Book*. Newton-Abbot, England: David and Charles, 1973.

Sterba, G. *Freshwater Fishes of the World*. London: Vista Books, 1974.

Warnecke (trans. by Robert Gooden). *The Young Specialist Looks at Butterflies and Moths*. London: Burke, 1961.

Woolham, F., Avon, D., and Tilford, T. *Aviary Birds in Color*. New York: Sterling, 1974.

Index